GERMAN WOMEN
In the Nineteenth Century

GERMAN WOMEN
In the Nineteenth Century
A SOCIAL HISTORY

Edited by
JOHN C. FOUT

HOLMES & MEIER
New York   London

First published in the United States of America 1984 by
HOLMES & MEIER PUBLISHERS, INC.
30 Irving Place
New York, N.Y. 10003

Great Britain:
HOLMES & MEIER PUBLISHERS, LTD.
131 Trafalgar Road
Greenwich, London SE10   9TX

Book design by Stephanie Barton

LIBRARY OF CONGRESS CATALOGING IN PUBLICATION DATA
Main entry under title:

German women in the nineteenth century.

1. Women—Germany—History—19th Century—Addresses,
essays, lectures. I. Fout, John C., 1937–
HQ1625.G467   1984   305.4'0943   83-18596
ISBN 0-8419-0843-5
ISBN 0-8419-0844-3 (pbk.)

Manufactured in the United States of America

Contents

Acknowledgments

One of the frequent complaints expressed in the essays that make up this book is that the male-dominated German historical profession has failed to write or show much interest in the history of German women. If this book was undertaken with any one intent in mind, it was to make a contribution to redressing that imbalance in German historiography. In turn, I can only hope that these essays will encourage others to join what is an ever-increasing number of scholars who are already publishing in the field. A second goal was to bring together a collection of essays that represented the best and most sophisticated work now being done on German women's history. I also wanted the collection to be cross-disciplinary and to bring together scholars from both sides of the Atlantic. In the case of the former, a number of disciplines are indeed included here (see "The Contributors" at the back of this book): history, political science, economic history, literature, and education. And there are scholars from the universities of Bielefeld, Cologne, Liverpool, and Perugia, as well as a number of American colleges and universities. (In this generation of disharmony in the relations between nations, scholars can set an example through the peaceful exchange of ideas between peoples.) Finally, with the cooperation and help of the contributors, I sought to organize this book in such a way as to make it interesting and informative to specialists and yet readable for an audience of undergraduates and general readers.

If I have succeeded in any of these goals, it is largely because of the many people who helped make this book possible and I would like to express my gratitude to them at this time. It is appropriate that I first acknowledge the contributors themselves, who, from the beginning to the end of the arduous process of getting this book off to press, have done everything possible to make my responsibility as editor less burdensome. All the contributors were prompt in turning in their essays—some kind of record for such a big book—and more importantly, all of them were supportive of the project and intent on its success. The spirit of cooperation and enterprise that prevails in the field of women's history should be a model for the behavior of the larger historical profession. I am especially indebted to Renate Möhrmann for acquiring a photographic copy of Erasmus Engert's "Hausgarten."

I am sorry that a host of other scholars who had hoped to contribute an essay to this collection could not do so—because of the constraints of time or other commitments—but I thank them for their interest in the project. Many others were helpful in various important ways. I am grateful to Richard Evans, who warned me of the pitfalls of essay collections; I can only hope I have met his high standards. I would like to thank the W.R.C.C. in London for including my call for papers in their *Newsletter* and also the *Women in German* newsletter, edited by Jeanette Clausen, for mentioning the book. I am indeed appreciative of the many scholars who suggested specialists in the field to me: Marilyn J. Boxer, Renate Bridenthal (an old friend and compatriot in the hallowed halls of the New York Public Library), Natalie Zemon Davis, Barbara Miller Lane, Otto Pflanze, Leila J. Rupp, Adelheid v. Saldern, Joan W. Scott, Peter N. Stearns, and Louise Tilly. My thanks also to my publisher, Holmes & Meier. Max Holmes was enthusiastic about the project from the start and the decision to publish in simultaneous hardback/paperback means that the book can enjoy a wider readership and the probability of adoption in undergraduate and graduate courses. Too often fine work is not often readily available because the increasing costs of hardbacks prohibits all but large libraries from purchasing new works. Elsa Dixler was helpful at an early state of the project and Barbara Lyons deserves considerable credit for her role as editor; she was supportive of my work and offered sound advice.

Many people at Bard College were incredibly positive and genuinely interested in my work and I want to acknowledge how important that was to me. I am grateful for the support from my colleagues on the women's studies committee and the two chairs of that committee—the former chair, Iska Alter, when she was at Bard (we miss her dearly)—and Suzanne Vromen, present director of the women's studies program who has done so much for the program. This book could not have been finished without the inordinate amount of information that I received from the Bard library staff, headed by Richard Wiles and David Tipple. My thanks to Connie Fowle, Evelyn Dayton, and Sharon Wiles—Sharon and Evelyn were both very helpful with the bibliography and Sharon often had to interrupt her own work on the computer to locate an obscure citation for me. I am most obligated to Jane Hyrshko; she assisted me at every point along the way by providing books and articles for my research. Surviving the double burden of teaching and writing and research at a small college would not be possible without the good sense of humor, friendship, and first-rate professional advice from my colleagues in the History Department. My thanks to Christine Stansell, whom I still think of as a colleague though she is now at Princeton, and Mark Lytle, Alice (and Timothy) Stroup, and Carol Karlsen. The Stroups "educated" me to work with a computer and they supported me with their love and gourmet chocolate desserts when I needed motivation and energy.

The terrible task of secretarial work fell upon a number of people and I want to thank "Betty" Shea and her staff in central services and Sheila Powers, the faculty secretary. Most of all I am indebted to my assistant Ann McTighe, whose efforts at every phase of this project were boundless. I thank my work-study students, Janet MacMillan, Allen Yates, Lisa Daniels, and especially Willie G. Pannell, Jr., who bore a heavy burden at the final stage of getting the manuscript ready for press. The students in my European women's history course were the first to have this material "tried out" on them and their comments were informative.

Finally I am appreciative of my children, Justine, Elizabeth, and John, who are always interested in my work and generous in not complaining about the time I spend on it. My friend Israel Rodriguez is always there when he is needed.

John C. Fout
Annandale-on-Hudson, New York
Spring 1984

GERMAN WOMEN
In the Nineteenth Century

Current Research on German Women's History in the Nineteenth Century*

JOHN C. FOUT

One of the most exciting results of the current deluge of publications on German women's history is that it has brought German scholars into the mainstream of research on women's history. They have demonstrated a sophisticated and in-depth knowledge of the literature on American and European women, published on both continents,[1] and they can now better translate the experiences of German women into language used by feminist scholars everywhere. In turn, American and British scholars have been publishing numerous articles and books on German women's history, thus making a large body of scholarship available in the English language. This interplay in the emergence of new work on German women's history is amply reflected in the articles brought together for this essay collection. Specialists on German women's history from the United States and Europe share their ideas here. Their research provides fascinating insights into the social history of German women in the nineteenth century. Moreover, given the diverse approaches to women's history represented in these essays, the new history contained therein, and the host of other articles and books that have appeared in the past

*My thanks to Alice Stroup and Kristine Martz for reading this essay and making helpful suggestions; I also appreciate the efforts of my work-study students, Jerad Day, William Space, Tony De Stefano, and Willie Pannell, Jr., who had the arduous task of proofing it. Finally, I must thank Erik Kiviat and Hudsonia Ltd. for use of their computer. I am especially grateful to my colleague Michele Dominy for her help at a crucial moment.

3

decade, we now have a reasonably coherent, though still sketchy picture of women in Germany in the nineteenth century. We better understand how the experiences of German women compare with those of other women in the West and how, also, their circumstances and responses differed, given Germany's peculiar social, economic, and political conditions. Scholars from outside Germany are for the first time offered some understanding of an important urbanized, industrialized country where the impact of the industrial revolution was delayed in comparison to Great Britain, for example, but where the impact on women's lives was massive nonetheless, especially in the latter half of the nineteenth century.

Of course, this is not the first time there has been an explosion of publications by German women. Just as in other Western countries, during the "first feminist movement," which began in the early decades of the nineteenth century, there were a host of works written on the history and contemporary experiences of German women; the period from the 1890s to the 1920s was exceedingly rich in women's writings. From the 1930s the publications on and by women slowed to a trickle, and though they never ceased entirely, it has only been since the 1970s that women's history has once again received considerable attention in Germany. There, as in the rest of the transatlantic community, most of the works have been written by women and it is questionable how great the impact has been on the larger male-dominated historical profession.[2] Certainly there are signs that attitudes are changing. Women's history has reached such a level of sophistication that it has drastically reinterpreted the social history of modern Germany; its implications can no longer be ignored. But only time will judge what the larger results will be.

Almost all aspects of women's history have been studied, although the modern era continues to receive most attention.[3] There are studies on social history, which is of course the focus of this collection, and on the history of the dynamic feminist movement that evolved in Germany in the nineteenth century. The latter is not the concern of this book, but in this introduction there will be an opportunity to comment at least briefly on some of the new literature. Interestingly, the German feminist movement was evidently more conservative than similar movements elsewhere in the industrialized West. The social history discussed here offers fascinating insights into why that German situation was different. There are implications, therefore, in this new scholarship for the political history of modern Germany as well; scholarly work on German women in the nineteenth century should force the larger historical profession to reconsider many facets of history and could result in considerable revision of standard interpretations of German history.

When the call for papers for this book was sent out early in 1981, the assumption was that there were indeed an adequate number of scholars working in the field to ensure the success of the project. The purpose of this book, as then conceived, was to make a contribution to that slowly emerging subfield in German studies. That perspective and the function of this essay collection have been altered just in the past two and a half years. In that period, an impressive number of new works on German women have appeared: journal articles, special issues of journals, document collections, reprints of older works, as well as important new monographs. Since most of the contributors to this collection have been able to use this new work, this book can now serve an additional useful function of a much-needed initial synthesis. Scholarly studies on women in Germany have appeared in the past at a slower rate than in Great Britain or the United States, but if the pace of publication continues at its present rate—and there is every reason to believe it will—there will soon be an impressive body of literature available; it is an exciting time to be working in the field.

Because the list of recent works is lengthy, only a small segment of that scholarship can be reviewed here; naturally, the best-researched and most original efforts will be given greater attention, but much good work will have to be ignored or cited only in the notes. This cross section will in the main be limited to publications that have appeared in the past half decade and will emphasize new approaches to German women's history. In almost all cases, there will be some discussion of the sources on which this new research is based. That will provide an opportunity to introduce the essays in this book and set them within the context of existing research. About one half of this essay will be concerned with publications on working-class women and the other half will be on middle- and upper-class women. The material will be subdivided topically for clarity of presentation. It should not be forgotten that although there is a large body of new literature (and some crucially important older standard works[4]) we are still only in the very early stages of the time-consuming process of reconstructing the history of German women in the nineteenth century.

It is appropriate to begin with sources on working-class women; fortunately, numerous works are being reprinted and, in addition, there are new anthologies of original documents. (Reprinting is vital to the future of the field of women's history; frequently earlier works by women were issued in limited editions and, furthermore, many were lost or are extant in only a very few libraries or archives.) Although books and periodicals of the period have been made available in recently published microfilm (or microfiche) collections, they are extremely expensive and have generally been purchased only by large research libraries.[5] Equally important, reprints have been done as individual volumes, many in paperback. Two important socialist women's autobiographies, Ottilie Baader's *Ein steini-*

ger Weg (*A Stony Road*—first published in 1921) and Adelheid Popp's classic *Jugend einer Arbeiterin* (*A Working Woman's Youth*—first published in 1909), and some other old and new works on socialist women have appeared.[6] Regrettably, the autobiographical sources written by socialist women were essentially designed by their authors to convert women to the movement. They are less valuable therefore for the social history of the working class[7] than for the history of organized labor and women's role in that movement. In the late nineteenth and early twentieth centuries, autobiographies of non-socialist women were given relatively little notice by either middle-class feminists or the socialist press; that continues to be the case in our own time. Thus, important works have been neglected, such as Doris Viersbeck's *Erlebnisse eines hamburger Dienstmädchens* (*The Experiences of a Hamburg Domestic Servant*), the anonymous *Im Kampf ums Dasein. Wahrheitsgetreue Lebenserinnerungen eines Mädchens aus dem Volke als Fabrikarbeiterin, Dienstmädchen und Kellnerin* (*The Struggle for Existence: Memoirs of a Girl from the People as a Factory Worker, Domestic Servant and Waitress*), and Mrs. Hoffman's *Aus der Gedankenwelt einer Arbeiterfrau* (*A Working Woman's Thoughts*); these books desperately need to be reprinted as well.[8]

A miscellany of autobiographical writings by working-class women is contained in a number of anthologies that have appeared in recent years. The two-volume work edited by Wolfgang Emmerich, *Proletarische Lebensläufe. Autobiographische Dokumente zur Entstehung der zweiten Kultur in Deutschland* (*Proletarian Lives: Autobiographical Documents on the Formation of a Second Culture in Germany*), has already become a standard work since it contains such a large number of sources; most excerpts are selections from autobiographies.[9] However, it is terribly biased in favor of the experiences of males. In volume 1, of 98 documents, only 11 are by women. In volume 2, of 98 again, only 6 are by women. Moreover, the collection is also biased in favor of "socialist women," rather than working-class women as a whole. Comparing the total number of women workers in Germany and Austria with the number of women involved in socialist unions (i.e., the Free Trade Unions) and the Social Democratic Party gives quite a different picture. It has been estimated that on the eve of World War I, there were 18.5 million men employed in Germany and 9.5 million women—approximately half of all adult women were wage earners (out of a total population of about 66 million). In 1914, of the 1,085,905 adherents of the Social Democratic Party, only 174,751 were women (16.1 percent); of the 2,052,377 members of Free Trade Unions, only 203,648 (9.9 percent) were women. In Austria (in 1910), the total population was 28,570,800, and of that figure 14,538,610 were women. There were 6,770,613 women employed, or 46.6 percent of all women (the highest percentage of any German-speaking country). Of the 114,316 members of the Social Democratic Party in Austria, 12,198 were women (10.7 percent); of 400,565 union members, 42,607 were women (10.6 percent).[10] These figures clearly indicate that only a relatively small segment of the female working-class population was associated with the Social Democratic Party or socialist unions. It is true that the socialists had already captured the loyalty of the working class. In 1890 a male worker in a machine factory (which employed only men) was quoted as saying, "Everything here is social democratic, even the machines."[11] Though only some of the workers in that factory actually belonged to a socialist union or the Social Democratic Party, the socialist leaders among the workers nonetheless influenced the behavior of all workers. Moreover, in many families where both husband and wife worked, which was common especially when the husband was unskilled, generally only one member of the family (because of budget constraints) could be allowed to pay union dues, most often the man. But even given such considerations as these, working-class women were in the main untouched by socialist agitation in the prewar period. Many male unions were antifeminist, and besides, given the character of women's work (for example, farm workers, domestic service, or home industry), most women were isolated from other workers, males especially. A monograph or a collection of original documents that takes into account only the activities of "socialist" women, as Emmerich's does, is certainly limited in perspective and does not acknowledge the reality of women's work experiences.

A more important anthology of original autobiographical documents relevant to working-class women is *Arbeiterinnen kämpfen um ihr Recht (Women Workers Struggle for their Rights)*, edited by Friedrich G. Kürbisch and Richard Klucsarits. This collection attempts to re-create through primary sources the experiences of working-class women, and it is the first to recognize tacitly the important contribution of the female work force in the nineteenth and early twentieth centuries.[12] Though there are documents ranging in time from the 1840s through the 1940s in the collection, the emphasis is on the late-nineteenth- and early-twentieth-century period. All German-speaking areas are represented (Germany, Austria, and Switzerland) and the documents are well chosen and represent a variety of significant autobiographical sources. There are selections from long autobiographies, and shorter pieces from contemporary socialist publications are cited in their entirety. Like the Emmerich volumes, this anthology is also biased in favor of the experiences of socialist women (though there are a few selections from the autobiographies of non-socialist women). A reader familiar with working-class women's autobiographies will be amazed at how different the tone of these sources is, given the way in which they have been edited by Kürbisch and Kluc-sarits. Collections which emphasize involvement in strikes, socialist labor unions, and the socialist party lose much of the important social history of everyday life. Future anthologies must not be so circumscribed; we must have a history of all working-class women, not just those involved in socialist organizations.

Nonetheless, the influence of "traditional" approaches to the study of working-class history is strong, as reflected by a surge of monographs on the organizational history of women's participation in German socialism in the nineteenth century. Of course, these new monographs are important, since together they make for a better balance in the literature; in the past most organizational histories have emphasized male activities. Equally important, a substantive history of socialist women is emerging at this juncture. Although socialist activists in the late nineteenth and early twentieth centuries wrote autobiographies and histories of the movement, the first recent quasi-scholarly study was Werner Thönnessen's *The Emancipation of Women: The Rise and Decline of the Women's Movement in German Social Democracy, 1863–1933*.[13] For some years this study stood alone as the only work on women in the socialist movement. Though it provides a useful (but brief) analysis of socialist theories on women's emancipation in the prewar period and a valuable history of socialist women in the Weimar period, it has now been completely super-seded by recent works. These include: Jean H. Quataert, *Reluctant Feminists in German Social Democracy, 1885–1917;* Gisela Losseff-Tillmanns, *Frauenemanzipation und Gewerkschaften (Women's Emancipation and Labor Unions);* and Sabine Richebächer, *Uns fehlt nur eine Kleinigkeit. Deutsche proletarische Frauenbewegung, 1890–1914 (We Are Lacking Just a Little Bit: The German Proletarian Women's Movement, 1890–1914).*[14]

These studies by Quataert, Losseff-Tillmanns, and Richebächer taken together provide us with valuable information about women in German trade unions and in the German Social Democratic Party, the largest socialist party in Europe in the late nineteenth century. Each is strong on different facets of that complex history. Quataert's study is the only one of the three based on extensive archival research in the Federal Republic and the German Democratic Republic. Well written and buttressed by a strong theoretical framework, it focuses on eight of the most prominent women leaders in Social Democracy in the period from 1885 to 1917. Using a host of archival and published sources—letters, autobiographies, government reports, trade union and socialist party minutes and pro-tocols—and extensive secondary works, Quataert has provided us with sophisticated biographical and intellectual portraits of Emma Ihrer, Ot-tilie Baader, Helene Grünberg, Gertrud Hanna, Clara Zetkin, Luise

Zietz, Lily Braun, and Marie Juchacz. Quataert analyzes feminist tactics in German Social Democracy to show how socialist and feminist ideas came into conflict, and that women could not always be loyal to both. "As a group within Social Democracy, these feminists had put their faith in socialism to redress sex inequalities. To achieve this goal, they accorded first priority to the struggle for a new society. Hence, they did not fight for feminism if the issue threatened the advancement of socialism."[15] The theme of "reluctant feminists" dominates this fascinating book, which is a major contribution to the literature on socialist women.

Gisela Losseff-Tillmanns' *Frauenemanzipation und Gewerkschaften* is also a significant new treatise. Though she evidently did not use archival material, she based her organizational history of women in trade unions on extensive published sources, both primary and secondary, and relied heavily on trade union periodicals and protocols. The book is divided into four parts—up to 1860, 1860–90, 1890–1914, and 1914–33. The first half of the book is devoted to the period down to the end of World War I; the second half is entirely cn the Weimar period. Losseff-Tillmanns emphasized the relationship between economic development and women's particular role in the economy and how that affected their involvement in unions. She described the evolution of women's unions— from the early period when middle-class women played an important role through the rapid growth of the Free Trade Unions when working-class women came to have control. Throughout she reiterated how difficult it was for women to achieve quality within the male-dominated unions and how women were in the end essentially given a secondary role. The first quarter of the book is rather encyclopedic, but later sections are increasingly well written and it becomes fascinating to read. There is no question that this monograph is a major study of trade union women in nineteenth- and twentieth-century Germany.

Sabine Richebächer's *Uns fehlt nur eine Kleinigkeit. Deutsche proletarische Frauenbewegung, 1890–1914,* like the study by Quataert, is a general history of socialist women in the Wilhelmine era, but with considerably less emphasis on a biographical approach. It relies on published sources, especially autobiographies and women's periodicals published by unions. It is quite significant in its own way because the first third of the book is concerned with "*der Lebenszusammenhang der proletarischen Frau*" (roughly translated: "the daily life of the working-class woman"). In other words, Richebächer has tried to show the "connections" *(Lebenszusammenhang)* between women's family life, work experiences, and their ultimate involvement with socialism. Though this section of the book is about one hundred pages long, it makes us realize just how little we know about the social history of working-class women. In this way she has broken the mold of the "traditional" approach to the study of labor history in a most effective way. There is only one weakness: Richebächer provides an introductory history of material life of the working class in general but she offers insufficient insight into the "social history" of that specific group of women who were active in socialism—obviously that history has yet to be written. The other sections of Richebächer's study, like both the Quataert and Losseff-Tillmanns treatises, are standard in their development. Thus there is a continuing tendency to write essentially a history of "feminist worthies"—a history of the women at the top of the socialist hierarchy.[16] We know almost nothing about rank-and-file women and relatively little about women in socialist organizations in specific cities.

Molly Nolan, in her fascinating article "Proletarischer Anti-feminismus. Dargestellt am Beispiel der SPD-Ortsgruppe Düsseldorf, 1890 bis 1914" ("Proletarian Antifeminism as Represented in the Case of the SPD's Local Organization in Düsseldorf, 1890 to 1914"),[17] had already reached the same conclusion; she too warned of the dangers of that approach to women's history. She criticized those historians who have adhered to that methodology:

> They remain in the well-trodden area of political or intellectual history instead of testing the new methods and insights of social history. They study exclusively the documents on the elite of the women's movement—Zetkin, Braun, Zietz, Baader, and a few other prominent leaders who had developed speaking and writing talents and whose ideas and activities are well documented. At the same time they are concerned only with how the leading male theoreticians, functionaries, and politicians have reacted to the women's question. The anonymous woman worker who worked day in and day out in the factory and at home and who attempted at the same time to be politically active appears only in the statistical tables.

Nolan also argues that the problems and methods chosen determine the sources used and those sources in turn have limited the perspective.[18]Nolan sought to move in a different direction by investigating the activities of one socialist local, especially in terms of working-class antifeminism. With this article she has made an important contribution to the literature.

Two other articles on socialist women deserve at least a brief commentary: Richard J. Evans, "German Social Democracy and Women's Suffrage, 1891–1918"; and Willy Albrecht et al., "Frauenfrage und deutsche Sozialdemokratie vom Ende des 19. Jahrhunderts bis zum Beginn der zwanziger Jahre" ("The Women's Question and German Social Democracy from the End of the Nineteenth Century to the Beginning of the 1920s").[19] Evans's essay provides us with a better understanding of the complex question of women's suffrage and the Social Democrats; he shows that both support for and opposition to women's suffrage were widespread within the party. Evans thereby also picks up on the question of antifeminism within the leadership and the rank and file of male socialists and illustrates how antifeminism was played out within the socialist movement over the issue of women's suffrage. Willy Albrecht and his colleagues challenge many assumptions about the proletarian women's movement and address questions not asked previously. To clarify the evolution of women's participation in unions, they examine the relationship between women's work experiences and their attraction to the socialist movement. The authors ask: Why were women more interested in the trade unions than in the party? Why were those trades in which women workers formed the majority the most active within the largely male-dominated union movement? Why, given the character of their work, were the majority of women largely uninvolved in the trade unions? Why was the road to unionization inherently more difficult for women than it was for men? Why is the correlation between increased female membership in the unions and the increased participation of women in strikes important? In asking and addressing such questions as these Albrecht and his colleagues have taken an important step toward directing research on the relationship between women and socialism in significant new directions.

It is appropriate to turn now to the paid employment of working-class women, both inside and outside the home. Some of the most original monographs that have appeared in the past decade have been written by American scholars. The study by Louise A. Tilly and Joan W. Scott, *Women, Work, and Family,* based on extensive published sources, has already become a standard work on the experiences of English and French women, primarily of the working class. Thomas Dublin, in *Women at Work: The Transformation of Work and Community in Lowell, Massachusetts, 1826–1860,* has reconstructed the development of the textile industry in Lowell after extensive archival research. David M. Katzman studied the history of domestic service in *Seven Days a Week: Women and Domestic Service in Industrializing America,* and Lee Holcombe's *Victorian Ladies at Work: Middle-Class Women in England and Wales, 1850–1914,* is the first major study of the work life of middle-class women, especially teachers, nurses, shop assistants, clerks, and civil servants.[20] The latter book should be listed under the section on middle-class women, of course, but many working-class women ended up in those positions as well.

Disappointingly little research has been done on the working life of working-class women in Germany or Central Europe in the nineteenth century. Though a number of fascinating articles on facets of women's work, and the relationship between work and family and private (single

and married) life, have come out recently, there is yet only one monograph specifically on work, and it is on Austrian rather than German
women: namely, Edith Rigler, *Frauenleitbild und Frauenarbeit in
Österreich vom ausgehenden 19. Jahrhundert bis zum Zweiten Weltkrieg
(Women's Image and Women's Work in Austria from the Late 19th Century to World War II)*.[21] It is a useful introduction, but like the Thönnesen
study, it will have to be "fleshed out" with extensive quantitative and
qualitative studies. The book is really just a short introductory overview
with far too little commentary on working-class women in the period up to
World War I, although the section on the interwar period is considerably
more detailed. There is an interesting discussion on the early period that
attempts to demonstrate how attitudes toward women shaped women's
work experiences and opportunities to a large extent, though her argument is insufficiently supported with data. The material on the decades
after World War I is more substantive since it is concerned with the
varieties of women's work in that era and it is the most interesting part of
the study. Rigler here speaks of specific occupations and provides much
helpful statistical information. There is one problem with the book; it too
readily mixes the experiences of middle- and working-class women,
which makes one question the author's theoretical assumptions.

A number of extremely well-researched articles on women workers in
certain large cities and the work and family life of workers in specific
occupational categories have appeared recently. Both of these approaches
are desperately needed in order for scholars to better understand the
lives of women in local communities; so such studies on working-class
women's work are indeed quite original in their approach. Of these, one
of the most fascinating is Robyn Dasey, "Women's Work and the Family:
Women Garment Workers in Berlin and Hamburg Before the First World
War."[22] Dasey based her work on extensive archival and published
sources, especially government statistics, and looked at a number of
significant issues, including the rapid growth in the numbers of women
employed in that sector of the economy, wages, hours, and working conditions. She compared factory work and home industry, and the employment of single and married women, and she discussed the fascinating role
of the *Zwischenmeisterinnen* (middlewomen), those female entrepreneurs of the garment industry who played such an interesting role in
home industry. Moreover, in the case of married women, she offers us
fascinating insights into their complex family and work responsibilities,
including the relationship between women's reproductive and productive
life cycles. She concludes:

> The gradual divorce of the sphere of production from the household
> under the conditions of nineteenth-century industrialisation in Germany
> severely limited the range of productive earning activities open to the

rapidly increasing number of poor women in the cities. Industries which did offer them employment in large numbers were able to exploit the characteristics of the female labour force which arose out of the socially-defined family role of women. Commitment to marriage and family on the part of women did not determine where they worked and under what conditions: the sexual division within the labour market arising out of the longer-term incorporation of women's family roles into the employment structure certainly did.[23]

Josef Ehmer also draws attention to the increasing participation of married women in the work force in his article "Frauenarbeit und Arbeiterfamilie in Wien. Vom Vormärz bis 1934" ("Women's Work and Working-Class Families in Vienna from the *Vormärz* to 1934").[24] Despite its chronological breadth, one should not assume the essay is too general. In fact, it deals primarily with the period of the late nineteenth and early twentieth centuries. Based on extensive published primary and secondary sources and government statistics, it recognizes that the daily life of the married working-class woman was in reality far from what the middle-class social scientist thought it was. Ehmer also emphasizes that women's work changed with the approach of the twentieth century and he shows how these changes affected women workers. He concludes by discussing the decline in the size of working-class families and he explains how that decline was shaped both by shifts in the character of work and by the desire of workers to live with an improved standard of living. Some important statistical information is provided in an appendix to the article.

Regina Schulte's elegantly written "Dienstmädchen im herrschaftlichen Haushalt. Zur Genese ihrer Sozialpsychologie" ("The Domestic Servant in the Master's Household: On the Genesis of a Social Psychology")[25] displays an incredible familiarity with the large body of published literature on the subject, especially contemporary nineteenth-century sources. She shows how the changing character of the bourgeois household, class attitudes, and big-city life created the circumstances for the master/servant relationship which were so typical (and so debilitating) for the domestic servant in the latter half of the nineteenth century. It is this analysis of the daily routine of the domestic servant in a typical upper- or middle-class household that makes this work so fascinating and valuable. Schulte's essay offers a better understanding of how and why so many lower-class women were forced into this type of employment and why, because of the conditions of their labor, they often left it as soon as it was possible to do so. Additionally Schulte has established a very useful model for evaluating the role of working-class women in the work force in the industrial age.

Many aspects of women's work remain to be explored. Karin Hausen's "Technischer Fortschritt und Frauenarbeit im 19. Jahrhundert.

Zur Sozialgeschichte der Nähmaschine," ("Technological Progress and Women's Work in the 19th Century: The Social History of the Sewing Machine")[26] addresses the neglected relationship between technological change and women's work. Peter Schneck, an East German scholar, wrote on "Die gesundheitlichen Verhältnisse der Fabrikarbeiterinnen" ("The Health of Women Factory Workers"); he is the only scholar that I know of who has examined the crucial question of women's health in the workplace, and his work is significant. Otherwise that subject has all but been entirely ignored.[27] Finally, Ingeborg Müller, in her "Damshagen: Aus dem Alltagsleben der Tagelöhnerfrauen" ("Damshagen: On the Daily Life of Women Day Laborers"), has investigated the changes in the lifestyle of rural women over the course of the nineteenth century, especially in the rural community of Damshagen.[28]

In concluding this review of the literature on working class women, I would emphasize that many aspects of their lives have yet to be researched; good examples are sexuality[29] and education. I should add that there has been considerable research done on working-class women in the Weimar and Nazi eras.[30] More appropriately, with this review of recent work in mind, it is the proper moment to introduce five of the essays in this collection to illustrate how they add to our understanding of the lives of poor women.

W. R. Lee, in his article "The Impact of Agrarian Change on Women's Work and Child Care in Early-Nineteenth-Century Prussia," sought an explanation for the high infant mortality rate in Prussia in the first half of the century. Having clearly demonstrated the inadequacies of earlier explanations, Lee, using extensive statistical sources and demographic indices, offers new and cogent arguments which make for a more sophisticated understanding of regional variations in Germany; he explains how the commercialization of agriculture affected women's work and indeed child care in Prussia. He argues that "the key weakness of existing studies of early-nineteenth-century trends in both maternal and infant mortality is their relative failure to explore the concrete framework of the family economy." For example, agricultural work outside the home was often a reason why women were unable to breast-feed their children. Moreover, regional variations in methods of agricultural production and in diet also affected the health of farm workers and their infants. With this entirely new way of looking at the role of women in peasant agriculture, Lee provides an interdisciplinary analysis and a cohesive interpretive framework.

Barbara Franzoi attacks many standard assumptions about the character of German industrialization in the nineteenth and early twentieth centuries in her essay "Domestic Industry: Work Options and Women's Choices." In her analysis, she argues that historians have emphasized the development of heavy industry and have failed to take into account the tenacious survival of domestic industry. This sector of the economy was still thriving in the early twentieth century and it was "women who benefited most from its persistence." She demonstrates how women, especially married or self-sustaining women with dependents, were able to take advantage of domestic industry in a way that allowed them to balance their family and paid employment needs in a reasonable way; many women in fact preferred work at home over factory employment. Of course, working and living at home in a crowded dwelling with children underfoot was difficult and debilitating and pay was generally incredibly low. Thus Franzoi, using a broad selection of published contemporary sources, has analyzed an important sector of women's work in the Imperial period and she will force scholars to rethink the character of the German economy in that era and women's role in it.

Jean H. Quataert, in "Social Insurance and the Family Work of Oberlausitz Home Weavers in the Late Nineteenth Century," has also taken a new look at women's employment in domestic industry in the late nineteenth century. Her work is based on extensive archival research in East Germany into an aspect of women's lives that has been, as of yet, all but totally ignored, namely, the impact of the implementation of "paternalistic social legislation." Quataert believes that the new protective labor laws were a compromise between production requirements (for cheap female labor) and a desire to safeguard working-class family life; they reflect as well the ruling group's preoccupation with women as reproducers. She also points out that "females worked in weaver families to provide both cash wages and the homegrown products immediately consumed by the family. Until the insurance law was extended to home weaving, they were relatively unaffected by the growing state regulation of labor relationships." Moreover, the general definition of work excluded housework and "the whole social climate of industrial society did not favor or ease women's productive activities because they were defined basically as men's tasks." Quataert argues: "The law assumed that women at best provided supplemental labor, but judged that work insufficient to qualify for a pension unless the women actively fought the ruling." Therefore, "with increasing industrialization, the whole climate in the textile industry of the South Oberlausitz had shifted to lower the valuation of women's work." Quataert has opened a new area of inquiry about women's family and work relationships and the attitude of the larger society toward them.

John C. Fout writes about "The Woman's Role in the German Working-Class Family in the 1890s from the Perspective of Women's Autobiographies." He emphasizes that numerous working-class women's autobiographies have either been overlooked or used mainly to write about the lives of women active in the socialist movement. He establishes the value of these autobiographies as a source for writing the social history of everyday life of women in the working-class family. The thrust of his essay is to demonstrate how crucial women were to the survival and well-being of these families. Looking at the lives of working-class women as they saw themselves, rather than from the perspective of middle-class social scientists, offers a radically different picture of the daily lives of these women. It shatters long-accepted views, such as the assumption that married women did not work for pay, either inside or outside the home. In fact, most married women in working-class families worked in various forms of paid employment almost all of their adult lives, but the jobs open to them were not of the kind that were generally recorded in government statistics. Women in poor homes had to be resourceful in acquiring the necessary food and clothing, often by inventive measures. Fout illustrates how much pressure there was on these women with their family, child-rearing, housekeeping, and employment responsibilities in an environment where basic food and housing needs were horribly inadequate.

In "The Civilizing Tendency of Hygiene: Working-Class Women under Medical Control in Imperial Germany," Ute Frevert argues that in the last two decades of the nineteenth century doctors and health agencies increased their efforts to extend their authority over working-class women. From the 1880s to World War I the medical profession took steps on both the local and state levels designed to change profoundly the behavior of the working-class family in regard to their health. Doctors and health officials hoped to reduce the high rate of infant mortality. They believed that in general the health of the working class was deteriorating, due to the "irrational" behavior of the common people. Doctors wanted women to raise the standards of health behavior in the working-class family. In a number of popular books and pamphlets doctors tried to "educate" working-class women in the "science" of health preservation; these texts also helped establish the hegemony of bourgeois values and morals. Women had to be concerned with cleanliness, healthy clothing, nourishing meals, and sanitation. Doctors believed that infant mortality resulted from artificial feeding, which working-class mothers obviously favored over breast feeding. Especially in the first decade of the twentieth century doctors sought to convince these mothers to breast-feed their children. Middle-class women took control of the implementation of this program in local health offices. These measures were designed to improve the health of the labor force, by encouraging women to adopt bourgeois values and habits, which they were told would improve the health of the family. Such health propaganda defined new roles for the working-class woman, roles modeled on the example of the bourgeois housewife. Frevert also demonstrates how this propaganda affected the actual reproductive behavior of these women and how it influenced their attitudes toward health and the medical profession.

The last essay to be discussed in this section will serve as a transition to the commentary on the literature on middle- and upper-class women; it is less concerned with the question of class. It addresses an important topic untouched by historians in the recent period; and yet it is quite a significant issue, namely, "The Female Victim: Homicide and Women in Imperial Germany." The authors, Randolph E. Bergstrom and Eric A. Johnson, rest their findings on a mountain of empirical data. They have coded all reported female murder and manslaughter victims, as well as females convicted of the offense of murder or manslaughter, over a period of several years, from the over 500 individual *Kreise* (counties) of Prussia and from the 90-odd larger administrative districts for all of Germany *(Regierungsbezirke)*. In addition, census data concerning relevant features of the social and economic life of these communities were coded (e.g., population figures, size of community, ethnic makeup of the community, taxes paid, death rates, occupational breakdown). Bergstrom and Johnson conclude that "German women were less likely to be murdered than were German men." Yet "women who broke away from traditional roles, either by getting married at an early age, by not getting married at all, or by moving off to the city, were in more danger of getting murdered than those who followed a traditional lifestyle."

Literature on middle- and upper-class women will be the focus of the remaining sections of this essay. There will still be a topical approach and there will be extensive citations in the notes. The publication and reprinting of sources will be emphasized as has been done throughout. Sources on the lives of middle- and upper-class women and the feminist movement are appearing at a rapid rate, both in English and in German-language editions. As was the case with works on working-class women, these include unrevised reprints, anthologies of sources by individual women or sources from a variety of individuals or organizations, and newly edited sources—especially by women who have been ignored in the past. This publishing is irrefutable proof of the strength of the current resurgence of German women's history in Germany and in the Atlantic community.

The first topic to be taken up will be sexuality. (Unfortunately I was unsuccessful in soliciting an essay on that subject for this collection despite considerable effort on my part.) A number of important new works on American and European women have appeared in the past few years, but again that scholarship has mostly been authored by American or British researchers—only a handful of articles and books have been done on German women and those too have been written or edited mainly by non-German scholars. An excellent example of this is a very recent work,

Powers of Desire: The Politics of Sexuality, edited by Ann Snitow, Christine Stansell, and Sharon Thompson, which should provoke a spirited discussion of sexuality and how its history can be adequately studied.[31] Most of the essays in that collection are on the twentieth century, rather than the nineteenth, and generally they are concerned with American experiences—but there is one very pioneering essay on Germany by Atina Grossmann, "The New Woman and the Rationalization of Sexuality in Weimar Germany."[32] Also very noteworthy is a monograph by Lillian Faderman, *Surpassing the Love of Men: Romantic Friendship and Love between Women from the Renaissance to the Present.*[33] Though this work attempts a comprehensive survey of attitudes toward women's sexuality in the modern period, the emphasis of this remarkable study is on lesbianism. The chapters on "The Rise of Antifeminism" and "The contributions of the Sexologists" are fascinating, as they connect the emergence of the feminist movement with antifeminist attacks focusing on lesbian sex. Faderman writes:

> Of course, love between women had been encouraged or tolerated for centuries—but now that women had the possibility of economic independence, such love became potentially threatening to the social order. What if women would seek independence, cut men out of their lives, and then find solace from loneliness by making what should have been "a rehearsal in girlhood of the great drama of a woman's life," the drama itself? Love between women was metamorphosed into a freakishness, it was claimed that only those who had such an abnormality would want to change their subordinate status in any way. Hence, the sexologists' theories frightened, or attempted to frighten, women away from feminism and from loving other women by demonstrating that both were abnormal and were generally linked together.[34]

A number of other studies on lesbian and gay men's history have also been done on nineteenth- and twentieth-century Germany. For example, James D. Steakley's *The Homosexual Emancipation Movement in Germany* was published as a volume in the Arno Press series *Homosexuality: Lesbians and Gay Men in Society, History and Literature,* edited by Jonathan Katz. Steakley's work is essentially on gay men's history but it is a useful introduction for anyone interested in the history of homosexuality in the last two centuries.[35] A valuable anthology of documents on lesbians has been edited and translated by Lillian Faderman and Brigitte Eriksson, *Lesbian-Feminism in Turn-of-the-Century Germany.*[36] The editors have provided a good introduction, though it is frustratingly short; the documents themselves are excerpts from autobiographical, literary, and lesbian liberation sources (by strict definition, all of these sources were concerned with lesbian self-liberation). Two selections are particularly welcome, one from Aimée Duc's novel *Are These Women?* and the other from Anna Rueling's "What Interest Does the Women's Movement Have in the Homosexual Question?"[37] Aimée Duc published her novel *Sind es Frauen? Roman über das dritte Geschlecht (Are These Women? A Novel about the Third Sex)* in 1901—it has now been reprinted in Germany[38]— and it is amazing how positive it was about lesbianism—in contrast, for example, to Radclyffe Hall's rather negative *The Well of Loneliness*, published in 1928. Duc's real name was Minna Wettstein-Adelt and another important work she wrote was *3½ Monate Fabrik-Arbeiterin. Eine praktische Studie (3½ Months as a Woman Factory Worker: A Practical Study)*.[39] Imitating the work of Paul Göhre, who was at that time a young social activist Protestant minister, she spent three and a half months working in a number of textile factories in Chemnitz (now Karl Marx Stadt) and then wrote about her experiences in this excellent firsthand observer's account; her middle-class bias is obvious but the work is nonetheless quite significant; given the paucity of sources on working-class women, it is an additional valuable resource that has all but been forgotten.[40]

The last major segment of this paper will be on the middle-class feminist movement, but before turning to that material, it is appropriate to delve into the intellectual and literary background and developments in women's education, issues important to the feminist movement in the nineteenth century and topics which are of current interest to scholars. In the past the feminist movement has been studied only within the narrowest organizational confines and its social context has been relatively ignored. Now a host of recent studies have begun to give equal treatment to the social history of middle- and upper-class women and this scholarship opens up a new world of exciting possibilities for future research. I should only caution that much of that work is still oriented to feminists rather than women in general and thus the same kind of imbalance exists in the literature on middle-class women that exists with working-class women, essentially for the same reason—the heavy reliance on "feminist" auto-biographies and periodicals which focus on the lives of eminent women.

In her essay in this collection entitled "Henriette Schleiermacher: A Woman in a Traditional Role," Gwendolyn E. Jensen takes a different approach. She investigates the life of a woman who was, to be sure, hardly "ordinary"; she could never have been that, given her husband's fame and busy public life. Yet like most middle-class women in that time and place, her world existed mainly in the private sphere of the family. In her study, Jensen does what feminist historians often have done, she uses old sources in new ways. She analyzes the extensive collection of letters between Henriette and her famous theologian husband, Friedrich Ernst Daniel Schleiermacher, as a basis for her study of Henriette. Her purpose was "to explore the two most important institutions in Henriette's life, marriage and religion." Interestingly, Henriette "did not consider motherhood pure, noble, holy, or any of the other qualities Ernst attached to being a parent"; ". . . her true vocation was marriage itself, rather than the work of the house or of parenting." In her conclusion Jensen rightly argues that marriage must be studied by historians as an institution in its own right because through such study we can learn more about the lives of the majority of middle-class women. "For Henriette, it was through marriage that she liberated herself." Jensen paints a picture of a woman who was satisfied, if not happy, with her "traditional" role in society. The subject matter of this essay should be a focus for further research.

A variety of sources, articles, and monographs have been published on the literary and intellectual history of women in the nineteenth century.[11] One monograph stands out as a model of good scholarship; it is well researched and it makes a major contribution by interpreting the intellectual and literary history of the *Vormärz* period (1815–48) from a feminist perspective. It is Renate Möhrmann's *Die andere Frau. Emanzipationsansätze deutscher Schriftstellerinnen im Vorfeld der Achtundvierziger-Revolution (The Other Woman: Emancipation Narratives of German Women Writers in the Period Immediately before the Revolution of 1848).*[42] Möhrmann begins by establishing the intellectual background; she reviews the status and the changes in women's education in the seventeenth and eighteenth centuries and then offers an overview of the *Vormärz* era in terms of attitudes toward women. But the main thrust of the book is a discussion of the "feminist" ideas of Luise Mühlbach, Ida Hahn-Hahn, Fanny Lewald, and Louise Aston. The study is additionally valuable because Möhrmann looks at the social and intellectual development of these women. She also explains why there were so many women writing in this particular period. Her analysis is sound from the point of view of both literary criticism and feminist theory. Möhrmann is certainly an expert on the literature of the period and the implications of her work are far-reaching. Her research sheds new light on the *Vormärz* period from a literary-history perspective; the role played by these women in the Young German Movement is fascinating. Just as importantly, Möhrmann has resurrected women writers of some distinction who have been forgotten or ignored by male scholars. Finally, she has provided a sophisticated analysis of the evolution of "feminist" ideas ("feminist" evidently means consciousness of women's unequal status in society and the yearning for new opportunities) which helps in understanding the coming of the "organized" feminist movement in the 1860s. Thus Möhrmann's work has more than re-created the world of literary women in the *Vormärz;* she has opened the way for a radical revision of German literary history and she has written an introduction to the "intellectual background" of the German feminist movement. This book will be a standard work for a long time to come.

Möhrmann has continued her research on the early nineteenth century in the essay she wrote for this collection entitled "The Reading Habits of Women in the *Vormärz*." She sought to reconstruct "the literary socialization of the female writer," and she went about that task by using autobiographies and memoirs of those early writers, the curriculum of upper-class girls' schools, the books on "advice to women" which were so common in that era, and finally the "aesthetics of literary criticism." This material was then evaluated dialectically and the result is a fascinating commentary on the circumstances that shaped the reading habits of middle- and upper-class women. Moreover, Möhrmann emphasizes that this group of writers was not chosen randomly but "represented the first generation of female writers in the history of German literature who no longer exercised their literary talent only occasionally or as an unrewarding hobby; they actually wrote on a professional basis." She discusses the family background of these women, the transition from a pre-industrial to an industrial economy and the impact of that evolution on the family, changing attitudes toward women and how that shaped the school syllabi, and perhaps most importantly, the actual literary works which society considered acceptable for young women to read. Möhrmann offers fascinating insights into literary socialization and the reading habits of this first generation of female writers.

Two other essays in this collection should be introduced at this time, as they are relevant to the preceding discussion; they are "Growing Up Female in the Nineteenth Century," by Juliane Jacobi-Dittrich, and "Hannah Arendt's Rahel Varnhagen," by Deborah Hertz. Both contribute to a better understanding of the social and intellectual history of German women. Jacobi-Dittrich looks at a most neglected aspect of women's history, namely, girlhood in the nineteenth century. She recognizes that it would be impossible to compare the experiences of middle- and upper-class girls with those of working-class origin, so she has limited her essay to the subject of the former. Relying on *Backfischliteratur* (manuals for girls written in the guise of novels) and autobiographies and autobiographical novels, she compares the lives of Fanny Lewald, Mathilde Franziska Anneke, Hedwig Dohm, Franziska Tiburtius, Helene Lange, Lily Braun, Marianne Weber, Gertrud Bäumer, and Elly Heuss-Knapp. She intentionally chose those women as she wanted to investigate women who led public lives and whose autobiographies "had a stated consciousness of the contradictions in their development." All these women were born between 1811 and 1881, and Jacobi-Dittrich argues that "between 1811 and 1900 the childhoods of middle-class girls exhibited similar patterns."[43] The essay takes up a number of issues, including socialization in the family, family relationships (with parents, siblings, and extended family), the emotional support provided by various family members, sexuality and relationships with their own and the opposite sex, searching for and selecting a husband, education, and a variety of childhood experiences. Jacobi-Dittrich draws fascinating conclusions about the childhood of these prominent German women, and the author maintains that "the identity of these women developed within a tension—between the accepted goals of socialization that were then prevalent and their intellectual interests—the tension between their desire for autonomy and their needs which conformed to the goals of socialization."

Deborah Hertz, in her "Hannah Arendt's Rahel Varnhagen," investigates both the life of Rahel Varnhagen and that of her famous twentieth-century biographer, Hannah Arendt. She thereby provides a double intellectual portrait, triple if one considers what it reveals about Hertz herself. It is a provocative approach to women's history. In so doing, Hertz offers new views of Arendt and of Varnhagen and her intellectual circle. Hertz seeks to renew interest in Arendt's work. She believes it is regrettable that the biography has remained obscure, because in her opinion the "reconstruction of the book's themes shows a crucial transition in Arendt's own intellectual history." Moreover, Hertz argues, "study of the book is useful in coming to terms not only with the author of the biography but also with its subject, Rahel Varnhagen herself. It is impossible to understand the significance of the Berlin salons for the female and the Jewish pasts in Germany without understanding Rahel Varnhagen."[44] Hertz has done interesting research on these two remarkable women.

A host of newly printed sources are now available on the literary and intellectual history of nineteenth-century women of the upper classes. These sources are being republished in a variety of forms that are not always satisfactory. Some have been merely reprinted in their original form, some have been put together around a particular theme, and others are selected works of an individual author; too often, however, with insufficient understanding or knowledge on the editor's part of the writer in question. Sometimes the excerpts are incomplete to the point of altering the meaning of the original work. Some have been introduced with brief editorial commentary and then no further information is provided. In other cases, there is more extensive introductory material but insufficient to make for a standard edition. Many lesser-known works are not being made available and few works are being printed in their entirety.

It is appropriate at this juncture to cite examples of such sources to illustrate these points; in turn, other examples will be discussed in the remaining pages of this essay. At one end of the spectrum, there is the new English-language edition of Ellen Key's biography of *Rahel Varnha-*

gen: A Portrait.[45] This volume is simply a photographic reprint of the 1913 edition. A biography of a prominent feminist, written by an equally prominent feminist from a later century, cries out for commentary. Ellen Key was incredibly influential in Germany and elsewhere in the West in her own time and it is remarkable that the present generation of feminist scholars have essentially ignored her; though that is perhaps understandable given Key's views on motherhood.

At the other end of the spectrum, a new anthology of the writings of Louise Otto-Peters has been edited by Ruth-Ellen Boetcher Joeres which is a model for future work. *Die Anfänge der deutschen Frauenbewegung. Louise Otto-Peters (The Beginnings of the German Women's Movement . . .)*[46] is a volume in the series published by the Fischer Taschenbuch Verlag, *Die Frau in der Gesellschaft. Texte und Lebensgeschichte (The Woman in Public Life: Texts and Life Histories)* edited by Gisela Brinker-Gabler—the quality of the volumes in the series is mixed but as a group they are extremely valuable. A number of factors make the Joeres volume useful. First, Joeres has devoted many years to the study of Louise Otto and this volume is the first product of that lengthy research.[47] (Extensive research is important so that an editor can acquire the expertise to judge which selections are indeed representative. There is too much of a rush to get original works by women in print to meet market demands.) Secondly, Joeres divides her material into logical chronological subdivisions and each section begins with a *Lebenstafel* (chronology), introductory biographical material, and some textual analysis. In turn, each document has its own brief introduction. Finally, there is a good bibliography of works published by Otto and secondary literature on her. Joeres notes in her introduction that she had wanted to include more of Otto's writings in this volume but could not because of the constraints of space. She hopes to publish a second volume and it would be helpful if the successor volume contains complete works, rather than excerpts as is the case with this effort.[48]

Yet another anthology is Renate Möhrmann's *Frauenemanzipation im deutschen Vormärz. Texte und Dokumente (Women's Emancipation in the German Vormärz: Texts and Documents)*.[49] The volume is valuable because it is a companion piece to Möhrmann's *Die andere Frau* and the selections were evidently chosen with her monograph in mind. It also has a good introduction and what the editor has called a "*Bio-bibliographischer Anhang*" (an appendix which contains biographical and bibliographical information); the latter makes the anthology a handy reference tool for further research. The volume has shortcomings. Because Möhrmann cites the writings of many women—Fanny Lewald, Malvida von Meysenbug, Louise Dittmar, Louise Otto-Peters, Louise Aston, Mathilde Franziska Anneke, Luise Mühlback, and Ida Hahn-Hahn—this short anthology can only be a brief introduction to their writings. Moreover, there is no additional explanatory material from the editor beyond the introduction—Möhrmann knows this material as well as anyone and her insights would have made for a well-rounded work.

A number of other recently republished works deserve notice. Fanny Lewald (1811–89), feminist, novelist, and political activist, published her autobiography in Berlin in 1861–62. Entitled *Meine Lebensgeschichte (My Life Story)*, it has now been reprinted by Fischer Verlag. Gisela Brinker-Gabler has edited it and she comments on the autobiography in a twenty-page introduction. Some explanatory footnotes are provided along with a bibliography. Another reviewer points out that there is a problem with this edition; it has been edited down to the point that its selections are not really representative. It is really asking too much to have complete editions if an author is that important?[50]

Using the same format as Joeres and Brinker-Gabler, Maria Wagner has edited a selection of the writings of Mathilde Franziska Anneke (1817–84), *Mathilde Franziska Anneke in Selbstzeugnissen und Dokumenten (Mathilde Franziska Anneke Through Her Own Eyes and Through Documents)*.[51] Clara Zetkin, as Lia Secci points out in her article "German Women Writers and the Revolution of 1848," called Anneke one of the three "Amazons of the German Revolution"[52] and Anneke was indeed a controversial figure in her own time because of her political activism in the revolution—she later went into exile in America. Extensive reprinting of women's writings such as these volumes is evidence of the current vitality of German women's history.[53]

Numerous new articles, many published in special issues of journals or in essay collections, have appeared recently that collectively are rewriting German literary history from a feminist viewpoint; equally important, these studies have brought neglected women writers into the limelight through the investigation of their writings. These developments should alter existing opinions about and interpretations of women's contributions to literature. Though this process is only in the early stages, these new works offer exciting options for future research. Two examples are a recent issue of *New German Critique* entitled *Women Writers and Critics*[54] and an essay collection edited by Susan L. Cocalis and Kay Goodman entitled *Beyond the Eternal Feminine: Critical Essays on Women and German Literature*.[55] Of the essays in *New German Critique*, two are quite representative of the new work being done on women and literature. They are: Ingeborg Drewitz, "Bettine von Arnim: A Portrait," and Kay Goodman, "Poesis and Praxis in Rahel Varnhagen's Letters."[56] Drewitz contends that Bettine von Arnim has generally been seen as the sister of Clemens Brentano, the wife of Archim von Arnim, and a devoted mother but has not been perceived as having a personality and a history in her own right. Drewitz seeks to rectify that injustice—she writes:

> But now, after the establishment of the Bettine von Arnim Archives, documents showed that she had used her energies not only for the cause of the "Göttingen Seven," but she had also initiated the first statistical account of the poverty-stricken in Berlin, championed the cause of the imprisoned Polish revolutionaries in Berlin, and fought against the censorship policies during the "Vormärz." The findings in the Archives have given rise to the profile of a highly modern and politically conscious woman—with all the difficulties that this entails in a woman's life.[57]

Bettine von Arnim is an excellent example of the countless political and literary women who have disappeared from history because of the bias of male historians and literary critics; Drewitz's reclamation history is indeed worthwhile. Kay Goodman makes another kind of contribution through her analysis of Rahel Varnhagen's letters. In her opening statement, she writes: "When German feminists trace their literary and cultural roots, they usually begin with the romantic women living around 1800."[58] Goodman, like Möhrmann, establishes the importance of these early-nineteenth-century women writers for the future of the organized feminist movement in the latter half of the century. In turn, Goodman, through her commentary on Rahel Varnhagen, illustrates the intellectual brilliance of her subject and by implication argues that the failure to investigate the ideas of these writers has left a significant gap in German literary and intellectual history. Her well-reasoned analysis makes a strong case for greater appreciation of Varnhagen's contribution to the intellectual life of her own time.

Cocalis and Goodman have brought together essays on the German literary tradition from the late eighteenth century to the present in their *Beyond the Eternal Feminine.* Only the introduction and a few of the seventeen essays can be evaluated here; readers are advised to consider some of the later essays in the collection for contemporary debates over literary and feminist criticism. In the introduction, "The Eternal Feminine Is Leading Us On," Cocalis and Goodman write:

> Traditional male views of women as Other, the Eternal Feminine, have formed the ideological foundations of Western patriarchal society and identified women as the natural repository of all the positive and negative attributes of the human race, the source of all hell or of any potential redeeming grace on earth. Insofar as they were postulated and received as universally valid laws of nature (biology as destiny) and insofar as they were essentially accepted as social norms by both men and women, such views served to locate any debate on the emancipation of women in an ahistorical context that often overshadowed the economic realities of

women's oppression. Moreover, even in its positive variants, the Eternal Feminine, as the locus of male visions of a humanitarian utopia, co-opts the subversive potential of women's oppression and denies women a positive utopian vision transcending patriarchy. Only insofar as women have been and are able to see themselves and the world without the blinding stereotypes that contribute to their exploitation, will they be able to envision a fundamentally radical and truly humanitarian utopia. We must therefore learn to recognize and analyze the images of woman that are propagated by patriarchal ideology so that we may begin to formulate alternative modes of living. The selection of essays in this volume reflects these concerns.[59]

The authors trace the evolution of such attitudes toward women in the late eighteenth and early nineteenth centuries that led to "a bourgeois system of values that accorded middle-class males the power in the private sphere that they had lacked in the feudal hierarchy."[60] Later sections of the essay follow the subdivisions of the essay collection as a whole: "New Voices in Mid-Century," "The 'Liberated Woman' of 1900," "Problematic Views," and "New Perspectives." Cocalis and Goodman have thus written more than just an introduction, they have provided a provocative commentary on women in the German literary tradition.

Other essays in the volume are equally interesting. Maria M. Wagner writes on "A German Writer and Feminist in Nineteenth-Century America: An Archival Study of Mathilde Franziska Anneke."[61] Wagner introduces her subject as the most prominent woman of the "Forty-eighters" (exiles to America after the 1848 Revolution), "who was well known among her contemporaries as a writer, educator, and feminist."[62] Wagner's main intent in the essay, after a brief discussion of Anneke's life in Germany, is to sketch out her career as a writer and politically active feminist in America. It is fascinating to reflect that this German woman was an early and staunch supporter of women's suffrage in America. Elke Frederiksen asks the question: "German Women Writers in the Nineteenth Century: Where Are They?"[63] She does not answer the question in a totally satisfactory way but she offers some explanations that are revealing. Part of the problem, she argues, stems from the failure of male scholars to include women writers in anthologies. Also, too many recent works emphasize analysis of female characters in works written by men; although that "constitutes an important part of feminist literary criticism and contributes decisively to the revisioning of traditional literary interpretation, we now must proceed a step further and begin research on the literature by nineteenth-century *women* writers."[64] Frederiksen advocates further a reevaluation of the lives and writings of writers such as Annette von Droste-Hülshoff and Bettine von Arnim, further research on the

Vormärz, and an examination of writers at the turn of the twentieth century, especially writers active in the feminist movement.

Three other important essays in the Cocalis and Goodman volume are contained in the section entitled "The 'Liberated Woman' of 1900." They are: "Laura Marholm and the Question of Female Nature," by Marilyn Scott-Jones; "Gabriele Reuter: Romantic and Realist," by Richard L. Johnson; and "Ricarda Huch and the German Women's Movement," by Miriam Frank. Only one of these literary figures is seen in a positive "feminist" light. Scott-Jones writes of Marholm: "Part of Marholm's ambivalent reception can be explained by her ambiguous interpretation of women in society and of female 'nature' and part of it by the fact that Marholm constantly contradicts herself. Although she was an elaborate and perceptive chronicler of female consciousness, she insisted that its function was submission to genuine maleness."[65] Miriam Frank says of Huch:

> She herself had broken through the sex barrier as a student, and in earlier writings had supported the movement towards professional equality. Now that she saw it as a part of the downfall of the patriarchal order, she judged it decadent and dangerous. Thus, she equated female emancipation with socialism; she was against them both because they sharpened the contradictions of an oppressive society. . . . Faith in the old values, maintenance of the patriarchal family system, and obedience to God and the State are the solutions she proposes.[66]

Only "Reuter," Johnson writes, "shared her vision of women's experience in over fifty years of fiction and nonfiction. If she has been neglected because she chose to write primarily about women, then in this second wave of feminism, she deserves to be taken seriously by feminist scholars who are reclaiming women's history and culture."[67]

Two essays in this collection further that reevaluation of women writers. Ruth-Ellen Boetcher Joeres writes of "Self-Conscious Histories: Biographies of German Women in the Nineteenth Century," and Lia Secci comments on "German Women Writers and the Revolution of 1848."[68] Joeres's essay is a study of biography writing of and by women during the years 1845–85; she is especially interested in Claire von Glümer, Louise Otto, Fanny Lewald, and Amely Bölte (among others). Joeres's comments on one of Louise Otto's works are representative of her essay as a whole. She writes:

> What is particularly significant here was Louise Otto's emphasis not only on the importance of telling women's lives, but on having women do the telling. She saw a clear distinction between the attitude of male and female biographers toward their female subjects, and in an echo of the middle-class (not to mention the early German feminist) emphasis in

the nineteenth century on the major importance of *Bildung* (education), there was at least an intimation that a more knowledgeable interpretation of women's lives by women would enable the female readers of such biographies to benefit from the newly-gained knowledge of their own heritage.

Joeres's study is unique because she has analyzed sources previously neglected; she brings them to life and in so doing provides a new focus for further research. In addition, Joeres offers new information on the evolution and intellectual development of the feminist movement.

Lia Secci's "German Women Writers and the Revolution of 1848" also investigates an area of women's history that has previously been inadequately studied. She argues that "in general, the part played by German women in 1848 has been ignored, partly because of the lack of attention given them in traditional histories and partly because of the intrinsic difficulty of finding original sources, many of which were destroyed by the censors, or kept in secret police archives." Her findings should radically revise many assumptions about women in the Revolution of 1848. Moreover, Secci's conclusions should shed some light on the question of why the German feminist movement was more politically conservative than other feminist movements in the West in the nineteenth century.[69] Essentially her essay is reclamation history at its best, detailing the political activities of women during the course of the revolution and reconstructing, through the use of autobiographies and early women's newspapers, the literary works of these remarkable women.

Three new volumes of sources on the first half of the nineteenth century should be mentioned at this juncture. Timothy F. Sellner has edited and translated Theodor Gottlieb von Hippel's *On Improving the Status of Women*, which was first published in Berlin in 1792 under the title *Über die bürgerliche Verbesserung der Weiber.*[70] Sellner wrote a useful introduction and he has provided important editorial commentary in extensive footnotes. Though Sellner has performed a real service with this edition, he has rightly been criticized for having deleted seventy-two pages of Hippel's writing and for having transposed many sentences in the text.[71] He has thereby undermined the validity of his own work. Ute Gerhard, Elisabeth Hannover-Drück, and Romina Schmitter have published selections from Louise Otto's newspaper—*"Dem Reich der Freiheit werb' ich Bürgerinnen." Die Frauen-Zeitung von Louise Otto* ("I Am Recruiting Women Citizens for the Empire of Liberty": Louise Otto's Women's Newspaper)[72]—the editors claim about a fifth of it (but only from the years 1849 and 1850; it was published until 1852, when it ceased publication because of the ban on women's political activities in Prussia). The editors wrote a solid introduction but provided no further editorial commentary on the material itself. Gerlinde Hummel-Haasis has edited an important anthology of women's sources on the Revolution of 1848: *Schwestern zerreisst eure Ketten. Zeugnisse zur Geschichte der Frauen in der Revolution von 1848/49 (Sisters, Break Your Chains: Documents on the History of Women in the Revolution of 1848–49).*[73] Hummel-Haasis offers a broad and representative array of women's writings from that period and she provides extensive footnotes and a bibliography. Her short two-page introduction is disappointing at best.

Joanne Schneider has done a study of "Enlightened Reforms and Bavarian Girls' Education: Tradition Through Innovation" for this collection, and it will serve to introduce a group of essays that is concerned with the education of German women in the nineteenth century. Schneider investigates one aspect of the reform era in Germany early in the century, "specifically, how the reforms in education related to public and private attitudes about women." Her research reveals more than just "attitudes towards women," however, as she comments on the curriculum of the first schools for women in Munich and she considers teaching training for females. She discusses as well the founding of the various girls' schools and how their emergence reflects the educational concerns of the bourgeoisie of that city in the first decades of the nineteenth century. Schneider's conclusions are fascinating. For example, she argues: "The stereotypes of amusing, charming but frivolous aristocratic females and the industrious, practical, hard-working middle class women were fixtures in Bavarian society. The reformed government under Montgelas and his successors sought to preserve many social continuities through modernized political institutions. Through more efficient means, traditional society with its limitations placed on women was strengthened."

A limited number of new monographs and journal articles have been written on women's education in Germany in the nineteenth century; the work is of high quality but it is disappointing that more has not been done.[74] Six articles deserve a brief mention, as collectively they serve as a useful and sophisticated introduction to the history of women's education. This material provides some understanding of why this issue was central to the feminist movement. The relationship between the reality of women's lives—the social history of their experiences—and the demands put forth by the organized feminist movement becomes quite evident. Most importantly, these studies reveal a dismal, if not depressing, history of discrimination that was shaped largely by an educational philosophy that was remarkably consistent and narrow-minded in its view of the role of women in society; a view that saw women's needs solely in terms of the family with no thought of educating minds for any manner of creative thinking. What is amazing is the number of women who managed to overcome these obstacles.

Karin Meiners has published excerpts from an interesting early-

nineteenth-century document, "'Plan und Einrichtung einer bürger-
lichen Töchterschule und Erziehungsanstalt.' Aus dem Testament der
Anna Barbara von Stetten" ("'A Design for and Construction of a Middle-
Class Girls' School and Educational Establishment': From the Will of
Anna Barbara von Stetten").[75] She has written a valuable introduction that
reviews the character of women's education in the eighteenth century.
Meiners also analyzes some aspects of the document itself, and she adds
extensive explanatory footnotes. The actual document is the 1803 will of a
widowed patrician of the city of Augsburg who left a generous bequest for
the establishment of a girls' school upon her death, which came in 1805.
The school opened in 1806. Her *Plan* was lengthy and Meiners has
selected substantive pieces of it (though only a small part of the whole). It
is a fascinating commentary on women's education seen from an early-
nineteenth-century vantage point. It also includes a detailed outline of
the staff, salaries, etc., as well as a discussion of the proposed curriculum.

Catherine M. Prelinger has written on "Religious Dissent, Women's
Rights, and the Hamburger Hochschule fuer das weibliche Geschlecht in
Mid-Nineteenth-Century Germany." Prelinger makes a number of "connections." She writes: "The German women's movement, like so much
else that was progressive in modern German history, had its origins during the decade culminating in the revolution of 1848."[76] She then traces an
important but forgotten link, "radical separatist congregations which appeared in both the Roman Catholic and Protestant communions during
these years."[77] So in addition to being about the origins of the feminist
movement and women's involvement in the church—a subject essentially
no one has written about—Prelinger's essay deals with education through
her analysis of this Hamburg college for women. In her conclusion Prelinger maintains:

> German-catholicism and the kind of feminism it fostered shared the
> ambivalence of the city. At the intellectual level, the movement was
> modern; rational values supplanted those of the supernatural. But wher-
> ever the separatists succeeded, they succeeded because their commit-
> ment to congregationalism won for them the support of local and
> traditional interests: representatives of the old Mittelstand who treas-
> ured individuality and feared the uniformity of the modern state and the
> intrusion of capitalism; town officials and tradesmen who wanted to
> continue to control their own affairs. The commitment to modernism in
> education coupled with a fine appreciation of the hazards of economic
> progress characterized the outlook of the Hamburg women.[78]

Two articles by George Bernstein and Lottelore Bernstein, "Attitudes
Toward Women's Education in Germany, 1870–1914," and "The Curriculum for German Girls' Schools, 1870–1914,"[79] are valuable for an in-

troduction to women's education in the latter part of the nineteenth and early part of the twentieth centuries. The first essay, "Attitudes Toward Women's Education in Germany, 1870–1914," is indeed that, a study of male attitudes toward women's education. The material is extremely informative, if not depressing; it makes one recognize just how reactionary male educators were in their thinking about women. There are few women in this story and so this work is more about men's views than women's experiences (that is not to deny that the former often was successful in shaping the latter). The Bernsteins write:

> In the context of German history and society, there was a strong consensus among the educated bourgeoisie that high priority be given to the individual personality. This enabled educated women to see themselves partially as heirs to the classical tradition. Beyond this, however, it made possible a strong emphasis on the individual without giving equal attention to any rigorous analysis of Germany's social system. The humanist tradition with which the bourgeois women's movement identified and from which it believed itself to draw sustenance made difficult, if not impossible, any identification with the educational aspirations of any social groups below the middle class. In some respects many of the participants in the educational reform movement clung to traditional views about women, but at the same time their energy and organizational abilities made possible the changes in women's education which appeared in the generation preceding World War I.[80]

The second article by the Bernsteins is the more valuable of the two, as it has women as the focus of the investigation. The essay "The Curriculum of German Girls' Schools, 1870–1914," discusses the growth of girls' schools, the actual curriculum of these schools, various conferences concerned with education for girls, and the eventual admission of women into the universities. The Bernsteins report that in the case of girls' upper schools *(höhere Töchterschulen)* there were perhaps 22 of them in Prussia before 1820; "by 1901, there were 869 private and public girls' schools in Prussia, out of a total in Germany of more than 1,133."[81] The Bernsteins do another service by discussing the status of women teachers in the schools. In the elementary schools, for example, by 1901 there were 13,866 women teachers and 76,342 men.[82] While women were dominant in private schools, the principals were generally male and in the public schools teachers and administrators were mainly men. As one might imagine, the salaries of women teachers were also much lower than men's. Finally, the essay also details women's enrollment in the universities in the period right before World War I when women were finally allowed to matriculate in German universities—a long overdue victory in higher education had been achieved.

Two articles by James C. Albisetti are also valuable. They are: "Could

Separate Be Equal? Helene Lange and Women's Education in Imperial Germany" and "The Fight for Female Physicians in Imperial Germany."[83] The first is the more important of the two, as it focuses on the role of Helene Lange in the fight to secure better educational opportunities for women, and Albisetti makes a strong case for a more positive evaluation of Lange's contribution to education and the women's movement. Albisetti reviews the evolution of women's educational institutions, especially in the period of Lange's influential pamphlet, the "Yellow Brochure," which she published in 1887. Lange was the first to admit "that the demands of the . . . 'Yellow Brochure' were conservative in nature, calling for a return to an earlier practice of girls being educated primarily by women. She also accepted at this time the traditional view of the woman's role in upper-class society. 'Create better teachers for us,' Lange argued, and 'we will have better mothers and, through them, better human beings.' "[84] But Lange's views continued to change and Albisetti sees that evolution in a favorable light. He emphasizes the positive impact of travel to England—where she met English feminists—on her thinking and her role in opening the *Realkurse,* a kind of substitute girls' Gymnasium. The essay also discusses various government decrees and how they affected women's education in the period before 1914. Albisetti concludes that, despite charges against Lange that she was too conservative,

> through her insistence that girls be educated for their own personal fulfillment rather than for the sake of their future husbands, her work for increased education and career opportunities, and her ultimate conviction that specifically feminine education could not be equal, Helene Lange contributed more to the improvement of the position of women in German society than did most of the more radical feminists of her day.[85]

Albisetti's second essay, "The Fight for Female Physicians in Imperial Germany," is also a fine piece of research but less useful only in that it deals primarily with the role of men in the struggle by women to study and practice medicine in Germany. Albisetti reviews how women were first forced to study medicine in Switzerland and then the fight that followed over whether they could practice in Germany. He reviews the growth of the feminist movement in Germany and how that related to the issue of women's work and the debate over whether medicine was a "suitable" occupation for women. "By far the most compelling and most influential argument for opening just the medical profession to German women was that made by Mathilde Weber: female physicians were needed to treat women. This stance did not make the issue one of women's rights, but of the right to choose their physicians rather than their careers."[86] Albisetti then highlights the various male arguments against women in medicine and how women used those arguments to advocate their cause. Moreover, he shows how women were able, because of the prevailing attitudes toward women and work, to use their admission to the medical profession as a rationale for access to other professions.

Before turning to new material on the feminist movement in the nineteenth century, it is appropriate to introduce the three essays in this collection that have not yet been discussed. They are concerned with women who sought solutions to social problems or who were active in women's politics; this material is important, as it provides a partial explanation of what motivated women to become involved in "feminist" issues. The intellectual origins of the organized feminist movement that have been discussed in the preceding pages and the insights into motivations that are contained in these three essays comprise the background history that is inadequately covered in the two monographs on the feminist movement that have appeared recently. They are: Richard J. Evans, *The Feminist Movement in Germany, 1894–1933*, and Barbara Greven-Aschoff, *Die bürgerliche Frauenbewegung in Deutschland, 1894–1933 (The Middle-Class Women's Movement in Germany, 1894–1933)*.[87] The discussion of these two books will conclude this essay, but it is interesting to observe that the three essays are about activist women who were involved in women's concerns; the authors of these essays explain what prompted the women in question to devote their lives to improving their own and other women's lives. These studies will have to be replicated many times over for the social history of the feminist movement to come into better focus; this will be necessary for both the leadership and the rank and file of the movement, the rank and file most of all.

Catherine M. Prelinger has done a study on "Prelude to Consciousness: Amalie Sieveking and the Female Association for the Care of the Poor and the Sick." Prelinger argues that "a perennial task for the historian of women is the reassessment of preconditions for the development of feminism and the identification of circumstances under which women can function independently to initiate social change in their own behalf." In this essay, which is based on extensive archival research in Hamburg, Prelinger has done just that in drawing her portrait of a remarkable woman from the first half of the nineteenth century, Amalie Sieveking (1794–1859). According to Prelinger, Sieveking has been ignored because her views seem inconsistent with modern feminist thinking. Yet Prelinger believes that Sieveking played an important role in the liberation of women by making philanthropic activities available to them at a time when there was no such tradition in Germany. Sieveking was a member of the Hamburg patriciate who became involved in charitable activities as a result of "a campaign launched by the press in 1830 to identify and publicize the failure of municipal poor relief in the city." The second reason "was the cholera epidemic of 1831." Sieveking had long been a critic of upper-class women who were only concerned with an endless round of social activities. She was of the opinion that their time "could be more profitably spent in charitable enterprise, a route to the kind of self-esteem denied them by the society of the period." Moreover, Sieveking had long been interested in establishing a religious order for Protestant women in Germany. Thus "on May 23, 1832, she was joined by twelve other women to found the Female Association for the Care of the Poor and the Sick, a society for benevolent visiting." In reviewing the history of that organization Prelinger shows how Sieveking was able to juggle two apparently incompatible social philosophies, one which upheld the contemporary exploitation of the poor, the other which rejected the contemporary oppression of women. In addition, she traces the growth of Sieveking's work and the creation of a small network of similar organizations across Germany. Prelinger has opened a fascinating area of inquiry into women's charitable and religious activities in the first half of the nineteenth century.

Stanley Zucker investigates "Female Political Opposition in Pre-1848 Germany: The Role of Kathinka Zitz-Halein"; his work grows out of extensive archival research in Mainz.[88] He is another in a chorus of voices that pushes back the date of the beginning of the feminist movement. He argues: "Writing the history of German women's political and civic activities around the middle of the nineteenth century has only recently begun. But already it is clear that the generally accepted thesis that the women's rights movement or women's political activism begins in the 1860s is in need of serious revision." In evaluating Zitz-Halein's life, Zucker seeks motivations. He emphasizes Zitz-Halein's middle-class family background and the fact that her home life became intolerable for her. He also looks at her work experiences and unhappy marriage; all of these circumstances, Zucker argues, helped awaken her to the injustices suffered by women. Finally, he discusses the social and political atmosphere in Mainz, which also helps explain her emergence as a political activist and writer. Zucker demonstrates that Zitz-Halein was not a radical feminist, but she was a prominent figure, and as a role model she probably did more to raise women's consciousness than many feminists. His conclusions should be a stimulus for further research. He writes:

> The examination of several main currents in Kathinka Zitz-Halein's life suggests that a pronounced feminist ideology was not a prerequisite to involvement in the struggle for political progress in Germany. And the widespread political activities by women in 1848–49 reinforce this conclusion. Zitz-Halein's world was formed not only by her sex but by her family, city, literary talent, and most of all by her character. It cautions us

not to ignore those women whose feminist consciousness does not seem to be highly developed but whose political awareness was.

This essay (and Zucker's "German Women and the Revolution of 1848: Kathinka Zitz-Halein and the Humania Association"[89]), like a number of others that have been reviewed in this introduction, point to an obvious conclusion: the failure of the 1848 revolution had an inordinately negative impact on the future course of the feminist movement in Germany, at least in political terms. The revolution and the post-revolutionary period will have to be studied further, and then the ramifications of other European revolutions in 1848 will have to be carefully considered as well, in order to understand the relationship between revolution and the emergence of the feminist movement.

Alfred G. Meyer's "The Radicalization of Lily Braun" is, as the title implies, concerned with her radicalization; the evolution of her political and feminist views. For twenty-five years Lily Braun (von Kretschmann) lived the sheltered life of an aristocrat's daughter. Her life was enmeshed in the social whirl of the aristocracy—her father was a Prussian general. The search for an eligible husband in the upper-class marriage market had to be, because of prevailing social norms, the focus of her existence.[90] But she rebelled against that world and became involved in a circle of people who supported radical causes, and she married out of her social class. Meyer says of these developments:

> This independence more and more alienated her from her family, and her family from her. While her parents doubtless rejoiced in her ability to earn money by writing, they were alarmed and offended by what she wrote and where she published. They disapproved of her new friends and associates and strongly objected to her marrying a professed atheist and socialist, and an impotent wheelchair patient to boot. They really expected her to stay at home as a dutiful daughter who would help her mother run the household.

She became interested in feminist issues and eventually joined the Social Democratic Party. Meyer seeks to answer a number of questions. What led her to opt for revolutionary feminism and socialism? Why did she give up a life of ease to take up revolutionary politics? What was it in her upbringing that might help explain that transformation? Meyer based his study on her published memoirs and unpublished diaries and letters; his conclusions are complex and fascinating. He displays great knowledge of his subject and a keen understanding of political and social life in Imperial Germany. His biography of the young Lily Braun, one of the most remarkable women of her time, brings her to life.

Before turning to the two monographs on the feminist movement, some other recently published sources should be mentioned. Two English translations of feminist works have been reprinted in their original form with no further editing—Kaethe Schirmacher's *The Modern Woman's Rights Movement: A Historical Survey* and Hedwig Dohm's *Women's Nature and Privilege.*[91] In Germany, a new anthology of documents goes a long way toward superseding the second volume of Margrit Twellmann's two-volume *Die deutsche Frauenbewegung. Ihre Anfänge und erste Entwicklung, 1843–1889 (The German Women's Movement: Its Beginning and Early Development, 1843–1889).*[92] Twellmann's second volume, a source book, has often been criticized for containing too many documents that are only partial versions of the originals. A new anthology is considerably more valuable; it is *Die Frauenfrage in Deutschland, 1865–1915. Texte und Dokumente (The Women's Question in Germany, 1865–1915: Texts and Documents),* edited by Elke Frederiksen.[93] Frederiksen's volume is unique, as it juxtaposes documents on the middle-class and working-class feminist movement, making for fascinating reading. All in all, the selections are well chosen and the volume as a whole is well organized. Frederiksen has written an excellent introduction and at the end of the volume she provides biographical and bibliographical information on the authors of the selections. Essentially the only fault with the volume is that individual sections and documents have no introductory material, making them more difficult to use for readers not familiar with all the material. Nonetheless, the anthology is perhaps the best available on the feminist movement.

It is fitting to complete this review of new literature with comments on the Evans and Greven-Aschoff volumes, two absolutely first-rate studies. Both are based on extensive archival research and are well written, and taken together, they offer a detailed and sophisticated introduction to the first feminist movement in Germany. Greven-Aschoff's study should be translated into English. The two volumes have a number of factors in common. They are essentially organizational histories, with only minimal discussion of the ideology of the movement and only brief biographical portraits of the most prominent leaders. Neither volume really offers detailed information on organizatons at the local level or their membership. Both have concluding sections on the Weimar period, and the collapse of the feminist movement with the establishment of Hitler's dictatorship, but neither volume covers that period from 1918 to 1933 adequately. Much additional work will have to be done on the Weimar era.[94]

There are differences between the two studies. As to the Evans volume, he was indeed the first to reconstruct the history of the feminist movement from the archival sources and he must be given credit for that remarkable achievement. However, his approach is "traditional" in terms of political history in Imperial Germany. He sees the emergence of the feminist movement within the framework of the politics of the authoritarian, militaristic state of the Bismarckian and Wilhelmine eras (1871–1918). Given that, he presents, it seems to me, male political history as the backdrop for women's history, which is inadequate to explain the ramifications of the women's movement; women's experiences should be the central causal factor. Placing women's political history within the framework of male political history is too much of an intellectual juggling act. Evans describes the purpose of his study:

> It seeks to contribute to the comparative study of feminism by showing, among other things, that feminism cannot be properly understood unless it is seen as an integral part of the social and political system within which it sought to achieve its aims. The closest ties of feminism in the 19th and early 20th centuries, it suggests, were to bourgeois liberalism, and it is to the success or failure of this creed, itself dependent on wider political and social circumstances, that its fate was linked. Too often, histories of feminism proceed as if feminists everywhere meant the same thing when they spoke of the emancipation of women, and assume that undifferentiated male prejudice was all that stood between them and the achievement of their aims.[95]

Perhaps Evans is entirely correct in what he argues but he has probably gone too far the other way by writing women's history without adequately describing the social history of women's experiences. He also places great emphasis on the ultimate failure of the feminist movement, which seems to overshadow its accomplishments in his thinking. In that vein, he asserts that the movement became ever more conservative after 1908 and he makes it appear rather monolithic in its ideology and actions.

Greven-Aschoff takes quite a different approach in her study; she was able to take advantage of Evans's work. She sought to integrate the social history of women's lives, especially family life and economic circumstances related to work and class; that background history (the first quarter of the text is devoted to explaining the social reality of women's position in society) makes later sections of her treatise more meaningful than Evans's work since he stressed strictly male political history. It has already been noted that there is far too little work on the issue of women and work; though that is not the central focus of Greven-Aschoff's study, her well-reasoned discussion of work-related problems makes her overall analysis of the feminist movement more rational. Her explanation of the emergence of the feminist movement in the latter half of the nineteenth century, given that it is framed by the social history of middle-class women, makes her treatise the most important study yet done. If one were to criticize her social history, that critique would be in the same vein as that leveled at Richebächer. Social historians in Germany today sometimes describe the impact of industrialization in terms of large social forces that they claim shape the lives of individuals. But they then do not adequately integrate into their analysis the more mundane issues revolving around daily living. Greven-Aschoff too tends to put insufficient emphasis on the lives of the central characters of her story, leaving the reader still in the dark about individual feminists and the reasons for their involvement in feminist politics. Yet when she discusses the organizational history of the movement, she makes a fascinating contribution through her division of women's organizations into three main types: occupational and educational, charitable and social reform, and "general" women's groups. In so doing, she clarifies many issues. She also makes the point (and she makes a good case for it) that the feminist movement was far more heterogeneous in its ideology than Evans's study has indicated. But criticisms aside, the books by Evans and Greven-Aschoff are both models of good scholarship.

In concluding this essay, a number of summary remarks are in order. The number of new works on German women in the nineteenth century that have appeared in the past decade (and especially in the past five years) is remarkable. Significantly the quality of that work is high, attesting to the emergence (one should say, reemergence) of a sophisticated and now well-established subfield of German and women's history. Research is being done on both sides of the Atlantic and there has been a real exchange of ideas—the field is truly international in scope, as is this essay collection. Moreover, a broad array of differing approaches to the study of German women's history are in evidence which reflect traditional, feminist, and new social history perspectives. These studies reveal that a fascinating variety of topics on many aspects of women's lives are being researched. They have been based on both published and archival sources. A host of sources have been reprinted or printed for the first time and, increasingly, scholars in the field are literally being overwhelmed with documents. Old myths about the lack of sources pertaining to women's history have been thoroughly debunked. Perhaps at no point has so much new and startling information been disclosed about German history in the nineteenth century.

One must be cautious nonetheless about the future of this field. It is questionable whether a true breakthrough has been made—is the field still a "ghettoized" discipline or has the larger male-biased historical profession been educated to recognize the inherent value of this material? Ways must be found to integrate women's history into the larger body of historical knowledge. In terms of the field itself, only the bare outlines of women's lives have been revealed; years if not decades of work will be needed to reconstruct and write a detailed history of German women. More often than not, only the experiences of "feminist worthies" are being studied; ordinary women still escape the purview of scholars. Many areas of inquiry have not been studied at all or have been given only minimal treatment; sexuality and women not congenial to contemporary twentieth-century feminists are good examples. The process of the reconstruction of source materials is a long way from being complete. Rare published sources and archival materials must be made available to scholars. The publication of those documents must be done in a more careful and purposeful way. Complete works must be published and anthologies must be organized and edited in a way to make them more useful to a variety of specialists and nonspecialists. These remarks should not be construed as overly negative. The discipline of women's history has made incredible gains and it has contributed in a most positive way to the larger discipline of history—Clio is not only having her consciousness raised, she must have a smile on her face.

NOTES

1. I would urge readers to consult the English-language bibliography on European and American women at the end of this volume for English-language works on German women, as well as the notes to all the essays that comprise this collection, as they cite an impressive array of German-language works.

Works by scholars in the United States and the United Kingdom are now readily available in Germany, and some works have been translated. See, for example, the essay collection edited by Claudia Honegger and Bettina Heintz, *Listen der Ohnmacht. Zur Sozialgeschichte weiblicher Widerstandsformen* (Frankfurt, 1981), which includes translations of writings by Joan W. Scott and Louise Tilly, Peter N. Stearns, Carroll Smith-Rosenberg, and Mary P. Ryan, among others. Some nineteenth-century feminist writings (American and European) have been edited and translated for a two-volume German documents book: Hannelore Schröder, ed., *Die Frau ist frei geboren. Texte zur Frauenemanzipation*, vol. 1: *1789 bis 1870*, and vol. 2: *1870 bis 1918* (Munich, 1979–81).

2. Nonetheless a number of volumes have grown out of conferences on women. See, for example, *Frauen und Wissenschaft. Beiträge zur Berliner Sommeruniversität für Frauen. Juli 1976*, ed. by Gruppe Berliner Dozentinnen (2nd ed.; Berlin, 1977); *Frauen als bezahlte und unbezahlte Arbeitskräfte. Beiträge zur 2. Berliner Sommeruniversität Okt. 1977*, Autorinnenkollektiv (Berlin, 1978); and *Frauengeschichte. beiträge 5 zur feministischen theorie und praxis*, Dokumentation des 3. Historikerinnentreffens in Bielefeld, April 81, ed. by "Sozialwissenschaftliche Forschung und Praxis für Frauen e. V" (Munich, 1981). These are general essay collections much like the earlier work done in America when there were not enough specialists in any one period to contribute to a more

defined set of essays. See, for example, *Clio's Consciousness Raised: New Perspectives on the History of Women*, ed. by Mary S. Hartman and Lois Banner (New York, 1974); and *Liberating Women's History: Theoretical and Critical Essays*, ed. by Berenice A. Carroll (Urbana, Ill., 1976). Two other important essay collections are somewhat more narrowly focused (but still too eclectic, it seems to me): *Frauen in der Geschichte I. Frauenrechte und die gesellschaftliche Arbeit der Frauen im Wandel. Fachwissenschaftliche und fachdidaktische Studien zur Geschichte der Frauen*, ed. by Annette Kuhn and Gerhard Schneider (2nd ed.; Düsseldorf, 1982); and *Frauen in der Geschichte II. Fachwissenschaftliche und fachdidaktische Beiträge zur Sozialgeschichte der Frauen vom frühen Mittelalter bis zur Gegenwart*, ed. by Annette Kuhn and Jörn Rüsen (Düsseldorf, 1982). Both of these works are published by Schwann Verlag and a third volume will be appearing shortly: *"Wissen heisst leben." Frauen in der Geschichte* (forthcoming, late 1983 or 1984); I understand that a fourth volume is underway as well. In addition, see Karin Hausen, ed., *Frauen suchen ihre Geschichte: Studien zum 19. und 20. Jahrhundert* (Munich, in press).

3. Even when German scholars began publishing actively on women, work on medieval and early modern women was slow to appear. In the essay collection edited by Susan Mosher Stuard, *Women in Medieval Society* (Philadelphia, 1976), only a little material on Germany was contained in the essays by David Herlihy, "Land, Family and Women in Continental Europe, 701–1200," and Jo-Ann McNamara and Suzanne F. Wemple, "Marriage and Divorce in the Frankish Kingdom." British and American medievalists have written articles on German women but no monograph examines early medieval German women; Suzanne Fonay Wemple has done a study of Frankish women, *Women in Frankish Society: Marriage and the Cloister, 500 to 900* (Philadelphia, 1981). There is a new book on the later period, Margret Wensky, *Die Stellung der Frau in der stadtkölnischen Wirtschaft im Spätmittelalter* (Cologne, 1980), and a number of articles: Peter Ketsch, "Aspekte der rechtlichen und politisch-gesellschaftlichen Situation von Frauen im frühen Mittelalter (500–1150)," in *Frauen in der Geschichte II*, ed. by Kuhn and Rüsen; Barbara Kroemer, "Von Kauffrauen, Beamtinnen, Ärztinnen— erwerbstätige Frauen in deutschen mittelalterlichen Städten," in ibid.; Barbara Händler-Lachmann, "Die Berufstätigkeit der Frau in den deutschen Städten des Spätmittelalters und der beginnenden Neuzeit," *Hessische Jahrbücher für Landesgeschichte*, 30 (1980), pp. 131–75; Edith Ennen, "Die Frau in der mittelalterlichen Stadtgesellschaft Mitteleuropas," *Hansische Geschichtsblätter*, 98 (1980), pp. 1–22. See also some English-language work: Leslie W. Rabine, "The Establishment of Patriarchy in Tristan and Isolde," *Women's Studies*, 7 (1980), pp. 19–38; Bernhard Scholz, "Hildegard von Bingen on the Nature of Woman," *American Benedictine Review*, 31 (1980), pp. 361–83; Charles T. Wood, "The Doctor's Dilemma: Sin, Salvation, and the Menstrual Cycle in Medieval Thought," *Speculum*, 56 (1981), pp. 710–27. There are also some studies of the early modern period (see the bibliography at the end of this book for English titles): Dagmar Birkelbach, Christiane Eifert, and Sabine Lueken, "Zur Entwicklung des Hebammenwesens vom 14. bis zum 16. Jahrhundert am Beispiel der Regensburger Hebammenordnungen," in *Frauengeschichte. Beiträge 5*; Joanna Hodge, "Hexen und die Enstehung der modernen Rationalität," in ibid.; Harmut

Lehman, "Hexenverfolgungen und Hexenprozesse im Alten Reich zwischen Reformation und Aufklärung," *Jahrbuch des Instituts für deutsche Geschichte*, 7 (1978), pp. 13–70; Brigitte Rauer, "Hexenwahn—Frauenverfolgung zu Beginn der Neuzeit—ein Beitrag zur Frauengeschichte im Unterricht," in *Frauen in der Geschichte II*, ed. by Kuhn and Rüsen; Gerhard Schormann, *Hexenprozesse in Deutschland* (Göttingen, 1981); Uta Ottmüller, "Mutter und Wicklekind in der vormedikalisierten Gesellschaft des deutschsprachigen Raums (ab ca. 500)," in *Frauengeschichte. Beiträge 5;* Lore Sporhan-Kremple, "Susanna Maria Sandart und ihre Familie: Eine Nürnberger Kupferstecherin und Zeichnerin im Zeitalter des Barock," *Archiv für Geschichte des Buchwesens*, 21 (1980), pp. 965–1004; Barbara Becker-Cantarino, ed., *Die Frau von der Reformation zur Romantik*, Modern German Studies, vol. 4 (Bonn, 1980). New work on literature is also being done: see, for example, Blanca-Maria Rudhart, *Die Frauen in Shakespeares Königsdramen* (Frankfurt, 1982). There are no anthologies of documents on German women such as *Women: From the Greeks to the French Revolution*, ed. by Susan Groag Bell (Belmont, Calif., 1973), or *Not in God's Image: Women in History from the Greeks to the Victorians*, ed. by Julia O'Faolain and Lauro Martines (New York, 1973).

Only a few review articles have been written on this massive new literature on German women—most of which, it would seem, have been penned by Richard J. Evans, that one-person library on German studies. As was the case with the essay collections mentioned earlier, these reviews have been too undifferentiated (including those by Evans). We now need topical reviews on such problems as women and work and the feminist movement, etc. See Ruth Schlette, "Neue Veröffentlichungen zur Geschichte der Frauenbewegung," *Archiv für Sozialgeschichte*, 14 (1974), pp. 631–36; Tim Mason, "Frauenarbeit im NS-Staat," *Archiv für Sozialgeschichte*, 19 (1979), pp. 579–84; Eleanor S. Riemer and John C. Fout, "Women's History: Recent Journal Articles," *Trends in History*, 1 (1979), pp. 3–22; Richard J. Evans, "Women's history: The Limits of Reclamation," *Social History*, 5 (1980), pp. 273–81; Richard J. Evans, "Modernization Theory and Women's History," *Archiv für Sozialgeschichte*, 20 (1980), pp. 492–514; Richard J. Evans, "The History of European Women: A Critical Survey of Recent Research," *The Journal of Modern History*, 52 (1980), pp. 656–75; a controversial article by Patricia Hilden, "Women's History: The Second Wave," *The Historical Journal*, 25 (1982), pp. 501–12; and an angry reply by Brian Harrison and James McMillan, "Some Feminist Betrayals of Women's History," *The Historical Journal*, 26 (1983), pp. 375–89; for East German literature, see Hans-Jürgen Arendt and Fritz Staude, "Forschungen zur Geschichte der Frauenbewegung," *Zeitschrift für Geschichtswissenschaft*, 28 (Sonderband, 1980), pp. 707–19.

For information on archival material, there is no German equivalent of Andrea Hinding et al., eds., *Women's History Sources: A Guide to Archives and Manuscript Collections in the United States*, 2 vols. (New York, 1979), but there is an important article by Richard J. Evans, "Feminism and Female Emancipation in Germany, 1870–1945: Sources, Methods, and Problems of Research," *Central European History*, 9 (1976), pp. 323–51. Important bibliographies on archival material give scant attention to women's sources, for example, *Archivbestände zur Wirtschafts- und Sozialgeschichte der Weimarer Republik. Übersicht über*

Quellen in Archiven der Bundesrepublik Deutschland, ed. by Thomas Trumpp, Renate Köhne, et al. (Boppard am Rhein, 1979).

For bibliographies on German women, the standard work is still Hans Sveistrup and Agnes von Zahn-Harnack, eds., *Die Frauenfrage in Deutschland. Strömungen und Gegenströmungen, 1790–1930* (Burg, 1934). A second edition was published in 1961 (Tübingen) but it was not revised. Though massive, that bibliography has many gaps. That is also true for successor volumes. The most recent is vol. 10 in the series, edited by the Deutscher Akademikerinnenbund, *Die Frauenfrage in Deutschland: Bibliographie*, vol. 10: *1931–1980* (Munich, 1982). (The volumes are not well known and the OCLC computer lists only vols. 1, 2, 3, 5, and 7 extant in U.S. libraries.) There are three recent short bibliographies: see Ute Frevert and Christian Oemisch, "Die Frau in der Alten Welt," and Hans Heinrich Kaminsky, "Die Frau in Recht und Gesellschaft des Mittelalters," in *Frauen in der Geschichte I*, ed. by Kuhn and Schneider. See also Barbara Maas, "Neuere Literatur zur Sozialgeschichte der Frau, 1978–82," in *Frauen in der Geschichte II*, ed. by Kuhn and Rüsen. For East German material, see Ingrid and Hans-Jürgen Arendt, eds., *Bibliographie zur Geschichte des Kampfes der deutschen Arbeiterklasse für die Befreiung der Frau und zur Rolle der Frau in der deutschen Arbeiterbewegung. Von den Anfängen bis 1970* (Leipzig, 1974). My thanks to Renate Bridenthal, who made that latter bibliography available to me.

4. Many important older works have been ignored. Just on the topic of women and work, for example, there are studies such as Gertrude Dyhrenfurth, *Die hausindustriellen Arbeiterinnen in der Berliner Blusen-, Unterrock-, Schürzen- und Tricotkonfektion* (Leipzig, 1898); Rose Otto, *Über Fabrikarbeit verheirateter Frauen* (Stuttgart, 1910); and Rosa Kempf, *Das Leben der jungen Fabrikmädchen in München. Die soziale und wirtschaftliche Lage ihrer Familie, ihr Berufsleben und ihre persönlichen Verhältnisse*. Schriften des Vereins für Sozialpolitik, vol. 135, pt. 2 (Leipzig, 1911).

5. One important collection of books on microfilm is *History of Women* (Research Publications, Inc., New Haven, Conn.) which includes many works by German women. A second collection which contains both books and many women's periodicals, including many German ones, is the Gerritsen Collection published by the Microfilm Corporation of America on microfiche. See Janet Sharistanin et al., "The (Dr. Aletta H. Jacobs) Gerritsen Collection: The University of Kansas," *Feminist Studies*, 3 (1970), pp. 200–6. What appears to be a very ambitious new collection on microfiche is being edited by Richard J. Evans. It will be on "Women's Movements in Germany" and will contain periodicals, printed sources, and unpublished archival materials. It is being published by IDC—Inter Documentation Company, Zug, Switzerland.

6. Ottilie Baader, *Ein steiniger Weg*, (3rd ed.; Bonn, 1979), and Adelheid Popp, *Jugend einer Arbeiterin*, ed. by Has J. Schultz (3rd ed.; Bonn, 1980). Dietz has also reprinted August Bebel's *Die Frau und der Sozialismus* (1929 ed.), Lily Braun's *Die Frauenfrage* (1979 [1st ed., 1901]), Rosa Luxemburg's *Ich umarme Sie in grosser Sehnsucht. Briefe aus dem Gefängnis, 1915–1918* (1980), and they published a German edition of Richard J. Evans, *Sozialdemokratie und*

Frauenemanzipation im deutschen Kaiserreich (1978). A reprint in English of Bebel's *Women Under Socialism* was published by Schocken (New York, 1971).

7. See my article "The Women's Role in the German Working-Class Family in the 1890s from the Perspective of Women's Autobiographies" in this volume for comments and a lengthy list of autobiographies and autobiographical material.

8. Doris Viersbeck, *Erlebnisse eines Hamburger Dienstmädchens* (Munich, 1910); [anonymous], *Im Kampf ums Dasein* (Stuttgart, 1908); and C. Moszeik, ed. *Aus der Gedankenwelt einer Arbeiterfrau,* von ihr selbst erzählt [Frau Hoffmann] (Berlin, 1909).

9. Wolfgang Emmerich, ed., *Proletarische Lebensläufe,* 2 vols. (Reinbek, 1974–75).

10. For these and other statistics, see Werner Thönnessen, *The Emancipation of Women: The Rise and Decline of the Women's Movement in German Social Democracy, 1863–1933* (London, 1973), pp. 57 and 116; and Friedrich G. Kürbisch and Richard Klucsarits, eds., *Arbeiterinnen kämpfen um ihr Recht. Autobiographische Texte zum Kampf rechtloser und entrechteter "Frauensperso-nen" in Deutschland, Österreich und der Schweiz des 19. und 20. Jahrhunderts* (2nd ed.; Wuppertal, 1981), pp. 27, 32, 34–35. See also Jean H. Quataert, *Reluctant Feminists in German Social Democracy, 1885–1917* (Princeton, 1979), p. 184. She notes that in 1912, in addition to the women in the Free Trade Unions, there were 4,950 women in the Hirsch-Duncker and 28,008 in the Catholic trade unions; finally, Gisela Losseff-Tillmanns, *Frauenemanzipation und Gewerkschaften* (Wuppertal, 1978), pp. 383–84.

Another anthology that contains both middle- and working-class (socialist) documents on the feminist movement (which I shall say something about later in this essay) is Elke Frederiksen, ed., *Die Frauenfrage in Deutschland, 1865–1915* (Stuttgart, 1981). See also two of the volumes in the series *Die Frau in der Gesellschaft. Frühe Texte,* published by Fischer Verlag and edited by Gisela Brinker-Gabler: *Frauenemanzipation und Sozialdemokratie,* ed. by Heinz Nig-gemann (Frankfurt, 1981), and *Frauenarbeit und Beruf,* ed. by Gisela Brinker-Gabler (Frankfurt, 1979). These volumes make an important contribution but it would also be helpful to do what Dietz has done and publish complete works. Most of the selections in *Frauenarbeit und Beruf* are by middle-class women (socialist and nonsocialist); there are only a few documents by working-class women. Some documents by working-class women in Germany are contained in the English language anthology I co-edited, Eleanor Riemer and John C. Fout, eds., *European Women: A Documentary History, 1789–1945* (New York, 1980).

11. Cited in Paul Göhre, *Three Months in a Workshop: A Practical Study* (New York, 1895), p. 112.

12. Kürbisch and Klucsarits, *Arbeiterinnen*—for complete citation see note 10.

13. Thönnessen, *The Emancipation*—for complete citation see note 10.

14. For complete citations of Quataert and Losseff-Tillmans, see note 10. Sabine Richebächer, *Uns fehlt nur eine Kleinigkeit. Deutsche proletarische Frauenbewegung, 1890–1914* (Frankfurt, 1982). See also Heinz Niggemann,

Emanzipation zwischen Sozialismus und Feminismus. Die sozialdemokratische Frauenbewegung im Kaisserreich (Wuppertal, 1981), and Richard J. Evans, *Sozialdemokratie und Frauenemanzipation im deutschen Kaiserreich* (Bonn, 1978).

15. Quataert, *Reluctant Feminists*, p. 240.

16. This notion of "feminist worthies" is, of course, a play on words of Gerda Lerner's "women worthies." She wrote: "The history of notable women is the history of exceptional, even deviant women, and does not describe the experience and history of the mass of women." Gerda Lerner, "Placing Women in History: Definitions and Challenges," *Feminist Studies*, 3 (1975–76), p. 5.

17. Molly Nolan, "Proletarischer Anti-Feminismus. Dargestellt am Beispiel der SPD-Ortsgruppe Düsseldorf, 1890 bis 1913," in *Frauen und Wissenschaft*, pp. 356–77.

18. Ibid., pp. 358–59.

19. Richard J. Evans, "German Social Democracy and Women's Suffrage, 1891–1918," *Journal of Contemporary History*, 15 (1980), pp. 533–57, and Willy Albrecht et al., "Frauenfrage und deutsche Sozialdemokratie vom Ende des 19. Jahrhunderts bis zum Beginn der zwanziger Jahre," *Archiv für Sozialgeschichte*, 19, (1979), pp. 459–510. Two other articles that "sound good" but are terribly disappointing because they are evidently written for high school students, are Bärbel Gudelius, "Proletarische Lebenserfahrung und sozialistische Frauenbewegung," in *Frauen in der Geschichte I*, ed. by Kuhn and Schneider, and Rosemarie Beier, "Zur Geschichte weiblicher Lebenschancen—Alltagsleben, gewerkschaftliche Organisation und Streik Berliner Bekleidungsarbeiterinnen, 1870–1914," in *Frauen in der Geschichte II*, ed. by Kuhn and Rüsen.

20. Louise A. Tilly and Joan W. Scott, *Women, Work, and Family* (New York, 1978); Thomas Dublin, *Women at Work: The Transformation of Work and Community in Lowell, Massachusetts, 1826–1860* (New York, 1979); David M. Katzman, *Seven Days a Week: Women and Domestic Service in Industrializing America* (New York, 1978); and Lee Holcombe, *Victorian Ladies at Work: Middle-Class Working Women in England and Wales, 1850–1914* (Hamden, Conn., 1973).

21. Edith Rigler, *Frauenleitbild und Frauenarbeit in Österreich vom ausgehenden 19. Jahrhundert bis zum Zweiten Weltkrieg* (Munich, 1976). See also Josef Ehmer, *Familienstruktur und Arbeitsorganisation im frühindustriellen Wien* (Munich, 1980).

22. Robyn Dasey, "Women's Work and the Family: Women Garment Workers in Berlin and Hamburg Before the First World War," in *The German Family: Essays on the Social History of the Family in Nineteenth- and Twentieth-Century Germany*, ed. by Richard J. Evans and W. R. Lee (Totowa, N.J., 1981). See also my forthcoming article "The Viennese Enquête of 1896 on Working Women" in the proceedings of an international conference on German women held at the University of Minnesota in April 1983 (Indiana University Press).

23. Dasey, pp. 248–49.

24. Josef Ehmer, "Frauenarbeit und Arbeiterfamilie in Wien. Vom Vormärz bis 1934," *Geschichte und Gesellschaft*, 7 (1981), pp. 438–73. See also Ehmer's "Familie und Klasse. Zur Entstehung der Arbeiterfamilie in Wien," in *Historische*

Familienforschung, ed. by Michael Mitterauer and Reinhard Sieder (Frankfurt, 1982).

25. Regina Schulte, "Dienstmädchen im herrschaftlichen Haushalt. Zur Genese ihrer Sozialpsychologie," *Zeitschrift für bayerische Landesgeschichte,* 41 (1978), pp. 879–920. See also Uta Ottmüller, *Die Dienstbotenfrage. Zur Sozialgeschichte der doppelten Ausnutzung von Dienstmädchen im deutschen Kaiserreich* (Münster, 1978).

26. Karin Hausen, "Technischer Fortschritt und Frauenarbeit im 19. Jahrhundert. Zur Sozialgeschichte der Nähmaschine," *Geschichte und Gesellschaft,* 4 (1978), pp. 148–69. See also Barbara Brick and Christine Woesler, "Maschinerie und Mütterlichkeit," in *Frauengeschichte. Beiträge 5.*

27. Peter Schneck, "Die gesundheitlichen Verhältnisse der Fabrikarbeiterinnen. Ausgewählte Aspekte der Situation in der sächsischen Oberlausitz im ausgehenden 19. Jahrhundert," *Jahrbuch für Wirtschaftsgeschichte,* 16 (III) (1978), pp. 53–72.

28. Ingeborg Müller, "Damshagen: Aus dem Alltagsleben der Tagelöhnerfrauen," *Jahrbuch für Volkskunde und Kulturgeschichte,* 20 (1977), pp. 85–103. See also Peter Taylor and Hermann Rebel, "Hessian Peasant Women, Their Families, and the Draft: A Social-Historical Interpretation of Four Tales from the Grimm Collection," *Journal of Family History,* 6 (1981), pp. 347–78, and three articles by Rosmarie Beier: "Berliner Heimnäherinnen und ihre Familien," *Journal für Geschichte,* 2 (1980): "Leben in der Mietskaserne. Zum Alltag Berliner Unterschichtsfamilien in den Jahren 1900–1920," in *In Hinterhof, Keller und Mansarde. Bilder von Wohnen,* ed. by Gesine Asmus (Reinbek, 1982); and "Proletarische Kindheit in Berlin um 1900," in *Hilfe. Schule. Ein Bilderlesebuch über Schule und Alltag* (Berlin, 1981). In addition see Gottfried Kössler, *Mädchenkindheiten im 19. Jahrhundert* (Giessen, 1979); Margarete Flecken, *Arbeiterkinder im 19. Jahrhundert. Eine sozialgeschichtliche Untersuchung ihrer Lebenswelt* (Weinheim, 1981); Aurel Ende, "Battering and Neglect: Children in Germany, 1860–1978," *Journal of Psychohistory,* 7 (1979–80), pp. 249–70; and Aurel Ende, "Bibliography on Childhood and Youth in Germany from 1820–1978: A Selection," in ibid., pp. 283–87. See also Wilfried Feldenkirchen, "Kinderarbeit im 19. Jahrhundert. Ihre wirtschaftlichen und sozialen Auswirkungen," *Zeitschrift für Unternehmensgeschichte,* 26 (1981), pp. 1–41, and Brigit Bolognese-Leuchtenmüller, "Unterversorgung und mangelnde Betreuung der Kleinkinder in den Unterschichtenfamilien als soziales Problem des 19. Jahrhunderts," in Herbert Knittler, ed., *Wirtschafts- und sozialhistorische Beiträge. Festschrift für Alfred Hoffmann zum 75. Geburtstag* (Munich, 1979).

29. See two articles by R. P. Neumann, "Industrialization and Sexual Behavior: Some Aspects of Working-Class Life in Imperial Germany," in *Modern European Social History,* ed. by Robert J. Bezucha (Lexington, Mass., 1972), pp. 270–98, and "Working Class Birth Control in Germany," *Comparative Studies in Society and History,* 20 (1978), pp. 408–28, and Stefan Bajohr, "Uneheliche Mütter im Arbeitermilieu: Die Stadt Braunschweig, 1900–1930," *Geschichte und Gesellschaft,* 7 (1981), pp. 474–506—also in English: "Illegitimacy and the Working Class: Illegitimate Mothers in Brunswick, 1900–1933," in *The German Work-*

ing *Class, 1888–1933*, ed. by Richard J. Evans (Totowa, N.J., 1982). See also Richard J. Evans, "Prostitution, State and Society in Imperial Germany," *Past and Present*, nr. 70 (1976), pp. 106–29; Chryssoula Kambas, "Frühsozialismus und Prostitution: Zum Verdacht unsittlicher Vergesellschaftung," *Ästhetik und Kommunikation*, 6 (1975), pp. 34–48; Ulrich Linse, "Arbeiterschaft und Geburtenentwicklung im Deutschen Kaiserreich von 1871," *Archiv für Sozialgeschichte*, 12 (1972), pp. 205–72; Arthur E. Imhof, "Die Übersterblichkeit verheirateter Frauen im fruchtbaren Alter," *Zeitschrift für Bevölkerungswissenschaft*, 5 (1979), pp. 487–510; Arthur E. Imhof, "Unterschiedliche Säuglingssterblichkeit in Deutschland, 18. bis 20. Jahrhundert," *Zeitschrift für Bevölkerungswissenschaft*, 7 (1981), pp. 343–82; and John Knodel and Susan de Vos, "Preferences for the Sex of Offspring and Demographic Behavior in Eighteenth- and Nineteenth-Century Germany: An Examination of Evidence from Village Genealogies," *Journal of Family History*, 5 (1980), pp. 145–66.

30. For English-language material, see the bibliography at the end of this volume. On the Weimar period see Hans-Jürgen Arendt, "Weibliche Mitglieder der KPD in der Weimarer Republik. Zahlenmässige Stärke und soziale Stellung," *Beiträge zur Geschichte der deutschen Arbeiterbewegung*, 19 (1977), pp. 652–60; Hans-Jürgen Arendt, "Das Reichskomitee werktätiger Frauen 1929–1932," *Beiträge zur Geschichte der deutschen Arbeiterbewegung*, 23 (1981), pp. 743–49; Stefan Bajohr, *Die Hälfte der Fabrik. Geschichte der Frauenarbeit in Deutschland 1914 bis 1945* (Marburg, 1979); Karen Hagemann, "Möglichkeiten und Probleme der 'Oral History' für Projekte zur Frauengeschichte am Beispiel meiner Arbeit zur sozialdemokratischen Frauenbewegung Hamburgs in der Weimarer Republik," in *Frauengeschichte. Beiträge 5*; K. Jursczyk, *Frauenarbeit und Frauenrolle. Zum Zusammenhang von Familienpolitik und Erwerbstätigkeit in Deutschland, 1918–1975* (Frankfurt, 1978); Silvia Kontos, *Die Partei kämpft wie ein Mann: Frauenpolitik der KPD in der Weimarer Republik* (Frankfurt, 1979); *Mutterkreuz und Arbeitsbuch. Zur Geschichte der Frauen in der Weimarer Republik und im Nationalsozialismus*, ed. by Frauengruppe Faschismusforschung (Frankfurt, 1981); Anneliese Seidel, *Frauenarbeit im Ersten Weltkrieg als Problem der staatlichen Sozialpolitik am Beispiel Bayerns* (Frankfurt, 1979); Gabriele Wellner, "Industriearbeiterinnen in der Weimarer Republik: Arbeit und Privatleben, 1919–1933," *Geschichte und Gesellschaft*, 7 (1981), pp. 534–54; Christl Wickert, "Biographische Methode und 'Oral History' in der Frauengeschichte am Beispiel einer Untersuchung über die führenden SPD-Frauen der Weimarer Republik," in *Frauengeschichte. Beiträge 5*.

For the period 1933–45 see Hans-Jürgen Arendt, "Grundzüge der Frauenpolitik des faschistischen deutschen Imperialismus 1933–39," *Jahrbuch für Geschichte*, 24 (1981), pp. 313–49; Stefan Bajohr, "Weiblicher Arbeitsdienst im 'Dritten Reich': Ein Konflikt zwischen Ideologie und Ökonomie," *Vierteljahresheft für Zeitgeschichte*, 28 (1980), pp. 331–57; Gisela Bock, "Frauen und ihre Arbeit im Nationalsozialismus," in *Frauen in der Geschichte I*, ed. by Kuhn und Schneider; Gisela Brinker-Gabler, ed., *Der alltägliche Faschismus. Frauen im Dritten Reich* (Berlin, 1981); Susanna Dammer und Carola Sachse, "Nationalsozialistische Frauenpolitik und weibliche Arbeitskraft," in *Frauengeschichte*.

Beiträge 5; L. Eiber, "Frauen in der Kriegsindustrie. Arbeitsbedingungen, Lebensumstände und Protestverhalten," in *Bayern in der NS-Zeit*, ed. by M. Broszat et al., vol. 3 (Frankfurt, 1978); Dorothee Klinksiek, *Die Frau im NS-Staat* (Stuttgart, 1982); Annette Kuhn, ed., *Frauen im deutschen Faschismus. Eine Quellensammlung mit fachwissenschaftlichen und fachdidaktischen Kommentaren*, 2 vols. (Düsseldorf, 1982); Margret Lück, *Die Frau im Männerstaat. Die gesellschaftliche Stellung der Frau im Nationalsozialismus* (Frankfurt, 1979); Annemarie Tröger, "Die Planung des Rationalisierungsproletariats. Zur Entwicklung der geschlechtsspezifischen Arbeitsteilung und des weiblichen Arbeitsmarktes im Nationalsozialismus," in *Frauen in der Geschichte II*, ed. by Kuhn and Rüsen; Dörte Winkler, *Frauenarbeit im "Dritten Reich"* (Hamburg, 1977). See citations in note 94 for material primarily on middle-class women in the Weimar and Nazi periods.

31. Ann Snitow, Christine Stansell, and Sharon Thompson, eds., *Powers of Desire: The Politics of Sexuality* (New York, 1983). See also "Part IV: Woman and her Body" in Riemer and Fout, *European Women: A Documentary History, 1789–1945.*

32. Ibid., pp. 153–71. See also a second important essay by Grossman, "Abortion and Economic Crisis: The 1931 Campaign Against §218 in Germany," *New German Critique*, 5 (1978), pp. 119–37.

33. Lillian Faderman, *Surpassing the Love of Men: Romantic Friendship and Love between Women from the Renaissance to the Present* (New York, 1981).

34. Ibid., p. 240.

35. James D. Steakley, *The Homosexual Emancipation Movement in Germany* (New York, 1975). See also Jonathan Katz, *Gay American History: Lesbians and Gay Men in the U.S.A.: A Documentary* (New York, 1976).

36. Lillian Faderman and Brigette Eriksson, eds., *Lesbian-Feminism in Turn-of-the-Century Germany* (Weatherby Lake, Mo., 1980).

37. Ibid., pp. 1–21 and 81–91.

38. It has been reprinted in its original form with very brief introductory remarks by Amazonen Frauenverlag, Verlag Gabriele Meixner (Berlin, 1976).

39. Frau Dr. Minna Wettstein-Adelt, *3½ Monate Fabrik-Arbeiterin. Eine practische Studie* (Berlin, 1893).

40. See note 11. See also three selections in *Historical Perspectives on Homosexuality*, ed. by Salvatore J. Licata and Robert P. Petersen (New York, 1981): Hubert C. Kennedy, "The 'Third Sex' Theory of Karl Heinrich Ulrichs"; Brigitte Eriksson, "A Lesbian Execution in Germany, 1721: The Trials Records"; and Louis Crompton, "The Myth of Lesbian Impunity: Capital Laws from 1270 to 1791." Two important works by John D'Emilio are a recent article, "Capitalism and Gay Identity," in *Powers of Desire*, ed. by Snitow, Stansell, and Thompson, and his monograph *Sexual Politics, Sexual Communities: The Making of a Homosexual Minority in the United States, 1940–1970* (Chicago, 1983).

See also an important review article by Martha Vicinus, "Sexuality and Power: A Review of Current Work in the History of Sexuality," *Feminist Studies*, 8 (1982), pp. 133–56, and an interesting essay by Gary D. Stark, "Pornography, Society, and the Law in Imperial Germany," *Central European History*, 14 (1981), pp. 200–29. Johann Albrecht von Rantzau has written a valuable essay, "Zur Geschichte der sexuellen Revolution. Die Gräfin Franziska zu Reventlow und die Münchener Kosmiker," *Archiv für Kulturgeschichte*, 56 (1974), pp. 394–446. In speaking about the sexual revolution he writes (p. 394): "Diese Revolution richtet sich gegen die überkommene, religiös begründete Geschlechtsmoral—die sie stark erschüttert hat. Sie durchdringt das ganze soziale Leben, sie wirkt sich in der Gesetzgebung und also in der Politik einschneidend aus. Sie deckt sich teilweise mit dem Kampf für die Emanzipation der Frau, ohne darin vollkommen aufzugeben. Die sexuelle Revolution umfasst auch die vergangenen Kämpfe um den vorehelichen Geschlechtsverkehr, um das Recht auf uneheleiche Mutterschaft, um die Erleichterung der Ehescheidung und wirkt sich jetzt in den Auseinandersetzungen über die Straflosigkeit der Abtreibung aus." For the Weimar period, see Renny Harrigan, "Die Sexualität der Frau in der deutschen Unterhaltungsliteratur, 1918–1933," *Geschichte und Gesellschaft*, 7 (1981), pp. 412–37.

41. For a biography of an essentially eighteenth-century woman, see the recently reprinted (in paperback) Hilde Spiel, *Fanny von Arnstein oder Die Emanzipation. Ein Frauenleben an der Zeitwende 1758–1818* (Frankfurt, 1962— most recent paperback, 1981). For all periods, but especially the nineteenth century, see a new list of course outlines, with bibliographies included, in *German and Women's Studies: New Directions in Literary and Interdisciplinary Course Approaches*, ed. by Sidonie Cassirer and Sydna Stern Weiss and prepared for the Coalition of Women in German (South Hadley, Mass., 1983).

There is no opporunity here to review the limited number of works that are concerned with middle-class women and work, but see Gisela Bock and Barbara Duden, "Arbeit aus Liebe—Liebe als Arbeit. Zur Enstehung der Hausarbeit im Kapitalismus," in *Frauen und Wissenschaft;* Gisela Brinker-Gabler, ed., *Frauenarbeit und Beruf* (Frankfurt, 1979); Ute Gerhard, *Verhältnisse und Verhinderung. Frauenarbeit, Familie und Rechte der Frauen im 19. Jahrhundert* (Frankfurt, 1978).

42. Renate Möhrmann, *Die andere Frau. Emanzipationsansätze deutscher Schriftstellerinnen im Vorfeld der Achtundvierziger-Revolution* (Stuttgart, 1977).

43. That argument somewhat contradicts the views about changes in family life that Möhrmann articulates and it should prompt some interesting discussion. There is extensive literature on the family: see, for example, the standard work by Ingeborg Weber-Kellermann, *Die deutsche Familie. Versuch einer Sozialgeschichte* (6th ed. Frankfurt, 1981), as well as Michael Mitterauer and Reinhard Sieder, eds., *Historische Familienforschung* (Frankfurt, 1982); Heide Rosenbaum, "Zur neueren Entwicklung der historischen Familienforschung," *Geschichte und Gesellschaft*, 1 (1975), pp. 210–25; Karin Hausen, "Familie als Gegenstand historischer Sozialwissenschaft. Bemerkungen zu einer Forschungsstrategie," *Geschichte und Gesellschaft*, 1 (1975), pp. 171–209; Heide Rosenbaum, *Formen der Familie. Untersuchungen zum Zusammenhang von Familienverhältnissen, Sozialstruktur und sozialem Wandel in der deutschen Gesellschaft des 19. Jahrhunderts* (Frankfurt, 1982); Wilfried Gottschalch, *Vatermutterkind. Deutsches Familienleben zwischen Kulturromantik und sozialer Revolution* (Berlin, 1979); Barbara Duden, "Das schöne Eigentum: Zur Heraus-

bildung des bürgerlichen Frauenbildes an der Wende vom 18. zum 19. Jahrhundert," *Kursbuch*, 47 (1977), pp. 125–42; Hannelore Schröder, "Die Eigentumslosigkeit und Rechtlosigkeit der Frau im 19. Jahrhundert," in *Frauen und Wissenschaft;* Karin Hausen, "Die Polarisierung der 'Geschlechtscharaktere.' Eine Spiegelung der Dissoziation von Erwerbs- und Familienleben," in Werner Conze, ed., *Sozialgeschichte der Familie in der Neuzeit Europas* (Stuttgart, 1976); Richard J. Evans and W. R. Lee, eds., *The German Family: Essays on the Social History of the Family in Nineteenth- and Twentieth-Century Germany* (Totowa, N.J., 1981); W. R. Lee, "Past Legacies and Future Prospects: Recent Research on the History of the Family in Germany," *Journal of Family History*, 6 (1981), pp. 156–76; Jürgen Reulecke and Wolfhard Weber, eds., *Fabrik. Familie. Feierabend. Beiträge zur Sozialgeschichte des Alltags im Industriezeitalter* (Wuppertal, 1978); Lutz Niethammer, ed., *Wohnen im Wandel. Beiträge zur Geschichte des Alltags in der bürgerlichen Gesellschaft* (Wuppertal, 1979); an important collection of essays on aging, especially the essay by Gudrun Wedel, "Bemerkungen zum Altwerden und Altsein von Frauen im 19. Jahrhundert als Themen in ihren autobiographischen Schriften," in *Gerontologie und Sozialgeschichte. Wege zu einer historischen Betrachtung des Alters*, ed. by Christoph Conrad and Hans-Joachim von Kondratowitz (Berlin, 1983)—my thanks to Christoph Conrad for making a copy of this book available to me. I would also recommend an interesting diary from World War I written by a middle-class girl about her family's experiences in the war: Jo Mihaly, . . . *da gibt's ein Wiedersehn! Kriegstagebuch eines Mädchens, 1914–1918* (Freiburg, 1982).

44. See also the following by Deborah Hertz: "Salonières and Literary Women in Late Eighteenth-Century Berlin," *New German Critique*, 14 (1978), pp. 97–108; her dissertation (which she is preparing for publication), *The Literary Salon in Berlin, 1780–1806: The Social History of an Intellectual Institution*, dissertation, University of Minnesota, 1979; and her forthcoming edition of Rahel Varnhagen's "censored" letters to Regina Frohberg between 1805 and 1810, which will appear in German in 1984, to be published by Kiepenheuer and Witsch. Unfortunately there will not be an opportunity here to review some important literature on Jewish women, but see the bibliography at the end of this volume. Note the works by Marion Kaplan, especially her *The Jewish Feminist Movement in Germany: The Campaigns of the Jüdischer Frauenbund, 1904–1938* (Westport, Conn, 1979), and her most recent effort, "Tradition and Transition: The Acculturation, Assimilation and Integration of Jews in Imperial Germany: A Gender Analysis," in *Leo Baeck Institute Yearbook*, 27 (1982), pp. 3–35. See also Julius Carlebach, "Family Structure and the Position of Jewish Women," in *Revolution and Evolution: 1848 in German-Jewish History*, ed. by Werner E. Mosse, Arnold Paucker, and Reinhard Rürup (Tübingen, 1981).

45. Ellen Key, *Rahel Varnhagen: A Portrait*, trans. from the Swedish by Arthur G. Chater (Westport, Conn., 1976). See the curious introduction by Havelock Ellis. This volume was published by Hyperion Press, which has done a number of reprints on women's history. See also Gisela Brinker-Gabler, ed., *Deutsche Dichterinnen vom 16. Jahrhundert bis zur Gegenwart* (Frankfurt, 1978).

46. Ruth-Ellen Boetcher Joeres, *Die Anfänge der deutschen Frauenbewegung. Louise Otto-Peters* (Frankfurt, 1983).

47. See also other work by Ruth-Ellen Boetcher Joeres, "Louise Otto and Her Journals: A Chapter in Nineteenth Century German Feminism," *Archiv für Sozialgeschichte der deutschen Literatur*, 4 (1979), pp. 100–29; "The Ambiguous World of Hedwig Dohm," *Amsterdamer Beiträge*, 10 (1980), pp. 125–54; and "Ein Dichter: An Introduction to the World of Luise Büchner," *German Quarterly*, 52 (1979), pp. 32–49; "The Triumph of the Woman: Johanna Kinkel's *Hans Ibeles in London* (1860)," *Euphorion*, 70 (1976), pp. 187–207. See also Marielouise Janssen-Jurreit, "Geschichte und Familiengeschichte: Die radikale Feministin Hedwig Dohm und Enkelin Katia Mann," in Marielouise Janssen-Jurreit, *Sexismus* (Munich, 1976), pp. 11–27. There is now an English translation of that work: Marielouise Janssen-Jurreit, *Sexism* (New York, 1982).

48. One other small fault with the book is that Joeres uses a few too many ellipses, making the reader wonder at times just how much material has been left out. More complete selections would be desirable.

49. Renate Möhrmann, ed., *Frauenemanzipation im deutschen Vormärz. Texte und Dokumente* (Stuttgart, 1978).

50. Gisela Brinker-Gabler, ed. *Fanny Lewald. Meine Lebensgeschichte* (Frankfurt, 1980). See the essay by Juliane Jacobi-Dittrich in this collection, "Growing Up Female in the Nineteenth Century," her note 4.

51. Maria Wagner, ed., *Mathilde Franziska Anneke in Selbstzeugnissen und Dokumenten* (Frankfurt, 1980). See also Mathilde Franziska Anneke, *Mutterland. Memoiren einer Frau aus dem badischen-pfälzischen Feldzüge* (Münster, 1982).

52. See Lia Secci, "German Women Writers and the Revolution of 1848," in this volume, especially the material in the text between notes 6 and 7.

53. There are a number of other important volumes published by Fischer—see, for example, Gisela Brinker-Gabler, ed., *Kämpferin für den Frieden: Bertha von Suttner. Lebenserinnerungen, Reden und Schriften* (Frankfurt, 1982), and Gisela Brinker-Gabler, ed. *Frauen gegen den Krieg* (Frankfurt, 1980).

54. *New German Critique*, no. 27 (Fall 1982). Two other essay collections are *Wolfenbüttler Studien zur Aufklärung*, vol. 3, ed. by Günter Schulz (Wolfenbüttel, 1976), and *Die Frau als Heldin Und Autorin*, ed. by Wolfgang Paulsen (Berne, 1979). Another important special issue of a journal dealing with women and literature is *Gestaltet und Gestaltend. Frauen in der deutschen Literatur*, ed. by Marianne Burkhard, *Amsterdamer Beiträge*, 10 (1980). See for example, Kay Goodman, "The Impact of Rahel Varnhagen on Women in the Nineteenth Century." See also Doris Starr Guilloton, "Rahel Varnhagen und die Frauenfrage in der deutschen Romantik: Eine Untersuchung ihrer Briefe und Tagebuchnotizen," *Monatshefte*, 69 (1977), pp. 391–403; Ruth P. Dawson, "'Der Weihrauch, den uns die Männer streuen': Wieland and Women Writers in the *Teutscher Merkur*," in *Christoph Martin Wieland, 1733–1813: North American Scholarly Contributions on the Occasion of the 250th Anniversary of His Birth*, ed. by Hansjörg R. Schelle (Tübingen, Niemeyer, forthcoming); Brigitte Wartmann, "Die Grammatik des Patriarchats. Zur 'Natur' des Weiblichen in der bürgerlichen Gesellschaft," *Ästhetik und Kommunikation*, 47 (1982), pp. 12–32; Gisela Dischner, *Caroline [Schlegel-Schelling] und der Jenaer Kreis. Ein Leben zwischen bürgerlicher Vereinzelung und romantischer Geselligkeit* (Berlin, 1979); Silvia Bovenschen, *Die imaginierte Weiblichkeit. Exemplarische Untersuchungen zu kulturgeschichtlichen und literarischen Präsentationsformen des Weiblichen*

(Frankfurt, 1978); Eda Sagarra, "'Echo oder Antwort.' Die Darstellung der Frau in der deutschen Erzählprosa, 1815–1848," *Geschichte und Gesellschaft,* 7 (1981), pp. 394–411.

55. Susan L. Cocalis and Kay Goodman, eds., *Beyond the Eternal Feminine: Critical Essays on Women and German Literature* (Stuttgart, 1982). My thanks to Kay Goodman for providing me with a copy of this work.

56. Ingeborg Drewitz, "Bettine von Arnim: A Portrait," pp. 115–22, and Kay Goodman, "Poesis and Praxis in Rahel Varnhagen's Letters, " pp. 123–39, in *New German Critique,* no. 27 (1982).

57. Ibid., Drewitz, pp. 115–16. See also Ingeborg Drewitz, *Bettine von Arnim: Romantik-Revolution-Utopie* (2nd ed.; Munich, 1979), and Edith Waldstein, *Bettine von Arnim and the Literary Salon: Women's Participation in the Cultural Life of Early Nineteenth-Century Germany,* dissertation, Washington University, 1982.

58. Ibid., Goodman, "Poesis and Praxis," p. 123.

59. Susan L. Cocalis and Kay Goodman, "The Eternal Feminine Is Leading Us On," in *Beyond the Eternal Feminine,* ed. by Cocalis and Goodman, pp. 1–2.

60. Ibid., p. 2.

61. Maria M. Wagner, "A German Writer and Feminist in Nineteenth-Century America: An Archival Study of Mathilde Franziska Anneke," in ibid., pp. 159–75—but the Table of Contents, not the title page of the essay, lists the complete title.

62. Ibid., p. 159.

63. Elke Frederiksen, "German Women Writers in the Nineteenth Century: Where Are They?" in ibid., pp. 177–201; in an appendix she provides a brief bibliography. See also her "Deutsche Autorinnen im 19. Jahrhundert. Neue kritische Ansätze," *Colloquia Germanica,* 14 (1981), pp. 97–113. For later material, see Gisela Brinker-Gabler, "Die Schriftstellerin in der deutschen Literaturwissenschaft: Aspekte ihrer Rezeption von 1835 bis 1910," *Die Unterrichtspraxis,* 9 (1976), pp. 15–27; Renny Harrigan, "The Limits of Emancipation: A Study of Fontane's Lower Class Women," *Monatshefte,* 70 (1978), pp. 117–28; Linda Schelbitzki Pickel, "Self-Contradictions in the German Naturalists' View of Women's Emancipation," *German Quarterly,* 52 (1979), pp. 442–56.

64. Frederiksen, "German Women Writers," in Cocalis and Goodman, eds., *Beyond the Eternal Feminine,* p. 179.

65. Marilyn Scott-Jones, "Laura Marholm and the Question of Female 'Nature'," in Cocalis and Goodman, eds., *Beyond the Eternal Feminine,* pp. 204–5. See also Marilyn Scott [-Jones], "Laura Marholm (1854–1928): Germany's Ambivalent Feminist," *Women's Studies,* 7 (1980), pp. 87–96.

66. Miriam Frank, "Ricarda Huch and the German Women's Movement," in Cocalis and Goodman, eds., *Beyond the Eternal Feminine,* p. 260.

67. Richard L. Johnson, "Gabriele Reuter: Romantic and Realist," in ibid., p. 244.

68. See Lia Secci, *Dal salotto al partito. Scrittrici tedesche tra rivoluzione borghese e diritto di voto (1848–1918)* (Rome, 1982).

69. Cocalis and Goodman maintain that the laws restricting women's political activities grew directly out of the revolution—passed in 1850, these laws in Prussia, Bavaria, and other states lasted until 1908. See Cocalis and Goodman,

"The Eternal Feminine," in Cocalis and Goodman, eds., *Beyond the Eternal Feminine*, p. 20. Frederiksen also emphasizes the conservative reaction—Frederiksen, "German Woman Authors," in ibid., p. 183.

70. Timothy F. Sellner, trans. and ed., *Theodor Gottlieb von Hippel: On Improving the Status of Women* (Detroit, 1979). See also Ruth P. Dawson, "The Feminist Manifesto of Theodor Gottlieb von Hippel (1741–96)," *Amsterdamer Beiträge*, 10 (1980).

71. See Sellner's comments in his "Translator's Note," p. 17. For criticism, see Evans, "The History of European Women: A Critical Survey of Recent Research," p. 665–66.

72. *"Dem Reich der Freiheit werb' ich Bürgerinnen." Die Frauen-Zeitung von Louise Otto*, ed. by Ute Gerhard, Elisabeth Hannover-Drück, and Romina Schmitter (Frankfurt, 1980).

73. *Schwestern zerreist eure Ketten. Zeugnisse zur Geschichte der Frauen in der Revolution von 1848/49*, ed. by Gerlinde Hummel-Haasis (Munich, 1982).

74. See Dagmar Grenz, *Mädchenliteratur. Von den moralisch-belehrenden Schriften im 18. Jahrhundert bis zur Herausbildung der Backfischliteratur im 19. Jahrhundert* (Stuttgart, 1981); Gottfried Kössler, *Mädchenliteratur im 19. Jahrhundert* (Giessen, 1979); Margarete Schecker, *Die Entwicklung der Mädchenschule* (Weinheim, 1963); Monika Simmel, *Erziehung zum Weibe. Mädchenbildung im 19. Jahrhundert* (Frankfurt, 1980); Gerda Tornieporth, *Studien zur Frauenbildung* (Weinheim, 1977).

75. Karin Meiners, ed., "'Plan und Einrichtung einer bürgerlichen Töchterschule und Erziehungsanstalt.' Aus dem Testament der Anna Barbara von Stetten," *Zeitschrift des historischen Vereins Schwaben*, 74 (1980), pp. 131–68. For a brief but well-written introduction to women's education in the eighteenth century, see Peter Petschauer, "Improving Educational Opportunities for Girls in Eighteenth-century Germany," *Eighteenth-Century Life*, 3 (1976), pp. 56–62.

76. Catherine M. Prelinger, "Religious Dissent, Women's Rights, and the Hamburger Hochschule fuer das weibliche Geschlecht in Mid-Nineteenth-Century Germany," *Church History*, 45 (1976), p. 42. See also Konrad Fuchs, "Katharina Kasper (1820–1898), Gründerin der Klostergenossenschaft der Armen Dienstmägde Jesu Christi. Ein Beitrag zur sozialen Frage im 19. Jahrhundert," *Nassauische Annalen*, 83 (1977), pp. 149–66.

77. Ibid.

78. Ibid., p. 55.

79. George Bernstein and Lottelore Bernstein, "Attitudes Toward Women's Education in Germany, 1870–1914," *International Journal of Women's Studies*, 2 (1979), pp. 473–88, and Bernstein and Bernstein, "The Curriculum for German Girls' Schools, 1870–1914." *Paedagogica Historica*, 18 (1978), pp. 275–95.

80. Bernstein and Bernstein, "Attitudes Toward Women's Education in Germany, 1870–1914," p. 486.

81. Bernstein and Bernstein, "The Curriculum for German Girls' Schools, 1870–1914," p. 279.

82. Ibid., p. 287.

83. James C. Albisetti, "Could Separate Be Equal? Helene Lange and Women's Education in Imperial Germany," quoted from a typescript copy gener-

ously provided by the author; the essay has been printed in *History of Education Quarterly*, 22 (1982), pp. 301–17. See also James C. Albisetti, "The Fight for Female Physicians in Imperial Germany," *Central European History*, 15 (1982), pp. 99–123. See also Ute Frevert, "Frauen und Ärzte im späten 18. und frühen 19. Jahrhundert. Zur Sozialgeschichte eines Gewaltverhältnisses," in Kuhn and Rüsen, eds., *Frauen in der Geschichte II*.

84. Albisetti, "Could Separate Be Equal? Helene Lange and Women's Education in Imperial Germany," pp. 8–9 of typescript.

85. Ibid., p. 25.

86. Albisetti, "The Fight for Female Physicians in Imperial Germany," p. 108.

87. Richard J. Evans, *The Feminist Movement in Germany, 1894–1933* (Beverly Hills, 1976), and Barbara Greven-Aschoff, *Die bürgerliche Frauenbewegung in Deutschland, 1894–1933* (Göttingen, 1981). For other work on the feminist movement, see Elfriede Bachmann, "Das kirchliche Frauenstimmrecht in der Stadt Bremen. Vorbereitung und Durchführung," *Hospitium Ecclesiae*, 9 (1975), pp. 55–132; Herrad-Ulrike Bussemer, "Bürgerliche und proletarische Frauenbewegung (1865–1914)," in Kuhn and Schneider, eds., *Frauen in der Geschichte I*; Barbara Greven-Aschoff, "Sozialer Wandel und Frauenbewegungen," *Geschichte und Gesellschaft*, 7 (1981), pp. 328–46; Elisabeth Helming, *Geschichte der bürgerlichen Frauenbewegung, 1865–1908* (Frankfurt, 1977); Marielouise Janssen-Jurreit, "Nationalbiologie, Sexualreform und Geburtenrückgang. Über die Zusammenhänge von Bevölkerungspolitik und Frauenbewegung um die Jahrhundertwende," in Gabriel Dietze, ed., *Die Überwindung der Sprachlosigkeit: Texte aus der neueren Frauenbewegung* (Darmstadt, 1979); Ulrike Prokop, "Die Sehnsucht nach Volkseinheit: Zum Konservatismus der bürgerlichen Frauenbewegung vor 1933," in ibid.

88. Stanley Zucker has written another article on Kathinka Zitz-Halein but unfortunately there is no space to review it here; it is quite an interesting essay: Stanley Zucker, "German Women and the Revolution of 1848: Kathinka Zitz-Halein and the Humania Association," *Central European History*, 13 (1981), pp. 237–54. See also Fritz Böttger, ed., *Frauen im Aufbruch. Frauenbriefe aus dem Vormärz und der Revolution von 1848* (Darmstadt, 1979), and Gustav Otruba, "Zur Frauenfrage im Revolutionsjahr 1848 im Spiegel Wiener Flugschriften," in Herbert Knittler, ed., *Wirtschafts- und sozialhistorische Beiträge. Festschrift für Alfred Hoffmann zum 75. Geburtstag* (Munich, 1979), pp. 395–409.

89. See citation for Zucker's article in note 88.

90. There is almost no material on upper-class women generally, but there is a group of essays on "royal" women, mostly in the early modern period, in a recent issue of the *Zeitschrift für bayerische Landesgeschichte*—see, for example, Giuseppe Pansini, "Violante Beatrix von Bayern, Prinzessin der Toskana," *Zeitschrift für bayerische Landesgeschichte*, 44 (1983), pp. 291–302, Peter Claus Hartmann, "Zwei wittelsbacher Prinzessinnen am Hof Ludwigs XIV.: Maria Anna Christina von Bayern und Elisabeth Charlotte von der Pfalz," ibid., pp. 269–89, and a nineteenth-century piece, Brigitte Hamann, "Kaiserin Elisabeth von Österreich," ibid., pp. 397–412.

91. These two volumes are in the Hyperion reprint series *Pioneers of the*

Woman's Movement. Dr. Kaethe Schirmacher, *The Modern Woman's Rights Movement: A Historical Survey* (Westport, Conn., 1976 [1912]), and Hedwig Dohm, *Women's Nature and Privilege* (Westport, Conn., 1976 [1896]).

92. Margrit Twellmann, *Die deutsche Frauenbewegung. Ihre Anfänge und erste Entwicklung, 1843–1889*, 2 vols. (Meisenheim am Glan, 1971–72). Volume 1 is now out of print; volume 2 is not.

93. Elke Frederiksen, ed., *Die Frauenfrage in Deutschland, 1865–1915. Texte und Dokumente* (Stuttgart, 1981). My thanks to Professor Frederiksen for providing me with a copy of her book.

94. The reader is reminded of citations in note 30 for material on working-class women in the Weimar and Nazi periods. The citations that follow deal primarily with middle- and upper-class women in the same periods. For English-language works, see the bibliography at the end of this volume. For the Weimar period, see Ute Frevert, "Traditionale Weiblichkeit und moderne Interessenorganisation: Frauen im Angestelltenberuf, 1918–1933," *Geschichte und Gesellschaft*, 7 (1981), pp. 507–33; Ute Frevert, "Vom Klavier zur Schreibmaschine. Weiblicher Arbeitsmarkt und Rollenzuweisungen am Beispiel der weiblichen Angestellten in der Weimarer Republik," in Kuhn and Schneider, eds., *Frauen in der Geschichte I*; Renny Harrigan, "Die Sexualität der Frau in der deutschen Unterhaltungsliteratur, 1918–1933," *Geschichte und Gesellschaft*, 7 (1981), pp. 412–37; Michael H. Kater, "Krisis des Frauenstudiums in der Weimarer Republik," *Vierteljahrsschrift für Sozial- und Wirtschaftsgeschichte*, 59 (1972), pp. 207–55; Helgard Kramer, "Veränderungen der Frauenrolle in der Weimarer Republik," in *Frauengeschichte. Beiträge 5*; Ilka Riemann, "Zur Diskrepanz zwischen der Realität sozialer Arbeit als Frauenberuf und dem Mythos dieser Arbeit als Karriereberuf von Mittelschichtsfrauen," in *Frauengeschichte. Beiträge 5*; Irmgard Weyrather, "Die Frau im Lebensraum des Mannes. Studentinnen in der Weimarer Republik," in *Frauengeschichte. Beiträge 5*. For the Nazi period, see Hanna Elling, *Frauen im deutschen Widerstand, 1933–45* (Frankfurt, 1978); Benedicta M. Kempner, *Nonnen unter dem Hakenkreuz* (Würzburg, 1979); Rolf Kralovitz and Brigitte Kralovitz, "Hedwig Burgheim oder die Reise nach Giessen: Bericht über das Leben einer Lehrerin in Nazi-Deutschland," *Mitteilungen des oberhessischen Geschichtsvereins*, 65 (1980), pp. 55–86; Hans Müller, "Frauen und Faschismus," in Kuhn and Schneider, eds., *Frauen in der Geschichte I*; Charlotte Mueller, *Die Klempnerkolonne in Ravensbrück. Erinnerungen des Häftlings Nr. 10787* (Frankfurt, 1981); Jill Stephenson, "Nationalsozialistischer Dienstgedanke, bürgerliche Frauen und Frauenorganisationen im dritten Reich," *Geschichte und Gesellschaft*, 7 (1981), pp. 555–71; Lucie Suhling, *Der unbekannte Widerstand* (Frankfurt, 1980); Annemarie Tröger, "Die Dolchstosslegende der Linken: 'Frauen haben Hitler an die Macht gebracht.' Thesen zur Geschichte der Frauen am Vorabend des dritten Reichs," in *Frauen und Wissenschaft*; Guste Zhorner, ed. *Frauen. KZ Ravensbrück* (Berlin, 1973); Gerda Zorn and Gertrud Meyer, *Frauen gegen Hitler. Berichte aus dem Widerstand, 1933–45* (Frankfurt, 1974).

95. Evans, *The Feminist Movement*, p. ix.

Enlightened Reforms and Bavarian Girls' Education

Tradition through Innovation

JOANNE SCHNEIDER

The reform era in Germany, especially as examined by American scholars, is often synonymous with Prussia and politics. Mention is usually made that Bavaria, Württemberg, and Baden also experienced periods of reform. But many interesting questions, particularly those related to social history, remain unexplored. It is the purpose of this essay to raise some of those questions, through an examination of one aspect of the reform era in Bavaria—specifically, how the reforms in education related to public and private attitudes about women. In the girls' schools created in the wake of the reforms of the early nineteenth century, the traditional image of women was cultivated and preserved. Girls were taught the virtues of being a good wife, mother, and housekeeper. But new themes such as patriotism and loyalty to the state also became important features of the proper education for young girls. What brought the Bavarian state and its leaders to concern themselves with the reform of girls' education?

Reform in the early nineteenth century was the child of the Enlightenment, which encouraged the systematic examination of human society. Problems were to be eliminated through the use of applied human reason. A monarch or his advisers, following enlightened ideas, were to effect reforms that would improve all aspects of life for ruler and ruled alike. One goal, achieved through the reforms, was the creation of a stronger, more efficient government. This new government needed a literate public, because the newly rationalized bureaucracy required a pool of qualified candidates from which to draw. Therefore, public education became a crucial concern for the state.

The growing interest in literacy and education brought problems on many fronts. Two sensitive areas were the following: the state would assume control of education from the Church, which had served as the source of primary education for centuries; and decisions had to be made concerning the distinctions between girls' and boys' education. As state governments took control of education, Church leaders warned about the impending decline of morality. Officials countered that the quality of education in some of the Church schools was questionable and it was necessary for the state to set standards and supervise educational facilities. The debate about girls' and boys' education and the qualitative differences between the two was no less problematic. Few people denied girls the right to basic literacy, but beyond that minimum most would not venture to go. Dire consequences were predicted if girls were too well educated. Life for their husbands would be miserable, since such women would rather read than keep house.[1] In addition, there was always the chance that too much education would overburden a girl's mind and incapacitate her or, worse, cause her to become infertile.[2]

The discussion about what was considered a proper education for girls, nevertheless, was an integral part of the reform era. The most widely accepted Enlightenment principle concerning girls' education was expressed by Jean Jacques Rousseau. In his novel *Emile*, Rousseau outlined the education of Sophie, Emile's intended bride. Her education was to be different in quantity and quality from his. The end product would be a woman/wife who would complement her husband. Her modest education would prevent her from boring him, but, of course, she was never to challenge him intellectually.[3] Within this tradition, a body of literature and debate about the nature of girls' education grew. How did Bavaria react to these ideas?

It is impossible to discuss the Enlightenment in Bavaria without mentioning Maximilian von Montgelas, Prime Minister from 1799 to 1817. He, more than any other person, was the architect of enlightened reforms there. Born in Munich, educated in France, he returned to Bavaria in 1799 when his patron Max Joseph became Elector, at the death of his cousin Karl Theodor. During the ten years prior to Max Joseph's accession, Montgelas formulated a reform plan to modernize the Electorate.[4] One of the plan's more drastic measures was the secularization of all monasteries and convents, the closure of their schools, and the confiscation of their land and property. In turn, the state was to establish a public school system based on enlightened principles which would instill the proper values in Bavaria's inhabitants.

Montgelas implemented his plan almost immediately. By 1802, the state instituted mandatory school attendance for boys and girls aged seven to sixteen.[5] In 1803, the government began the secularization of the convents and monasteries. As a result, most of the girls' schools in Bavaria ceased to function. Since nuns were prohibited from teaching unless they left their orders, there was a critical shortage of qualified women teachers.

The state was not wholly unresponsive to this problem. In 1803, it founded a Teacher Training Institute for Men, and allowed a few female candidates to enroll.[6] But this handful of lay teachers could not fill the gap left by the absence of teaching nuns. It is difficult to attribute outright malice on the part of the Montgelas government against women's education, as its anticlerical policies took precedence over others. The problems facing girls' schools and the teacher shortage were unfortunate results. When questions of education reforms were directly addressed, the government's greater concern lay with improving boys' education rather than girls'.

Part of the reason for the low priority given girls' education was connected with current debates about citizenship. The reformed government was responsible for the education of its citizens. But could girls and women be considered citizens, since they were forbidden by law or custom from serving in public office?[7] To refute this argument, it was suggested that, as mothers, these women would bear and rear the state's future citizens and were therefore entitled to state-sponsored education. Proponents also praised the female nature, which was supposedly very patriotic and conservative.[8] Such characteristics were of benefit to the state, which desired a contented populace. "Properly" educated young women were expected to have a calming influence on the male members of their families, which would promote stability in society.

Following that argument, the Bavarian government issued various directives about the establishment and proper management of girls' schools.[9] It was understood, by all concerned, that these schools would be sex-segregated. The justification was that girls should be sheltered from the rowdiness of boys, to say nothing of the possibility of immoral behavior if the children were not separated.[10] In Bavaria, the goal of sex-segregated schools was accomplished at the equivalent of the junior and senior high school level, but elementary schools, especially in the rural areas, remained coeducational. The special regulations associated with the girls' schools were delineated in the Bavarian Teaching Directive issued in 1804. From Article 25 of that document:

> Male and female instructors will have less difficulties in implementing the teaching directive in the girls' schools. Teachers, in all classes, are to use uniform instruction methods that are related to the nature, at-

titudes, and orientation of young women. Any examples and comparisons made to explain a concept should be taken from the everyday experiences of the girls. Many topics which should be thoroughly explained to the boys can be dealt with in a more superficial manner with the girls. But teachers should also recognize what topics the girls would desire more information about.[11]

The new girls' schools were supposed to have all-female teaching staffs. Although this aspiration was never met, the state began to secure qualified lay female teachers through two facets of the education reform plan. To assure the caliber of prospective teachers, the state instituted qualifying examinations. Candidates who presented themselves for the examination either had gone through a teacher training course or had prepared themselves by other means, often by private study. Some of those examinations make interesting reading, in terms of the questions asked and the responses. In Kreszenz Rapp's examination, which she wrote in 1807, comes the following:

> Question: Why are women chosen to teach at girls' schools?
> Answer: Girls require a softer, gentler treatment than boys, because nature plants in the girls' hearts the seed of gentleness and timidity, a noble gift of their sex. (This timidity is the companion of feminine propriety.) Who can understand/manage these feminine feelings, whose delicacy envelops the entire being of the girls, better than one of their own sex? A woman teacher understands how to cultivate these feelings, because she herself carries them in her bosom. She can control the girls' passions more effectively and help develop their noble feelings into pure virtues. Male teachers are less effective because their knowledge of female delicacy only comes from books.[12]

There is little doubt that this young woman would instill the proper virtues in her charges.

Another means by which the Montgelas government secured qualified female teachers was through the founding of a state-sponsored Teacher Training Institute for Women. As mentioned above, shortly after the secularization, the government allowed some female candidates to enroll in the Teacher Training Institute for Men. But their numbers were restricted to three or four students per year. In 1814, the government commissioned a school where female teacher trainees could study. The new facility had a two-year course plan and expected to graduate twelve or so lay teachers every other year. Young women between the ages of fifteen and twenty-four could enroll in the program. Entrance requirements included, among other things, baptismal certificates and vaccination records, which attested to the candidate's legitimacy and good health. Letters of recommendation written by local officials acquainted with the girls were also to address the issue of moral character. Also,

prospective students were to submit records or evidence of their needlework capabilities. Once enrolled, the students learned skills which prepared them to teach at the elementary level. They studied teaching
methods and practice-taught.[13]

In 1818, sixteen young women attended the Training Institute. They
ranged in age from fifteen to twenty-seven. Five candidates received government scholarships, which had been awarded on the basis of a competitive examination.[14] Such financial assistance was undoubtedly necessary if
these women were to continue their studies. The overwhelming majority
of these students were of lower-middle-class and middle-class backgrounds. Their fathers were either artisans or civil servants.[15] Both occupational groups had particular social images to live up to, which was often
difficult when incomes did not meet expectations. It is reasonable to
assume that the Institute's students viewed teaching as a respectable
occupation for women of their social standing. Such an attitude cannot be
glossed over lightly, especially in a traditional society in which women
were not expected to seek employment outside the home. Economic
need and/or the absence of marriage prospects caused women of the
middling social layers to seek a suitable means by which to support themselves. The state-sponsored teacher training course was one method to
achieve that end.

The Teacher Training Institute for Women functioned for eleven
years. Its pedagogical duties were taken over by Munich's Höhere
Töchterschule (Advanced Girls' School), to be discussed below.[16] Also, in
1825, the critical shortage of female teachers was eased somewhat when
the new king, Ludwig I, rescinded the secularization policies of his
predecessor and encouraged religious orders to resume teaching duties.

Under the direction of the Montgelas government, what kind of girls'
schools were established? The school reform plan called for the creation of
secular schools for boys and girls throughout Bavaria. In Munich, two
state-sponsored girls' schools were founded: the Max Joseph Institute in
1813 and the Nymphenburg School in 1817.[17] Each of the county seats
(Kreisstädte) was to have its girls' school as well. Unfortunately, this goal
was not realized because of lack of funds.[18]

The Max Joseph Institute was Bavaria's premier girls' school. It was
the preserve of upper-class girls ranging in age from seven to sixteen.[19]
During the debates that preceded the school's dedication, even Montgelas expressed his views about the purpose of the institution:

If the Institute is to fulfill the task envisioned, it cannot restrict itself to
pure formalities and simplistic instruction; rather it must concern itself
with the inner development (Bildung) of its charges, always keeping in
mind their future lives. The Institute must educate the inner and outer
person. Its major responsibility is to promote virtue in the girls. Such

training should help the girls in their future duties as overseers of households, wives, mothers, and as members of this society. Every attempt should be made to awaken and maintain in the girls pure sentiments and noble feelings. . . . [20]

The Institute, its teaching staff and students, early on experienced, in microcosm, the political and cultural tensions of the day. The school's first director, Madame Chardoillet, brought with her ten French women to aid in managing the school. Before the Institute opened its doors, government officials and some parents expressed concern about how this "French influence" would harm the girls' essential German qualities. [21]

Madame Chardoillet and her teachers used the Écouen, the largest girls' school founded in Napoleonic France, as their model. Students spoke French outside of class, during handiwork activities, meals, and whatever free time they had. This occurred despite the fact that the Provisory Laws of the school stipulated that the girls should have equal exposure to the German and the French languages. [22] The ebb and flow of complaints about the French influence in the Institute were obviously tied to the current state of political affairs between the two countries and the interest, or lack thereof, in French culture. [23]

Despite the debate about the school's French orientation, many of Bavaria's upper-class girls were educated under its auspices. The goal of the Institute's instructors was to instill deep religiosity and a sense of responsibility in the girls. The school's curriculum included religious instruction (Catholic or Lutheran), as well as German, French, history, geography, natural history, arithmetic, drawing, music, dancing, and handiwork. Girls in the upper grades could take English or Italian if they wished. [24] Although there was quite a selection of courses, the school's graduates were expected to become good housewives and mothers, according to the dictates of their social standing. To develop the domestic abilities of the girls, the school was run as a large household:

> With special care, the girls were to be instructed in household management and prepared for their responsibilities as wives and mothers. They must care for their clothes and linen. The older girls are to care for and dress the younger ones. The former are personally responsible for the cleanliness of their younger charges. [25]

The Max Joseph Institute was Bavaria's answer to the French finishing school. Since it was restricted to the daughters of the upper class, it preserved the class distinctions and attitudes prevalent in a pre-industrial traditional society. [26] These young women were trained for their proper sphere. They attained the necessary social graces and accomplishments and were also capable of supervising a large household and its servants. These girls were the products of one attitude regarding women extant in Bavarian society.

The history of the Nymphenburg School represents another example of government involvement in girls' education. Originally a convent school founded in 1730, Nymphenburg was closed in 1816 and reopened under state administration a year later.[27] The school was designated as Bavaria's "Höhere Mädchenschule" (Advanced Girls' School) for girls from the middle class. Its specification as such was an appeasement offered to members of the upper middle class who were not pleased with the exclusivity or the orientation of the Max Joseph Institute.[28] The school's educational policy was to reflect typical bourgeois values such as piety, pragmatism, and patriotism.

The school's charter, issued in 1817, announced that Nymphenburg would accept students of middle-class origins (aus den mittleren Stand) between the ages of six and fifteen. Through the proper education of body, spirit, and heart, the students would become valuable members of society.[29] The charter then outlined the curriculum and the weekly schedule of classes. The most important courses were instruction in the Christian religion, German language, reading comprehension, and the ability to memorize. Also included in the class schedule were arithmetic, botany, and some history and geography. French, needlework, and music lessons were reserved for late afternoons, Sundays, and holidays. Parents had to pay an additional fee if they wished their daughters to take French or music lessons.[30]

Despite the fact that Nymphenburg was now a state school, the carefully chosen course material stressed "die heilige Religion" ("the holy religion"), that is, Catholicism.[31] Students were encouraged to think about God and the harmony he created in the universe. Because of this emphasis, religion class and reading comprehension were given highest priority by the instructional staff.[32] The deep-seated religiosity of the people could not be weakened, regardless of Montgelas' anticlerical policies with regard to education.

The pragmatic nature of the Nymphenburg School is evident in its policies regarding needlework. The school offered courses in various needle arts. The students did not learn fancy embroidery, but were taught the basics of sewing, knitting, and crocheting. Once these skills were mastered, the girls could learn more decorative needle art, but this was not encouraged. Also, needlework was not part of the daily class schedule, in contrast with most girls' schools, which included it as a legitimate aspect of the curriculum.[33]

The graduates of Nymphenburg were expected to be patriotic supporters of the Bavarian state. Awareness of their native land was instilled in the students through a careful choice of courses. They studied the geography of Upper and Lower Bavaria, Bavarian history, and some aspects of German history. The history the girls were taught, however, was always specially selected. The predominant opinion was that females should be aware of dynastic and anecdotal history, but not much else. Political concerns and military exploits were not seemly subjects with which to occupy the girls' minds.[34]

Nymphenburg's administrators exuded confidence about the future of its graduates. From the yearly report of 1829 comes the following:

> One can feel great joy and happiness for these young girls, who will probably have a happier future because of the sound education they received at this school. We can hope they will reflect all the feminine virtues our Creator endowed them with, while bringing joy, peace, and happiness to their homes. Nothing can be more rewarding at the end of an arduous school year than this hope, which will be fulfilled with the blessing of Heaven![35]

Within this quotation is the express acknowledgment of the woman's crucial position at the center of private life. The education Nymphenburg's students received prepared them to fulfill the time-honored role accorded women in the private sphere of life. In this respect, Bavaria's bourgeoisie was in step with its European counterparts.

To illustrate another direction girls' education took in early-nineteenth-century Bavaria, a discussion of Munich's Höhere Töchterschule is in order. This school was organized at the behest of several concerned citizens. They complained that the Max Joseph Institute and the Nymphenburg School were too restrictive in their admissions policies. A good school for the daughters of the remainder of Munich's bourgeoisie was needed. In 1820, the Local School Commission granted permission to found a Höhere Töchterschule. The school would not be allowed to open, however, unless its sponsors could guarantee a certain enrollment.[36] Some commission officials feared that the school might become a financial liability to the School Fund unless such precautions were taken.[37]

The Höhere Töchterschule opened in December 1822. It was the first city-affiliated school of its kind in Bavaria. Closely associated with the city's Bürgerschule (young men's school), the two schools shared faculty. This was considered a great advantage for the girls' school, because of the caliber of the teachers at the Bürgerschule:

> The Töchterschule (because of its close association with the Bürgerschule) has the following advantages: 1. a very efficient teaching staff; 2. an excellent arithmetic class, equivalent to instruction in the Bürgerschule; the students also receive excellent classes in the funda-

mentals of geometry, drawing, history, geology, and natural history; 3. also, the caliber of the student body is enhanced because of the required entrance examination.[38]

To be accepted as a student at the Höhere Töchterschule, girls had to be twelve years old and have completed elementary school with very good grades, in addition to passing the entrance examination. Seventy students enrolled the first year. A subsequent year-end report from the school's administration stated that, of the initial student body, eighteen withdrew from school, while twenty-seven completed their work with very good grades.[39]

The faculty at the Höhere Töchterschule cooperated with the students' parents in directing the girls' educational progress. In fact, parents were invited to attend school and sit in on classroom instruction. Later, in conference with the teachers, parents were to discuss their daughters' accomplishments. This was an attempt to integrate values from the home into what was taught at school.[40] Such parental concern was certainly praiseworthy, but one school inspector warned the School Commission that many parents stressed household skills to the detriment of the girls' basic education.[41] At the end of the school year, oral examinations were held and prizes were awarded to the best students. At the Höhere Töchterschule, such festivities were restricted to the girls' parents, in contrast to the Bürgerschule, where the boys' families and friends could attend the year-end celebrations.[42]

In several respects the courses taught at the Höhere Töchterschule were similar to those taught at the Max Joseph Institute or the Nymphenburg School, especially when one discounts the former's French orientation. The core curriculum at the city school consisted of religion, German, penmanship, geography, history, arithmetic, natural history, and handiwork. In addition, though, the girls were taught gardening skills, the handling of flax and hemp, and basic pedagogical methods. There was no question that this curriculum would produce industrious middle-class women destined to be good wives and mothers. Yet it was also recognized that these girls would profit from teaching skills.[43] These were important for two reasons. First, this training would allow these girls, as mothers, to be more effective when helping their children with school work. Second, if necessary, these young women could become elementary school teachers.[44]

The progressive tendencies within the Höhere Töchterschule are associated with the efforts of city magistrate Simon Spitzweg, the father of Biedermeier painter Carl Spitzweg. He helped found the school and encouraged quality education for its students. He criticized conservatives who feared that too much education would harm young girls. At the Höhere Töchterschule, the students were to receive a solid academic education, whereas household skills such as cooking were to be learned outside of school.[45] His was a very open-minded opinion about girls' education.

> I do not need to fear that our future citizenesses will be too educated and therefore unsuited for their appointed vocations. There is no question that knowledge becomes a woman just as well as a man. It is important to recognize that these women will be the first teachers of their children and also could, because of their education, help the youngsters with homework.[46]

Spitzweg campaigned tirelessly on behalf of the school and a quality education for its students. His death in 1828 left the school without its most ardent spokesman. Its standards weakened over the next decade. In order to keep up enrollment figures, the school abolished the required entrance examination.[47]

The graduates of Munich's Höhere Töchterschule probably received the most thorough education allowed young women in Bavaria at that time. The goals of its students, in part, justify Spitzweg's confidence in them and their capabilities. A document included in the school's yearly report for the year 1824–25 illustrates this point. Recorded therein are the aspirations of some of the students upon completing their studies. Out of a class of sixty students, seven wished to teach, fifteen wanted to manage dry-goods shops, and one wished to use her French-language skills in some way.[48] Although these statistics are not overwhelming, there is indication that some young women considered a career outside of the family. In this respect, the Höhere Töchterschule is the direct heir of the Teacher Training Institute for Women, whose students also prepared themselves for paid employment.

The Max Joseph Institute, the Nymphenburg School, and the Munich Höhere Töchterschule are noteworthy products of Bavaria's reform era. What conclusions can be drawn from a study of these schools that help explain prevailing attitudes about women and their place in society? All three schools wished to graduate young women who would become good wives and mothers. Except for the slight acknowledgment that girls might seek employment outside the home, as seen in the evidence from the Höhere Töchterschule, the prevailing attitude was that women would find their sense of well-being in the home, the private sphere of life. The differences among the schools are explained by the fact that each served a specific group within the social hierarchy. Girls were educated according to the dictates of their social class.

In spite of the turmoil and upheaval associated with the French Revolution era, Bavaria's social structure remained static in the first half of the

nineteenth century. The upper class, civilian and military alike, preserved the outlook of a traditional aristocracy. True to that mentality,
Bavaria's upper class followed in French high society's footsteps. Nowhere is this more evident than in the education of this group's daughters. The Max Joseph Institute was patterned after a French model, down
to the fact that many of the teachers were French women. Its graduates
were trained in the fine accomplishments of ladies of the high society.
Their education was thorough, but nevertheless it had an air of superfici-
ality about it.

Bavaria's middle class was not as homogeneous as the upper class. Yet
a common ethic of piety and pragmatism is evident, whether professionals, civil servants, or artisans are discussed. This solid practicality is dis-
cernible in the schools that middle-class girls attended. The
Nymphenburg School definitely catered to the daughters of the upper
middle class of professionals and high civil servants, whereas the students
at the Höhere Töchtershcule were girls from the lower civil service and
artisan ranks. Both the schools stressed hard work and approached education of the girls from a serious perspective. The graduates were expected
to become useful productive members of society. The ideal of the woman
as homemaker, wife, and mother dominates this picture. Yet these
women were also expected to be patriotic Bavarians as well. There is no
clamor for political rights or careers for women, but there is a tacit recognition that women should be aware of the public world around them.

Bavaria in the early years of the nineteenth century was a pre-
industrial society. Therefore it retained many of the values commonly
associated with eighteenth-century aristocratic life, such as that of pre-
revolutionary France. The stereotypes of amusing, charming, but frivolous aristocratic females and industrious, practical, hardworking middle-
class women were fixtures in Bavarian society. The reformed government
under Montgelas and his successors sought to preserve many social continuities through modernized political institutions. Through more
efficient means, traditional society, with its limitations placed on women,
was strengthened. The static condition of Bavaria's women at this time
bears witness to the shortcomings of enlightened thought when confronted with the problems facing women. Real change could only come in
the aftermath of the midcentury revolutionary period and the advent of
industrialized urban society. Such radical events challenged tradition-
bound beliefs and forced the re-evaluation of many. The proper position
of women in society was not exempt from scrutiny. It was only during the
second half of the nineteenth century that Bavaria, along with other
German and European states, instituted legal and educational reforms
that helped women on the path toward equality.

NOTES

1. "Die Leserinnen." *Morgenblatt für gebildete Stände*, 2 (1830), pp. 1045–46.

2. F. H. C. Schwarz, *Grundsätze der Tochtererziehung für die Gebildeten* (Jena, 1836), pp. 214–15. J. Wychgram, "Geschichte des höheren Mädchenschulwesens in Deutschland und Frankreich," in *Geschichte der Erziehung vom Anfang bis auf unsere Zeit*, ed. by K. A. Schmid, (Stuttgart, 1901), vol. 5, pt. 2, p. 268. It is interesting to note that similar dire predictions that too much education would harm girls' health were also used by French educators in the second half of the nineteenth century. See Linda L. Clark, "The Molding of the *Citoyenne:* The Image of the Female in French Educational Literature, 1880–1914," *Third Republic*, nos. 3–4 (1977), p. 94.

3. Jean Jacques Rousseau, *Emile* (New York, 1974), pp. 321–444, passim.

4. Eberhard Weis, *Montgelas, 1759–1799. Zwischen Revolution und Reform* (Munich, 1971). This is the first volume of Weis's monumental biography of Montgelas. It details his life and the political plans he had for Bavaria before he actually took office.

5. Rudolf Hindringer, *Das kirchliche Schulrecht in Altbayern. Von Albrecht V. bis zum Erlasse der bayerischen Verfassungsurkunde, 1550–1818* (Paderborn, 1916), p. 130.

6. Joseph Heigenmooser, "Geschichtliche Nachrichten über weltliche Lehrerinnen in Bayern," in *Jahresbericht der königlichen Kreis-Lehrerinnenbildungsanstalt für Oberbayern in München pro 1887–1888* (Munich, 1888), p. 63.

7. Friedrich Faber, *Ueber weibliche Bildung. Drei Reden an Heranreifende und Gereifte dieses Geschlechts* (Nuremberg, 1820), p. 22.

8. Elisabeth Blochmann, *Das "Frauenzimmer" und die "Gelehrsamkeit"* (Heidelberg, 1966), pp. 54–55. As a means to ensure the proper education of both boys and girls, the Montgelas government established a network of school inspectors. These men, usually Catholic or Lutheran clerics, would visit the various schools and then file reports with the Local School Commission. They were not only to observe the teachers and the content of the instruction but also to determine if the teachers or the students showed any unpatriotic tendencies. See Michael Doeberl, *Zur Geschichte der bayerischen Schulpolitik im 19. Jahrhundert. Sitzungsbericht der königlichen Bayerischen Akademie der Wissenschaften* (Munich, 1812), p. 27; and Hindringer, p. 137.

9. Joanne Schneider, "An Historical Examination of Women's Education in Bavaria: Mädchenschulen and Contemporary Attitudes about Them, 1799–1848," unpublished Ph.D. dissertation, Brown University, 1977, pp. 32–35. On the cited pages is a list of directives issued by the Montgelas government pertaining to girls' schools. The directives are primarily from the years 1802 to 1809.

10. Maria Liobgid Ziegler, *Die armen Schulschwestern von unserer Lieben Frau* (Munich, 1935), pp. 4–5; Berta Sachs, *Pläne und Massnahmen der Regierung des Königs Max I Joseph Mädchenschulen Altbayerns. Ein Beitrag zur Geschichte der Aufklärung in Bayern* (Munich, 1914), p. 15.

11. *Lehrplan für alle churpfalzbayerischen deutschen Elementarschulen in*

Städten sowohl auf dem Lande. Nebst einer dazu gehörigen Instruktion für Lehrer und Lehrerinnen. Vom churft. General-Schulen- und Studien Direktorium entworfen und von Sr. churfürst. Durchlaut gnädigst bestättigt (Munich, 1804), p. 46. Artikel 25: "Weit weniger Schwierigkeiten in Anwendung des neuen Lehrplans auf die weiblichen Schulen werden jene Lehrer und Lehrerinnen finden, denen nur Mädchen zu unterrichten obliegt. Diese werden in allen Zweigen des Unterrichts ein einförmigere, ganz auf die Natur, Verhältnisse und Bestimmung des Mädchens berechnete Lehrart befolgen; alle Beyspiele und Gleichnisse zur Erläuterung ihrer Lehren und Versinnlichung schwerer Begriffe aus dem Lebens und Geschäftskreise des Mädchens hernehmen; manchen Gegenstand, der für Knaben ausführlich behandelt werden muss mit Wenigern berühren, um sich dagegen über andere, das Mädchen oder Weib, als solches mehr interessierende oder näher angehende Dinge weiter verbreiten zu können, worüber in dem, seiner Zeit nachfolgenden allgemeinen Methodenbuche mehrere und deutlichere Winke werden gegeben werden."

12. Nymphenburgisches weibliches Erziehungsinstitut, Schriftliche Beantwortung und Ausarbeitung folgender Prüfungsfragen (bey Lehramtskandidatin Kreszenz Rapp), 16 Oktober 1807, Nr. 14542/1, Regierungsakten, Stadtarchiv München, Munich. "Warum wählt man für Mädchen-Schulen weibliche Lehrerinnen? Die Mädchen erfordern eine sanfte, etwas zartere Behandlung als die Knaben: weil ihnen die Natur den Keim der Sanftmuth und der Schüchternheit, als die edleste Gabe für ihr Geschlecht, in ihr Herz gepflanzte/ :versteht sich solche Schüchternheit, die die weibliche Sittsamkeit zur Begleiterin hat:/ Wer kann also diese weiblichen Gefühle, die seine Delikatesse, welche in ihr ganzes Wesen verwebt ist, besser behandeln als eine selbst von ihrem Geschlechte? Diese weiss jene Gefühle am besten zu entwickeln: denn sie trägt sie selbst in ihrem Busen. Sie kann daher den Mädchen ihre Leidenschaften mehr bezähmen, ihre edlen Gefühle mehr zur reinsten Tugend bilden, als ein Lehrer, der nur aus Büchern weibliche Delikatesse kennt."

13. Bericht der königlichen Lokal Schulkommission im Auftrag von dem königlichen Ministerium des Innerns von Zentner, betr. die Präparandinnenschule, 19 Juli 1813, Nr. 1327, Schulamt 134/I, Stadtarchiv München, Munich; Kammer des Innern and die Lokal Schulkommission betr. die Präparandinnenschule, 12 Oktober 1819, Nr. 19749/14619, Schulamt 134/I, Stadtarchiv München, Munich; *Königlich-Baierisches Intelligenz Blatt für den Isarkreis 1815* (Munich, 1815), p. 715. All of these sources specify requirements for entrance into the Teacher Training Institute.

14. Verzeichniss der Präparandinnen am Ende des 1. Semesters 1818, no number, Schulamt 134, Stadtarchiv München, Munich.

15. Ibid. Here is the information from that document:

Studentin	Alter	Stand der Eltern
1) Loehere, Josepha	24	Schäftler Meister
2) Frank, Anna	22	Zimmermann
3) Ebenbeck, Josepha	15	Salz-Conducteur
4) Haslander, Mariana	19	Tuchmacher

Studentin	Alter	Stand der Eltern
5) Gerstner, Sophie	18	Klaviermacher
6) Kneuttinger, Elise	18	Kanzellistner (pensioniert)
7) Versch, Barbara	16	Kriegs-Raths
8) Niedermayr, Anna	16	Nadler
9) Lieber, Susana	15	Büman Diener
10) Bode, Anna	16	königlicher Holzinspektor
11) Bonin, Elenore	18	Krämmer
12) Hörl, Kunigunde	19	Cantor und Mädchenlehrer
13) Zeichenberger, Josepha	18	Bildhauer
14) Spicker, Amalia	18	Stadt Gerichts Bote
15) Sedlmayr, Anna	18	Kleidermacher
16) Griebl, Francisca	27	königlicher Mauth Direktions Rechnungs Commissär

See also Sachs, p. 69.

16. Joseph Heigenmooser and Alfons Bock, eds., *Quellenbuch und Überblick der Geschichte der Pädagogik: Mit besonderer Berücksichtigung der bayerischen Erziehungs- und Schulgeschichte* (Munich, 1901), p. 198. Schneider, pp. 137–60.

17. Nymphenburg School was founded in 1730 by the Chorfrauen de Notre Dame. It was closed in 1816 and then reopened under government auspices in 1817. It remained a state-sponsored Mädchenschule for twenty years, when King Ludwig I gave it to the order of the Englisches Fräulein. See Johanna Gaab, *Das höhere Mädchenschulwesen in Bayern* (Munich, 1931), p. 33.

18. Ziegler, pp. 8–9.

19. Allgemeines Erziehungshaus des Max Joseph Stifts, 1813–1939. Bericht über die Eröffnung der Anstalt, 27 May 1813, Nr. 56414, Regierungsakten, Stadtarchiv München, Munich; *Max-Josef Stift. 150 Jahre. 1813–1963* (Munich, 1963), pp. 11–12; M. Sculteta, "Nach 90 Jahren (90. Jubiläum des Max Joseph Stifts in München)," *Bayernland*, 14 (1903), p. 412.

20. Max Josephstift. Oberrealschule für Mädchen: Weibliches Erziehungsinstitut zu München: Errichtung, Dotation, Gebäude, Einrichtung. Zweck des Max Josephstiftes, 4 Februar 1812, Nr. 21532, Ad. 2545, 2619, 2693, 2895, 3080, 3453, 3573, Kultus Ministerium, Hauptstaatsarchiv München, Munich. "Wenn der Plan des Instituts dem Zwecke desselben entsprechen soll, so darf es sich nicht bloss auf äussere Formen und auf Unterricht beschränken, sondern er muss die innere Bildung der Zöglinge, die eigentliche Erziehung derselben, mit steter Rücksicht auf ihre künftige Bestimmung, zugleich damit vereinigen. Das Institut muss eine Unterrichts- und zugleich eine Bildungs-Anstalt seyn, die ganze Verfassung und Einrichtung des Hauses muss zu jenen Tugenden führen, welche die jungen Frauenzimmer in ihren künftigen verschiedenen Beziehungen als Vorsteherinnen des Hauswesens, als Gattinnen, als Mütter, als Mitglieder der bürgerlichen Gesellschaft auszuüben haben, jeder Anlass muss benutzt werden, gute Gesinnungen und edle Gefühle zu erwecken und erhalten. . . ."

21. Ibid. See also Joseph Heigenmooser, *Überblick der geschichtlichen Ent-*

wicklung des höheren Mädchenschulwesens in Bayern bis zur Gegenwart (Berlin, 1905), p. 43.

22. Marie von Schulze, "Zum 100 jährigen Bestehen des königlichen Max-Joseph-Stiftes in München," *Bayerischer Kurier* (24 May 1913); Gaab, p. 33;*Max-Josef Stift* . . . , pp. 7, 14–15; *Provisorische Gesetze und Einrichtungen des weiblichen Erziehungs-Instituts der höheren Stände. Max Joseph Stift* (Munich, 1813), pp. 10–11.

23. The debate about the French influence exerted in the school by the teaching staff continued during the first half of the nineteenth century. Discussions about this problem even occurred in the Chamber of Deputies when the annual debates about school finances took place. But by the middle of the century, only references to the German character of the education are found. *Verhandlungen der zweiten Kammer des Ständesversammlung des Königreiches Baiern* (Munich, 1819), vol. 8, p. 84; vol. 11, p. 447; and, vol. 14, p. 334. Bericht des königlichen Rektors der hiesigen Lateinschule Dr. J. G. Beilhackpetre betr. das Erziehungsinstitut für Töchter aus der höheren Stände in München. 24 Februar 1847, Nr. 56414, Regierungsakten, Stadtarchiv München, Munich.

24. Heigenmooser, *Überblick der geschichtlichen* . . . , p. 43.

25. Ibid., p. 55. "Mit besonderer Sorgfalt wird man zur Hauswirtschaft anleiten und für jene Verrichtungen vorbereiten, welche die Mädchen einst als Gattin und Hausmutter zu besorgen haben. Sie müssen Kleider und Weisszeug selbst anfertigen. Ältere Zöglinge müssen jüngere pflegen und ankleiden, sind für Ordnung und Reinlichkeit derselben verantwortlich."

26. In the early years of the Max Joseph Institute, daughters of officers who had loyally served in the Bavarian army were allowed to enroll in the school. Their fees were paid by royal subsidy. Some of these girls could not be regarded as coming from Bavaria's highest social circles.

27. Gaab, p. 33.

28. Sachs, pp. 51–52.

29. The charter of the school is found in the first volume of its yearly reports. The information referred to is in the first paragraph of Die Verfassung der weiblichen Erziehungs- und Unterrichts Anstalt. *Nachricht von der gegenwärtigen Einrichtung der königlichen weiblichen Erziehungsanstalt in Nymphenburg* (Munich, 1817).

30. *Nachricht* . . . (1817), n.p.n., paragraphs 3 and 6; *Nachricht* . . . (1846), pp. i–v; Sachs, p. 52.

31. *Nachricht* . . . (1824), p. 8; *Nachricht* . . . (1826), p. 9.

32. *Nachricht* . . . (1820), p. 14; *Nachricht* . . . (1832), p. 8; *Nachricht* . . . (1824), p. 10.

33. *Nachricht* . . . (1817), n.p.n., paragraphs 3 and 6; *Nachricht* . . . (1846), pp. i–v.

34. *Nachricht* . . . (1820), p. 14; *Nachricht* . . . (1832), p. 8; *Nachricht* . . . (1824), p. 10.

35. *Nachricht* . . . (1829), p. 14. "Wenn nun eine glückliche Zukunft mit den Grundlagen der Erziehung des Instituts sich verbindet, so könnte man freylich über die weibliche Jugend der süssen Hoffnung sich erfreuen, dass sie dereinst

durch ihre Tugenden jener Bestimmung entspreche, die der Schöpfer und die Natur diesem Geschlechte angewiesen haben, und die Zierde, die Freude, das Heil und das Glück des häuslichen Lebens werde. Nichts kann aber auch am Schlusse eines mühsamen Schuljahres belohnender seyn, als eben diese Hoffnung, welche der Segen des Himmels rechtfertigen und erfüllen wolle!"

36. Töchterschule, höh-Luisenstrasse, Lehrpläne, Gehalter der Lehrer, Verbesserungsvorschläge der Lokal Schulkommission von der Regierung genehmigt, Polizey Direktor und Lokal Schulkommissar und die königliche bayerische Regierung des Isarkreises betr. eine Töchterschule; 26 Dezember 1819, Nr. 1026/I, Schulamt, Stadtarchiv München, Munich; G. Dostler, *1822–1922.* *Hundert Jahre Höhere Mädchenschule* (Munich, 1922), pp. 11–12.

37. Töchterschule, höh-Luisenstrasse, Lehrpläne, Gehalter der Lehrer, Verbesserungsvorschläge der Lokal Schulkommission von der Regierung genehmigt, königliche Regierung und die Lokal Schulkommission betr. eine höhere Töchterschule, Gründung derselben, 14 Juli 1820, Nr. 1026/I, Schulamt, Stadtarchiv München, Munich.

38. Sachs, pp. 60–61. "Die Töchterschule erhält dadurch 1. einen tüchtigen Lehrerstand, 2. einen guten Arithmetikunterricht mit gleichem Stoffausmass wie die Bürgerschule; sogar die Grundbegriffe der Geometrie, Zeichnen und Realien, dass ist, Geschichte, Erdkunde, Naturlehre, werden gelehrt; 3. ein ausgewähltes Schülerinnenmaterial durch Einführung einer Aufnahmeprüfung."

39. Bürger- und Töchterschule, Beilage zu Nr. 348, Jahresbericht der höheren Bürger und Töchter Schule, 1822–1823, Nr. 1184/II, Schulamt, Stadtarchiv München, Munich: G. N. Marschall, *Die Städtische Höhere Töchterschule in München. Eine Gedächtnissschrift zur Feier des 50 jährigen Verstandes derselben* (Munich, 1873), p. 4.

40. Töchterschule, höh-Luisenstrasse, Lehrpläne, Gehalter der Lehrer, Verbesserungsvorschläge der Lokal Schulkommission von der Regierung genehmigt, königliche Regierung und die Lokal Schulkommission betr. eine höhere Töchterschule, Schulinspektor Reflinger an die königliche Lokal Schulkommission über die höhere Bürger- und Töchterschule, 23 Januar 1823, Nr. 1026/I, Schulamt, Stadtarchiv München, Munich.

41. Ibid.

42. Bürger- und Töchterschule, Beilage Nr. 313, die königliche Schulkommission und die königliche Regierung über die Prüfungen am Ende des Schuljahrs und die Preisen, 28 April 1823, Nr. 1184/I, Schulamt, Stadtarchiv München, Munich.

43. Töchterschule, königlicher Regierungskreis an die Lokal Schulkommission, die Töchterschule sollte die Schülerinnen für den Lehramt bereiten, 17 Dezember 1824, Nr. 1026/I, Schulamt, Stadtarchiv München, Munich; Heigenmooser, p. 58; Wilhelm Muehlon, *Die rechtliche Stellung der Kirche auf dem Gebiet des bayerischen Volksschulwesens* (Munich, 1904), p. 6.

44. Ibid.

45. Töchterschule, höhere Generalakt des Kollegiums der Gemeinde Bevollmächtigten, 1820–1919. Simon Spitzweg betr. Mädchenerziehung, 19 Oktober 1825, Nr. 127, Schulamt, Stadtarchiv München, Munich.

46. Töchterschule, Stadtrat Simon Spitzweg an die höhere Töchterschule über die Wichtigkeit der weiteren Ausbildung der Mädchen, 2 August 1823, Nr. 1026/I, Schulamt, Stadtarchiv München, Munich "Ich glaube nicht befürchten zu müssen, dass dadurch die künftigen Bürgerinnen zu gelehrt, und für ihre eigentliche Bestimmung unbrauchbar werden möchten; denn unstreitig kleideten Kenntnisse die Frau eben so gut, als dem Mann; und ausserdem wird es jeder Bürgerin namhaft zu statten kommen ihre Kindern die erste Lehrerin werden, und denselben in den verschiedenen Schulgegenständen zu Hause nachhelfen zu können."

47. Dostler, pp. 23–24.

48. Bürger- und Töchterschule, Beilage Nr. 2192, Jahresbericht 1824–1825 der höheren Bürger- und Töchterschule, 16 Oktober 1825, Nr. 1184/II, Schulamt, Stadtarchiv München, Munich.

Hannah Arendt's
Rahel Varnhagen*

DEBORAH HERTZ

When female intellectuals become celebrities in America, much of their notoriety seems to derive from their sex. The female intellectual is packaged as a personality. Publicists and the public feel no shame in gossiping about such women's lives, condescendingly slighting their intellectual accomplishments.[1] Hannah Arendt became such a celebrity in the United States in the second half of her life. But however fascinating her life story was, it was not at all easy to neglect her work. She was just too formidably serious. Taking her seriously was therefore hard work. To be sure, in part this was because her contributions could not be easily pigeonholed. Her writings created classificatory dilemmas for specialized scholars, if not for the general public. Had she been a philosopher? A historian? A political theorist? Her ideologies were as hard to pin down as was her intellectual discipline. Had she been a conservative? An anarchist? A Zionist? A "self-hating" Jew? A feminist?

Exactly which sections of Arendt's corpus either the general public or the scholarly public has found to be the most provocative have changed over time. In the 1950s, it was her comparison of Stalinism to Nazism which attracted the most attention.[2] In the early 1960s, it was her thesis that Adolf Eichmann had been evil in a banal rather than in a sadistic fashion and her harsh judgment of the Jewish Councils which mightily aroused her readers.[3] Just after her death in 1975, it was her final, par-

*I am grateful to the State University of New York at Binghamton for a 1982 Summer Faculty Grant which made it possible to complete the research for this essay. Professors Elizabeth Young-Breuhl, Lotte Kohler, and David Biale were kind enough to comment on an earlier version of the essay.

tially unfinished work in metaphysics which captivated scholars, especially philosophers.[4] But in recent years yet another aspect of Arendt's work has come to the fore. Now debate on Arendt's narrower position on the role of the Jewish leadership during the Holocaust years is being inspected in the light of a wider perspective. Her views on the Holocaust are currently seen as a smaller part of a larger body of Arendt's work on the long sweep of Jewish history throughout the last two centuries. Yes, finally, almost a decade after her death, Arendt has been discovered as a Jewish historian.[5]

Arendt never wrote anything resembling a systematic history of the Jews in modern Europe, or even of the Jews in Germany. But from the very outset of her publishing career she was obsessed with and wrote about the Jewish past. The times and places she covered in these writings ranged widely, and her perspective was always thoroughly comparative. This breadth was hardly surprising, since neither narrowly national histories nor simple narrations of events were what Arendt found interesting about the Jewish or about any other part of the past. As was fitting for a scholar with an unusual commitment to political engagement in the present, Arendt sought nothing less from the past than to learn its lessons. This meant a search among the facts and the dates for patterns, for meanings, for moral lessons. Only discovery of such larger historical contexts would make it possible for the historian, or anyone needing to act politically in the present, to judge past behavior. The research in Jewish history necessary to fulfill Arendt's own triple injunction—to learn in order to judge in order to act—was above all focused on the twin burning questions of Jewish existence in the modern era: assimilation and nationalism. Both her studies and her political experiences led her to reject the first, but by no means to conclude that any ordinary version of the second was acceptable. She did become a Jewish nationalist, all right, but one of a very particular sort. It was her own process of coming to reject assimilation and her eventual enthusiasm for an unusual brand of Zionism which became the crucial themes in her writing on Jewish history.

For the American scholarly public, Arendt's contributions to Jewish history first became accessible when her *Origins of Totalitarianism* was published in 1951. Her years of celebrity with a broader public began only with her *Eichmann in Jerusalem* in 1963. But in fact her absorption, research, and writing on Jewish themes went back to the first book-length manuscript Arendt wrote after completing her dissertation in 1929. That post-dissertation manuscript was a biography of Rahel (née Levin) Varnhagen, the Jewish *salonière* whose Berlin home had been a famous intellectual center during the late eighteenth and early nineteenth centuries. But the biography remained unpublished until 1957, when an English translation was published in London. The book appeared in its original

74 DEBORAH HERTZ

German in 1959. A slightly revised American edition was published in 1974.[6]

In spite of the fame of its author, its several editions, and a full gamut of not totally unfavorable reviews, the book really did fall stillborn from the press.[7] Many Arendt aficionados quietly confess that they could never finish the book, that the book whetted but did not satisfy an interest in Rahel Varnhagen. Part of the problem was that the book was devoted to a person who was utterly obscure in an American context. The book presumed a familiarity with the literary personalities and debates of the romantic era in Germany, which was largely absent here. Moreover, Arendt's prose was dense, difficult, and altogether too abstract for a biography.

The fact that Arendt's biography has remained as obscure as its subject is a terrible shame, for the book is a fascinating one. Detailed examination of the book—the aim of this essay—repays handsomely in two respects. First, reconstruction of the book's themes shows a crucial transition in Arendt's own intellectual history. It was with this project that she moved from philosophy to history, from concern with the universal human fate to concern with Jewish fate in particular. Second, study of the book is useful in coming to terms not only with the author of the biography but also with its subject, Rahel Varnhagen herself. It is impossible to understand the significance of the Berlin salons for the female and the Jewish pasts in Germany without understanding Rahel Varnhagen. She was at the center of salon society and her life was a dramatic example of how far and how quickly a Jewish woman could travel away from tradition, family, and the Jewish community. She is important, and Arendt's biography of her is far and away the most complex and empathic portrait of her. Arendt's startling conclusion was that Rahel Varnhagen was, underneath it all and contrary to established opinion, proud and not ashamed to be Jewish. This conclusion badly needs scrutiny. Therefore it is fitting that we apply Arendt's emphasis on judgment to her own work, and judge whether her biography correctly interprets Rahel Varnhagen's life.

In the best tradition of German philosophy, Arendt's biography of Varnhagen was at once both a continuation of and a departure from the intellectual passions of her university years. Arendt's first serious mental work was philosophical, and especially the movement in twentieth-century philosophy later called existentialism. While in *Gymnasium* (advanced secondary school) in Königsberg and as a precocious auditor at the University of Berlin, her intellectual obsessions were the newest works in theology and philosophy.[8] She read Kierkegaard, Heidegger, and Jaspers, thinkers who rejected idealist or formalist systematic philosophical systems in order to turn their close attention to the unique individual's estrangement from the modern world. Appropriately enough, Arendt began university in 1924, at the University of Marburg, where Martin Heidegger was teaching. After a year of intensive study in his seminar, and a secret love affair with Heidegger, Arendt departed Marburg.[9] As was typical for German students, Arendt migrated to continue her studies, going first to Freiburg and then to Heidelberg. She wrote her Ph.D. under Karl Jaspers at Heidelberg. Her topic was St. Augustine's concept of neighborly love. Arendt was fascinated by Augustine's notion of love because it represented for her a desirable alternative offered in an earlier age to the alienation of the individual which was the moral and intellectual problem posed by the existentialist thinkers.[10]

Although neither the Jewish past in general nor Rahel Varnhagen in particular played any role in Arendt's intellectual life in these years, Arendt was aware of Varnhagen's existence since at least 1925. It was in that year that Arendt's friend Anne Mendelssohn bought the entire multi-volume series of Rahel's husband's memoirs for pennies a volume from a book dealer who had gone bankrupt during the inflation.[11] At that time Arendt paid little attention to her friend's find. But by the time Arendt had completed the Augustine thesis in 1929, a variety of non-academic events and friendships during the preceding five-year period effected a definite shift in her interests, and she finally decided to borrow and actually read the Varnhagen memoirs.

The most decisive event in the chain that turned Arendt away from philosophy was her growing involvement in the Zionist movement. In a fashion utterly consistent for someone who ardently believed in the importance of friends, Arendt's affiliation with Zionism grew out of her closeness to Kurt Blumenfeld. Blumenfeld was a prominent Zionist intellectual whose Zionism was "post-assimilatory." Blumenfeld acknowledged the success at social integration which generations of Jews had achieved in Germany since the emancipation era of the late eighteenth century. Blumenfeld's point was that twentieth-century Jews should be honest about the sharp limits of even the seemingly most complete assimilation. His conclusion was that Jews should therefore formulate their identity in proud, self-consciously Jewish terms.[12] The growing power of the Nazi Party in Germany after 1929 also played a role in Arendt's new concerns. Her perception that most Jews, even some of her closest friends, displayed a willed ignorance about Nazi plans for Jewry fueled Arendt's Zionist convictions.

While at Heidelberg in 1927, Arendt also began to pay more attention to the scholarly study of literature, especially that of the Romantic era. She grew close to Benno von Wiese, a young literary historian, and attended the lectures of von Wiese's mentor, Friedrich Gundolf. It seems to have been at this point that Arendt decided to embark on post-dissertation research on the Romantic period.[13] But the move to narrow her concentration to one singular Romantic woman seems to have been the result of some very non-intellectual experiences. It could not have been irrelevant in Arendt's shifting interests that she herself came to participate in the lively Sunday-afternoon salons which had become a tradition for Heidelberg's intelligentsia. A cousin who was on the scene then in Heidelberg later remembered Arendt, complete with pipe, in the role of an emancipated latter-day Rahel Varnhagen, amidst a swarm of prominent Gentile admirers.[14]

Few knew it at the time, but, according to Arendt's biographer, the parallels between Arendt's and Rahel Varnhagen's situations went far deeper, right down to their love lives. No doubt this perceived similarity was one of the more powerful reasons why Arendt confessed that Rahel Varnhagen was her "closest friend, although she had been dead for one hundred years."[15] Rahel Varnhagen's first affair had been with one Count Karl von Finckenstein, a dashing blond nobleman who had ultimately been unable to resist his family's opposition to his marriage to a Jew. After another rejection by a Spanish diplomat, she remained single until she was forty-three, when she converted and married Karl August Varnhagen von Ense. Karl August was extremely dedicated to his wife's literary projects and her potential literary fame. But Rahel never loved him as passionately as she had loved either of the two men who had rejected her. In her biographer's opinion, Heidegger's 1924 rejection led Arendt to empathize with Rahel's pain at her rejections by her first two lovers. When Arendt married Gunter Stern (Anders) in 1929, the parallels deepened. Stern was Arendt's intellectual comrade and daily companion. But she never trusted him with her melancholic, stormy side, which she had revealed only to Heidegger.

Because Arendt felt a deep empathy with Rahel Varnhagen's love experiences, it by no means follows that this empathy was Arendt's only or most important motive for choosing to write about her or that this motive explains the content or the style of the biography. Once her interest in Zionism, her exposure to Gundolf, and her own triumphs in Heidelberg's salons awakened her interest in Jewish history and in the Romantic era, several other factors besides the paralle⁻ in their love lives drew Arendt to concentrate on Rahel Varnhagen. Her motives for choosing Varnhagen as a subject were actually many in number and various in kind.

Arendt saw in Rahel Varnhagen's final comments on her Jewishness a microcosm of the post-assimilatory Jewish identity she herself had come to endorse. When Rahel Varnhagen lay dying in 1833, she proclaimed that "the thing which all my life seemed to me the greatest shame, which was the misery and misfortune of my life—having been born a Jewess—

this I should on no account now wish to have missed."[16] This claim and other statements and actions Arendt discovered throughout Varnhagen's life were evidence for Arendt that, at the very outset of Jewish emancipation in Germany, this woman had already learned to be suspicious of the seductions of the Gentile world. Thus Arendt had a political as well as a personal empathy with her subject.

But entangled with the personal and political empathy which Arendt felt for Varnhagen were some more generalized intellectual concerns which made writing her biography a perfect project. In 1930, while her husband was pursuing an advanced degree in sociology, the couple moved to Frankfurt. Arendt had received a grant to work on the biography, which left her free to live where she chose.[17] While in Frankfurt, she participated actively in the university's intellectual life and attended Karl Mannheim's seminars. One of these seminars was devoted to the epoch of "early liberalism" in Germany during the beginning of the nineteenth century.[18] The seminar gave Arendt a chance to acquaint herself with the social and political history of the period, as well as with the sociology of knowledge methodology pioneered by Mannheim. But for Arendt, acquaintance by no means meant agreement. As summarized in a review of Mannheim's *Ideology and Utopia*, which she published in 1930, Arendt came to reject definitively Mannheim's approach. Although she by no means accused him of being a "vulgar" or reductionist Marxist, in her view his approach to ideas still robbed the realm of intellect of its rightful autonomy.[19]

Arendt's rejection of Mannheim for being too much of a materialist did not arise from an idealist position on her part. Rather, her critique of materialism followed from her existentialism, which she took with her when she moved from philosophy to history. Arendt found in the Romantics' enthusiasm for the individual, for feelings, for friends, and for the irrational an early version of existentialism, just as she had found a far earlier version of it in Augustine.[20] More specifically, she found in Rahel Varnhagen a very clear example of this Romantic version of existentialism. Varnhagen had a high conception of her own individual mental powers, in spite of her haphazard education and her unwillingness to write for publication.[21] In Rahel Varnhagen's loneliness Arendt found an analogue to modern experiences of alienation, and in her practice of "self-thinking" she found an analogue to modern notions of individualism. Moreover, Arendt decided that it would be fitting to employ a highly romantic and expressive method in her telling of Rahel Varnhagen's story. Arendt announced at the outset of the book that she had written the biography as if it were an autobiography, so convinced was she that she understood Varnhagen's own perspective.[22]

Arendt's enthusiasm for Varnhagen's romanticism was also linked to her critique of assimilationism. Like so many other central issues in modern life, the fundamental position one held on the Jewish "question" could be traced back to one's views on the eighteenth-century dialogue between the Enlightened and the Romantics.[23] The former celebrated reason, progress, and secularism. Following Christian Wilhelm von Dohm, enthusiasts of the Enlightenment tended to believe that Jewish political and economic emancipation would and should be followed by assimilation so successful that Jewry as a cohesive ethnic group would disappear.[24] Those on the Romantic side of the debate celebrated emotion, history, and ethnic difference. Following Johann Herder, they opposed the ultimate radical assimilationist consequences of the Enlightened position. Arendt was not the only twentieth-century Jewish thinker whose views on assimilation were self-consciously grounded in a position on the classic debates between supporters of the Enlightenment and supporters of Romanticism. Hermann Cohen and Walther Rathenau stood on the side of the Enlightenment; Martin Buber and Gershom Scholem stood with Arendt on the side of Romanticism.[25]

Nor were the rich set of intertwined personal, political, and intellectual motives which drew Arendt to Varnhagen the only reasons why her project on Varnhagen became so exciting. While using the Varnhagen Collection at the Prussian State Library in 1932, Arendt discovered a set of letters which Rahel Varnhagen had written to the novelist Regina Frohberg (née Rebecca Solomon, married Rebecca Friedländer) between 1805 and 1810. Karl August Varnhagen von Ense had liberally edited his wife's published correspondence to remove references to her Jewish family and friends and to her pain and anger at the social costs of her Jewishness. He never allowed these letters to Frohberg to be published, because they were written in a very bitter period in Varnhagen's life to a woman with whom she could be very frank, since Frohberg's problems were all too similar to her own.[26] For Arendt, these letters to Frohberg were the perfect evidence for the theme of her biography, which was that Rahel Varnhagen saw through the mystique of assimilation and had a deeply rooted Jewish identity. By the end of 1932, Arendt had published three articles about her work on Varnhagen, and had written eleven chapters of the biography.[27] She planned to supplement her text with a selection from the letters to Frohberg and a corrected version of other letters which had never been published in their entirety.[28]

But political events intervened, in the form of Hitler's appointment as Chancellor in January 1933. Arendt herself belonged to no political parties. But her husband was friendly with prominent members of the Communist Party, and she was doing secret ideological work for the Zionists at the Prussian State Library.[29] Gunter Anders left for Paris in February 1933, and she joined him there in the fall.[30] For many years to come,

Rahel Varnhagen must have been very far indeed from Arendt's mind. Arendt was faced with problems of a pressing practical nature. She had to find work as a refugee in Paris, undergo the ordeal of divorce and remarriage, endure temporary incarceration in an internment camp, fight to procure a visa for the United States, and then settle and find employment in New York City.[31] To be sure, at the urging of her new husband, Heinrich Blücher, and her friend Walter Benjamin, Arendt did complete the last two chapters of the biography in the summer of 1938.[32] Still, her papers show no record of any attempt to publish the biography throughout the 1930s or 1940s. The only reference of any kind to the manuscript is a 1942 letter from Jerusalem from Arendt's friend Gershom Scholem, who mentioned his plans for delivery of his copy of the Rahel Varnhagen manuscript to Arendt.[33] Whether or not his was the only surviving copy is not known.

During the late 1940s and early 1950s, Arendt's intellectual energies were devoted to writing *The Origins of Totalitarianism*. In the first section of that book, "Antisemitism," Arendt incorporated many of the same themes she had first worked through in the biography: the sad futility of so many individual attempts at assimilation, the privileged Jews' betrayal of their less fortunate brethren in eighteenth-century Berlin, the choice each Jew had to make between becoming a pariah, a "conscious" pariah, or a parvenu.[34] The only record of any interest Arendt showed during these years in her long-neglected manuscript is an exchange of letters about it in 1952 with her ex-mentor and lifetime friend, Karl Jaspers.[35] Arendt had sent Jaspers the manuscript for his advice about its content and whether and where she might publish it. His response was bracing. Although he did like much about the biography, Jaspers thought that Arendt's work needed much stylistic and other revision. Fundamentally, Jaspers judged that the biography was more about Arendt's own process of becoming a self-conscious Jew than a true portrait of the complicated Rahel Varnhagen herself. Jaspers could not agree that the essence of Varnhagen's life could be reduced to her Jewishness. Arendt responded that she had decided, after all, not to publish the biography. Some of Jaspers's minor criticisms she accepted. But Arendt stood by her emphasis on the utter centrality of Jewishness in Varnhagen's life. Arendt and Jaspers simply disagreed about how crucial a factor Jewishness was in the lived experience of Jews in modern Germany, either for this one woman at that time or for German Jewry as a whole over time. Arendt did explain that she had not meant to impose her own values on Varnhagen's experience. Rather, she wrote Jaspers, she had meant to express in Rahel Varnhagen's own terms Varnhagen's conflicts about how to balance her inner feelings about being Jewish against the way others treated her because of her Jewishness.

Evidently, Arendt changed her mind eventually, for within the next several years she did decide to publish the biography, without substantial changes in the text.[36] The publisher for the English edition, which appeared in 1957, was the East and West Library in London, which published it for the Leo Baeck Institute. Leo Baeck had been a leading rabbi in Berlin during the Holocaust years, and the L.B.I. is an international research institute dedicated to the history of the Jews in Germany, which Arendt had helped to establish in New York City after the war.[37] One scholar has suggested that the publisher hoped to use proceeds from the sale of the book for progressive political projects in Israel.[38] The German edition followed two years later, published by Piper in 1959.[39]

Up until now this essay has steadfastly remained loyal to its first goal, examining the history of Arendt's biography of Rahel Varnhagen for the light it sheds on her own intellectual history. This reconstruction of the history of the book has attempted to provide a description of the book's "context of discovery," or the reasons why it came to be written. But the time has come to move quickly to the essay's second goal, the analytic task of providing the "context of justification." This is necessary because a full enumeration of Arendt's reasons for writing the biography can and should remain distinct from evaluating the book as a work of scholarship. Stylistic problems with Arendt's prose aside, there are many such analytic angles from which the book can be viewed. Although Arendt was explicit that her contribution was not a work of social history, it is not at all inappropriate to ask whether the social-history claims which she makes in the book are accurate or not.[40] There are other pertinent questions which must be asked too, such as whether the primary evidence Arendt offers actually demonstrates her thesis about Varnhagen, whether her decision to write the biography as if in the first person was a correct one, and whether Arendt's model for categorizing Jewish behavior is an adequate one. It is also fair to ask whether Arendt gives a useful portrait of Rahel Varnhagen as a female as well as whether she gives a useful portrait of her as a Jew. An efficient way to answer this string of questions would be to separate out the aspects of the book which are correct and useful from those which are wrong or problematic.

Even though Arendt did not conceive of her biography as a work of social history, one of the book's most useful features is the way that Arendt embedded her analysis of Varnhagen as an individual in descriptions of the changing material situation of larger social groups in Berlin at the time. Without providing the details required for a thorough economic analysis, Arendt did sketch the long-term historical reasons for the temporary capital shortage of the Prussian nobility, for the unusual wealth of Berlin's Jewish community, and for the relative absence then and there of a Gentile bourgeoisie.[41] Arendt's thesis that the nobility was the only group with which Berlin Jews had real social and economic ties is convincing and original, although she did not explain the chronological irony of the lag between the social and the economic ties.[42] In Arendt's view, Varnhagen's fate with her lovers and friends could partially be explained by the changing situation of these larger groups. She described how the nobility and the sections of the intelligentsia dependent on noble patronage turned anti-Semitic when the need for Jewish capital decreased in the first decades of the nineteenth century. Arendt tried to show that when in 1807 Prussia lost Polish lands populated with many poor Jews, which had made the rich Berlin Jews appear to be exceptions, nobles and intellectuals found additional reasons to become anti-Semitic.

Arendt's analysis of the milieu of these wealthy Jewish families, into one of which Varnhagen was born, was especially penetrating. According to Arendt, the richest Jews in Berlin had absolutely no solidarity with poor Jews elsewhere in Prussia, whose sole use had been to provide them with a background against which they could be tokens. In spite of the high taxes and wide gamut of restrictions from which these rich token Jews suffered, Arendt judged that many preferred this situation to an emancipation which would deprive them of the conditions which allowed them, as exceptional tokens, to become so rich and powerful. Arendt saw exceptional Jews as preferring to escape from Judaism altogether by conversion and intermarriage, rather than struggle to reform Judaism or achieve political rights as Jews. She went so far as to condemn them for lacking any principled commitment to anyone, including their fellow Jews, knowing only the questionable ties binding those who sought an individual road away from family and from heritage. In a passage that well sums up one of the themes she would develop in her later work, Arendt compared the exceptional Jews' willingness to separate themselves from the rest of Jewry to some of the Gentile friends' willingness to accept them as their token, "exception" friends while remaining anti-Semitic.[43] A less sentimental picture of the first generation to experience the emancipation process would be difficult to imagine.

In spite of the attempted balance between the social and the individual, the biography goes wrong insofar as neither side of the equation gets enough or the right kind of attention. The lack of attention to the individual is the more problematic in terms of the goals of any biography, and thus of simply following Arendt's narrative. In many passages, to be sure, Varnhagen herself is very much with us, in exceedingly concrete terms. We are treated to long quotes from her letters and diaries; one entire chapter is devoted to one of Varnhagen's recurrent dreams. Her emotional relationships with each of her lovers receive exquisitely detailed attention. Yet we are often deprived of the most mundane, yet utterly necessary details. Although historically well versed readers might be able to fill in the details themselves, Arendt often does not reveal the crucial facts. Was Herr Bokelmann, her lover in Paris in the summer of 1800, Jewish or not? Was it she who rejected Count von Finckenstein in 1799, or really he who rejected her? Was Alexander von der Marwitz actually willing to marry her if she had broken with Karl August Varnhagen von Ense?[44] At some times in her life Varnhagen is described as having been rich, at other times as having been poor. Yet her precise place on the city's social hierarchy at various times in her life is never made clear. The complaint is not that one needs such facts for social history "background." Rather, it is that the lack of these details makes it difficult, if not impossible, to be sure of the exact kinds of pressures Varnhagen herself was under when certain decisions had to be made.

There are equally serious problems on the other side of the individual-social equation. And all of them stem from the odd mixture in Arendt's approach of the comparative and systematic methods of social history with the causally idealist and individualist constructions of an existentialist philosopher new to history. In truth, Arendt only flirted with taking the aggregate, slow-moving fate of large groups seriously. When it came to explaining the truly important things in life or history, it was will and personality and spirit that made things happen. As an example, take Arendt's treatment of the birth and death of the salon as a social institution, an institution which was crucial for Rahel Varnhagen's ability to mix with and marry into prestigious Gentile society. On the one hand, Arendt acknowledged that the nobility's post-1806 boycott of the exceptional Jews was a key cause of the decline in the Jewish salons. Yet elsewhere she also maintained that the salon was nothing but a "chance constellation in an age of social transition" or that "only the power of Rahel Varnhagen's personality" held the salon together.[45] In other words, just where her own evidence suggests a large-scale social explanation of short-term institutional change, Arendt abandons the systematic and the collective explanation for the random and the individual explanation.

Arendt's failure to provide the right balance between the individual and the social shows up very clearly when she applied her pariah—"conscious" pariah—parvenu model of Jewish behavior to Rahel Varnhagen. In her classificatory schema, the pariah was the outcast Jew rejected from prominent Gentile society, and the parvenu was the opportunist who sought acceptance by the prominent, undeterred either by modesty or by ethnic solidarity. The only way out of these two distasteful alternatives was to become a conscious pariah, a Jew who accepted the fact of rejection but based a conscious political solidarity with other pariahs—Jewish and oppressed Gentile alike—upon clear-eyed recognition of that rejection. Arendt first published an essay outlining the notion of the conscious pariah in 1944.[46] But in fact her notion of the conscious pariah was first developed in the last chapter of the biography where she tried to show that Varnhagen had become conscious of her pariah status by the end of her life. Sometimes Arendt made the stronger claim that she had never really been a "real" parvenu. The full text of Varnhagen's famous deathbed utterance casts doubt on her ultimate transformation into a conscious pariah.[47] As for Arendt's stronger claim that Varnhagen had never been a parvenu, the problem is that the bulk of the evidence, including most of Arendt's own citations throughout the earlier chapters of the book, just does not support this classification of Rahel Varnhagen as a conscious pariah. On the contrary, most of Varnhagen's own versions of her marital plans, her social encounters, and her experiences with getting and losing male and female friends suggest that, if classifiable at all, she was a "conscious parvenu" rather than a conscious pariah.[48] Again and again, she tried her best to enter the charmed noble circle, aware of how she must shun other Jews to succeed in this attempt, aware of how limited her success always was. It seems obvious that for all of her methodological preference for examining heroic individuals rather than groups, the reason that Arendt's labeling of Varnhagen is so wrong is that it is not really Rahel Varnhagen's process of coming to be a conscious pariah Arendt was describing but rather her own. It is this that makes her decision to write the book in the first person so deceptive. She believed in the particular and the individual, but could not manage to break away from the abstraction of a philosophical approach, which led her to portray a flesh-and-blood individual in an idealized fashion. She moved much of the way from philosophy to history, but the move was really never complete. Her perspective and her new sources allowed her to depict a Rahel Varnhagen who was undoubtedly closer to the real Rahel Varnhagen than the picture provided either by her husband or by previous biographers.[49] Nevertheless, her picture was still recognizably Hannah Arendt's Rahel Varnhagen.

It seems fitting to conclude with a preview of how future work might both continue and alter Arendt's work on Varnhagen. It was Arendt's view that all studies of German-Jewish history written before the Holocaust would have to be rewritten after this terrible conclusion to the German-Jewish symbiosis.[50] Her reasoning, no doubt, was that the events of the far past only acquire their meaning when seen in the perspective of the end of the story. Yet it does not seem that the end of the German-Jewish story is in fact the perspective from which Arendt's work on Varnhagen should or will be analyzed anew. On the contrary, the post-Holocaust historiography of German Jewry has only underscored Arendt's own alertness to the existential nuances and personal bankruptcy often involved in the radical assimilationist stance. Rather, future work is likely to reconceptualize Rahel Varnhagen, not as a Jew, but as a female. Arendt never concerned herself politically with feminism, and except for a few minor asides about Varnhagen's lack of beauty and lack of a dowry, she did not analyze Varnhagen's experiences as a woman. There is no doubt at all that her identification with Rahel Varnhagen qua female played a large role in her context of discovering Varnhagen, but this identification played no major role in the book's substantive themes. In fact, one of the weaknesses of the biography is Arendt's high-handed dismissal of many of Rahel Varnhagen's female Jewish friends.[51] Yet as Arendt's own abbreviated discussion of these friends and much other evidence suggests, Jewish women in Berlin had a far greater chance to assimilate through intermarriage than Jewish men had to assimilate through either intermarriage, education, or employment. Newly discovered conversion and intermarriage records have made it possible to show the aggregate contrast between female and male rates of assimilation in Berlin.[52] The rediscovery of Rahel Varnhagen's letters to Regina Frohberg will make it possible to reconstruct this friendship, and the publication of these letters will definitely alter the picture Arendt painted of Rahel Varnhagen's ties to her Jewish women friends. But whatever new research will show, it will be much indebted to Arendt's contribution. For it is not just that Rahel Varnhagen helped Arendt to become a conscious pariah, with decisive consequences for Arendt's political future. At the same time, Arendt allowed Varnhagen to live on into the twentieth century, with decisive consequences for our ability to understand Varnhagen's meaning for our own day.

NOTES

1. See, for example, Alfred Kazin's review of the new biography of Arendt (Elisabeth Young-Bruehl, *Hannah Arendt: For Love of the World*), entitled "Woman in Dark Times," in *The New York Review of Books* (June 24, 1982), pp. 3–5.

2. For discussion, see Stephen Whitfield, *Into the Dark: Hannah Arendt and Totalitarianism* (Philadelphia, 1980), and Margaret Canovan, *The Political Thought of Hannah Arendt* (New York, 1974).

3. Arendt's book was *Eichmann in Jerusalem: A Report on the Banality of Evil* (New York, 1963). For an introduction to the response to the book, see Jacob Robinson, *And the Crooked Shall Be Made Straight: The Eichmann Trial, the Jewish Catastrophe, and Hannah Arendt's Narrative* (New York, 1965).

4. See Hannah Arendt, *The Life of the Mind* (New York, 1978); vol. 1 is entitled *Thinking*, and vol. 2 is entitled *Willing*.

5. See Ron H. Feldman's edition of Arendt's essays, *The Jew as Pariah: Jewish Identity and Politics in the Modern Age* (New York, 1978). A conference entitled "History, Ethics, Politics: A Conference Based on the Work of Hannah Arendt" was held at New York University in October 1981; one panel was devoted to "Questions of Jewish Identity." For information about the eventual publication of the proceedings of the conference, contact Prof. Reuben Garner, Empire State College, Buffalo, New York. A recent review of Young-Breuhl's biography noted the importance of discovering "the source of her [Arendt's] inspiration to elevate a particular perception of the 'Jewish question' into a universal theory—at once metaphysical and concrete—of 'World History'" in order to grasp Arendt's "creative and controversial brilliance." See Gilbert Allardyce's review of *Hannah Arendt: For Love of the World* in the *American Historical Review*, 88 (1983), p. 75.

6. The American edition was published in both hardback and paper by Harcourt Brace Jovanovich: Hannah Arendt, *Rahel Varnhagen: The Life of a Jewish Woman* (New York, 1974).

7. A complete file of the reviews of the book can be found with Arendt's papers at the Library of Congress in Washington, D.C. I am grateful to Martin Bunzl for technical assistance in obtaining copies of the reviews. Among the reviews of interest, see Heinrich Schnee's in *Historisches Jahrbuch*, 80 (1960), pp. 458–59; Vivian Gornick's in *The Village Voice*, January 6, 1975; Lore Dickstein's in *The New York Times Book Review*, November 24, 1974, pp. 27–28; and Brigitta Hilberling's in *Des Hochland*, 52 (August 1960), pp. 569–76.

8. See Elisabeth Young-Breuhl, *Hannah Arendt: For Love of the World* (New Haven, 1982), pp. 35–36.

9. Ibid., pp. 50–55.

10. A good summary of the Augustine dissertation can be found in chap. 1 of Robert Meyerson's dissertation, "Hannah Arendt: Romantic in a Totalitarian Age, 1928–1963," unpublished dissertation, University of Minnesota, 1972.

11. Young-Breuhl, p. 56. It is not known precisely which set of Varnhagen memoirs Mendelssohn bought. It was probably either Karl August Varnhagen von Ense, *Denkwürdigkeiten des eignen Lebens* (6 vols; Leipzig, 1871), or his *Denkwürdigkeiten und vermischte Schriften* (9 vols.; Mannheim, 1837–59).

12. Young-Breuhl, p. 71. For an eloquent statement of this position, see Gershom Scholem, *On Jews and Judaism in Crisis* (New York, 1976).

13. Young-Breuhl, p. 68.

14. Ibid., p. 68.

15. Ibid., p. 56.

16. Hannah Arendt, *Rahel Varnhagen: The Life of a Jewess* (London, 1957), p. 1. Unless otherwise noted, all citations are from the 1957 London edition.

17. Arendt's grant was from the Notgemeinschaft der deutschen Wissenschaft; see Young-Breuhl, p. 77.

18. On Mannheim's seminar, see Ülrich Hermann's introduction to the reissue of Hans Gerth's *Bürgerliche Intelligenz um 1800. Zur Soziologie des deutschen Frühliberalismus* (Göttingen, 1976). I am grateful to David Kettler of Trent University in Canada, author of a forthcoming biography of Karl Mannheim, for sharing some unpublished material on Mannheim with me.

19. See Arendt's "Philosophie und Soziologie. Anlässlich Karl Mannheim, *Ideologie und Utopie*," *Die Gesellschaft*, 7 (1930), pp. 163–76. For a useful summary of Arendt's position on Mannheim, see Meyerson, pp. 54–59.

20. On the parallels between Arendt's project on Romanticism and Rahel Varnhagen and her earlier work, see Meyerson, pp. 75–77.

21. One of Varnhagen's quotes to this effect can be found in Arendt, *Rahel Varnhagen*, p. 79. One of the most frustrating aspects of all editions of the biography is that there are no references for specific quotations.

22. Arendt, *Rahel Varnhagen*, p. xi.

23. I found Meyerson's discussion of this theme most helpful, on pp. 64–69 of his thesis. For Arendt's own version, see "Aufklärung und Judenfrage," in *Zeitschrift für die Geschichte der Juden in Deutschland*, 4 (1932), pp. 65–77.

24. A good introduction to Dohm's position is Jacob Katz, *Out of the Ghetto: The Social Background of Jewish Emancipation, 1770–1870* (Cambridge, Mass., 1973), chap. 2.

25. Meyerson, p. 60.

26. Arendt had not finished her work on these letters when she left Germany in 1933. After the war, she believed that they had been destroyed in the course of the war. However, the letters survived the war and are now at the Jagiellonian Library in Krakow, Poland. I will publish an edition of the letters (in German) in 1984 with Kiepenheuer and Witsch in Cologne, West Germany. For details on the rediscovery, see my "The Varnhagen Collection Is in Krakow," *American Archivist*, 44 (1981), pp. 223–28.

27. "Berliner Salon" and "Brief Rahels an Pauline Wiesel," in *Deutscher Almanach für das Jahr 1932* (Leipzig, 1932), pp. 175–84 and 185–90, and "Rahel Varnhagen. Zum 100. Todestag," in *Kölnische Zeitung*, March 7, 1933, reprinted in *Jüdische Rundschau*, April 7, 1933.

28. Arendt's notes for the corrected version of these letters are in the Archive of the Leo Baeck Institute in New York City.

29. Young-Breuhl, p. 102.

30. Ibid., p. 103.

31. Ibid., chap. 4.

32. Arendt mentioned the completion of the last two chapters in a letter to Karl Jaspers which she wrote in 1952. See note 35 below.

33. Scholem's letter is dated February 6, 1942; it can be found with Arendt's papers at the Library of Congress, File 12.

34. See Hannah Arendt, *The Origins of Totalitarianism* (Cleveland, 1951), chap. 3.

35. I am grateful to Mary McCarthy, Arendt's literary executor, and to Dr. Hans Saner, Jasper's literary executor, for their permission to refer to these as yet unpublished letters. I am grateful to Prof. Lotte Kohler for making copies of this exchange of letters available to me. Jasper's letter is dated August 23, 1952; Arendt's is dated September 7, 1952. The letters will eventually be published in the Arendt-Jaspers correspondence, which Prof. Kohler and Dr. Saner are preparing. The German edition of the correspondence will be published by Piper in Munich; the English edition, by Harcourt Brace Jovanovich in New York.

36. See Arendt, *Rahel Varnhagen*, preface.

37. The Leo Baeck Institute was founded in 1955 by the Council of Jews

from Germany; since that year, the Institute has published an annual yearbook devoted to this theme.

38. See Meyerson, p. 78.

39. There were apparently conflicts with the Leo Baeck Institute over the timing of the German edition, as suggested by two of Arendt's letters to Dr. Siegfried Moses at the Jerusalem L.B.I. The letters are dated January 28, 1957, and April 29, 1958, and are in File 11 of the Arendt papers at the Library of Congress.

40. Arendt, *Rahel Varnhagen*, p. xi.

41. Ibid., p. 100 on the nobility; p. 145 on the Jewish community.

42. Ibid., pp. 146–47.

43. Ibid., p. 69.

44. On Bokelmann, see ibid., p. 59; on von Finckenstein, see pp. 27–40; on von der Marwitz, see p. 133.

45. The first quote comes from Arendt, *Rahel Varnhagen*, p. 45; the second from p. 46.

46. Hannah Arendt, "The Jew as Pariah: A Hidden Tradition," *Jewish Social Studies*, 6 (1944), pp. 99–102.

47. The final four sentences of the quote are in fact evidence of her strong *Christian* allegiance. See the Schnee review cited in Note 7 above.

48. For example, see the quotes Arendt cites on pp. 105, 107, 131, 132, 144, 147, 151, 164, 171, and 179 of the biography for evidence which better fits the label "conscious parvenu" than that of "conscious pariah." I am grateful to the students in my seminar "Jews and Other Germans," taught in the fall semester of 1981 at the State University of New York at Binghamton, for their thoughtful discussion of this aspect of the book. Sharon Muller's article "The Pariah Syndrome," in *Response*, 39 (1980), pp. 52–57, was also useful. I am indebted to Betsy Platkin Teutsch for bringing this article to my attention.

49. Some of the more important biographies include Otto Bedrow, *Rahel Varnhagen: Ein Lebens und Zeitbild* (Stuttgart, 1902); Ellen Key, *Rahel Varnhagen: A Portrait* (New York and London, 1913); Jean-Edouard Spenlé, *Rahel, Madame Varnhagen von Ense: Histoire d'un Salon Romantique en Allemagne* (Paris, 1910), and Bertha Badt, *Rahel und ihre Zeit* (Munich, 1912).

50. Arendt, *Rahel Varnhagen*, p. xii.

51. Ibid., p. 87 on Regina Frohberg; on Henriette Herz, p. 24; on Dorothea (Mendelssohn) (Veit) Schlegel, p. 25. It is also possible to interpret Arendt's failure to discuss Rahel Varnhagen as a woman in the light of her decision to write the biography as Rahel Varnhagen herself thought, and not to have any more awareness than she could have had. I am grateful to Dr. Elizabeth Kamarck Minnick for sharing her views on this issue with me, although I received them too late to make major changes in the essay. Minnick's own essay, "Hannah Arendt: Thinking As We Are," will appear in *Between Women: Biographers, Novelists, Critics, Teachers and Artists Write about Their Work on Women*, Sara Ruddick, Carol Ascher, and Louise DeSalvo, eds. (Boston, 1984)

52. I summarize the results of this research in chap. 7, "Seductive Conversion," of my monograph-in-progress, *Mixed Company: The Jewish Salons of Eighteenth-Century Berlin.*

Henriette Schleiermacher
A Woman in a Traditional Role

GWENDOLYN E. JENSEN

Henriette von Mühlenfels was born in Pomerania and in 1804, when she was sixteen, married Ehrenfried von Willich, a pastor serving as chaplain in the war against Napoleon. She was widowed two years later and left with a daughter and a son, who was born after his father's death. She lived for a time near her late husband's relatives on the island of Rügen, off the Pomeranian coast, and within a year and a half became engaged to another pastor, a bachelor over twice her age who had been a friend of her late husband's. They were married in 1809, and set up their home in Berlin, where they lived until his death in 1834. They had three children of their own, including one son who died when he was nine years old.

Because her second husband was Friedrich Ernst Daniel Schleiermacher, the most distinguished German theologian of the time, many of her letters have been available in published form for over a century.[1] These letters have been standard source material for scholars working on Schleiermacher. What is proposed in this essay is to use these letters once again, not for what they reveal about her second husband, but rather see what can be learned from them about Henriette.

Most of the letters were written in the first decade of the nineteenth century during a period of military and political turmoil and intellectual and religious regeneration. In both these spheres Schleiermacher played a major role. The army of Prussia was defeated by Napoleon at Jena and Auerstädt in 1806, and the royal family and government had to flee east to Königsberg. Within that government there emerged leadership demanding reform of the state along lines that had been proposed before but had never been supported by the force of military disaster. Therefore, the era of Prussian reform (1806–19) began in the shadow of military defeat, promising many reforms but delivering only on some of them. Serfdom was abolished, the church was revitalized, a new university at Berlin was established, and a constitution was promised, though not granted. These great events took place in an atmosphere of renewed cultural vitality in Berlin and other German cities, with the ideals of Romanticism and nationalism giving serious, intelligent people a renewal of hope and confidence in a time of great trouble. Ernst was a central figure in the reform movement, and the time of his courtship and marriage was for him the time of greatest influence in the political and religious affairs of Prussia. He traveled back and forth to the government-in-exile, worked for the establishment of the university, and framed the constitution of a new state church. His earlier successes as a theologian and a man of persuasive sermons were now rounded out by his becoming a man of affairs.

The correspondence has the advantage of being ample. It begins just before Henriette's first marriage to Ehrenfried von Willich, Ernst's friend, in 1804. Their friendship during her first marriage was carried on almost entirely through letter-writing, and his consolation after her husband's death in 1807 was also by letters only. In the months after her bereavement and the birth of her second child, their letters grew warmer as Ernst—himself recovering from an unhappy love affair—gradually made a commitment to her and her children. Though he proposed to her in person, in 1808, their fear of the danger in Berlin led them to postpone their marriage until the following year. For this reason, their engagement was conducted entirely by the post. This correspondence, therefore, constituted their relationship, almost in its entirety, for a crucial time in their lives, and they each recognized that fact. When in 1813 they were separated by the war, Ernst wrote Henriette when it appeared that Berlin itself was threatened. He told her that he had pulled together his most important papers for special safekeeping; her letters were among them. In 1814, when she went on an extended holiday with the children to Rügen, she took along the letters he had written her for comfort.[2]

The correspondence has the further advantage of being written in an age in which expression of feeling was considered appropriate. Henriette's characterization of her joyous life with Ehrenfried after the birth of their first child is representative of the tone on the whole, a tone that is unembarrassed by feeling.

> How I feel when I hold my little daughter in my lap, or lay her to my breast, you will not expect me to describe—how could I? It is such an all-absorbing love, deep, deep in my heart—a longing desire to screen the little creature from every pain, every suffering, and to take all upon myself . . . One evening, in particular, I felt so strange. I was still somewhat weak; H. B. was playing softly but sweetly on the piano. I felt

as if my whole being was dissolving, and floating toward heaven with the child.[3]

Another example of this tone is to be found in a letter to Ernst a few months later, in which she described her "joy at the spring" and her child's joy at her first spring. The baby "is inhaling its fragrance, and is blossoming forth in it." She went on:

> This morning we put a nosegay in her little hand while she was still asleep; her first look fell lovingly upon the flowers. . . . Early in the morning I go into the garden with her, and her eyes rest so seriously and thoughtfully upon every object, that she can hardly find time to play and laugh with me.[4]

This tone is to be found in Ernst's letters too. Consider his summing up of their relationship, written in 1813, when war had separated them:

> The anniversaries of the most important epochs of our lives are drawing near—the day on which I saw you for the first time, when you gave me a touching impression of a pious, gentle girl, under the influence of a first and holy love, such as I had never before witnessed. How tenderly attached to you I was! I looked upon it as the highest happiness left to me, to be near you and to witness and to bless your wedded life. Then again, the time when I felt such an irresistible desire to see you again as a sorrowing widow, and when gradually a deeper love still was developed. Yes, Jette, it was Divine guidance that led me to you; and I feel it now as deeply as ever. I could never have loved any other woman as I love you.[5]

Subtlety was not considered to have the advantages that our age attributes to it, and though the contemporary historian may occasionally smile at such enthusiastic expression of tender feelings, Ernst and Henriette—in wearing their hearts upon their sleeves—have made the task of historical reconstruction easier.

The purpose of this essay is to use these letters to explore the two most important institutions in Henriette's life, marriage and religion, and to try to find out what functions each had for her. It must be said at the outset that this has been a most difficult task, and that the author is well aware of the dangers inherent in this particular single source. The title of my essay characterizes Henriette as playing a "traditional role," and this is certainly true. Yet it must be noted that I do not claim that Henriette was in any sense typical or representative of all such women. Her son by her first marriage considered her a bit excessive in her religious enthusiasms,[6] and even if this was not important or even untrue, she was married to a remarkable man, and the tone and content of her correspondence certainly were affected by his reputation and the quality of the letters she received from him. The task was also made difficult by the temptation offered by these letters, the temptation to interpret them in an ideological light and to describe her life as one of coping in a world especially difficult for women. This approach would do violence to her understanding of herself. Henriette did not believe herself to be discriminated against, and though she had a very difficult life as a young girl, she met her problems with a dignity and seriousness that deserve respect.

So this essay has a modest purpose. It is to use the letters to discover what Henriette considered the functions of marriage and religion to be for her. An effort will be made to understand these matters on her terms, not on Ernst's, and to do so with sympathy for and understanding of the sense of integrity she had about herself and her role.

> In the sweet vocation that had been allocated to me in the world of love in which I live, all the powers that dwell in me will freely develop themselves, but otherwise I am poor and weak.[7]

She wrote these words to Ernst upon the occasion of her first marriage, and the sentiments of this bride of sixteen did not change throughout the correspondence in the years that followed. Marriage was her vocation, and however much she struggled to understand the meaning and proper content of that vocation, there was no question that it was within marriage that her existence was centered.

Ernst considered himself an expert on the subject of marriage and the role of women, and his letters to her were filled with philosophical expositions on the subject, which held a great fascination for him. He spoke often on the exalted place of the woman, on the home as a sanctuary in a difficult world, on the noble nature of women, on the spiritual powers of motherhood, on the natural differences between the sexes, and on the equality of the sexes. He did not hesitate to explain how she was to feel on these matters, and where appropriate, he referred her to his writings on the subject.[8]

Though Henriette was extremely deferential to him when he expounded on such matters, her view of her vocation was different from his. In spite of his fame (how many brides had that sort of philosophical and intellectual uplift as a part of their dowries?), and despite the great age differential (she was after all still a young girl), she knew more about marriage than he did. He had never married, and had for some time been in love with a married woman, Eleanor Grunow. His efforts to persuade Eleanor to leave her husband and marry him were unsuccessful. He was unhappy, leading what he called "a disjointed life,"[9] which he believed marriage would integrate. Since Eleanor was at the end of her childbearing years, he assumed that even if he succeeded in marrying her, their marriage would be childless.[10] These personal circumstances, coupled with his romantic views on the subject of marriage, produced an outlook that was idealistic in the extreme.

Henriette, for her part, did not regard household management as a particularly interesting vocation, though in fact she was the head of a household (and that was what they both called her) from the time she was sixteen, and it was from this position that her authority in society was derived. In the early months of her first marriage, he asked her about this work, and she replied:

> The feeling of being the housewife, who takes care of the whole house-hold, and who may arrange everything according to her own will and pleasure, is, I think, always precious to a woman, and I also value it very much, and am proud of the dignity. But the special household occupations do not afford me particular pleasure, though they are by no means irksome to me.[11]

Being a housewife provided her with status, power, and work. In this sense, it was her vocation, but she hardly mentioned it again, despite Ernst's belief that it was noble and ennobling.

Similarly, her perception of what it was to be a parent was her own, not Ernst's. As with her role as housewife, here too she accepted what she had to do, and took seriously the responsibility for her children, most poignantly after her first husband's death. Unlike her position in the house, however, this was a role she spoke of often in her letters. She worried about the children, she loved them, and she did all the things she had to do. What emerges from the letters is a clear sense of purpose and commitment.[12]

Nonetheless, she did not consider motherhood pure, noble, holy, or any of the other qualities Ernst attached to being a parent. She was delighted with the birth of her first child, a daughter, but found this joy was mixed with other feelings. She became jealous for the first time, jealous of her daughter's love for anyone other than herself. Later, while widowed and rearing the children without a father, she was resentful of them because they were a tie to this earth that kept her from feeling free to follow her husband in death. She found her life empty, and believed herself to be only a servant of the children. During her engagement to Ernst, she complained that the children would be in the way in Berlin when they established their home there, keeping her from fully enjoying adult company. Her vocation as a parent, therefore, though real enough, was a questionable blessing for her.[13]

Her true vocation was marriage itself, rather than the work of the house or of parenting. Here she agreed with Ernst's views that marriage had a vital place in private development and public well-being. Marriage was a joint enterprise, freely entered into by both partners, and of vital importance to both. This joint vocation was important in both her marriages and remained so. In letters to Ernst, Henriette described the daily routine of her life with Ehrenfried. They intended to arise at five in the morning, but this intention "has very rarely been carried out." She continued:

> When we have got lights, and have dressed, we go into the parlour, where we find the fire burning in the stove and the breakfast table ready laid. . . . The early morning is in itself so delightful, everything without so dark and tranquil, but the mind of man so revived and wide awake.[14]

Henriette and Ehrenfried worked together on self-improvement during these early morning hours. At breakfast Ehrenfried read to her, first from the Bible, followed by something else; in the above instance they were reading Ernst's *Discourses on Religion*.

Henriette expected that in her marriage to Ernst she would have once again an intimacy in which personal growth and mutual support would be understood by both to be a goal. She described their domestic arrangements, in which the sitting room would be next to his study. She wanted all his books to be in that study; she wanted to dust them, read them, and discuss them with him. She then imagined their conversations, saying of him: "I could speak to you about anything and everything. You are not to me as a man, but like a delicate maiden, so innocent, so like a child, and this to me a delicious feeling."[15] And then, in the evening after the children were in bed, Henriette imagined the time when they would be alone together: "You live for me alone, and we sit a good while longer in confidential chat, you telling me about former times, before I knew you."[16] Ernst shared this goal for marriage, which apparently was realized to some extent, for he wrote her nearly a decade after their marriage: "When I consider how much wiser we have already grown, and how much better I have become through you, I despair of nothing that may still lie before us."[17]

Both husbands treated Henriette as an intellectual partner, albeit in a somewhat condescending manner, or so it seems to a twentieth-century reader. Henriette, however, gave no indication that she was offended by the clear implication that, though her opinion was sought after eagerly in matters of theology and the weekly sermons, they believed she could not be expected to understand these matters without some help. Quite the contrary was the case. She expected to be included, she sought further instruction, and she relished the personal growth that this participation encouraged. Ernst wrote her early in her first marriage, asking her to describe her married life, and she wrote him of how they read out loud and discussed material for Ehrenfried's sermons. They were also reading and discussing Ernst's current translation of the Dialogues of Plato. Ernst wrote her husband, cautioning him to explain Plato to her ahead of the reading and to select passages so that it would not be too difficult for her.[18] In her marriage to Ernst these joint endeavors continued, as he promised her in their engagement that they would. He asked her opinion of his work in a most genuine manner. She kept current with his work of translation, and together they attempted to keep up with the literature of their day. At one point she observed humorously that her neighbors called her "the little pastoress."[19] The label certainly was appropriate. Through her marriages she was able to participate in the theological controversies of the time, something she clearly enjoyed.

Marriage's importance to her went beyond the life of the mind. It enabled her to participate in the larger events of her time, both personal and public. It is interesting to note that she was not protected from the fact of Ernst's courtship of Eleanor. Later generations found this aspect of his life shocking. She did not, and no effort was made to keep her other than fully informed. Similarly, he kept her apprised of the work he was doing in the reform of the Prussian government. Ernst observed in 1808, when things in the country were not going well, that he wished she were there to discuss matters with him. He said some men did not confide in women, arguing that women could not keep a secret, but he had never felt that way.[20] Ernst made Henriette feel important. Through him, she was part of the reform of the government, the establishment of the university, and preparations for war.

Seen in this context, her bereavement was especially devastating. With her first husband's death she had lost more than a father for her children or a part of the household she headed. She had lost her entrée into the world outside that household. She wrote Ernst: "I am terrified at the misery and emptiness of the life that is left to me. Months go by without having an opportunity of hearing one forcible, elevating thought—one deep and striking truth from the lips of a cultivated man. . . ."[21]

What we see of her life work, then, is that she accepted the work of the house and the children, but that her true vocation, her freely chosen one, was in her marriages. Though a sense of purpose derived from marriage might seem offensive in our time, it should be remembered that she chose the men she married, and through those marriages, chose a vocation that she clearly found suitable and even joyous.

> Widespread and cheerful activity in the midst of the world was never included in the pictures of life which accompanied my steps up its ascent; quiet retirement from the world and its affairs—renunciation of the sweetest joys of life—longing looks towards heaven, seeking for love *there*—high enjoyment in spiritual intercourse with the living and the

dead—such were the tendencies early developed in me, and most in accordance with my nature.[22]

If marriage was her vocation, religion enabled her to function within it. It is important to note the distinction here. Since her vocation was marriage, and since she chose to marry pastors, it must be said that religion and marriage were inseparable for her. Through marriage she was involved in the theological issues that accompanied the reform of the state church. In her marriage to Ernst she became informed of and occasionally was a participant in the organizational changes that created this new unified Protestant state church. Furthermore, she was in a privileged position in her marriage to Ernst, knowing more about the reality of religious revival and new beliefs than most others of her time. In no small measure due to Ernst's theological views and his hard work, religion in Prussia had changed. The Enlightenment had held religious enthusiasm in low regard. At the end of the eighteenth and the beginning of the nineteenth century, religion had once again become an urgent matter, an important part of the well-integrated life, a vital affair of both heart and mind. The polite and rational beliefs of the eighteenth century were no longer considered polite or rational in the nineteenth. Henriette knew of these developments firsthand.

In considering the role religion played for her, what is important to understand is that it was a force in her life that would have been there whomever she married. In an early letter to Ernst she described how habits of devotion had developed when she was a child. She would not go to services on Sunday morning but instead would go to the schoolroom, "where I could hear the tones of the organ and of the human voices from the church close by." During those quiet times she would read devotional books she had selected.[23]

She explained that the reason for this habit of private devotion was her loneliness. It is clear that she had an unhappy childhood, though she was unusually reticent in her letters to Ernst when this subject came up for discussion. She wrote an autobiography describing her childhood, but she destroyed it without giving it to him. Her father died (or possibly left home) when she was very young, and she was quite explicit about her need to find another father. She spoke of a father figure coming into her life before she left home, gaining her love, and then dying, leaving her once again alone and without love. As a child she had decided that she had to accept unhappiness and learn how to live without human love. She spoke as a young woman of resignation; she would not be one of those fortunate people whose life was characterized by "widespread and cheerful activity in the midst of the world."[24]

Religious devotion enabled her to deal with this lack of love. In her devotion she transformed loneliness into what she later called "quiet retirement" and "renunciation of the sweetest joys of life."[25] Those hours she spent in the classroom, listening to sounds of the service from the church and reading, helped her, she said later: they "elevated my being" and "inspired me with an earnestness that followed me through the bustle of the whole ensuing week."[26] Religion in her childhood, therefore, gave her solace. Early on she had turned away from this world, with "longing looks toward heaven, seeking love there."[27]

The comfort and strength that religion had provided her as a child continued to be important to her as an adult, for her life had many unhappy times. The circumstances of war made her life difficult. Her first husband sent her to Rügen, to be with his family while he stayed with the troops as chaplain. She went with her daughter, missing him desperately, and comforting herself that through God he was hers, even though absent. There was no escape from the war, even in Rügen. There had been a poisoning, and one Swedish officer had died. "Peace and innocence seem departed from the world," she wrote Ernst.[28] She worried about her child, longed for a better time, and pregnant for a second time, sought solace in God. When her husband died, leaving her pregnant with their second child, she found it difficult to mourn and in a letter to Ernst characterized her strength in the loss as an insult to the dead. She rejected those who sought to comfort her, telling Ernst that she felt "as if I must tear myself away from all those who cling to me." She felt able to grieve only when she gave herself "up entirely to God," for then "thought ceases, and solemn light and darkness seem at one and the same time to veil my eyes." When her son was born shortly after his father's death, she found the strength she needed through the communion service, which freed her "to attain to all that my soul beholds in its visions." She wrote Ernst that her religious experiences as a child had prepared her for the loss of happiness in her husband's death. Because of her past history, it "seemed neither strange nor unexpected."[29] Religion, therefore, helped her accept the unhappiness and loneliness of her life; for these purposes religion served her very well.

As she grew older she looked to religion for a second purpose, to help her learn how to be happy. This was important in her engagement to Ernst, as she had the good fortune to find a second husband who suited her very well. He was a father figure to her, as well as a lover, and she needed both. That he was famous and successful made her very happy, and that his work was in a field she respected and enjoyed herself was personally rewarding. Furthermore, he wanted her and her children and longed himself for a life that provided private as well as public satisfaction. Yet this good fortune in a time of great sorrow created a problem for Henriette. Her childhood and her faith had prepared her to be unhappy, not happy.

This circumstance was the single most important theme of their letters in the year of their engagement. She believed that her lonely childhood had made her an unfeeling person and she remembered that as a child she had been "dull, and without sentiments of affection." As she matured, this sense of insufficient feeling remained with her, a problem she defined as a lack of "quick sensibilities and lively emotions."[30] Even in what she described to Ernst as the very happy marriage she had had with Ehrenfried, even then she worried that she seemed not to enjoy life as much as others did, and she let opportunities for happiness "escape."[31]

When she and Ernst became engaged, this sense of lack of feeling only intensified and to these feelings were added an intense sense of unworthiness. A wife, she wrote him, should not have an impoverished heart, but even after they were married, she continued to feel the same way. "My outward life seems to drag on slowly and sullenly, and my inward life seems sunk in profound sleep.– . ." She worried about the effect of this on her children. She feared that the "icy crust around their mother's heart had chilled the tender babes."[32]

She was determined to come to terms with this part of her nature and conquer it. She wanted to be content with herself. She wrote Ernst a few months before their marriage that her goals were: "to understand myself thoroughly, to be contented with my own nature, and to live with you and the children, without heeding myself."[33] She sought her husband's help, and Ernst comforted her by saying that he had the same problem. He too felt dissatisfied with his feelings about religion and human affection. He found himself full of torpor, unwilling to work hard all the time and unable to feel life's joys and sorrows as deeply as others did. He also comforted her on the matter of the children, saying that the three of them had been to a "severe school" together and that she had reared them as best she possibly could.[34]

She looked to religion to help her with this problem, and though the evidence of the correspondence suggests that she never learned how to accept her own nature and enjoy life as she wanted to, the moments when she came closest all took place within a religious context. Communion, for example, made her happy, and in times of sorrow gave her the capacity to mourn. She described for Ernst the communion at her first marriage. It transfigured her life that she had found so hard into "a quiet, peaceful, sunny day, tempered by a balmy breeze from heaven." Religious music had a similar function for her, enabling her to express her feelings freely. She wrote Ernst: "I often shed the most delicious tears over a simple hymn of Gellert's, or when singing to an andante or adagio on the piano words of my own composition, which were always of a religious character."[35]

She had discovered, in part, a cure for torpor, for self-doubt, and for insufficient love. Religious devotion was "a heavenly gift," and in the religious instruction she gave her children—most particularly her first child—she was determined that the early development of religious feelings be encouraged. Heavenly love would come first, as a "first love—love to the invisible Father," and through this new life, her daughter would be "born anew," as she had been. Though she never was satisfied, she believed that "could I but lead a really pious life, I think I would be cured."[36]

Henriette was a pre-industrial, pre-Victorian woman who participated directly and indirectly in Prussia's decade of liberation. Liberation did not go as far for Henriette as it did for other women in Ernst's circle of friends in Berlin, since she did not become a writer or a woman around whom writers gathered, in the salon tradition of the time. Ernst chose in her a person from outside that circle, a person with whom marriage was far more conventional than the marriage he had hoped for with Eleanor. Nonetheless, this age of liberation liberated Henriette too, in the sense that she held herself to its standards of independence and self-understanding.

Henriette expected to be her own person, and did not define herself in terms of her work in the home. In this opinion she was encouraged by Ernst, who wrote her upon the occasion of the birth of her first child that because she was a strong and independent person, she would not make the mistake of making the fact of her motherhood the central point of her life, of devoting herself "exclusively to the life and duties of a mother."[37] She took up this theme often and with a vigor reinforced by the reality of her child-rearing responsibilities, which lay heavily upon her, especially after Ehrenfried's death. It was only when the child was asleep, she said, that her true self could be free. "But when she is resting in sweet slumber," Henriette wrote Ernst in 1806, "then my cares also go to rest, and with my whole free soul, I give myself up to the occupations I like best— to writing, reading, and needlework."[38] And in the following year, after Ehrenfried's death and before her engagement to Ernst, she lamented the fact that her child-rearing responsibilities had become far too important in her life, and she had been denied what she characterized as her "higher enjoyment," "to strive after light and truth."[39] Thus, though her life's work was the rearing of children and the making of a home, neither she nor Ernst defined her person in those terms.

The marriage that she entered into with Ernst rested upon a belief in equality between the sexes. It was Ernst who spoke most often about equality. His views of equality rested upon the belief that men and women were fundamentally different, but equal, and that marriage was a joining of two halves of human nature.[40] Henriette had difficulty accepting Ernst's insistence that she was his equal. She believed herself to be inferior to him in her education and in her standing in society, and her letters are filled with expressions of doubt and self-deprecation. "I see clearly what a woman should be, to be worthy of being your wife, but, alas! . . . the emptiness of my mind, and the poverty of my heart," she said, made her worry about whether she could ever be worthy of him.[41] Ernst never gave up in his efforts to persuade her of her equality. In a most serious moment he spoke in anger, saying that if her low opinion of herself was correct, then they should not marry.[42] More typical of his response was the exhortation to feel better about herself: "Let it be so, and place yourself on a level with me, as it beseems man and wife. . . . And thus we shall ever be as one, and will not inquire if or why the one is superior or inferior to the other."[43]

Though Henriette had difficulty accepting Ernst's belief in their equality, the correspondence reveals that she grew toward greater self-confidence, and that this growth was one of the benefits that marriage had for her. In the early months of her first marriage, she wrote Ernst that her "intellect is expanding and is being enriched."[44] What she saw happening within that first marriage can also be seen in her correspondence with Ernst. At first, she was extremely deferential and self-deprecating, but signs of her spirit and strength showed themselves early. In 1807, in response to a criticism he made of her concerning her lack of self-worth, she said that he should understand that since there were great differences between individuals, naturally those who were more limited than others would feel sad when they recognized those limitations.[45] Another example of her growing ability to speak her mind to him occurred after he re-proved her for her gratitude toward him. She asked why did he "make so little of" that gratitude which—she observed—is not what she said any-way.[46] In the matter of Eleanor, Henriette also learned to speak up and be confident. At first, she sought reassurance that he really wanted her and was not marrying her simply on the rebound. Later she became confident and wise in her handling of him, recognizing and helping Ernst to recog-nize that his relationship with Eleanor had been quite one-sided.[47] By 1809, the year of their marriage, they each continued the conventional expressions of inadequacy, and then each reproved the other. At one point she proudly said to him after one such exchange that she would adopt "a pride and presumption that shall make you wish the meekness back again."[48] Thus the reality of their relationship had changed, and though she still had moments of doubt, she was no longer a child being educated by her father. She became his mother, and was so called, offering him advice, information, and occasional chastisement, just as he offered her the same. Their relationship—if not equal—was at least one where mutual growth was expected.

The place of religion in her life is also best understood within the context of a time of liberation. Religion was more than a promise of eternal life, just as marriage was more than an economic or sexual relationship. Religion was a source of energy, energy for the state in its efforts to "liberate" itself from the French and from an outmoded form of government, and energy for the individual. Her eager and in the end only partly successful effort to feel deeply through religion appears to be a characteristic of her time.

These ideas infuse the whole of their correspondence. Henriette wrote Ernst upon the occasion of her marriage to Ehrenfried, thanking him for his blessing, and promising to have a Christian marriage.[49] This notion of a Christian marriage was more than a figure of speech. She meant it, and what she meant by it was well expressed by Ernst, in writing to Ehrenfried, warning against a marriage that was too close, too much "a pretty snug little room in the great palace of God . . . a snuggery in which one may bury oneself deeply, and feel around one its narrow, cozy limits." This is dangerous, Ernst said, for "every family . . . must from the beginning adopt the missionary spirit, and be on the look-out for some soul that it may draw towards itself and save from the desolate waste of life."[50] Religion was a reality, the source of good and of the energy to enjoy the good. When Henriette said to Ernst that she hoped things would be better for him, and that he would find joy as she had, she wrote: "Dearest, I feel as if a good angel must come to you one day, and plant in your heart new joy and the hope of new happiness. . . ."[51] When Ehrenfried died and she was left alone to rear the children, she prayed for strength to do so.[52] In 1808, after their engagement, she wrote of the dead Ehrenfried to whom she prayed "as a patron saint, and thus it is I live with him."[53] In this Ernst was in complete agreement, and for him the identification of love and religion was a recurring theme.[54] Religion was more than metaphor, it was a search for emancipation, energy, and content to live in the full way that was expected.

What is to be learned from this? First of all, that through marriage and religion Henriette participated in a modest way in the great events and ideas of her time. Second, that if the historian is to understand early-nineteenth-century Prussian history, an effort must be made to take seriously and thereby better grasp the reality of religious belief. Finally, and in the same vein, those historians concerned to celebrate—or at least recognize—the role of women in history will need to study marriage as an institution. For Henriette, it was through marriage that she liberated herself. Though she never was self-supporting, and though her social standing was always derived from her husband, she was fortunate that the dominant view of marriage when she was a young woman permitted—nay required—that she grow and seek her own character.

NOTES

1. These letters are available in three collections: *Friedrich Schleiermachers Briefwechsel mit seiner Braut*, ed. by Heinrich Meisner (2nd ed.; Gotha, 1920). *Aus Schleiermachers Leben, in Briefen*, ed. by Ludwig Jonas and Wilhelm Dilthey (4 vols.; 2nd ed.; Berlin, 1860). Portions of this last collection have been translated into English: *The Life of Schleiermacher, as Unfolded in His Autobiography and Letters*, trans. by Frederick Rowan 2 vols. (London, 1860). The author expresses appreciation to Dorothy Jeanne Martin for her excellent and patient assistance in the preparation of this essay.

2. Ernst to Henriette, 17 May 1813, Jonas and Dilthey, 2, pp. 272–73, and Rowan, 2, pp. 230–32. Henriette to Ernst, 29 July 1824, Jonas and Dilthey, 2, pp. 389–90, and Rowan, 2, pp. 290–91.

3. Henriette to Ernst, October 1805, Jonas and Dilthey, 2, pp. 40–41, and Rowan, 2, pp. 39–40.

4. Henriette to Ernst, May 1806, Jonas and Dilthey, 2, p. 59, and Rowan, 2, p. 53.

5. Ernst to Henriette, June 1813, Jonas and Dilthey, 2, pp. 298–99, and Rowan, 2, p. 246.

6. Ehrenfried von Willich, *Aus Schleiermachers House* (Berlin, 1909), pp. 2–3.

7. Henriette to Ernst, 7 September 1804, Rowan, 1, pp. 385–86.

8. It is difficult to find an extended letter from Ernst in which he does not speak of at least one of these matters. Particularly interesting is a letter written during their engagement. Ernst to Henriette, 26 January 1809, Jonas and Dilthey, 2, pp. 210–11, and Rowan, 2, pp. 173–74.

9. Ernst to Henriette and Ehrenfried von Willich (her first husband), 17 October 1804, Jonas and Dilthey, 2, pp. 6–8, and Rowan, 2, pp. 5–7.

10. Ernst to Henriette, 19 October 1808, Meisner, pp. 169–71.

11. Henriette to Ernst, 25 November 1804, Meisner, pp. 24–25; Jonas and Dilthey, 2, pp. 12–14; and Rowan, 2, pp. 11–13.

12. See, for example, Henriette to Ernst, 28 April 1807, Meisner, pp. 79–81; Jonas and Dilthey, 2, pp. 93–95; and Rowan, 2, pp. 85–87.

13. Henriette to Ernst, October 1805, Meisner, pp. 53–55; Jonas and Dilthey, 2, pp. 40–41; and Rowan, 2, pp. 39–40. Henriette to Ernst, 21 January 1806, Meisner, pp. 58–60; Jonas and Dilthey, 2, pp. 51–52; and Rowan, 2, pp. 45–46. Henriette to Ernst, 28 April 1807, see note 12. Henriette to Ernst, 12 October 1807, Meisner, pp. 86–90; Jonas and Dilthey, 2, pp. 99–100; and Rowan, 2, pp. 91–92. Henriette to Ernst, 15 November 1808, Meisner, pp. 203–4; Jonas and Dilthey, 2, pp. 163–64; and Rowan, 2, pp. 150–52.

14. Henriette to Ernst, 25 November 1804, see note 11.

15. Henriette to Ernst, 1 November 1808, Jonas and Dilthey, 2, p. 156, and Rowan, 2, pp. 144–45.

16. Henriette to Ernst, 17 November 1808, Rowan, 2, pp. 152–54.

17. Ernst to Henriette, 30 August 1817, Jonas and Dilthey, 2, pp. 330–32, and Rowan, 2, pp. 266–68.

18. Henriette to Ernst, 25 November 1804, see note 11. Ernst to Henriette and Ehrenfried, 6 January 1805, Meisner, pp. 27–29; Jonas and Dilthey, 2, pp. 14–15; and Rowan, 2, pp. 13–14.

19. Henriette to Ernst, 13 March 1806, Meisner, p. 62; Jonas and Dilthey, 2, pp. 57–58; and Rowan, 2, p. 52.

20. Ernst to Henriette, 15 December 1808, Jonas and Dilthey, 2, pp. 180–83 and Rowan, 2, pp. 161–63.

21. Henriette to Ernst, 12 October 1807, see note 13.

22. Henriette to Ernst, 30 January 1808, Meisner, pp. 99–100; Jonas and Dilthey, 2, pp. 107–8; and Rowan, 2, pp. 99–101.

23. Henriette to Ernst, 25 November 1804, see note 11.

24. Henriette to Ernst, 30 January 1808, see note 22.

25. Ibid.

26. Henriette to Ernst, 25 November 1804, see note 11.

27. Henriette to Ernst, 30 January 1808, see note 22.

28. Henriette to Ernst, 4 August 1806, Meisner, pp. 69–70; Jonas and Dilthey, 2, pp. 64–65; and Rowan, 2, pp. 59–60.

29. Henriette to Ernst, 13 March, n.d. April, 28 April, n.d. (summer) 1807, Meisner, pp. 72–74, 77, 79–81, 82–85; Jonas and Dilthey, 2, pp. 86–88, 91, 93–95, 96–99; and Rowan, 2, pp. 77–80, 83, 85–87, 88–91. Final quotation from Henriette to Ernst, 30 January 1808, see note 22.

30. Henriette to Ernst, 17 November 1808, Meisner, pp. 204–6, and Rowan, 2, pp. 152–54. Henriette to Ernst, n.d. (summer) 1807, see note 29.

31. Henriette to Ernst, 4 August 1805, Meisner, pp. 46–50; Jonas and Dilthey, 2, pp. 32–34; and Rowan, 2, pp. 32–34.

32. Henriette to Ernst, 24 August 1808, Meisner, pp. 119–22; Jonas and Dilthey, 2, pp. 125–27; and Rowan, 2, pp. 116–18. Henriette to Ernst, 23 September 1811, Jonas and Dilthey, 2, pp. 258–59, and Rowan, 2, pp. 221–22.

33. Henriette to Ernst, 3 March 1809, Meisner, pp. 357–58; Jonas and Dilthey, 2, pp. 227–28; and Rowan, 2, pp. 185–86.

34. Ernst to Henriette, 4 December 1808, Meisner, pp. 234–41, and Rowan, 2, pp. 159–61.

35. Henriette to Ernst, 3 September 1804, Meisner, pp. 19–20; Jonas and Dilthey, 1, p. 404; and Rowan, 1, pp. 383–84. Henriette to Ernst, 17 November 1808, see note 30 above.

36. Henriette to Ernst, n.d. (summer) 1807, see note 29; 15 November 1808, see note 13; 23 September 1811, see note 32.

37. Ernst to Henriette, 13 June 1805, Meisner, pp. 42–43; Jonas and Dilthey, 2, pp. 25–26; and Rowan, 2, pp. 25–26.

38. Henriette to Ernst, 21 January 1806, see note 13.

39. Henriette to Ernst, 12 October 1807, see note 13.

40. Ernst to Henriette, 25 March 1807, Meisner, pp. 74–76; Jonas and Dilthey, 2, pp. 88–90; and Rowan, 2, pp. 80–82.

41. Henriette to Ernst, 24 August 1808, Meisner, pp. 119–22; Jonas and Dilthey, 2, pp. 125–27; and Rowan, 2, pp. 116–18.

42. Ernst to Henriette, 29 January 1809, Meisner, pp. 319–25; Jonas and Dilthey, 2, pp. 212–15; and Rowan, 2, pp. 174–78.

43. Ernst to Henriette, 11 September 1808, Meisner, pp. 134–38; Jonas and Dilthey, 2, pp. 134–37; and Rowan, 2, pp. 123–26.

44. Henriette to Ernst, 4 August 1805, see note 31.

45. Henriette to Ernst, n.d. 1807, Jonas and Dilthey, 2, pp. 102–4, and Rowan, 2, pp. 94–96.

46. Henriette to Ernst, n.d. (August) 1808, Meisner, pp. 124–26; Jonas and Dilthey, 2, p. 129; and Rowan, 2, pp. 120–21.

47. Henriette to Ernst, 7 October 1808, Meisner, pp. 159–61; Jonas and Dilthey, 2, pp. 141–42; and Rowan, 2, pp. 132–33.

48. Henriette to Ernst, 13 February 1809, Meisner, pp. 336–38; Jonas and Dilthey, 2, pp. 220–21; and Rowan, 2, p. 181.

49. Henriette to Ernst, 7 September 1804, see note 7.

50. Ernst to Henriette, 30 October 1804, Meisner, pp. 22–24; Jonas and Dilthey, 2, pp. 9–11; and Rowan, 2, pp. 8–10.

51. Henriette to Ernst, November 1805, Meisner, p. 55; Jonas and Dilthey, 2, p. 41; and Rowan, 2, p. 40.

52. Henriette to Ernst, 28 April 1807, see note 12.

53. Henriette to Ernst, 4 September 1808, Meisner, pp. 128–30; Jonas and Dilthey, 2, pp. 129–30; and Rowan, 2, pp. 121–22.

54. Ernst to Henriette, 4 December 1808, Meisner, pp. 234–41, and Rowan, 2, pp. 159–61.

The Reading Habits of Women in the *Vormärz*

RENATE MÖHRMANN

"I can't help it," said Alice very meekly: "I'm growing."
"You've no right to grow here," said the Dormouse.
"Don't talk nonsense," said Alice more boldly: "you know you're grow-
ing too."
"Yes, but I grow at a reasonable pace," said the Dormouse: "not in that
ridiculous fashion."
—Lewis Carroll, *Alice in Wonderland*

Picture of a summer's day: she is sitting in the left corner of the arbor in
the small sunlit back garden, which is enclosed and walled off by the back
of the house and by the ivy-covered trellis. Wearing a frilly lace bonnet,
her eyes lowered on the Bible lying in her lap, her arms bent slightly
outward as if to make room for her knitting, she is both reading and
working with her hands; in short, a familiar picture to all. The Biedermeier artist Erasmus Engert captured this scene in his picture entitled
"Hausgarten" ("The Garden"), painted in 1825. Two aspects of this painting lead to the following observations. The woman reading, portrayed
with the utmost attention to realistic detail, is not the focus of the picture.
She occupies only a small corner seat, and is a part of the garden—a
summer accessory just like the hedge, the bushes, and the flowers. The
reader herself, lacking any trace of individuality, is assimilated into the
still life. And a further striking feature: Bible and knitting are depicted in
such a way that they appear to the observer to be of equal size and
importance. Manual work is elevated by the written word and reading is
kept in check by useful labor. Imagination is put on a utilitarian chain held

taut by the woolen tow rope of the knitting. Even the reading of the Holy Scriptures must be combined with useful labor or it cannot be justified— the artistic message can be iconographically deciphered in this way. The whole adds up to a faithful picture of the everyday life of a woman. Thus one can read the following account in Sophie Alberg's *Letters on the Education of Young Ladies:* "Skill in needlework is an integral part of a woman's life and, as such, should not be taught for the first time to the adolescent girl but at an early age, when it should be made pleasant and familiar to the child and done as a natural daily activity."[1]

An authoress of the *Vormärz* period (1815–48) recalled:

> It struck him [my cousin] that I still clung fast to my old habits, that I regarded it as my duty to do sewing and mending because this had formerly been my task. . . . And while I made a conscious decision not to depart from the practices and rules of the parental home under any circumstances, more accustomed to dependence and subordination than I myself realized, I continued to regard my literary career as a concession which had been granted me but which could at any time be withdrawn. Simon shouted at me almost every day: "Devote yourself totally to your work! Don't sew: read and learn instead!"[2]

The reference to such diverse sources is no random montage. On the contrary, it serves as a methodological preamble. For a reconstruction of the process of literary socialization of the female writer in the *Vormärz*, it is necessary to work on different levels and to consult diverse sources. Also, it must be remembered that, as a rule, no mention at all or, at best, only a brief one is made of the authoresses themselves in the relevant literary histories.[3] It may even be worth considering whether the analysis of their reading habits may not be doomed to failure, since such analysis must inevitably be speculative.

To preclude such failure, recourse has been made in this study to four different categories of material, which will be consulted and evaluated dialectically. The most obvious category is that of the autobiographies and the memoirs of the *Vormärz* authoresses themselves. In addition, there are informative references to the general reading habits of young girls and women in the first half of the nineteenth century in the curriculum of the upper-class girls' schools, as well as in the innumerable books that offered advice to young women. Such "advice" was based on a very definite notion of femininity; thus the findings of modern sociology in the fields of family and role theory must also be taken into consideration. And, finally, observations made in conjunction with the aesthetics of literary criticism will be incorporated.

Each of these sources taken on its own would provide us with only partial insights. To draw conclusions from the social imperatives of the advice to women alone, without reference to social reality, would result in a repetition of the old errors of the traditional history of ideas. But neither does analysis of *Rezeptionsforschung* (research into literary reception) with respect to the reading habits of women convey much information about female readers if it does not take into account the concrete context of feminine life and the ideology in which it was embedded. When Günter Häntzschel, in his research into the literary reception of Heine, quite rightly pointed to a largely female public, and saw "the greater affinity between lyric poetry and women" first and foremost as a phenomenon of the time ("they had, of course, more time and opportunity for it than men"),[4] he combined a correct observation with an unsatisfactory explanation. For middle-class girls and ladies of the nineteenth century could just as well have invested their leisure time in the reading of dramas and novels. The fact that they did not usually do so can be more correctly accounted for by the nineteenth-century tendency to attribute characteristic features to the sexes, and by the "psychological 'sex characteristics' conceived as a contrast,"[5] according to which the male seems better suited to rational and the female to emotional matters: this, rather than theories of the normative affinity between lyric poetry and women, is a logical explanation. Thus, the female reception of lyric poetry was in the main due to a middle-class ideology which thought it could best bridge the widening gap between working life and family life, and between public life and private life, by forming a dichotomy of the sexes and, in so doing, by attributing emotional qualities to the woman.[6]

Similarly, exclusive reliance on autobiographical materials would be equally problematic as well. All too often, the autobiographies of the *Vormärz* authoresses were stylized apologia, in which the disciplinary measures they experienced were interpreted, in retrospect, as humanitarian, as a result of many years of internalization; therefore, the assertive discourse should be taken with a grain of salt. The autobiographies cannot be used as sufficient proof in their own right, but must always be compared and contrasted with the empirical evidence. Typical of such autobiographies is Fanny Lewald's claim in her *Life Story* that she had, as a child, an unlimited stock of literature at her disposal and that she was, on the whole, brought up very liberally. Contradictory evidence is found in her concrete descriptions of everyday events, from which we learn that every book had to be approved beforehand by her father, and that she could make no move on her own until she was well into her thirtieth year. In fact, this surveillance was hardly ever relaxed. What is more, it was sanctioned by parents, neighbors, and teachers alike.

> The little girls were dressed by the older girls, and sometimes, when you least expected it, Herr Ulrich [the headmaster] was standing on one of the street corners to see whether we stopped on the way, whether we raised our voices, or whether we displayed any other signs of careless-

ness. One girl, who had once thrown her needlework bag over her shoulder and strolled home in this manner, was scolded for it for a long time afterwards.[7]

Such unpretentiously written passages illustrate the conditioning process to which middle-class girls were all too frequently exposed.

So much for the methodological preamble. As the following account will show, the German authoresses of the *Vormärz* do not represent an arbitrary generation of female writers. Women such as Fanny Lewald, Luise Mühlbach, Mathilde Franziska Anneke, Louise Otto-Peters, Ida Hahn-Hahn, Louise Aston, Therese von Bacheracht, or Luise Dittmar—just to mention the most committed and the most important few—represented the first generation of female writers in the history of German literature who no longer exercised their literary talent only occasionally or as an unrewarding hobby; they actually wrote on a professional basis. Before that time, according to a study by Sophie Pataky (herself one of the great exceptions who by the end of the previous century had rendered outstanding service by publishing women's literature), "the female urge to write was, with few exceptions, visibly expressed and satisfied in the drafting of books on cookery, housewifery, and needlework."[8]

The female writers of the *Vormärz* were consequently rebellious and revolutionary women, and the question of their literary socialization could perhaps provide information about the part played by literature in such a process of emancipation. And the social origin of the respective writers must be considered. They all, without exception, came from the upper classes, the middle classes, or—as in the case of Ida Hahn-Hahn and Therese von Bacheracht—from the aristocracy. The fathers of the middle-class writers were, more often than not, civil servants; this was true for Mathilde Franziska Anneke, Luise Mühlbach, and Louise Otto-Peters. Fanny Lewald's father was a businessman, and Louise Aston's father was a clergyman. However, such classification is of only limited significance. Of decidedly greater influence on feminine socialization was the particular family type in which the daughters grew up, for the institution of "the family" was undergoing a process of radical change between 1825 and 1855 caused by the transition from a feudal to a capitalist society.

In this connection, it should be emphasized that, in the course of the history of civilization, the process of female emancipation has by no means been a continual progression, especially in the field of general education. This process did not commence with a *tabula rasa,* the initial state of the woman, so to speak, followed by the overcoming of her illiteracy, and ending, for example, with female Nobel Prize winners. The idea of a progression should, in this respect, be used with care, because during the transition from the eighteenth to the nineteenth century, blockages and even a regression of the egalitarian attitude toward the sexes can be observed. Such retrogressive "advances" were closely related to fundamental changes in family structure in Germany during the second quarter of the nineteenth century.

> Running *parallel* to the liberation of man as a "citizen" whose whole existence and energies are devoted to "society" and its daily economic, political, and social struggles, is the commitment of woman and her whole being to her house and family, and the utilization of the family as "refuge" from daily struggles.[9]

With the transition from a pre-industrial to an industrial economy and "the increasing production of all wares and consumer goods outside the home, and with the exclusion of working life from the home, the sphere of activity of women was limited to a very small domain which was now devoted, to a large extent, to the creation and maintenance of a quite specialized product, namely household service and care of children and husbands."[10] During this transitional period, woman was reduced from the all-round efficient mother figure to the more emotional side of her character, that of mother of the nuclear family. "The family is no longer the center of joint home economy, but rather the domestic core—apparently freed from all work—in which the man, on returning home from work, expects loving service for himself and the children. In the course of this change in values, all the wife's formerly equal economic capabilities are transformed into 'female nature,' into psychologically rooted sexual characteristics."[11]

This is a completely new idea. In earlier statements on the differences between man and woman, the only allusions made were to "the social status" and to "the virtues expected of people in these positions."[12] The change in the system of reference—that is, the replacement of class criteria by character criteria and the establishing of woman as the one concerned with matters of the heart, while the man was concerned with matters of reason—happened at a time when "the social structures outside the family unit were changing and for the man committed to success in that arena, such qualities had lost all value and were eliminated as disruptive factors."[13]

It is necessary to recognize such changes in the family structure in order to comprehend the significance of the new imperatives and all their inconsistencies—imperatives which, in the course of the nineteenth century, were increasingly laid down for women and which decisively determined the female reading program at that time. And, over and above the ideologized rationale for patriarchal rule, the reduction of woman to her emotional qualities must be understood as "structurally necessary for the middle-class social system."[14] The contradiction inherent in such thinking is that the female sexual character is derived from the female nature itself, and yet has to be developed by means of special didactic strategies. Thus, the concentration on the largely aesthetic and educational content was symptomatic of the new literature for girls in the nineteenth century. "The educated man can and must . . . know and read everything," wrote Christian Oeser in his *Ceremonial Gift for German Maidens,* one of the most popular and most widely read guides of the second quarter of the nineteenth century; "it is only fitting for educated women to know that which can afford true poetic delight."[15]

The school syllabi bore this out. Boys at the state grammar schools were chiefly given instruction in genres such as the drama and the epic, while pupils of the upper-class girls' schools received instruction in lyric poetry, and no more than a random sample at that. Günter Häntzschel has drawn attention to the many anthologies of lyric poetry which were "rendered harmless" and "pruned" before being placed in "tender feminine hands."[16] Thus, even in the field of poetry there was considerable "censorship." Dagmar Grenz's investigations demonstrate that all the special literature for young girls of the nineteenth century was subjected to such pruning; common to this category were "the moral tale," "the sentimental didactic novel" *(Prüfungsroman),* and "stories of conversion" *(Umkehrgeschichte).* "As regards content, the common characteristic feature of girls' literature during the first half of the nineteenth century . . . is a strong Christian-religious orientation, on the basis of which all suffering is seen as a trial sent by God, and a clearly conservative picture of society."[17] All erotic elements were carefully removed from the girls' literature. Hence, the warning in Betty Gleim's book of advice to women that contact with Greek mythology should be avoided, for the "mention of procreation and reproduction" was all too frequent.[18]

Concealed behind such postulations was the opinion, so widespread in middle-class circles of the nineteenth century, that the prolonging of a girl's childishness was the best way to guarantee her spiritual purity. "One of the superstitious axioms of a normal education was the conviction that innocence, grounded in ignorance and destroyed during the first hour of marriage, represents the true spiritual beauty of a young girl and her greatest charm, and for that reason, any reading capable of infringing upon this gem of ignorance should be avoided." To say "My daughter is still no more than a child"[19] was the highest praise a mother could bestow when describing her already grown-up, marriageable daughter.

Furthermore, there was a continuous call for the exclusion of contemporary literature from the reading programs of young ladies. There were vivid warnings of the powers of such literature to destroy harmony; and from that view came the conviction that any reference to reality should be carefully kept away from the adolescent girl. Indeed, allowing girls to read was, if anything, generally considered to be a risky business. In many guides it was ranked immediately after obsession with cleanliness and was described as "a craze for reading." It represented a vice apt to lead a girl astray from her womanly virtues and one which would certainly reduce her value on the marriage market. Such assessments and the ideologies which produced them form the system of reference against which the writings and autobiographical accounts of the female *Vormärz* writers must be measured and their literary socialization examined. We can assume that their reading habits were not established outside the reading programs already described, but rather were shaped by them to a large extent. Also, the fact that not one of the *Vormärz* authoresses seems to have been a bookworm, greedily consuming international literature in secret, by candlelight—like many of their literary brothers—is only significant if seen against the background outlined above. Yet we may presume that they did indeed all read in secret and more often and more widely than the later official report would have us believe. Doubtless here too, we see the effect of their specific socialization, according to which disobedience and disorder in young girls were strictly disciplined.[20]

In Fanny Lewald's *Life Story,* one of the most informative documents of that period on the subject of female socialization, particularly the literary aspect, the same maxims as those in the guides can be found. Lewald described a phase in her development when at the age of fourteen, having completed her school education, she devoted herself increasingly to her reading: "Few days went by without my mother reproaching me that nothing is more objectionable or more useless than an educated, impractical female, and that I had every prospect of becoming one."[21] Her father reacted by taking countermeasures against her growing "craze for reading" and drew up a timetable for her with a view to leading her back to womanly virtues. "Every day I sat for five hours in the living room in a particular spot at the window and learned how to darn socks, mend clothes, and lend a hand with the dressmaking and other work."[22]

In *Pages of Recollections from the Life of Luise Mühlbach,* the reports by Therese von Bacheracht, or Ida Hahn-Hahn's *Picture of Life,* few references to the literary stimulation of the daughter are to be found. Classroom education for middle-class girls was often inadequate and shortened, and the occasional governess or private tutor for the daughters of aristocratic origins proved equally barren. In this respect, the case of the Countess Hahn-Hahn is a particularly gloomy one. Her literary tools were limited, in her early youth, to the *Illustrated Newspaper, Diezmann's Fashion Journal,* and *The Brockhaus Encyclopedia.*[23] In comparison, the books owned by Fanny Lewald during her "seven and a half years at school" appeared little short of impressive. She was at least able to call her own *A History of Prussia* by Heinlein, *Biblical Stories* by Kohlrausch,

Campe's *Discovery of America*, a kind of anthology by Betty Gleim, and, later on, some comedies by Frau von Genlis.[24]

In accordance with the demands of the books offering advice to women, we find indications in most of the authoresses' biographical and autobiographical reports that novel-reading was, for them, forbidden fruit. Even a writer like Fanny Lewald, herself able to refer to a wide range of novels, has quite clearly internalized these maxims to such a degree that even she described the reading of novels as a dangerous activity likely to corrupt a girl's character.[25] Indeed, there are other sources as well. We have in Louise Otto-Peters's *A Woman's Life in the German Empire: Recollections of the Past,* an extremely informative document on the everyday life of women and their reading habits. It is interesting that there was no ban on reading. Quite the contrary, novel-reading is a totally integrated part of feminine life. "The world of poetry was never and nowhere pushed into the background by housework," Louise Otto-Peters reported, and she gave the following detailed account:

> When vegetables were being cleaned or fruit being prepared for bottling, there was always a recitation from English as well as German novelists, whether they liked it or not: Walter Scott, Cooper and Bulwer, Wilhelm Hauff, Ernst Wagner, Henriette Hanke, Caroline Pichler, Rellstab, Sealsfield, and others lost none of their dignity in the process. The characters seemed to us more lifelike and left their mark upon us when we, as it were, shared their lives and spoke about them in earnest and in jest. Likewise there were recitations while everyone sewed together— and there was, of course, plenty of sewing to do in such a large and well-managed household.[26]

How can we interpret such diverging statements about novel-reading? What do they imply about the *Vormärz* authoress as a reader? At this point, we can formulate our first theory. As already discussed at the outset, the middle-class family was undergoing considerable change during the period in which the *Vormärz* authoresses were enjoying their youth. The large, pre-industrial domestic family, characterized by the unpaid labor of all members—related and unrelated alike—under the supervision of the mother, begins to give way to a new type of family community. We can ascertain that, as a result of this change, the woman's functional purpose was altered considerably. With the gradual phasing out of male activity in the domestic sphere, with the family's transformation from a production center into a consumer group, where the man became the sole breadwinner, the cultural task of the woman had to be defined anew.

Not until this situation had arisen was the polarization of the sexes ratified and the separation of woman's expressive role and man's instrumental role made theoretically sound; only then did the woman become the true governor of the heart and the "beautiful property" of the husband.[27] Now women's new roles were derived from the female psyche itself and were therefore interpreted as natural. The countless number of books offering advice to women which suddenly emerged were the consequence of this development and reflected the pedagogical attempts to justify the new demands being made on women as ones compatible with their nature. In this context, novel-reading also fell into the prohibited category of the perilous, capable of leading the female imagination out of its allotted inner chambers and into the freedom of the outer chambers. It is clear from Louise Otto-Peters's memoirs that her family background was that of the pre-industrial home economy, that is, the old family type, where there was still no reason to restrict the woman to the emotional sector and where the demarcation line between the sexes and their sexual characteristics had not yet been drawn. Work and reading went hand in hand; this much we can conclude from Otto-Peters's reports. A pre-selection of reading material for girls had evidently not taken place. Thus, the first conclusion may be formulated as follows: The literary socialization of the female *Vormärz* writer was largely determined by the particular family type in which she grew up. It could result either in the freedom to select her own reading material or in a restriction of that choice.

The counter-example to Louise Otto-Peters is Fanny Lewald. The family type to which she owed her development was the new family unit based on inwardness, where the division of labor was, to a large extent, institutionalized. Her literary upbringing accordingly followed a strict regimen. The father became the arbiter of the literary tradition, and this became the rule in the middle-class family of the progressive nineteenth century. This situation led to completely new areas of conflict which had had no impact on the daughters of the pre-industrial home economy, as the example of Louise Otto-Peters demonstrated. The fact that fathers used to tutor their daughters is, in itself, problematic; after all, the whole socialization of scholarly daughters in the eighteenth century had always followed this pattern. The conflict arose out of the confrontation of two diametrically opposed sets of norms which can be outlined—albeit rather roughly—as the new male and female characteristics. While the eighteenth-century paternal arbitration of knowledge for daughters was not really influenced by the consideration of the formation of specific sexual characteristics—we have only to consider the father of Sophie Laroche—this consideration became a guiding principle in the nineteenth century for the new generation of the fathers of the female *Vormärz* writers. The victims of these double standards were, of course, the daughters.

An eloquent example of such a function for literature—that is, shaping the feminine role—is found in Fanny Lewald's memoirs. One of the first dramas she had read at the instigation of her father, who was clearly quite fond of this literary work, was Goethe's *Natural Daughter*. Fanny, however, was reluctant to comply. "The secret thought that my father's preference for Eugenie stemmed mainly from his view that every woman should wed and that the more educated the woman, the more willing she might be to enter into an inadequate and undesirable marriage—this thought made the natural daughter's resignation even more abhorrent to me.[28]

One thing is clear: paternal authority found its resonance in the cultural heritage. Goethe's *Natural Daughter* represented a literary work which served as a role model that emphasized the sacrifice of love making way for the marriage of convenience. In addition, there were situations where the conflict arose, in quite the reverse manner, out of the clash between the norms of the already completed feminine socialization and the clinging of the fathers to a traditional set of norms. An example of this is the dispute between Fanny Lewald and her father over her rejection of the poet Homer. Already sufficiently conditioned to feminine virtues such as gentleness, consideration, and compliance, Fanny was incapable of deriving pleasure from the Greek heroes. She gave, as the reason for her disapproval, the character traits of the heroes. She rebelled against their warlike elements and this brought her father's disapproval. He would not admit such a judgment was valid, on the ground that it was of an aesthetic nature, and he gave Fanny a dressing down, calling her "a foolish child" incapable of appreciating her cultural heritage.[29]

Interestingly, the Countess Hahn-Hahn also referred to Homer in the accounts of her travels. But the Greek poet was one of her favorites. This is partly to be explained by a domestic situation very different from that of the Lewald family type. The noble family type, characteristic of the first half of the nineteenth century just as it was of the period before, differed considerably from the new middle-class family. It was characterized first and foremost by its prestigious place in society and by its "lack of inwardness."[30] The dichotomy of male and female characteristics was, therefore, scarcely necessary and this resulted in the much less marked specific feminine socialization of the Countess Hahn-Hahn. For her, literature in no way served the new form of femininity. Indicative of this was her familiarity with Homer. He was not—as in Lewald's case—merely on the literary program drawn up by her father. Countess Hahn-Hahn was actually present when her mother and other ladies were reading aloud the *Iliad* and the *Odyssey* and she listened "from start to finish with the utmost attention and interest, with her heart in her mouth . . . to the inspired poetry."[31]

The reading situation thus far was, as we have seen, closely connected with feminine socialization based on the "supplementary theory" (*Ergänzungstheorie*), which became increasingly common in the course of the nineteenth century. The next question is: What other existing literary works outside these restricted confines were relevant to the female writers of the *Vormärz?* The Young German Movement (Das Junge Deutschland), so often considered disreputable, must be considered first, and with it, we introduce our second argument. The Young German writers could bring to their female colleagues of the *Vormärz* that which the books of advice to women, the school curricula, the carefully pruned anthologies, and their fathers acting as literary arbitrators deliberately kept from them: modern contemporary literature. The women reacted to the Young German Movement in completely different ways and occasionally even with disapproval, as in the case of Ida Hahn-Hahn. Yet this "tumultuous" generation of writers made these women familiar with that which was so stubbornly withheld from them: unstylized, contradictory, and sometimes unattractive reality.

Luise Mühlbach was the first to show an interest in the Young Germans. She had, in her youth, already had the chance to adopt numerous external ideas in the course of her frequent travels,[32] and to discover the writings of Heine, Gutzkow, and Mundt. Her lengthy correspondence with Theodor Mundt led to their marriage in 1839. Therese von Bacheracht had been the companion of Gutzkow for many years, and almost all were regular visitors to the Mundt household.

Via the *littérature engagée* of the Young Germans, the female writers of the *Vormärz* received information which the feminine socialization had not meant them to have: the reflection of concrete historic reality and everyday political life. Through the writings of the Young Germans they were allowed a glimpse beyond the inner chambers of the home designated to them; they could look out over the garden wall into the world of ideas that governed their time. "Heine's pictorial accounts of his travels and of the state of affairs in France, Börne's reports from Paris, Gutzkow, Laube, Theodor Mundt, Gustav Kühne, and Wienbarg spoke a language as yet unknown in Germany," Fanny Lewald reported. "All of us, still young in those days like them, have to . . . confess that we greeted wholeheartedly the Wally and the Madonna, the letters of a foolish man to a foolish woman, indeed all those early works of the so-called *Junges Deutschland,* with surprise and enthusiastic approval."[33]

There is a further point. The complete rejection of standard classical aesthetics by the Young Germans and their turn toward that which I would like to term everyday aesthetics was not an insignificant stimulus for the literary careers of the *Vormärz* authoresses. The participation of women in cultural life had always been possible by the inclusion of everyday life and at the moment when the term "everyday life" was promoted to one worthy of art, women too could make their creative contribution.[34]

There were, in addition to the Young Germans, other writers who spurred on many of the female writers of the *Vormärz*, principally other women writers who served as shining examples: Mme. de Staël, George Sand, Rahel Varnhagen von Ense, and Bettine von Arnim. The fact that they were women and that concrete feminine experiences were being written about was of great significance. It was also important that all the authoresses mentioned had strayed from the "straight and narrow" prescribed for women and led a life diametrically opposed to the existing conventional morality. Because of this, they were able to present an alternative picture of femininity. Here was the particularly problematic aspect of girls brought up in the new middle-class family type: cut off from any contact with the public, they had to learn *alone*, the hard way. They had to bury their frustrations deep inside and regard themselves as possibly the sole "wayward" feminine exception. Thus, the discovery of the letters of Rahel Varnhagen in 1834 was nothing short of liberating to Fanny Lewald. Because of her refusal to enter into a marriage of convenience, she had fallen out with her family and was greatly troubled.

> The posthumous letters of this woman were, for me, a revelation and my redemption. That which, above all others, is capable of the most complete destruction of a human being is the idea of suffering a unique fate. . . . That which one perceives other enduring, one can more easily endure. . . . What I had encountered, all the uncomfortable, the embarrassing, the painful experiences I had borne and suffered, Rahel Levin [Varnhagen] had known them all; she had survived them, every one, and had emerged victorious from all her struggles. With the help of her inherent strength, she had finally reached the point where she could recognize what she had always longed for, the opportunity to satisfy her inborn need for enjoyment and achievement.[35]

It is striking, of course, that not one of the female writers of the *Vormärz* had the courage to write about her own career in her fiction.[36] Despite the examples which female writers represented for them and their own literary careers, there is no *Vormärz* novel written by a woman which has a female writer as its heroine, with the exception of Luise Mühlbach's *Aphra Behn* (1849). Female socialization had clearly left a deeper mark than one would have expected on these female writers, even though many were unconventional. Therefore, the counter-example of Luise Mühlbach is interesting. Her literary socialization and her personally chosen models showed a shift of emphasis. She dealt extensively with English literature—as none of the other female writers had—and, in doing so, she discovered the enigmatic figure of Aphra Behn (1640–89), the very first female playwright in the history of European literature to write on a professional basis. Mühlbach devoted her major literary work of light fiction to the reconstruction of Behn's life. Through the medium of a historical character, she examined this new species of professional female writer and, more than any other female writer of her time, stressed Behn's career as a shining example to others.[37]

NOTES

1. Sophie Alberg, *Briefe über Mädchenbildung* (Leipzig, 1852), p. 57.

2. Fanny Lewald, *Meine Lebensgeschichte. Befreiung und Wanderleben* (Berlin, 1862), 1, pp. 260–61.

3. See Renate Möhrmann, *Frauenemanzipation im deutschen Vormärz. Texte und Dokumente* (Stuttgart, 1978), p. 3.

4. Günter Häntzschel, "Ein entdornter Heine. Zur Sozialgeschichte der Lyrik des 19. Jahrhunderts," *Heine Jahrbuch*, 21 (1982), p. 101.

5. Karin Hausen, "Die Polarisierung der 'Geschlechtscharaktere.' Eine Spiegelung der Dissoziation von Erwerbs- und Familienleben," in *Sozialgeschichte der Familie der Neuzeit in Europa*, ed. by Werner Conze (Stuttgart, 1976), p. 367.

6. See Hausen, especially pp. 365–75.

7. Fanny Lewald, *Meine Lebensgeschichte. Im Vaterhause* (Berlin, 1861), 1, p. 117.

8. Sophie Pataky, *Lexikon deutscher Frauen der Feder* (Bern, 1971), pp. viii–ix.

9. Herbert Marcuse, "Autorität und Familie in der deutschen Soziologie bis 1933," in *Studien über Autorität und Familie*, ed. by Erich Fromm (Paris, 1936), p. 738.

10. Ute Gerhard, *Verhältnisse und Verhinderungen. Frauenarbeit, Familie und Rechte der Frauen im 19. Jahrhundert* (Frankfurt, 1978), p. 94.

11. Barbara Duden, "Das schöne Eigentum. Zur Herausbildung des bürgerlichen Frauenbildes an der Wende vom 18. zum 19. Jahrhundert," *Kursbuch*, 47 (1977), pp. 125–40.

12. Hausen, p. 370.

13. Ibid., p. 381.

14. Brigitte Wartmann, "Die Grammatik des Patriarchats. Zur 'Natur' des Weiblichen in der bürgerlichen Gesellschaft," *Ästhetik und Kommunikation*, 47 (1982), p. 13.

15. Christian Oeser [Tobias Gottfried Schröer], *Briefe an eine Jungfrau über die Hauptgegenstände der Ästhetik. Ein Weihgeschenk für Frauen und Jungfrauen* (Leipzig, 1892), p. 48.

16. Häntzschel, p. 102.

17. Dagmar Grenz, *Mädchenliteratur. Von den moralisch-belehrenden Schriften im 18. Jahrhundert bis zur Herausbildung der Backfischliteratur im 19. Jahrhundert* (Stuttgart, 1981), p. 194.

18. Betty Gleim, *Erziehung und Unterricht des weiblichen Geschlechts. Ein Buch für Eltern und Erzieher* (Leipzig, 1810), p. 114.

19. Fanny Lewald, *Meine Lebensgeschichte. Leidensjahre* (Berlin, 1862), 1, pp. 122–23.

20. See Gottfried Kössler, *Mädchenliteratur im 19. Jahrhundert* (Giessen, 1979), p. 57.

21. Lewald, *Im Vaterhause*, 1, pp. 219–20.

22. Ibid., 2, p. 9.

23. Marie Helene, *Gräfin Ida Hahn-Hahn* (Leipzig, 1869), p. 5.

24. Lewald, *Im Vaterhause*, 1, p. 115.

25. See Fanny Lewald, *Gefühltes und Gedachtes* (Dresden, 1906), p. 147.

26. Louise Otto, *Frauenleben im Deutschen Reich. Erinnerungen aus der Vergangenheit* (Leipzig, 1876), pp. 7–8.

27. See Duden, pp. 125–40.

28. Lewald, *Im Vaterhause*, 2, p. 53.

29. Ibid., 2, p. 33.

30. See Gerhard, p. 80.

31. Ida Hahn-Hahn, *Jenseits der Berge* (Leipzig, 1840), 2, p. 116.

32. See Renate Möhrmann, *Die andere Frau. Emanzipationsansätze deutscher Schriftstellerinnen im Vorfeld der Achtundvierziger-Revolution* (Stuttgart, 1977), p. 61.

33. Lewald, *Leidensjahre*, 1, pp. 115–16.

34. See Renate Möhrmann, "Beruf: Künstlerin," *Frau und Kultur*, 2 (1982), p. 15.

35. Lewald, *Leidensjahre*, 2, pp. 20–21.

36. See Regula Venske, *Alltag und Emanzipation. Eine Untersuchung über die Romanautorin Fanny Lewald*, unpublished M.A. thesis, Hamburg, 1981, p. 7.

37. See Möhrmann, *Die andere Frau*, pp. 81–83.

Prelude to Consciousness

Amalie Sieveking and the Female Association for the Care of the Poor and the Sick

CATHERINE M. PRELINGER

A perennial task for the historian of women is the reassessment of preconditions for the development of feminism and the identification of circumstances under which women can function independently to initiate social
change in their own behalf. Women's historians have increasingly rejected models of victimization and recognize women's responsibility in
shaping their own lives. Occasionally what appears to the historian to be
no more than cooperation in support of patriarchy is in fact the innovative
pursuit of self-interest, autonomy, and power as women themselves perceive it within the possibilities of contemporary circumstances.[1] This essay examines the work of one such woman, Amalie Sieveking (1794–1859).

Sieveking was a member of the Hamburg patriciate, daughter and
granddaughter of senators, niece of a syndic, and cousin of another syndic
who was one of Hamburg's principal early-nineteenth-century diplomats.
Because her outlook is and was uncongenial to feminists, her role as a
liberator of women has been neglected, but, within the German context,
she was a pioneer. She made philanthropic activity available to women at
a time when, unlike the situation in England, organized Protestant charity was monopolized by men, and she did so not simply to improve the
quality of charity but to improve the quality of women's lives. As she
indicated in a speech before an audience in Bremen in 1841, nearly a
decade after she had founded the Female Association for the Care of the
Poor and the Sick (Weiblicher Verein für Armen- und Krankenpflege):

To me at least as important were the benefits which [work with the poor] seemed to promise for those of my sisters who would join me in such a work of charity. The higher interests of my sex were close to my heart.

For, she continued:

I have long since expressed my own view that in a great many cases, namely those of the upper classes, household and other domestic responsibilities do not offer the female side of the family a sufficient arena for the sum of their energies.[2]

Sieveking was convinced that the time upper-class women devoted to theaters, concerts and dances, parties and social calls, could be more profitably spent in charitable enterprise, a route to the kind of self-esteem denied them by the society of the period. The association which she founded in 1832 was an institutional innovation. More important, it provided a model and initiated a network for women throughout Germany which engaged them in an exchange of skills and strategies for social leadership, mutual support, and the creation of a female consciousness. It is this latter aspect of Sieveking's accomplishment and its roots in the personal experience of conquering societal prescriptions that this essay addresses. For it is here rather than in the institutional impact of her career—the one touched in conventional histories of German Protestant philanthropy, where she appears as the single woman in the array of male philanthropists[3]—that one can examine what was distinctively female in her experience and its relation to the lives of other women.

The politicization of the personal was an important aspect of Sieveking's success. Amalie's mother died when she was four years old; she lost her father when she was fifteen. Raised in close companionship with her brothers, she and the three boys habitually played together and were tutored as a homogeneous group. The absence of a mother and the undifferentiated sibling experience may have assisted Sieveking in rejecting the conventional role of the Hamburg matron. When her father died in 1809, his fortune eroded by the French occupation and the severance of trade with England, Amalie and her brothers were separated and placed to board in the homes of relatives and friends. Her own school lessons—but not her brothers'—were discontinued. Later, in her adult years as a proselytizer for women's entrance into public charity, she made much of the disparity in educational opportunities for women and men. She discovered her own talent as a teacher in the household where she lived, and instituted a series of six-year instructional programs for girls which she continued throughout her life. They became a major source of her influence because her former pupils were dedicated disciples and ardent correspondents.[4] This project also established the mode of her subsequent activism: the marshaling of influence derived from her family to advance the interests of women.

A protracted period of personal turmoil and self-examination absorbed Sieveking's attention during her early twenties, a crisis evoked in part by the evident contradictions between contemporary expectations and the option of the single life for which she yearned. Religious implications were always closely interwoven with personal considerations for Amalie, and themes of autonomy and subordination recur in both domains of her speculation. Much later she described those years to the girls who came to her pension as pupils:

> It must have been about the year 1818 when I started to reflect on the specific fate of women, and when my inner calling began to be clear to me. The fatherly advice of Campe [the moralist Joachim Heinrich Campe, 1746–1818] to his daughter made a profound impression on me at that time and was, as I only later grasped, truly useful. Marriage was presented there [in Campe's book] as the only course for a girl, which contradicted an inner voice in me. . . . More and more it seemed clear to me that it was impossible that the bountiful Lord would bestow his blessing on one estate alone. Rather he would look with favor on all estates, even that of the ill-reputed old maid.[5]

In her moral diary of the period, the Sunday Conversations (*Sonntagsunterhaltungen*), she wrote defiantly: "If not a happy wife and mother, then founder of an order of Sisters of Charity!"[6] This goal was to dominate her thinking for the next decade.

The widespread collaboration of women in charity as it had so elaborately unfolded in Catholic Europe had no counterpart in early modern Protestantism. The absence of a tradition of female philanthropy, particularly in Germany, was intrinsic to the nature and development of the Lutheran Church. In his insistence upon clerical marriage, on the one hand, and the centrality he gave the Word of God as articulated by the male clergy, on the other, Luther left little room for the development of women's service, except for wives of the clergy. Pietism introduced a new dimension to German Protestantism in the eighteenth century; in the Pietist community of Herrnhut, the opportunities for practical Christian service implicit in Pietism were extended to include women. The disciplined communal life required of single women and the custom of marriage by lot, however, meant that the Herrnhut experience did not create a usable past for most women in subsequent generations. During the War of Liberation women created clubs to care for the injured and abandoned, but when peace returned they dispersed. Children's shelters (*Rettungshäuser*), the philanthropic innovation of the war and postwar period, increasingly assumed a heavily pedagogical character and hence involved women in only the most menial capacities. It is against this background, one marked by the absence of Protestant female philanthropists, that Sieveking's achievement must be understood.

Sieveking's fantasy, the creation of an order for Protestant women in Germany, was shaped by the religious awakening Hamburg experienced during and after the French occupation. Patriotism stimulated an enormously emotional revival, one which obscured confessional distinctions and sustained subjective forms of religious expression. The Sieveking family and many of their closest associates among Hamburg's religious and political elite were profoundly caught up in this movement. The pastor of the French Reformed Church, the mystic Henri Merle d'Aubigné, exercised a powerful influence in this circle, preaching that the one true Catholic Church embraced all Christians who had experienced conversion.[7] Amalie's religious sensibilities resonated with those of Merle and she wrote to a mentor in Leipzig: "The difference between Catholicism and Protestantism appears now not nearly so great as in former years"; to a woman friend and former pupil she confessed that during these years she had indeed been in love with Merle.[8] The Catholic legacy became particularly accessible to the Sieveking circle through Count Friedrich Leopold Stolberg and Pastor Johannes Gossner, the one a recent convert to Catholicism, the other newly won to Protestantism. Both frequented Hamburg in the postwar years. Stolberg's biography of St. Vincent de Paul introduced Amalie to the historic milieu of the Catholic Sisters of Charity. When Gossner departed Hamburg for a post in Berlin, Amalie accepted his blessing which formally solemnized her vow to make a reality of the Protestant Sisters of Charity.[9]

Nevertheless, in the end she moved in a very different direction, one determined by personal as well as social developments. Careful scrutiny of the statutes of the Bavarian order of Sisters of Charity which Gossner sent her piqued a sense of skepticism. "The yoke is too slavish, the chains too restrictive. The free spirit would be struck dead by the multiplicity of little legalisms,"[10] she wrote to Baron vom Stein, the most notable contemporary committed to the implementation of women's philanthropy. To her brother she had once confessed: "From the bottom of my soul I hate all human organizations of authority in matters of faith, and I acknowledge evangelical freedom as one of the most exalted attributes of our church."[11] The Hamburg awakening was fed from English evangelicalism as well as from the Catholic renascence of the South; as one writer suggested, English ideas like English wares flooded the city after the war.[12] Johann Wilhelm Rautenberg, pastor of Trinity Church, introduced the institution of the Sunday school along English lines, and his annual report of 1831 called upon the men of his congregation to adopt another English practice, that of benevolent visiting. Amalie Sieveking never acknowledged a specific indebtedness to this report, but her membership in this circle makes it a probable source of inspiration for the kind of society she ultimately founded.[13]

Two events in the life of contemporary Hamburg propelled Sieveking from speculation to action. The first was a campaign launched by the press in 1830 to identify and publicize the failures of municipal poor relief in the city. The second was the cholera epidemic of 1831. At a time when only seventy cities in the German Empire had counted more than 10,000[14] residents, Hamburg's population numbered 110,000;during the decades after the peace settlement, the population increased at a rate of approximately 6 percent annually. The restoration of commerce after the war acted as a magnet to the rural population; inordinate growth of the city kept wages low and drew the poor into increasingly miserable housing as the extension of wharfs and warehouses impinged upon their traditional quarters.[15] The poor relief administration was unable to accommodate these changes. At the end of the eighteenth century Hamburg supported a system of relief which was the envy of the European continent. Designed by Kaspar von Voght (1752–1834) it combined public and private resources with the goal of eliminating the conditions which produced poverty. The system depended upon close involvement with the poor, on training as well as penal provisions, and on the personal commitment of ranking government officials. Disrupted by the war when occupying officers banished poor people from the city, the poor relief administration never recovered its earlier character. In 1832, 2,846 families were regularly registered with the administration; the increase of a mere 850 since 1788 in no way corresponded to increases in the impoverished population; the facilities of public relief had rather become inadequate to the demand.[16] These people received the dole and virtually nothing in the way of preventive intervention. When the cholera epidemic struck, 5,800 families applied for support on one occasion, 15,000 on another. A more accurate indication that a permanently impoverished and alienated class was in the making was the record of illegitimacy, which in the years 1826–35 numbered one in every five births. Residency requirements to meet the qualifications for legal marriage were, in other words, increasingly beyond reach. Many people were beyond the reach of the Church as well; seldom were more than thirty or forty persons in attendance at any one of the city's five major churches.[17]

At the beginning of the nineteenth century, citizens of Hamburg believed that theirs was a city of mutuality and interconnectedness. One of them boasted: "We have no nobility, no patriciate, no slaves, even no subjects. All true residents of Hamburg acknowledge the existence of just one status and that is the status of citizen."[18] This was a euphemism. Nevertheless, the guilds in their day served as a source of bonding among their members. Before the middle of the century, however, their hold on the economy was no longer secure. In 1838, for example, guild restrictions on the building of ships were lifted when it became clear that the industry, critical to the city's survival, was stagnating. The postwar decades witnessed a rapid expansion of non-guild-controlled manufactures, among them tobacco wares, sugar products, umbrellas, and walking sticks. By 1856, 85 percent of all goods manufactured in Hamburg for export came out of factories rather than guild-controlled shops, a development accompanied by the appearance of a class of independent entrepreneurs as well as one of unaffiliated workers, many of whom lived on the borders of poverty.[19]

Baron von Voght returned to the city in 1830 after a twenty-year absence, and in a series of newspaper articles and privately distributed reports he attacked the poor relief administration for its failure to deal with contemporary issues. He targeted the erosion of individual involvement, particularly on the part of ruling circles, and the substitution of almsgiving for work and supervision. Conceding that the situation was beyond restitution, the poor relief administration called for a decisive delineation between public and private responsibility, so far as services rendered to the poor beyond minimal relief were concerned; only where no private agency was in a position to intervene with nursing care, vocational training, child support, or whatever would the public administration endeavor to provide these services.[20]

Amalie Sieveking took this announcement as an invitation and a challenge. During the autumn of 1831 she had earned a public reputation when she entered the infirmary of St. Ericus as a volunteer to care for female cholera patients. The medical service at first resented her intrusion; her social circle suspected her of courting deliberate martyrdom. She persevered, and when she completed her tour of duty, she had established credentials with the officialdom on which her future work would depend and won the reverential support of her peers.[21]

On May 23, 1832, she was joined by twelve other women to found the Female Association for the Care of the Poor and the Sick, a society for benevolent visiting. The aim of the association was to visit the households of impoverished invalids and their families in accordance with recommendations from the public administration, and to provide practical and material help as well as spiritual guidance. The statutes of the association recognized that the numbers of clients the association could expect to serve and the nature of its commitment would necessarily depend both on the number of members recruited and on the financial resources at its disposal. No woman was to consider membership unless she could expect to devote herself to at least one and preferably two house calls each week, and to at least one meeting each week with other members of the association to assess the results of their visits.[22]

Socially as well as spiritually and morally, Sieveking conceived of the charitable function as one of amelioration and integration, not one of change. Poverty, as she represented it, was one dimension of an educative plan ordained by God to improve the souls of the poor and instruct the rich in the virtues of mercy. Benevolent visiting took both dimensions of this plan into account. The visitor was expected to make a full assessment of the material and spiritual inventory of the household visited. She might donate goods and services but most important she must instruct the visited in the virtues of cleanliness, parsimony, sobriety, and the fear of God. Every visit included prayer and Bible reading. At the center of Sieveking's personal faith was a strong commitment to the doctrine of individual immortality, and in her own visits she tried to awaken her clients to the promise of eternal life, which, she believed, offered them an incentive to conduct better lives. As she wrote in the instructions to her colleagues: "Christian love . . . points the way to future salvation but also recalls the condition to which the attainment of it is tied."[23] Sieveking, in other words, enlisted the supernatural in the service of social compliance.

Beyond the personal interaction of the visit itself, visits were the means the Female Association used to identify more extended commitments to its clientele: the distribution of clothing, of food donated by local provisioners, of coupons for the city's soup kitchen, and, most important, the assignment of work. The association functioned as an employer; it organized work among its own clientele, such as repairs and maintenance, and it assigned put-out work, particularly to homebound women. Sieveking operated within what for Hamburg was an increasingly obsolete household economy and she acted to save rather than to change it. The workers her association usually supported were displaced artisans, such as carpenters dislocated by the new construction trades and spinners put out of work by the mechanization of the textile industry. The poor Sieveking applauded in her annual reports were those who displayed "the fear of God" and accepted aid "within the bounds of modesty."[24] In the economic crisis of the 1840s Sieveking recognized that, however virtuous, the male worker could scarcely support a family, and she believed that the cause lay in the relentless drive of manufacturers to lower prices in order to seize the market. The surplus of laborers facilitated this practice. Sieveking barely contained her anger at the new bourgeoisie. Given the constraints of her own education and position, Sieveking's observations were often acute, but strategies of change completely eluded her. "I see no way in the realm of human power and wisdom," she wrote, "to mitigate this poverty. But I should at least like to draw it to the attention of the upper classes as an evil."[25] In one of the messages she wrote to her "friends among the poor"—this time after violence had erupted in Paris and Berlin early in 1848—she equated the destruction of factories with the destruc-

tion of jobs. She reassured her ostensible audience that "our first states-
men" were seeking a solution to the crisis and urged the oppressed to
forgo the temptation to take the law into their own hands.[26]

Particularly when the association was first founded, it met with resistance at many levels. Sieveking herself had not anticipated the extent of
the opposition—particularly, in the light of her own example in the cholera infirmary, the initial reluctance of women to join her. Baron von Voght
actually doubted whether a society of "wives, mothers, housekeepers,
sisters, and daughters" could undertake the requisite services: "The work
of sisters of charity is suitable only to persons who are completely alone in
the world and can devote themselves exclusively to their calling," he
wrote to her.[27] Relations between the association and the public administration remained fragile for years and demanded Sieveking's constant
attention.

> You have to know our local situation [she wrote in 1837]; the multitude
> of civic bureaucrats, the frequent changes among them, a prevalent
> republican spirit, and each one of them wishing to conduct his own area
> of competency with a kind of independent hegemony over which he is
> very jealous; then in the majority of our doctors a powerful partiality
> against the revived evangelical spirit, which they equate with mys-
> ticism.[28]

Allusions to opposition reappear in her correspondence. Neither the support of an influential family circle nor the extent of the crisis in Hamburg
and the concomitant response on the part of comparable male societies
insulated the Female Association against contemporary prejudice.[29]

Ultimately, however, the Sieveking association met with a strong and
positive response among the women it was designed to enlist. From the
original twelve members the society expanded to include fifty-three during its first decade, seventy on the eve of the revolution, and eighty-five
at the time of Sieveking's death in 1859.[30] Sieveking published no formal
membership list; her handwritten notes and the annual reports of the
association make it apparent that the women who joined her came from
her own constellation—families engaged in the religious and political
leadership of Hamburg. In 1847, of the seventy members Sieveking recorded in her personal notebook, at least thirteen besides herself were
wives and daughters of senators.[31] As the membership grew the caseload
expanded from an original 85 families to 256. Funded by voluntary contributions, the expendable income of the association increased from 1,332
banco marks the first year to 47,000 in 1859.[32] In 1837 a large anonymous
endowment made possible a significant addition to the society's enterprises in the form of the Amalienstift, which allowed for the construction
of a building to provide both low-cost housing to the poor and a children's

hospital. After the fire of 1842, advantageous funding made possible an extension of housing to familes who had been burned out.[33]

Originally Sieveking viewed the society as an expedient until such a time as she could mount an initiative to implement the earlier goal of an order. Apart from success and "the affection I have come to feel for the association in its present form,"[34] a number of developments intervened to induce her to abandon the original plan. Of singular importance was her decision, one which engaged her the better part of a year, to refuse an offer from Pastor Theodor Fliedner to superintend the institution which he founded and directed at Kaiserswerth near Düsseldorf. Fliedner was involved in introducing women as deaconesses into the Prussian church; Sieveking would have acted as his immediate subordinate. Her refusal reinforced her commitment to female leadership independent of both male and ecclesiastical direction. At the same time it marked a conscious recognition on her part of her role as a philanthropic pioneer, the founder of an innovative institution which departed decisively from Catholic antecedents, of which vestiges were evident in Fliedner's deaconessate.[35]

As early as 1837, as Sieveking indicated to Fliedner, the Female Association was generating interest and imitation elsewhere in Germany. At least four similar societies had been established in other cities and more were anticipated. Sieveking's imitators found in her work not only the precedent for benevolent visiting as such but also the legitimation for a systematic recruitment of lay volunteer women, married as well as single, into the charitable enterprise. By 1842 there were more than fifteen associations which identified themselves as affiliates; on the eve of the revolution, fifty-nine such affiliates were in operation, forty-five of them in Germany.[36] Johann Hinrich Wichern, on the way to becoming Germany's most prominent philanthropist through the Inner Mission, applauded "this voluntary effort of Christian women" in the pages of the *Fliegende Blätter (Flysheets)* as "one of the most distinctive evidences of social regeneration of our times."[37] The absence of a formal structure associating the several societies disturbed Wichern, but it was precisely this informality which proved the strength of the Sieveking coalition. Personal networking created the impetus to organize that permitted women with little or no public exposure to come together without embarrassment and develop their talents through experience. There was a loose bond forged primarily by correspondence with Sieveking and subscriptions to her annual report.

The initial overture to Sieveking was usually a request for copies of the statutes of the Hamburg association or for her instructions to benevolent visitors or for annual reports. Women such as Bertha Lack of Magdeburg believed that the recruitment of colleagues and the implementation of a program would be facilitated by adhering to current practice in

Hamburg. Charlotte Ahlefeldt-Lindau identified herself as a cloistered woman in Preetz who was hoping to extend the nature of her work by creating a society like Sieveking's. Fredericka Plau from Danzig wrote of her own familiarity with visiting societies in England and her pleasure to learn through her mother that Sieveking had demonstrated that the practice could be adapted to German circumstances.[38] By 1850 the society in Danzig had twenty members and made 1,500 visits annually; its members believed that their lives had been enriched by their "closer acquaintance with the poor."[39] Sieveking's visit to Bremen in 1841 stimulated a surge of correspondence, for it was on that occasion that she formally and in person carried her message outside of Hamburg. Henriette von Gruber, writing from Stralsund after reading Sieveking's Bremen address, described herself as the mother of five children; she was inspired to found a visiting society nevertheless, and wrote for the continued guidance of the annual reports.[40]

Many of the letters to Sieveking sought very practical forms of advice. Frau Pastor Noltensius, for instance, asked for the title of prayer books particularly suitable for the sick and she inquired about the wages the Hamburg association paid its homebound workers. Bertha Lack wanted to know how many visits each member should make. Experience bred confidence. Doris Esselbach in Schleswig reported twenty-five families cared for by her society in 1845. From Hanover, Ida Ahrenhold reported the purchase of a house providing cheap rentals to twenty families in 1843. Annual reports were increasingly exchanged rather than simply requested. The Bremen association invited Sieveking's critique of their statues in 1844.[41] From Stettin in 1847, Emilie Behrens wrote:

> It gives me particular pleasure to be able to send you, my dear lady, the enclosed report. For indeed your activity to relieve the need of the poor preceded ours; I owe you our gratitude, for your sleepless nights permitted our success. . . . You, in contrast to us, suffered in much greater measure than we, for you founded your society at a time when much greater resistance prevailed. My sister workers ask you to accept their heartfelt thanks . . . in community with you they wish to pray and to work.[42]

One woman spoke of the society at Cologne as a "little daughter" of the one at Hamburg.

In the course of their correspondence many of the women writing Sieveking were candid about their sense of personal inadequacy to deal with the problems they confronted, usually as chairwomen of their associations. "A greater expansion under my aegis will be difficult, for my energies are insufficient for it," Marianne von Voigt wrote from Celle in 1835. Sophie Behrens called herself "still so inexperienced" in her situation in Kiel. Leadership was the recurrent problem. In Ludwigslust,

Helene Schultze wondered if she was following instructions accurately. Emmy Pauli apparently accepted the chair of her society in Lübeck against her better judgment and wrote of her "very difficult hours" entailed by the development of an opposition group within the association.[43]

There was a certain uniformity in the kind of issues which Sieveking's correspondents raised, and it was these recurrent themes that were addressed by the anonymous little volume *The Work of Women in Associations for the Care of the Poor and Sick. An Exchange of Letters between Two Friends (Arbeit der Frauen in Vereinen für Armen- und Krankenpflege. Ein Briefwechsel zweier Freundinnen)*. The authors were friends of Sieveking's and the purported exchange of letters echo authentic letters in Sieveking's file; they were designed as a guide to women in club work. The correspondence opens with "Clara's" election to the chair of her club and successively examines such issues as the best time and place for meetings, meeting strategies, procedures for visitations, personal qualities necessary for the successful interchange with clients, characteristic client problems, work suitable for home manufacture, and finally the management of club affairs as such: finances, records, and annual reports. The authors hoped to supply a resource and a source of reassurance. At one point Clara deplores the fact that, while her co-workers acknowledge the importance of reading one another's reports of visits in the official bluebook each society kept, "how often is nothing read and virtually nothing written. . . . [Yet] how necessary it is that I don't lose my patience and bring upon myself the charge of pedantry in the service of orderliness."[44] *The Work of Women* delivered more substantive counsel as well:

> Intervention on our part into the domestic and marital relations of our clients is something special and often much more sensitive than our clients themselves behave as though it were. We cannot always entirely avoid involvement; the naïveté with which our poor commonly disclose their intimate relations and the motives of their conduct requires as great candor as it does caution in our ways of approaching such issues.[45]

A compendium of often sound observation, *The Work of Women* offered a hidden agenda. It reminded the reader that other Christian women were out there coping with similar problems and seeking bonds of mutual support. For Sieveking the value of collective action over the "isolated effects of individuals" had become an article of faith.[46]

This was the real achievement of the Sieveking network. Sieveking herself believed that the introduction of female benevolent visiting and the implementation of female leadership and sisterhood were singular accomplishments. Defending her record against the articulated feminism of 1848, she argued that she, too, championed a kind of female emancipation—as indeed she did.[47] Sieveking tried to extend opportunities for women while at the same time she accepted the oppression of the poor as an unalterable condition of society. She was able to embrace these contradictions through her essentially backward-looking view of society, one which centered in the functional, patriarchal rationale of the household rather than in the more modern view of the dichotomous nature of the sexes underpinning the bourgeois family. In her public speeches she cajoled fathers and husbands to allow the women of their households to engage in charitable activities; she never questioned their authority to do so. The concept of woman's nature and a sphere in which women might be autonomous was totally alien to her. Private and public were one. To legitimate women's charity she used the analogy of a court whose high moral tone penetrated the conduct of the entire *Residenz*.[48]

On Christian premises Sieveking mounted a significant opposition to the nascent bourgeois women's movement, one which her own work had in fact anticipated.[49] When, in the wake of the revolution, the reaction proscribed most women's public activities, her own coalition of organizations survived to become a fixture of the post-revolutionary urban scene. They too, however, also fell victim to the anti-feminism of the reaction. As the Inner Mission advanced with uniformity, efficiency, and funds to extend and coordinate all dimensions of German philanthropy, female compliance with the standards of male institutionalism supplanted the cultivation of female leadership as the goal for women's charity.[50]

NOTES

1. For this formulation, I am grateful to the review essay of Carolyn Lougee, "Modern European History," *Signs: Journal of Women in Culture and Society*, 2 (1977), p. 648.

2. Amalie Sieveking, "Vortrag in Bremen, gehalten am 25. Oktober 1841," Weiblicher Verein für Armen- und Krankenpflege, *10. Bericht* (Hamburg, 1842), pp. 73, 80.

3. For instance, Gerhard Uhlorn, *Die christliche Liebestätigkeit* (Neukirchen Kreis Moers, 1959), pp. 732–33; Franz Schnabel, *Deutsche Geschichte im neunzehnten Jahrhundert* (4 vols.; 3rd ed., Freiburg i.B., 1955), 4 pp. 420, 425, 429.

4. [Emma Poel], *Denkwürdigkeiten aus dem Leben von Amalie Sieveking in deren Auftrage von einer Freundin derselben verfasst mit einem Vorwort von Dr. Wichern* (Hamburg, 1860), pp. 2–25. This work was assembled shortly after Sieveking's death and contains extensive excerpts from her letters and diaries before they were deposited with the family archives in Hamburg. See, for exam-

ple, StArHmbg, Familie Sieveking III: Schriftliche Nachlass von Amalie W. Sieveking, Verzeichnis IIIB, Die Schülerinnen. I am grateful to Dr. Kurt Sieveking for permission to use this archive.

5. *Denkwürdigkeiten*, pp. 116–17. See Joachim Heinrich Campe, *Vaeterliche Rath für meine Tochter. Ein Gegenstück zum Theophon. Der erwachsenern weiblichen Jugend gewidmet* (Braunschweig, 1791), especially pp. 85, 172.

6. StArHmbg, Nachlass A. W. Sieveking VI, Sonntagunterhaltungen, entry of 18 April 1819.

7. Rudolf Kayser, "Henri Merle d'Aubigné und die Anfänge der Erweckung in Hamburg," *Zeitschrift des Vereins für Hamburgische Geschichte*, 30 (1929), p. 125 (hereafter cited as *ZVHG*).

8. StArHmbg, Nachlass A. W. Sieveking IA$_2$, A. Sieveking to Senator Dr. Volkmann, fall 1825; to Caroline Bertheau, 13 May 1836.

9. *Denkwürdigkeiten*, pp. 85, 117, 131–34. StArHmbg, Nachlass A. W. Sieveking IB$_2$, A. Sieveking to Volkmann, 25 July 1828; Rudolf Kayser, "Friedrich Perthes und seine katholischen Freunde," *ZVHG*, 34 (1933), pp. 9–10; Hermann Dalton, *Johannes Gossner. Ein Lebensbild aus der Kirche des neunzehnten Jahrhunderts* (Berlin, 1874), pp. 297–98.

10. StArHmbg, Nachlass A.W.S., IA$_2$, A. Sieveking to Freiherr v. Stein, 14 September 1830.

11. *Denkwürdigkeiten*, p. 167.

12. Kayser, "Henri Merle d'Aubigné," p. 129.

13. Martin von Gerhardt, *Johann Hinrich Wichern. Ein Lebensbild* (3 vols.; Hamburg, 1927–31), 1, pp. 118, 257.

14. Karl Obermann, "Die deutsche Bevölkerungsstatistik und die Bevölkerungsstruktur des Deutschen Bundes in den Jahren um 1815," in *Bevölkerungsgeschichte*, ed. by Wolfgang Köllmann and Peter Marschalck (Cologne, 1972), p. 196.

15. Antje Kraus, *Die Unterschichten Hamburgs in der ersten Hälfte des 19. Jahrhunderts. Entstehung, Struktur und Lebensverhältnisse* (Stuttgart, 1965), pp. 34, 36, 31.

16. Kaspar Freiherr von Voght, *Account of the Management of the Poor in Hamburg since the Year 1788* (reprinted, London, 1817); Joachim Hermann, *Historische Arbeiten aus seinem Nachlass* (Hamburg, 1936), p. 127; Paul Kollmann, *Die Wirksamkeit der Allgemeinen Armenanstalt der Stadt Hamburg von 1788–1870* (Hamburg, 1871); Krause, pp. 48–49.

17. Elisabeth Haupt, *Amalie Sieveking als Gründerin des weiblichen Vereins für Armen- und Krankenpflege in Hamburg* (Berlin-Spandau, 1933), pp. 20, 22, 77; Ingrid Lahrsen, *Beiträge zum kirchlichen und religiösen Leben Hamburgs zur Zeit der Erweckungsbewegung*, dissertation, Hamburg, 1957, pp. 98–100.

18. Percy Ernst Schramm, *Hamburg, Deutschland und die Welt. Leistung und Grenzen hanseatischen Bürgertums in der Zeit zwischen Napoleon und Bismarck* (Munich, 1943), p. 29.

19. Ernst Baasch, *Geschichte Hamburgs 1814–1918* (2 vols.; Gotha-Stuttgart, 1924–25), 1, p. 20; Kraus, pp. 1, 21, 51.

20. Haupt, pp. 20–24.

21. Ibid., pp. 19–20; Martin Hieronymus Hudtwalcker, *Ein halbes Jahrhundert aus meiner Lebensgeschichte* (3 vols.; Hamburg, 1862–64), 3, pp. 387–88.

22. Haupt, p. 32; "Statuten des Vereins," W. Verein, *2. Bericht*, pp. 1–5.

23. W. Verein, *2. Bericht*, pp. 27–29; *9. Bericht*, pp. 50–66, quotation from pp. 62–63.

24. Ibid., *12. Bericht*, pp. 40–41; *17. Bericht*, p. 19, *22. Bericht*, p. 24; *11. Bericht*, pp. 33, 35 for quotations.

25. Ibid., *16. Bericht*, pp. 47–48; *6. Bericht*, pp. 42–45, quotation from p. 43.

26. Ibid., *16. Bericht*, pp. 48, 58.

27. *Denkwürdigkeiten*, p. 209; Voght is quoted in Heinrich Sieveking, "Zur Geschichte der geistigen Bewegung in Hamburg nach den Freiheitskriegen," *ZVHG*, 28 (1927), pp. 141–42.

28. Fliedner Archiv, Rep. II Kb3, A. Sieveking to Theodor Fliedner, 28 August 1837.

29. StArHmbg, Nachlass A.W.S., IA$_2$, A. Sieveking to "Geehrte Vorsteherinnen des Cellischen Frauenvereins," 27 May 1836, and note 42 below; A. Sieveking to Eduard and Louise Sieveking, 25 April 1832, in which she mentioned the support of Senator Hudtwalcker among others and her belief that the exposure of the public administration would assure acceptance of her idea. H. Segelmann, *Die Gegenwart der evangelisch-Lutherischen Kirche Hamburgs . . .* (Hamburg, 1862), Beilage II: Vereine, Stiftungen und Unternehmungen . . . ohne Zuthun des Staates und der Kirche gestiftet, pp. 293–94.

30. W. Verein, *10. Bericht*, p. 11; *15. Bericht*, p. 39; Richard Remé, *Amalie Sieveking. Eine Vorkämpferin der christlichen Frauenbewegung* (Hamburg, 1911), p. 28.

31. StArHmbg, Archiv des weiblichen (Sievekingschen) Vereins für Armen- und Krankenpflege, small notebook in Sieveking's hand dated 1847, which unfortunately includes only last names. Dirk Bavendamm, *Von der Revolution zur Reform. Die Verfassungspolitik des hamburgischen Senats 1849–50* (Berlin, 1969), pp. 284–85, for a chart indicating familial relationships among senatorial members.

32. W. Verein, *1. Bericht*, pp. 6–7; Remé, p. 28.

33. Haupt, pp. 48–50.

34. Ibid., pp. 58–59, for a reprint of a letter of Sieveking's to Prof. Karl von Raumer, 18 January 1832; W. Verein, *10. Bericht*, p. 77 for quotation.

35. Fliedner's original invitation and Sieveking's first response of 27 March 1837 are transcribed in Anna Sticker, *Friedericke Fliedner. und die Anfänge der Frauendiakonie. Ein Quellenbuch* (2nd ed.; Neukirchen-Vluyn, 1963), pp. 331–34, 109–110; for final letter, see note 28 above. Also StArHmbg, Nachlass A.W.S., IA$_2$, A. Sieveking to Eduard Sieveking, Jr., 8 April 1855.

36. W. Verein, *10. Bericht*, pp. 28–29; StArHmbg, Nachlass A.W.S., Verzeichnis, pp. 60–63: Nach dem Muster des hamburger Vereins an anderen Orten gegründete Frauenvereine.

37. *Fliegende Blätter aus dem Rauhen Haus*, 4 (1847), p. 228.

38. StArHmbg, Nachlass A.W.S., IB, Bertha Lack to A. Sieveking, 16 Feb-

ruary 1848; Charlotte Ahlefeldt-Lindau to A. Sieveking, 7 November 1841; Fredericka Plau to A. Sieveking, 19 April 1849.

39. "Weiblicher Verein für Armen- und Krankenpflege in Danzig," *Armen- und Krankenfreund. Eine Zeitschrift für die Diakonie*, 3 (March–April 1851), p. 20.

40. StArHmbg, Nachlass A.W.S., IB, Henriette von Gruber to A. Sieveking, 1 June 1847.

41. StArHmbg, Nachlass A.W.S., IB, Frau Pastor Noltensius to A. Sieveking, 23 December 1842; Bertha Lack to A. Sieveking, 20 January 1848; Doris Esselbach to A. Sieveking, Montag Abend; Ida Ahrenhold to A. Sieveking, 25 January 1843; Elise Hunicke to A. Sieveking, 14 December 1844.

42. StArHmbg, Nachlass A.W.S., IB, Emilie Behrens to A. Sieveking, 23 February 1847.

43. StArHmbg, Nachlass A. Sieveking, IB, Emilie Lehman to A. Sieveking, 22 November 1849; Marianne von Voigt to A. Sieveking, 20 August 1835; Sophie Behrens to A. Sieveking, 17 September 1845; Helene Schultze to A. Sieveking, 9 November 1843; Emmy Pauli to A. Sieveking, 10 February 1848.

44. [Emma Poel and Sophie Wattenbach], *Arbeit der Frauen in Vereinen für Armen- und Krankenpflege. Ein Briefwechsel zweien Freundinnen*, introduction by Amalie Sieveking (Berlin, 1854), p. 33.

45. Ibid., p. 145.

46. W. Verein, *19. Bericht*, p. 21.

47. A. Sieveking, "Vortrag gehalten in Berlin den 25 April 1849, über die Stellung des weiblichen Geschlechts auf dem Gebiete der inneren Mission," W. Verein, *17. Bericht*, pp. 53–79.

48. Ibid., p. 66; *Denkwürdigkeiten*, p. 350; A. Sieveking, "Aufruf an die christliche Frauen und Jungfrauen Deutschlands," W. Verein, *18. Bericht*, p. 27; *5. Bericht*, p. 14.

49. I have discussed these connections in papers delivered at the Missouri Valley History Conference, March 9–11, 1978; at the Fourth Berkshire Conference on the History of Women, August 23–25, 1978, at Mount Holyoke College; and, cursorily, in "Religious Dissent, Women's Rights and the Hamburger Hochschule fuer das weibliche Geschlecht," *Church History*, 45 (1976), pp. 42–55.

50. *Fliegende Blätter*, 11 (1854), pp. 307–8; Haupt, pp. 12, 86.

Female Political Opposition in Pre-1848 Germany

The Role of Kathinka Zitz-Halein*

STANLEY ZUCKER

Writing the history of German women's political and civil activities around the middle of the nineteenth century has only recently begun. But already it is clear that the generally accepted thesis that the women's rights movement or women's political and social activism begins in the 1860s is in need of serious revision.[1] The decade from 1840 to 1850 was rich in such activities by women: the philosophical writing and lectures of Louise Dittmar, the social novels and journalistic work of Louise Otto, the radical feminist views and actions of Louise Aston, and the educational endeavors of Hamburg's Hochschule für das weibliche Geschlecht (College for the Female Sex). Organized activities by women in 1848–49 raised money for a German fleet and supported the participants in the spring 1849 uprising, while politically motivated acts by individual women included building and fighting on barricades, decorating the graves of executed revolutionaries, and wearing black to mourn the defeated revolution.

Of the German women whose efforts had an impact on her contem-

*The writer wishes to thank the American Philosophical Society and the Deutscher Akademischer Austauschdienst for their financial support which helped make possible a research trip to the BRD. He also wants to express his gratitude to Prof. Dr. Winfried Baumgart, chairman of the History Department, Johannes Gutenberg University, Mainz, for his many kindnesses during my stay in the BRD.

poraries, probably none was greater than that of Kathinka Zitz-Halein. As the founder and first president (May 1849–June 1850) of the Humania Association, the largest women's organization formed during the revolution (1,600 members), she managed a wide-reaching program of support for political refugees and prisoners as well as their dependents during the aftermath of the spring revolt of 1849. She traveled widely through southern Germany, Switzerland, and France visiting prisoners and refugees and negotiating for the release of or for improved conditions for those incarcerated. Besides directing this politically motivated relief program she could be considered the poet laureate of the German revolution. She used her literary and journalistic talents in poems, short stories, novellas, and newspaper articles to advocate a German republic, democracy, and unification. She was a regular contributor to Louise Otto's *Frauenzeitung* and helped get the work of other female writers such as Malvida von Meysenbug and Johanna Kinkel published. No other woman was more active politically in such a wide variety of ways.[2]

Her midcentury roles, in order to be fully understood and evaluated, need to be viewed against the backdrop of her pre-1848 activities. Even before the Revolution of 1848 briefly opened the door to political activities by women, Kathinka Zitz-Halein had sought to advance the cause of Germany's freedom and unity. This essay will examine her pre-March activity and try to understand how she could step outside the social parameters in which women were normally required to operate.[3]

The most useful keys to understanding Kathinka Zitz-Halein's pre-1848 political activism are found in the influence of her hometown, Mainz, her family life, marriage, attitude toward a woman's place in society, literary activity, and religious beliefs. Her interest in political issues as well as her views on them were perhaps most affected by the political culture of Mainz. This Rhenish Hessian city, an integral part of France from 1798 to 1814, experienced the impact of her modernizing legislation, and during the French occupation of 1792–93 Mainz was the center of a significant Jacobin movement. Annexed by the Grand Duchy of Hesse after 1815, Mainz remained a democratic and liberal bastion in Germany with a politically active population. The Mainzers opposed the annexation, believed their economic growth was retarded by the Hessian government, and feared that the government would substitute a more retrogressive Hessian law code for the progressive French legal codes still in force in Mainz. The citizens of Mainz felt little loyalty to their new rulers, and this made them more sympathetic to German nationalism and unity.[4]

It was in this highly charged political atmosphere that Kathinka Zitz-Halein was raised. She wrote in her autobiography that from her "mother's milk" she was "patriotic and republican" but in a "classical sense," similar to Bismarck's comment that when he left the *Gymnasium* he was convinced that the republic was the most rational kind of state. She recalled learning Greek and Roman history from her mother and hearing of George Washington, the "noble Washington." Her familiarity with the Jacobin period of Mainz's history, in which her grandparents played minor roles, is demonstrated by her novel *Magdalene Horix*, which is set in the 1790s. The participants in her story and the quotations she assigned them were based on their speeches in the Jacobin Club and the Rhenish National Convention. She owned copies of their protocols, which she later sold to the Mainz city library. Her portrayal, although sympathetic to the Jacobins, was not uncritical of them, while her major criticism was reserved for the aristocracy. A reviewer found the book so realistic that he called it "scarcely a novel."[5]

While Mainz shaped her political outlook her familial situation influenced her in other ways. Born on November 4, 1801, into a prominent Mainz business family, Kathinka Halein's first twenty-three years were marked by the economic decline of the family, her mother's death in 1824, and her father's insanity.[6] Her education was as good as could be obtained by a female. She attended three private schools in Mainz and Strassburg until she was about fourteen, and except for a year at a school run by the Order of English Ladies, her schooling was secular, in the French language, and enlightened. She was introduced to seventeenth-century French writers such as Corneille and Racine, and read the works of Voltaire. She also stressed her interest in history and believed she was well prepared to understand nineteenth-century society.[7]

While her patrician birth gave her access to a decent education, the breakdown of her family's existence forced her to make use of it to survive economically. Because of her father's growing mental instability, she left home in 1825 and for more than three years worked as a governess and teacher in Darmstadt and Kaiserslautern. When her younger sister's illness forced her to return to Mainz in 1829, she lived on her income from embroidery—which was a major part of the curriculum at girls' schools—and from French lessons.[8] Barely able to support her sister and herself at first, she eventually achieved a "respectable" standard of living by the time of her marriage in 1837. These experiences shaped her character and outlook. Plagued by adversity, she overcame it due to her "industry, sense of order, and frugality." Her social views were also affected. As she wrote in 1850:

> I lived once from the work of my hands; consequently I belong to the proletarian class and consider it an honor to belong to it. I do not feel myself attracted to the privileged classes but to the people, the poor,

suffering, oppressed, industrious people upon whom, nevertheless, the well-being of the state rests, and who substitute for a lack of intellectual culture the culture of the heart.[9]

Her strength of character and ability to overcome misfortune would be needed and evidenced in her turbulent relationship with her husband, Franz Zitz. Zitz, a lawyer, first became a prominent political figure in Mainz as the president of the Carnival Society. In 1847 he was elected to the Hessian state legislature, and in 1848 to the Frankfurt Assembly. The following year, as a result of his participation in the spring uprising, he was forced into exile. Kathinka Halein met Zitz in 1833, became engaged within a year, and married him on June 3, 1837, shortly after he had been licensed to practice law. Their marriage was a failure from the start. Zitz, as he explained it, could not be satisfied with one woman. After eighteen months she left him and lived in Paris until November 1840, when she returned to Mainz. The next two years were marked by a bitter divorce suit which he initiated and she contested successfully, even after being warned "not to *claim* your *rights*, for, believe me, the wife never has rights and even the laws are too weak to protect the weak woman." Unable to get an ironclad guarantee of support if divorced, she believed her prospects for financial support were better as his wife. The long process was made more unpleasant by the apparent loyalty of her first lawyer to her husband's case.[10]

Although bitter about love and marriage, she refused to fall prey to discouragement and apathy. As she expressed it in "Not So Dumb, or the Philosophy of a Young Woman": "When the husband seeks other hearts, silly is the one who complains; when the spouse denies us love, silly is the one who is consumed by sorrow; when he plagues us with stupid moods, silly is the one who doesn't fight and dare." The toughness she demonstrated during the long struggle with her spouse was also reflected in her poem "Confession of Faith." She was not the one, she wrote, who would follow the cowardly biblical injunction to turn the other cheek. "Whoever can do this has no self-esteem; . . . whoever slanders me without cause, to him I say: an eye for an eye, a tooth for a tooth."[11]

Finished with the divorce process, she was free to resume her literary career. Her talent had developed early and by the time she was in her twenties her poems were being published in a variety of literary journals and newspapers throughout Germany.[12] In spite of her promising beginning she never became a major literary figure. To what extent her sex as well as the related familial, marital, and financial problems played a role is difficult to estimate, but her literary output clearly diminished during periods of domestic crises. As a secondary figure she struggled to find publishers, and received meager financial rewards. Nowhere did she express the frustrations of a literary career better than in a letter to her lawyer during the divorce proceedings.

> If he [Zitz] now seems to be of the belief that I could earn a significant income through my literary work that is a colossal error. Germany, which lets even its greatest poets half starve, makes no exception with us insignificant lesser lights. Most of the periodicals, particularly the local ones, pay at best with a thank-you [and] don't even give you a free copy. . . . Only the *Didaskalia* [Frankfurt] pays an honorarium, eight gulden for 960 lines. . . . and you will concede that the lowest of your clerks earns as much with copying work without straining his brain. My literary income goes almost penny for penny for writing materials . . . and if one is lucky to make something today one can also sniff around in vain for years with a wide-open mouth after the dried corpse of an honorarium. Believe me, the existence of the writer is the most precarious of any.[13]

Regardless of her difficulties and disappointments, writing was her profession. Not even the hostility she experienced, from women and men, could deter her. Once again she fought against it. In "Harpar und Tulisant," for example, she warned that the woman writer, though she may win fame and fortune under the cloak of anonymity, will still have to face criticism, "for one finds her humor too biting, her mournful passages too gloomy, . . . her depictions of love and passion unsuitable for her sex; in short she should only publish what is thoroughly insignificant."[14] But the social intimidation would not work, because where once the "demon of poesy has been awakened it no longer falls asleep so easily again." The "most excellent women of this century have taken pen in hand."[15]

Her attitudes on the proper role of women are difficult to categorize or reconcile with some of her activities. She was clearly inclined toward a traditional view, believing women were cut out for the domestic sphere. The title of her work on the question of female emancipation, "The Woman within the Limits of Her Destiny," suggests her point of view. Her ideal of emancipation, she claimed, was nothing more than the "nobler recognition of the feminine existence within its own limits," and these were the family and home. Outside them the woman could not find "real and lasting happiness." Moreover, she explicitly condemned emancipation understood in a political or economic sense. It was an "absurdity," a "monster from the depths." Women who took part in "Frauenmeetings" (sic), she believed, wanted to be eligible to participate in military and political matters, to hold public office, study at a university, in essence to place women on the same footing as men and where possible to surpass them. This she opposed, while women who adopted male dress or smoked cigars only made themselves objects of ridicule. Even a woman who devoted herself to scholarship, she stressed, usually went beyond the "limits of her sex."

Notwithstanding this conservative stance, she balanced it with other views which reflected her independence and pride. If women were destined to find the center of their happiness in the home, this did not mean that they should play an inferior or subordinate role, but rather one worthy of respect and based on equality. A woman, she maintained, should be the "co-regent in the realm of domesticity," and her "natural rights" within this sphere should be acknowledged. Running a house required "demanding qualities," especially since they were demonstrated privately and "seldom acknowledged." "Domestic heroism," she called it, "which, hidden under dark duties, flows on and loses itself without having viewed the light of day. It is something sublime; it is to be compared to a clear spring, which, hidden under the grass, nourishes and refreshes the plants." Unfortunately, in her eyes, most men did not realize this. Because of the tyranny of their pride, and "the injustices of their laws," men made women's virtues into liabilities; "one condemns them for their tenderness, belittles their talents, and regards them as incapable of great things." Men, she continued, claimed a monopoly of all great virtues. But what they "in their egoism call character," she noted sarcastically, "they regard as stubbornness and disobedience in the woman." Moreover, even if women needed the protection of men, she emphasized, they were not to be slaves of their "despotic power, servants of their moods, mere housekeepers or educators of their children." She granted extremely talented women the right to enter an "alien area" if they did not marry. For "lesser lights" she agreed with the English writer Elizabeth Gaskell that one could be both homemaker and writer. Moreover, she granted women the right to form organizations to deal with the problems of poverty and moral decline. And most unexpected of all, she suggested that women should take part in public issues concerning the German nation such as the struggle for civil rights. But their role, she added without further elaboration, was to be passive, not active.[16] It was within this framework that she would create a role for herself before and during the Revolution of 1848.

A final element in shaping her social and political pursuits may have been contributed by her sympathy for German Catholicism, which emerged in the 1840s under the leadership of Johannes Ronge. Many German Catholics were found in the democratic camp and they sought to transfer the democracy of their Church to the larger secular society. They also tended to be socially progressive and accorded women larger roles in the Church. Ronge was strongly committed to female emancipation and sought to organize women during the Revolution of 1848.[17] Out of sympathy with the Roman Catholic Church, as a result of her upbringing and schooling, the already democratically inclined Kathinka Zitz-Halein supported the German Catholic community which was active in Mainz. Her involvement in it may have encouraged her to play a more active public role.[18]

Political opposition in pre-March Germany was risky. In 1819 and again in 1832 the Frankfurt Diet passed legislation increasing press censorship and setting up a central investigating committee to ferret out subversives. As a writer who was interested in social and political themes, Kathinka Zitz-Halein was bound to be affected by such restrictions on freedom of expression. Throughout her writing career, both before and after 1848, she had run-ins with the censor, and repeatedly expressed her opposition to the "disfigure[ment]" caused by his red pencil. Literary property, she pointed out, was the only kind that could be easily "confiscated without negotiation, without defense," and "destroyed by the sole will . . . of the censor." For this reason writers learned to write and readers to understand "half words."[19] Instructive, because it offers us an insight into her character as well as the political and social milieu in which she operated, was her public quarrel with a fellow writer, Ludwig Kalisch, in 1843–44. Believing she had been attacked by him in a satirical journal at the instigation of her estranged husband, she exchanged public insults with Kalisch. What angered her even more was the fact that her open letters had been censored by the authorities. This impelled her to write to the Hessian government in a way which was designed to sting both Kalisch and the government. She complained of Kalisch's misconduct and his disrespect for the Bavarian and Russian rulers, threatening to write the former, who had already banned his journal. She then charged that she, "a citizen of Mainz," was forced to delete several lines from her open letters while Kalisch, an "outsider," could say what he wanted. She continued:

> I believe that in a state where unconditional freedom of the press does not rule, where the censor cuts in so quickly with his thought-killing scissors when an enlightened idea wants to surface, but who shows himself overly considerate when one endeavors to ruin the fortune and honor of harmless people [Kalisch had also attacked certain business people in Mainz], I believe that where the censor generally has sway, the life and activity of peaceful citizens must be protected from the intrusions of unrestrained, insolent caprice.

The Hessian government, although it did not at first take the affair seriously, apparently feared the reaction of the German rulers. On February 7, 1844, it banned Kalisch's journal.[20]

Kathinka Zitz-Halein's earliest political act occurred in 1825 with her "first visit" to the grave of Karl Ludwig Sand, whose assassination of the conservative playright August Kotzebue was the occasion for the Karlsbad

Decrees.[21] Her next, more serious step occurred around 1830–32. She met the young Prussian officer and aspiring author Friedrich von Sallet, and helped get his first work published. It so offended some of his fellow officers that he was brought before a court of honor. She offered to take the blame by claiming that she had had the story printed without his knowledge. He refused and ultimately spent two months in fortress confinement.[22]

The first taste of the political consequences of literary activity did not deflect her from her inclination to express herself on political and social themes. She used a variety of devices: translations of plays with social or political messages, poems which addressed similar themes, fairy tales into which one could insert criticism of political and social conditions, novellas, and newspaper articles. Her works appeared in at least forty journals and newspapers throughout Germany and were also published as collections.[23] She expressed no entirely uniform or integrated political and social outlook—probably because she had none. She remained the writer of the moment who shared the not yet sharply defined or differentiated liberal-democratic constitutional views of her progressive contemporaries, and who was also sensitive to emerging social problems. Moreover, her works, which frequently involve women, show them politically or socially engaged but also suffering due to the injustices of society. Nothing better illustrates this than her translations of three of Victor Hugo's plays: *Marion Delorme* (1833), *The King Amuses Himself* (1835), and *Cromwell* (1835). The first two, which were banned shortly after their opening in France, have women as the central characters and as heroines. They show them overcoming the experiences of rape and prostitution and emerging as courageous figures, willing to make demanding sacrifices. Blanche saves the king who had dishonored her, while Marion Delorme offers herself to the king and then appeals to the crowd in a vain attempt to save her lover's life. In both plays the monarchs appear as immoral and deceitful. The third play, *Cromwell*, sees the English ruler as corrupted by his dictatorial power.

In her poetry she covered a wide variety of political and social subjects. As early as 1822–23 her poems contained support for Germany's unity and freedom. In "Soldier," she saluted his "victory and death for the fatherland." In "Eighteenth of October," she commemorated the battle of Leipzig, which marked the beginning of the end of "France's venal yoke." In "A Voice of the Age," written to honor the industrial fair in Mainz (1842), she hoped to hear a prince proclaim: "'No Austria, no Prussia. A single, free German land' . . . constitution, free speech, open legal proceedings . . . an end to intellectual slavery. . . . Listen, Germany, to the spirit of the age, and be strong in unity." Three years later, in "Let There Be Light," she sought to encourage the reawakening reform movement.

"Many fools," she warned, "dream of Germany's freedom and fancy themselves free from slaves' chains. Yet their freedom is not yet born." Rather one ought to recognize that

> free speech is kept in chains, the rights of the press suffer under pressure and compulsion, legal proceedings continue in their old beaten track. O German land . . . when does the day come when your hymn echoes, no longer mocked by princely yoke? It comes for sure . . . don't retreat . . . whoever wants to win cannot avoid the battle.[24]

Perhaps her favorite poem, one which also sums up her life, was "Farbenwechsel" ("Change of Colors"). In it she identifies the various phases of her life by the color of her clothing: white for childish innocence, red and green for awakening impulses and hope, blue for married life, violet for anger, black for a failed life, and brown for indifference. But when one expects a melancholy ending she finishes instead on a note of activism and defiance. "Indifference! have I forgotten everything, buried every elevated feeling? Oh no! For the Fatherland, for the great interests of the age, my heart will never again be indifferent."[25]

She also used her poetry to call attention to social and economic abuses. It might be a plea against gambling as in "Number Thirteen," a poem about the notorious gambling den in the Palais Royal. It could focus on the "aristocracy of wealth," "as pernicious as the political aristocracy," or in "Thirst for Gold" on the wealthy to whom fatherland and God are of no value. In "Taxes of the Poor" a father and son discuss what to do when faced with the choice of feeding the family or paying taxes.

FATHER: The tax collector waits no longer.
Soon his agent knocks.
My last funds are these coins.
I'll buy you dark bread with them.

SON: Pay the taxes, good Father.
We'll eat if it pleases God.

The father then condemns the prince and court, who "only vote the taxes," live in luxury, and erect splendid monuments "with the sweat of the poor."

SON: O father, father, pay the taxes.
The collector is at the door.

FATHER: No! No! To still your hunger
I'll keep the last coins.

The same format of father and son is used to criticize aristocratic society. In "Appearance and Reality," a boy's first visit to the theater is the occasion of the father's lesson in the ways of the world. He cautions the child not to be enchanted by the glitter. "Behind it cold reality is hidden. The palaces are only painted screens; the princesses, so beautiful to look at, are shriveled made-up women, and those in royal crowns . . . are pupils who say by heart the lessons they have learned." "We all believe too easily," he tells his enlightened son.[26]

In addition to her poems and translations, her stories, especially the fairy tales, provided a means of calling attention to existing political and social abuses. Often she wove in experiences from her life and made her characters resemble her acquaintances in Mainz. In "Felizian," a kind of Candide, she used his adventures as a vehicle to criticize existing injustices. Orphaned while a boy, he becomes an assistant to a journalist who is willing to serve any party, permitting her to refer to that kind of journalism as the "disability ward" of literature. Disillusioned, Felizian continues on his way to Belgium, where he meets many Germans whom the "shameful" law code has forced out of Germany, but who, she added for the benefit of the censor, "do not call themselves political refugees." France is quiet, she wrote, lacking a Mirabeau, Marat, or Desmoulins, which shows her attempt to cover the revolutionary spectrum. On to Russia, the "police state," "the classic land of absolutism," Felizian finds the bootlicking of the courtiers beyond all limits. The trip continues to exotic lands where she uses the strange customs of the natives to call attention to the equally strange costumes and functions of the courtiers and to assert that a person's worth should be "based only on his moral and intellectual ennoblement." Observing the relationship between man and woman, she asserts, "During five thousand eight hundred and so many years our female ancestors have sighed under the biblical decision which condemned them to original sin." Women will soon receive a patent of "completion," she hears. Tossed about by a storm at sea, Felizian finally reaches land and sees a gallows. "'Thank God I am in a civilized land!' He was right, he was in Germany." He finally reaches Dunkelheim, where lanterns are seen as a protest against the moon and banned, and where nepotism, prisons, torture, and a too powerful clergy are the bane of the inhabitants. Felizian decides to become a journalist but seeks to avoid "hypocritical, deceitful optimism, which only helps the despots." She ends in an oration of praise for the press, which "enriches the people because it enlightens them," and a condemnation of censorship, the most gruesome institution," which commits "intellectual murder." It is a

> blind absolute power which works in insidious ways against authors. . . .
> Here there is no appeal or reversal. Everything is done silently in the
> dark. . . . It takes its pointiest scissors, its sharpest blades, its most
> penetrating scalpel. It cuts blindly without understanding, without
> mercy . . . until [the work] is a skeleton, . . . the little flesh remaining
> hangs down in bloody pieces.[27]

Her other stories from the 1840s showed similar tendencies. In "Master and Slave," a tyrant is overthrown and replaced by a constitutional monarchy, *libertas nobilitas*, while the hero of the story, Populus, goes in search of democracy, *libertas communus*. She made her point indirectly when she asked:

> Has he been successful? The news of it has not reached me. Yet I believe that if he should succeed . . . it will be possible only in the country of fantasy, for although here on earth [democracy] has many secret supporters, these cannot yet make known their support. The mighty one [Metternich?] of this earth is and remains in all eternity a hated and feared personage.[28]

Whether she favored a particular political system is not clear. In "The Empire of the Stars," which describes the struggle between the Sun and the Moon, Queen Sun rules in an enlightened way. She recognizes the need to awaken the "national spirit" in the direction of "unity," to be firm with neighboring states, but to tolerate no "national hate" against foreign countries. She permits the progressive spirit of her subjects to develop freely. She introduces courts with public procedures; a state without such a system "must be fled from like the plague." A free press emerges; if one suppresses the press, "nothing remains but to go around on all fours and live off acorns." The Sun, we are told, initiated these reforms because she wanted to avoid revolution, which arises out of general dissatisfaction with the pressure of the laws. A revolution, Zitz-Halein implied, should be avoided because of the danger of "anarchy," which would have to be fought with military power.[29] In "Hausgenossen" ("Lodgers"), which also deals with the theme of a good political system, an aristocratic government in the land of "somewhere" aims to pump out the last penny and the last bit of freedom. There ruled the "negative": "negative ministers, a negative parliament," and the inhabitants had a "negative freedom." The strength of good government, she emphasized, rested, not on its arbitrariness, but on the "intelligent harmony of rights and obligations." In order to be strong, a government did not need

> to be able to do everything it wants; it suffices that it can do all that is necessary. A strong government should resemble those strong natures who command respect because one recognizes their strength in their powerful constitution. Freedom must be the end of government, and it is erroneous to believe that authority can be strong only at the cost of freedom. Nothing is so weak as absolute power, nothing so much like anarchy as dictatorship. The extremes touch.[30]

Although most concerned with political issues in her stories, she often had women as central characters. In "The Tumult in the Empire of the Plants," the king mistreats his wife; when he dies she seizes power and decides to introduce female emancipation. But as "with most women's governments the queen ruled according to favoritism and not strict justice." An uprising occurs and she is saved by a prince who marries her and in effect takes over the government. His unjust rule produces a new revolt. The people, now triumphant, reject the idea of a republic and return power to the queen on the condition that she governs, not rules, grants civil liberties, and accepts a "constitutional consort" according to the choice of the people.[31] Her attitude toward women's role in society is perhaps most sharply expressed in "Rumpelstiltskin." The princess, after unhappy marital experiences, no longer believes in marriage and asks for the opinion of Rumpelstiltskin. He advises her not to be so slavish, and to show less love, more energy and strength of character. But as he begins to leaf through her papers he makes one amazing discovery after another. He finds songs by Hoffman von Fallersleben and copies of the *Rheinische Zeitung (Rhenish Newspaper)*. "You take part in politics," he cries. "Why shouldn't I?" she replies proudly.

> I am indeed only a woman but I love my fatherland not less than the best man and if I were one I would be brave as one of the Maccabee brothers. . . . I am a child of the century . . . the instinct to all great things lies in me. But I am no Titan; I don't want to storm the heavens. I am sorry not to have been made a man. If I were, I'd call to my brothers: "Rally around the banner of true freedom—bury your dead but not your freedom, for as free as we are we are still slaves enough. . . ." If I were a man, [freedom] would be the mistress to which I would sacrifice blood, life, and goods. O my beautiful fatherland which is not only my little principality but all Germany . . . when will the great idea of unity rule in all your districts? And you know, I would have become a democrat, for the true democrat . . . must be ready for every sacrifice.[32]

This thoroughly politicized woman, shortly before the Revolution of 1848, used journalism in order to influence the citizens of Mainz. Her actions represent, along with Louise Otto's work for the *Vaterländische Blätter* and Louise Dittmar's public lectures, one of the few efforts of this kind before 1848.[33] As early as the 1840s Kathinka Zitz-Halein was in contact with South German liberals such as Adam Itzstein, Heinrich von Gagern, and Friedrich Daniel Bassermann, and she had conceived a plan to help political refugees by donating the proceeds from the sale of her literary works. Nothing seems to have come of this clever plan to combine patriotism with business. She was also asked to contribute a novella or correspondence to the *Veilchen* (Bautzen), whose editor, Bruno Theobold, announced that he intended to follow an "enlightened socialistic tendency."[34]

Her major political activity before 1848 consisted of her reports about

Mainz in the democratic and widely read *Mannheimer Abendzeitung*.[35] Mannheim was in the Grand Duchy of Baden and not subject to the severe censorship that existed in Hesse. In the mid-1840s the Hessian government made a determined effort to introduce a common legal code for its three provinces. When it became clear that the government's unified law code would introduce significant departures from the Napoleonic codes then in force in Mainz, especially in matters of church-state relations, the role of the state in family questions, and the powers of the police, some Mainzers began to organize a campaign of opposition—in which Kathinka Zitz-Halein played a significant role. At stake were the laws regarding marriage, divorce, and guardianship, which had special significance for her. It is not possible to identify all of her reports; some are found in her papers, which give us an indication of the symbols under which she wrote; others can be identified with confidence because of style and phraseology; still others can be recognized because of her comments in her "Skizzen" about the subjects of some of the articles. Zitz-Halein's reports began in September 1846 on the occasion of the city council election, which she described as a contest between progressives and conservatives (gentlemen of darkness). She criticized the mayor's censorship of election literature, stating that "Germany now knows how it would go with all such modern expressions and words when the mayor of Mainz has the exclusive right to decide." But she was also very critical of the citizens of Mainz, whom she accused of being brave behind their wineglasses or united only when it was a question of organizing the pre-Lenten carnival. The Mainzers were too sunk in their carnival revelry to pull themselves out of the "morass of effeminacy." They forgot they had a fatherland; patriotism like Barbarossa was asleep in the Kyffhäuser. She hoped the Mainzers would regain their sense of civil esteem and "manly duty." Only a few seemed courageous enough to express liberal views, and she called on that "small band of men" who still had a spark of true patriotism to continue the work of "progress and enlightenment." Otherwise, she wrote, there would be more city councilmen like the one who bragged he was poor at reading and writing but endowed with physical strength. "Such intellects," she warned, "are made for the men of darkness; when one pulls on the right string, the puppet bows."[36] She cautioned that attitudes would change if the principles of the French codes were threatened.

When the government's bill did this, the Mainzers began to stir. In October the city councilmen voiced their opposition to the projected changes in the legal code. A petition with 300 signatures was sent to the Grand Duke. Copies of it were sent to the other Rhenish cities which sent petitions of support.[37] In November a similar petition received 2,000 signatures. The Carnival Society decided to forgo certain festivities, and the women of Mainz began to wear black to protest the threat to the principle of civil marriage.[38] Zitz-Halein's writings many have helped stimulate the movement. Several times she attacked the provincial governor, Reinhard von Dalwigk, who later came to symbolize the authoritarian Hessian government. She reported his efforts to prevent the city council from protesting the proposed legal codes. She charged him with trying to intimidate electors in Mainz during the elections for the state parliament, as well as being unwilling to recognize the popular will. She also criticized him for banning a performance of *William Tell* and for instituting house searches. She even pointed out that the only Mainz daily, the *Mainzer Zeitung*, was controlled by the censor.[39]

As for the projected law code, she claimed it would push the Rhenish Hessians back to the Middle Ages; it would be preferable to bring the blessings of the Rhenish codes to the other provinces. She stressed the threat to the principle of civil marriage and civil control of the registration of vital statistics, while the new police regulations would make citizens prey to police excesses. She further charged that Mainz was being exploited by the Hessian government in the sense that necessary economic improvements were not being undertaken, and that far too many local jobs were in the hands of outsiders.[40]

What impact did her articles have? Clearly the Hessian government was disturbed. The editor of the paper was sued and requested to identify the correspondent, but he refused and paid the fines. Finally, the sale and distribution of the newspaper was banned in Hesse in December 1846.[41] Nevertheless, in spite of the ban, the *Mannheimer Abendzeitung* continued to be distributed there until the outbreak of the Revolution of 1848.[42]

In her memoirs Kathinka Zitz-Halein claimed that she wrote about Hessian conditions with "a courageousness such as no man would have written at that time," that she attacked Dalwigk "from all sides," that she called on the Mainzers to rise from the "muck" of the carnival societies, "shake off their wine stupor," and show that "they were men." Perhaps she exaggerated when she claimed that "the spark was lit . . . and to me belongs the credit of having first awakened the slumbering sense of manhood in my hometown."[43] But only a few had a right to claim as much. In any case, the state elections of 1847 resulted in a major victory for the opposition forces. And within Rhenish Hesse there was a decided move to the left, including the election of her husband for the Mainz district.

Eda Sagarra has recently argued that there was no sharp dichotomy between conservative and progressive female authors during the pre-March period with regard to their views of women's roles in society.[44] The examination of several main currents in Kathinka Zitz-Halein's life suggests that a pronounced feminist ideology was not a prerequisite for involvement in the struggle for political progress in Germany. And the widespread political activities by women in 1848–49 reinforce this conclusion. Zitz-Halein's world was formed not only by her sex but by her family, city, literary talent, and, most of all, by her character. It cautions us not to ignore those women whose feminist consciousness does not seem to be highly developed but whose political awareness was. It may not be inappropriate to label these efforts as a kind of "feminism by deed."[45]

NOTES

1. Fritz Böttger, ed., *Frauen im Aufbruch. Frauenbriefe aus dem Vormärz und der Revolution von 1848* (Darmstadt, 1979); Ute Gerhard et al., eds., *"Dem Reich der Freiheit werb' ich Bürgerinnen."* Die Frauen-Zeitung von Louise Otto (Frankfurt/M, 1980); Gerlinde Hummel-Haasis, ed., *Schwestern, zerreisst eure Ketten. Zeugnisse zur Geschichte der Frauen in der Revolution von 1848–49* (Munich, 1982); Ruth-Ellen Boettcher Joeres, "Louise Otto and Her Journals: A Chapter in Nineteenth Century German Feminism," *Internationales Archiv für Sozialgeschichte der deutschen Literatur,* 4 (1979), pp. 100–29; Renate Möhrmann, *Die andere Frau. Emanzipationsansätze deutscher Schriftstellerinnen im Vorfeld der Achtundvierziger-Revolution* (Stuttgart, 1977); Catherine Prelinger, "Religious Dissent, Women's Rights and the Hamburger Hochschule für das weibliche Geschlecht in Nineteenth Century Germany," *Church History,* 45 (1976), pp. 42–55; Margrit Twellmann, *Die deutsche Frauenbewegung. Ihre Anfänge und erste Entwicklung 1843–1889,* Marburger Abhandlungen zur politischen Wissenschaft, vol. 17, pts. 1 and 2 (Meisenheim am Glan, 1972); Maria Wagner, ed., *Mathilde Franziska Anneke in Selbstzeugnisse und Dokumenten* (Frankfurt/M, 1980); Sigrid Weigel, *Flugschriftenliteratur 1848 in Berlin* (Stuttgart, 1979).

2. Stanley Zucker, "German Women and the Revolution of 1848: Kathinka Zitz-Halein and the Humania Association," *Central European History,* 13 (1980), pp. 237–54; Hummel-Haasis, *Schwestern,* pp. 259–327, has published relevant documents.

3. Elke Fredriksen, "Deutsche Autorinnen im 19. Jahrhundert. Neue kritische Ansätze," *Colloquia Germanica,* 14 (1981), pp. 105–6.

4. *Deutsche Jakobiner* (3 vols.; Mainz, 1981); Karl-Georg Faber, *Die Rheinlande zwischen Restauration und Revolution* (Wiesbaden, 1966); Werner Schubert, "Der Code Civil und die Personenrechtsentwürfe des Grossherzogtums Hessen-Darmstadt von 1842 bis 1847," *Zeitschrift der Savigny Stiftung für Rechtsgeschichte. Germanistische Abteilung,* 88 (1971), pp. 110–71.

5. Kathinka Zitz-Halein (hereafter cited as KZ-H), *Magdalene Horix* (Mainz, 1858); *Mainzer Zeitung,* June 16, 1858.

6. Information about Zitz-Halein's early life can be found in the manuscript of her autobiography, "Skizzen aus meinem Leben," pp. 1a–2a, 8a–9b, 53ab, 54a, 55b, 56a, 58b–60a. Two basically identical copies are in the Kathinka Zitz-Halein Nachlass, HS 122, Hessische Landesbibliothek, Wiesbaden (hereafter cited as "Skizzen," KZN-W). Both were written during the early 1850s (KZ-H to ?, July 5, 1850, KZN-W); Karl Georg Bockenheimer, *Geschichte der Stadt Mainz während der zweiten französischen Herrschaft 1798–1814* (Mainz, 1890), pp. 333, 338–43, 365.

7. "Skizzen," pp. 2ab–3ab, 53b–54b, 56a, KZN-W; Elizabeth Blochmann, *Das Frauenzimmer und die Gelehrsamkeit* (Heidelberg, 1966); Jürgen Zinnecker, *Sozialgeschichte der Mädchenbildung* (Weinheim, 1973); Maria Rudolph, *Die Frauenbildung in Frankfurt am Main* (Frankfurt, 1978), pp. 52–58, 74–79.

8. "Skizzen," pp. 9b–10b, 60b–66b, KZN-W. In the *Wegweiser der Stadt Mainz, 1830* she is listed as an "embroiderer"; in 1833 she appears as a "writer."

9. Skizzen," pp. 66ab, 77a, KZN-W; KZ-H, *Einige Worte an das Publikum* . . . (Mainz, 1850), Stadt bibliothek Mainz, Mog m3163.

10. The material relating to her relationship with Franz Zitz is found in her "Skizzen," pp. 13a–28b, 64a–100a, KNZ-W; in her correspondence with her lawyers, Lehne and Kramer, Kathinka Zitz-Halein Nachlass, Stadtarchiv Mainz (hereafter cited as KZN-M); and in her poetry, which she called the "diary of my life"; KZ-H, *Herbstrosen in Poesie und Prosa* (Mainz, 1846), pp. 159–60, 168–69, 176–78, 182, 183–84, 190–92, 203, 302, 305, 306, 323, 327.

11. KZ-H, *Herbstrosen*, pp. 196–97; see also KZ-H, "Notizen," t, KZN-W. "Notizen" are notes she prepared for her divorce trial; although they are uncatalogued, the writer has labeled his xerox copies a, b, c, etc.; KZ-H, *Dur- und Molltöne* (Mainz, 1859), pp. 59–61.

12. Carl von Schindel, *Die deutschen Schriftstellerinnen des neunzehnten Jahrhunderts* (Leipzig, 1823–25), 1, p. 187; 3, pp. 144–49, has the best bibliography of her early works; KZ-H to Schindel, June 8, 1824, Carl Schindel Nachlass, Oberlaustizische Bibliothek der Wissenschaften, Görlitz; "Skizzen," pp. 2b–7b, KNZ-W.

13. KZ-H to Paul Kramer, May 19, 1842, KZN-W; see also the folder "Verhandlungen mit Verleger," KZN-M, for her literary career; successful writers like Fanny Lewald and Ida Hahn-Hahn received six times as much (Möhrmann, *Die andere Frau*, p. 2); K. Halein to Schindel, July 25, 1830, Schindel Nachlass, for the relationship between her familial responsibilities and literary productivity.

14. KZ-H, "Harpar und Tulisant," in her *Variationen* (Mainz, 1849), p. 405.

15. KZ-H, "Ulrike," in her *Donner und Blitz* (Mainz, 1850), pp. 29–30. What Michelangelo was to artists, she wrote, George Sand was to female writers (KZ-H, *Weltpantheon* [Mainz, 1858], p. 134).

16. For the above, see KZ-H, "Das Weib in den Grenzen seiner Bestimmung," *Herbstrosen*, pp. 330–41, 257, 258, 271; KZ-H, "Die Schriftstellerin," in her *Quodlibet* (Mainz, 1857), p. 61; KZ-H, "Mokka di Cheribon," *Variationen*, pp. 72–76; KZ-H, "Die Männer- und Frauenrepublik," in her *Kaiserin Josephine* (Mainz, 1855), pp. 43–48; KZ-H, "Aus den Papieren einer Unglücklichen," *Der Rheinische Telegraph*, no. 29, April 10, 1842, p. 114; KZ-H, "Schattenspiele an der Wand," *Letzte Rheinsandkörner* (Mainz, 1854), pp. 381–84.

Female Political Opposition in Pre-1848 Germany   149

17. Ronge to ?, August 1849, Johannes Ronge Nachlass, M.S.C.R., Dresden
App. 131, Bl. 55, Sächsische Landesbibliothek Dresden; Günter Kolbe, "Demo-
kratische Opposition in religösen Gewande. Zur Geschichte der deutschkatho-
lischen Bewegung in Sachsen am Vorabend der Revolution von 1848–49,"
Zeitschrift für Geschichtswissenschaft, 20 (1972), pp. 1102–12; Catherine Prelinger, "The German-Catholic Church: From National Hope to Regional Reality,"
Consortium on Revolutionary Europe. Proceedings (Athens, Ga., 1976), pp. 88–
101.

18. See the material in the folder "Beziehungen zu Deutschkatholizismus,"
KNZ-M.

19. Friedrich Sieger to KZ-H, November 20, 1835, ? to KZ-H, October 8,
1840, Z. Rehnert to KZ-H, March 26, 1843, Lasker to KZ-H, December 12, 1844,
Heribert Rau, to KZ-H, February 6, 1848, KZN-M, and her comments in the
introduction to her *Variationen;*KZ-H, "Schattenspiele," *Letzte Rheinsandkörner,*
pp. 384–85.

20. "Skizzen," pp. 102b–103a, KZN-W; *Narrhalla,* 1844, pp. 14, 39–44, 81–
83; *Neue Mainzer Narrenzeitung,* January 14, 1844, pp. 28–29; Alexander Burger,
"Aus der Geschichte des Mainzer Karnevals," *Heim und Welt,* no. 73 (March 1,
1924); Fritz Saurmann, "Ein karnevalistisches Literatengeplänkel aus Alt-Mainz
und seine Folgen," *Mainzer Warte,* nos. 5, 7, 8 (February 2, 16, 23, 1929); Leonore O'Boyle, "The Democratic Left in Germany, 1848," *Journal of Modern
History,* 33 (1961), pp. 374–83.

21. KZ-H, *Rahel oder Dreiunddreissig Jahre* (6 vols.; Leipzig, 1864), 6,
p. 85 n.

22. "Skizzen," p. 11a, KZN-W; *Allgemeine deutsche Biographie,* 33, pp. 717–
26.

23. The best collection is in the Stadtbibliothek in Mainz. See also Karl
Goedke, *Grundriss zur Geschichte der deutschen Dichtung* (Dresden, 1938), 3,
pp. 295–98; and the list she prepared for Brummer (Nachlass Brummer, Briefe II,
Zitz), Staatsbibliothek, Handschriftenabteilung, Berlin, BRD.

24. Kathinka Halein, *Phantasieblüthen und Tandeleien* (Mainz, 1825),
pp. 76–77, 180–81, 252–53; KZ-H, *Herbstrosen,* pp. 221–23, 242–43.

25. KZ-H, *Herbstrosen,* pp. 243–44.

26. KZ-H, *Herbstrosen,* pp. 230–41, 296–97; see also KZ-H, *Dur- und
Molltöne,* pp. 19–20, 273–75.

27. KZ-H, "Felizian," *Donner und Blitz,* pp. 225–77; see also "Narziss das
Wandelbare," *Variationen,* pp. 201–51, where she uses a similar format to stress
the necessity of parliamentary opposition in a representative system.

28. KZ-H, "Herr und Sklav," *Variationen,* pp. 1–34.

29. KZ-H, "Das Reich der Sterne," *Variationen,* pp. 177–200.

30. KZ-H, "Hausgenossen," *Donner und Blitz,* pp. 400–49; see also "Adler
Eier," "Der Metallkönig," "Chikander," and "Die heilige Schäfer und sein Assist-
ent," in KZ-H, *Variationen.*

31. KZ-H, "Die Aufruhr im Pflanzenreich," *Variationen,* pp. 34–52; see also
"Die Konigen der Geizigen" and "Bärenpratz," *Variationen,* pp. 278–335.

32. KZ-H, "Rumpelstilzchen," *Variationen,* pp. 150–76.

33. Ruth Götze, "Louise Ottos Beziehungen zum Proletariat in Vormärz und

in der Revolution von 1848/49," *Sächsische Heimatblätter,* 27, pp. 154–56; Louise Dittmar, *Vier Zeitfragen* (Offenbach, 1847); Louise Dittmar to Lorenz Dieffenbach, July 30, 1847, Lorenz Diffenbach Nachlass, Universitätsbibliothek Giessen.

34. "Skizzen," p. 83b, KZN-W; Itzstein to KZ-H, December 3, 1844, KZN-W; Bruno Theobold to KZ-H, July 11, 1846, KZN-M; the *Veilchen,* for which Louise Otto wrote, was a non-Marxist socialist weekly (Karl Marx and Friedrich Engels, *Werke* [Berlin, DDR., 1977], 4, pp. 268–70).

35. Andreas Lück, *Friedrich Hecker* (Berlin, 1979), p. 140; *Mainzer Zeitung,* December 30, 1846.

36. *Mannheimer Abendzeitung,* September 4, 22, October 4, 7, 1846, November 10, 1846, pp. 946, 958, 1029, 1078, 1091, 1226 (hereafter cited as *Mann. AZ*).

37. "Allerdurchlauchtigsten Grossherzog . . . ," October 1846, Stadtbibliothek Mainz, Mog m: 40/443; "Bürger von Frankental . . . ," November 1846, ibid., 66: 2°/30.

38. *Mann. AZ,* November 29, December 1, 1846, pp. 1301, 1309; Veit Valentin, *Geschichte der deutschen Revolution 1848–1849* (2 vols.; Berlin, 1930), 1, pp. 175–80.

39. *Mann. AZ,* October 23, December 23, 31, 1846, pp. 1153, 1398, 1425, January 13, September 26, 28, 1847, pp. 109, 1045, 1053.

40. *Mann. AZ,* October 21, 23, 25, 26, November 29, December 5, 1846, pp. 1145, 1153, 1162, 1166, 1301, 1326.

41. *Grossherzoglich Hessisches Regierungsblatt,* no. 42 (December 30, 1846); *Mainzer Zeitung,* January 1, 1847; *Sicherheitspolizei,* 1846, XVIII/I n. 968: 2220, 2269, Stadtarchiv Mainz.

42. See material from Hessian foreign ministry files regarding attempts to stop the newspaper's distribution (Acta ministeriale betrd. der Versendung und Verbreitung der *Mannheimer Abendzeitung* und des *Deutschen Zuschauer* innerhalb des Grossherzogthums, 1848, Abt Gl/Konv. 156/5, Hessisches Staatsarchiv, Darmstadt). Karl Buchner, *Das Grossherzogthum Hessen in seiner politischen und sozialen Entwicklung von Herbst 1847 bis zum Herbst 1850* (Darmstadt, 1850), p. 8, refers to the muzzling of the local press and the consequently important role played by the non-Hessian press.

43. "Skizzen," p. 104b, KZN-W.

44. Eda Sagarra, "Echo oder Antwort. Die Darstellung der Frau in der deutschen Erzählprosa 1815–1848," *Geschichte und Gesellschaft,* 7 (1981), pp. 394–411.

45. On defining women's consciousness, see Gerda Lerner, "Politics and Culture in Women's History," *Feminist Studies,* 6 (1980), pp. 49–54.

German Women Writers and the Revolution of 1848

LIA SECCI

We already have some understanding of certain German women writers who were directly committed to the cause of the Revolution of 1848, but a further examination of their work still has to be done to complete the picture. In general, the part played by German women in 1848 has been ignored, partly because of the lack of attention given them in traditional histories and partly because of the intrinsic difficulty of finding original sources, many of which were destroyed by the censors or kept in secret police archives. A first attempt, only partially successful, to re-evaluate the female contribution was made by Leo Busch in a 1926 study done on women in the Rhineland.[1] In 1928 Anna Blos wrote *Die Frauen der deutschen Revolution von 1848. Zehn Lebensbilder (Women in the German Revolution of 1848. Ten Biographical Portraits)*, which was a one-volume study. The book dealt with Louise Otto-Peters, Mathilde Franziska Anneke, Louise Aston, Malvida von Meysenbug, Johanna Kinkel, Jenny Marx, Emma Herwegh, Amalie Struve, Wilhelmine Schröder-Devrient, and Maria Kurz. But the portraits were more hagiography than reliable sources because precise chronological and bibliographical references were lacking.[2]

Veit Valentin, in his history of the 1848 German revolution, written in 1930–31, but still indispensable (it was in fact reprinted in 1977), gave some accounts of women's participation, particularly intellectuals like Malvida von Meysenbug, Emilie Wüstenfels, and Louise Otto.[3] Louise Aston was mentioned briefly but only in a footnote.[4] Valentin dealt only a little with the revolutionary activities of working-class women. According to him, the six unknown women who fell on the Berlin barricades were struck down more by "cruel chance" than conscious intent. He noted, in fact, that German women at that time, except perhaps for a very few, did not have the political preparation necessary for autonomous action; they served only as spectators and collaborators with men. This was why the prominent women in 1848 were the wives of the best-known revolutionaries, such as Emma Herwegh, Amalie Struve, and Johanna Kinkel.[5] Clara Zetkin's reductive judgment weighed, and continues to weigh, on these women. With her view of the class struggle—she was a Marxist Socialist—she saw no reason to take the revolutionary activity of bourgeois women seriously: "On the whole it seems that the above-mentioned women's presence in the revolution has been more the target of moral indignation and banal witty epithets from moderate German philistines, rather than the object of serious consideration or of actual fear by the counterrevolutionaries."[6] Zetkin called Amalie Struve, Mathilde Franziska Anneke, and Emma Herwegh the three most famous *Amazonen der deutschen Revolution* (the Amazons of the German revolution), not doubting the sincerity and courage of their revolutionary zeal, but she found limitations in what they were willing to do:

> If, however, we examine the lives and work of these women, it is evident that wifely love was the strongest impulse that led them to engage in political activity and in the revolutionary struggle. From that point of view, what the *Amazonentum* of 1848/49 did was more window dressing than action.[7]

Clara Zetkin seems to share with Valentin the conviction that the main impetus behind female political commitment was loyalty to their husbands. Therefore, it may well be very difficult to have a true understanding of the role played by the *Amazonentum* (all the unknown but active women in 1848) simply because what they did has been ignored, since it was not legitimized or publicized by their husbands. The exceptional case of Louise Dittmar is a good example of this. Author of revolutionary pamphlets and poetry, editor of a newspaper published in 1849, she has been only recently rediscovered and it has not yet been possible to reconstruct the details of her life. It may well be that her notoriety has been forgotten and she has remained anonymous because she did not have a husband.[8]

On the other hand, some of Valentin's remarks about newspapers edited by women, about a democratic *Frauenklub* (women's club) in Berlin, about *Kundgebungen* (demonstrations and/or proclamations) by Rhenish women in Elberfeld, Cologne, and Bonn, about proclamations made to the women of Berlin, Potsdam, and Dresden by revolutionaries and counterrevolutionaries, lead us to conclude that the political role played by women must not be underestimated.[9] A whole series of satirical *Flugblätter* (pamphlets) attacking the idea of the implementation of improvements for women demonstrate how every emancipatory tendency was misunderstood or obstructed.[10] The widespread resistance to any change in the traditional role played by women was so deeply rooted that not only did reactionary authors like Wilhelm Heinrich Riehl[11] condemn every initiative of the *Emanzipierten* (the emancipated women), but even democrats like Johannes Scherr criticized women's political activities in the strongest terms:

> You can be sure that the contingent of women who are pushing themselves unasked into public life is made up either of old, ugly, and hysterical spinsters—who might be forgiven for physiological reasons—or else slovenly housewives and mothers who have forgotten their duty, whose housekeeping books—if they have any—are in disorder, whose rooms, kitchens, pantries, and linen cupboards are in a state of chaos, whose milliner's bills are high and unpaid, and whose children are physically and morally unwashed.[12]

Recent studies on the beginning of female emancipation in Germany, reprints of earlier works, and the publication of documents are bringing to light a number of independent personalities who made clear and conscious contributions, who took drastic positions, and whose actions were as rational as they were courageous. What they did cannot be labeled "female emotionalism," a term which even contemporary historians have often used to write off the work of the "Amazons" of the revolution.[13] One of the best and most comprehensive new works on German women in 1848–49 is Gerlinde Hummel-Haasis's *Schwestern, zerreisst eure Ketten*[14] (*Sisters, Break Your Chains*), which is a collection of original documents. The emphasis here in this essay will be on women writers who were only partially accounted for in her work. As research is still in progress, I do not pretend to have provided exhaustive documentation and I leave to the historians the task of verifying the value of these writings as sources.

The most immediate contribution which German women intellectuals made in the day-to-day course of the revolution was through journalism. Some women were already professional writers (Mathilde Franziska Anneke, Louise Otto), others experimented as collaborators with their fathers or male companions (Claire von Glümer, Johanna Kinkel), or they improvised and founded revolutionary papers on their own (Louise Aston, Louise Dittmar). Mathilde Franziska Anneke, who was active in Rhenish political circles, was well known for having collaborated on various newspapers, and she published the *Neue Kölnische Zeitung (New Cologne Newspaper)* from September 10 to December 23, 1848, in place of her husband, who had been arrested. On September 27 and 28 she edited the *Frauen-Zeitung (Women's Newspaper)*, the first women's political newspaper in Germany. It was immediately suppressed by the censors owing to its revolutionary content. It reported on the state of emergency in Cologne, on the political situation in Berlin, Koblenz, Prague, and Naples, and it incited revolt: "The struggle is growing ever more serious—it is either a republic or despotism. All the provinces must lend a hand and rise up like one man."[15]

In the same way the following year, Johanna Kinkel directed the *Neue Bonner Zeitung (New Bonn Newspaper)* in place of her husband and in addition, on March 21, 1849, published the only issue of *Spartacus. Wochenzeitung für sociale Fragen (Spartacus. A Weekly Newspaper for Social Questions)* as a supplement to the Bonn newspaper. The paper discussed the debates taking place in the upper house of the Prussian Diet concerned with social questions, had articles that attacked political absolutism, and offered very provocative descriptions of the miseries of the workers as well as news of democratic uprisings. The writer Louise Aston managed to publish independently in Berlin seven issues of the weekly *Der Freischärler. Für Kunst und sociales Leben (The Insurgent. For Art and Social Life)* between November 1 and December 16, 1848. "Art" was just a pretext for the publication of political poems and articles, satirical verses, fictitious reviews that attacked conservatism; and reports on parliamentary activity, the state of emergency, the meetings of democratic clubs, and the expedition of the *Freischaaren* (the insurgents) to Schleswig-Holstein in which the author herself had participated. Veit Valentin mentioned another *Frauen-Zeitung* published in Berlin, but apparently only the *Probenummer* (the first issue) of December 12, 1849, is still in existence.[16]

Claire von Glümer and her father were regular correspondents for the *Magdeburger Zeitung (Magdeburg Newspaper)* from the Frankfurt Parliament.[17] We know from indirect sources that the philosopher and moralist Louise Dittmar had the monthly review *Sociale Reform* published by the Leipzig editor Otto Wigand in 1849. No issues are in existence but it is mentioned in the *Neue Kölnische Zeitung* (No. 40, February 17, 1849) and in Louise Otto's *Frauen-Zeitung* (May 19, 1849, and September 15, 1849). It must have been a political-philosophical publication for a cultured readership, both male and female. At least that is what we can surmise from the headlines of the first issue: "*Die monarchische Weltanschauung*" ("The Monarchical Outlook"), "*Der Selbstzweck der Menschheit*" ("Humanity's End in Itself"), and "*Das Ideal und die Wirklichkeit*" ("Ideal and Reality").[18]

The only *Frauen-Zeitung* which managed to survive censorship, even after the counterrevolutionary victory that ended the revolution in 1849, was that begun by Louise Otto on April 1, 1849, at Grossenhain, in Saxony. It appeared weekly for four years (until 1852), when it too succumbed to the prohibition on political activity for women. Rather than accept male control of the editing, Louise Otto and her colleagues preferred to give up the publication. The first two years' issues are extant in the Dresden Library and those from 1851–52 are in the University Library in Mainz. Only the issues of the first two years were reprinted in 1980, edited by Ute Gerhard, Elisabeth Hannover-Drück, and Romina Schmitter.[19] Though it upheld the ideals of 1848 in its motto, "*Dem Reich der Freiheit werb' ich Bürgerinnen*" ("I Am Recruiting Women Citizens for the Empire of Liberty"), beginning with the first issue it was clear that the *Frauen-Zeitung* would be moderate, advocating, as it did, limitations on women's political activities, reducing their involvement to indirect action in the family and in cultural affairs. This explains how the magazine managed to elude reactionary censorship for so long.

This journalistic activity clearly represents considerable initiative on the part of German women intellectuals in the public sphere. There is other evidence of their political commitment that has been documented in the more private and traditional form of letters and diaries. A collection of letters, *Frauen im Aufbruch. Frauenbriefe aus dem Vormärz und der Revolution von 1848 (Women's Awakening. Women's Letters from the Vormärz and the Revolution of 1848)*, edited by Fritz Böttger, was published in 1977.[20] Also, the memoirs of writers who took an active part in revolutionary events—Emma Herwegh, Amalie Struve, Mathilde Franziska Anneke—as well as those who served more as spectators—Fanny Lewald, Malvida von Meysenbug, Johanna Kinkel—are no way inferior in their depiction of what happened, especially in terms of specific events, shrewdness of judgment, or reports on their companions and colleagues. In fact, these women showed in some cases a humorous detachment and a capacity for self-criticism which was lacking in the actions of the rebellious hotheads involved in the military expeditions and in the confused parliamentary sessions. Emma Herwegh in her history of the German Democratic Legion in Paris, published anonymously in 1849, and Amalie Struve in her reminiscences of the war of liberation in Baden, written in London in October 1849, described (with an attitude of humorous indulgence) the infantile romanticism and the inadequate preparation of the revolutionaries:

> [Hecker] brought me upstairs to the guest room. It was quite a spectacle, just like Wallenstein's encampment. One group here, one group there, some were lying on the floor, others sitting around a table talking animatedly, others were standing, meditating as they leaned against the doorposts. As far as their clothes and weapons, it was complete anarchy,

but the best part, at least what I liked best, was the fact that despite the forthcoming battle which everyone knew was approaching, there was a placid serenity and not one gloomy face.[21]

Amalie Struve wrote in the same vein:

The republicans spent the night in the village. I saw my husband there again and he had not lost his sense of humor. The romantic and childishly original character of the liberation force had grown stronger and stronger. Struve and Hecker, to confound the enemy, no longer used their own names. Struve took the name Nord (North) and Hecker something else. The leaders, so as not to give the impression of being soft, spent the night undressed, were quite content with the simplest food, and refused the better lodgings offered them. . . . With infantile naïveté, young and old alike marched toward imminent dangers. They had left their homes joyously to join the liberation force. Perfect harmony reigned among the freedom fighters. They all called each other brother and addressed each other informally.[22]

Both Emma Herwegh and Amalie Struve say they took part in the unfortunate campaigns in Baden so as to not be separated from their husbands,[23] but their participation was certainly not passive. It involved courageous actions, often risking their own lives. Emma Herwegh crossed the German frontier many times in April 1849 to keep in contact with the German Legion in Paris, which was waiting for the signal to cross the Rhine from the leaders in Baden. Even though Georg Herwegh was not given military responsibilities, Emma delivered a much-needed cache of gunpowder to the rebels. In the same period Amalie Struve transported cases of ammunition across enemy lines. Her *Erinnerungen aus den badischen Freiheitskämpfen (Memoirs of the Struggle for Freedom in Baden)* offers a complete picture of the developments in Baden, from the earliest beginnings to the final defeat in July 1849—with the alternating exhilaration and failure, liberation and imprisonment, flight and exile. Compared with *Geschichte der drei Volkserhebungen in Baden (History of the Three Rebellions in Baden)*, written by Gustav Struve in Bern in 1849, Amalie's memoirs, dedicated to her German sisters, offer a "feminine" version of the same events. But as we have already said, that does not mean emotionalism and sentimentality. Amalie's history provides a lucid analysis of the revolution's problems, especially the disparity between the rebels and the people and the political immaturity of the provisional government. Moreover, the writer gave proof of a capacity for independent decision making, as evidenced in the charges made against her by the grand-ducal minister in Baden and by the fact that soldiers of the regular army asked her advice on whether or not to join the republican forces.[24]

Among the "Amazons of the revolution," the most picturesque figure is that of Mathilde Franziska Anneke, who has frequently been written about in recent studies.[25] She edited the *Neue Kölnische Zeitung* until May 20, 1849, and then joined her husband in the Palatinate. She took part in the resistance against the Prussians until the fall of Rastatt and the flight beyond the Rhine of July 23. Her *Memoirs of a Woman from the Campaigns in Baden and the Palatinate* were written shortly thereafter but were not published until 1853 in Newark, New Jersey, where she was in exile.[26] A big, athletic woman, Mathilde served as a horseback-riding messenger with virile efficiency. She took care, however, to defend her femininity, as the censors often made charges against her and the other *Freischärlerinnen* on that point. But their opponents were generally more concerned with their masculine clothing than with their courageous efforts in the cause of liberty. Mathilde Anneke wrote:

> Here I want to mention, if only in passing, an honor which as far as I can make out has been conceded to me by my old friend the *Kölnische Zeitung*. At the time of the campaign in Baden-Pfalz, they pictured me wearing the most fanciful costume a woman must have ever worn. It was a pack of lies but they actually said I had donned a massive cavalry saber, a hunting pike, a musket, and men's clothing. In actual fact, though I participated in the expedition as I have said, I was at my husband's side, unarmed, and in my usual woman's clothing, with only the addition of linen trousers for riding. I certainly did not expect the male editors of that old gossipy newspaper to understand the real reasons why I had left the sphere originally assigned to me to become involved in the war.[27]

She emphasized that though she was a woman, she was driven by political motives:

> Many of you, whether at home or in foreign lands, will despise me because I, a woman, have apparently answered the call of war. Especially you women at home will discuss this question, asking what a woman may do or should do. So did I once, until I realized that a woman must act when the moment presents itself. Women, I appeal to your finest virtue, have mercy on me and do not pass jugment. You know it was not war that called me but love; yet I must confess—hate, too, a burning hate generated in the struggle against tyrants and oppressors of sacred human rights.[28]

As for the women at home, many felt the need to get involved in the events going on around them, perhaps not in the fighting but with an increased awareness and a willingness to write about what was happening. Among that group it was not just women who were concerned about their male companions, although Johanna Kinkel, who was in Bonn, did travel to Karlsruhe to visit her husband; he had been wounded in the encounter of the *Freischaar* of Willich at Durlach. He was imprisoned in the tower of the City Hall and she fought with great strength of spirit to free him from a death sentence. Just as importantly, she wrote about her experiences in those days of July 1849; her *Erinnerungsblätter aus dem Sommer 1849*, (Memories from the Summer of 1849), published earlier in fragments, was published in its entirety in 1929.[29]

There were other intellectuals who also held revolutionary ideals and principles who, on their own—they were unmarried—left their homes to attend the parliamentary sessions in St. Paul's Church in Frankfurt and the National Assembly in Berlin. They only returned home when the state of emergency was over, democratic resistance had proven useless, and the reactionary right was victorious. Malvida von Meysenbug, whose courageous political commitment was the cause of her being exiled from her country, wrote about her experiences in 1848–49 but sent it to press only later; her *Memoirs of an Idealist* was published for the first time in Switzerland in 1869.[30]

Fanny Lewald managed to reconcile sincere adherence to the democratic cause with a rational detachment from excessive enthusiasm and rash initiatives. Her *Erinnerungen aus dem Jahre 1848 (Memoirs from the Year 1848)* is a collection of her letters written in the course of the revolution, during which time she had made several journeys. She went from Oldenburg to Paris, passing through Bremen, Düsseldorf, Cologne, and from Aachen to Brussels. She stayed in Paris from March 12 to the beginning of April, when she was called to Berlin by the news of the uprising in the Prussian capital. She spent the summer in Hamburg and Helgoland and in October attended sessions of the Parliament in Frankfurt. From November 8 until the end of December the writer followed the political situation in Berlin day by day and was present at the forced dissolution of the National Assembly and the suppression of democratic elements.[31]

Fanny Lewald's memoirs were published in Braunschweig in 1850, and it is surprising that her work managed to elude the censor and did not bring on a response from the reactionaries. Perhaps, as she herself bitterly commented, a cry of protest against social injustice was considered "extravagant" and pardonable since it came from a woman.[32] But Fanny Lewald never definitively broke with the conservatives and even in the most heated moments in 1848, her political interests were always balanced by her artistic and cultural concerns. She was really a writer of *Tendenz* (current trends) in the style of the Jung Deutschland (Young Germany Movement), but substantially more moderate. In March, when she was in Paris, she was informed about popular demonstrations and the fighting on the barricades, but she also went to the Opéra, the Opéra Comique, the Gymnase, and the theater of Alexander Dumas. She visited Heine and Herwegh, but she was also often to be seen in the homes of aristocrats and bankers. She went to the Club Centrale des Républicains but also found time to describe monuments and works of art. While in

Hamburg she heard the echo of war in Schleswig-Holstein but also savored the famous oysters at Wilken's restaurant and she dedicated a whole letter to the paintings of Heinrich and Rudolf Lehmann. In Frankfurt she collected information about the killing of Prince Lichnowsky and followed the debates in the Parliament, but also visited museums, Goethe's house, and historic buildings. Only in the last phase of the revolution in Berlin did political commitment predominate over all of her other interests. Despite everything, her disappointment and disdain were overcome by a sense of hope in a better future; eventually she believed that this very repression would bring German democracy to maturity. It is this optimism—which did not give rise to the positive radicalism exhibited by many other women—that provides us, through her memoirs, with important commentary on the revolution from two sides.

Kathinka Zitz-Halein, founder of the Humania Association, a woman's organization in Mainz, wrote her memoirs, which she called "Skizzen aus meinem Leben" ("Sketches from My Life"), but the manuscript, dated December 10, 1853, is still unpublished; it is kept in the State Library in Wiesbaden. Both Stanley Zucker and Gerlinde Hummel-Haasis have quoted excerpts from it in their works.[33]

It can be presumed that further research in libraries and public and private archives will bring more personal testimony to light concerning women's activities during the revolution. Moreover, two developments were taking place at about the same time in Germany. Women writers were producing literary works that were professional, rather than amateurish,[34] and there was now real political commitment in the activities of these women; both cases led to a form of writing that was far more elaborate than letters or diaries. We have examples of two extremes; Emma Herwegh, in the preface of her historical report, stated that she had no literary ambitions,[35] while Fanny Lewald's letters were written with a cultured reading audience in mind rather than for private consumption. Equally, the memoirs of Malvida von Meysenbug were very refined, and the works of Mathilde Franziska Anneke, Amalie Struve, and Johanna Kinkel reveal, despite their directness, the expert hand of the writer as well. Amalie Struve and Johanna Kinkel wrote prose and poetry.[36] In fact, revolutionary poetry was another important contribution made by these women in the course of the struggle, just as was the case with their male colleagues.

In a volume of collected works kept in the Bavarian State Library in Munich, the poetry of Louise Aston and Louise Dittmar is bound together with the verses of Alfred Meissner, Wilhelm Cornelius, Rudolf Gottschall, Adolf Glasbrenner, Ferdinand Freiligrath, Ernst Herold, and other writers either anonymous or pseudonymous. Louise Otto had begun to compose political poems even before 1848, and she included a selection of her works in her 1893 collection, *Mein Lebensgang (My Life)*.[37] In particular, she included poems dedicated to Georg Herwegh and Alfred Meissner. In March 1848 she exalted revolt, in November she wrote a eulogy upon the death of Robert Blum, and in 1849 uttered a cry of grief at the failure of the revolution. Her position was somewhat contradictory. She was a moderate who idealized rebellion but yet she considered the aggressive behavior of the *Emanzipierten* unbecoming of ladies. This is evident in the title of a poem she composed in March 1848, "Und ich bin nichts als ein gefesselt Weib!" ("And I Am Only a Woman in Fetters!"). That line is a quotation from *Die Jungfrau von Orleans (The Virgin from Orleans)*, but unlike Schiller's heroine, Louise Otto did not consider it her responsibility to take up arms. She limited herself to inciting others to fight for justice and liberty.

The poems of Louise Dittmar and Louise Aston express more radical and enterprising personalities. Dittmar published two collections of poems in 1848: one signed, *Brutus-Michel* (it was also reprinted); and one anonymous, *Wühlerische Gedichte eines Wahrhaftigen (Subversive Poems of a Truthful Person)*.[38] There is little difference, in content or tone, between her verses and those of the other political poets of that period. She sometimes addressed herself to the leaders of the revolution: "Hecker und Gagern," "Hecker," "Die Männer von Darmstadt" ("The Men from Darmstadt"), "Der erste deutsche Volkstribun" ("The First German Leader of the People"—Robert Blum). She also praised the uprisings in Germany: "Germania" ("Germany"), "Deutsches Bundeslied" ("German Federation Song") and in Vienna: "Wien"; and she applauded the philosophical theories of Feuerbach, the man who liberated them from "the despotic theological folly": "An Ludwig Feuerbach" ("To Ludwig Feuerbach"). Often she directed satirical attacks at her adversaries: "Der deutsche Kaiser" ("The German Emperor"), "Der Zopf der Ordnung" ("The Pedantry of Orderliness"), "Versteigerung" ("Auction"), and she criticized demagogy, Prussian legitimism in "Dom und Flotte" ("Cathedral and Fleet"), "Volksthümlich" ("Of the People"), inexperienced parliamentarians and the ingenuity of the people in "Volkslied" ("Song of the People"), "Die Schwarzgelben" ("The Black and Yellow"), "Unverantwortlich" ("Unresponsible"). Yet whatever the subject of her writing, Louise Dittmar's voice was not particularly feminist.

Louise Aston's *Freischärler-Reminiscenzen (Memoirs of an Insurgent)*[39] on the contrary, introduced into the political arena the specific question of female emancipation, and it reappears in all her writings. In her first volume of poetry, *Wilde Rosen (Wild Roses)*, which was published in Berlin in 1846, she rejected the institution of marriage and bourgeois morality, championing instead, following the example of George Sand, theories of free love and *femme libre* (the liberated woman). Because of her recklessness of spirit, which she put into practice by frequenting liberal circles in Berlin, she was expelled from the Prussian capital. From her exile in Switzerland, she published her self-defense, *Meine Emancipation, Verweisung und Rechtfertigung (My Emancipation, Exile and Justification)*, and an autobiographical novel, *Aus dem Leben einer Frau (From the Life of a Woman)*.[40] In March 1848 she returned to Berlin and took part in the fighting on the barricades. Then she joined the Berlin *Freischaar* expedition in Schleswig-Holstein against Denmark. Contemporaries and biographers speak somewhat ironically about the part she played in the revolution, emphasizing only her "feminine" readiness to look after the wounded; they were not particularly impressed by the fact that she was injured too.[41] Back in Berlin after the Armistice of Malmö, she founded the newspaper *Der Freischärler. Für Kunst und sociales Leben.* In it she published seven of her poems, which, together with five others, made up the collection she published two years later. These poems were political, as their titles imply: "Im October," "Berlin am Abende des 12. November 1848" ("Berlin on the Eve of November 12, 1848"), "Den Mördern Robert Blum's" ("To the Murderers of Robert Blum"), "In Potsdam," "Der Linken" ("To the Left")—these poems appeared in *Der Freischärler,* issues 1, 3, 4, 5, and 6, respectively. In her volume *Freischärler-Reminiscenzen,* she included "Barrikadenklänge" ("Sounds of the Barricades") and "Nach der ersten Vertreibung der Berliner Volksvertreter" ("After the Representatives of the Berlin People Were First Driven Out"). It is strange (Varnhagen von Ense also noted this in his diary[42]) that the author was allowed to publish these poems since she openly sided with the rebels, criticized political reaction, deplored the defeat of the revolution, and advocated the continuation of the struggle. It may be that, as in the case of Fanny Lewald, Louise Aston was not taken seriously in a political sense because she was a woman. Moreover, in this particular book she was mainly interested in the condition of women. In the *Freischärler,* that theme had not been emphasized so strongly as in the book, and the newspaper was already censored in December 1848.

Louise Aston's ideological position and her personal views were certainly more provocative than either Fanny Lewald's or Louise Otto's. Publicly they intentionally kept their distance from her.[43] Louise Otto and Louise Aston agreed on only one issue, namely, the double exploitation of female labor—because it was underpaid and because these working women often fell victim to prostitution. Thus they expressed similar views on the question, Louise Otto in "Klöpplerinnen" ("Bobbin Women"), which she first published in 1847, and Louise Aston in "Lied einer schlesischen Weberin" ("Song of a Silesian Woman Weaver"). Heinrich Heine had already written about the misery of the weavers in *Vorwärts!* (Forward) in 1844 (he was in exile in Paris at that time). Now Otto and Aston did the same, but from a woman's perspective. Aston wrote:

> *Der Fabrikant ist kommen*
> *Sagt mir: "Mein Herzenskind,*
> *Wohl weiss ich, wie die Deinen*
> *In Noth und Kummer sind;*
> *Drum willst Du bei mir ruhen*
> *Der Nächte drei und vier,*
> *Sieh' dieses blanke Goldstück!*
> *Sogleich gehört es Dir!"*

> The factory owner has come,
> And he says to me: "My darling child,
> I know your people
> Are living in misery and sorrow;
> So if you want to lie with me
> For three or four nights,
> See this shiny gold coin!
> It's yours immediately!"[44]

In other poems Louise Aston returned to other, more personal themes. In "An die Frauen" ("To Women") she launched an appeal for liberation from repressive morals and she idealized the joys of *freie Liebe* (free love), and in "Die Türkin" ("The Turkish Woman")—which also appeared in *Freischärler*, no. 7—she likened the destiny of all women to that of the slave who commits suicide to avoid the harem. The concluding poems in that issue, "Die wilde Rose" ("The Wild Rose") and "Hinaus!" ("Out!"), express the proud self-awareness of the author, left alone and about to leave the country where she was denied liberty:

> *Nirgends* bett' ich mein heimathslos Haupt.

> Drum denn hinaus in's Freie! in's Weite!
> *Nichts* nenn' ich mein, drum gehört mir das *All;*
> Jubelnd begrüssen mich, die Befreite
> Wandernde Stürme mit Donnerschall.

> Hoch von der Felsen gigantischen Spitzen
> Seh' ich das Dunkel des Lebens erhellt;
> *Wenn mich die ew' gen Gedanken durchblitzen*
> *Baut sich im Busen die eigene Welt!*

> *Nowhere* can I lay down my homeless head.

> So out in the open air! free!
> *Nothing* can I call mine, only *space* belongs to me;

Jubilantly they greet me, the liberated woman
Wandering storms with claps of thunder.

From high upon the rock's gigantic peaks
I see the darkness of life enlightened;
When eternal thoughts flash through my mind
It is in the breast that one's own world is built![45]

Before Louise Aston left Germany, she recorded her experiences in a political novel, *Revolution und Contrerevolution*, which was published in Mannheim in 1849. Some authors used the novel as a means of putting into print those ideas that others expressed more directly in letters and diaries. In so doing, they had a greater probability of reaching a wider circle of readers and they ran less risk of being censored. Then there were those who, like Louise Otto, waited a long time before they wrote about the "fatal years" between 1847 and 1849. She was certainly accustomed to clashes with the censors since her *Schloss und Fabrik (Castle and Factory)* was published in 1847, but only after many cuts were made.[46] For whatever reason, it was only in 1867 in Altona that she published her two-volume novel *Drei verhängnisvolle Jahre* (1847–49) *(Three Fateful Years)*.

Another writer, Claire von Glümer, also had a remarkable career: she was the translator of George Sand, Swift, and Turgenev; she was a correspondent for the *Magdeburger Zeitung* at the Frankfurt Parliament; she was imprisoned for three months in the castle of Hubertusburg; she was banned from Saxony for having tried to help her brother escape from prison, where he was serving a life sentence—he was involved in the May uprising in Dresden in 1849—and in Leipzig, in 1851, she published a novel entitled *Fata Morgana. Ein Roman aus dem Jahre 1848 (Fata Morgana. A Novel from the Year 1848)*. Because of the active role she played in the revolution, one would expect a novel animated by complex political events. Instead the author, perhaps to evade the censor, diluted her political discourse. Though she advocated democracy and social justice and was anti-Catholic, the novel was mostly concerned with lengthy romantic entanglements spiced with inflamed love affairs, contested inheritances, German aristocrats locked up in their castles, and passionate Italian women and plotting friars. Nonetheless, *Fata Morgana* did end with the militant defense of the Frankfurt Parliament in September 1848 and the assassinations of Auerswald and Lichnowsky. Gertrud, the young German protagonist, who had had a rational education in France and who evidently reflects and represents the author's ideas,[47] commented calmly but with a tone of bitterness on the immaturity of the people and a meaningless revolt: "What did the enraged crowd want? Where was its leader? What was its aim? It is like an angry child, Gertrud thought, who does not know how to use his own strength, nor the weapons he finds in his hands."[48]

In Louise Aston's *Revolution und Contrerevolution,* the ending is much the same. In this case also, the protagonist, Alice, was bitter about the foolishly ambitious rebellion of the citizens of Frankfurt:

> During the violent struggle Alice sat in her room on Allerheiligen Street, where it runs into Ziel Street. Right under her window there was a large barricade which was being assaulted by Austrian soldiers. She thought of that March night in Berlin and sighed deeply. What a difference between *now* and *then!* Joyously and with the courage that comes with certainty of victory, she had gone down into the street to encourage the brave fighters. But today she was afraid and troubled as she looked out on that unfortunate battle in the street. Unconsciously tears ran down her face. . . .[49]

It was really as early as the dawn of March 18 in Berlin when Aston had recognized the political immaturity of the German people, who were caught between the bourgeoisie and the state and were unable to make any headway against an authority that was determined to hold on to its power. She wrote:

> The 18th of March is as innocent as a newborn child. The people of Berlin proved it well enough, as they played with it as one would play with a child. Of course, one has to realize that the people of Berlin are like a child. Though on this day their cradle no longer seemed—as Schiller said—like an infinite space, as it had been before, and so the child tried to get out of it. But the attempt failed. Later the strict master arrived and the child dragged himself back into the corner of passive resistance and he let himself be wrapped up again in his swaddling clothes and put back in the old cradle. That comes quite naturally to a child who has been shown the rod.[50]

Compared to Claire von Glümer's novel *Fata Morgana,* Aston's *Revolution und Contrerevolution* is considerably more dynamic and certainly closer to political reality. The action moves from Vienna to Berlin, from Schleswig-Holstein to Frankfurt, and all the characters were actively involved in the revolution. However, the author did not describe the events in which she participated in a realistic way: for example, the rebellion and the state of emergency in Berlin and the expedition of the *Freischaaren* to Schleswig-Holstein. Historical facts are mixed up with fictional events and the narrative is worthy of a serialized magazine story: love affairs and kidnappings, betrayals and conspiracies, deception and detection. An obvious example of that is the treatment of Prince Lichnowsky. All through the story he is called Lichninski and in the end he is stabbed, not by the anonymous crowd, but by his son, the young Salvador, who was incited to revenge by his mother, Ines, a Spanish woman seduced and abandoned by the Prince. Therefore, Lichnowsky became a betrayer of women as well as the popular cause.

It may be supposed that in this case, too, the romantic plot served to elude the censor. In addition, the author was still convalescing from her injury and she was banned from Berlin. She needed money and so, to attract a larger audience, she wrote in the sensationalist style of contemporary novels. In the preface, the author insisted she intentionally chose the *Tendenzliteratur* (literature written with a specific purpose in mind) approach, forsaking a more perfect form:

> As far as the poetic side is concerned, instead of criticizing it for its deficiencies, keep in mind that it is easy to write novels when the *Zeitgeist* [spirit of the time] is so bored that he lets the chalk, which he is using to write on the blackboard of history, fall from his hand. It is very difficult when, drawn into the center of cataclysmic events, he is obliged to dress history itself in romantic, even fictitious clothing.[51]

By far the most interesting aspect of the novel is the creation of a new literary type, an emancipated and politically active woman. Alice, the protagonist, is a conspirator in the revolutionary struggle, she was an ardent supporter of the Voigtland workers, and she was so active and influential in democratic circles that she was readily able to criticize men who were not organized or energetic enough. Alice fights her own battles, rather than just carrying out men's ideas, she acts with determination, and her behavior is lucid and rational. Interestingly, literature in 1848 launched other female types, ranging from the slandered *freche Dirne* (shameless prostitute)[52] to the idealized *Barrikadenbraut* (bride of the barricades), the woman in love who follows her fiancé or husband to battle; Pauline in the short story with the same title by H. B. Haberland and Flora in *Die Freischärlerin* by Friedrich A. Karcher are good examples.[53]

Finally, when one compares Alice with similar heroines, such as those of Claire von Glümer's *Fata Morgana* and the short story "Auf rother Erde" ("On the Red Earth") by Fanny Lewald,[54] one finds that Alice has original characteristics. She acts according to personal conviction, not just according to the dictates of the man she loves, and she throws herself into the fray, not being content with observing the revolution from the sidelines. She does not so much represent an eccentric woman's search for adventure as she does the avowed goal of German women to free themselves from the restricted private sphere, in order to be able to contribute to the reform of social and political conditions in the larger world.

In the December 28, 1851, edition of Louise Otto's *Frauen-Zeitung*, she mentioned a few other writers who were politically active in those years, writing and giving lectures: Ida Frick, Ida von Düringsfeld, and Minna Zimmermannn.[55] There is very little information on them in biographical dictionaries or literary histories. They serve as proof that the field is still open to further research—research that must continue to unearth original documents, further analyze the texts discussed in this essay, explain in greater detail the relationships among these German intellectual women and between them and their male counterparts, and, finally, evaluate this material as a historiographical source.

NOTES

1. Leo Busch, "Die Anteilnahme der rheinischen Frauen an den politischen Bestrebungen der Jahre 1848 und 1849," *Rheinische Heimatblätter,* 3 (1926), pp. 463 ff.

2. Anna Blos, *Die Frauen der deutschen Revolution von 1848. Zehn Lebensbilder* (Dresden, 1928).

3. Veit Valentin, *Geschichte der deutschen Revolution von 1848–1849* (Berlin, 1930–31; reprinted, Cologne-Berlin, 1977), 2, pp. 579–80.

4. Ibid., p. 684, note 56.

5. Ibid., pp. 581–82.

6. Clara Zetkin, "Die Forderung der Frauenemanzipation in der deutschen Revolution 1848–49," in *Zur Geschichte der proletarischen Frauenbewegung Deutschlands* (Frankfurt/M, 1971), p. 19. (The essay was written in Moscow in 1928.)

7. Ibid., p. 18.

8. Between 1845 and 1848 Louise Dittmar published, in Darmstadt and Offenbach, three anonymous pamphlets and three others signed, in which she dealt with philosophical and religious problems and morals and customs connected with conferences held by her in the *Mannheimer Montag-Verein.* Her writings have been rediscovered by Renate Möhrmann and Lia Secci during the preparatory research for the anthologies *Frauenemanzipation im deutschen Vormärz. Texte und Dokumente* (Stuttgart, 1978) and *Dal salotto al partito. Scrittrici tedesche tra rivoluzione borghese e diritto di voto (1848–1918)* (Rome, 1982).

9. Valentin, 1, p. 369; 2, pp. 236, 580–82.

10. Ibid., p. 581 and p. 684, note 55. See also the documentation in Gerlinde Hummel-Haasis, ed., *Schwestern, zerreisst eure Ketten. Zeugnisse zur Geschichte der Frauen in der Revolution von 1848–49* (Munich, 1982), pp. 59–82.

11. Wilhelm Heinrich Riehl, "Die Frauen. Eine sozialpolitische Studie," *Deutsche Vierteljahrsschrift,* 15 (1852), pp. 236–96.

12. Johannes Scherr, *Von Achtundvierzig bis Einundfünfzig. Eine Komödie der Weltgeschichte* (Leipzig, 1868), 2, pp. 188–89.

13. One of the first collections of documentary material on the history of female emancipation in Germany was published by Margrit Twellmann, *Die deutsche Frauenbewegung. Ihre Anfänge und erste Entwicklung 1843–1889* (Meisenheim-am-Glan, 1972). It consists of two volumes, one a monograph and one with texts. Renate Möhrmann's monograph is especially concerned with women writers, *Die andere Frau. Emanzipationsansätze deutscher Schriftstellerinnen im Vorfeld der Achtunvierziger-Revolution* (Stuttgart, 1977). This is also true for the anthology mentioned in note 8 above. Various German editors have published texts on the feminist movement, such as the series *Die Frau in der Gesellschaft*, edited by Gisela Brinker-Gabler for Fischer Verlag. See, for example, Fanny Lewald, *Meine Lebensgeschichte* (Frankfurt/M., 1980), ed. by Gisela Brinker-Gabler, and *Mathilde Franziska Anneke in Selbstzeugnissen und Dokumenten*, ed. by Maria Wagner (Frankfurt/M., 1980).

14. See note 10.

15. *Frauen-Zeitung*, ed. by Mathilde Franziska Anneke, no. 2, Donnerstag den 28. September 1848, p. 7. Through the publishing house of the *Neue Kölnische Zeitung*, Mathilde Franziska Anneke printed the records of the trial against her husband in December 1848, protesting against his brutal arrest and the delay in legal proceedings. Anneke and the others accused, Gottschalk and Esser, were acquitted because the charge against them was based on false information.

16. Valentin, p. 580.

17. Twellmann, p. 20, note 45.

18. According to Margrit Twellmann, Louise Dittmar's newspaper may have been edited in Darmstadt. The *Neue Kölnische Zeitung*, in announcing the first issue of *Sociale Reform*, mentioned that the editor was Wigand of Leipzig.

19. "*Dem Reich der Freiheit werb' ich Bürgerinnen.*" *Die Frauenzeitung von Louise Otto (Jge. 1849–50)*, ed. by Ute Gerhard, Elisabeth Hannover-Drück, and Romina Schmitter (Frankfurt/M., 1980).

20. Fritz Böttger, ed., *Frauen im Aufbruch. Frauenbriefe aus dem Vormärz und der Revolution von 1848* (East Berlin, 1977). The collection was reprinted in Darmstadt in 1979.

21. Emma Herwegh in *Zur Geschichte der deutschen demokratischen Legion aus Paris. Von einer Hochverräterin* (Grünberg, 1849), p. 32. Emma Herwegh's report is mentioned as a source in Wolfgang Dressen's document collection, *1848–1849: Bürgerkrieg in Baden. Chronik einer verlorenen Revolution* (Berlin, 1975), pp. 26 ff.

22. Amalie Struve, *Erinnerungen aus den badischen Freiheitskämpfen. Den deutschen Frauen gewidmet* (Hamburg, 1850), pp. 34–35.

23. Herwegh, p. 21. For biographical material on Emma Herwegh, see Blos, pp. 61–66, and Hummel-Haasis, pp. 185–202. Struve, pp. 5–6, 10–11, 68–69: "Why shouldn't a wife who has shared danger with her husband not also share in his work? If traditional prejudices are followed, even in the midst of a revolution, the yoke of tyranny will never be broken"; (pp. 109–10): "In reality, my crime was

only that of faithfully carrying out my wifely duties. My husband's public trial was postponed until March 20. I was not allowed to stand at his side before the jury. I, who had followed him in the fight, just as a wife should, was presented to the court together with a few young people, some of whom I did not even know." For biographical material on Amalie Struve, see Blos, pp. 67–70, and Hummel-Haasis, pp. 203–20.

24. Struve, pp. 45, 71, 78, 131, 137, 144, 146, 148–49, 163.

25. Martin Henkel and Rolf Taubert have written a monograph, *Das Weib im Conflict mit den socialen Verhältnissen. Mathilde Franziska Anneke und die erste deutsche Frauenzeitung* (Bochum, 1976). The work takes its title from a pamphlet that Mathilde F. Anneke wrote in 1847 in defense of her colleague Louise Aston, who was banned from Berlin. An excerpt has been published in Renate Möhrmann's anthology, pp. 82–87; she worked it out from an unedited manuscript kept in the State Historical Society of Wisconsin. Maria Wagner is dealing with the *Nachlass* by Mathilde F. Anneke and she has already edited an anthology (see note 13 above).

26. *Memoiren einer Frau aus dem badisch-pfälzischen Feldzuge* was reprinted in America by Albert Bernhardt Faust: "Mathilde Franziska Giesler-Anneke. 'Memoiren einer Frau aus dem badisch-pfälzischen Feldzüge' and a Sketch of Her Career," *German-American Annals*, 16 (1918), nos. 3–4, pp. 73–140, and in Germany by Henkel and Taubert, pp. 63–121; and recently in Mathilde Franziska Anneke, *Mutterland. Memoiren einer Frau aus dem badisch-pfälzischen Feldzüge* (Münster, 1982). See Hummel-Haasis, pp. 223–35.

27. Anneke, in Henkel-Taubert, pp. 86–87.

28. Ibid., pp. 64–65.

29. Johanna Kinkel, *Erinnerungsblätter aus dem Sommer 1849* (Darmstadt, 1929). This publication is based on the manuscript acquired from the Universitätsbibliothek Bonn. Before that, two different versions of Johanna Kinkel's memoirs had appeared: in the *Monatsschrift für Politik, Wissenschaft, Kunst und Leben*, 2 (Bremen, 1851), and in the *Deutsche Revue*, 19 (1894). See Kinkel's biography in Blos, pp. 47–54.

30. Malvida von Meysenbug, *Mémoires d'une idéaliste (entre deux révolutions 1830–1848)* (Geneva-Basel, 1869). The German version in three volumes, *Memoiren einer Idealistin* (Berlin-Leipzig, 1876), was expanded with the years between 1848 and 1861. For Meysenbug's biography, see Blos, pp. 33–46.

31. Fanny Lewald, *Erinnerungen aus dem Jahre 1848* (Braunschweig, 1850); vol. 1: *Reise von Oldenburg nach Paris. Der März in der französischen Republik;* vol. 2: *Berlin im Frühjahr 1848. Hamburg. Helgoland. Frankfurt am Main. Berlin in November und Dezember 1848*. A selection from Fanny Lewald's memoirs was published by Dietrich Schaefer (Frankfurt/M., 1969).

32. Lewald, pp. 346, 348–49.

33. Stanley Zucker, "German Women and the Revolution of 1848: Kathinka Zitz-Halein and the Humania Association," *Central European History*, 13 (1980), pp. 237–54; see, in particular, note 17 on p. 245, for relations between Zitz-Halein, Otto, Meysenbug, Lewald, and Kinkel during the years of the revolution. Hummel-Haasis, pp. 259–327.

34. Möhrmann, *Die andere Frau*, pp. 60 ff.; Möhrmann, *Frauenemanzipation im deutschen Vormärz*, pp. 9–12.

35. Herwegh, pp. iii–iv: "All the other doubts which at any other time would convince me *never* to take the path of literature—at a moment like this disappear. It is not necessary to have talent or a professional writing style to raise one's *own* voice for liberty, to energetically oppose calumny. . . . I am writing this long preface to a work that is short and insignificant perhaps, to defend myself in advance against any suspicion of wanting to increase in some way, even temporarily, the number of women writers (called by the technical term *bas bleus*). I have been protected from this career by everything that can protect one: a lack of professionalism, inclination, and, above all, the best guard against the literary plague, a good and loving destiny. Today I take my pen in hand, as I have already said, the only weapon available to me at this moment, to do something even quite modest, in the interest of truth and in the interest of poor imprisoned friends. The German, as far as I can figure out, is more willing to spend money on the written word than living things. . . ."

36. Struve, *Erinnerungen aus den badischen Freiheitskämpfen*, *Widmung* (dedication) and pp. 48, 103–4, 167. Johanna Kinkel, *Erinnerungsblätter aus dem Sommer 1849*, p. 37. Amalie Struve wrote several novels, in particular the trilogy *Historische Zeitbilder: Westminster, Heloise Defleurs*, and *Der Fall von Magdeburg* (Bremen, 1850). She also collaborated with her husband in compiling the third, fourth, and fifth volumes of the *Weltgeschichte* during her exile in America. Johanna Kinkel, writer and musician, wrote short stories, musical theory, and an autobiographical novel about the life of exiles in London, published posthumously: *Hans Ibeles in London. Ein Familienbild aus dem Flüchtlingsleben* (Stuttgart, 1860).

37. Louise Otto, *Mein Lebensgang. Gedichte aus fünf Jahrzehnten* (Leipzig, 1893); *Abteilung I: aus den Jahren von 1840–1850*: "An Georg Herwegh," pp. 46–49; "An Alfred Meissner," pp. 63–64; "Und ich bin nichts als ein gefesselt Weib!", pp. 136–39; "Robert Blum. November 1848," p. 140; "Am Schluss des Jahres 1849," p. 142. Louise Otto is considered the founder of the German feminist emancipation movement, and there is a vast bibliography on her. For her activities in the period of the revolution, see Blos, pp. 9–15.

38. Louise Dittmar, *Brutus-Michel. Gedichte* (Darmstadt, 1848); *Wühlerische Gedichte eines Wahrhaftigen*, ed. by L. D. (Mannheim, 1848).

39. Louise Aston, *Freischärler-Reminiscenzen. Zwölf Gedichte* (Leipzig, 1850).

40. Louise Aston, *Meine Emancipation, Verweisung und Rechtfertigung* (Brussels, 1846) and *Aus dem Leben einer Frau* (Hamburg, 1847). For information on Louise Aston, see Lia Secci's essay Louise Aston: A German George Sand "Louise Aston: Una George Sand tedesca *(Studi Tedeschi)*, 31 (1978), pp. 23–59, and Blos, pp. 25–31. See also Germaine Goetzinger, ed. *Für die Selbstverwirklichung der Frau. Louise Aston in Selbstzeugnissen und Dokumenten* (Frankfurt/M., 1983).

41. The most unfavorable description is to be found in the *Grenzboten*, no. 24 (1848): "The 'Freie Berliner' ['free Berliners'] distinguished themselves

because each one of them carried a black tailcoat and a pair of *glacé* boots in his knapsack and spent all his pay on gloves. When they arrived at the garrison, the first thing they did that very evening was to organize a ball or a torchlight serenade. From every perspective they were privileged men; also the well-known Madame A. . . . had joined them. This lady brought some of her 'Wilde Rosen' ['Wild Roses'] to our expedition—she was always faithful to the idea of a 'free life and free love.' She is a languid woman with interesting eyes—*voilà tout!* But as the only feminine figure among thousands of savage warriors she knew how to get everyone's attention. Moreover, she assumed with the greatest dedication and *sans gêne* the care of the wounded, and that deserves full acknowledgment. Indeed, she was even injured, grazed by a rifle shot, and willingly made use of the occasion to show the wound and, with it, the loveliest white arm. Such a heroine should not have had much need of male protection, but a woman is always a woman, in spite of any emancipation." (See Blos, pp. 28–29.) But even the democrat Otto von Corvin, who had taken part in Herwegh's expedition, noted in *Erinnerungen aus meinem Leben* (Leipzig, 1861), 3, p. 19: "She showed this wound willingly, if for no other reason than to show off her beautiful hand." In the second volume of Corvin's reminiscences there are descriptions of Emma Herwegh, Amalie Struve, and other *"Freischärlerinnen."*

42. Varnhagen von Ense's diary is mentioned by Helene Nathan, "Louise Aston. Ein Lebensbild aus den Anfängen der Frauenbewegung," *Die Frau. Monatsschrift für das gesamte Frauenleben unserer Zeit,* 21 (1913–14), p. 654.

43. Louise Otto, in the *Frauen-Zeitung,* criticized Louise Aston and the Berlin *Emanzipierten* many times, repeating the condemnation already made in the article "Die Teilnahme der weiblichen Welt am Staatsleben," *Vorwärts!* (Leipzig, 1847), p. 49: "I recognize that with a woman like Louise Aston, you have someone who is the antithesis of that aspiration that seeks the elevation of German women." Fanny Lewald, in *Erinnerungen aus dem Jahre 1848,* 2, pp. 44–45, also criticized the women of Berlin who exposed themselves through their political involvement: "However much we may wish to recognize the spiritual legitimation of women, their appearance in the public sphere is alien to the German character. Therefore, this should not be provoked intentionally, because in this way nothing essential is gained for women, nor for the people, indeed it may be lost."

44. Aston, *Freischärler-Reminiscenzen,* pp. 18–9. *Klöpplerinnen* by Louise Otto appeared in the *Vorwärts!* of Leipzig in 1847 and was reprinted in *Frauen-Zeitung,* 3 (February 5, 1851), nr. 1/2, p. 7. *"Lied einer schlesischen Weberin"* and *"Potsdam"* by Louise Aston have been reprinted by Bruno Kaiser in the anthology *Die Achtundvierziger. Ein Lesebuch unserer Zeit,* (Weimar, 1952), pp. 11–13.

45. Aston, *Freischärler-Reminiscenzen,* p. 28.

46. Since her first novel *Ludwig der Kellner* (1842), Louise Otto had dealt with difficult social questions. *Schloss und Fabrik* (Leipzig, 1847) at first was confiscated for "subversive content"; after a hearing with the young writer, the Minister of Culture for Saxony allowed the novel to be published after the incriminating passages were deleted.

47. Claire von Glümer, daughter of a political exile, lived in Switzerland and France.

48. Glümer, *Fata Morgana*, p. 399.

49. Aston, *Revolution und Contrerevolution*, 2, p. 267.

50. Ibid., p. 2.

51. Ibid., *Vorrede*, pp. 1–2.

52. For comparisons of *Freischärlerinnen* and *freche Dirnen*, see Hummel-Haasis, pp. 109–10.

53. The short story "Pauline" by Haberland appeared in the *Frauen-Zeitung* of Louise Otto, June 2, 1849. *Die Freischärlerin. Eine Novelle aus der Pfälzer Revolution 1849* by Friedrich Albrecht Karcher appeared in Kaiserslautern, 1851; it was reprinted by Hellmut G. Haasis (Frankfurt/M., 1977) for the Verlag Roter Stern with an accurate and interesting commentary.

54. Fanny Lewald, "Auf rother Erde" (Leipzig, 1850). See Möhrmann, *Die andere Frau*, pp. 148–49.

55. *Frauen-Zeitung*, 3 (December 28, 1851), pp. 358 ff., and Twellmann, p. 20, note 45.

Self-Conscious Histories

Biographies of German Women in the Nineteenth Century

RUTH-ELLEN BOETCHER JOERES

In 1868 and 1869 in Leipzig two volumes were published that contained biographical sketches of personages whose roles in history ranged from the sensational to the utterly obscure.[1] At a time when biography had become widespread as a version of personal history, easy to read and immensely adaptable to a variety of forms, from full-length tomes to brief contributions in anthologies, from obituaries (necrologies) of all shapes and sizes to sketches of still-living figures, such a publishing event could hardly have been considered unique or even worthy of particular notice. The fact that the books were labeled volumes 2 and 4 of a series entitled *Privatgeschichten der Weltgeschichte (Private Lives from World History)* also would not have aroused any special interest, since by the 1860s the earlier Brockhaus *Conversations-Lexikon* definition of biographies as, first and foremost, depictions of persons distinguished "by their social position" was no longer necessarily valid:[2] minor figures had already gained the attention of a readership that at least on occasion consented to accounts of lesser lives. What was significant were the subjects of the volumes: Louise Otto, the biographer who wrote these sketches, directed her attention exclusively to women. More than that, with few exceptions, her subjects were not members of royal families, and indeed often represented the other extreme, the forgotten women of the murky past whose anonymity she wished to remedy.

Women had not been excluded from biographical attention before the appearance of Louise Otto's volumes. The Brockhaus definitions of biography during the course of the nineteenth century were usually careful in their choice of neutral words to describe the subjects of such works: they were labeled "person" (1814) or "individual" (1851) or "human being" (1851), and the most wide-ranging of the century's entries, that of 1851, also listed both Carl Schindel's *Die deutschen Schriftstellerinnen (German Women Writers, 1823–25)* and Abraham Voss's *Deutschlands Dichterinnen (Germany's Women Writers, 1847)* in its bibliography.[3] The tone of earlier biographies, however, often resembled that found in Christian August Wichmann's *Geschichte berühmter Frauenzimmer (The History of Famous Females)*, a three-volume anthology of women's lives assembled in the 1770s. After a series of less than complimentary comments on women in his foreword—Wichmann acknowledged, for example, that women did indeed suffer from an inadequate formal education, but asserted that their brains were smaller and thus could not be expected to absorb what men could learn—the author wrote alphabetically arranged descriptions of women from around the world, many of them listed by their first names alone, whom he found worthy of mention. The following entry is a sample in its entirety:

> Alexandra. Daughter of Aristibulus, wife of Philippion, son of Ptolemy Menneus, the King of Chalcis, a province located on the Mount of Lebanon. She possessed such an extraordinary beauty that her stepfather developed a culpable love for her and, in order to satisfy this passion, had his son murdered and married her.[4]

Like many others, Wichmann found women worthy of biographical interest because of their royal heritage or physical beauty, not because of their own purposeful action. And it was against this prevailing attitude that Louise Otto thundered in her prefaces to the two volumes she published in the 1860s. The first of them was entitled *Merkwürdige und geheimnissvolle Frauen (Remarkable and Mysterious Women)* and comprised biographical accounts of the lives of twelve women whom she characterized as witches. But just as she emphasized that her interest was in those "from a more private world, but for all that no less worthy of augmenting the portrait of any era," (p. 1), she also saw the label of witch in revisionary fashion: her subjects were called witches, she admitted, but: "In intoning such a word, their contemporaries could most rapidly discard everything that was unusual or noticeable in a female being. . . ." (p. 3).

The preface to the 1869 volume, *Einflussreiche Frauen aus dem Volke (Influential Women among the Common Folk)*, was more adamant. After reconfirming that the female subjects of most biographers have been those who through royal birth or "chance royal attention" (p. 3) had merited notice, she described her own subjects as women who needed neither blood nor favors to gain fame: ". . . who, despite all the unfavorable circumstances that exclude the female sex from public activities and efforts everywhere and at all times, still participate in the work of their age" (p. 3). She concluded with a heated polemic statement justifying both her choice of subjects and her approach to them:

> . . . but it was our purpose to present a female figure who has always existed, who had an influence on the times in which she lived, and to portray such a woman in a living relationship with her times, so that we could show that women are capable of such influence. Either by fulfilling a dark impulse or in conscious awareness of what they are doing, they also have the power and the right—despite the fact that it is so often denied them—to participate actively in the course of general evolution. And doubly important for us was the use of a female pen and viewpoint to compose these life portraits, because men can least correctly judge precisely *those* women and at best cannot sympathize with those who are driven by the desire to emerge from the narrowness of the family role in which one has wanted forcefully to confine them. The fact that this desire is alive in the hearts of countless women and indeed exists there as a completely justified *human* desire will not and cannot be admitted or understood by so many men who still allow themselves to be ruled by old prejudices—yes, most of them could not be expected to be capable of placing themselves in the position of a being that feels a holy craving for knowledge and influence and yet finds no opportunity to fulfill such a craving—and for that reason it happens that they attribute quite different motives to women for their behavior than those which they actually have. Completely ruled by the assumption that women have only a natural function and possess a cultural function only indirectly through the power of their influence on men, those male historians attribute what are usually completely false motives even to the women who have accomplished something extraordinary in any area, intellectual or otherwise.[5]

What is particularly significant here is Louise Otto's emphasis not only on the importance of telling women's lives but on having women do the telling. She saw a clear distinction between the attitude of male and female biographers toward their female subjects, and in an echo of the middle-class (not to mention the early German feminist) emphasis in the nineteenth century on the major importance of *Bildung* (education), there was at least an intimation that a more knowledgeable interpretation of women's lives by women would enable the female readers of such biographies to benefit from the newly gained knowledge of their own heritage. If we indeed define biographies as a version of popular history, often anecdotal in nature and thus usually more readable and accessible than the dry accumulation of facts and numbers found in standard histories, then we can assume that nineteenth-century German women, excluded from the realms where more formal, traditional history was taught, might well have been avid readers of biographies. And if we can in turn assume that their view of history could have been shaped by biographical accounts, then it seems logical that an increased emphasis on the narration of women's lives such as that which Louise Otto and others propounded might well be significant in changing the woman reader's view of history and her role in it.

In order to investigate this thesis, one would benefit most from statistics that are not available, from the sorts of surveys that are used today to determine reader reaction to certain types of texts. Since such data do not exist, however, another method of approach might concentrate less on the reception than on the texts themselves that appeared with ever-greater frequency in the nineteenth century, among them the accounts of what Jean Strouse has called "semiprivate lives," for women as subjects of biographies were often immortalized because they had famous husbands or fathers or brothers—or, as in the case of a frequently treated subject in the last century, Rahel Levin Varnhagen von Ense, because they had husbands who were also biographers.[6] The fact that women were the subjects of male biographers as well can help to clarify the differing perspectives of each author, less in terms of the sources, which were often the same, than as to the attitude toward the subject and the selection among available materials. The following discussion will proceed on the assumption that has already been put forth: biographies as a form of popular history were frequently read by women who, as the century progressed and their literacy, if not their access to advanced education, became more and more an accepted fact, in all probability formulated much of their sense of history on the basis of such biographical accounts. Louise Otto's appeal to a female readership seems to be predicated precisely on this assumption, as well as on her assertion that by describing the lives of women, she as a female author might create a perception of historical worth in her female readers that would enlighten them more accurately and meaningfully than male authors could or would. Because she urged women biographers to write on women, it is important to determine any recognizable differences between their assumptions about women's lives and the attitude of male biographers toward the same. Various subject areas worth investigation come immediately to mind:

1. Subject matter: Who is selected? What changes are evident in the choices of female biographers in contrast to their male counterparts? What is the balance between contemporary figures and figures from the past? What social classes are most often depicted?

2. Method of approach: What elements of a life are concentrated

upon? If there are leitmotifs, what are they? Is the story simply told, from birth to death, or is there a stress on highlights? How is history perceived, and what elements of history are important to the biographer?

3. Standpoint of biographer: How frequently and in what ways does the biographer interject herself or himself into the narrative? What sorts of comments are made? Is there any sense of bonding between biographer and subject of the sort that Louise Otto claims is present only when women write about women? Is there dialogue with the readers as well? How much of the biographer is revealed? What sorts of values does the biographer stress: is there, for example, the emphasis on *Bildung* that one finds elsewhere in nineteenth-century writings?

4. Choice of source materials: Are the sources different with women and men? How are the sources used? How important are the actual utterances of the subject: are they reported directly, or only reported upon? Are others quoted, male or female? Are more impersonal sources, such as newspapers or journals, employed, and if so, does this remove any sense of intimacy evident, for example, in an account based entirely on subjective recollection or the personal literary sources such as diaries or letters?

Comprehensive answers cannot be provided in an essay. What follows is a discussion of selected texts that, by giving substance and illustration, can begin to answer some of the questions suggested above. The increasing number of biographies by and about German women in the last century is only one facet of the issue; what must also be examined is whether such texts varied significantly from male biographers' interpretations of their female subjects. A knowledge of these texts as sources for women's views of themselves, their heritage, and their role models, can broaden and deepen our perception of the German women who in the course of the nineteenth century experienced the formation of the first national organizations that were to speak for their rights as women.[7] If these new biographies made an impression on them, then the attitudes and values that were stressed in the texts may well have played a role in formulating the philosophy that shaped German feminism.

It was said above that Rahel Levin Varnhagen von Ense was a popular subject for nineteenth-century biographers. In 1833, the year of her death, she was already depicted in a number of portraits, initially by her biographer husband, whose *Rahel. Ein Buch des Andenkens für ihre Freunde (Rahel. A Book of Remembrances for Her Friends)* appeared in its first version that spring.[8] The lengthy biographical sketch that introduced this collection of diary and letter excerpts concentrated perhaps understandably on the specifics of her death; later portraits, dependent more or less on the letters which Varnhagen chose to share with the public, increasingly gained perspective and provided a more comprehensive detailing of her life. In the mid-1850s, when one might have expected to find a lessening of interest in a woman whose fame rested on little besides posthumously published letters, two new biographies appeared, one by a male, the other by a female author. Thus a useful comparison can be made between texts that, aside from the sex of their authors, shared both subject matter and sources as well as a similar time perspective. Claire von Glümer's "Rahel," a sketch in volume 6 of her series *Bibliothek für die deutsche Frauenwelt (Library for German Women)*, was overtly addressed to a female readership and was published in 1856; Eduard Schmidt-Weissenfels brought out his *Rahel und ihre Zeit (Rahel and Her Times)* the following year.[9] From the outset—Glümer began with the words "A woman" and Schmidt-Weissenfels with "The husband"—it is apparent where the focus was to be placed; indeed, the title of each study already provided a clue as to its author's intentions. Both biographers used Rahel to a certain degree as a paradigm illustrative of an era, but whereas Schmidt-Weissenfels concentrated on the latter part of his title, using his subject as a vehicle to allow him to disseminate his views of the predominant male figures of the day as well as to present his concepts and generalizations about an entire age, Glümer's concentration pinpointed Rahel herself as a symbol of her sex and time, as the passive, waiting, often purposeless, ill woman who, it was indicated, was immensely uncomfortable in her inactivity. The biographer as interpreter was clearly present in both cases, yet the resulting portraits were noticeably different. One need only compare the summarizing passages that each author provided; see, for example, Glümer's appraisal toward the end of her sketch:

> Here is the summation of her life: the recognition of the uselessness and inadequacy of our social conditions; the painful yearning for improvement; the restless search for an activity that can raise us above personal sufferings—she has all that in common with the lives of everyone and she expresses all that in her letters.[10]

In contrast, Schmidt-Weissenfels, after a nervous passage in which he criticized women who write, was relieved to return to Rahel, who wrote only letters:

> She was a private writer and, without ever denying the most uncompromising femininity, she was moved and enlivened by all the great issues of intellect and speculation. Through words, through letters to the greatest minds and poets of her time, she utilized her talent and her natural intellect without ever misusing it or without stepping into unfeminine areas and damaging the chastity of that femininity. Perhaps Rahel would not have been what she really was if she had indulged

humanity or her own egotism as a poet or a philosopher or a diplomat; but she was none of these and was instead a torch that illuminated much that was beautiful and saw her light constantly fed by thousands of precious sparks, a queen who captivated all men of intellect; she is an epic figure of her time.[11]

The fact that these and other biographers chose to portray a woman who was as private as Rahel Varnhagen was significant. She, along with Bettina von Arnim and Charlotte Stieglitz, formed a triad that many of her contemporaries saw as characteristic for a particular time and place in German history.[12] Schmidt-Weissenfels' motivation for idealizing such a woman, whose life was so often marked by inactivity and seclusion, seems related to his unhappiness with the women of his own time and his longing for a past that kept women in what he perceived as their serene and passive place. Glümer, however, saw in Rahel not the satisfaction of a placid existence, but rather a disturbed and angry woman who was confined because of the sexual and social limitations of her time and who was far from content with her lot. The fact that both biographers had access to a similar set of source materials does not imply a similar use of those materials. Indeed, it is here that the significant role of the biographer becomes apparent: not only through overt commentary but also through the deliberate decision as to which materials to choose. Claire von Glümer, for example, in her report on the breaking off of Rahel's first engagement, provided the letter detailing that occurrence and added as well both the private diary entry and Rahel's angry railing against her own vulnerability as evidenced in a further letter written to a female friend. The reader can comprehend the proud, strong anger of the public acknowledgment, the exhaustion and despair of the private thoughts, and finally the openness possible only with a friend (pp. 20–23). What is omitted from both biographies is also important: whereas Schmidt-Weissenfels devoted considerable energy to drawing a broad historical framework for his portrait, Glümer included only those events that were immediately meaningful and illustrative for her study of the individual Rahel Varnhagen: the 1830 July Revolution was therefore not mentioned, although there was some discussion of the cholera epidemic in the following year, since Rahel reacted to it with fear and apprehension (p. 94). A woman's history—and possibly even women's history—was shown to be markedly different from the usual accounting of wars, revolutions, and matters of state.

Glümer was not alone in her interpretation of Rahel Varnhagen. Louise Otto's 1869 volume also included a chapter on her in which the biographer/narrator played an active role, and here too one finds sentences like the following:

She is also not responsible for the fact that she submerged herself so subjectively in her own being, listening to every single stirring of her soul as if it were of special importance, to every single impulse of her nerves, whereby she only made herself more ill than she already tended to be—for she lacked a great deal because of the inactivity and the absence of a profession, a condition to which she saw her sex condemned. . . . If such an activity had been offered to her earlier, then she would perhaps have been less ill, but certainly less dissatisfied and self-tormenting than she was forced to be, living a life that had no meaning for her.[13]

Editorializing is characteristic of many biographies, and indeed creates part of the fascination of the genre, for double portraits are thereby given, thus adding an entirely new dimension to that found in autobiographies with their confinement to a single subjective perspective. In the case of Rahel Varnhagen, the commentary by the two biographers shaped the general effect of their portraits; Schmidt-Weissenfels' soothing characterization of an intelligent, yet placid woman contrasted sharply with the unhappy figure Glümer and Otto saw imprisoned in the social controls of her era. The message of the female biographers was directed harshly against the enforced inactivity of women; the impression left by Schmidt-Weissenfels, on the other hand, was more a reinforcing of a role that he labeled "*weiblich*" ("feminine"), whose principal trait for him was passivity.[14] Indeed, he seemed to find no irony in making the following statement: "Her accomplishments, her greatness, and, yes, we do not deny it, her existence did not become known to thousands until she had died" (p. 21)—a sentiment that apparently consigns women to an existence so private and isolated that it is publicized only when it has ceased to be.

A later biography, the 1898 portrait of Louise Otto that appeared three years after her death, offers another clear, if more problematic chance to compare the differing techniques of male and female biographers. In this case, the biography, *Louise Otto-Peters, die Dichterin und Vorkämpferin für Frauenrecht (Louise Otto-Peters, Writer and Pioneer for the Rights of Women)*, was jointly produced by Hugo Rösch and Auguste Schmidt, two close associates who individually signed the chapters which each wrote.[15] At a first superficial glance, the differences are clear-cut and, on the basis of the Glümer/Schmidt-Weissenfels example, expected. Whereas Rösch tended to idealize his subject, thereby often passing over important individual facets of Otto's life and personality, Schmidt was far more precise and realistic, frequently commenting herself on the significance of Louise Otto's sex as a determining factor in the way in which her life developed. Rösch was too facile in his assumptions: the fact that he uncritically stated that Louise Otto and her sisters had little time together after their parents' death because of their preparation to fulfill "the calling of the woman" (p. 20) is an example of a specific, confining message. As a female poet, Louise Otto was not allowed to be present at the Saxon *Sängerfest* (poetry festival), but instead had to publish her poem of welcome in the local Meissen newspaper; Rösch reported this incident, but again did not comment upon it. Equally vague and non-reflective was his statement that, with increasing age, Louise Otto retreated fully from public life and "dedicated herself in the latter decades solely to the women's movement and the National Organization of German Women" (p. 38). Considering such an activity as removed from public life was not an opinion which Otto would have shared. Finally, there were two revealing definitions of that elusive and inexact term *"Weiblichkeit"* ("femininity"):

> Her joyful response to nature which rose to a level of inner well-being when the sun shone or a nightingale sang, which allowed her to be satisfied living for weeks on bread, milk, and fruit, the moving attachment to her little bird, which began to sing gratefully every time she approached his cage—all of these are purely feminine traits. In addition, her faithful and deep devotion to the members of her own family, which she never let slacken despite all her sacrifice, should be mentioned.[16]

A further explanation of the term appears shortly thereafter: "Truly feminine as well were her energy, her tireless determination in pursuing goals she established, and her basically feminine aversion to showiness or impropriety" (p. 39).

To dismiss such generalizations as the product of a male biographer describing women whom he, by the mere fact of being a man, cannot fully comprehend, becomes problematic when one approaches the chapters written by Auguste Schmidt, for here too one discovers less overt, but equally strong statements about women and their role in life. Louise Otto, she tells us, remained "feminine" even in her political activities: "But here too she preserves the nature of the woman, for her inspired poems for freedom are always filled with the divine breath of humanity."[17] *"Weiblichkeit"* was imbued by her with exceptional moral behavior, a quality she also found in Otto. The fact that Otto married allowed her, according to Schmidt, to be "fully developed" (p. 48). To see such apparent agreement among male and female biographers causes one to recall Carolyn Heilbrun's nine questions for future women biographers, the first of which asked: "Have so-called 'female' and 'male' points of view or standards of 'normality' led you into judgments of behavior different from those you would have applied had your subject been of the other sex, or had such standards been ignored altogether? . . . Words like 'feminine' and 'virile,' if they once were convenient, are no longer useful or appropriate."[18] Another apt modern comment at this juncture is that made by Patricia Meyer Spacks in a 1977 article describing the dilemma of women as a subculture that views itself in the same way as the male, dominant, albeit minority culture judges it: "Women are trained to think of themselves, to describe themselves, in certain ways. The stories they tell about their lives take shape partly from their presuppositions about what stories they are *supposed* to tell."[19] Put in terms of the text at hand, Auguste Schmidt had been taught that femininity was in some way synonymous with morality and a married state, and thus in her effort to portray her honored associate in the best possible light, she realized the necessity of describing her in similar fashion as feminine. Hugo Rösch's more simplistic method resembles Schmidt's, yet as a member of the dominant culture he by definition was reciting traits that it was in his interest to further and praise. He clearly wished to view Louise Otto as essentially reserved, controlled, and always willing to give way to a stronger, male power, to reduce her indeed to the level of a little old lady who ate sparsely, remained modest, and liked and was liked by relatives and birds. Again, the role of the biographer/narrator was decisive; here, however, the ambivalence of Auguste Schmidt's intention and the more complex message that she imparted have added another element to the portrait of female subject by female biographer.

Among female biographers in the nineteenth century, few seem to have concentrated on book-length studies of their female subjects. Ludmilla Assing, whose portraits of Varnhagen von Ense and Fürst Pückler-Muskau were supplemented by studies of Sophie von La Roche and Elise von Ahlefeld, among others, and who, unlike the other biographers referred to here, considered the writing of biographies as her primary task, should be mentioned, but the following discussion will concentrate on a lesser-known author.[20] Amely Bölte's 1865 study of her aunt, the writer Fanny Tarnow, was remarkable in its scope, its choice of subject matter, and its approach to that subject.[21] Fanny Tarnow was a popular writer, the author of a number of sentimental novels that sold well. She never married, and in an age when the worth of a woman was often intimately related to her marital status, she suffered accordingly. Her niece's portrait was based on Tarnow's diaries; the restrained preface, unlike the polemical forewords of Louise Otto, nevertheless contained a revealing dedication: "This book is dedicated to all those women who are destined to struggle for their existence." Bölte's narrative closely followed the chronological course of Tarnow's life amidst frequent editorializing, whether through her choice of what diary entries or aphorisms to include or through the more direct means of open commentary.

Like the other subjects mentioned thus far, Fanny Tarnow belonged neither to royalty nor to those with great public reputation; she was a middle-class writer whose novels afforded her only a limited degree of fame. Bölte's account of her life evidences a tone that has already been identified in Auguste Schmidt's description of Louise Otto, for Bölte concentrated on Tarnow's unhappiness at not being able to fulfill the profession which was understood to be that of all women, that of wife, if not mother.[22] There was a painful emphasis on the dissatisfaction that plagued Tarnow, a sense of a life not properly led, and the theme was consistent throughout, even in the volume's concluding paragraph: "A warm heart had ceased beating, a heart that only wanted to live and to bring happiness and never found the right illumination or the right place for its energies" (p. 295).

Despite the sense of vulnerability, weakness, and frustration that was imparted, however, an emphasis no doubt made all the more effective by the facts of Bölte's own life (she too was a writer, a governess, a traveler, and unmarried), there were other, more revealing sides to the portrait. There was indeed a balance of sorts between the agonies of a single woman who felt that society viewed her as incomplete, and the frequent statements of both biographer and subject on such topics as freedom, independence, and the ability to manage for oneself. Diary excerpts such as Tarnow's happy comment about a move to the country ("I am looking forward immensely to the quiet of a country life. I want to be intimate with myself, and reflection, reading, and energy should restore lost elasticity to my soul" [p. 107]), her aphorisms ("True freedom is being independent of the will of others" [p. 35]), or her agonized outbursts ("Ah! Why am I a woman! Why does this intellect exist in this fragile husk!" [p. 92]) peppered the text, and despite Bölte's message that a woman alone is bound to suffer and to lose, there was an undercurrent of solidarity, understanding, and anger that united narrator and subject. Here, more than in any of the texts thus far mentioned, the bonding between women was emphasized, and the biographical text was clearly double-sided, a portrait of both narrator and subject.

One interesting example of this was the description of the ill-fated friendship between Tarnow and another writer, Helmine von Chezy. In a chapter entitled significantly "The Search for a Home," Bölte portrayed the first meeting of the two women in Berlin during the summer of 1816; a later chapter depicted the flowering and problematic conclusion of the relationship. The initial phase in Berlin came at a time when Tarnow, according to her biographer, was particularly vulnerable: "She had completed her 37th year, she stood at the turning point in a woman's life when she must tell herself: it is over!" The explanation of such obscure language followed in an outburst by the narrator:

> She had been neither wife nor mother and that which she had not become, perhaps because of her own wishes, was now to be pushed aside and made impossible, like a point of view that has been overridden. A man is not aware of this cliff and thus cannot imagine these emotions that creep up on a woman when she approaches this border point—indeed, nature has set no milestone for him, for him there is still a future, there is always a way to go forward—there is no dreadful task assigned to him to stop in the midst of his existence, at the peak of his strength, and to say to himself: you have completed your life; from now on no going forward will be possible; from now on there is stagnation, a truce, and because there can be no such thing, you must begin your retreat—from now on you, still possessed of all your senses, all your strength, have begun to outlive yourself. Dying has begun, and so try to see to it how you can confront your gradual disintegration courageously.[23]

The friendship with Helmine von Chezy, granddaughter of the poet Anna Louisa Karschin, seemed initially to represent a solution to Tarnow's dilemma. Chezy, emerging from an unhappy marriage, welcomed the chance for new companionship. Bölte made an effort to describe the considerable differences between the two—Tarnow's fastidiousness and efficiency, Chezy's scatterbrained nature, her impatience with prosaic matters—but the friendship developed and was clearly of use to both women. The description of the unhappy end in 1820 revealed not only a less propitious side of the relationship, but also its narrator's clear regret at the fact that even here Tarnow could find no permanent base. A summer stay in the town of Schandau near Dresden, during which the two women complemented one another in their shared desire to write, and where even a circle organized by the townspeople entertained readings by both of them, also brought about their estrangement. This was described with such tact by Bölte that the reader is not sure exactly what the cause of the break was, although it evidently was tied in some way to professional jealousy. In the excerpts from Tarnow's diary that conclude the episode, there was a particularly strong portrait of a woman torn between the pleasures of independence and the awkwardness of a single existence:

> If a woman would just once decide to write her Confessions, what totally new views of nature would be revealed to us. I am considered one of the most intellectually endowed women of our age, I possess knowledge, mind, inspiration, I can think, feel—I can perceive everything that is great and beautiful—can perceive it in the purest idealism, can be happy

in contemplating nature, joyful in the pleasure of art—I am magnanimous in personality and character—all petty impulses of envy and hate are foreign to me—and all that sinks into insignificance in face of the impression that the kiss of a beloved man makes on me—and in that fact there is material for introspection and contemplation.[24]

Again, the ambivalence of a single woman's lonely and angry existence was transmitted, made all the more bitter by the inability to find any kindred soul with whom to share her life. The highlighting of this particular episode was enhanced by Bölte's own point of view, revealed through her deliberate choice of illustrative materials and her own commentary. As in the case of Auguste Schmidt, however, the apparent imperative to reinforce the necessity of a woman's partnership with a man as her ultimate purpose in life remained paramount. What makes Bölte's portrait more interesting is the other aspect of her aunt's existence which she underlined by using Tarnow's autobiographical writings to illustrate the welcoming of independence, the joy at the fact of her own existence that allowed her to write: "I am grateful to God now that he let me remain single, for in every marriage I see a limiting of inner cultivation that I now can uninterruptedly make the highest purpose of my life, but that must be reduced in a relationship with a man—men being as they are" (p. 74). It is this dual message—the frequent helplessness of the single woman in confronting society to convince it of her individual worth as well as her stubborn belief in her own value—that provides the remarkable and interesting effect of Bölte's biography.

Shorter biographical sketches, ranging from the ever more common necrologies of and by women that appeared in the organ of the National Organization of German Women, *Neue Bahnen (New Paths)*, or in more broadly based journals like the popular *Gartenlaube (Arbor)*, to chapters in anthologies or articles in other journals, were far more the rule than the exception represented by Bölte's study of Fanny Tarnow.[25] Many are worthy of mention, and four have been singled out to illustrate particular aspects of their depictions.

Among the biographies of George Sand, a forceful biographical interpretation published during her lifetime that had as its impetus the appearance of Claire von Glümer's translation of Sand's *Histoire de ma vie (The Story of My Life)* is virtually unknown today.[26] Although the essay was published anonymously in 1856 in the *Deutsches Museum (German Museum)*, it was later established to have been written by the conservative and reclusive novelist Louise von François, who had just begun tentatively to publish and who, in a practice commonly employed by women in the last centuries, did not supply her name and signed her article instead "by a lady."[27] Like Bölte, François frequently interjected her own commentary into her account of Sand's life and she was both opinionated and forcefully self-confident. Aside from the stress that she placed on the image of Sand as mother,[28] the need to verify her subject's femininity is not strongly felt, nor is the advertising of marriage as an essential part of a woman's life particularly noticeable. François's narration was critical, direct, and revealing; for example, despite her own conservatism, she displayed no negative feelings about Sand's move to Paris with her daughter in order to write, and her tone remained neutral, perhaps even supportive:

> . . . she is her own servant, seeks no connections other than those with a few young students from her area, does without many things, and works, tries this and that with a miserable degree of success, until finally her lucky star rises with the appearance of *Indiana*. So that she can observe the life styles of various social classes without being recognized and without the ostentation of clothes, so that she can sit in the pit of the theaters, on the advice of her mother and remembering the riding parties of her youth, she dons men's clothes and feels endless pleasure in her rough gray jacket and her boots bound with iron at the often amusing confusions that this little masquerade results in.[29]

Although François validated Sand's behavior by adding that her subject's husband knew and approved, her own unquestioning acceptance of the wearing of trousers was in contrast to the attitude of many other portraitists. As a biographical sketch of a living figure, François's essay perhaps was not obliged to idealize. She was critical on occasion, but she was primarily intent upon painting an accurate portrait that would inform and influence her readers to see Sand as an independent, competent woman, to view her as "the greatest poetic genius in France today and the greatest female genius in all of France's history" (p. 692). The emphasis on sex as a decisive factor in establishing the course of a life was a message that François obviously wanted her readers to absorb.

Fanny Lewald's *Zwölf Bilder nach dem Leben* (*Twelve Portraits Drawn According to Life*, 1888), an anthology of biographical sketches of both women and men, reinforced in its dedication the idea of a biography as a double-sided portrait: "In memory of them *and me* dedicated to their *and my* friends."[30] Although the majority of her subjects were men, and the few portraits she drew of women are of varying quality,[31] the importance of her own editorializing and commentary must not be overlooked. If one is searching for well-rounded depictions of Lewald's contemporaries, one will in most cases be disappointed, since she dealt above all with those single aspects of a life that were of interest to her and that in some way involved her personally. If, on the other hand, one seeks illumination about Lewald herself, there is much to be gained by studying these portraits, for Lewald's own point of view was revealed in every utterance, every choice of source materials. As an example of her technique, there is her sketch of Johanna Kinkel, a close friend of Lewald's and a talented writer and musician whose short life ended in exile in London in 1858. Her many letters form the basis of this characterization, and in most instances Lewald was content to let Kinkel speak for herself. The few comments of the narrator (e.g., "One forgot that she was an important writer and a great musician because one was always thinking about what a woman and what a character she was" [p. 3], and ". . . a blessing for her family, that elevated portrait of a nobly tried and tested woman" [p. 31]) provided little more than accompaniment to the letters. Although Lewald's decision to share the often personal, highly revealing letters was clearly a move on her part to paint an accurate portrait unsullied by her own opinions, the choice of texts whose themes stressed Kinkel's great variety of activities seems deliberate. All of the women who were Lewald's subjects were professionally active, a point which she emphasized; if indeed they had children, that appeared to be of little consequence. There was scant mention of the normally understood tasks assigned to women: these figures were instead the exceptions, noteworthy, not as wives or mothers, but rather for whatever else they accomplished in life. When one recalls similar contemporary biographical efforts by men, such as Karl Frenzel's *Dichter und Frauen (Poets and Women*, 1859–66), Ludwig Geiger's 1896 collection by the same name, or Carl Vogel's *Frauenliebe und Dichterleben (Women's Love and Poets' Lives*, 1873),[32] the differing intent becomes all the more apparent. In a Germany where femininity was defined as somehow connected to home and hearth and children, to an image of obliging conformity, it is significant that Lewald did not follow the usual path. It is true that Johanna Kinkel's letters often spoke of her four children and her husband; the emphasis, however, was on her composing, her piano teaching, the controlling of her energies so that there was time for more than what was understood as women's work. By choice of subjects and by the highlighting of active accomplishments rather than passive reflection, Fanny Lewald made an important statement about women and the expansion of their normally viewed role.

If the impression one wishes to leave of women writing about women in the nineteenth century is one of vulnerability, helplessness, and passivity, then this essay should end with the following discussion. Its penultimate position, however, is an indication that the text under question should not be considered any more paradigmatic as the ultimate woman's biography than should the far more positive portrait that follows it. In the first of Louise Otto's biographical anthologies, there is a sketch that might be viewed as a metaphor of impotence and fearfulness; its title, "The Unknown Woman from Hildburghausen, 1804–1845," already introduces that element of anonymity that so often characterized women and their endeavors in the past.[33] Otto's subject was an unknown woman, a historically verified figure without a name whose story contains no solution, no answer to the mystery of her existence; indeed, the major source for information was a text by a man who stressed not her in his account, but rather the male who accompanied her. The biographer's frustration is evident; the lack of information indeed caused Otto to engage in considerable polemics that, from a twentieth-century vantage point, make her sketch all the more intriguing. The tale—and it is, at least at the outset, more like a detective story than a biography—begins with a depiction of a veiled woman who arrived in the small town of Ingeldingen in 1804 with an unnamed count: the sketch thus immediately departed from the expected narrative by providing not the birth date of its subject, which was unknown, but the date of her first appearance. After disappearing for a period of time, she reappeared in Hildburghausen, where she remained until her death. It is never made clear why she almost always stayed indoors, why she was never seen without her veil, why she never conversed publicly with anyone, and why indeed her woman servant was forced to turn away every time the woman emerged into her garden. An incident in which she apparently tried to speak with that servant's son ended in similar mystery, when the count pulled her away (*Remarkable Women*, p. 194). Again, the mention of the dates in the title takes on an ironic tone: 1845 does not represent the date of her death, which occurred in 1837, but rather that of her male companion.

What is most interesting, however, are the biographer's openly expressed frustration at not being able to determine a solution to the mystery and her overt attack on the male biographer who, she felt, had sorely neglected the woman in his account. The final pages of the sketch are tendentious: Otto railed against the fact that any individual could live for that length of time in a town without her identity becoming known to the authorities. In addition, she condemned the political favoritism shown; because the count was rich, she asserted, he was allowed to remain silent. Like any biographer, she longed for completion, for information, and chafed at the missing revelation that she desired. Here there is no exposure of the subject except through the words of the biographer, who took the occasion to say something as well about the woman as a sacrificial victim, as a helpless creature at the mercy not only of what she viewed as uncaring, perhaps even evil men, but of an indifferent biographer as well, whose lack of interest in his subject condemned her to irreversible anonymity. Her attack on the male biographer for his carelessness served, of course, to underline the argument Otto made in her preface for having women biographers treat women subjects; the implication is that women would not ignore the details or miss the insinuations or ramifications that men skim over. As subject, an anonymous, unidentifiable woman seems quite the opposite of the normal focus of biographies: the fact that she was selected by Otto, and that Otto made the decision to intrude so liberally and to provide such a strong message, makes this sketch interesting and useful.

In her recent documentary study of the German-American activist writer Mathilde Franziska Anneke, Maria Wagner[34] pays less than careful attention to a biographical sketch by Anneke of the radical writer Louise Aston, one in a series under the general heading *Das Weib im Conflict mit den socialen Verhältnissen (The Woman in Conflict with Social Conditions)*.[35] Wagner's omission, as well as that of Henkel and Taubert in their 1976 portrait of Anneke,[36] is perhaps understandable, for Anneke's essay was awkwardly written, wordy, obviously in need of revision. Nevertheless, as an example of women writing about women from a vantage point of strength and optimism, it is worth mention here. More a polemic tract than an objective biographical text, Anneke's portrait overflowed with personal comment, using Aston's writings as appropriate illustration of the author's own beliefs about the need for women to be independent and her horror at what she perceived as women's *"Selbstverläugnung"* ("self-repudiation"). That last motif is important proof of the heightened awareness of self among socially critical women that began to emerge in the decade of the 1848 revolution, but it is not often as overtly expressed as it is here. Anneke clearly had a didactic purpose in mind; her aim was to influence women to be strong and independent, as well as to know themselves, and her method of proceeding was through the biographical portrait of a woman whose life and work provided a useful example. Aston was by no means viewed as an entirely positive role model, since Anneke accused her of greed and opportunism in the publication of her novel *Aus dem Leben einer Frau (From the Life of a Woman)*, which Anneke found weak and vain; nevertheless, the readers of this biography were obviously meant to learn from mistakes as well as accomplishments. And it is women who constitute the exclusive audience addressed: Anneke's message was directed toward a female public whom she wanted to inform and educate about the way in which a woman of this new era should live and think. In a particularly powerful outburst in response to Aston's statement of belief not in God but in the finite world, the biographer essentially replaced her subject and used Aston's statement to illustrate her own convictions:

> Why is such a confession so utterly condemned particularly when it is made by a woman? Why should the truth remain concealed from a *woman*, truth that is the inheritance of our times and that in its battle with falsehood has begun to be victorious over it? Why are the opinions that have been allowed to men for centuries viewed by the state as

dangerous precisely when they are held *by women?* Perhaps because women are more powerful at propagating these opinions than men are, and if they are propagated more, these opinions might shake the nation and the world today? Because women in their very hearts are approaching a belief in a new development of human beings that in the coming generation can leave you a healthier, freer sex that will never again let itself be cowardly enslaved? *For that reason?* Yes, for that reason: because truth, as it is represented by women, goes forth as a victor who will overturn the thrones and altars of tyrants and despots. Because truth alone will make us free and release us from the bonds of self-repudiation, from the chains of slavery. Because truth will free us from the delusion that we shall be rewarded up there for our loving and suffering, for our patience and service; because truth brings us to the realization that we are as equally entitled to the pleasures of life as are our oppressors; that it was they alone who made the laws and gave them to us, not for our use and profit, but for theirs. Because truth shatters these tables of the law and from now on stands there as victor, and needs nevermore to be the hunted fugitive who knocks on doors everywhere and finds refuge nowhere. Because this truth, as soon as women's hearts are entirely open to it, prepares the eternal hoard, and the inheritance of humanity has been secured.[37]

The biographical essay takes on a new dimension with Anneke's text: that of a polemic that not only tells of a subject and a biographer, that is written by and about a woman, but that is directed exclusively at a female audience that is expected to learn and to benefit precisely from other women as role models. Louise Otto's assumption that such a configuration was signifiant and useful was thus illustrated long before she assembled her anthologies some twenty years later.

In an 1837 description of a visit with the Romantic poet Betinne von Arnim, Karl Gutzkow, the rebellious Young German writer, commented on the manner in which one depicts the lives of others:

> But when we couple a personal acquaintanceship with a philosopher whose moral law is self-control with an exchange of words with him, during which noise and squabbling are present, a dog is barking, the housewife breaks a tureen, and the children yell—then one can probably say that great people are like landscapes, better viewed from a certain distance, and that a genius would also look small if one wrote his story according to the information provided by his valet.[38]

If we substitute "woman" for "valet," we can see a parallel between this description of life and the elements which we have encountered in women's biographies of women. A woman might well understand that a philosopher who stressed self-control had more practical than aesthetic reasons for doing so. Gutzkow, on the other hand, echoing here the school that believed in the search for an organic whole, was obviously uncomfortable at the thought of being too close to his subject, for fear of making the extraordinary ordinary again, and thus by his definition banal and unimportant. Barking dogs, shrieking children, and women breaking things have no place, he asserted, in a depiction of the great and exceptional. It is apparent that he would not be sympathetic to Amely Bölte's detailed portrait of Fanny Tarnow, with its careful accounting of facts and events that could not by any stretch of the imagination be called earthshaking or profound, nor to Louise Otto's fascination with a nameless, even faceless woman whose life lacked all evidence of outward significance. Perhaps Friedrich Sengle and Helmut Scheuer would reinforce Gutzkow's viewpoint: the former mentioned women only briefly in his *Biedermeierzeit* (the term used to describe the emergence of middle-class values and attitudes in the period 1815–1848) discussion of biography; the latter's otherwise splendid discussion of the genre essentially ignored women as biographers or even as subjects of biographers.[39] Jean Strouse, whose recent biography of Alice James has gained critical attention, has been mentioned previously as the author of a useful essay on women who by dint of their relationship to the famous become the subjects of biographers; Carolyn Heilbrun has delivered a very good paper on women as biographers.[40] But only rarely, as in a recent issue of the University of Hawaii journal *biography*, is there a critical discussion of women biographers: Margot Peters's essay on the subject is useful and welcome in its effort to categorize the types of biographies written by and about women.[41] Still, she, like most feminist critics, does not mention German literature, nor does she provide any thoughts on the possible differences between the manner in which female and male biographers approach their female subjects.

Women as biographers or as subjects of biographies should not be neglected, not only because their studies provide the insights of both narrator and subject which have been illustrated in this short discussion, but also because biographies such as these emphasize that violation of the norm, as Peters terms it, of the expected, that element of individuality and uniqueness that biographers particularly want to stress. No clear-cut pattern, no easy categories can or should be established; in fact, the interest accorded to the subjects of the works investigated has a great deal to do with their variety. Schmidt-Weissenfels was eager to conceptualize, to objectify, to generalize about Rahel Varnhagen and her era, to find some pattern that would give his portrait a satisfying and comforting wholeness and completeness; Claire von Glümer was far more intent upon extracting that which was unique and individual in her subject, at the same time seeing the many facets of Rahel's life as a comment not only on the era in which she lived but also and more importantly on her assumed role as a woman in that era. Although there are leitmotifs present in women's studies of women—Fanny Tarnow's conflict between independence and loneliness, Johanna Kinkel's strong professional interests, Rahel's enforced passivity—the women biographers centered on the subjects as women, indeed tended to focus on them alone and to place them against a backdrop of historical occurrences that played a role in their lives only insofar as the subjects were shaped and often limited by those events. The fragmentation of women's lives seems highly appropriate to the genre of biography, with its emphasis on all facets of a single human existence. Especially in centuries preceding this one—where the setting of professional goals by middle-class men was rarely an exercise engaged in by women and where fragmentation continued indefinitely for them, whether because of the biologically determined interruptions of any continuum they might establish or the unpredictable search for adequate employment by those not involved in marriage and childbirth—it would seem that the personal, subjective biography might best circumscribe their lives. Women's history has never had the same rhythms as men's, has only tangentially been marked by the same world events, and the transitory periods that are the exceptions in male histories may indeed always be present in one form or another in a woman's life. And the personal nature of a biography, allowing for the inclusion of facts, details, and thoughts that have had no place in the statistics of standard history, is appropriate to reflect this individuality and fragmentation.

In addition, not only were women like the unknown woman from Hildburghausen or Fanny Tarnow discovered in the nineteenth century to be worthy of attention, but the telling of their lives by women gave the readers knowledge on two levels: a picture of the subject whose life might otherwise, in a more patriarchal circle, be ignored, as well as a view of a female author who commented, intruded, shared her own thoughts and perceptions with her readership. The personal involvement with their subjects was particularly evident in women's biographies of women and augments in an important way our understanding of nineteenth-century German women and the ways in which they contemplated themselves. The self-repudiation that Anneke so strongly condemns was struck a blow every time a German woman reader had the opportunity to read of other women and thus to see women's history, her history, in a perspective far more meaningful and alive for her.

In the early twentieth century, the author who is often considered the definitive biographer of his time, Lytton Strachey, commented in the preface to his *Eminent Victorians* that biography is "the most delicate and humane of all the branches of the art of writing . . .; we do not reflect that it is perhaps as difficult to write a good life as to live one."[42] German women biographers often reflected that delicate humaneness and that involvement, that emphasis on the uniqueness and importance of their subjects. It is time that we resurrect them as commentators and personal historians who bore witness to their times, and more importantly to the women of those times.

NOTES

1. Louise Otto, *Merkwürdige und geheimnissvolle Frauen* (Leipzig, 1868), and Louise Otto, *Einflussreiche Frauen aus dem Volke* (Leipzig, 1869). *Privatgeschichten der Weltgeschichte*, vols. 2 and 4. In the following discussion, lengthy quotations will be cited in the notes; for shorter quotations or references, page numbers will be given in parentheses following the reference.

2. *Conversations-Lexicon oder encyclopädisches Handwörterbuch für gebildete Stände* (3rd ed.; Leipzig, 1814), 1, p. 715.

3. Voss and Schindel are mentioned in no later editions nor are any other references to sources of information about women included. The editions referred to here are the 1814 edition mentioned in note 2 and the *Allgemeine deutsche Real-Encyclopädia für die gebildeten Stände. Conversations-Lexicon* (10th ed.; Leipzig, 1851), 2, pp. 703–4.

4. [Christian August Wichmann], *Geschichte berühmter Frauenzimmer. Nach alphabetischer Ordnung aus alten und neuen in- und ausländischen Geschichts-sammlungen und Wörterbüchern zusammen getragen* (3 vols.; Leipzig, 1772–75), 1, p. 141. All translations from the German are my own.

5. *Einflussreiche Frauen*, pp. 10–11.

6. Jean Strouse, "Semiprivate Lives," in *Studies in Biography*, ed. by Daniel Aaron (Cambridge, Mass., 1978), pp. 113–29.

7. It is middle-class German women who are the subject of this essay, since it is they who were initially involved both in writing and publishing and in the organizing of a German women's rights movement.

8. [Varnhagen von Ense, ed.], *Rahel. Ein Buch des Andenkens für ihre Freunde* (Berlin, 1833). The biographical sketch is signed by Varnhagen and dated April 1833.

9. Claire von Glümer, *Bibliothek für die deutsche Frauenwelt*, vol. 6: *Berühmte Frauen* (Leipzig, 1856), pt. 1, pp. 7–102. The second essay in the volume is a biographical sketch of the life and work of Elizabeth Fry. Eduard Schmidt-Weissenfels, *Rahel und ihre Zeit* (Leipzig, 1857). Short citations from both volumes will be provided, with page numbers given in parentheses after the cited text.

10. Glümer, pp. 101–2.

11. Schmidt-Weissenfels, pp. 26–27.

12. An investigation as to why these three women were selected as symbols

for their era and were, in fact, of particular interest to the Young German movement in the early 1830s, is needed. My own jaded theory is that all three represented certain traits that were attractive and comforting to the dominant sex. Rahel Varnhagen was liked by and attracted and fascinated males and male biographers precisely because she did not write and was thus no threat to them; she was, at least according to Schmidt-Weissenfels, among others, the ideal woman, entertaining, conversational, and pliable. Bettina von Arnim, on the other hand, did write, but her penchant toward calling herself "*das Kind*" ("the child"), a name often applied to her by the males who wrote about her once she had published the 1835 *Goethes Briefwechsel mit einem Kinde,* also reduced her to a harmless level. And Charlotte Stieglitz—whose fame was based upon her suicide, committed so that her husband, the inferior poet Heinrich Stieglitz, might receive sufficient shock to become a great writer—was hardly remembered for positive, assertive accomplishments.

13. *Einflussreiche Frauen,* p. 232.

14. This problem of identifying women with non-action has not yet been resolved. See, for example, Carolyn G. Heilbrun, *Reinventing Womanhood* (New York, 1979), p. 31. In her prefatory remarks on a generation coming into adulthood in the post-World War II years, she comments: "The ideal condition of womanhood remained passivity."

15. Auguste Schmidt and Hugo Rösch, *Louise Otto-Peters, die Dichterin und Vorkämpferin für Frauenrecht. Ein Lebensbild* (Leipzig, 1898). Brief references to this text will have their page numbers given in parentheses after each citation.

16. Rösch, p. 39.

17. Schmidt, p. 47.

18. I quote from p. 4 of an unpublished talk given by Carolyn Heilbrun at a "Forum on the Problems in the Definition of Feminist Criticism" at the yearly meeting of the Midwest Modern Language Association in the fall of 1973. The talk was entitled "Biographies of Women: An Uncharted Area."

19. Patricia Meyer Spacks, "Women's Stories, Women's Selves," *The Hudson Review,* 30 (1977), p. 33.

20. Ludmilla Assing is best known for her biographical work on Varnhagen von Ense; she also edited letters and diary entries of Rahel Varnhagen. Her work on Pückler-Muskau is *Fürst Hermann von Pückler-Muskau. Eine Biographie* (Hamburg, 1873). I have not yet found her studies of women; pertinent biographical information has, however, been assembled: *Aus Rahels Herzensleben. Briefe und Tagebuchblätter* (Leipzig, 1877). *Gräfin Elise v. Ahlefeld, die Gattin Adolphus von Lützow, die Freundin Karl Immermanns* (Berlin, 1857). *Sophie von la Roche, die Freundin Wielands* (Berlin, 1859). The subtitles of the latter two lead one to suspect that Assing also exhibits a somewhat ambivalent perspective in her depictions.

21. Amely Bölte, *Fanny Tarnow. Ein Lebensbild* (Berlin, 1865). Page numbers for brief quotations are provided in the text of the essay.

22. In both Auguste Schmidt's study of Louise Otto and Bölte's text it is perhaps worth noting that the concentration is on the value of wifehood. Since neither woman was a mother, the explanation may be entirely straightforward, but

the standard male glorification of motherhood is found in neither. Indeed, Bölte describes Tarnow's disinterest in, even dislike of motherhood, citing it as a barrier to her creative ambition. One example of such a thought appears quite late in Bölte's text, in a diary entry of Tarnow's: "*I have no talent for raising children.* A child needs love and sacrifice; I could never detach myself sufficiently from myself to descend into the little world of these little people. . . ." (p. 285). See also the later discussion of Fanny Lewald as biographer: she too said surprisingly little about women as mothers or even as wives and stressed instead their other accomplishments. In Bölte's case the narrator felt justified in commenting as well. In the process of describing Tarnow's chosen profession, she made the following observation: "Besides, people with the education attained by Fanny Tarnow are not useful in the field of teaching; for them the petty ordering of facts has no value, the eternal repetition of small bits of knowledge tires them, generally they have a too active need for self-involvement, they are eager to work on their own development, so that they cannot tarry for long in the presence of others and their ideas. Thus in her there was a continual need to pull children up to her level instead of descending into their small world of thoughts to order, explain, and elucidate things" (pp. 28–29). Further remarks on the profession of teaching are given in great abundance in chap. 5, entitled "Die Unbeständigkeit der Menschen" ("The Fickleness of People"), pp. 98–101 in particular.

23. Bölte, pp. 187–88.

24. Bölte, pp. 242–43. The many interjected remarks of Bölte add considerably to the interest of her portrait. In the chapter preceding the description of the initial meeting of Tarnow and Chezy, for example, Bölte remarked on friendship among women and comments: "Friendship among women is generally a rare flower that easily wilts and dies whenever a man intrudes, and where on this earth are there no such intruders?" (p. 162). As contrast, one might look at Kurt Schleucher, *Das Leben der Amalia Schoppe und Johanna Schopenhauer* (Darmstadt, 1978), which includes many references to Tarnow and Chezy. But whereas Bölte seems firmly determined to understand and portray her aunt accurately, but never viciously, Schleucher, whose point of view wavers between sneering cynicism and weak efforts at wit, describes Chezy as a "literary spider" (pp. 44, 154) whose nets were everywhere, Tarnow as a hysterical female, and even his subject Schoppe as someone who frequently exhibited a hissing hysteria (p. 202).

25. *Neue Bahnen* is particularly rich in obituaries of women by women, as well as in sketches on living women. Especially in the 1870s and 1880s there is rich material to be found, articles often written by the journal's co-editor, Louise Otto, but also by many others. See also the later journal *Die Frau (The Woman)*, ed. by Helene Lange, which from the start of its publication in 1893 included a section entitled "Biographien." Although the *Gartenlaube* is not as rich as these two journals, essays on and about women occasionally appear: see, for example, the essay on G. A. Bürger's wife, Elise Hahn, by E. Laddey (*Gartenlaube*, 8 [1872], pp. 126–28). A particularly monumental effort to illustrate the lives of women was put together in the late 1880s and early 1890s by Lina Morgenstern: *Die Frauen des 19. Jahrhunderts* (Berlin, 1888–91) comprises three large volumes

of biographical material as well as essays on the history of German women, but by that time the pattern had been established.

26. [Louise von François] ["von einer Dame"], "Das Leben von George Sand. George Sand, 'Geschichte meines Lebens,' deutsch von Claire von Glümer. Leipzig, O. Wigand," *Deutsches Museum*, 45 (November 6, 1856), pp. 680–93.

27. See Fritz Oeding, *Bibliographie der Louise von François* (Weissenfels, 1937), p. 21 and elsewhere, where this essay is credited to Louise von François.

28. See François, pp. 690–91: ". . . we shall repeat it: in that closest and holiest of relationships, as a mother, Aurore Dudevant was a heroine of unshakable courage, patience, and ardent, untiring love; all her gratifications stream out of this source."

29. François, p. 689.

30. Fanny Lewald, *Zwölf Bilder nach dem Leben. Erinnerungen* (Berlin, 1888). Italics added.

31. The women Lewald included, in addition to Kinkel, were Wilhelmine Schröder-Devrient, Caroline Ungher-Sabatier, and Hortense Cornu. The last-named is poorly drawn: the portrait is more of Napoleon III than of its subject, with much in the way of distracting anecdotal material about others.

32. Karl Frenzel, *Dichter und Frauen. Studien* (Hannover, 1859–66); Ludwig Geiger, *Dichter und Frauen. Vorträge und Abhandlungen* (Berlin, 1896); also his *Dichter und Frauen. Abhandlungen und Mittheilungen* (Berlin, 1899); Carl Vogel, ed., *Frauenliebe und Dichterleben. Ein literarisches Album für die deutsche Frauenwelt* (2nd ed.; Leipzig, 1873).

33. In her *Merkwürdige und geheimnissvolle Frauen*, pp. 181–210.

34. Maria Wagner, ed., *Mathilde Franziska Anneke in Selbstzeugnissen und Dokumenten* (Frankfurt, 1980). Wagner includes some minor bibliographical information about this series, but says very little about it.

35. Mathilde Franziska [Anneke], *Das Weib im Conflict mit den socialen Verhältnissen. Deutsche Dichter der Neuzeit II. Louise Aston.* Typescript from Box 6, folder 7, Wisconsin State Historical Society Archives, Madison, Wisconsin.

36. Martin Henkel and Rolf Taubert, *Das Weib im Conflict mit den socialen Verhältnissen. Mathilde Franziska Anneke und die erste deutsche Frauenzeitung* (Bochum, 1976).

37. Anneke, pp. 11–12.

38. Karl Gutzkow, *Gesammelte Werke*, vol. 9: *Oeffentliche Charaktere*, "Ein Besuch bei Bettinen 1837" (Jena, n.d.), p. 230. Preceding this essay is an equally interesting critical comparison of Rahel Varnhagen, Bettina von Arnim, and Charlotte Stieglitz: "Rahel, Bettina, Charlotte Stieglitz. 1835," pp. 215–29.

39. There are innumerable critical works on biography as genre in the nineteenth century; I have mentioned only two that were useful for me, and should perhaps add a third, which, however, also says very little about women biographers. The three texts are: Friedrich Sengle, *Biedermeierzeit. Deutsche Literatur im Spannungsfeld zwischen Restauration und Revolution 1815–1848*, vol. 2: *Die Formenwelt* (Stuttgart, 1972), pp. 306–21. Helmut Scheuer, *Biographie. Studien zur Funktion und zum Wandel einer literarischen Gattung vom 18. Jahrhundert bis zur Gegenwart* (Stuttgart, 1979): an excellent book, and thus

it is all the more surprising that women remain outside of Scheuer's consideration. Recommended by Scheuer and useful for basic information on biography is Jan Romein, *Die Biographie. Einführung in ihre Geschichte und ihre Problematik* (Bern, 1948).

40. See notes 6 and 18.

41. Margot Peters, "Biographies of Women," *biography,* 2, 3 (1979), pp. 201–17.

42. Lytton Strachey, *Eminent Victorians* (New York, n.d.), p. viii.

Growing Up Female in the Nineteenth Century*

JULIANE JACOBI-DITTRICH

I

Könnte ich nicht auch ein Wolkenschwimmer werden?
(Couldn't I become a cloud swimmer, too?)
— *Bettina von Brentano*

The history of women is not only the history of adult women. It has its roots in the history of women as children. In the research on socialization there is no less a controversial proposition than that which propounds that socialization is determined by sex. Varying opinions are held as to the importance and reversibility of sex-determined aspects of socialization; none, however, questions the basic fact. Historians who for the past twenty years have been investigating historical aspects of the conditions for childhood socialization have been primarily concerned with the circumstances of boys' socialization. And aspects determined by sex have rarely been considered, or if they have, it has not yet led to the inclusion of sex (gender) as a category for research. An example of this is Philippe Ariès's telling statement that well into the nineteenth century boys in their early childhood wore the lower-status clothing of women.[1]

In this article I seek to shed some light on the history of female childhood. I shall attempt to present a picture of the childhood of middle-class girls throughout the entire nineteenth century. That is a long period of time but justifiable for this topic nonetheless, since from all our knowledge of the history of the family, it can be assumed that the changes that took place during this period were limited in scope. I would even argue

*This article was translated with the help of Lynn Hattary-Bayer.

that between 1811 and 1900 the childhoods of middle-class girls exhibited similar patterns. In fact, from the point of view of socialization, one might argue that individual differences were only secondary. Yet these individual differences in each girl's childhood should not be overlooked. They will be important for our examination of changes that were occurring generally in girls' socialization in the nineteenth century.

The following criteria were used in the selection of source material: (1) the source material is available in published form; (2) childhood and youth must be described in considerable detail in the autobiographies, *Schlüsselromane* (novels in which living people appear with assumed names), and/or letters; (3) the author must have described her childhood in a reasonably conclusive manner—for this reason many autobiographies were not considered if the description of childhood never went beyond the sentimental discussion of Christmas celebrations; (4) the autobiographical material had to be written by women who led public lives, as it is important to analyze sources where the authors had a stated consciousness of the contradictions in their development and where, nevertheless, it can be assumed that normal girls' socialization patterns existed.

I am limiting my selection to girls from the middle class and the nobility, since the inclusion of descriptions of working-class girls' childhoods proved to be problematic in establishing a common framework for interpretation. All the authors were born between 1811 and 1881. Their dates of birth are distributed relatively evenly throughout the whole time frame under consideration. The greatest differential in age between two authors is seventeen years (Helene Lange was born in 1848 and Lily Braun was born in 1865), and the smallest is three years (Marianne Weber was born in 1870 and Gertrud Bäumer was born in 1873). The dates of publication of the autobiographies expand the time frame; they were published between 1860 and 1948.

Some of the authors were married: Fanny Lewald, Hedwig Dohm, Mathilde Franziska Anneke, Marianne Weber, Lily Braun, and Elly Heuss-Knapp. Three never married: Franziska Tiburtius, Helene Lange, and Gertrud Bäumer. Whether the status of Lewald, who at the age of forty-four married the man she had loved for years, is comparable to that of Dohm, who at nineteen entered into an unhappy marriage, is a difficult question. The women whose lives are examined here had the following professions: author and journalist, teacher, politician, and scientist (without academic position).

Girls' childhood experiences changed little in the course of the nineteenth century. Even the fact that in the second half of the nineteenth century many young middle-class women faced the prospect of having to go out and earn a living, had no direct consequences for the developmental patterns of childhood and youth. In addition to the obvious educational and socio-historical relationships, one specific aspect of family history interests me in my study of female autobiographies that are concerned with childhood; namely, with whom might these women have identified? The answer to that question may help us understand what enabled or forced them to escape from the anonymity of the private sphere. The question cannot be answered, given the limited number of autobiographies used for this study, but individual autobiographical statements do help us identify or understand the process within each emotional context. Therefore nine autobiographies are to be interpreted individually in order to examine this problem.

The question asked by Bettina von Brentano at the beginning of the century: "Couldn't I become a cloud swimmer, too?"—where she tried to compensate for the differentiation between the sexes in a romantic, imaginative way—was no longer asked by the authors in this selection. Woman's role as "housewife, wife, and mother," a notion that was deeply embedded in German society, was not a goal which these authors chose as a focal point for their lives. However, this deviation from the norm created discontinuities in their lives and probably in their personalities. Although I have previously stated (here I agree with Theodor von Hippel) that nineteenth-century middle-class biographies depict *Lebensläufe nach aufsteigender Linie* (upwardly mobile lives), I must now state that generally this model does not hold true for the female autobiographies examined here.[2]

In the next section of this essay I shall provide brief biographical sketches which will serve as background information in the course of the evaluation of the source material. The third section of this essay will be concerned with various aspects of the childhood experiences of these nine women. I do this so that I can better represent the concerns of my research and I can combine individual with generalized facets of my work, without giving preferential treatment to one or the other.

II

La réalité ne se forme que dans la mémoire.
(Reality is not shaped but in the memory.)
—Marcel Proust

Fanny Lewald (1811–89)[3]

Fanny Lewald wrote her autobiography when she was nearly fifty years old. She is considered one of the most important first-generation authors of the feminist movement. She consciously modeled her memoirs on Goethe's. In selecting material for her autobiography, she evidently chose to write about experiences that were directly related to the question of women's emancipation. She was quite successful in that. It can be said, without irony, that Lewald was able to delineate all the inconsistencies which females had to confront in the nineteenth century. For example, one sees in her writing the issue of sex stereotyping (and its insolubility in that century) and how that phenomenon influenced her enlightened education in a Jewish family that was undergoing the process of emancipation. This woman experienced the contradictions of middle-class emancipation in a twofold manner: as a woman and as a Jew. In looking back on her childhood it seemed possible to her to overcome these contradictions in a pragmatic, middle-class manner. Humor and the writing of prose were her individual solutions to the problem. The pain that nonetheless came with that is not concealed but it is not overly stressed either. If I could confront the actual woman, I would ask her questions about this dark side of her life, which she in her old age, having had a successful life, would not be able to answer. Hypothetically one might argue that a certain liberal pragmatism was the female strategy for survival practiced by a talented woman in her social situation. Childhood and youth were described in the first volume of her three-volume memoirs.[4]

Mathilde Franziska Anneke (1817–84)[5]

Anneke wrote a scanty autobiographical sketch for her friend Mary Booth when she was in her fifties. It is an unfinished autobiography which tells of her childhood. Written in a romantic style, it supplies very little information about her girlhood and education. It may be argued that the character of the manuscript was shaped by her personal experiences; she was forced to emigrate following the Revolution of 1848. The extensive collection of letters in her literary *Nachlass* (remains), most of which date from the period 1847 to 1870, clearly shows that she never accepted her forced emigration, even though it was impossible for her ever to return to Germany. Her fate was a typical one for many emigrants; it was characterized by an unhappy consciousness of not being at home anywhere. Given that situation, she wrote about her childhood in a very positive light. Nonetheless, she did describe some aspects of her family history which are not unimportant to the question of girls' childhood.

Hedwig Dohm (1813–1919)[6]

When Hedwig Dohm was sixty-five, she wrote the first part of a three-volume novel, which it is assumed is quite autobiographical. It presents a detailed picture of childhood and youth, with special emphasis on the psychological conditions under which she grew to adulthood. Dohm's goal was to show how from earliest childhood women were trained to become good wives and mothers and how, therefore, every individual feeling, be it of an aesthetic, intellectual, or social nature, was suppressed. The memoirs were written in a very programmatic manner, as were Fanny Lewald's, although there is considerably more differentiation on the psychological level. Dohm understood very clearly the problematic, destructive, and suppressive aspects of her childhood. Implacable, she attacked parents and society alike for allowing a girl to grow up in that fashion.

Franziska Tiburtius (1843–1927)[7]

Franziska Tiburtius wrote her memoirs relatively late, after World War I and as an eighty-year-old woman. They are written in a very conventional manner. Going far back in history, including general historical events that took place on the island of Rügen and aspects of family history, the memoirs offer a picture of a very upright Pomeranian-Prussian family whose values prejudiced her political judgment in a catastrophic way. Naturally, she considered herself to be absolutely divorced from politics. Questions such as why women could not study at German universities or why it was so difficult to establish that right, were never raised, although Tiburtius was one of the first German women to study at a university. Equally conspicuous in their absence are remarks about her personal life, especially as an adult. No comments are made about Miss Lemus, her friend and colleague of many years. According to her autobiography, there were no men in her life, other than her brother and younger friends and pupils. She described her childhood, youth, and university years in a very positive manner, despite the adverse conditions under which she lived.

Helene Lange (1848–1930)[8]

Helene Lange wrote her memoirs at the age of seventy and a large segment was devoted to her childhood and youth. Her preference for the impersonal subject, *man* (one), in many of her sentences is quite conspicuous. She stated in the preface that she wrote with the following criteria in mind: "If I have refused to have anything to do with that often recurring desire, I did so with the conviction that my whole life has been dedicated to and concerned with *one* thought, *one* interest, in order to realize it in the real world."[9] It may be assumed that that one main thought and interest was women's cultural task. The entire presentation is dry, much like Tiburtius's, but it is representative of a middle-class environment of the second half of the nineteenth century. The struggles of her youth are described with considerable understatement. Childhood and youth were far back in her past and were presented in a soft light.

Lily Braun (1865–1916)[10]

Lily Braun wrote the first volume of her *Memoirs of a Socialist Woman* at the relatively young age of forty-five. In this first volume she described in great detail her childhood and youth as the daughter of a Prussian general. That work ends with the death of her first husband, whom she married at the age of twenty-six and with whom she lived for only a short period. Braun's autobiography is probaby most like that of Fanny Lewald, as it was obviously also modeled on Goethe's. In the introduction, she writes: "The people who have spent some time with me get angry and call me a deserter; it appears to me they are the disloyal ones."[11] She does not glorify her childhood but it is depicted in the context of problematic family relationships which are presented with psychological and sociological understanding. There is nothing *bürgerlich* (bourgeois) in this autobiography, if one understands *bürgerlich* to mean middle-class. A dissertation done on Lily Braun in the 1930s had an appropriate title: *Lily Braun: A Journalist of Sentiment.*[12]

Marianne Weber (1870–1954)[13]

Marianne Weber wrote her memoirs during World War II and probably completed them right after the German capitulation—at the age of seventy-five. They are very long and begin with a description of her mother's life, who died when she was a very young child. In fact, the detailed descriptions of both her mother's and her father's life that frame the childhood memoirs are quite remarkable. Autobiographical material on how she chose her husband is not found in her memoirs but in the biography of her husband.[14] Weber essentially saw herself as a small part of a "whole." That probably results from her sociological training or possibly from her individual character. It should be emphasized that this woman specialized in describing other people's lives. She seemed to live her life through the lives of other people. Given that, and the fact that she was a social scientist, meant she rarely reflected on her own personal feelings. Her memories of childhood play an unimportant role, since the main themes of the autobiography are "women's emancipation," "the relationship between the sexes," and the "political development of Germany after World War I." Her childhood in a protective middle-class environment in provincial East Westphalia seemed hardly reconcilable to her with her later life with Max Weber, the famous social scientist who taught in Berlin, Freiburg, Munich, and Heidelberg. The central theme of the memoirs is the political crisis of the enlightened upper middle class in Germany from the onset of the twentieth century through the Nazi period; therefore, her remarks about childhood were merely preliminary.

Gertrud Bäumer (1873–1954)[15]

Gertrud Bäumer minutely described the stages of her childhood in three large sections of her memoirs. The first two deal with the period up to the age of nine, when her father died; that included her early childhood in Pomerania and the family's short stay in the booming industrial city of Essen. After her father's death, Bäumer lived in her grandmother's upper-middle-class home in Halle/Saale and she described the life style, the social and family relationships, and the educational possibilities for young girls in great detail. This part of her memoirs was written in a very emotional but conventional style. Although certainly not intended, the passages where she awkwardly attempted to describe her inner feelings evoke for the reader associations with trivial late-nineteenth-century women's novels. Up to the moment when she decided to attend a university and join the fight for women's right to study and the women's emancipation movement in general, her childhood is described at great length, and it is quite apparent how the family and other friends influenced her. For that reason, Bäumer's memoirs are a valuable source for the examination of girls' childhood experiences in the second half of the nineteenth century.

Elly Heuss-Knapp (1881–1950)[16]

Elly Heuss-Knapp's *Ausblick vom Münsterturm (View from a Münster Tower)* is a very short retrospective which she wrote while relatively young; it only covers the first forty years of her life. The writing style is quite interesting. It is emotionally reserved (compared to Gertrud Bäumer's memoirs—they were about the same age) but at the same time not intellectually stiff. The fact that the two hundred pages are replete with many quotes attests to her high-quality education. The whole text is full of self-irony but yet is witty and light. The main theme is her life as a German, first as a child and then as a young woman, in Strassburg after 1870. She felt at home there and evidently wanted to attest to that fact. She was quite aware of the political and historical context of her life, which is atypical for female autobiographies. In this respect, although she was middle-class and utterly bourgeois, she went beyond the boundaries of the middle-class women's movement of her time. She probably considered it self-evident that the "personal" is political That linkage of the personal with the political is certainly also a result of the influence of her father, the economist Georg Friedrich Knapp.

III
GIRLS IN THE FAMILY

Es ist Menschenunkunde, wenn sich die Leute einbilden, unser Geist sei anders und zu anderen Bedürfnissen konstituiert, und wir könnten z.E. ganz des Mannes oder Sohnes Existenz mitzehren.

It is ignorant of people to imagine that our spirit is different and suited to
other needs and that we can live only through the existence of a husband
or a son.

—Rahel Varnhagen

All nine women, whose autobiographies I have described, wrote
about their lives after having become active in public life. In entering the
limelight, they all left the sphere prescribed for women in the nineteenth
century. That subject was constantly discussed either directly or indirectly in these memoirs. The fact that their lives were "unique" must have
affected their perception of childhood experiences and the way they
viewed their position in their families. It certainly acted as a filter for their
memories. The next section of this essay will examine these and other
questions from the vantage point of the autobiographies. Several general
hypotheses about nineteenth-century concepts of education for girls
which I have made will be integrated into the analysis.

Research on socialization has shown that firstborn children (as well as
the single child in a family) are more highly motivated than those born
into a different position within the sibling sequence.[17] Of these nine
women, five were firstborn children: Lewald, Anneke, Braun, Weber,
and Bäumer. In all these women's lives, their father's support and influence was a primary factor in the process of socialization. They all
portrayed their fathers in a positive way, even when they were hurt by
them, as was the case with Lily Braun. Some of the women offered a very
romanticized description of their fathers, for example, Anneke and especially Bäumer. She spoke of her father as if he were an idolized and
inaccessible lover. That may be explained by the fact that he died when
she was nine years old and therefore her image of him was not affected by
puberty or adulthood. Of the other four women, who were not firstborn
children, Heuss-Knapp and Lange also harbored tender, loving feelings
for their fathers. Lange viewed her father as a liberal educator who,
during her motherless childhood, protected her from the tyranny of conventions about education for girls. Heuss-Knapp said she was indebted to
her father for his contribution to her intellectual development. The relative freedom from convention that she enjoyed while growing up almost
motherless was largely due to the influence of her well-educated father.
She wrote: "When I weigh what we learned from my father and grandfather and what we learned at school, the scale is out of balance, as we
were not just raised at home, we were educated."[18]

Lewald loved her father dearly, as is evident in her moving description of him. Most importantly, he was concerned about her intellectual
development. Dohm felt that her father was completely unimportant and,
accordingly, said little about him. This is also true for Tiburtius, who, in a
restrained way, described her father as difficult and a hypochondriac. Due

to his mental instability, Weber was no longer able to live with her father after her mother's death. She grew up in her paternal grandmother's home.

Relationships with mothers cannot be as easily delineated. Weber, Lange, and Heuss-Knapp lost their mothers at an early age. Lewald had a very difficult relationship with her mother, as she objected to Fanny's early deviation from the generally accepted female mode of behavior. For Fanny, her mother represented the conventional middle-class Jewish woman. Braun had an extremely bad relationship with her mother, which she attributed to her mother's conventionality and the arrogance and emotional reserve of the Prussian nobility. Bäumer's mother was described as weak and as having little influence on the child. Tiburtius wrote about her mother with great warmth, but Heuss-Knapp implied that her mother remained a stranger to her because she was often ill and spent little time with her. Dohm hated her mother and said explicitly that her mother saw her as an unloved child and she admitted that fact openly. One might assume that, in the case of firstborn daughters especially, there might be competition between mothers and daughters for the father's attention. Heuss-Knapp described her family as one where the mother and older daughter, and the father and younger daughter, were quite close and where there was a substantial social and cultural rift between the parents.

The importance which the girls occasionally attached to a grandmother, aunt, or grandfather is conspicuous. Braun loved her maternal grandmother very much and was strongly influenced by her. Bäumer's grandmother acted as a matriarch; Gertrud, her mother, and her siblings lived in this grandmother's home for many years following her father's death. Anneke adored her paternal grandfather, and Weber, an orphan at an early age, saw her paternal grandmother and aunt as her "parents," although her maternal grandfather, a middle-class nineteenth-century patriarch, also "fathered" her. For Lange, living in her grandfather's house with her many unmarried aunts was the most important part of her childhood following her mother's death. Heuss-Knapp said of her paternal grandfather, in whose home she spent the first year and a half of her life, "The passionate (leidenschaftliche) love between my grandfather and me began when I was four months old."[19] Even Dohm, who was unable to say much of anything good about her family, wondered if she did not possibly inherit her sensitivity from her grandfather.

Relationships with siblings varied with these women. Dohm is very negative; her brothers constantly teased her, making her childhood hell. Lewald evidently considered herself in an exceptional position as the oldest daughter and she hardly mentioned her younger brothers and sisters. Braun, who essentially grew up as an only child, played the roles of mother and teacher for her beloved younger sister. Bäumer, like Lewald, said very little, again perhaps because she was the oldest child. Lange loved both of her brothers deeply and wrote a great deal about them. Many of her social contacts and friends came about through their help. Heuss-Knapp reported little but often wrote using the "we" form, which was probably meant to include her sister, who was two years older than she. Tiburtius, even at the age of eighty, was still the "wonderful little one" who is always allowed to participate but never forgets the gap separating her from the "older" ones. Her brother played a decisive role in her life. The women who had brothers perceived the differences in girls' and boys' socialization more critically and noted it in their memoirs.

Extending beyond the close-knit parent-child relationship in the majority of the families, there was a strong material and emotional relationship with other family members, which was very important for the girls. In this limited sampling, general trends in sibling relationships cannot be determined. The father usually played a decisive role in the families where the women left the private household sphere to enter public life as doctors, authors, scientists, teachers, and politicians. With this kind of source material, it is difficult to know whether the statements are based in reality. The society in which these women grew up reserved the public sphere for men. Therefore, it is likely that these women's fathers, through their support, paved the way for their entrance into public life. These same women were very critical of their mothers because they saw in them all the limitations on women as wives, housewives, and mothers.

The extended family was not unimportant even though almost all the women lived in "nuclear" families. Grandparents and unmarried aunts accepted important responsibilities for the girls' upbringing and education. Less can be said about sibling relationships. This is due to the fact that in the autobiographies "childhood" is viewed in conjunction with later adult life; memories are selected accordingly. Siblings necessarily played a less important role than the adults in the family.

SEXUALITY AND EROTICISM BEFORE AND AFTER PUBERTY

It may be assumed that the onset of menstruation is a very important experience in the life of every female child. It may also be assumed that, with the taboo on sexuality, this topic would not be mentioned in autobiographical sources. Quite surprisingly, there was one exception in my selection. Braun devoted a small section to it.[20] In several of the women's descriptions of that period in their lives, the similarities stood out; they were hostile, discontented with themselves, and at odds with their traditional role and their families' expectations (Lewald, Braun, Dohm). They felt uncomfortable with their constantly changing bodies (Braun, Tiburtius). They all wanted to read more books than they were allowed to read, since reading was not suitable for a young lady (Lewald, Dohm, Braun). In short, they all remembered this period as an extremely unpleasant one. After having turned fourteen, they seemed to accept the fact that people considered them as future women. As Lange put it, the *Wartezeit* (the waiting period) begins at that age.

There was little mention of sexuality and eroticism during this "waiting period"; almost nothing was said about their relationships with their own sex or with the opposite sex: Lewald is adored by a student whom she loves but he constantly provokes her wrath. Dohm, who was a beautiful girl, had several uncomfortable encounters with brash men and she worshipped a young hero whom she saw dying in the street during the Revolution of 1848. Anneke's memoirs break off at an earlier point, as she married when she was only seventeen years old. Lange consciously excluded this period of her life from her memoirs. Tiburtius is also silent, but Bäumer wrote unbelievably bombastic descriptions of experiences she supposedly had in this period of her life; the reader wonders if the good woman knew what she was talking about. She described going ice skating on two occasions with a Norwegian student and she spoke of exhilaration on one February night in that same year. Both obviously served as a substitute for erotic and sexual desires, although neither really had anything to do with that aspect of life. This approach clearly demonstrates nineteenth-century prudishness. In contrast, Braun, who became sexually mature at an early age, gave full rein to her desire for adulation, love, and playful eroticism. She thereby broke the strict code of etiquette of the Prussian nobility on numerous occasions. Since she was completely at odds with society, her memoirs are quite different in this regard than the other autobiographies. Somewhat comparable is Dohm's description of her young heroine's need for love, but Dohm portrayed that as a weakness. Braun, however, considered love and eroticism to be rightful desires which were undeniably hers. Weber used an unmistakably matter-of-fact style. She described in a very dispassionate way her school crushes, her poor chances of marriage, and the desolation of the *Wartezeit*. Her life was shaped by her encounter with one man—Max Weber—and so at seventy-five, she looked upon the loves of her youth as meaningless. Heuss-Knapp was totally discreet. Here is how she described those years: "We slowly grew out of childhood. One attended confirmation classes and wore long robes."[21] She spent the *Wartezeit* in a more meaningful way than the others (namely, Dohm, Lange, Lewald, Weber)—as a teacher and volunteer in Strassburg's relief programs for the poor. She wrote:

> When I think back on this period it seems like a rich and happy time, but youth is too restless to be happy and in many diary entries and letters there is much written about wounds and scars. But people often deceive

each other and I had the very girlish feeling that everything was not yet real life. Sometimes I felt like I was sitting in a waiting room.[22]

Heuss-Knapp's life was the least influenced by the admonition that a woman is supposed to fall into a man's lap and become a wife, housewife, and mother. She also did not have to be concerned about earning her own living. Therefore, she was able to make many friends and have time for many activities. She described her youth in such a way that it could have been written by a young man. Female influence on her life seemed to be minimal in her youth; it only became a factor later in her life when a career and marriage were important to her.

From puberty onward, some of the women had close friendships with other girls. Lewald devoted a whole chapter to her friend Mathilde and Mathilde's family. Dohm had a girlfriend with whom she shared her enthusiasm for the Revolution of 1848. Braun corresponded with her cousin Mathilde and often quoted these letters to document how she felt at that particular time. Adult friendships played an even more important role for these women. Having read many other autobiographies (especially by twentieth-century men, e.g., Sperber, Canetti, K. Mann), I believe that these women considered these friendships unimportant. In writing, none of them was searching for a "lost past." Rather, they sought to portray their lives in terms of their successful emergence into public life—out of their minority status within the family. To them, their friendships with other girls were not important to that development. That says nothing, of course, about the actual existence of friendships these women had with girls when they were ten to eighteen years old. Relationships with their own sex were simply not a topic of conversation. Only Lewald wrote about her friendships with other girls, and she said somewhat warningly: ". . . and when you have not disclosed sensuality in children's love, you should respect it and leave it alone."[23]

From research on the middle-class women's movement, we know that the sexual repression of women, or the discovery of specifically female repression, was not discussed in the nineteenth century. These autobiographies support that finding. Only the more "radical" women, Dohm and Braun, mentioned the topic explicitly. They describe incomprehensible taboos and sexual repression and exploitation. All of the women perceived puberty as an unhappy time. Only with their later education and marriage did they overcome that and make the adjustment to family and societal expectations.

SEARCHING FOR AND SELECTING A HUSBAND

Some of the autobiographies included stories about crushes and love affairs; some did not. There were some borderline cases. For example, Tiburtius's relationship with her brother went beyond normal boundaries. The fact that some autobiographies had dramatic descriptions of love affairs and some were more *bürgerlich* was not just a matter of style; it is related to social environments. The non-Jewish women did not include love stories (Lange, Tiburtius, Bäumer, Weber, Heuss-Knapp), but the autobiographies of Jewish women and women of noble birth did (Lewald, Dohm, Braun); the latter believed that the "great loves" of their lives contributed to their development and they spoke highly of these men in their memoirs. One wonders if the other women did not have experiences such as these, or if they did, perhaps they were too disappointed by the men to include them in their memoirs. They could have been lacking in self-confidence, fearing that the men they loved in their youth would not be happy about being mentioned in an autobiography. Of course, discretion might have been the reason these women concealed or merely hinted at the loves of their youth.

In all of the autobiographies it was clear that there was a direct relationship between the search for a husband and their education. In this respect, stories about men are not a private matter but rather an important part of their public life. Those women who could not be expected to marry because of their family's financial situation (Bäumer, Tiburtius) hardly mentioned searching for a husband. They began preparing for their careers, as teachers, at an early age. Those women with adequate finances, who therefore could count on getting married, had to struggle to get an education and did not put as much emphasis on the search for a mate. Lange spent much of her time at balls and the like but did not specifically complain about such inactivity. Weber suffered the life style of an unmarried daughter in a secure middle-class family. Dohm hated the *Wartezeit* and latched on to the first man she found. Lewald regretted the time she had spent in meaningless social activities looking for the right man and at twenty-six consciously decided to remain single and devote her life to her career as a writer. Her later marriage was a marriage of love which was against all conventions. Looking back, Anneke, viewed her marriage at seventeen as a conventional one, which it probably was.[24] Braun, at the age of twenty, was not permitted to marry her great love, as he did not meet the standards of her aristocratic family; thereafter she turned to writing and teaching. Although her intelligent grandmother thought she would have to earn her own living since the family was destitute, Braun's parents still hoped that, with her good looks, the prestigious family name, and the promise of a later inheritance, she would be able to find a suitable husband. She was not, however, at all willing to enter a marriage of convenience. For her, marriage had to be based on love and, moreover, she credited her husbands for the role they played in her education and intellectual development.

Heuss-Knapp chose her husband in a "modern" way. While studying in Berlin, she met him as a result of their shared political work in the

Naumann circle. The letters she wrote to Theodor Heuss at that time demonstrate that she considered herself an equal partner in their marriage.[25] Actually the marriage did have consequences for her education and career, but it was her own "free" decision.

Three of these nine women were able to plan their professions without problems. For two of the three, the impetus was their poor marriage chances. All of the others had to fight for their education, which would give them intellectual and possibly financial independence. Lewald, Dohm, and Braun were the only women who found the conditions for marriage completely disgraceful and denounced society for it. Heuss-Knapp, the youngest of the authors, was almost a unique case, probably one of the first in her generation. Her life stands as a symbol of the revolutionary tendencies in women's education. Of these nine women, only two were "married off"—Dohm and Anneke. But both rebelled against their fate; Dohm primarily in an intellectual way, through writing, and Anneke got a divorce and dared thereafter to be a social outcast.

Girlhood ended for these women either with marriage or with their decision to pursue higher education or a career (Tiburtius, Bäumer, Lange, Weber, Braun, Heuss-Knapp). There was clearly an opposite pattern for middle-class men in the nineteenth century. The search for a wife seldom coincided with education. The only general exception to this was a variety of government positions which paid poorly and therefore not only limited the choice of prospective wives considerably but also postponed marriage to a later age. I emphasize this point because obviously there was a real difference between the way girls and boys conceived of their own identity and development. This point will be examined further in the discussion of school and education.

SCHOOL AND GIRLS' EDUCATION

Girls had limited educational possibilities in the nineteenth century and this can be illustrated with the nine women under discussion here. Normally girls attended a private (sometimes coeducational) preschool, elementary school, and after that private *Töchterschulen* (girls' schools). Of the nine, only Bäumer attended a public elementary school, but that was made possible by the fact that her father was a school administrator; otherwise it would have been quite unusual, given her social status. Lewald, Dohm, Tiburtius, Lange, Weber, and Heuss-Knapp attended private girls' schools. Private tutors were used for Anneke, Tiburtius (as long as her parents lived in the country), and Braun (depending on the situation in the garrison where her father was stationed). Lewald and Lange attended private elementary schools that were coeducational.

Dohm and Heuss-Knapp went to teachers' colleges, and Tiburtius studied for her *Abitur* (required university entrance examination) on her own. Weber attended a well-known boarding school in Hannover for two years, and Lange boarded in a pastor's home in southern Germany. All the women wrote extensively about their schooling. In almost all cases the education they received was unmethodical, often of poor quality, and not especially broad. The main emphasis was always on literature, religion, foreign languages, and history. Science, mathematics, and ancient languages, the core of higher education for boys in the nineteenth century, were never included.

While reading what these women wrote about their education, I felt a certain sense of tragedy that their childhood had been so poorly utilized. This was often true for boys as well, but the quality of girls' education was certainly lower. Lewald, of all the women, had the most ambitious ideas about girls' education. She said of her father: "I do not believe that my father ever devoted much time to books on education or even thought much about it, with the possible exception of Jean Paul's *Levana*, which I know he had read quite early. What should you do to give your children a good education?"[26] Although Jean Paul perfected the idea of sex stereotyping in his *Levana*, it is an ambitious book on education. From the point of teaching, Heuss-Knapp's intellectual education went far beyond that offered in the schools. Both she and Lewald were taught by their fathers on a daily basis.

Bäumer and Braun also documented social experiences at school. Bäumer attended a public *Volksschule* (elementary school) and encountered class distinctions at an early age. A lower-class girl enunciated these differences, which Bäumer's liberal middle-class parents would never have done. Braun was attracted to a Jewish child who, in the anti-Semitic atmosphere of her exclusive girls' institute in Berlin, had been labeled an outcast. Lily's parents forbade her to have contact with these "rich social climbers." In general, life in the private girls' schools of Oldenburg, Stralsund, Strassburg, and Lemgo must have been undisturbed by the social tensions of the *Kaiserreich* (Imperial Germany).

Teachers, both female and male, were influential people. Lewald admired her principal's talent for teaching. During her puberty, Braun had a tutor who obviously did a good job teaching her German and history, as it gave her a framework for her intellectual development. Most of the teachers, however, were described in a colorless way in the autobiographies. Dohm was the only one who was critical, especially on the question of the sexual exploitation of schoolgirls. By doing that, she courageously discussed an aspect of violence against children which it was taboo to discuss. Tiburtius, Lange, Bäumer, Weber, and Heuss-Knapp, all graduates of the *höhere Töchterschulen* established in the nineteenth century for middle-class girls, had nothing exciting to report. Truly relevant experiences in their education usually came after ten or more years in school. When Tiburtius was seventeen, she began teaching children of the nobility on the eastern bank of the Elbe and she gained considerable insight into people. At twenty-three she went to England to continue her teacher training. She had planned on establishing her own private *höhere Töchterschule*. But her studies went in another direction, mainly due to her brother; he wanted her to study medicine and helped her prepare for her university entrance examinations.

Lange spent a year as a "boarder" in a parsonage in southern Germany, where she was allowed to listen in on intellectual discussions of a kind which never would haven taken place in Oldenburg. Looking back, she was convinced that the impetus for her later involvement in the fight for women's right to study was developed then. Tiburtius also worked as a tutor for a family and then taught in a French girls' boarding school while completing her own education. Only after having come of age was she able to fulfill her dream and pass her teaching examinations. Bäumer's situation was similar to that of Tiburtius; her family raised her with the idea that she would be able to earn her own living. Given the thirty-year age difference, by the time Bäumer went to school, there was a formalized system and so she was able to go directly from a *höhere Töchterschule* to a teachers' seminary and she became an elementary-school teacher. She later taught at a *höhere Mädchenschule* in Magdeburg and then, after gaining some experience, went to Berlin to prepare for her *Oberlehrerin* (advanced teacher) examinations. She passed them and became actively involved in the women's movement and began studying the social sciences and eventually received her doctor's degree.

As mentioned earlier, Weber was allowed to spend two years at a boarding school, which she wrote enthusiastically about, but she certainly did not receive a systematic education there. At the age of twenty-two she was allowed to leave home to pursue her musical training in Berlin. She was not under any economic pressure to earn her own living. Only after her marriage to Max Weber did she seriously begin to educate herself in a systematic way in philosophy, law, and sociology. Heuss-Knapp also attended a *Töchterschule* but she spent her girlhood in a way that was quite different from the others (the others would not have been allowed to do this). She was involved in social politics, both through her work in a boys' home and also intellectually through working on plans for relief programs for the poor. She wrote about that and she studied economics for a couple of semesters in Berlin and Freiburg. In other words, she represented a new type of woman. She was not limited to being a *höhere Tochter,* which was the fate of the other eight women. Therefore she was neither an object of prestige nor a financial burden. Because she had a very intelligent father and a very unconventional mother and given the specific political and cultural atmosphere in Strassburg, she had many educational experiences which the other women had to fight for or missed completely. It is certainly not a coincidence that she was the youngest of the authors.

From what we have seen, it is not possible to establish any standardized educational pattern for women before 1900. Education was organized by the family and it was only in the period between 1902 and 1908 that Prussia, for example, made all children's education equal; university education was not open to women until 1908. Before that time, all women had to fight for what education they received, as the schools were not organized for that purpose.

In their description of school education many of the women were inclined to compare themselves to boys or men. Women who were later publicly active had to make such a comparison. Lewald even reported that Prussian Privy Councillor Dinter, an influential school administrator, once said to her during an examination: "'With your brain, you should have been a boy!' But then he added, in a friendly tone: 'If you turn out to be a fine woman, that's all right too!' "[27] She was happy with that. Dohm wrote: "I don't know why my brothers never learned anything. They attended good schools and the most gifted one successfully made it to the third form. I know why we girls never learned. In those days there was hardly anything taught that went beyond the most elementary. The boys had it good. They had gymnastics and they were allowed to romp freely in the streets. . . . At that time I had the idea that boys were real boors who never washed and for them school meant nothing."[28]

Tiburtius obviously adored her older brothers and male cousins more than her older sisters. Anneke portrayed herself as a wild horseback rider. Lange suffered because she was made to knit while the boys were allowed to play outside. Because of the way Heuss-Knapp carried on, other girls were not allowed to play with her and her sister. Braun played with a farm boy in Garmisch and she was also a reckless horseback rider. Bäumer and Weber both grew up in an environment without a strong male presence and either did not experience the trials and tribulations of being compared to boys or did not think it was worthy of mention. Almost all the women had to suffer through long, boring hours of fancy needlework. Though their personalities were oriented in a different direction, family and school clearly trained them to perform typical female tasks. When they were young, they identified themselves with such figures as "the female professor in Bologna" (Lewald), a "fairy princess," or a "revolutionary heroine." As they grew older, they were more realistic and dreamt of becoming "well-traveled teachers." Lange, Tiburtius, Bäumer, and

Weber were the product of the changes in the second half of the nineteenth century and of their social class and made no mention of their dreams.

IV
NORMAL CHILDHOOD EXPERIENCES

Gottfried Kössler, in his book *Mädchenkindheiten im 19. Jahrhundert (Girls' Childhood in the 19th Century)*, attempted "to find indices for a correlation between the intentions of the producers of ideologies and their theories and the socialization agents—mothers, fathers, school—on the one side and those who were socialized on the other but they could not be produced."[29] In other words, he was looking for "breaches" out of which emancipatory movements might have originated. He suspected these would appear in "dreams, friendships, games, adventures, and other non-genital forms of sexuality." But he found little evidence in his sources. His conclusion that these breaches existed, nonetheless, is far-fetched, as far as I am concerned. In my opinion, these deviations were not just hidden, as Kössler argued, they were nonexistent. I will cite three examples from the autobiographies I have examined to refute Kössler's thesis.

Lewald said of her first young love: "Female nature is such that it is so instinctively independent of men that even in youth it automatically feels unwilling to be the property of the man who claims her."[30] Here she justified her early engagement—though it was against her will—it was right in line with prevailing opinion. The sense of the contradictions and even rebellion against socialization practices are evident here but they were not associated with "female nature." Tiburtius, to cite a second example, does not mention the fact that she wanted to study medicine. The reader is given the strange impression that her family planned this for her, but that is not very plausible. That is especially true since she enjoyed studies and was a very innovative and involved doctor. She evidently did not see this contradiction in her memoirs. The only woman who had an exaggerated sense of happiness in her autobiography was Braun. It is fairly easy to understand that. When compared with the other autobiographers, she spent her childhood in a non-middle-class, elite environment where she was the only daughter of a father who adored her. She was thereby forced into opposition, since her milieu was so extremely contradictory. If economic necessity had not arisen, she might not have aspired to a career as a journalist. Rather, she might have sought happiness in the private sphere.

In reality, most of these women's childhoods were without dreams, adventures, other forms of sexuality, or any close friendships other than what was acceptable. Lewald's dream of the female professor in Bologna is moderate and even realistic in comparison to Brentano's *Wolkenschwimmer*. The women who largely shaped the women's movement in the period of the second half of the nineteenth century and up until World War I (Lange, Bäumer, Weber, Tiburtius) did not dream of any "new worlds."[31] The main criticism of their childhoods was the poor education they received. Almost all these women perceived their childhood as a harmonious time. Sexuality was definitely not a subject which a nineteenth-century woman was able to write about without risking her social status. Most of the women examined here felt no such restriction.

To summarize, it may be said the childhood of these women is not distinguished by anything out of the ordinary. That they were able to plan their own lives was made possible by family circumstances, being Jewish, early intellectual interests, and economic necessity. By abandoning the prescribed way of life for women, they were able to fight for women's rights and for life styles outside conventional marriages. In later life, they all were active in the fight to improve women's education, which proves that they had reflected critically on their childhood. It was not really until the twentieth century that some successes were achieved, namely, a change in girls' childhood development, but we know now that the work is not yet finished. There are barriers which none of them foresaw except Marianne Weber.

The identity of these women developed within a tension—between the accepted goals of socialization that were then prevalent and their intellectual interests—a tension between their desire for autonomy and their needs which conformed to the goals of socialization. There was no set pattern for life. That is also the reason why love affairs with men played such an important role in the lives of some of these women—more important than in the lives of men. That is also the reason why these women's career goals were usually derivatives of "motherhood." We cannot simply attribute that to patriarchal influence. As women, we must ask ourselves if our childhood as girls—which had these same tensions—did not also shape our lives with all the corresponding ambiguous identities?

NOTES

1. Philippe Ariès, *Centuries of Childhood* (New York, 1969), pp. 50–61.

2. Dittrich Eckhard and Juliane Dittrich-Jacobi, "Die Autobiographie als Quelle zur Sozialgeschichte der Erziehung," in *Aus Geschichten lernen*, ed. by

Dieter Baacke and Theodor Schulze (Munich, 1979), pp. 99–119. I have not included a discussion of pedagogical theories of girls' education. I would refer to Elisabeth Blochmann, *Das "Frauenzimmer" und die "Gelehrsamkeit"* (Heidelberg, 1966), where the topic is covered thoroughly. For more recent work, see Gerda Tornieporth, *Studien zur Frauenbildung* (Weinheim, 1977), and Monika Simmel, *Erziehung zum Weibe* (Frankfurt, 1980).

3. Fanny Lewald, *Meine Lebensgeschichte*, ed. by Gisela Brinker-Gabler (Frankfurt, 1980); *Römisches Tagebuch 1845–56* (Leipzig, 1927).

4. My interpretation is limited since I was unable to find the original and thus I relied on Brinker-Gabler's edition. Regula Venske pointed out to me that Brinker-Gabler was very selective and thus did not give the complete picture of Lewald's complex life.

5. Mathilde Franziska Anneke, "Autobiographisches Fragment," in *Mathilde Franziska Anneke in Selbstzeugnissen und Dokumenten*, ed. by Maria Wagner (Frankfurt, 1980), pp. 20–26.

6. Hedwig Dohm, *Schicksale einer Seele* (Berlin, 1899); see also Elisabeth Heimpel, "Hedwig Dohm," *Neue Deutsche Biographie* (Berlin, 1952–80), 4, pp. 41–42.

7. Franziska Tiburtius, *Erinnerungen einer Achtzigjährigen* (Berlin, 1925).

8. Helene Lange, *Lebenserinnerungen* (Berlin, 1927).

9. Ibid., p. 7.

10. Lily Braun, *Memoiren einer Sozialistin. Lehrjahre* (Munich, 1909); see also Elisabeth Heimpel, "Lily Braun," *Neue Deutsche Biographie* (Berlin, 1952–80), 2, pp. 546–47.

11. Braun, p. 3.

12. G. Gärtner, *Lily Braun. Eine Publizistin des Gefühls*, Ph.D. dissertation, Heidelberg, 1935.

13. Marianne Weber, *Lebenserinnerungen* (Bremen, 1948).

14. Marianne Weber, *Max Weber. Ein Lebensbild* (Tübingen, 1926).

15. Gertrud Bäumer, *Lebensweg durch eine Zeitenwende* (Tübingen, 1933).

16. Elly Heuss-Knapp, *Ausblick vom Münsterturm* (Tübingen, 1952); *Bürgerin zweier Welten. Ein Leben in Briefen und Aufzeichnungen* (Tübingen, 1961).

17. Jaques Vontobel, *Leistungsbedürfnis und soziale Umwelt* (Bern, 1970), pp. 81–84.

18. Heuss-Knapp, *Ausblick*, p. 36.

19. Ibid., p. 23.

20. Braun, pp. 105–6.

21. Heuss-Knapp, *Ausblick*, p. 36.

22. Ibid., p. 66.

23. Lewald, p. 82.

24. According to Wagner, this was not merely a marriage of convenience. I do not agree with her argument. This applies to her comment on the Aston review, in which Anneke accused Aston of marrying a man she did not love. In my opinion, this does not prove that Anneke could not have criticized herself for the same reason. Wagner, p. 28.

25. Heuss-Knapp, *Bürgerin*, pp. 81–109.

26. Lewald, pp. 55–56.
27. Ibid., pp. 59–60.
28. Dohm, pp. 28–29.
29. Gottfried Kössler, *Mädchenkindheiten im 19. Jahrhundert* (Giessen, 1979), p. 91. To a certain extent, Kössler and I use the same source material.
30. Lewald, p. 112.
31. They belonged to the *Bildungsbürgertum* (the educated middle class). This specific German social class was defined by Klaus Vondung in *Das wilhelminische Bildungsbürgertum* (Göttingen, 1976), but Vondung did not include the women's movement.

The Radicalization of
Lily Braun[1]

Alfred G. Meyer

Lily Braun,[2] born 1865, was the daughter of Hans von Kretschmann
(1832–99), who served with great distinction in the Prussian Army, rising
to the rank of General of the Infantry. He was authoritarian father, stern,
irascible, and punitive, yet generous and even tender at times—an im-
pulsive man who was lavish in giving and spending, and totally inept in
handling money. Politically he was reactionary, Prussian rather than German in his loyalties, opposed to Bismarck and to the Reich. As a child,
Lily feared him; as a young adult, she had contempt for him; in later life,
she revered his memory.

Her mother, Jenny von Kretschmann, was descended from an age-old
baronial family *(Uradel)*. She too was a stern disciplinarian, but, in contrast to her husband, looked on life with profound pessimism. She felt
herself to be a victim and believed that women were born to be victims.
In the family she was the voice of practicality and common sense; she
preached and practiced self-control. The relationship between her and
Lily became very warm; but in the daughter's memoirs the figure of the
mother is cold and forbidding.

Lily von Kretschmann received the conventional upbringing of an
aristocratic daughter; she was taught French and English, reading, writing, and reckoning, but got little formal training of an academic sort. She
took piano and drawing lessons, and was introduced to literature and
history by private tutors. But her principal training was in being a future
lady and housekeeper. Cooking, sewing, needlework, and related skills
were stressed. Sex education, of course, was not included in this curriculum, although she did receive it, at age thirteen, from a chamber-

maid. Religious instructions were given sporadically by her mother, and more systematically by a pastor in preparation for confirmation in the Protestant Church. Her mother's teachings seem to have concentrated on the message that it is women's duty to serve, to suffer, and to be silent. As a child of nobility, Lily was also given the service ideology of her class, according to which aristocratic privilege carried obligations. The early effects of this message made her incredibly arrogant.

Lily was a sickly child and, perhaps because of this, often lonely. A certain willfulness and rebelliousness, probably related to her arrogance, further contributed to her frequent withdrawal into fantasy worlds of her own. All her life she would love fairy tales and myths, and the first book she wrote, in her late teens, was a collection of children's stories, published under a male pseudonym.[3]

She also very early displayed a philosophic disposition and a high moral conscience. She took the ethical commands of Christianity seriously but questioned some of its dogmas and already in her early teens convinced herself that the behavior of confessed Christians by no means matched their professed beliefs. When she voiced these doubts, she was quickly scolded for her impious questions, which naturally deepened her doubts. Although she took the teachings of Christianity seriously, she found hypocrisy abominable. At the age of fourteen, when she was to be confirmed, she refused, arguing that she could not perjure herself before God's altar. Her parents nonetheless made her go through the ceremony in order to maintain proper appearances.

One year later the exasperated parents sent their unruly child, now fifteen, to her father's oldest sister, the widow of a very rich Augsburg nobleman, in whose salon Lily had a chance to mingle with the intellectual and aristocratic elite of southern Germany and Austria. Two years of harsh finishing in Aunt Clothilde's home seemed to have tamed the rebellious teen-ager into a proper young lady. In reality she harbored deep resentment against all the most important principles underlying her upbringing. She believed these principles to be pretense of the same kind that she had detected in Christian practice; emphasis on proper form, polite phrases and manner to mask personal ambition, greed, and lust— this seemed to her to be the lesson all children were taught. Conventional child-rearing, in short, was training children how to lie. Significantly, her first serious work, which remained unfinished, was a treatise on child-rearing inspired by Nietzsche's philosophy; its title was *Wider die Lüge (Against All Lies)*.[4]

If her mother and her aunt had sought to make of her a proper young lady who would make a good catch in the marriage market, her maternal grandmother tried to give her a thorough humanist education. Born Jenny von Pappenheim, Lily's grandmother was the illegitimate daughter of Jérôme Bonaparte, the King of Westphalia. Her mother, the Alsatian countess Diana (see note 3), had moved to Weimar after the collapse of the Napoleonic state, and young Jenny, when she was fifteen, caught the eye of the aging Goethe, became a member of his extended household, and was appointed *Hoffräulein* (young lady-in-waiting) at the ducal court. Her association with the court and the Goethe family lasted until her death, and the opportunities it brought to Lily, the ideas it generated in her, were important in shaping her thinking. The grandmother was steeped in the spirit of Weimar—cosmopolitan, tolerant, humane, and unconventional—and Lily seems to have absorbed this spirit thoroughly.

Even as a child she was a voracious reader, and her reading from age eleven included "adult" literature, including authors then considered avant-gardist or controversial. By the time she was thirteen she had read Goethe's *Werther, Faust, Die Wahlverwandtschaften,* and *Iphigenie.* Within a few years, the authors she had sampled included Ruskin, Browning, Shelley, William Morris, Nietzsche, Ibsen, Wagner, and contemporary defenders of Darwinism.

At the age of seventeen Lily von Kretschmann returned to her parents after two years of rigid training by her aunt. She was well mannered and well connected. She dazzled men with her wit and intelligence, her beauty, her flirtatiousness, and her arrogance. She puzzled those around her by her sharp opinions, her interest in intellectual pursuits, her wild horsemanship, and her unconventional behavior, such as smoking. For the next eight years she was to play two principal roles. At home she was the dutiful daughter who relieved her mother of some of the household drudgery and child care (there was a sister thirteen years younger then Lily). Equally to be taken seriously was her duty to entertain and to be entertained, to cultivate a very active social life with the young officers and the noble families of the garrison. This had two purposes. First, her father, as commander, considered it his duty to open his home to his officers; and as he explained to her, the presence of an attractive daughter would make this much easier for him, never noticing that this made her feel like a whore.[5] Second, and more importantly, the social games this young woman was to play for the next eight years were designed to help her make a catch. The social life in the garrison was, among other things, a marriage market for aristocratic daughters.

For young women of her own social set, the basic purpose in life was to catch a husband whose nobility and wealth were sufficient to make him worthy of marriage. Daughters of the wealthy bourgeoisie and of rich estate owners might rely on their dowries to attract suitable men; and in the highest reaches of the nobility marriages may still have been arranged in conformity with dynastic politics. But a poor officer's daughter (and Hans von Kretschmann was poor) who did not wish to end up as a spinsterish lady-in-waiting at some small court or as an Evangelical deaconess caring for the sick or the insane, had to use all her talents and skills to get a husband, if she did not wish to remain dependent on the charity of more or less distant relatives. Until she had succeeded in this, life for her would essentially be a market in which she was to display herself as eminently desirable merchandise.

The first rule of this marketing game was that she had to make herself seductive. In her memoirs, Braun tells us that she was seven or eight when older relatives introduced her to this role of women: to be pretty, to be seductive, to dominate others through sexuality, and to learn that these love games are intriguing and enjoyable.[6] Rule number two commanded chastity, unapproachability, and untouchability. Women were to be seen but not to be touched, and to be seen only under controlled conditions. The code made clear when a woman might or might not be viewed by a man, and which parts of her were open to view. It allowed some slight and fleeting touch only under the most ceremonious circumstances. Violation of this code was a serious, often unpardonable offense against respectability; and it was the woman who suffered the worst punishment even if the man had been the offender. She should not have allowed the man an opportunity to overstep the bounds of propriety.

The code of chastity also demanded that a young woman be equally charming, seductive, and unapproachable to all young gentlemen of her circle. The slightest deviation, the gentlest hint that she preferred one over all others, would cause the gossip mill—an important social institution—to regard her as promised, engaged, i.e., a particular man's exclusive property. A young woman forced to issue a denial of such an engagement was considered compromised; she should not have allowed things to reach the gossip stage. The rule of conduct demanded asexual coolness until a woman had fully committed herself. A single kiss was enough to pledge her to a man.

The clothes women wore symbolized seduction as well as touch-me-not virginity. The formal ballroom wear bared the neck, the arms, and the upper part of the breasts, and by forcing the women into an exaggerated hourglass shape it accentuated feminine curves. But the dresses also kept the lower extremities hidden, and the stiff corset functioned as an armor plate against lecherous hands during the dance. In short, the clothing of upper-class women symbolized the ambiguity of their situation. Moreover, women's formal attire was designed ingeniously so that they could not dress themselves. All the hooks and buttons were in the back, and the gowns fitted so tightly that a lady needed help getting into them. Upper-class clothing thus reminded the woman of her dependency on others, even if they be only servants.[7]

These two rules of behavior, of course, were incompatible. To be seductive and chaste at the same time was a dilemma in which a young women could hardly do anything right. What the young ladies of the nobility were forced to do in this dilemma was to flirt, i.e., to play with a strange mixture of seductiveness and chastity which made coy pretense of both. Flirting conceived as a serious pursuit—and indeed it was the most serious one a woman could pursue under the circumstances—was a dangerous game in which losing was easier than winning. If the young woman was not seductive enough, she would remain an old maid, cheated of all conventional sexual experience and, much worse, economically dependent on father, uncles, brothers, or charitable institutions, unless she found demeaning employment in a higher servant role. In any event, she would become a physical, intellectual, and social cripple, an object of ridicule. If she flirted too much, she might suffer the same fate because many serious suitors would not risk getting engaged to a woman who appeared to have sexual desires of her own; or she might even slide down into the category of loose woman and become a social outcast. Virgin, old maid, whore, and wife were in fact the only roles society reserved for women in this system. Lily von Kretschmann, in the final analysis, found all four alternatives distasteful, even though for a long time she took it for granted that she would end up as some aristocrat's wife. It is clear from her correspondence, however, that every time this possibility threatened to become reality she saw to it that, through some unconventional behavior, she would turn the suitor away; her favorite means seems to have been to be too openly flirtatious.[8]

What made this man-hunting game, requiring seductiveness and chastity, so devilish was that it demanded cool, dispassionate control over some of the most uncontrollable human urges—sexual desire and related emotions, including jealousy, ambition, rage, and the like—even while artfully arousing and feeding them in flirtation. The young woman's art was supposed to consist in generating desire without fanning it into flames of passion, for once passions flared up the game turned into disaster. In the final analysis, the code of behavior obviously was designed to train men and women, and especially the latter, for frigidity, for only a negative attitude toward sex, arising from fear, from disgust, or from disdain of the opposite gender. This made is possible to play the game without breaking down under it. Lily von Kretschmann, however, was too sensual a woman to lapse into frigidity. Instead, she often was close to collapse, and many times she expressed envy of the whore or of the lower-class girl not caught in this infernal code.[9]

She rebelled with equal stubbornness against the restrictions which conventions placed on her choice of career. She hated housework and had no wish to become either a governess or a lady-in-waiting. Intellectually she sensed her superiority to many men who were entering interesting careers in public life, and she envied them their opportunities. She wished to become *somebody*, to make her mark in the world, to assume a leadership position. Those were forbidden ambitions; even her purely intellectual and artistic interests, pursued as hobbies, tended to give her the reputation of a bluestocking.

Her unpublished papers contain a wealth of letters which she wrote during these years to her best friend and confidante, a distant cousin named Mathilde von Colomb (born 1854). A number of themes recur and predominate in these letters; first, a love of flirting is expressed in a variety of ways: burning sensuality; hedonism; delight in her ability to reduce men to fools through use of her sexuality; a cult of youth and a dread of old age, when all these games would be over; deep resentment of the double moral code; and, as mentioned, envy of lower-class women and prostitutes. "Every person," she wrote when she was twenty-one, "has a wild beast inside which will come to the fore sooner or later, and mine perhaps is the wildest of all; its name is sensuality. Almost since my childhood it has driven me from passion to passion; I have never been able to master it." This sensuality, she suggested in the same letter, was the secret of her many successes with men.[10] "My feverish senses often are attracted by men whose minds and heart repel me; and conversely, my own mind and heart often are captivated where my physical senses almost feel disgust. *If I were ashamed of my instincts,* if I therefore were to cover them with the fig leaf of mendacious amorousness—how many unfortunate marriages I would already have allowed to bind me!"[11]

As mentioned, Lily von Kretschmann deliberately rebuffed many men who in the eyes of her parents and her society would have been good catches. She dreaded marriage, not only because she recognized it as a financial bargain from which considerations of love and affection were to be excluded, but also because it would spell the end of youth. Marriage, she knew, was forever, and she could not make peace with that fact. "I will," she wrote to her cousin, "be allowed only a marriage of convenience, so I probably won't marry at all. Because of this I am tired of life and poor of hope and have ceased to dream of happiness. I entered life with excessive expectations."[12]

The expectations here referred to are, of course, the expectations that "Mr. Right" would come along. The ludricous situation in which the husband-catching business placed a young woman easily led her to dream about her future husband as Prince Charming, with whom she would live happily ever after. Braun thus had described her future husband; he would be "beautiful as Apollo, intelligent as the Seven Wise Men, faithful as Toggenburg, brave as Alexander the Great, and rich as Croesus."[13] Her educators' warnings against such dreams apparently had remained without effect. And in fact Prince Charming did not arrive, at least not for a very long time; and Lily turned down one eligible suitor after another.

This indecision, and the mixture of feelings in which it was grounded, her envy of men's societal privileges, her fear of being crushed by conventions, her sexual ardor and her strong sense of propriety, her intellectual pursuits and her fear of becoming a bluestocking, her enjoyment of parties and balls together with her knowledge that these pleasures were empty—all this increased her tendency toward profound self-contempt. She felt herself to be useless, a parasite. "Most people," she wrote to Tilly, "complain because they are suffering; I probably am living much too well. I have no position to fill; no heavy burdens have been placed on my shoulders; everyone spoils me. I think of myself as a lap dog who does her tricks and gets petted for that, but is useful for nothing else. And I would have the strength to accomplish something. Or should it be some sort of duty to contribute to the amusement of others?"[14]

From early on, this assessment of herself as a useless parasite, as a doll, was mixed in with contempt for her entire class. When at the age of eleven she first ventured into the slums of Posen during a disastrous flood, she reacted to the sight and the smell of poverty with disgust; poverty offended her aesthetic sense. But five years later, this had turned into shame over being privileged, and contempt for those, like her Augsburg aunt, who practiced charity for self-indulgence and also because they hoped it would woo the poor away from Social Democracy. By the time she was twenty-four, her letters to her cousin begin to contain criticisms of capitalism and the social problems it had created;[15] and in the wake of the Ruhr coal miners' strike of May 1889, which she observed from her father's garrison in Münster, she expressed the hope that the nobility and the working class might form a coalition to defeat the bourgeoisie. "The power of capital must be broken. We will live to see the marvelous spectacle of nobility and workers marching together."[16]

From year to year her attempts at self-appraisal became more desperate and unmerciful, ending at last in almost incoherent outbursts that expressed arrogance and self-contempt, shrewd self-analysis and shrewd self-deceptions—desperate cries for help of a young woman totally at sea because her desire to become a personality came into ever sharper conflict with the conventions of her society. Here is one of these incoherent outbursts, written on New Year's Eve 1889/90.

> . . . when I rise in the morning I see—well, what?—a face, pale, with tired veiled eyes which on rare occasions emit a strange flash, a deep furrow in the brow, and, if I look quite sharply, a tiny crease around the mouth. That's me! There is a picture of me, a portrait of some time ago: a wooden figure, bony shoulders, the arms long and slim—all that no

longer fits, though my waist is slim, 20½ inches, impressive, isn't it! The shoulders have become full, the arms round, but, strange, the face has remained almost the same. A child's face it never was. But was I ever a child? A happy child? If so, it must have been a very long time ago, because I do not remember it. Nor do I wish to rummage in my memory because it shows only ugly pictures; to be sure, most of them are framed in gold and painted on ivory in the brightest colors, but take a closer look at these devil's tricks—was fate not a foolish and wasteful painter to take such precious colors for painting such—trash? Or was it anything better than that? What of all this has remained whole? Love, perhaps? You poor creature! There was a time when you dreamt of the future which you thought would bring you happiness and glamour and love. Where is happiness? It passed me by, I saw only enough of it to retain the feverish hot longing for it. And glamour? How quickly the excessively perceptive eye saw that there is nothing genuine about it—fool's gold, carnival mummery, fireworks, the rockets crackle and shine, and once they are burnt out it is much darker than it was before. But love? Once it freely flew to me, and I treated it the way children treat a new toy, it delights for a while and then is thrown away. And later? Later love entered my heart and wounded me deeply, and—went away, the wounds healed, but there are times when the scars burn with pain. They say it is caused by change in the weather, that is true, for the closer autumn comes, the more I feel them, man.[17] There was one who talked to me of love, of eternal love indeed, and what became of it? It went away or passed on to every—pretty face! Don't get the illusion that there is even one who loves you, your own self, your innermost personality which ceaselessly struggles to become better, ceaselessly works to become more intelligent—nobody knows anything about this, they love only with their bodies, their heart is not involved in this, it is only a muscle, the people say, but the body's senses are there, they are alive, yes indeed, they are so alive they cannot be ignored! Stop yearning for love, it is a fairy tale from long ago. Do look at yourself carefully, soon no one will love you anymore, not even with that modern love. Then—people will respect you! Pooh, I am shivering!—You are talented, you have learned a lot, they will exploit that thoroughly, as much as they can. Then what will you have? You have pursued learning as if it were an illicit affair, otherwise the dear neighbors would have made fun of the "bluestocking,"—that will stay with you! You have loved art, shyly, in order not to besmirch the noble Muse with your amateurish efforts, that also will stay with you. Is that enough? Learning is endless and yet so limited—there is a point beyond which we cannot go, and at that point we run against a wall and bloody our heads and hearts; and does science teach anything that goes beyond the human being? Everything carries the human stamp, everywhere you run into yourself, your own miserable little self. But art? Where it is pure and great, the real world looks all the more filthy, and the harmony of art glaringly reveals the disharmony of reality; but if it is like the world, what good is it? Or perhaps despite everything you will still have the future? You have sinned, more grievously than anyone has ever suspected, and you have been punished, not an atom of punishment was spared you, every punishment was murderously hard, and you took it because you considered it deserved. But what now? You know that you have become better, that you are worth more than many of those around, and yet darkness continues to envelop you while those others walk in the bright light. Are you remembering biblical sayings from previous habit? God punishes those whom he loves—is that just? What is the use of becoming better if life gets worse all the time? A nice image of the future! Then I would rather plunge into the wildest mael-strom of life and perish in ecstasy than carry a burdensome existence on my back and suffer hunger and thirst with the "elevating" idea of becom-ing better, hunger and thirst, those are the right words! Hunger and thirst for happiness and glamour and love—just as in previous times! When I was a child, it was a wish which, in childish manner, carried the certainty of fulfillment: the little Christ child will bring it. Later, in the religious mind, a longing which clung to the hope: God is kind and will reward those who are good, I want to earn it. By now, old Tantalus, you know the score! Where is that sweet quiet happiness, the mild sunlight, where is love—not that admiring slavish love, but a gentle, compassion-ate one which softly presses me to its heart, saying, come and rest, you poor tired child! For what purpose are you alive? Would anyone miss you if you quietly went away? Your parents, your sister, your friends. But for how long? You have remained a stranger to them after all, have caused a lot of trouble to all of them, they won't miss you so very long, not even your little achievements. You have looked around for those very painfully in order to kill time, in order to be doing something. Who is going to be truly missed? A good father, a faithful mother spreading her blessings!—Cut it out! Look in the mirror—pfui, you have been crying, quickly put on the mask, who these days shows her face? With-out masks there would be too many wrinkles, too many tears!

Several blows hit Lily von Kretschmann in quick succession in her mid-twenties and jolted her out of the passivity with which she had endured her unendurable existence as a not quite proper young lady. Her father was dismissed from military service; her grandmother died, leaving her a rich legacy of Goethiana; and the one great love of her life, her own Prince Charming, came—and went.

General von Kretschmann's retirement was ordered by the new Em-peror Wilhelm II, effective at the end of 1889. Two years before, at the Imperial maneuvers of 1887, the general had been in charge of a mock army which had administered a decisive defeat to a division ineptly led by the then Prince Wilhelm; and at the Imperial maneuvers of 1889 the general and his sovereign had got into an argument about the relative importance of infantry as against cavalry. But the young emperor had no use for people who disagreed with him. For the Kretschmann family this was a major disaster; the father's brilliant career had been destroyed, the family's finances seriously impaired—far more than the general's wife and daughters could guess, because they had no inkling of the fantastic debts he had incurred. They did not know that the situation was bad; and Lily tried dutifully to add to the family's income by making and selling useless but pretty little artifacts in leather and textile—a commercial activity which only added to her self-contempt.[18]

While the Kretschmann family was preparing to move into a modest apartment in Berlin, Lily's grandmother died, and Lily inherited her collected papers and memorabilia: letters and poems written by Goethe; correspondence with his family and the Weimar court; her grandmother's own literary efforts; pictures; and presents she had received from Goethe. This inheritance gave Lily an opportunity to engage in some scholarly and editorial work, and she promptly set out to erect a monument to her grandmother by publishing selected papers and excerpts from these treasures.

Prince Charming arrived at that very same time. Lily's one great, overwhelming love in her life was a distant cousin, twenty years older than she, recently widowed, with two teen-aged daughters. Colonel Gottfried von Pappenheim, commander of a regiment of *Jäger* (chasseurs, i.e., a type of light cavalry), whom she had known since her childhood, appeared to love her as deeply and passionately as she loved him. But the courtship ended abruptly after a few months because his family objected to the match; Lily von Kretschmann for some unknown reason was not considered good enough for Count von Pappenheim.[19] She never forgot or forgave him; in various careful disguises he appears in her memoirs, in her novels, and in her bitter essays on the evil institution of marriage. And toward the end of her life, he was reborn for her in the flesh when her only son joined a regiment of chasseurs, rose to officer's rank, and came home on furlough wearing the green tunic of a *Jägerleutnant* (chasseur lieutenant).

These events at last forced Lily von Kretschmann to take her life into her own hands, to educate herself, and to establish her autonomy. She did this with determination and increasing boldness, rapidly testing ideas and activities of ever-increasing unconventionality and radicalness, until, five or six years later, she broke uncompromisingly with her entire past and joined the Marxist movement.

Her self-education as a radical began with two projects that were well within the bounds of aristocratic respectability, even though they were unconventional. The first was her work in editing and publishing her grandmother's papers. In order to do this properly, she got in touch with the keepers of the Goethe archive in Weimar and with the grand-ducal court; and, as the granddaughter of Jenny von Gustedt, she at once received red-carpet treatment by both institutions. With her charm, her wit, her youth, and her beauty, she swept the grand duke and his family as well as the Goethe scholars off their feet. She was offered free access not only to the archive but also to the secret archives of the grand-ducal family. The scholars invited her to join them permanently and suggested that she undertake a major historical work on the history of Weimar society during the last decade of Goethe's life. The grand duke offered her a position as lady-in-waiting.[20]

Between 1891 and 1893, she published selections from her grand-mother's literary legacy and a number of monographs based on research she had done in Weimar.[21] The money she received for these publications was dutifully turned over to her family and was given to a young cousin who as a cadet *(Fähnrich)* was living way beyond his income. As an associate of the Goethe archive she would have been a member of one of the most prestigious clubs in the German literary elite. She turned all these offers down. The life they would have provided her was too tame, too bookish, too conventional to suit her; and there is no indication that she ever regretted this decision.[22]

Her scholarly work as a Goethe specialist may seem a detour in her path toward radicalization, but the other project in her early self-education was a more direct road toward her final destination. In the summer of 1890, during her courtship with Gottfried von Pappenheim, the latter introduced her to a fellow cavalry officer, Major Moritz von Egidy. Egidy was just then in the process of discovering and formulating his ideas about a humane and socially conscious practical Christianity (ideas for which not much later he was forced to leave the military ser-vice), and Lily von Kretschmann immediately recognized their similar views. They quickly became friends and began to correspond with each other. The correspondence culminated, about five years later, in an ex-change of "open letters" published in a journal of which she was co-editor.[23] The correspondence, private as well as open, shows that Egidy was the more timid reformer, while Lily became increasingly more radical until it was more apparent that he aimed toward a society in which genuine Christianity might be applied, while she had convinced herself that Christianity must be overcome; her attitude toward the religion she had been taught had become thoroughly Nietzschean, and one could say that it was partly through Nietzsche that she eventually found her way to Marx.

I have suggested that Lily von Kretschmann's work in the Goethe archive may seem a detour on her road to radicalization. However, it could be argued that it was not a detour at all. One effect of this work was that she began to move in the highest literary circles; another, that she took a very active interest in the arts and letters of her time. Berlin in the early 1890s was one of the centers of literary activity and literary controversy; censorship and stage gossip were in the news; and Lily threw herself into this world with enthusiasm. Her beauty, her intelligence, her connections, and her publications opened all doors for her. Soon she had befriended the leading lights of this world, and equally quickly she began to take sides in the literary disputes then reigning. A series of about twenty articles she wrote on literary themes between 1893 and 1902 shows a determined trend to move to the left.[24] In the conflict between the established writers and the young rebels—*Tendenz* (ideological) writers and Naturalists—she more and more sided with the young against the old, even while criticizing the young for excesses, immaturities, or rude manners; but just as often she criticized them for not going far enough in their denunciation of social evils. For indeed, in her survey of literature, the stage, and the arts in general, she more and more focused on social themes, especially poverty and capitalism, the hypocrisies of sexual morality, and the oppression of women.

Moreover, the circles in which she moved in Berlin not only included writers and critics but more and more comprised the entire radical elite of the capital—religious reformers like Egidy, controversial writers like Hermann Sudermann and Gerhart Hauptmann, feminists such as Minna Cauer (with whom before long she would team up to form the far left wing of the German feminist movement), radical Russian exiles like Peter Struve, and *Kathedersozialisten* (academic socialists) like her close friends Ferdinand Toennies and Werner Sombart. With all these and many more she became good friends, at least until she moved further to the left.

Among the *Kathedersozialisten* she befriended, one must be singled out as all-important: Georg von Giżycki, *Extraordinarius* (associate professor) in moral philosophy at the University of Berlin. Paralyzed from the waist down as the result of a childhood illness, Giżycki was one of the most radical intellectuals outside the Marxist movement in Germany at the time. He preached religious skepticism and materialism, democratic socialism, absolute freedom of inquiry, and the emancipation of women, on the basis of a humanitarian philosophy which was a blend of Bentham and John Stuart Mill, Rousseau and Condorcet, Fourier and Marx, Goethe and Nietzsche, Wollstonecraft, Chernyshevsky, and Ibsen. He did so from his university lectern and in the organization he had helped create, the German Society for Ethical Culture, a branch of the Ethical Culture movement founded some years earlier in the United States. Together with Lily von Kretschmann, whom he married in the summer of 1893, he owned and edited a weekly journal, *Ethische Kultur,* which allowed her to publish her own contributions freely. Giżycki died in March 1895, but in the brief years that he and Lily had together, he became her tutor, not only introducing her to a wide range of works in history, economics, philosophy, and politics, but also training her in re- search methods, the use of libraries, and in statistics. Most important, he encouraged and helped her to make herself independent intellectually.

This independence more and more alienated her from her family, and her family from her. While her parents doubtless rejoiced in her ability to earn money by writing, they were alarmed and offended by what she wrote and where she published. They disapproved of her new friends and associates and strongly objected to her marrying a professed atheist and socialist, and an impotent wheelchair patient to boot. They really ex- pected her to stay at home as a dutiful daughter who would help her mother run the household. There were countless ugly scenes, and in the end, when her father in mindless rage ran at her with a pistol in his hand, she moved in with Giżycki even though they were not yet married.

One should not underestimate the difficulty with which the daughter made this break and the seriousness of her repeated attempts to smooth relations with her parents. What made the rupture so painful for her was not only genuine love for her family but also the knowledge that she was designated to become the heir of her Augsburg aunt's great wealth; a total break would mean forfeiting this comfortable cushion of financial security.

The break, however, became unavoidable when, toward the end of 1895, she publicly declared her membership in the Social Democratic Party. She had hesitated a long time before taking this step, not only because she had wished to avoid a total rupture with her family, but even more because she recognized serious flaws in the politics and ideology of the S.P.D. Under the organizational dictatorship of August Bebel and the ideological orthodoxy of Karl Kautsky, the German Marxist movement incorporated a good deal of that same Prussian spirit against which Lily von Giżycki had rebelled much of her life. Moreover, as she explained at length to Kautsky, her effectiveness as an agitator and as a missionary would be over as soon as she joined; as an outsider she could generate sympathy and mobilize people for cooperation, but once she was inside she would no longer be able to communicate with any radical sympathiz- ers.[25] Why then did she join?

Several answers suggest themselves, and I will summarize them, not necessarily in order of their importance. First, in the summer of 1895 she attended the world congress of the Women's Christian Temperance Un- ion, in London. At this important feminist gathering she not only met prominent English and American feminists but also befriended the lead- ing lights of British socialism, including George Bernard Shaw, Sidney and Beatrice Webb, Alys Russell, and Lady Somerset. One of the lessons this seems to have impressed on her was the realization that noble origin and high culture were quite compatible with being an active socialist.

Second, Georg von Giżycki's death had made her once again dependent; indeed, her parents suggested that she return home to share her mother's household duties; and in her grief and her loneliness, the friends she had made in the S.P.D., August Bebel, Wilhelm Liebknecht, Karl Kautsky, Paul Singer, and their wives, including some prominent S.P.D. women, such as Ottilie Baader, seem to have shown her the warmest sympathy. They also were the only ones who tried to find financial support for her, by referring her to one of the party's most effective fund raisers, Dr. Heinrich Braun, whom she married in August 1896.

This marriage was considered a scandal. He was twice divorced; in fact, he had married his second wife only a few months before he met Lily. He was a Social Democrat and a Jew. By marrying him, Lily offended not only her aristocratic class and her family but also many people in the leadership of the S.P.D. For she not only demonstrated her commitment to the Marxist movement but also publicly proclaimed her disdain for the prevalent sexual morality, which many of the Marxist leaders took for granted. With this she completed the first phase of her radicalization. From now on her spirit of rebelliousness would be directed against the narrowness and the inanities of Marxist orthodoxy.

NOTES

1. This article is a condensation of the early chapters of a biography of Lily Braun on which I have been working for a few years. The sources for this article include Braun's own fictionalized autobiography (Lily Braun, *Memoiren einer Sozialistin*, vol. 1: *Lehrjahre* [Munich, 1909]); a large number of articles and monographs she published between 1890 and 1896; but primarily her unpublished letters deposited in the archive of the Leo Baeck Institute, New York. I wish to express my deep appreciation to the staff of the Leo Baeck Institute for their courtesy and helpfulness in making this *Nachlass* (literary remains) available to me even before it was fully sorted and catalogued.

2. Her actual baptismal name was Amalie. I have seen only one legal document—a petition to the Prussian Ministry of Education—in which she used it. Reference: SG Darmst.ZK 1896(s) Lily Braun. Staatsbibliothek Preuss. Kulturbesitz. Berlin.

3. I know about the book only from her letters, but have never seen a copy and therefore will not cite it. The pseudonym she used was Ludolf Waldner, the last name being the maiden name of her favorite great-grandmother, Countess Diana Waldner von Freundstein.

4. The manuscript does not appear to be contained in her *Nachlass*. We

have to rely on the portions of this fragment which she published in her memoirs.
See *Memoiren,* 1, pp. 328–29.

5. Letter to Mathilde von Colomb, Summer 1882.

6. *Memoiren,* 1, pp. 41–43. Since it was customary to begin the torture of
tight lacing at this age, it is plausible to assume that the adult women made the
first lacing into some sort of initiation rite to mark the girl's passage into female
sexuality.

7. See Katharine Anthony, *Feminism in Germany and Scandinavia* (New
York, 1915), pp. 70–71.

8. Letter to Tilly von Colomb, 26 September 1886.

9. This is a persistent theme not only in her letters to her cousin but also in
published essays and novels written during the last twenty years of her life,
especially *Die Liebesbriefe der Marquise* (Munich, 1912) and the opera libretto
Madeleine Guimard, in Lily Braun, *Gesammelte Werke,* vol. 5 (Berlin, 1922).
Braun also lectured on the theme of the courtesan; thus in the fall of 1907 she
presented a cycle of five lectures on the *grandes amoureuses,* according to the
following outline: (1) The courtesan in antiquity and today; (2) Female Maecenases
in the Renaissance; (3) The *grande amoureuse* as ruler and inspirer; (4) The
grande amoureuse as artist; and (5) Death and resurrection of the *grande
amoureuse.* Reference: Pr. Br. Rep. 30 Bln C Pol. Pras. Nr. 16082 Bl. 55.
Deutsches Zentralarchiv, Potsdam. I would like to express my appreciation to the
archival services of the German Democratic Republic for making these and other
police files on Lily Braun available to me.

10. Letter to Tilly, 11 September 1886.

11. Letter to Tilly, 31 January 1889. Emphasis added.

12. Letter to Tilly, 13 January 1889.

13. Letter to Tilly, 26 July 1883.

14. Letter to Tilly, 29 August 1886. See also letter of 21 September, 1888.

15. Letters to Tilly, 16 April 1889, 24 April 1889.

16. Letter to Tilly, 12 May 1889.

17. ". . . desto mehr fühle ich sie, Mensch."

18. *Memoiren,* 1, pp. 433 ff.

19. Letters to Tilly, 11 May 1890, 14 June 1890, 26 December 1890, and 27
January 1891, provide the sketchy outlines of this romance. In her memoirs it has
been fictionalized beyond recognition; and in her sister's unpublished autobiographical sketch, the fictionalized version is reported as if it were fact. Maria von
Kretschmann's autobiographical sketch was written in 1918–19 when she was
spending a year in federal detention on Ellis Island as a German spy. It is in the
possession of the Leo Baeck Institute.

20. Letters to Tilly, 24 May 1891, 18 October 1891, 25 May 1892.

21. *Aus Goethes Freundeskreise. Erinnerungen der Baronin Jenny von Gustedt* (Braunschweig, 1892); George Westermann, "Erinnerungen von und an
Jenny von Pappenheim (Freifrau von Gustedt)," *Goethe-Jahrbuch,* 12 (1891); "Ottilie von Goethe und ihre Söhne. Aus den Erinnerungen einer Zeitgenossin."
Westermann's Monatshefte, 71 (1892), pp. 235–64; "Briefwechsel zwischen
Goethe und Minister von Gersdorff," *Goethe-Jahrbuch,* 13 (1892), pp. 98 ff.; "Die
literarischen Abende der Großherzogin Maria Paulowna," *Deutsche Rundschau,*

75 (1893), pp. 442–48, and 76 (1893), pp. 58–89. See also Lily von Giżcki, *Deutsche Furstinnen* (Berlin, 1893).

22. Letters to Tilly, 20 September 1891, 22 December 1894.

23. *Ethische Kultur,* 1895. See also various letters between Braun and Egidy in the Lily Braun archive, Leo Baeck Institute. For Egidy's views, see also his *Ernste Gedanken* (Berlin, 1890).

24. These include a series of twelve articles under the title "Streifzüge durch die moderne Literatur," published in 1895 and 1896 in different issues of *Ethische Kultur;* several theater reviews, some brief, some of article length, in the same journal; "Die neue Frau in der Dichtung," *Neue Zeit,* 14 (1895–96), pp. 293–303; and three articles published in Maximilian Harden's *Die Zukunft:* "Die Frauenfrage auf der deutschen Bühne," *Zukunft,* no. 2, (1897), pp. 26–33; "Ein Frauendrama," ibid., no. 24 (1898), pp. 511–17; and "Die Lieder der neuen Frau," ibid. (1902), pp. 494–505. I could have included essays on Wagner and articles about contemporary painting, but the above citations sufficiently show the volume and range of her work. I have translated these and many other works by Braun into English and hope to publish a selection of them.

25. Braun's letter to Karl Kautsky, 16 May 1895, in which she expresses these fears, is in the hands of the Institute of Social History, Amsterdam. I gratefully acknowledge their courtesy in giving me access to this and other documents.

The Impact of Agrarian Change on Women's Work and Child Care in Early-Nineteenth-Century Prussia*

W. R. LEE

The nineteenth century witnessed significant changes in the sphere of the family. It is frequently argued that the increasing separation of work from the family home and the functional separation of production from reproduction in the process of early industrialization in Europe led to a redefinition of the family, its function, and the nature of interfamily relationships. At least within a middle-class context, historians can point toward increasing family intimacy, and "emotionalization" of family relations, and a redefinition of women's work.[1] This was increasingly viewed as being confined to domestic matters and the rearing of children. It is also argued that these changes benefited children in two distinct ways: through greater family attention and through the discovery of childhood.[2]

However, the propagation of this essentially middle-class ideal of family life took place at a time when maternal mortality rates in Germany remained excessively high and infant mortality was on the increase. Certainly in the case of four specific German communities maternal mortality for the period 1780–1899 stood at 924.2 per 100,000, in contrast with a

*Certain aspects of this paper have benefited from the contributions of colleagues and discussants at the International Symposium on Mortality Decline (Lund, 1981) and at the Pollard-Wehler Colloquium at the University of Bielefeld (1981).

TABLE 1
Infant Mortality in the Prussian Provinces

PROVINCE	1819–33	1834–48	1849–63	1864–70
East Prussia	17.08	19.29	20.78	22.83
West Prussia	18.01	19.28	21.60	24.18
Brandenburg*	15.95	17.25	18.67	18.95
Pomerania	14.03	15.30	16.43	19.30
Posen	18.19	19.47	21.69	23.83
Silesia	22.66	24.02	24.36	26.27
Saxony	17.52	18.44	19.68	20.61
Westphalia	13.59	14.21	13.73	16.24
Rhineland	15.09	15.10	15.78	17.89

*Excluding Berlin.

Source: F. Prinzing, "Die Entwicklung der Kindersterblichkeit in den europäischen Staaten," *Jahrbücher für Nationalökonomie und Statistik*, 17 (1899), p. 587.

figure of only 45.9 for West Germany in the early 1970s.[3] Moreover, at the end of the nineteenth century infant mortality in Germany was among the highest in western Europe. A rate (per 100 live births) of 28.28 in Saxony, 27.90 in Bavaria, and 26.24 in Württemberg stood in marked contrast to the significantly lower levels of infant mortality in Norway (9.51) and Ireland (9.63).[4] More significantly, not only did infant mortality continue to rise within the various regions and provinces of Prussia throughout the first half of the century, but its divergent spatial incidence became increasingly pronounced (Table 1). Infant mortality was consistently higher in the eastern provinces, in contrast to predominantly lower rates in a fairly homogeneous geographical region of northwestern Prussia, which embraced the provinces of Schleswig-Holstein, Hannover, Hessen-Nassau, and most parts of Westphalia and the Rhineland.[5] This situation was compounded by the fact that the eastern regions of Prussia suffered from inflated child mortality rates. An east-west differential also existed in relation to mortality rates in the age group 5–14 years, although it was not as pronounced. These regional differences also tended to increase during the early decades of the nineteenth century.

Previous attempts to explain both the trend and the spatial distribution of Prussian infant mortality during this period have been generally unsatisfactory. Earlier commentators often recognized the connection between high infant mortality rates and the absence of breast feeding, but relied on such factors as height above sea level and temperature differences to explain this phenomenon.[6] Alternatively, racial differences and clothing styles were the critical factors.[7] The credibility of more recent hypotheses, however, is just as tenuous. Imhof, for example, has recently emphasized the importance of different mental attitudes toward infants and their survival, with two extremes standing out: a system of wastage and a system of conservation of human life. These differences were apparently the result of religious and confessional factors, as well as the impact of various military campaigns on individual communities and regions within Germany.[8] Unfortunately, the spatial correlation between different *mentalités* and regional infant mortality rates is seldom convincing, and the role of religion as a means of justifying, rather than causing, human behavior is seldom explored.

The key weakness of existing studies of early-nineteenth-century trends in both maternal and infant mortality is their relative failure to explore the concrete framework of the family economy. Attention is seldom directed toward the interrelationship between changing economic conditions, particularly in agriculture, and the sexual division of family labor, which arguably influenced both contemporary attitudes toward children and the trends in infant mortality. The apparent discrepancy between the middle-class emphasis on the emotional bond between the mother and child and the empirical evidence of increasingly excessive rates of infant mortality in Prussia can only be resolved through an examination of the impact of agrarian change on the family role of peasant women. This essay will focus attention on the specific nature of agrarian change in the different Prussian provinces. The ramifications of the process of agrarian change on the family economy and the sex-specific division of labor will be examined theoretically. An attempt will be made to relate the empirical evidence of regional trends in infant mortality to the impact of agrarian change on the role of women in the peasant economy. It will be argued that the variegated nature of agrarian change, by affecting the relative economic role of women in peasant society, was the key factor in influencing relative levels of infant and child care and the age-specific mortality rates of these groups within Prussian society.

Within the different regions of Prussia the pattern of peasant emancipation and the structural reorganization of the primary sector took a markedly different path. The nature of the Prussian reform legislation of 1807 and 1811, together with the enclosure edict of 1821, has already been dealt with extensively in German historiography.[9] The actual effect of this legislation varied significantly in the different provinces of Prussia. A critical difference between the eastern and western provinces lay in the extent of land transferences. Peasant land losses, as a result of the reform legislation, were most acute where peasants traditionally had enjoyed weaker tenurial rights.[10] As a result, a high proportion of the post-1811 regulation cases in the east involved substantial land compensation by the peasantry. The net loss of peasant cultivable land was often considerable: In Pomerania in the period between 1816 and 1859 the number of peasant holdings fell by 7.4 percent and the area under peasant cultivation by 13.2 percent. In the western provinces, however, land compensation was much rarer. In Westphalia there was a net increase in the extent of peasant landholding of 9.9 percent during the same period.[11]

The impact of the enclosure edict of 1821 also varied considerably. In the western provinces, enclosure benefited a broad spectrum of peasants. In the east, however, the enclosure movement was severer in uprooting peasants.[12] It benefited large-scale peasant cultivators and served to accentuate the existing degree of polarization within the peasant class.

Admittedly the origins of this divergent pattern of development are to be found in earlier centuries. The export orientation of the eastern provinces was well established by the late eighteenth century and this had been facilitated by the extension of Junker estates, peasant land appropriation, and the retention of feudal controls. Most of western Prussia, by contrast, had been turned over to de facto peasant occupation before the end of the eighteenth century, a process that had been stimulated by the growth of urban markets and by the fact that the feudal system was relatively weaker in this area. The agrarian reform legislation, however, both accentuated and accelerated the divergent development of the primary sector within Prussia. Although the process of restructuring was seldom complete before the 1860s, by the 1840s the differences in the regional pattern of landholding were very marked. The early nineteenth century therefore witnessed a divergent pattern of structural transformation in agriculture. This was reflected not only in the nature of land ownership and distribution but also in the very system of regional agricultural production.

The liberal reforms reinforced the role of Junker estate owners and large-scale peasant cultivators in the eastern provinces.[13] The predominance of grain monoculture was also strengthened. The mechanism by which this was achieved is of critical importance to the central argument of this essay. The rise in arable output in the eastern provinces was achieved through an expansion in arable cultivation, which involved an increasing incorporation of marginal land, and through continuous increments in labor inputs at practically constant levels of productivity. In the northeastern provinces the amount of cultivable land expanded from 3.2 to 7.4 million hectares during the first half of the century [14] and at least during the 1820s, 1830s, and 1840s labor input rose at a faster rate than output per worker.[15] The framework of agricultural production remained largely unaltered except for two features. There was a significant growth in potato cultivation, specifically on peasant smallholdings.[16] Increased grain exports were therefore facilitated by the substitution in the peasant diet of wheat and rye by potatoes, which implied a growing dependency on this crop on the part of smallholders and *Häusler* (cottagers). There was also a marked decline in livestock holding among the peasantry as a function of the land redistribution brought about by the liberal reform legislation and the increasing emphasis on grain monoculture.[17]

It is important to note that many of the adverse aspects of agrarian development in the eastern provinces were less pronounced, or at least less evident, in the western regions of Prussia. Particularly in Westphalia, the first half of the nineteenth century witnessed the end of grain monoculture. Although there was an expansion in arable cultivation, the increase was relatively marginal. Equally, although there was a shift to potato cultivation, the growth rate for this crop was very low indeed, between 1800 and 1840.[18] By the 1840s fodder and commercial crops had been adopted on a far larger scale than in the east.[19] Land enclosure in Westphalia had also encouraged the retention of livestock on small- and medium-sized peasant holdings and facilitated a substantial increase in livestock numbers.[20] At the same time this was accompanied by an improvement in milk yields, as a result of the widespread adoption of new fodder crops. Although there can be no doubt that the position of the landless element in rural Westphalia did deteriorate in the early decades of the nineteenth century,[21] the process of structural change in agriculture in this region would clearly have affected peasant livelihoods and work patterns in a significantly different and arguably less adverse way than in the eastern provinces of Prussia.

The framework of primary sector production evolved along markedly different lines in the eastern and western provinces of Prussia during the early nineteenth century. This affected not only the class structure of the peasantry but also the net demand for labor and the sex-specific division of labor in the family economy. It is generally accepted that agricultural reform during this period was labor-intensive, but there has been relatively little analysis of the regional pattern of agrarian change or of its impact on the division of labor within the family economy. Increasing commercialization in agriculture supposedly led to a rising demand for male labor.[22] The introduction of the scythe and the gradual shift to a heavier hand-tool technology apparently displaced female labor from harvest work, pushed women into less well-paid jobs, as followers and rakers, and threatened them with severe seasonal unemployment.[23] In total contrast Duden and Hausen have argued that the intensification of agricultural production was largely achieved by women shouldering a significantly increased work load, which, in turn, contributed to a deterioration in the feminine condition during the century.[24]

Certainly in the case of Prussia a clear distinction existed by the early twentieth century between the *Gutswirtschaften* (estate farms) of the northeastern provinces and the rationalized family production units of the northwest.[25] The nature of female farm work was also conditioned by whether employment was located on small-scale holdings, on a larger *Hof* (farmstead), or in the context of a rural wage economy.[26] Social, as well as economic, stratification therefore was an important factor affecting the nature of female work in the family economy and this was primarily related to the actual size of the peasant holding. In the continuing absence of adequate empirical data relating to structural and technological change in the regional agrarian regimes of nineteenth-century Prussia, I would like to emphasize three broad facets of the impact of increasing agricultural commercialization on the role of peasant women.

Firstly, land redistribution, particularly after the liberal reform legislation, affected the degree of socioeconomic stratification within the peasantry in a markedly different manner in the eastern and western provinces of Prussia.[27] This almost certainly impinged on family fertility strategy and the task-specific use of female labor within the peasant family. Secondly, it is probable that increasing regional differentiation in the type of agricultural production influenced the sex-specific division of family labor. The sexual delineation of work spheres was often determined by the relative economic importance of specific activities.[28] The nature and extent of female non-household work would therefore have reflected the underlying trend in agricultural specialization in each region of Prussia. Thirdly, the increasing predominance of specific crops, on a regional basis, would have affected not only the level of demand for female labor, but also its seasonality. Root crops and sugar beets, for example, had an inordinately large demand for labor per unit of land and an excessively seasonal demand cycle.[29] The combined effect of these factors, I would argue, was to significantly determine the overall nature of women's work in Prussian agriculture and to influence substantially the relative amount of time and care that would be given to newborn infants and young children. The regional fluctuations in infant and child mortality evident within Prussia during this period can only be explained within this context.

Various commentators have sought to establish a link between the recorded trend in nineteenth-century infant mortality and the nature of contemporary economic development. Infant mortality was often highly sensitive to economic fluctuations, and purely demographic variables affecting relative levels of infant mortality, such as the average age at first marriage for women, cannot explain the magnitude of regional divergence in Prussian nineteenth-century infant mortality rates. Certainly Prinzing envisaged some connection between the high rates of infant mortality in the eastern provinces of Prussia and the nature of peasant emancipation, although he failed to explain the mechanism through which this

TABLE 2
Land Distribution in the Prussian Provinces (1849)

PROVINCE	TOTAL AREA IN MORGEN* (MAGDEBURG)	HOLDING SIZE										AVERAGE SIZE OF HOLDING
		600 M. +		300–600 M.		30–300 M.		5–30 M.		– 5 M.		
		No.	%	No.	%	No.	%	No.	%	No.	%	
Pomerania	12,345,400	2,275	3.05	1,317	1.76	24,808	33.27	21,489	28.82	24,677	33.10	166
Prussia	25,316,100	3,456	2.08	4,232	2.55	82,677	49.91	34,987	21.13	40,307	24.33	153
Posen	11,529,800	2,445	2.61	956	1.00	44,852	47.97	27,190	29.08	18,083	19.34	123
Brandenburg	15,708,200	1,877	1.38	1,754	1.29	45,346	33.23	36,635	26.85	50,827	37.25	115
Silesia	15,940,300	2,323	0.93	1,241	0.50	43,503	17.40	92,882	37.15	110,040	44.02	64
Saxony	9,899,100	835	0.48	1,153	0.66	36,399	20.80	57,274	32.72	79,345	45.34	56
Westphalia	7,907,600	594	0.29	1,447	0.69	45,836	21.98	68,096	32.65	92,579	44.39	38
Rhineland	10,468,800	886	0.13	1,362	0.19	46,523	6.78	181,669	26.48	445,835	66.42	15
State	109,115,300	14,691	0.82	13,462	0.75	369,944	20.67	520,212	29.06	871,693	48.70	61

*1 hectare = 4 Morgen

Source: W. Sombart, Die deutsche Volkswirtschaft im 19. Jahrhundert (Berlin, 1921), p. 518. G. Franz, "Landwirtschaft 1800–1850," in Handbuch der deutschen Wirtschafts- und Sozialgeschichte, ed. by H. Aubin and W. Zorn (Stuttgart, 1976), 2, p. 295.

operated.[30] An attempt will now be made to examine both the direct and indirect links between the pattern of regional agrarian change in Prussia and the recorded trends in infant mortality.

Agrarian reform in early-nineteenth-century Prussia had an immediate influence on regional infant mortality levels by affecting the class structure of the peasantry. Later-nineteenth-century surveys pinpointed the significance of socioeconomic status as a factor determining infant mortality rates, and this was equally the case in the earlier period.[31] Agrarian reform affected the overall structure of regional agricultural production, the pattern of landholding, as well as the relative role of day laborers within the local economy. It therefore had a direct impact on regional infant mortality trends. In the eastern provinces the effect would appear to have been entirely negative. There was an increasing degree of polarization within peasant society (Table 2), a disproportional rise in the number of smallholders and landless laborers, and an extended exploitation of these groups by Junker estate owners and large-scale peasants. In the western provinces, on the other hand, and specifically in Westphalia, agrarian reform helped to produce a more balanced pattern of land distribution. The growth of an increasingly large group of peasants holding medium-sized tenements (5–30 *Morgen*—a land measure with local variations from 0.6 to 0.9 acre) and therefore with an improved economic status could well have had a beneficial effect on infant mortality trends.

The process of regional agrarian change also affected infant mortality rates by determining the extent and nature of female participation in the agricultural work force. Although it is difficult to estimate female participation rates in the primary sector for the period under consideration, there was a clear difference in the extent of involvement between the eastern and western provinces. The pattern of agricultural development, particularly in the eastern provinces, extended the level of direct female employment in agriculture. The rapid extension in the cultivable area, together with an increasing emphasis on commercialized grain production on the large estates, created a regional demand for female labor. Indeed female participation in heavy agricultural work in the east was often necessitated by the low level of wages paid to agricultural laborers in this region.[32] Evidence from the 1840s indicates that a high proportion of peasant families failed to meet minimum subsistence requirements and were therefore vitally dependent on the additional earning capacity of women. Moreover, many of the "new crops" of the early nineteenth century, such as potatoes and sugar beets, were highly labor-intensive. They required greater general care, deep digging, and continuous weeding and necessitated a higher level of labor input than harvesting itself.[33] The shift to these "new crops", and particularly to extensive potato cultivation on peasant smallholdings, accentuated the importance of female agricultural work, as it was largely women who were employed in their cultivation. Although the western provinces were also affected by these general trends, particularly in relation to the cultivation of commercial crops, the pattern of agrarian development was arguably less exploitive of female labor. The expansion of potato cultivation was least pronounced in the west, and in contrast to the reinforced emphasis on grain monoculture in the east, this region benefited from the further development of livestock farming, which was by definition less labor-intensive.[34]

The increased exploitation of female peasant labor in the course of the early nineteenth century, particularly in the eastern provinces, arguably influenced relative rates of infant mortality. At one level the increasing necessity for peasant women, in particular the wives of day laborers, to undertake agricultural work in the fields would have minimized the amount of maternal care available for newborn infants. Women were now obliged to resume agricultural work almost immediately after delivery, and the pressure of contributing to the family economy frequently limited adequate maternal care to the first few weeks of an infant's life.[35] The increasing utilization of female labor in agricultural cultivation would also have had an exhausting and debilitating effect on the general health of peasant women, which, in turn, would automatically have influenced neonatal mortality rates.[36] At another level the imposition of additional work burdens on peasant women would have served to reduce both the extent and the duration of breast feeding. Despite the early recognition of the central importance of breast feeding in limiting infant deaths,[37] and official attempts to propagate this practice throughout Germany, significant regional differences were still evident at the end of the nineteenth century. Breast feeding was very common in the western provinces of Prussia, with only a small proportion of infants being artificially fed. By contrast, although breast feeding did occur in the eastern provinces, it was less commonly practiced and the average duration was far lower than in the west.[38] Although the incidence of breast feeding was probably influenced historically by a number of sociocultural factors, there is increasing evidence to indicate that the regional pattern of breast feeding within Prussia, and perhaps within Germany as a whole, was directly connected with the nature of agrarian development in the early nineteenth century and the impact of agrarian change on the functional role of women within the peasant economy.

Agricultural work outside the home was frequently an important reason why infants were not breast-fed, or were breast-fed for too short or too irregular a period.[39] The increasing utilization of female labor in the agrarian regime of the eastern provinces, particularly in the cultivation of labor-intensive crops, such as potatoes, had an adverse effect on the practice of infant feeding. Peasant women were not only directly prevented from breast feeding their infants by the increased level of outside work, but their physical capacity to extend breast feeding for an adequate period was arguably impaired by the nature of their additional economic function.[40] In addition to their traditional work in the kitchen and the garden, the nature of agrarian development in the eastern provinces meant that women were inexorably drawn into full-time agricultural work. Agrarian reform, therefore, by stimulating in the east a greater employment of women in the primary sector, would also have encouraged by necessity an increased reliance on artificial feeding of infants. The adverse effects of these developments in the primary sector on relative rates of infant mortality would have been significantly less in the western provinces, given the nature of the regional agrarian regime and the changes that took place in the period under consideration. The more limited growth in potato production, the extension of livestock farming, which was traditionally a sphere of female responsibility close to the peasant holding, and the retention of a significant element of domestic craft production would all have facilitated the retention of customary breast-feeding practices. To this extent, therefore, the regional pattern of infant-feeding practices within Prussia, which has perplexed many historians, would seem to be explicable in relation to the specific form and development of the regional agrarian regimes. The nature of agricultural development in the course of the early decades of the nineteenth century impinged directly on infant-feeding practices by affecting the role of peasant women within the labor force. In those regions of Prussia where the level of female participation in heavy agricultural work increased significantly during the course of the early nineteenth century, breast feeding was comparatively rare and infant mortality correspondingly high. It is not surprising, therefore, that given the nature of regional agrarian change in the nineteenth century, infant mortality should have remained excessively high in the eastern provinces of Prussia.

Finally, the divergent pattern of agricultural development in the eastern and western provinces of Prussia could also have affected regional infant mortality rates by influencing the nature of the peasant diet. The debate over the significance of the introduction of potato cultivation is still unresolved. However, considerable doubt now surrounds the overall contribution of the potato to improved dietary levels in western Europe as a whole.[41] Certainly in the case of Germany it has been argued that the substitute value of the potato was far lower than its grain equivalent and that the crop had a limited importance for day laborers and smallholders in years of grain scarcity because of shifts in purchasing patterns to potatoes by more weighty income groups. But even if widespread potato cultivation increased the overall supply of food, the dietary consequences of an increasing reliance on this crop would have been determined by the continued availability of important nutritional supplements. This was probably not the case as far as the eastern provinces of Prussia were concerned. The rapid expansion of grain monoculture was accompanied by a marked decline in livestock farming. The redistribution of land following the emancipation of the peasantry and the enclosure edict of 1821 meant that many peasant smallholders were no longer able to maintain cattle, particularly milk cows. Moreover, the quality of livestock in the east remained poor throughout this period.[42] The increasing reliance of the bulk of the peasantry in the east on the potato, in the absence of adequate nutritional supplements, amounted to a significant deterioration in their diet. Moreover, dietary conditions in the east remained unsatisfactory even at the end of the nineteenth century.[43] A combination of increased exploitation of female labor and a noticeable deterioration in regional nutritional standards would help to explain the pattern of infant feeding in the eastern provinces and the inability of many peasant women to afford extensive breast feeding to their offspring. Peasant women on a low diet, just as in the case of many contemporary Third World countries, would have been forced to stop breast feeding after the first few weeks.[44] Low-quality food, which reflected the consequences of a specific form of agrarian development in the eastern provinces, was therefore directly associated with above-average infant mortality levels.[45]

The low priority given to livestock and dairy farming in the eastern provinces of Prussia during the nineteenth century had further ramifications as far as regional trends in infant mortality were concerned. The system of agricultural production in the east remained both traditional and extensive. The increasing concentration on grain cultivation meant that fodder supplies tended to remain scarce. As a result, there is evidence in the early decades of the century of a fall in local milk supplies. Particularly during the winter months, milk yields were very low.[46] To this extent the divergent trends in agricultural production within the individual provinces of Prussia affected the supply of substitute milk where breast feeding, for whatever reason, could not be made available, Whereas the decline in both the availability and the quality of cow's milk in the eastern provinces would have prompted the use of even more dangerous food substitutes, such as sugar or meal pap,[47] infants in the western provinces would arguably have benefited considerably from the impressive growth in livestock and dairy farming which was evident in this region as a whole.

Significant differences in child mortality rates between the eastern and western provinces are also evident in Prussian demographic data (Table 3). Age-specific mortality for the age groups 1–2, 2–3, 3–4, and 4–5 remained consistently higher in the east throughout the century. Although it is difficult to determine the precise reasons for this, there would seem to be some indication once again that the structure and development of agricultural production during the course of the early nineteenth century played a major role in influencing the registered trends in regional child mortality rates. If the eastern Prussian diet was nutritionally deficient, particularly in dairy produce and meat,[48] protein malnutrition would have contributed to inflated child mortality levels. Indeed this would have been aggravated during the course of the century as potato cultivation was extended to more marginal land with limited short-term yields. Moreover, the increasing polarization within the peasant class after the liberal reform legislation and the disproportional growth of peasant smallholders and landless laborers meant that housing conditions in the east remained very poor.[49] Furthermore, an increase in

TABLE 3

Age-Specific Mortality Rates in Various Regions of Prussia and Germany

AGE GROUP	DEATH RATE PER 1,000 IN EACH AGE GROUP (BOTH SEXES)					
	Prussia (1859–64)				(1855–59)	(1855–64)
					Schleswig-	
			Hohenzollern	*Eastern*	*Holstein &*	
	State	*Westphalia**	*& Rhineland*	*Provinces*	*Lauenburg*	*Oldenburg*
0–1	236.03	162.32	186.82	255.19	135.34	135.34
1–2	77.23	73.36	73.73	78.40	49.69	49.69
2–3	42.66	40.11	39.88	43.64	27.66	27.66
3–4	29.00	26.32	24.47	30.34	20.08	20.08
4–5	20.76	19.17	18.47	21.51	14.30	14.30
5–10	10.13	10.73	9.47	10.24	10.07	10.07
10–15	4.91	6.09	5.03	4.76	6.09	6.09
15–20	5.26	6.24	5.96	4.94	6.85	6.85
20–25	7.41	–	–	–	8.47	8.47
25–30	7.94	–	–	–	9.86	9.86
30–40	10.39	11.77	10.68	10.15	12.52	12.52
40–50	14.51	15.71	14.21	14.45	16.95	16.95
50–60	24.81	27.18	23.66	24.79	26.78	26.78
60–70	48.98	54.02	47.78	48.66	54.45	54.45
70–80	110.43	123.17	117.16	107.05	117.38	117.38
80–90	205.36	232.25	211.32	200.56	226.98	226.98
90+	275.36	297.62	306.36	266.39	306.36	306.36
20–30	7.67	8.69	8.14	7.44	9.15	9.15

*Including the Jadegebiet.

Source: Ministerialrath Becker, "Preussische Sterbetafeln, berechnet auf Grund der Sterblichkeit in den 6 Jahren 1859–64, auch Vergleich mit fremden Sterbetafeln," *Zeitschrift des Königlich Preussischen Statistischen Bureaus*, 9 (1869), p. 136.

the mother's work load, together with a diminution in the seasonality of leisure, may well have reduced her ability to carry additional domestic burdens or to provide adequate care to dependent children in the case of serious illness. The primacy of work obligations increasingly overrode any more sensitive appreciation of the health requirements of individual children. In the eastern provinces, for example, it was common for all the family, including infants and very young children, to sleep outside in the fields during summer work, irrespective of climate or comfort.[50] In every case, however, conditions affecting young children would have been significantly worse in the eastern provinces of Prussia, where the role of women in the agrarian economy became increasingly pronounced during the early part of the century, than in the west.

Despite the preliminary nature of this study, it is clearly evident that the liberal reform legislation in early-nineteenth-century Prussia was an important factor in determining the pace of structural change in the agrarian regimes of the eastern and western provinces, as well as the long-term trend in regional economic specialization. This process of structural change affected the role of women in the agrarian economy and the sexual division of labor within peasant society. The divergent regional trends in infant and child mortality within Prussia during the century was a clear reflection of this important change in the pattern of women's work. Indeed, the general rise in overall infant mortality rates in the early decades of the century can be directly attributed to this factor. Certainly in the eastern provinces the increasingly excessive rates of infant mortality during this period were probably influenced to a great extent both by the enforced adoption of an inferior nutritional diet and by the increased utilization of female labor in agriculture. This was evident within the framework of a growing emphasis on grain monoculture and the cultivation of "new crops," such as potatoes. The increasing employment of women on a labor-intensive basis in the agrarian regime of the eastern provinces also inevitably increased the risk of fetal abortion and the incidence of prenatal mortality. Moreover, the changes that took place in the pattern of women's work in the east reduced the ability of the mother to adequately breast-feed her offspring, with obvious ramifications as far as the regional trend in infant mortality was concerned. In total contrast, the underlying structural changes in the agrarian regime of the western provinces of Prussia during this period had significantly different consequences for the pattern of women's work. The more balanced redistribution of peasant land, following the legislation of 1807, 1811, and 1821, the continuing development of a more diversified agrarian economy, with a significant expansion of livestock and dairy farming, together with the retention of domestic craft production, meant that the level of female employment in heavy agricultural work outside the home in the west was far less significant than in the case of the eastern provinces. The path toward increased commercialized production in the primary sector of the Western provinces differed markedly from that of the east and had different repercussions as far as the sexual division of family labor within peasant society was concerned. In total contrast to the comparatively low rates of infant and child mortality in the western provinces, the eastern regions of Prussia as a whole continued to suffer from inflated numbers of infant and child deaths throughout the period under consideration. The nature of agrarian change, therefore, by affecting the sexual division of labor and the degree of active exploitation of female labor in the primary sector, was arguably the critical factor in accounting for the prevalence of high infant mortality rates in the eastern provinces of Prussia. This was also to have long-term ramifications for the demographic development of the region as a whole, as high levels of infant mortality probably contributed to the maintenance of correspondingly high fertility levels and therefore functioned as a key variable in determining the central reproductive behavior of the indigenous peasant population.

Finally, on the basis of this analysis, I would like to conclude by reassessing the attitudes toward child care and child rearing which are generally assumed to have been prevalent in peasant society in the early nineteenth century. It is often assumed that patterns of work orientation determined human relationships and that the contemporary harshness of the working environment precluded the investment of emotional capital in young infants and children.[51] High infant mortality rates were therefore indicative of inadequate care and attention and evidence of parental indifference to the fate of offspring. However plausible this hypothesis may appear to be, a word of caution is necessary. It is arguably premature to argue that high infant mortality rates are indicative of a conscious absence of parental care, when the critical factor determining the recorded trends in infant and child mortality in Prussia before the period of industrial takeoff and sustained industrial growth, was the relative structure and development of the primary sector. The nature of agrarian change in the first half of the century in the different regions of Prussia, by affecting the sexual division of labor and the relative labor function of women in peasant society, was the key factor in determining rates of infant and child mortality. Increasing field work for peasant women reduced the possiblity of breast feeding and precluded the provision of adequate care and attention for young infants and children. However, it is one thing to appreciate the causal mechanism behind the regional trends in infant and child mortality; to argue from this that the attitude of peasants toward infants and children in the eastern provinces was in essence harsher and less emotional than in the west seems unwarranted and unfounded. Life for the bulk of the Prussian peasantry, whether in the eastern or western provinces, remained harsh and demanding throughout the first half of the century. The critical difference lay in the fact that the nature of structural change in the agrarian regime of the east during this period affected the key dependent variable, the nature of women's work outside the home, in a markedly more negative manner as far as the purely domestic role of peasant women was concerned than in the west. Given the adverse effects of agrarian development in the eastern provinces of Prussia on internal family welfare provision, peasant families in the east may well have had to rely on a greater reserve of emotional capital to cope with the frequent casualties in wasted infant and child lives that occurred with such increasing regularity.

Inevitably the recorded trends in Prussian infant mortality in the nineteenth century were influenced by a broad spectrum of individual factors; socioeconomic, environmental, demographic, medical, and confessional. Research into the causes underlying the temporal and regional variations in infant and child mortality within the different Prussian provinces is still at a comparatively early stage. However, it is already apparent that any meaningful analysis must concentrate on the critical relationship between the nature of women's work, contemporary infant-feeding practices, and the recorded mortality trends. Recent evidence would seem to suggest that the seasonal pattern of weaning in Germany may well have been linked to the cycle of the agricultural year and the demands made on women's time by agricultural activities.[52] Indeed, the critical importance of women's work outside the home in determining patterns of infant care and the probability of infant survival was already recognized intuitively by earlier writers. High infant mortality was inextricably caused by socioeconomic factors. Female work outside the home made breast feeding difficult and the premature death of infants was often related to various types of female work.[53] This was particularly the case as far as smallholders were concerned, where married women were expected to perform extensive field work in addition to the usual household jobs.[54]

However, in order to explore the inherent interrelationship between women's work, child care, and infant mortality in a historical framework a far more integrated interdisciplinary approach is necessary. We are dependent not only on the increasing availability of hard demographic data, obtained by family reconstitution,[55] but also on the extent to which this information can be combined with relevant social, economic, and ethnographic material. The present study has sought to illustrate the extent to which the pattern of agricultural development in the eastern and western provinces of Prussia in the early nineteenth century affected the economic role of peasant women and the nature of women's work in a significantly different way. Regional trends in infant and child mortality reflected quite closely the degree to which the local agrarian regime determined the extent of female involvement in the agricultural work force. The process of agricultural change in the east in the decades following the reform legislation of 1807–21 had a markedly negative effect on the work role of peasant women, and contributed both directly and indirectly to the increasingly high rate of infant mortality in this region, particularly in comparison with the western provinces. Confirmation of this general hypothesis, that trends in regional infant and child mortality levels reflected the underlying impact of economic and specifically agricultural development on the nature of women's work, must be sought through a more systematic study of different peasant ecosystems. Attention must be focused at the local level on the different structures of production, labor requirements, and the relative level of technological development.[56] More importantly, research should be centered on specific peasant subgroups, such as smallholders and landless laborers, in order to examine the class-specific ramifications of changes in the structure of local agricultural production on women's work and the pattern of child care.[57] Indeed, existing studies on the organization of peasant society in Germany which pay particular attention to the nature and extent of women's work within both the family home and the local agrarian economy,[58] provide a useful analytical framework which historical ethnological studies will hopefully reinforce and extend.[59] Only on the basis of such an interdisciplinary approach will the historical interrelationship between agrarian change, women's work, child care, and infant mortality be more fully understood.

NOTES

1. D. Langewiesche and K. Schönhoven, "Zur Lebensweise von Arbeitern in Deutschland im Zeitalter der Industrialisierung, in *Arbeiter in Deutschland. Studien zur Lebensweise der Arbeiterschaft im Zeitalter der Industrialisierung*, ed. by. D. Langewiesche and K. Schönhoven (Paderborn, 1981), p. 22.

2. I. Weber-Kellermann, *Die Deutsche Familie* (Frankfurt, 1977), passim. Phillipe Ariés, *L'Enfant et la vie familiale sous l'ancien régime* (Paris, 1960).

3. Arthur E. Imhof, "Women, Family and Death: Excess Mortality of Women in four Communities in Nineteenth-Century Germany," in *The German Family: Essays in the Social History of the Family in Nineteenth- and Twentieth-Century Germany*, ed. by R. J. Evans and W. R. Lee (London, 1981), p. 101.

4. F. Prinzing, "Die Entwicklung der Kindersterblichkeit in den europäischen Staaten," *Jahrbücher für Nationalökonomie und Statistik*, 17 (1899), pp. 577–635.

5. V. Behr-Pinnow and F. Winkler, *Statistische Beiträge für die Beurteilung der Säuglingssterblichkeit in Preussen* (Charlottenburg, n.d.), p. 8.

6. A. Würzburg, "Die Säuglingssterblichkeit im Deutschen Reiche während der Jahre 1875 bis 1877," *Arbeiten aus dem Kaiserlichen Gesundheitsamte (Beihefte zu den Veröffentlichung aus dem Kaiserlichen Gesundheitsamte)*, 2 (1887), pp. 208–22, 343–446, and 4 (1888), pp. 28–108. A. Geissler, "Über die Sterblichkeit der Neugeborenen im ersten Lebensmonat," *Zeitschrift des Königlich Sächsischen Statistischen Bureaus*, 31 (1885), pp. 248–49. H. Bernheim, "Die Intensitäts-Schwankungen der Sterblichkeit in Bayern und deren Factoren," *Zeitschrift für Hygiene*, 4 (1888), pp. 525–81.

7. F. W. Müller, *Über die Ursachen des Nichtstillens auf der schwäbisch-bayerischen Hochebene* (Munich, 1890), p. 27. G. Seiffert, "Das Nichtstillen in Bayern, seine Ursachen und seine Bekämpfung," *Münchner Medicinische Wochenschrift*, no. 28 (1930), p. 1197. J. G. Klees, *Über die weiblichen Brüste* (Frankfurt, 1906).

8. A. E. Imhof, "Unterschiedliche Säuglingssterblichkeit in Deutschland, 18. bis 20. Jahrhundert—Warum?" *Zeitschrift für Bevölkerungswissenschaft*, 6 (1981), pp. 343–82.

9. F. Lütge, *Geschichte der deutschen Agrarverfassung vom frühen Mittelalter bis zum 19. Jahrhundert* (Stuttgart, 1963).

10. H. Harnisch, "Statistische Untersuchungen zum Verlauf der kapitalistischen Agrarreformen in den Preussischen Ostprovinzen (1811 bis 1865)," *Jahrbuch für Wirtschaftsgeschichte*, 14 (1974), p. 169.

11. C. F. W. Dieterici, *Handbuch der Statistik des preussischen Staates* (Berlin, 1861), pp. 318–27. H.-J. Teuteberg, "Der Einfluss der Agrarreformen auf die Betriebsorganisation und Produktion der bäuerlichen Wirtschaft Westfalens im 19. Jahrhundert," in *Entwicklungsprobleme einer Region. Das Beispiel Rheinland und Westfalen im 19. Jahrhundert*, ed. by F. Blaich, Schriften des Vereins für Socialpolitik, 119, (Berlin, 1981), pp. 243–76.

12. L. Schofer, "The Formation of a Modern Industrial Labor Force: The Case of Upper Silesia, 1865–1914," Ph.D. dissertation, University of California, Berkeley, 1970, p. 79.

13. F. Lütge, p. 225. S. Korth, "Die Entstehung und Entwicklung des ostdeutschen Grossgrundbesitzes," dissertation, Göttingen, 1952. G. Heitz, "Bauernwirtschaft und Junkerwirtschaft," *Jahrbuch für Wirtschaftsgeschichte*, 4 (3) (1964), p. 86.

14. J. R. Mucke, *Deutschlands Getreide-Ertrag. Agrarstatische Untersuchungen.* (Greifswald, 1883), p. 20. In the Kurmark and the Neumark, to provide a further example of this trend, the amount of agricultural land under cultivation was increased by 32 percent and 43 percent, respectively, between 1801 and 1878.

15. R. A. Dickler, "Labor Market Pressure. Aspects of Agricultural Growth in the Eastern Region of Prussia, 1840–1914: A Case Study of Economic-

Demographic Interrelations during the Demographic Transition," Ph.D. dissertation, University of Pennsylvania, 1970, p. 84. Figures on per capita output were
calculated from H. W. Graf Finckenstein, *Die Entwicklung der Landwirtschaft in
Preussen und Deutschland und in den neun alten Preussischen Provinzen von
1800–1930* (Bern, 1959), vol. 3. In Brandenburg there was a fall in output per
capita in the arable and dairy sectors of farming between 1816 and 1855 of 9.14
percent. This was symptomatic of the general trend in many of the eastern provinces of Prussia.

16. I. Ballwanz, "Der Zusammenhang zwischen der Produktions-
entwicklung und der Betriebsgrösse in der deutschen Landwirtschaft von 1871 bis
1914," *Jahrbuch für Wirtschaftsgeschichte*, 18 (3) (1978), p. 86.

17. H. Plaul, *Landarbeiterleben im 19. Jahrhundert. Eine volkskundliche
Untersuchung über Veränderungen in der Lebensweise der einheimischen Land-
arbeiterschaft in den Dörfern der Magdeburger Börde unter den Bedingungen
der Herausbildung und Konsolidierung des Kapitalismus in der Landwirtschaft.
Tendenzen und Triebkräfte* (Berlin, 1979), p. 63. F. W. C. Dieterici, "Statistische
Übersicht der landwirtschaftlichen Productions- und Consumptions-Verhältnisse
im Preussischen Staate," *Annalen der Landwirtschaft in den Königlich Preussischen Staaten*, 1 (1843), p. 73. F. W. C. Dieterici, "Statistische Nachrichten über
den Viehstand in Preussischen Staate nach den Zählungen am Ende der Jahre
1819, 1831, 1843, 1852, und 1855," *Mittheilungen des Statistischen Bureaus in
Berlin*, 9 (1856), p. 292. In complete contrast to the western provinces of Prussia,
the number of cattle per head of population declined markedly in the east during
the early decades of the nineteenth century.

18. The increase in potato cultivation in Westphalia of approximately 50
percent between 1800 and 1840 was the lowest recorded in all the individual
provinces of Prussia. By contrast there was an increase of 1,196.79 percent in
West Prussia (1816–55).

19. A. V. Lengerke, *Entwurf einer Agricultur-Statistik des preussischen
Staates nach den Zuständen in den Jahren 1842 und 1843 (Berlin, 1847), p. 170*.

20. E. Engel, "Die Viehhaltung im Preussischen Staate in der Zeit von 1816
bis 1858," *Zeitschrift des Königlich Preussischen Statistischen Bureaus* (1861),
p. 220. The number of cattle held in Westphalia, for example, rose by over 23
percent between 1816 and 1849.

21. J. Mooser, "Bäuerliche Gesellschaft im Zeitalter der Revolution 1789–
1848. Zur Sozialgeschichte des politischen Verhaltens ländlicher Unterschichten
im örtlichen Westfalen," dissertation, Bielefeld, 1978, p. 543.

22. B. Ankarloo, "Agriculture and Women's Work: Directions of Change in
the West, 1700–1900," *Journal of Family History*, 4 (1979), pp. 111–20.

23. K. D. M. Snell, "Agricultural Seasonal Unemployment, the Standard of
Living and Women's Work in the South East: 1690–1860," *Economic History
Review*, 34 (1981), pp. 407–37. A. Lühning, "Die schneidenden Erntegeräte,"
dissertation, Göttingen, 1951. A. Fenton, "Sickle, Scythe and Reaping Machine:
Innovation Patterns in Scotland," *Ethnologia Europaea*, 7 (1973–74), pp. 35–47.

24. B. Duden and K. Hausen, "Gesellschaftliche Arbeit-
Geschlechtsspezifische Arbeitsteilung," in *Frauen in der Geschichte*, ed. by
A. Kuhn and G. Schneider, (Düsseldorf, 1979), p. 22. See also A. E. Imhof, "The

Amazing Simultaneousness of the Big Differences and the Boom in the 19th Century: Some Facts and Hypotheses about Infant and Maternal Mortality in Germany, 18th to 20th Century," paper presented to the International Symposium on Mortality Decline, Lund, 1981, p. 123.

25. G. Wiegelmann, "Bäuerliche Arbeitsteilung in Mittel- und Nordeuropa. Konstanz oder Wandel?" *Ethnologia Scandinavica*, 5 (1975), pp. 5–23.

26. R. Pedersen, "Die Arbeitsteilung zwischen Frauen und Männern in einem marginalen Ackerbaugebiet. Das Beispiel Norwegen," *Ethnologia Scandinavica*, 5 (1975), pp. 37–48.

27. In the east smallholders were undoubtedly the main losers in the process of agricultural reform, as they were increasingly downgraded from peasant smallholders to landless wage laborers. H. Plaul, p. 147. K. Bielefeldt, "Das Eindringen des Kapitalismus in die Landwirtschaft unter besonderer Berücksichtigung der Provinz Sachsen und der angrenzenden Gebiete," dissertation, Berlin, 1910, p. 13.

28. G. Wiegelmann, *Frauenarbeit in der Landwirtschaft* (Zender, 1959–64), pp. 37–83. "Erste Ergebnisse der ADV-Umfragen zur alten baüerlichen Arbeit," *Rheinische Vierteljahrsblätter*, 33 (1969), pp. 208–62. M. Mitterauer, "Geschlechtsspezifische Arbeitsteilung in vorindustrieller Zeit," *Beiträge zur Historischen Sozialkunde*, 3 (1981), p. 77. Non-household work by women was arguably more easily adapted to both short-term and seasonal needs, as well as to changes in local hand-tool technology. Whereas the husband's work was often relatively well defined, the peasant wife was frequently expected to modify the nature and extent of her work in step with changing economic conditions. Any shortfall in the supply of family labor would frequently result in a higher overall work load for female family members. W. R. Lee, *Population Growth, Economic Development and Social Change in Bavaria, 1750–1850* (New York, 1977), pp. 284–85. A. Hauser, "Der Familienbetrieb in der schweizerischen Landwirtschaft. Eine historische und sozio-ökonomische Analyse," *Zeitschrift für Agrargeschichte und Agrarsoziologie*, 26 (2), (1978), p. 208.

29. As a general rule whereas the ratio of labor input between winter and summer work stood at I: 1.71 for traditional grain crops cultivated under a three-course rotational system, the equivalent for the Norfolk four-course system stood at I: 3.88 and for sugar-beet cultivation at I: 5.73.

30. F. Prinzing, p. 587.

31. J. Eröss, "Über die Sterblichkeitsverhältnisse der Neugeborenen und Säuglinge," *Zeitschrift für Hygiene und Infektionskrankheiten*, 19 (1895), p. 387.

32. A. Neumann, *Die Bewegung der Löhne der ländlichen "freien" Arbeiter im Zusammenhang mit der gesamtwirtschaftlichen Entwicklung im Königreich Preussen gegenwärtigen Umfangs vom Ausgang des 18. Jahrhunderts bis 1850* (Berlin, 1911). H. Plaul, p. 224.

33. B. H. Slicher van Bath, "The Rise of Intensive Husbandry in the Low Countries," in *Britain and the Netherlands*, ed. by J. S. Bromley and E. H. Kossmann (London, 1960), pp. 130–53.

34. Certainly in southern Germany dairy and livestock farming was normally associated with lower levels of infant mortality. A. Groth, "Über den Einfluss der beruflichen Gliederung des bayerischen Volkes auf die Entwicklung der Sterb-

lichkeit und Fruchtbarkeit der letzten Jahrzehnte," dissertation, Munich, 1912, pp. 77 ff.

35. This is confirmed by contemporary evidence from southern Germany. Schleiss von Löwenfeld, *Medizinische Topographie vom Landgerichtsbezirke Sulzbach in der obern Pfalz* (Nuremberg, 1806). W. Brenner-Schaeffer, *Darstellung der sanitätlichen Volkssitten und der medicinischen Volks-Aberglaubens im nordöstlichen Theile der Oberpfalz* (Amberg, 1861), p. 14.

36. The relationship between the poor physical constitution of parents, the absence of breast feeding, and high infant mortality was touched upon by earlier writers. Dr. v. Vogl, *Die Sterblichkeit der Säuglinge in ihrem territorialen Verhalten in Württemberg, Bayern und Oesterreich und die Wehrfähigkeit der Jugend mit besonderer Rücksichtsnahme auf die Anforderung an die Marschfähigkeit* (Munich, 1909), p. 15. F. W. Müller, p. 14.

37. G. F. C. Wendelstadt, *Über die Pflicht gesunder Mütter ihre Kinder selbst zu stillen, nebst einem Versuch der Geschichter der Säugammen* (Frankfurt-Leipzig, 1792). L. Kunze, "'Die Physische Erziehung der Kinder.' Populäre Schriften zur Gesundheitserziehung in der Medizin der Aufklärung," dissertation, Marburg, 1971.

38. The village of Saalhausen in Westphalia, for example, was typical of the high level of breast feeding in the western provinces in the late nineteenth century. Only 2 percent of all infants were fed artificially and the average length of breast feeding was 12.4 months. By contrast, in Danzig, in 1880, only 5 percent of infants were breast-fed. C. Röse, "Die Wichtigkeit der Mütterbrust für die körperliche und geistige Entwicklung des Menschen," *Deutsche Monatsschrift für Zahnheilkunde*, 23 (1905), p. 165.

39. Evidence from the case of Petalax in Sweden confirms this. U. B. Lithell, "Breast-Feeding Habits and Their Relation to Infant Mortality and Marital Fertility," *Journal of Family History*, 6 (1981), pp. 182–94.

40. J. B. Roetzer, *Die Säuglingssterblichkeit in Altbayern und deren Bekämpfung* (Munich, 1913), p. 41.

41. G. Fridlizius, "Some New Aspects of Swedish Population Growth. I: A Study at Country Level," *Economy and History*, 17 (1975), p. 25. M. Drake, "Norway," in *European Demography and Economic Growth*, ed. by W. R. Lee (London, 1979), pp. 294–95. D. Saalfeld, "Handwerkereinkommen in Deutschland vom ausgehenden 18. bis zur Mitte des 19. Jahrhunderts," *Handwerksgeschichte in neuer Licht*, ed. by W. Abel, Göttingen Handwerkswirtschaftlichen Studien, 16, (Göttingen, 1970), pp. 100–1.

42. A. v. Lengerke, p. 46.

43. H. Plaul, pp. 267–68.

44. S. Chandrasekar, *Infant Mortality in India 1901–55* (London, 1959), p. 120. It was not until after the 1870s that average calorie consumption in Germany finally reached adequate levels. M. R. Haines, "Economic-Demographic Interrelations in Developing Agricultural Regions: A Case Study of Prussian Upper Silesia, 1840–1914," Ph.D. dissertation, University of Pennsylvania, 1971, p. 44.

45. R. A. Dickler, p. 126.

46. G. H. Gholamiasllari, "Zur Geschichte der künstlicher

254 W. R. LEE

Säuglingsernährung in Mitteleuropa dargestellt am Werdegang verschiedenenSäuglingsernährung in Mitteleuropa dargestellt am Werdegang verschiedenen
Milch- und Nährmittelfirmen," dissertation, Erlangen-Nuremberg, 1975, p. 7.

47. Dr. Geissler, "Sterblichkeit- und Krankheitsverhältnisse in Meerane
während der Jahre 1835 bis 1869," *Vierteljahrschrift für öffentliche Gesundheits-pflege*, 9 (1877), p. 39, W. R. Lee, p. 69. Poor-quality milk, white bread, and
coffee were also sometimes used as substitutes.

48. M. Rubner, *Wandlungen in der Volksernährung* (Leipzig, 1913), p. 66.
R. A. Dickler, p. 126.

49. R. Pape, *Die Entwicklung des allgemeinen Wohlstandes in Ostpreussen
seit dem Anfang des 19. Jahrhunderts* (Königsberg, 1909), p. 67. A. Freidländer,
"Über die Wohnungs-verhältnisse der ärmeren Classen der ländlicher
Bevölkerung in hygienischer Beziehung," *Vierteljahrschrift für Öffentliche
Gesundheitspflege*, 9 (1877), p. 127. There were few signs of any significant im-
provement in rural housing conditions until after the 1870s.

50. R. Pape, p. 69.

51. I. Weber-Kellerman, "Die Familie auf dem Lande in der Zeit zwischen
Bauernbefreiung und Industrialisierung," *Zeitschrift für Agrargeschichte und
Agrarsoziologie*, 26 (1) (1978), p. 70.

52. J. Knodel, "Seasonal Variation in Infant Mortality: An Approach with
Applications. Research Report," August 1982, p. 19.

53. H. Fakler, "Einwirkungen lokaler und sozialer Art auf die Entwicklung
der Geburtlichkeit und Säuglings-Sterblichkeit in Bayern von 1900 bis 1923,"
dissertation, Eichstätt, 1926. A. Spreti, *Die Säuglingssterblichkeit in den altbay-
erischen Landesteilen* (Munich, 1916). Dr. Presl, "Die Säuglingssterblichkeit in
Oesterreich," *Statistische Monatsschrift*, 29 (1903), p. 656.

54. J. B. Roetzer, pp. 36–37.

55. J. Knodel, *Demographic Behavior in the Past: A Study of 14 German
Village Populations in the Eighteenth and Nineteenth Centuries* (forthcoming).

56. The importance of hand tools and implements in determining both the
sex-specific division of work and key elements of peasant culture as a whole has
been explored by W. Jacobeit, *Bäuerliche Arbeit und Wirtschaft* (Berlin, 1965).
In the case of Britain there are already a number of studies which deal directly
with the impact of changing harvest technology in the nineteenth century on labor
supply and women's work. E. J. T. Collins, "Harvest Technology and Labour
Supply in Britain, 1790–1870," *Economic History Review*, 22 (1969), pp. 453–73.
M. Roberts, "Sickles and Scythes: Women's Work and Men's Work at Harvest
Time," *History Workshop*, no. 7. (1979), pp. 3–28.

57. See the work of H. Plaul; also C Heinrich, "Lebensweise und Kultur der
in- und ausländischen landwirtschaftlichen Saisonarbeiter von der Mitte des 19.
Jahrhunderts bis 1918," in *Bauer und Landarbeiter im Kapitalismus in der Mag-
deburger Börde. Zur Geschichte des dörflichen Alltags vom Ausgang des 18.
Jahrhunderts bis zum Beginn des 20. Jahrhunderts*, ed. by H.-J. Rach and
B. Weissel (Berlin, 1982), pp. 117–62.

58. M. Bidlingmaier, *Die Bäuerin in zwei Gemeinden Württembergs* (Stutt-
gart, 1918). H. Scharnagl, "Straussdorf. Eine sozialöknomische und soziologische
Untersuchung einer oberbayerischen Landgemeinde mit starken
Flüchtlingsanteil," dissertation, Erlangen, 1952. G. Wurzbacher and R. Pflaum,
Säuglingsernährung in Mitteleuropa dargestellt am Werdegang verschiedenen
Milch- und Nährmittelfirmen," dissertation, Erlangen-Nuremberg, 1975, p. 7.

47. Dr. Geissler, "Sterblichkeit- und Krankheitsverhältnisse in Meerane
während der Jahre 1835 bis 1869," *Vierteljahrschrift für öffentliche Gesundheits-pflege*, 9 (1877), p. 39, W. R. Lee, p. 69. Poor-quality milk, white bread, and
coffee were also sometimes used as substitutes.

48. M. Rubner, *Wandlungen in der Volksernährung* (Leipzig, 1913), p. 66.
R. A. Dickler, p. 126.

49. R. Pape, *Die Entwicklung des allgemeinen Wohlstandes in Ostpreussen
seit dem Anfang des 19. Jahrhunderts* (Königsberg, 1909), p. 67. A. Freidländer,
"Über die Wohnungs-verhältnisse der ärmeren Classen der ländlicher
Bevölkerung in hygienischer Beziehung," *Vierteljahrschrift für Öffentliche
Gesundheitspflege*, 9 (1877), p. 127. There were few signs of any significant im-
provement in rural housing conditions until after the 1870s.

50. R. Pape, p. 69.

51. I. Weber-Kellerman, "Die Familie auf dem Lande in der Zeit zwischen
Bauernbefreiung und Industrialisierung," *Zeitschrift für Agrargeschichte und
Agrarsoziologie*, 26 (1) (1978), p. 70.

52. J. Knodel, "Seasonal Variation in Infant Mortality: An Approach with
Applications. Research Report," August 1982, p. 19.

53. H. Fakler, "Einwirkungen lokaler und sozialer Art auf die Entwicklung
der Geburtlichkeit und Säuglings-Sterblichkeit in Bayern von 1900 bis 1923,"
dissertation, Eichstätt, 1926. A. Spreti, *Die Säuglingssterblichkeit in den altbay-
erischen Landesteilen* (Munich, 1916). Dr. Presl, "Die Säuglingssterblichkeit in
Oesterreich," *Statistische Monatsschrift*, 29 (1903), p. 656.

54. J. B. Roetzer, pp. 36–37.

55. J. Knodel, *Demographic Behavior in the Past: A Study of 14 German
Village Populations in the Eighteenth and Nineteenth Centuries* (forthcoming).

56. The importance of hand tools and implements in determining both the
sex-specific division of work and key elements of peasant culture as a whole has
been explored by W. Jacobeit, *Bäuerliche Arbeit und Wirtschaft* (Berlin, 1965).
In the case of Britain there are already a number of studies which deal directly
with the impact of changing harvest technology in the nineteenth century on labor
supply and women's work. E. J. T. Collins, "Harvest Technology and Labour
Supply in Britain, 1790–1870," *Economic History Review*, 22 (1969), pp. 453–73.
M. Roberts, "Sickles and Scythes: Women's Work and Men's Work at Harvest
Time," *History Workshop*, no. 7. (1979), pp. 3–28.

57. See the work of H. Plaul; also C Heinrich, "Lebensweise und Kultur der
in- und ausländischen landwirtschaftlichen Saisonarbeiter von der Mitte des 19.
Jahrhunderts bis 1918," in *Bauer und Landarbeiter im Kapitalismus in der Mag-
deburger Börde. Zur Geschichte des dörflichen Alltags vom Ausgang des 18.
Jahrhunderts bis zum Beginn des 20. Jahrhunderts*, ed. by H.-J. Rach and
B. Weissel (Berlin, 1982), pp. 117–62.

58. M. Bidlingmaier, *Die Bäuerin in zwei Gemeinden Württembergs* (Stutt-
gart, 1918). H. Scharnagl, "Straussdorf. Eine sozialöknomische und soziologische
Untersuchung einer oberbayerischen Landgemeinde mit starken
Flüchtlingsanteil," dissertation, Erlangen, 1952. G. Wurzbacher and R. Pflaum,

Das Dorf im Spannungsfeld industrieller Entwicklung. Untersuchung an den 45 Dörfern und Weilern einer westdeutschen ländlichen Gemeinde (Stuttgart, 1954). H. Caesar-Weigel, *Das Tagewerk der Landfrau* (Berlin, 1941).

59. See, for example, the work of O. Löfgren, "Family and Household among Scandinavian Peasants: An Exploratory Essay," *Ethnologia Scandinavica*, 4 (1974), pp. 17–51, and G. Wiegelmann, "Zum Problem der bäuerlichen Arbeitsteilung in Mitteleuropa," in *Aus Geschichte und Landeskunde. Festschrift Franz Steinbach* (Bonn, 1960), pp. 637–71.

Domestic Industry
Work Options and Women's Choices

BARBARA FRANZOI

In Breslau, a mother and her sixteen-year-old daughter worked together sewing petticoats by hand. They earned 11.50 M. a week, but the work was not steady. A widow who made wicker plaits for straw hats was paid 50 pf. per 100 meters of plaiting. She had worked for the same firm in Breslau for ten or eleven years where the work season lasted five months. There were three adults in the household. They lived in two rooms, one of which was used as the kitchen. In Niedernberg, a small village in Bavaria, a nineteen-year-old single girl rented sleeping space from a farm family. She worked alone sewing vests. In season she worked eleven hours a day and earned about 13 M. a week. In summer she did agricultural work with the family.[1]

These women and members of their households were employed in German domestic industry and the descriptions of their work experience were recorded in the first decade of the twentieth century. Factories, which took an increasingly larger share of the production process, did not squeeze home industry out of existence. Surprisingly, domestic production survived and in some instances actually thrived. And it was women who made the most use of its persistence. The kinds of work women did before, during, and after the expansion of factories and mechanization remained rather consistent. Domestic industry deserves separate treatment in a study of German industrialization in the period from 1871 to 1914 because it is the best refutation of the stereotypic model which stresses factory production in heavy industry.[2] Further, women's work in domestic industry demonstrates the multi-faceted and irregular nature of the female experience with work that often included a period in the factory, a time in domestic service, and in domestic industry.

This essay is an effort to make women workers visible, to reach the actual relationship between the female labor force and the production process. It is not merely an expanded dimension to labor history, but a new way of looking at the impact of industrialization on the lives of women who worked. It will attempt to show that conventional emphasis on changes in the organized, highly mechanized factory sector has had a distorting effect. Because factories were primarily employers of male labor, industrial history that focuses on factory work tends either to ignore women's work entirely or to subsume it under a set of generalizations that do justice to neither sex. Since Germany's industrialization was even more rapid than that of other European countries, its history has been particularly burdened by this misconception.[3]

Mechanization of production and concentration of work in factories was only part of the capitalist economic growth pattern. That process was neither uniform nor linear.[4] The tasks in many industries were a combination of both mechanized factory work and handicraft production. Some work processes involved both factory labor and home work in a sequential or interrupted schedule of operation. And factory work in almost every industry experienced periods of irregular employment because production was often subject to the demands of a seasonal market. This was particularly true in consumer goods industries and construction. Seasonal, highly labor-intensive production methods were not curious survivals of past time, but integral parts of the burgeoning capitalist economy.[5] Employers sought the cheapest production methods available, and the cheapest was not always factory work. In many instances, the factory was a burden, an unacceptable cost, and because it meant a concentration of workers, a threat to labor discipline.

Many industries, even some of the most highly mechanized, involved operations that were left to hand labor and home work.[6] This was true for metals and machines, chemicals and electrical products, as well as textiles and other consumer goods industries. There were discrepancies in the growth potential among industries and time lags in certain industries in adoption of mechanization. Most apparent was the difference between capital goods and consumer goods industries. There was no master plan in German capitalist development. German industrialization should not be conceptualized as a smooth and steady adoption of more machines and more factories. Rather, it is useful to view the process as a probing one— an experiment with various methods of organizing production that resulted in the combination of machine and hand labor and an assimilation of traditional work forms to the needs of production. Only by doing so can we understand the labor that thousands of women performed. They were rarely employed in factories on a steady basis, but this does not mean that their work was "pre-industrial" or that their productivity was incidental to Germany's economic growth. This gender division of labor was fundamental to capitalist development, and thus a study of women's work is an important contribution to the history of industrialization.

To understand women's work, it is necessary to move beyond the narrow definition of conventional labor history and investigate a much wider range of occupations. Most women's work was labor-intensive, low-skilled, irregular, and low-paid. They folded cartons, sorted parts, sewed dolls' clothes, plaited wicker, knotted fishnets, and rolled tobacco. The customary picture of the mill girl was true for only a small number of Germany's industrial working women, even among young single women. Almost 50 percent of the industrial female labor force was employed in the clothing industry; another third worked in foods and tobacco.[7] Both industries were heavily concentrated in home production.

When women worked in a factory setting, it was often seasonal and irregular. Women moved in and out of the factory as both industrial demand and personal necessity dictated. Most women who did factory work were young and single. Married women chose other ways to earn money. Women changed jobs frequently; they combined work in agriculture, in domestic service, in factories, and in domestic industry. Women juggled their various roles as earners, daughters, wives, and mothers, supplementing the family income when necessary, sometimes supporting themselves and their families entirely. Women worked in times of need or emergency. Multiple earnings were required in many working-class families, not as a cash reserve or savings for the future, but to meet immediate needs. If children could be used to supplement family income, their labor and earnings were commonly used before mothers went out to work. Women's experience with work, therefore, was irregular and cyclical. The combination of these factors produced an extremely fluid female labor force. The world was precarious, but there was some measure of safety in the opportunity to do something else. The significant point is that women workers did have the chance to choose, and the pattern of their work experience proved that they exercised that option.

While domestic industry retained a considerable share of the production process in Germany well into the twentieth century, it had always been recognized that home workers were elusive. They had always been counted in the national occupational censuses, but they had not been counted accurately. The problem of identifying and recording the extent of home work was complicated both by the mechanics of the German census and by the home workers, either inadvertently or with the full intention of escaping notice. Of more crucial importance was the "loss" of home workers due to the essential character of domestic production. Examination of these factors will point up the rhythm of home work that made this form of production almost an underground economy.

In was inherent in the pattern of home work for many workers to go uncounted. The time of year the census was taken contributed in part to the confusion. For a large number of home workers, notably those in non-urban areas, domestic industry was a part-time occupation, most usually coupled with agriculture. Since the census was taken in June, there was some confusion regarding identification of major occupation. Mitigating against this situation, however, were instructions to disregard temporary employment if it differed from the major occupation.[8] What effect this directive had on the outcome of the counting is difficult to determine, particularly for women, because many were only part-time family help. In addressing the problem of underrepresentation of family help in domestic industry, the *Statistik des Deutschen Reichs (Statistics of the German Empire)*, which was responsible for the official count, stated that probably large numbers of persons employed in home work were never registered.[9]

Another problem arose from employers deliberately reporting false figures to avoid the mandatory matching payments for workers' insurance. Women could be hidden most easily; employers simply neglected to count family members.[10] In many cases it was the workers themselves who intentionally omitted telling about home employment. This was especially true in cities, where the domestic industry of wives and daughters was deliberately concealed to avoid paying taxes.

Efforts to obtain an accurate record of the numbers of persons employed and the kinds of tasks they performed were short of satisfactory. The unreliability of numerical data can be disappointing. However, it was this very lack of preciseness that reflected most clearly the life style of large numbers of persons, mostly women, who moved relatively freely on the edges of more visible and more structured employment. Bringing domestic industry into focus was not an easy task. There were numerous conflicting interests involved, not the least of which were the home workers themselves. Although proposals concerning the issue of home work regulation were advanced in the Reichstag in 1906, the Home Work Act did not become law untiil 1911.[11] As late as 1911, then, domestic industry remained not only unregulated, but undefined as well.

Domestic industry declined in the late nineteenth and early twentieth centuries. The decline was steady and theoretically represented the transfer of production from a pre-industrial to an industrial pattern, i.e., from home to factory. In 1882 there were approximately 475,000 persons recorded as domestic workers; in 1907 that figure had diminished to a little more than 400,000.[12] However, the total picture does not tell the same story for men and women. While it is easy to assume a transfer from home work to factory work, there is evidence that this picture was not completely true, and much less true for women. Industries that had traditionally employed large numbers of home workers, old home industry, had declined. These were predominantly textile-related and situated in non-urban locations. However, focusing on one branch of home industry, even a very significantly large one, is misleading. An important exception to the decline in rural home industry was tobacco (cigar and cigarette manufacture). Because of the coincidence of geographic location between textiles and tobacco, many persons left the declining textile industry to take up domestic production in tobacco.[13] Urban home industry thrived, particularly the various branches of clothing manufacture. What is significant about German home production is that it was marked by clear industrial and geographic patterns that affirm regional rather than national economic development.[14]

The number of persons working in home industry, excluding textiles, increased, and the increase reflected a pattern of adjustment that included both geographic mobility and mobility from one kind of industry to another. Where gains were indicated, the increase for women was considerably more significant than that for men. In 1907, there were 235,000 women registered as domestic workers compared with 209,000 in 1882, representing an increase of 12 percent. For men the numerical profile is different. In 1907, 170,000 men were employed, while in 1882, 266,000 were recorded, a reduction of 36 percent.[15] What happened was that industries that were male-intensive showed a strong percentage increase for women, and industries that had been female-intensive became even more so. This transition resulted in a gender reversal in virtually every branch of domestic industry and brought about dramatic feminization of domestic production.

Part of the answer to the continuing viability of domestic industry lay in the material advantages it held for the employer. While regulations regarding conditions of employment had been spelled out for factory work in the 1890s, home industry remained beyond the constraints and protections mandated by law into the twentieth century. Compliance with factory regulations added to production costs. The myriad provisions regarding women in factories, particularly the maximum daily work time, cut into the amount of production the employer could expect from a traditionally cheap source of labor. Where the directives of the worker protection laws could be circumvented, employers did so, and home work was the alternative choice.

Using home workers also freed the employer from having to deal with the trade unions. Domestic workers were notoriously difficult to organize, a situation the unions deplored. Because domestic industry constituted competition for wages and jobs, the unions, especially the socialist trade unions, demanded legal restrictions on home work and actually went so far as to demand its abolition.[16] For the employer, the absence of worker organizations allowed access to an unprotected labor force. Home workers were a cheap, flexible, available labor source. As long as home work filled a need in German industry, employers continued to utilize this form of manufacture parallel to or in place of factory production.

Changes in Germany's employment and education laws acted to preserve traditional forms while underscoring industry's need for female labor. In 1891 child labor in factories was prohibited. In addition, children between the ages of fourteen and sixteen could not be employed in factories more than ten hours daily. Children also were required to attend school for eight years, usually between the ages of six and fourteen. Textiles and tobacco were especially affected by the new regulations because both industries employed child labor extensively. Several states chose to circumvent the national law by passing local ordinances permitting the factory employment of children under the age of fourteen if they had completed the required number of years in school.[17]

> Employers and parents of youngsters find the [new law] extremely difficult because thirteen-year-old children who are finished with school cannot take regular factory employment until fourteen. Older children seem reluctant to take work in the factories, and the parents do not know what to do with their children who are at home and not earning.[18]

There is overwhelming evidence that the major repercussion of the child labor law was expansion of child labor in domestic industry.[19] Factory inspectors noted large numbers of children working in a slipper factory in Zwickau in 1890; after 1891, they disappeared. "The children now work at home; they or their brothers and sisters pick up the cloth at the factory and deliver the finished slippers back."[20] Inspectors in Pirmasens in the Pfalz also reported increased numbers of children working at home. In Arnsberg, most needle manufacturing switched from factory to home production. Many mothers moved into domestic production when their children were forced to leave the factory. The effect of the law in the tobacco industry was most obvious. The regulations had wide repercussions in cigar making because large numbers of children were employed in factories as helpers. "When rollers cannot have their helpers in the factory, they move into home work so as not to lose the cheap labor."[21] There is no precise way to measure the cause-effect relationship between prohibition of child labor and the increased employment of women. It can be suggested that the new regulations on child labor and compulsory education pushed children into domestic industry and created more dramatic need for women to work to compensate for the deficit caused by loss of earnings.

For women it was the rhythm of work that gave domestic industry its uniqueness as an industrial work form. Home work intruded into the time and energy a women could devote to household tasks, but the intrusion was perceived as less harsh than factory work. More importantly, home work served as a base for the preservation of a family economy, especially for women and children, in which members not only contributed wage but frequently worked together to secure that wage. Women attempted to make the job fit their family circumstances instead of the reverse. This is a primary reason for the continuation of traditional work choices. It is also a fundamental explanation of how women endured the impact of industrialization without profound disruption. Women's family roles defined their work identity. Decisions were made within this framework governed by a constant attempt to balance family needs with economic demands.

Lack of precise figures complicates the problem of arriving at a definite picture of marital status and age category for women working at home. While married women comprised 21 percent of the total female industrial labor force including both factory and home work in 1907, married women, widows, and separated women made up about half the number working at home. Because there are fairly accurate figures only for those women listed as independent home workers, and because less than half the number of women home workers in 1907 listed themselves as independent, there remains the problem of trying to draw conclusions about the rest.

In 1907, 60 percent of all married women in industry were working as helpers. Most of these were concentrated in four industry branches: textiles, foods and tobacco, wood products and clothing. Seventy-three percent of all married working women were employed in these four industries, and industries that had large numbers of family members assisting were also heavily home work. These data suggest that at least half and probably more than half the number of women working at home were married.[22] The 1895 census indicated that 48 percent of the women over sixteen working at home were married, separated, or widowed.[23] A similar distribution appears in a survey of women home workers taken by the Christlicher Gewerkverein der Heimarbeiterinnen (Christian Union of Women Home Workers), published in 1906: 56 percent were married, 24 percent single, and 19 percent widowed or separated. Most of the women questioned worked in textiles and clothing.[24]

More definite information regarding marital status was available for women listing themselves as independent home workers.[25] More than half the women were married or formerly married in 1907. Forty-two percent were single. While the number and percentage of independent women home workers who were widowed remained constant between 1895 and 1907, there were significant changes in the composition of the work force between single and married women. A decrease in the number of single women was paralleled by an increase in the number of married women working at home. Expressed in percentages, in 1895, 53 percent were single; in 1907, 42 percent. Age categories for both single and married women remained about the same for both census years. While these data may indicate a slightly increased tendency to marry earlier, most probably they reflect the increasing availability of factory work. Young women without family responsibilities could more readily move into the factory. For married women, factory work was not so easily handled, and many preferred to remain at home.

Home work was at once both flexible and constricting. Because domestic industry generally was seasonal work, it could easily be combined with agricultural tasks, especially in rural areas. In cities, however, there were periods of unemployment and underemployment when *Pfennigs* (pennies) had to be stretched over months of layoff. The seasonal schedule also demanded short periods of rather intense energy when it was not unusual for work to continue for fourteen or fifteen hours a day, often without pause on the weekend. Because of the pressures on time management during the season, home workers had to juggle a varied and elastic schedule.

Wages in home work were not sufficient for economic independence. Perception of an annual wage was difficult for most home workers. Pay was usually reckoned on price per piece, and the intensity of work was personal. Most workers could respond to a question of piecework price, but when it came to figuring weekly wage, it was not unusual to get approximations and averages. At best, yearly wages could only be estimated because of the irregularity of work and seasonal fluctuations.

It is not surprising that figures for self-supporting home workers were sparse. Wage data were usually expressed as part of the family economy, testifying to the situation of most female home workers. Earnings derived from one source were not usual. Earnings of home workers overwhelmingly represented a share of the family wage, and women home workers belonged to families that relied on numerous sources of income in order to get by. The wife's contribution was necessary and recognized as an important share of the family income. Not infrequently, statements such as "She at the very least pays the rent"[6] were appropriate commentary on the value placed upon a wife's earning capacity. The irregularity of home work both allowed and demanded a flexibility in work schedule to take advantage of all chances to earn a wage. The concept of a one-wage-earner family relying on a one-job wage is an impossible one to apply to German home workers in the late nineteenth and early twentieth centuries.

In Baden, for example, while domestic industry was not large, it was diversified and intimately related to agriculture. Silk winding and wool spinning were jobs done only in the winter months. Women who did silk-ribbon weaving worked an average of two hundred days a year; chain makers working at home were employed for five months during the winter. Women who worked in the porcelain factory in Freiburg lived in the surrounding countryside; they made up the slack in factory work by sewing on the porcelain doll heads during the winter. This Freiburg factory employed over 1,300 women as home workers. Large numbers of agents went into the countryside to deliver the materials and pick up the finished work. Straw-hat workers were hired only in the winter, but the brush industry, which employed all year, lost many of its female home workers to agriculture in the summer. Brush manufacture in Baden was a revealing example of how an industry was forced to adapt to the pressure of a reluctant labor force. Women would not work in the factories, so plans for future expansion were scrapped in favor of enlarging the network of women working at home.[27]

In cities, domestic industry was no more regular than in rural areas. The kinds of jobs available were seasonal, mostly in clothing, and women did home work when men's wages were low or irregular. Men in construction were especially caught in the constraints of good wages during season and no wage or marginal income during the winter months. In Neustadt, a thirty-eight-year-old woman and four of her six children made artificial flowers with the help of her husband, a construction helper, who was unemployed. The six persons working together were able to earn 10 M. 20 pf. for two weeks' work.[28] In another family, where the father was employed only six months a year in construction, the wife and children also made artificial flowers. The woman had been a home worker for twelve years. With the help of her two oldest children and two other children whom she hired, the group made 6 M. a week for ten to twelve hours of work daily. The family paid 295 M. rent for a two-room apartment with a kitchen. All the flower work was done in the kitchen as well as cooking, eating, and washing.[29] A Berlin home worker employed in the highly "style-conscious" fine feather industry commented on the rhythm of her work experience.

> My husband is a bricklayer and he earns an average of 30 M. weekly in the summer. We have four children from one to six years old and a mother to care for. We pay 270 M. yearly for the apartment, which has two rooms and a kitchen. I work in the kitchen. I have worked six years for the same middleman (*Zwischenmeister*) and earn 3 to 6 M. a week for six or seven hours daily when there is work.[30]

There were certain continuities in job opportunities in many industries where factory work blended with home work. This fluidity created broader economic options for working-class families. Factories were not alien to home workers. There were close links between home work and factory work that tended to diminish the perception of work as a fixed condition. Instead of factories eliminating home work, many large establishments maintained a putting-out system for jobs that could better and more cheaply be done at home. This connection between factory and home work facilitated a relatively easy transition between the two work forms. More importantly, the work experience of many women included both factory and home production, representing a kind of cycle of employment that paralleled the demands of their lives.

Until 1908, when the practice was forbidden by law, it was possible to take work from the factory to be finished at home. It is difficult to obtain accurate information regarding the number of persons who took work out because employers were reluctant to divulge the figures to factory inspectors out of fear of being caught in non-compliance. There were only scattered and conflicting responses concerning the prohibition. In Bautzen, single women responded differently from married when questioned about their reactions. Married women welcomed the prohibition, stating that they were no longer under pressure to work overtime at home and could devote more time to taking care of the house. Single women resisted, indicating that they could not understand why they were being prevented from earning a little extra.[31] Württemberg women working in textile and clothing factories reacted to what they claimed was an infringement on their personal freedom to work. They remarked that it was unfair not to be able to use Saturday afternoons and Sundays, when the factories were closed, to get additional wages.[32]

Textiles maintained a fairly substantial putting-out system despite the increase in factory production. In Württemberg, for example, the factory inspector reported that more and more linen cloth weaving was done in factories, but home work was still done by women and children.

> The majority of the female home workers are wives and daughters of factory workers, home weavers, and small hand weavers. The young girls are employed for a time in one of the home-work-related factories and find that they are not suited to the regularity of factory work and for this or other personal reasons, they go over to *Hausarbeit* (homework).[33]

An industry where there were especially close ties between factory and home work was tobacco. Home workers were considered part of the factory establishment to the extent that employers usually did not even separate the two in their records. Structural changes in the tobacco industry increased decentralization and hand work, which created the need for additional labor outside factory premises. That demand was filled primarily by women who could not or would not enter the factory. Where tobacco manufacture was situated in rural areas, factories were often too far from the home to make travel back and forth reasonable. In Saxony, Leipzig was a center for tobacco products. To seek out sources of cheap labor, a system of small branch factories, distribution centers in reality, reached the home workers directly. Sorting was done in the main factory, with only minimal manufacturing jobs retained. In Saxony, the factory served as the school for training women who took up similar jobs at home after marriage. In Westphalia, where about 26,000 persons were employed in the tobacco industry, training for work was accomplished in the factories, with most women workers entering domestic manufacture as soon as they learned enough to do their job.[34]

Evidence of the easy transition between factory and home work in tobacco was clearly present in comments of women who were questioned about the conditions of their work by the Christian Union of Women Home Workers. An eighteen-year-old girl reported that she went into the factory only when she wanted to earn more money. She made inexpensive cigars during the high season between November and February; the rest of the time she worked at home cutting tobacco. Another eighteen-year-old declared that she worked at home when she was overwhelmed with work at the factory. A twenty-nine-year-old married woman complained about dust in her apartment when she rolled cigarettes at home, indicating she preferred factory work, but she had to care for her children. Still another married woman, aged thirty-six, indicated she would return to the factory as soon as her child finished nursing. Interestingly, she had worked at home for four years.[35]

Clothing was another industry that experienced decentralization in the late nineteenth century. Cities were the centers for women's clothing: Berlin and Breslau in the north and Munich in southern Germany.[36] As was the case in the tobacco industry, many women learned the job in the factory or workrooms, then upon marriage or the birth of children, switched into home work. Work in clothing factories reduced many of the disagreeable features of domestic production: there were opportunities for better training; conditions were cleaner; seasonal fluctuations were not as severe; wages were higher; and work time was more regular. Yet home industry thrived while in many locations machines in factories remained idle. The cyclical pattern appeared frequently in the reports of factory inspectors commenting on home work in their districts. In Oberamtsbezirk Baligen, the inspector described what he observed to be the usual pattern of employment in hosiery manufacture:

> Most sewers become familiar with hosiery work at an early age. As schoolchildren and sometimes even earlier they must help at home, and

after confirmation, with a few exceptions, they go to the hosiery mills. Usually when they go back to home work they perform similar jobs, often for the same factory where they were employed.[37]

Industrial work required adjustments in the lives of women, but women came to terms with the necessity to work by imposing an irregularity on the work experience. It was an irregularity based on the opportunity to select among various forms of work. The presence of a large, viable domestic industry in twentieth-century Germany can only be understood by viewing German industrialization as a complex process that expanded in many directions and into various work forms. Despite rapid and extensive industrialization, women in prewar Germany could still perceive work as multi-faceted. Agriculture could be combined with domestic industry, and domestic industry had close ties with factory production. The level of skill required for earning a wage was minimal. Women could take on jobs as easily as they could leave them. The persistence of home industry gave women a way out—a way out of an unmanageable economic situation and a way to circumvent the undesirable aspects of work in a factory. Ultimately, the real picture of the impact of industrialization emerges most clearly by looking at women who worked. Their lives were testimonies of hardship and scarcity, but also affirmations of adjustment and coping. Women changed jobs to fit the conditions of their lives. They worked when they had to, going into the factory only when there were no better options in terms of time or money. Work provided neither a life-defining activity nor a lifetime occupation.

The most important statement that should be made is that continuity prevailed over change in the lives of working women because women continued to select work options that were familiar to them. These choices established a pattern of adjustment that preserved a uniquely female response to work, even during a time of rapid economic transformation. The picture that emerges reveals a significant time lag between external circumstances, such as changes in the mode of production, and changes in the lives of women. The German situation gives ample evidence that this contention is valid for working women. It is time to move beyond generalizations about the impact of industrialization on women to take a more sensitive look at how women handled the multiple demands on their time and energy, demands which seemed to change very little over time. Women's work in Germany has dramatic implications that need to be evaluated in the broader context of European history and the history of women.

NOTES

1. C. Heiss and A. Koppel, *Heimarbeit und Hausindustrie in Deutschland* (Berlin, 1906), pp. 180–229.

2. David S. Landes, *The Unbound Prometheus* (Cambridge, 1970), p. 222.

3. J. H. Clapham, *The Economic Development of France and Germany, 1815–1914* (Cambridge, 1955), p. 278.

4. Wolfram Fischer, *Wirtschaft und Gesellschaft im Zeitalter der Industrialisierung* (Göttingen, 1972), pp. 251–53.

5. Raphael Samuel, "Workshop of the World, Steam Power and Hand Technology in mid-Victorian Britain," *History Workshop*, no. 3 (1977), p. 10.

6. Fischer, pp. 345–46.

7. "Die Frauenerwerbsarbeit im Deutschen Reich nach den Ergebnissen der Berufszählungen von 1882–1910," *Statistische Beilage des Correspondenz-Blatt*, 3 (April 27, 1912), pp. 68–77.

8. Frank Tipton, *Regional Variations in the Economic Development of Germany during the Nineteenth Century* (Middletown, Conn., 1976) p. 163.

9. *Statistik des Deutschen Reichs*, 220–221 (1914), p. 164.

10. *Protokoll der Verhandlungen des Ersten Allgemeinen Heimarbeiterschutz-Kongress* (Berlin, 1904), p. 61.

11. Heinrich Koch, "The New Homework Act," *Office International du Travail Domicile*, 6 (n.d.), p. 1.

12. *Statistik des Deutschen Reichs*, p. 165.

13. E. Jaffe, "Hausindustrie und Fabrikbetrieb in der deutschen Cigarrenfabrikations," *Schriften des Vereins für Sozialpolitik*, 84 (1899), p. 306.

14. "Das Hausgewerbe in Deutschland nach der gewerblichen Betriebszahlung vom 12 Juni 1907," *Reichs-Arbeitsblatt*, 2 (1910), p. 110.

15. *Statistik des Deutschen Reichs*, p. 167. These figures are rounded off to the nearest thousand.

16. Walther Frisch, "Die Organisationsbetrebungen der Arbeiter in der deutschen Tabakindustrie," *Staats und Sozialwissenschaftliche Forschungen*, 24 (Leipzig, 1905), p. 246.

17. *Amtliche-Mittheilungen aus dem Jahresberichten der Gewerbeaufsichtbeamten und Bergbehörden* (1893), p. 56.

18. Ibid., p. 52.

19. In March 1903, regulations regarding employment of children in industry were extended to home work.

20. *Amtliche-Mittheilungen*, p. 57.

21. Ibid.

22. *Statistische Beilage des Correspondenz-Blatt*, p. 93.

23. *Statistik des Deutschen Reichs*, 111 (1899), p. 226.

24. Heiss and Koppel, computed from charts on pp. 190–229.

25. *Statistik des Deutschen Reichs*, 221 (1913), p. 227.

26. Karl Bittmann, *Hausindustrie und Heimarbeit im Grossherzogtum Baden* (Karlsruhe, 1907), p. 45.

27. "Hausindustrie und Heimarbeit im Grossherzogtum Baden zu Anfang des XX Jahrhunderts," *Reichs-Arbeitsblatt*, 2 (1907), p. 125.

28. *Protokoll*, p. 24.

29. Ibid.

30. Ibid., p. 191.

31. *Amtliche-Mittheilungen*, 3 (1911), p. 24.

32. Ibid., 4, p. 33.

33. Ibid., 4 (1913), p. 41.

34. Jaffe, p. 311.

35. Heiss and Koppel, pp. 226–29.

36. Erhard Schmidt, *Fabrikbetrieb und Heimarbeit in der deutschen Konfektionsindustrie* (Stuttgart, 1912), p. 102.

37. *Amtliche-Mittheilungen*, 4 (1913), p. 34.

Social Insurance and the Family Work of Oberlausitz Home Weavers in the Late Nineteenth Century*

JEAN H. QUATAERT

In 1894, the German *Bundesrat* (Federal Council) extended disability and old age insurance to the self-employed in home weaving. Germany was the first industrializing country to adopt national pension plans for wage earners. Factory workers obtained health insurance in 1883 and accident insurance in 1884; five years later, the old-age pension scheme was passed. The specific political motive for this initial step to welfare capitalism is clear. Bismarck sought to wean workers from socialism through state welfare.[1] But the legislation reflected broader social concerns. Imperial officials also were seeking to influence labor conditions in the factories and workshops of the newly emerging industrial world. The ruling classes of agrarians and industrialists which Bismarck had forged by his tariff policy rejected laissez-faire capitalism and substituted a policy of state paternalism through industrial codes and detailed protective laws. In 1878, they even refashioned a Factory Inspectorate with powers to watch over and enforce the new labor legislation. Germany's rulers expected

*Research for this chapter was made possible by a National Endowment for the Humanities Research Fellowship (1980–81), an American Council of Learned Societies Grant-in-Aid, and a German Academic Exchange Service "Study Visit" Grant (DAAD) (summer 1982). I gratefully acknowledge the support of these foundations.

tangible benefits. Supervising the extent and character of women's and children's factory labor, for example, would secure working-class family life (and still guarantee a pool of cheap labor for a German competitive edge); values learned on the job such as sobriety and moral rectitude would find their way back into working-class homes; and a pension scheme, too, would insure poorer families against some of life's hard knocks and moderate social discontent.[2] Such broad, regulatory policies essentially were designed to promote socially integrative and conservative sentiments. In short, social insurance and state regulation of work were twin pillars of Imperial Germany's social policy. Thus, when home weavers were included in the insurance plan, the requirement elicited no special commentary; it seemed to fit an emerging pattern.

In reality, the decision to embrace home weavers represented something new. Both the insurance plans and the protective laws initially had been geared to laborers in factories and larger workshops. In contrast, the 1894 law was one of the first—and the most important until 1914—to extend insurance into the home of the self-employed, the so-called *Hausgewerbetreibende*, a work category that confounded even judicial experts in Imperial Germany.[3] In essence, these workers depended on distributors and factory owners for raw materials and/or assignments yet were in control of their work schedules and personnel. At times, they were on their own and realized an "entrepreneurial" profit or loss. Significantly, in mandating insurance for this category of worker, the law forced a collision of two worlds. The one was the new world of the factory, and insurance laws were attuned to its bases: an identifiable work force, place and length of work, method of payment, and employer. The second world was equally honorable and in the case of weavers it extended back centuries. It represented the survival of an older family work community, with its own traditions, work rhythm, and worker relations. When the two worlds met, the ambiguities centered on the issue of assessing women's work or, in the law's parlance, the work of so-called family members. How was the state to understand the wife who wove (*Weberin*) or wound the warp spools (*Treiberin*), watched the goats and tended the vegetables, and took primary care of running the home? Which labor was insurable and thus seen as real work? What about the husband and wife who both wove—on one loom or on two looms? Much of women's wage work in industrial capitalism actually did center in the home. Recent research has established a typical pattern of female employment in industrial and craft occupations.[4] Women's work life in factories tended to follow life- and family-cycle patterns. As single women, they took on factory work and later, after marriage and children, swelled the ranks of home industry labor in consumer goods production. A husband's illness or a protracted strike might send them back to the factory again; and, to be sure, women enriched the family fund by taking in lodgers or washing. But by extending insurance to work done in the home, as was envisioned in 1894, the German state might have begun to offer women the benefits of insurance, which they relinquished when they left the factory for the hearth.

By the mid-1890s, mechanization of textile production in Europe had proceeded sufficiently to undercut any serious prospects for handweaving. But German industrialization had its own pace. Some areas had been thoroughly mechanized, so only remnants of hand production existed, while in other, more remote regions a significant proportion of the population still made its livelihood in handicrafts. This was true of Saxony, one of the first German states to industrialize and the one associated in popular consciousness with wrenching mechanization and urbanization as well as worker militancy. Yet real handweavers continued to eke out a marginal existence well into the twentieth century in the mountainous regions of Saxony, such as the Erzgebirge and the South Oberlausitz. Furthermore, by the late nineteenth century, handweavers had been transformed into symbols of an older age and way of life that was disappearing in the new industrial world of factory labor. The plight of handweavers figured prominently in the corpus of social commentary written by middle-class critics of industrial capitalism.[5] And weavers had been active in history; memories of the Silesian revolt of 1844 lived on in the lithographs of Käthe Kollwitz and in the naturalist theater of Gerhard Hauptmann. Understandably, then, handweavers exercised a strong fascination on German thinking. Among the many pre-industrial work categories fighting a losing battle for survival, the *Bundesrat* appropriately singled them out. Passage of the insurance law changed in dramatic ways the lives of weaving families in the South Oberlausitz, an area of mixed factory and hand-textile production at the end of the nineteenth century.

The Oberlausitz is little known in the historic literature.[6] Yet for historians of work and family life it offers an instructive and highly fascinating story of rural textile manufacturing extending over centuries. It was a borderland between Saxony and Bohemia and today demarcates the southeastern extension of the German Democratic Republic on both the Polish and Czechoslovak borders. Despite shifting political fortunes, its ties to weaving have been long and continuous. Rural home weaving emerged during the Thirty Years' War when the urban guilds lost their monopoly over textile production. Weaving spread rapidly, offering peasants alternative employment in the hilly and only moderately fertile province. By the early nineteenth century, the South Oberlausitz had one of the densest populations in all of central Europe.[7] Production was decentralized, in the homes of weavers, and organized by commercial capital (the *Verlagsystem*). The Oberlausitz, in short, had become a classic example of proto-industrialism—a rural area manufacturing for a distant market.[8] And its whole material culture reflected the crucial position of weaving. Weaving determined the layout of the numerous long, narrow villages that emerged on both sides of small streams. It accounted, too, for the unique structure of weaver cottages, the *Umgebinde* house that today still stamps the landscape. It is a four-sided, square wooden structure enclosed by a larger wooden dwelling. The smaller structure contained the loom and had its own foundation so that the shaking of the loom would not extend throughout the home. And the area had its myths and heroes, among them Karasek, "The Praguer Kid," an early nineteenth-century Oberlausitz Robin Hood who stole linen and cotton goods, both raw and finished, from the rich distributors and gave them to poorer weavers. Karasek and his band hid out in the pockets of Austrian jurisdiction that until midcentury extended deep into Saxon territory. So strong was the weaving tradition that the area never developed an adequate spinning industry; the few spinning mills in the South Oberlausitz could not attract indigenous workers and had to employ Bohemian girls from Reichenberg (today Liberec). Unlike other areas in Germany, such as Berlin, that once had been important pre-industrial textile regions but subsequently developed other specialties, the Oberlausitz after 1900 became a leading producer of machine-made cloth for the national market. And today it is a center of terry-cloth and cotton goods production in the German Democratic Republic.

Industrialization had come late to the Oberlausitz, in part due to the tardy introduction of a railroad network. The first line to connect Löbau and Bautzen with Dresden opened only in 1846; several years later the two major South Oberlausitz cities, Löbau and Zittau, were linked, but construction of subsidiary lines connecting the various weaver valleys continued into the 1890s. The railroad expanded market opportunities and spurred mechanization. So did the discovery of lignite near Zittau, and the factory, with its large chimney and saw-shaped roof for natural light control, intruded into the landscape. But hand textiles played a surprisingly important role in these early enterprises and they existed independently. Factory owners continued to employ handweavers into the twentieth century in rather significant numbers for linen and colored cotton cloth. Such workers offered flexibility in meeting sudden shifts in market demand. In addition, much of the preparatory work in weaving—winding the warp spools and the bobbins—was done in workers' homes. Also, the first factories used both hand and mechanical looms, which kept handweaving skills alive. A major survey of work completed in the decade prior to 1894 documented concretely the continued importance of handweaving as a source of family livelihood.[9] In the administrative district of Zittau, comprised of 61 municipalities (but excluding the urban center of

Zittau itself), handweaving in 1885 represented 12 percent of a total population of 73,750. The percentage does not include family members supported by the occupation or those engaged in textile-related handicrafts. In some villages, the numbers far surpassed the average: in Middle and Lower Oderwitz, for example, 28 percent and 35.3 percent, respectively, of each total population worked in handweaving. The comparative backwardness of the South Oberlausitz, then, can be used to good advantage: a meaningful proportion of handweavers existed in the South Oberlausitz when the *Bundesrat* passed the old age insurance addendum.

Taken together, the history of the South Oberlausitz at the end of the nineteenth century offers a fascinating case study of the impact of social insurance on one category of worker. To be sure, these home weavers were a social group dying out. But the world of home production was connected closely to the victorious factory era by workers themselves. The Oberlausitz textile factory recruited its work force almost exclusively from former home industry weavers, and these weavers and their daughters and sons brought into the factory the values and attitudes toward work that had been fashioned in the preceding decades. In addition, it was public policy that had come to play an increasingly important role in this process of work definition and experience. While labor historians long have been concerned with the effect of factory jobs on labor consciousness, they have neglected the ways in which labor legislation and social insurance, too, fundamentally affected work and family life in the modern era.[10] The influence, however, was not simply unidirectional; workers actively participated in shaping their world. The Oberlausitz case is a telling example. Worker resistance to social insurance was immediate and dogged; the handweavers successfully frustrated state intentions. Amidst the controversy, however, it was women's work that was manipulated, and the crucial role of women in the labor force was downplayed.

Social commentators in late-nineteenth-century Germany loved to contrast the "traditional" and "new" domestic industries.[11] By this they meant the composition of the work force, not home industry's inherent association with capitalism. In their conception, women—especially wives and mothers in urban areas—dominated the new form; in contrast, family men—the true heads of households—were central figures in the traditional mode, although they relied on the periodic assistance of family members. These same observers would have been amazed at the extent of women's steady and important involvement in the older form of home industry production. A historian in the 1970s, Hans Medick, has noted correctly that work life in traditional home industry relied heavily on female labor and it broke the bonds of sex role divisions.[12] But such a pattern of labor can be reconstructed only with archival materials, since the published studies at the end of the nineteenth century seriously misrepresented the role of women in home industry households. Archival materials for the Oberlausitz are rich and unambiguous and affirm Medick's claim. To develop this intricate labor pattern in full detail, however, would require a separate study. Only a general examination of the evidence is offered here; it shows clearly that many productive tasks were shared by males and females and that work labels associating certain operations with gender, such as male weaver and female warp winder, are misleading. And remember, it was this household structure, characterized by a relative absence of labor assignment by sex, that the German government chose for its first efforts to extend social insurance.

In 1638, three years after the Saxons acquired the Oberlausitz, the Zittau city council permitted villagers to spin and weave for the market. The decision permanently broke the monopoly of the urban linen guilds; they already had been weakened in the disruptions of the Thirty Years' War and no longer could meet demand. In return, each village weaver had to pay a loom tax, a feudal levy that continued until 1848. Production outside guild control offered distinct advantages to women; guilds restricted female labor, and it appears that organized training in general discriminated against women. For well over two centuries, in raw and bleached linen weaving and in the cotton cloth goods industry that began to encroach on indigenous linen production after 1800, any "lad or girl" could learn the trade. The verb *erlernen*, or training through practice, was applied equally to men and women. A girl would take a short apprenticeship with a weaver and then return home to "work as" *(agieren)* a "master." The new weaver, in turn, would teach others, including family members. In the main, these work skills were survival tools, passed on in the home from generation to generation.[13]

Other documents establish work patterns in the home. In the early nineteenth century, the Oberlausitz home weavers had received special rights to hawk their wares. The weavers had to petition for permission and the Saxon government issued official permits. In these requests, family members described their living and work relationships. This unique glimpse into weavers' homes shows a pattern of shared "teamwork." Husbands were given permits; so were wives and daughters. Roles were exchangeable and not defined by sex. The documents, in fact, affirm the crucial importance of role sharing, ironically in part by reverse example. A few cases exist (although they are by no means typical) in which a survivor petitioned the Saxon government to assume the peddling rights of a wife who had died unexpectedly. Johann Scholze from Haynewalde was such an individual. In his petition of 1850 he described sex division of labor in his home: he "finished the goods and [his] wife alone undertook the selling and hawking." While the municipal officials supported Scholze's request, they predicted the family's imminent downfall. Due to rigid sex role divisions, Scholze was ill-informed about customers along the hawking circuit and was unable to maintain the household.[14] Role sharing, then, was a matter of practical necessity in this era of high mortality and economic deprivation.

The pattern of shared work roles continued throughout the century and was rooted partially in technology. Typically, weavers picked up the warp spools already wound and chained off; so, too, the bobbins. Much of the so-called preparatory work in weaving was done elsewhere, in other homes geared to the textile industry.[15] Thus, role divisions by age and sex were less likely to materialize among weavers; but even where these jobs were done in one home, the tasks were not assigned exclusively by gender. Municipal officials in the late nineteenth century, confounded by what they saw in the home, painstakingly sought to piece together the fluidity of jobs in home-weaving households. At times, adult male weavers wound the bobbin (so-called children's work); at other times, they commissioned an adult neighbor. True, wives might prepare the warp; so would husbands and often husband and wife wove one piece alternately. Furthermore, insurance records late in the century document an amazing relationship that appeared in the later stages of a family cycle. This evidence turns stereotypes totally upside down. Among the elderly, men who tended to age earlier prepared the warp and wound the bobbins (to save money) for their more healthy wives who continued to weave![16] Despite the myriad patterns, one stands out most clearly; among home weavers in the Oberlausitz, as in other cases of "traditional" home industry, women were highly productive participants in the joint family venture throughout their and the family's life cycle.

To leave the impression, however, that life remained pretty much the same for weavers during the nineteenth century would be erroneous. The joint family venture was subjected to new and constraining pressures by the late nineteenth century. In the first place, it had become much more intricately entwined in the money economy. Taxes had to be paid; the church required support; but more importantly, there were new levies, for schools as of 1873, expenditures for school clothing, and in the next decade even insurance premium deductions. Furthermore, coal, wood, and oil cost dearly at a time when handweavers' incomes went plummeting. Mechanization not only took jobs away; goods could be produced more cheaply and in greater quantities. To remain competitive, handweaving reduced wages to the point of impoverishment. Wage-earning handweavers in the Oberlausitz were so poor that they had been exempted from health insurance because their daily wage was far below the average in their locality. One inquiry concluded that weavers rarely made even 350 marks per year.[17] The figure alone is not revealing. Wage levels varied greatly, depending on the quality of labor and the hours worked; for a meaningful picture, gross income from handweaving must be related to family size, other sources of income, and expenditures. But no doubt remained that these handweavers survived in good measure because they owned homes with small amounts of land to grow vegetables and potatoes and to keep goats and chickens or they rented small agricultural plots. Those who did not own homes had been the first to migrate to the emerging factory towns and comprise the early factory work force.

The alternative job opportunities, as in the new factories, were the second major change in home weavers' experiences. In the early nineteenth century the whole family worked in weaving. Traveler and municipal accounts are unambiguous on that score.[18] Over time it became increasingly possible for family members to work in different occupations. The process of job differentiation had begun in the mid-nineteenth century and it accelerated with the spread of factories in the area. Poverty induced weaver families to diversify, although the change from domestic to other work initially was easier for men than women. Government-sponsored public works such as railroad construction, road building, and maintenance opened up seasonal jobs—for men. So did the flurry of urban building in the province in the second half of the nineteenth century. In the 1870s, construction workers in the summer made two to three times more per week than handweavers.[19] Such alternative opportunities simply did not exist for women before the spread of textile factories that relied so heavily on female hands. Agriculture was weak and the local towns were and remained socially working-class communities, unable to support domestic service. The few women who moved for work to Dresden or Berlin were exceptions. Thus, the women of the area remained at home in weaving while many of their husbands and brothers took on seasonal work in the summer and returned only in the winter to weave. This had become a familiar pattern by the time the insurance officials made their detailed study of handweaving in the 1890s. And it is captured by a common nickname in the Oberlausitz: "*Maurerweber*" (literally "builder-weaver").

The deepening poverty and the handweavers' actual dependence on other employers persuaded the *Bundesrat* to make disability and old age insurance compulsory. Home weavers were not given a choice, as in the case of health insurance. The decision to make protection mandatory reflected still another condition: an increasingly aged work force in a dying industry. In the last several decades of the nineteenth century, young people tended to look for other jobs but, confounding stereotypes again, some young people did choose handweaving, and these were the most vehemently opposed to insurance. According to the district school inspectors, the number of continuing education students *(Fortbildungsschüler)* in handweaving actually rose steadily between 1875 and 1880; in 1883, 11 percent of 1,241 graduates went into handweaving. But older home workers, as the government anticipated, could be persuaded to accept the notion of pension benefits. They had trouble finding other jobs, employers preferred younger workers, and many of the laborers refused to make the transition to unfamiliar and threatening factory jobs. As early as 1895 the administrative district of Bautzen *(Kreishauptmannschaft)* had the highest percentage of disability and old age pensioners in Saxony, although they represented, and continued to represent, but a small fraction of potential recipients.[20] But given the rising proportion of older home weavers, the insurance money was designed to prevent these workers from becoming public charges.

The statute of 1894 consisted of thirteen rather straightforward paragraphs. Considering the novelty of the plan and its clientele, the legislation was remarkably sketchy, perhaps reflecting the German government's lack of experience in regulating home industry. The category itself only had been added to the national census in 1882. The Industrial Code of 1869, which became the basis for labor regulation in the new unified *Reich,* made no explicit mention of home industry or its work force. Just one paragraph spoke of persons who manufactured goods for entrepreneurs outside the businessman's place of work. This phrase, then, became the foundation for incorporating home industry into national legislation, but the extension occurred in judicial commentary and by interpretation, which varied greatly. Thus, considerable ambiguity existed over the legal position of home industry in Imperial Germany. The Industrial Code had defined three types of manufacturing: so-called permanent *(stehende)* businesses (the typical form of modern enterprise) but also those oriented toward peddling *(Hausieren)* as well as those involved in selling at markets *(Marktverkehr).* Home industry enterprises were seen to fall under the first and third type (and the latter explicitly applied to linen yarn and cloth produced by peasants as supplemental agricultural activity). As such, the businesses had to register with the municipality, and the general provisions in the national labor code regulating work relations—Sunday rest, continuing education for youths, the illegality of the truck system, freedom of contract—applied to its work force. This left undetermined if the self-employed home worker was to be considered independent or "dependent" *(gewerbliche Arbeiter).* Laws regulating the trade courts as well as the growing protective legislation applied only to the latter. The implementing ordinances of 1869 and 1893, however, qualified the applicability of labor regulation more explicitly.

They exempted from *all* regulation two kinds of workers. The first were those engaged in the female domestic arts of spinning, knitting, needlework, and washing and ironing, not because of their ties to home industry but rather because the legislators tied them to housework. Supplemental wage work done not as a permanent occupation but next to everyday housework was not considered labor. The second exempted group consisted of assistants of the self-employed home workers who were family members. Family members did not qualify as industrial labor assistants *(gewerbliche Hilfspersonen)* unless they had a separate work contract that stipulated wages.[21] Thus, in the transition to welfare capitalism, legal definitions ignored the economic cooperation among family members and did not acknowledge the family as a work unit, beyond rewarding the member of the family identified as the producer.

These regulations, then, comprised the legal setting for the extension of social insurance into weavers' homes. As seen, the Industrial Code did not recognize joint family work. To qualify for insurance, furthermore, workers had to be engaged in activity recognized as real work by the Code. Yet, critically, there existed no guidance on the thorny question of family members' *wage* work in family enterprises. And it was precisely these small, semi-independent family weaving businesses that the insurance law of 1894 had incorporated. Thus, in order to implement the law in the South Oberlausitz, municipal officials had to determine four major issues. The first concerned the characteristics of work. What were the attributes that the law recognized as work? Second, would the law differentiate between husband's and wife's work? Third, how would premium deductions be determined—by output or hours of work? The fourth issue concerned employers. The old age and disability insurance required a one-third contribution by employers, a one-third by the insured, and for the first time it provided for public assistance (a fixed contribution by the state). If home weavers worked for several firms, how was the employer's contribution determined? Among those affected by the new law, the first issue involving the very definition of work provoked no open or explicit controversy. As will be seen shortly, the law simply exempted activities that might truly have qualified for labor. Over the other three issues at stake, however, implementation induced serious confrontation, direct protest, and successful resistance. Reconstruction of these patterns of response is possible because municipal officials in 1895 undertook a detailed, systematic survey of home weavers in the province, asking about work, family relationships, wages, hours, and employers. In addition, they kept records on problems that arose over the next several decades.

The insurance law defined work unambiguously; it was *paid* labor, the "free economic exchange of labor and wage."[22] Insurable work had to be characterized by receipt of a wage or salary *(Lohn* or *Gehalt)*, including payment in kind. Laboring for "room and board" did not qualify for work except in the case of apprentices who were considered wage earners. This definition implicitly affected countless members of the surviving family work unit in the Oberlausitz. The survey of 1895 omitted young people in the family who worked in weaving but received no wage. Their work officially was discounted; they neither appear in the statistics (and are therefore lost from the record) nor could they accumulate time to apply for a future pension. Some surfaced in history only because an official got wind of their labor and made a formal inquiry. Thus, their cases exist among the documents accumulated after 1895. In October 1898, Wilhelm Döring in Mittelweigsdorf, for example, testified before the insurance office that his daughter (unnamed) helped him weave but received no cash, merely maintenance. The Dresden executive ruled in November that she was not self-employed but a "helper to her father" and since she received only room and board she need not be insured. The same applied to Karl Bayer from Oberweigsdorf, a self-proclaimed *Hauskind* who wove periodically and did the agricultural work as well and received no cash wage. This was also the case of Karl Ernst Steudtner in Niederoderwitz. Auguste Köhler in Spitzkunnersdorf described her family work relations more fully. Her father and one sister worked in the mill; two brothers were construction workers and wove at home in the winter. To be sure, she helped her brothers wind the bobbins, but she worked the fields and gardens and never received cash for "this employment."[23] But someone did; money had been earned by the textile labor of these young people but the cash became part of the communal, family pool. One cannot help wondering how these family work relationships might have been described if the outcome had not been a new financial burden on the already hard-pressed weavers. In light of the next dispute over the wage work of wives, this becomes a highly intriguing question.

The Oberlausitz families employed an understandable and in the short run clever stratagem in the question of husband's and wife's labor. The survey of 1895 records the *wives* of male home weavers as "mere assistants of their husbands" (*bloss Gehilfin des Mannes*). In Spitzkun-nersdorf, for example, a village barely touched by the factory mills, one survey counted 342 handweavers. The list included males in weaving, weaving families whose men, however, worked in the factory, in construc-tion, or as day laborers, and 112 house-weaving couples. In 110 cases the wife was listed as the husband's assistant. In one example, the pollster's scribbles indicated that August and Friederike Böhm, both handweavers, worked together. Yet officially she appeared on the list as bobbin winder (*Spulerin*) and assistant (*Gehilfin*). In Wittgendorf, another rather isolated and backward village, in all cases the wife was her husband's helpmate. In Oberweigsdorf, the picture varied slightly: among handweaving couples, 18 recognized the wife, too, as an independent weaver (three of whom were remarried widows), and 15 recorded the wife's labor as just supplemental. Three husbands wove only in the winter and their wives were recognized as full-time weavers, but, more typically throughout the survey, a wife whose husband wove only in winter became his helpmate, even if she wove alone the rest of the year. In Mittelweigsdorf, 32.5 percent of the families in handweaving used the labor of both husband and wife but in a variety of combinations. Most typically and in 62 percent of the cases (38 in number), responses indicated that the wife assisted the husband, although in 19 examples her occupation was acknowledged as handweaver. In three cases she was the weaver and he wound the warp spools, several couples shared these preparatory stages, and in two cases the wife appeared as full-time weaver and her husband as part-time.[24] The details of the survey could be multiplied but the pattern remains the same; women tended to appear as men's helpers. This picture of course, corresponded to the portrait of traditional home industry given by contemporary social analysts. It reflected, more generally, a specific definition of the family that was spreading in the new industrial world: a residential unit comprised of husband—head and chief breadwinner—and his dependents, whose labor, particularly in the lower class, was needed to help make ends meet. The insurance survey itself assumed such a relationship quite explicitly. Several questions were directed especially to wives. One openly asked whether a husband worked in home industry *so that* the wife provided just supplemental labor (*so dass die Ehefrau nur Gehilfin ist*); another questioned how much time *she* spent in housework (and many surveyors wrote in the column a description similar to that given of Auguste Heinze's husband: "The guy is in construction and does the housework *for his wife*," who was a full-time weaver at home).[25] The law excused "assistants" from the insurance requirement and also those who worked "irregularly" or whose work was insufficient to provide a livelihood. In short, the law itself made it much simpler for a wife to be exempted; if she claimed status as an independent wage earner, she had to provide substantial proof.

The insurance legislation, then, clearly embodied middle-class assumptions about proper sex roles, family relationships, and women's labor that were crystallizing in late-nineteenth-century Germany. The norms had developed out of the bourgeois social world in the previous century.[26] They reflected material changes in family life (the breakdown of the extended household) as well as growing professionalization of bureaucratic and university careers. In these educated families, the wife's role was supportive at home; the husband's was productive outside. This description, however, became prescriptive and part of industrial ideology. In the nineteenth century, such beliefs increasingly spread throughout society and one mechanism was the promulgation of social legislation. The insurance law affirmed, in principle, that no distinction would be made on the basis of sex or marital position. But its implementing instructions qualified this ideal so heavily as to destroy its spirit. The legislators explicitly argued that the traditional *(herkömmliche)* position of the female sex in economic life or the housewife in the family made her labor *(ausgeübte Tätigkeit)* distinct from superficially similar employment by men. In other words, because women were held responsible for running the home, their wage labor was to be judged differently from men's. Furthermore, the legal guidelines essentially denied the possibility of a work relationship existing between two persons in a family (defined here as a conjugal and kin unit only).[27] The net result, as the survey had proven, was a prevailing depiction of the woman's labor as merely supplemental; many subsequent analyses failed to mention her work at all.

The outcome of disputed insurance claims in the Oberlausitz reflected these assumptions about sex roles. Three types of cases came before insurance officials in the two decades after promulgation of the law. The first concerned weaving families with one loom; only the husband's labor was seen as real and insurable. The second involved those couples in which the wife essentially wove throughout the year. If the husband worked summers in agriculture or construction but wove *on the same loom* in winter, then she was judged helping him (more realistically, of course, he was helping her) and his work alone was acknowledged by eventual receipt of a pension. The final case dealt with families with at least two looms.[28] If the husband and wife worked for one employer and shared an account, he—but not she—was required to join the insurance plan. The legal guidelines required that direct contact between worker and boss be present for any acknowledged work relationship. The trend in the last decades of the nineteenth century had been to give women their own separate accounts, but this had not yet become universal practice. Historically, joint family employment had been organized under one account and it was most typically in the husband's name. This method of payment reflected the pooled labor of all members of the family. Now this traditional custom was used to dismiss the serious nature of women's labor. And it led, although not necessarily logically, to the notion, as an employer by the name of C. A. Frenzel put it, that because of the one account the man was "responsible for everything."[29] A market economy in effect atomizes its workers; each is independent of the other, and paid separately. It does not recognize joint labor and society elevates the status of the one who is given the money. The final issue ruled on by officials concerned earnings. If the woman on her own loom made very little money (less than one-third the average daily wage) she automatically was exempted from the insurance requirement.

A crucial element of the transformation of women's work remains to be explained. The weaver families themselves had colluded in the designation of women as labor aides. To be sure the very assumptions in the law of women's merely supplemental labor roles had predisposed the outcome. The municipal officials taking the survey, too, shared these notions. But men and women in the home-weaving family sought to have the wife rather than the husband labeled assistant. They knew that state officials would more readily accept such a designation. Karl Köhler summed it up beautifully: "My wife is a mere helpmate, as it says in the Imperial law."[30] The motive is clear; the implications are much more clouded. These families were dirt-poor, barely surviving in the developing industrial world. As one group from Weigsdorf plaintively protested, "How could we possibly pay deductions when they may be for two or three family members?" The municipality in Oberweigsdorf, recognizing dire poverty, actually paid some women's financial contributions out of poor-law monies.[31] Thus, it was economic necessity that encouraged these families to engage in the verbal deception. By publicly downplaying women's work roles, they tried to get out of paying the weekly insurance premiums that cut deeply into their meager incomes. They were willing to manipulate the public account of women's labor, so it appears, to ensure the family's survival. Their designation, however, was a subterfuge and it became a central part of the home industry family's resistance to the encroachment of state capitalism. The reality continued to be one of shared work roles. The proof rests not only in the historic evidence offered earlier in this essay. Weavers often referred to other families' deceptions when they were trying to justify their own exemptions. Even more telling were the numerous cases argued before the insurance board by women who, later on in life, sought designation as independent weaver so as to qualify for a pension. As they aged, they came to realize the advantages of insurance. They argued their case and, more importantly, they won it. Among the most naturally eloquent and persuasive was Marie Louise Endert from Spitzkunnersdorf, who had appeared on the survey of 1895 as mere *Gehilfin* to her husband because, as it later came out, she earned very little money. Two years later, by then sixty years old, she set out to prove her inherent worth and the crucial meaning of her labor for her family. Her own life history is worth recording because such personal testimony is relatively rare for lower-class people.[32] Her case, too, mirrors that of other women who also sought to challenge narrow interpretation of the law.

Frau Endert had worked as a handweaver from the time she left school; this added up to about forty-six years in continuous employment. For the last fifteen years, she had been working for Ernst Bortsch in Neu-Eibau under her own account. Her husband was also a home weaver (the couple was childless) who had found work in Grosschönau for over twenty-five years. Four years before the case came to court, his employer, the Brothers Föhrmann, opened a factory and he lost his job; his wife's employer, Bortsch, offered him work. Both now wove on two separate looms for the same employer. Each had an independent account "although previously my wage book [*Lohnbuch*] was in my husband's name. This was the commonly accepted practice." Endert offered an intriguing explanation for the custom. Employers, she said, sought to safeguard their property rights by holding males responsible for the amount of yarn distributed. Weavers notoriously skimped, wove the saved material, and sold it for extra money. The distributor apparently could hold a husband legally accountable, but not a wife, whom the court did not consider a responsible adult. She admitted that couples typically helped one another out. "It could happen that my husband would work on my loom or I on his if a piece had to be delivered quickly." But this was exceptional, she maintained, and stated in no uncertain terms that she "is to be seen as an independent weaver for Bortsch [*selbständige Weberin*]" and "am still independent of my husband." Then she turned to the question of her earnings; she made roughly 60–70 marks per year.

> I weave the whole year through. In the summer, though, I work less because I'm caring for our garden and hay harvest and I also tend our little potato patch. This keeps me busy for about six weeks but I always have the loom dressed and weave on it now and then and particularly in poor weather.

Her earnings were skimpy, she admitted, but with the decline in wages it was hard to earn much in handweaving anyway. Nonetheless, her wage contribution was crucial. "Our needs are simple. Except for one pound of beef we buy for Sundays, we subsist on our grain and potatoes." "It is self-evident," she stressed carefully, "that in such conditions the earnings of the wife—even if as in my case they are 65 marks per year—play a very important role [*eine grosse Rolle spielt*]. These 65 marks are necessary to live on." What if her husband became ill or died? Many widows must get by on such low earnings. And here Endert was not alone. Other women who described their lives to insurance officials also stressed the value of their work: it "paid the rent," "gave the children milk," "went for clothing."[33] In the family work community operating at near-subsistence level, all wages paid in cash were critical to survival even if they appeared ludicrously small to the more privileged outsider. These women could describe exactly how important their wages were in their own lives. Endert ended her case by stressing, again, the difficulty of earning more, given the low wages, and by mentioning housekeeping tasks. These she described in the passive, so as not to make them gender-specific. "Housework must be done too in home weaving, which takes around 3–4 hours per day. This does not make weaving secondary. On the contrary, one cannot live from housework alone." In short, Marie Endert felt that her life entitled her to the full benefits of the old age pension. The court agreed.

Frau Endert had brought up a very important point. To the extent that home industry families were embroiled in a cash, not subsistence, economy, they were conscious of the differences in paid and unpaid work. Even home weavers in previous times, in proto-industrialism, had thought of "time as money" and were fully cognizant of the time that generated cash and time that did not.[34] Clearly, as money had become more important for survival, the distinction became more real. Housework, while necessary, was private, unpaid labor (and as such not even recognized as real work). And Marie Endert's casual remarks help clarify how lower-class families perceived the differences, although this says nothing about how these families valued housework. While housework helped the families live, Endert noted self-evidently that "one cannot live from housework alone." To these home-weaving families, housework was unpaid time. The very survey forced them to describe their workday in terms of hours spent in housework and hours spent in wage work. While housework was not as clearly "women's sphere" in these families as the dominant ideology on proper roles would have it, nonetheless during the insurance controversy the issue of time assessment emerged as a woman's issue. Remember, the question of time was the third point of controversy in implementing the law and women were the protagonists. They defended their interests collectively and effectively, and their arguments simply were one more reason why the Oberlausitz families resisted being drawn into the insurance plan. If the deductions were geared to the time it took to produce a product, as the law stipulated, then those persons doing other work as well—housework, child care, tending gardens— would be disadvantaged. So would old people who worked more slowly. Numerous protests were lodged immediately and in one case 41 wives in Wittgendorf appeared before the municipal insurance office with a joint petition.[35] They correctly complained that the reality of their lives as wage workers, mothers, and housewives required reassessment of the planned deduction scheme. They hoped to be fully exempted but, barring such a decision, sought a more equitable levying policy. Employers, however, sought to turn the reality of housework to their advantage. Again, due to complaints by weavers themselves, the Löbau district officials began an inquiry, for example, on the factory owner Hoffmann. They ruled he was paying a terribly small contribution for cotton cloth woven *by females.*[36] Hoffmann refused to take into consideration the question of actual time, arguing that a woman's workday was taken up anyway by housework and by summer field chores and the employer had no responsibility for this labor whatsoever. He only paid a predetermined amount of time— "uninterrupted" time that he said was necessary to produce a product. But the municipality agreed that he had set his contribution far too low.

The conflict over time never was solved satisfactorily because no "normal" workday could be agreed on. The two positions on time assessment were at loggerheads. The Zittau Chamber of Commerce, as late as 1904, favored establishing a piece rate for both employers and weavers. But by then the issue was moot. In the Lausitz, employers were not voluntarily paying their share, as the regional insurance bureau admitted in a memorandum in June 1914.[37] Extension of insurance to home weavers had included a modification of the original insurance law. It made weavers responsible for paying employer contributions, and they were to be reimbursed. The law hoped in this fashion to facilitate identification of employers, which was more problematic in home industries than factories. Village home weavers in the Oberlausitz typically worked for more than one person, as the survey definitely had established. This offered whatever flexibility these poor people might have had, but it added to the burdens of implementation. Many weavers worked for separate employers simultaneously on two or more looms because work contracts came in so infrequently, others alternated, and all sought to keep their actual work relations obscured, for financial reasons. But placing the burden of registration and deduction squarely on home weavers, who were powerless to compel their employers to contribute, reinforced worker resistance. In 1902, the treasurer of the insurance bureau admitted serious difficulties (bedeutende Schwierigkeiten) due to poverty.[38] Younger weavers had simply failed to register, despite repeated enjoinders by local officials. When asked about it, he noted with some alarm that they actually had responded "scornfully" or stated that "we don't earn anything." No threats or coercion could produce results. Only those who were becoming disabled looked favorably on the program, but then they had to contribute retroactively and employers matched the figure only when the weavers had paid in full. Clearly, the welfare state and home weavers had reached a stalemate. Over time, the conflict lost its intensity and faded into the background as the number of home weavers continued its inexorable decline.

The members of home weaving families in the South Oberlausitz employed a series of strategies after 1894 to keep from being drawn into the disability and old age insurance plan. Their reactions ranged from outright, open defiance to collective and personal protest to a series of verbal deceptions that masked real home-work relationships. This resistance essentially reflected the conditions of life among the surviving home

weavers in a rapidly developing industrial society, their poverty and pow-
erlessness. Besides, the insurance scheme opened up complex questions
about work time and puzzling relationships with several employers. All
added up to the weavers' deep suspicion of newfangled notions of state
pensions that required deductions from current labor earnings.

The controversy had unanticipated, negative consequences for the
valuation of women's wage labor in the family. From the beginning, the
insurance legislation failed to recognize the significance of family work, in
this case among poor groups marginally subsisting in the encroaching
industrial order. In practice, this meant the devaluation of *women's* wage
labor in the family (and the labor of other family members who did not
explicitly receive cash). The law assumed that women at best provided
supplemental labor, but judged that work insufficient to qualify for a
pension unless the women actively fought the ruling. And in the early
twentieth century, insurance officials were openly unsympathetic to the
growing number of requests for recognition by wives. They discouraged
wives from applying and only the most persistent among the women, such
as Marie Endert, actually went so far as to take their cases to court.[39]
Officials predicted dire consequences if family members were drawn into
the plan, such as serious depletion of insurance funds and overburdening.
It appears that the economic health of national insurance required downplaying women's work in the family just as the national economy itself
rested on the unpaid labor of women. Thus, the major prewar extension
of welfare legislation to the homes of workers, in the Oberlausitz at least,
failed to acknowledge women's productive work in the family as a basis for
the right of a pension.

The net result has implications for the usefulness of collected statistical data. The 1894 survey was the fourth major study of Oberlausitz
home weaving in a series of inquiries in the second half of the nineteenth
century. The first two investigations, in 1861 and 1879, failed even to raise
the question of family work. Thus, only male weavers were counted. The
third survey of 1885 sought to rectify this omission but did not distinguish
weavers by sex and lumped "family assistants" together without specifying
their labor contribution.[40] The original intent of the 1894 law promised to
revise the inherited notion of home-weaving relationships by doing
greater justice to women's productive roles. After all, the pollsters went
into the home to explicitly find out about family work. But the published
statistics did not challenge stereotypes because the very questions assumed, and then found, women to be "mere assistants." And these insurance statistics were not isolated.[41] They fed into larger pools of data that
the modern state collected and used to fashion legislation or determine
reforms. They formed, too, the basis of many factory inspectors' judgments and partially underpinned scholarly analysis of domestic industry

at the end of the nineteenth century. And in the publication of these statistical series, women, first mere assistants, later were dropped from the tables.

Evidence exists that the weaver families valued highly women's productive contribution but for purely economic reasons played down its importance in contacts with authorities. This finding, of course, leaves open the longer-term meaning of such an action. The implications are difficult to trace with certainty, but several tentative conclusions can be offered. The label "assistant" fit into dominant assumptions about gender work roles; this is one reason, of course, why the term was attached in so many cases to wives. It was perfectly reasonable, from the standpoint of ruling ideology. Does a label become reality? The opportunity to answer the question over time is complicated because home weavers were a dying breed. For many, such as Frau Endert, the label did not correspond to the real world. Yet the family members were asked to describe each wage contribution in specific arithmetic terms (the husband contributed two-thirds and the wife one-third) and such precision must have had an upsetting impact on family relationships. It certainly drew attention to time not paid and to society's principle to reward only paid labor. Granting the husband a pension but not the wife, when both had work experience spanning many years, elevated his status. And once others argued that a man had total "responsibility for everything" because he received the joint wage, such an abstract claim might, of course, be translated into reality. Certainly, notions of women's labor as merely assistance were used to pay women less. The practice in effect created a real breadwinner–supplemental earner relationship. Wages paid according to gender (and not by the piece) were introduced into home weaving in the South Oberlausitz apparently first around the time of this controversy (although the practice characterized factory pay scales developed earlier). The first archival reference to a distributor speaking of "light" cotton cloth (and calling it women's work and paying a small insurance deduction) and "heavy" linen cloth (men's work and worth a bit more) was in 1895.[42] To be sure, distinctions had been made in traditional home industry between fine, simple, and patterned cloth, but no one had paid by gender but rather by type of woven cloth. Yet with increasing industrialization, the whole climate in the textile industry of the South Oberlausitz had shifted to lower the valuation of women's work. And such notions came into lower-class homes as they were being incorporated into the industrial economy and affected by state policy.

A theoretical problem of how to assess the historic pattern of joint family work lies at the root of this analysis. Central to Marxist theory on women is a fundamental critique of pooled family wage labor. Socialists argued for the progressive nature of women's wage work in factories precisely because such labor outside the home freed women from economic dependency on husbands and fathers. In socialist symbolism, the weaver family stands out as the prototype of isolated living, economic oppression, and sex inequality. Feminists concurred and later pointed up the high incidence of violence and abuse inherent in private family living.[43] But the issues must perhaps be sorted out more carefully by analyzing the stages in the family's incorporation into the market economy. This essay, it is hoped, will stimulate such analysis. The problem might not be family wage work *per se* and certainly not the wage work in proto-industrial households, relatively independent of both state and guild control. But rather the roadblock to women's equality lies partially in the tension between work and family life that became acute in the developing industrial era. Well into the late nineteenth century, women home weavers in the Oberlausitz made money and by their own testimony valued it highly because it gave them a deep sense of independence and worth (which was not, however, recognized by the external society dispensing rewards). Females worked in weaver families to provide both cash wages and the homegrown products immediately consumed by the family. Until the insurance law was extended to home weaving, they were relatively unaffected by the growing state regulation of labor relationships but they were facing a generalized definition of work. This understanding excluded housework and other non-wage-producing labor activities at a time when such work effectively was assigned to women. Furthermore, the whole social climate of industrial society did not favor or ease women's productive activities because these were defined basically as men's tasks. Industrial production, however unevenly divided, might permit for the first time in history a lower-class family to survive on the income of one member (the male breadwinner). These changes gave a new context to work and family life, a reality that defined the former as man's world and the latter as woman's sphere and resulted in enormous constraints. In time, even women's wage work in industrial factories would be geared to *family* needs and requirements and the daughter's wage, for example, might support her brother's apprenticeship training program. Such assignments help explain why socialist theory of the inherently liberating role of wage labor in women's lives proved disappointingly simplistic in practice during industrialization and the transition to high capitalism. The varied patterns of family work relationships as they evolved over time require far more empirical analysis before their theoretical implications can be formulated.

NOTES

1. The interpretation is commonly accepted in the literature. See Sidney B. Fay, "Bismarck's Welfare State," *Current History*, 18 (1950), pp. 2–3; also Gordon A. Craig, *Germany, 1866–1945* (New York, 1978), pp. 150–51; and Hajo Holborn, *A History of Modern Germany, 1840–1945* (New York, 1969), pp. 291–93.

2. I develop this argument in an article entitled "A Source Analysis in German Women's History: Factory Inspectors' Reports and the Shaping of Working-Class Lives, 1878–1914," in *Central European History*, 16 (1983), pp. 99–121. At a time when ideological notions began to define the family as "private" and unconnected to the busy, competitive world of work, inspectors knew better. Their campaign to supervise employment and enforce morality at work was designed to raise the moral standards at home and at play.

3. In December 1891, old age and disability insurance had been extended to the self-employed in the tobacco industry. *Deutsches Reichs-Gesetzbuch für Industrie, Handel, Gewerbe*, 1, no. 2 (Berlin, 1903), pp. 1491–93 (hereafter *Gesetzbuch*). It was not until 1914 that health insurance was extended to the self-employed workers in general. Staatsarchiv Dresden, Aussenstelle Bautzen (hereafter B), Amtshauptmannschaft Zittau (hereafter AZ), Nr. 8083, Bl. 1–18: extension of health insurance, 5 December 1913.

4. See, among others, Louise Tilly and Joan Scott, *Women, Work, and Family* (New York, 1978); also Robyn Dasey, "Women's Work and the Family: Women Garment Workers in Berlin and Hamburg Before the First World War," in *The German Family*, ed. by Richard J. Evans and W. R. Lee (Totowa, N.J., 1981), pp. 221–55; Virginia Yans-McLaughlin, "Patterns of Work and Family Organization: Buffalo's Italians," in *The Family in History: Interdisciplinary Essays*, ed. by Theodore K. Rabb and Robert I. Rotberg (New York, 1971), pp. 111–26.

5. Among two typical works, see Robert Wilbrandt, *Die Weber in der Gegenwart. Sozialpolitische Wanderungen durch die Hausweberei und die Webfabrik* (Jena, 1906), and by the same author, *Die Frauenarbeit. Ein Problem des Kapitalismus* (Leipzig, 1906).

6. The area is known best as the land of the Wends, a Slavic minority that survived in German territory. The Wends were peasants and lived in the northern part of the province. German migrants had settled the southern districts (Zittau and Löbau) and they undertook weaving. For a general introduction to the area see, among others, Edmund Gröllich, *Die Baumwollweberei des sächsischen Oberlausitz und ihre Entwickelung zum Grossbetrieb* (Leipzig, 1911); Heinrich Gebauer, *Die Volkswirtschaft im Königreiche Sachsen. Historisch, Geographisch und Statistisch dargestellt*, vols. 2 and 3 (Dresden, 1893); Karl Haupt, "Sagenbuch der Lausitz," *Neues Lausitzisches Magazin*, 40 (1863); Johann Köhler, *Bilder aus der Oberlausitz, als ein Beitrag zur Vaterlandskunde* (Boudissin [Bautzen], 1855); and Rudolf Lehmann, "Niederlausitz und Oberlausitz in vergleichender geschichtlicher Betrachtung," *Jahrbuch für die Geschichte Mittel- und Ostdeutschlands*, 7 (1958), pp. 93–139.

7. Gröllich, *Die Baumwollweberei*, pp. 1–2; G. Korschelt, "Beiträge zur

Geschichte der Webindustrie in der sächsischen Oberlausitz," *Oberlausitzer Rundschau*, 11 (1964), p. 293 (reprint of an 1867 article); also *Die Südöstliche Oberlausitz mit Zittau und dem Zittauer Gebirge* (Berlin, 1970), pp. 165–66.

8. Recently, historians have shown considerable interest in pre-industrial rural production of goods for the international market. In today's literature, it is called "proto-industrialism," although earlier Marx, for example, had recognized the importance of bringing the countryside into the market economy: he called it the period of *Manufaktur*. Historians see it as a major transition phase of feudal, agrarian society and they have analyzed it in terms of population growth and density, fertility strategies, household formation, and family labor. See, for example, Peter Kriedte, Hans Medick, and Jürgen Schlumbohm, *Industrialisierung vor der Industrialisierung. Gewerbliche Warenproduktion auf dem Land in der Formationsperiode des Kapitalismus* (Göttingen, 1977); also David Levine, *Family Formation in an Age of Nascent Capitalism* (New York, 1977); too, the interesting study of ribbon makers in the West Lausitz by Bernd Schöne, *Kultur und Lebensweise Lausitzer Bandweber 1750–1850* (Berlin, 1977); and the classic work by Rudolf Braun, *Industrializierung und Volksleben. Die Veränderungen der Lebensformen in einen Industriegebiet vor 1800* (Zurich, 1960).

9. Richard von Schlieben, "Untersuchungen über das Einkommen und die Lebenshaltung des Handwebers in Bezirke der Amtshauptmannschaft Zittau," *Zeitschrift des Kaiserlichen Sächsischen Statistischen Bureaus*, 31 (1885), pp. 156–90.

10. Labor historians have concentrated on the effect of factory jobs on workers' consciousness and the extent of adaptation to the new factory world. They have focused on such issues as living standards, wage levels, and forms of protest. Considerable attention, too, has been given workers' organizations—both union and party history. A recent historiographical trend has merged labor and social history. Here, historians are concerned with the daily lives of workers on and off the jobs. For an overview and critique of new trends in the writing of labor history, see Tony Judt, "Minerva's Owl and Other Birds of Prey: Reflections on the Condition of Labor History in Europe," *International Labor and Working Class History*, no. 16 (1979), pp. 18–28. In the late nineteenth century, however, the industrial work world was also shaped by labor laws, and definitions and understanding of work have been affected by social insurance. Most historians of the emerging welfare state are concerned with the politics surrounding passage of such legislation and the financial and other details of the programs. They have not analyzed the actual effect of such legislation on workers. This is true of a recent conference in West Berlin, 1981, celebrating 100 years of welfare policy in Germany. See Peter H. Köhler and Hans F. Zacher, eds., *The Evolution of Social Insurance, 1881–1981* (New York, 1982).

11. Considerable attention was given home industry in the literature sponsored by the historical school of economics and other middle-class reform organizations in late-nineteenth-century Germany. The historical economists were interested in home industry as a form of economic organization. The authors generally distinguished old from new domestic industries. In their conception, the old were the households of weavers, spinners, nail makers, clog makers, and other

pre-industrial occupations that were performed essentially by male masters in their homes. In contrast, the new home industry was urban, female-dominated, and a product of mass consumption in industrial capitalism. The authors meant particularly the ready-made garment industry that emerged in Germany's larger cities after the mid-nineteenth century. See the series *Hausindustrie und Heimarbeit in Deutschland und Österreich*, vols. 1–4, Shriften des Vereins für Sozialpolitik (Leipzig, 1899); *Heimarbeit und Hausindustrie in Deutschland. Ihre Lohn und Arbeitsverhältnisse*, Herausgegeben im Zusammenhange mit der Deutschen Heimarbeit-Ausstellung 1906 in Berlin vom Bureau für Sozialpolitik (Berlin, 1906). Also, consult such specific investigations as Johannes Feig, *Hausgewerbe und Fabrikbetrieb in der Berliner Wäsche-Industrie* (Leipzig, 1896), and Gertrud Dyhrenfurth, *Die hausindustriellen Arbeiterinnen in der Berliner Blusen-Unterrock-Schürzen- und Tricotkonfektion*, Staats- und sozialwissenschaftliche Forschungen, vol. 15, no. 4 (Leipzig, 1898).

12. "Haushalt- und Familienstruktur als Momente des Produktions- und Reproduktionsprozess," in *Seminar: Familie und Gesellschaftsstruktur. Materialien zu den sozioökonomischen Bedingungen von Familienformen*, ed. by Heidi Rosenbaum, (Frankfurt, 1978), pp. 295–96.

13. *Praktische Darstellung der Oberlausitzer Leinwand-Fabrikation nebst ihren Mängeln, zum Beweis dass verschiedene Abhülfe und Verbesserungen dabei höchst nöthig sind, sowie wo dieselben anzuwenden*, von einem Fabrikanten (Herrnhut, 1837). Archival documents on hawking use the verb *erlernen* in describing both male and female weavers. For example, Staatsarchiv Dresden (hereafter StAD), Nr. 6257, 1840: the hawking trade among Oberlausitz, Sebnitz, and Zwönitzer weavers.

14. Materials on hawking are in both the Dresden and Bautzen archives. StAD, Nr. 6257, Bl. 41–43, 120–22, and 274–77: reports by the Bautzen district officials, 1842, 1844, and 1848; Nr. 6258, Den Hausirhandel . . . 1850–53; Nr. 6259, Den Hausirhandel . . . 1855–62. Also B, Kreishauptmannschaft Bautzen, Nr. 11236, hawking permits 1810–43; Nr. 11237, hawking permits, 1846–52, in particular Bl. 171–75 for Scholze's case.

15. This was true first in cotton weaving and it became typical with the spread of the warping frame in the area, Gröllich, *Die Baumwollweberei*, pp. 19, 76.

16. B, AZ, Nr. 8082, Bl. 70–76: report on work life among handweavers, 21 April 1902. The insurance reports are in the following collection: AZ, Nr. 8208 . . . Invaliditäts- und Alters-Versicherung des Hausgewerbetreibenden der Textilindustrie in . . . 1895–1914. The documents cover 31 weaver municipalities in the district of Zittau. See, particularly, Nr. 8225, Niederoderwitz.

17. Ibid., Nr. 5513, Bl. 89: determining the yearly incomes of the self-employed in textiles, 1900–14. Also Carl v. Rechenberg, *Die Ernährung der Handweber in der Amtshauptmannschaft Zittau* (Leipzig, 1890), p. 3. In contrast, a miner in the district in 1896 made on average 656 marks yearly. For further comparison, that year a metalworker (mechanic) made 16 marks per week; a male weaver in a mill, 9 marks per week; and a male handweaver, 3.50 marks per week. Edmund Fischer, *Die Lage der Arbeiter in der Sächs. Oberlausitz* (Zittau, 1898), pp. 10, 15, 29, 31.

18. Christian Pescheck, "Geschichte der Industrie und des Handels in der Oberlausitz," *Neues Lausitzisches Magazin*, 29 (1852) p. 8; StAD, Nr. 6257, Bl. 274–77: detailed report on conditions among Oberlausitz weavers, 1848; Konrad Sturmhoefel, *Illustrierte Geschichte des Albertinischen Sachsen*, 2 (Leipzig, n.d. [1908]), p. 639; Fritz Hauptmann, *Woher wir Kommen. Ein Buch von Heimat und Vorfahren* (Privatdruck Marburg, 1970), 1, p. 138; 2, pp. 117, 167.

19. B, AZ, Nr. 3643: survey of living standards and work, 1877.

20. For reports of the school officials, von Schlieben, "Untersuchungen," p. 158; *Jahres-Bericht des Handels und Gewerbekammer zu Zittau* (Zittau, 1896), p. xxvi.

21. *Gesetzbuch*, 1, no. 2, pp. 1493–96; W. Kähler, "Materialien zur Beurteilung der rechtlichen Stellung der Hausindustrie in Deutschland," *Hausindustrie*, pp. 2, 5, 11–12. Also Zentrales Staatsarchiv, Potsdam, RMdI, Nr. 6731, Bl. 75–77: clipping of *Reichs-Arbeitsblatt*, 1906, on insurance.

22. *Gesetzbuch*, 1, no. 2, pp. 1392, 1428–29, 1458.

23. B, AZ, Nr. 8223, Bl. 97–98: Mittleweigsdorf; Nr. 8228, Bl. 89: Oberweigsdorf, 1896; Nr. 8225, Bl. 5–12: Niederoderwitz, 1898; Nr. 8238, Bl. 127–28: Spitzkunnersdorf, 1896.

24. Ibid., Nr. 8238, Bl. 6–54: 1895 survey of Spitzkunnersdorf; Nr. 8241, Bl. 92–102: survey of Wittgendorf; Nr. 8228, Bl. 17–28: survey of Oberweigsdorf: Nr. 8222, Bl. 3–27: survey of Mittelweigsdorf.

25. (My italics.) These were columns 13 and 14 of the survey. For the remarks about Heinze, Nr. 8223, Mittleweigsdorf, #97 on the survey. The pollster internalized notions of proper roles and assumed that women were responsible for the housework.

26. Karin Hausen, "Family and Role Divisions: The Polarisation of Sexual Stereotypes of Work and Family Life," in Evans, *German Family*, pp. 51–83 (translated from the German); Birgit Panke, "Bürgerliches Frauenbild und Geschlechtsrollenzuweisungen in der literarischen und brieflichen Produktion des 18. Jahrhunderts," *Frauengeschichte. Beiträge 5. Zur feministischen Theorie und Praxis* (Munich, 1981), pp. 6–11.

27. *Gesetzbuch*, 1, no. 2, p. 1425. Also B, AZ, Nr. 8238: copy of an appeal decision on the labor of wives in Spitzkinnersdorf.

28. Specifically, see the following document: B, AZ, Nr. 8208: measures to implement extension of disability insurance to the self-employed, 1894–1902, particularly the decision by local Zittau officials of 9 July 1896.

29. For Frenzel's remarks, ibid., Nr. 8223, Bl. 67: 19 June 1897 memorandum from the Hirschfelde-based firm.

30. Ibid., Nr. 8238: Bl. 109: petition of August and Pauline Köhler, 16 July 1896.

31. Ibid., Nr. 8223, Bl. 54: report from local Mittelweigsdorf officials to the Zittau district, March 1897.

32. Ibid., Nr. 8238, Bl. 135: February–November 1897 for Endert's case; also Nr. 8222, 12 July 1896, petition of Frank Lischoff, Mittelweigsdorf, describing deception.

33. For various petitions by women: Nr. 8233, Reichenau, Johanne Apelt, 1901, and Bl. 101–2: collective protest by *Treiberinnen*, July 1896; Nr. 8225,

Niederoderwitz, Bl. 118, 1–16: petition by Johanne Schneider, 19 December 1897; Nr. 8235, Seifhennersdorf, Bl. 117: interview with Johanne Röthig and Bl. 130: interview with Ernestine Lehmann; Nr. 8210, Bertsdorf, Bl. 46: Marie Emalie Hamann; and B1. 49: Anna Hauptmann; Nr. 8214, Grossschönau, report by the local health insurance on the Tannert family in 1904; Nr. 8217, Jonsdorf, interview with weaver Anna Engler, 1906.

34. H. Rosenbaum, *Familie*, p. 43, discusses different interpretations on the implications of these distinctions.

35. B, AZ, Nr. 8241, Bl. 1–34: September 1894. The documents contain a detailed investigation of the 41 protesters.

36. Ibid., Nr. 8208, Bl. 54–57: correspondence between municipal officials in Alt-Eibau, officials in Löbau, and those in the province, November 1895.

37. Ibid., Nr. 5513, Bl. 96–108: 29 June 1914.

38. Ibid., Nr. 8082, Bl. 70–76: report on insurance in the area, Zittau, 21 April 1902.

39. Ibid., and also Amtshauptmannschaft Löbau, Nr. 2260, Bl. 110–16: annual report for 1903, specifically on the insurance controversy.

40. The first was the census of businesses taken for the German *Zollverein* on 3 December 1861, "Die Baumwollweberei der sächsischen Oberlausitz," *Der Textil-Arbeiter*, v. 24, no. 6 (1912). Gustav Schmoller, *Zur Geschichte der deutschen Kleingewerbe im 19. Jahrhundert* (Halle, 1870), pp. 500–3, warns that earlier investigations of businesses, as, for example, in 1846, totally omitted children and women's labor. The 1879 survey was conducted by the Zittau Chamber of Commerce, "Erhebungen über die Verhältnisse des Handweberei im Kammer-Bezirke," *Jahres-Bericht des Handels- und Gewerbekammer zu Zittau für das Jahr 1879* (Zittau, 1880), pp. 46–53. The 1885 survey was conducted by the district Amtshauptmannschaft von Schlieben, "Untersuchungen," pp. 171–72.

41. For example, Fischer, *Die Lage der Arbeiter*, pp. 6 ff., bases part of his analysis of the situation of the working class in the Oberlausitz on the reports of the old age and disability insurance office.

42. B, AL, Nr. 8208, Bl. 56: description of the insurance payments set by the mill owner Hoffmann, 28 November 1895: 5 pennies for "light" goods and 10 pennies for better-quality linen goods.

43. Frederick Engels, *The Origin of the Family, Private Property and the State* (New York, 1942), section on "The Monogamous Family"; Lenin, "The Development of Large-Scale Machine Industry," *Emancipation of Women* (New York, 1934), pp. 15–16. See also Amy Swerdlow et al., eds., *Household and Kin: Families in Flux* (Old Westbury, N.Y., 1981), pp. 74, 93.

The Woman's Role in the German Working-Class Family in the 1890s from the Perspective of Women's Autobiographies*

JOHN C. FOUT

The study of labor history has largely been shaped by the character of the labor movement itself in the nineteenth century. That is, the development of labor unions, conflicts between workers and factory owners, the evolution of a theoretical socialist ideology, the organization and growth of socialist parties, the phenomenon of revolution, and even the labor union leaders and party theoreticians have been the central focus of labor history; often that history was written by the participants themselves.[1] With time, professional historians took over the task but the format remained much the same. In recent decades, the 1970s especially, the "new social historians" have gradually recast that original mold and their writings have provided us with sophisticated new insights into the social history of the working class. Many scholars have adopted the research techniques

*An earlier version of this essay was presented at the Annual Meeting of the American Historical Association, meeting in Washington, D.C. on December 27, 1982. I am indebted to the members of the panel for their comments. My thanks also to Professor Ira M. Lapidus of the University of California, Berkeley. Early research for this essay was undertaken in Berkeley for his N.E.H. summer seminar in 1980 and I am grateful to Professor Lapidus for his sound advice at that time.

and theoretical models of other social science disciplines in order to expand the concerns of labor history. They often use quantitative research methods to study social mobility, demographic change, workers' incomes, family history, and a host of other issues relevant to certain groups of workers or workers in specific cities. Studies of these types are being published both inside and outside Germany.[2]

Yet these works are characterized by two inherent weaknesses that are a legacy from that earlier period in labor history. First, they tell us too little about the daily lives of workers. All too often in the quantitative approach, which tends to be a dominant feature of current research, historians anchor their research entirely in statistical analysis and what emerges is the worker in "aggregate"; the individual is lost. Second, even the most recent works are quite traditional in that they are male-centered. It is true that some works are concerned with industries that employed only male workers, nevertheless, labor history as a whole continues to operate on the false assumption that the experiences of males are representative of all workers. There were millions of women who worked for pay inside and outside the home in Imperial Germany whose experiences differed from those of their male counterparts in important ways.

Fortunately, feminist historians are seeking to redress that imbalance in labor history, and important new works on working-class women have been written in the last decade. Thomas Dublin's work on American women, *Women at Work: The Transformation of Work and Community in Lowell, Massachusetts, 1826–1860*, and Louise A. Tilly and Joan W. Scott's study of the experiences of English and French women, *Women, Work, and Family*, are seminal works in the field.[3] Within the specific area of German working-class women's history, there are numerous examples of recent work: Gisela Losseff-Tillmanns, *Frauenemanzipation und Gewerkschaften (Women's Emancipation and Labor Unions)*; Sabine Richebächer, *Uns fehlt nur eine Kleinigkeit. Deutsche proletarische Frauenbewegung 1890–1914 (We Are Lacking Just a Little Bit: The German Proletarian Women's Movement 1890–1914)*; Edith Rigler, *Frauenleitbild und Frauenarbeit in Österreich vom ausgehenden 19. Jahrhundert bis zum Zweiten Weltkrieg (Women's Image and Women's Work in Austria from the late Nineteenth Century to World War II)*; Josef Ehmer, "Frauenarbeit und Arbeiterfamilie in Wien. Vom Vormärz bis 1934" ("Women's Work and Working-Class Families in Vienna from the Vormärz to 1934"); Jean H. Quataert, *Reluctant Feminists in German Social Democracy 1885–1917*; Robyn Dasey, "Women's Work and the Family: Women Garment Workers in Berlin and Hamburg Before the First World War"; Regina Schulte, "Dienstmädchen im herrschaftlichen Haushalt" ("Domestic Servants in the Master's Household"), and Peter

Schneck, "Die gesundheitlichen Verhältnisse der Fabrikarbeiterinnen" ("The Health of Women Factory Workers").[4]

This essay is intended as a contribution to the new literature on the social history of working-class women (of course, much additional work will have to be done to offset the long standing emphasis on male-centered working-class history). Feminist historians have shown that it is methodologically crucial to place women at the center of women's history, rather than studying male "attitudes towards women," the old-fashioned way of doing women's history. Labor historians in turn must recognize that it is essential to place workers and sources on workers (rather than studies by middle-class social scientists) at the forefront of working-class history. And, it must be recognized, the experiences of working women are just as important as those of working-class men in the study of labor history.[5]

The analysis that follows depends on a group of rare and seldom cited autobiographies of working-class women, over a dozen published works in all.[6] Nine are relatively long, between one hundred and two hundred pages (one is over four hundred pages), two are just over fifty pages, two are about twenty-five pages, and the last is a collection of about eighteen short autobiographies that range in length from three to fifteen pages. Most of the authors signed their names, but a few did not and their identities are to date unknown.[7] Family life and work-related experiences dominate these accounts and fortunately for the sake of balance in this analysis almost all the major occupations of working-class women in the late nineteenth century are represented in this group.

The nine longer autobiographies deserve a brief introduction. *Im Kampf ums Dasein (The Struggle for Existence)*, one of the most informative and least well known, was written anonymously by a woman who never married. She provides a rich, detailed commentary on her life as a factory worker, domestic servant, and waitress in a large unnamed city on the North German coast. Annelise Rüegg, a Swiss woman born in 1879, published her autobiography in 1915, entitled *Erlebnisse einer Servier-tochter. Bilder aus der Hotelindustrie (Experiences of a Waitress* [or service girl]: *Portraits from the Hotel Industry)*. She candidly discusses her poverty-stricken youth and then her life as a single woman working as a well-paid waitress in elegant resort hotels. Hating factory work, she began working in the industry at sixteen. German was her native tongue and she taught herself a speaking knowledge of French, Italian, and English; as a result she found employment in a string of hotels in Switzerland, Germany, England, and Italy. She was a remarkably free-spirited, feisty woman, who journeyed from place to place, especially when working conditions were not to her liking. If her employers did not treat her right, she simply told them off and quit. Her autobiography ends as she sets sail for America. *Erlebnisse eines Hamburger Dienstmädchens (Experiences of a Domestic servant in Hamburg)* by Doris Viersbeck, begins in 1888 when at the age of twenty, she arrived in Hamburg from a small village in Holstein. She had already worked for two and a half years for a teacher and his family. Like so many women before her who came to a large city from a rural area, she followed an aunt and a sister who helped her find her first position. Viersbeck worked for a number of middle- and upper-class families for the next half dozen years before she married. She then left domestic service. Sadly, the account ends at that moment.[8] Marie Wegrainer entitled her autobiography *Der Lebensroman einer Arbeiterfrau (The Biographical Novel of a Working-class Woman*—which she described as "written by herself"—*von ihr selbst geschrieben)*. Born in 1852 in Bavaria, where she would live her entire life, she died shortly before World War I. Marie and her brother were the illegitimate children of an unmarried domestic servant. Because Marie's mother was in domestic service, Marie was raised mostly by a *Pflegemutter* (a foster mother). Marie also became a domestic servant and had an illegitimate child that died shortly after birth. She eventually married and had four more children. Though her husband was a skilled worker, a carpenter, he never earned enough money to support the family and Marie more often than not had to find paid labor. *Aus der Gedankenwelt einer Arbeiterfrau (A Working Woman's Thoughts)*, tells the story of a sixty-nine-year-old married woman, Mrs. Hoffman, who was a rural farm worker and domestic servant in East Prussia. Her account is especially valuable as there is little information available on rural women. *The Autobiography of a Working Woman,* by Adelheid Popp, is one of only two German texts available in English. It is a poignant history of her brutal childhood, work in various factories, married life as wife and mother, and early political involvement in socialism. Her story stops there although she eventually became one of the first women elected to the Austrian Parliament. Phyllis Knight eventually left for Canada and her autobiography, *A Very Ordinary Life,* was written with her son. Much of the work is concerned with her later life there, but in the first part she discusses her youth in Berlin and it is most valuable for that reason. Verena Conzett started writing her autobiography when she was sixty-five, after the death of both her husband and her two sons. Entitled *Erstrebtes und Erlebtes. Ein Stück Zeitgeschichte (Endeavors and Experiences: A Fragment of Contemporary History)*, it is the longest and most literate of the autobiographies. It describes in detail her youth in Zürich and the poverty of her family. She then writes about her own adult working and family life and involvement with politics and socialism in the late nineteenth and early twentieth centuries. It was published in 1929. Ottilie Baader's *Ein steiniger Weg. Lebenserin-*

nerungen (A Stony Road: Memoirs) portrays the odyssey of a single woman, who as a home worker supported herself, her widowed father when he could no longer work, and (at various times) nieces and nephews when there were deaths in the family. She goes on to explain how she became a prominent prewar leader in the Social Democratic Party. These are some of the women whose life histories are the backdrop for this essay. (It should be noted that few of these autobiographies are extant in American libraries.[9]) Most of the accounts are poorly written. Not by any stretch of the imagination are they literary masterpieces. But they are woman-centered autobiographies and taken together they represent one of the most important collections of published sources for writing the social history of working-class women.

Though the time frame for each autobiography was slightly different, they intersect in the main in the 1890s. The authors were German or from the German-speaking parts of the Austro-Hungarian Empire and Switzerland. Some wrote about their childhood and the period in their lives when they were young, single working women; others who married emphasized their experiences as married women and mothers. Moreover, they talked at length about their own mothers and grandmothers and many other single and married women they knew. They all worked for pay outside the home, although the majority worked for part of their lives as home workers, mostly during childhood and as married women. None had much formal education, and all held unskilled, low-paying jobs. (The writings and experiences of middle- or lower middle-class women are not considered in this study.[10]) Some became active participants in socialist labor unions and the Social Democratic Party. Their writings offer fascinating accounts of how and why they became politically conscious and involved in socialism.

Most significantly these autobiographies are an incredible source of information on the daily lives of this particular group of women. They lived desperate lives of misery and deprivation. They hated their jobs and the people they worked for, and generally they were cynical and bitter about the way they had to live. They could not comprehend why, when they worked long hours at demanding jobs, they were rewarded with brutality, sexual harassment, and low pay. Fortunately, they also tell us about other more meaningful moments in their daily affairs. We learn about courtship and marriage, their limited free time, and the few pleasures they enjoyed when they found the opportunity. We come to realize that they relied heavily on other women in the family and on the job for mutual aid and consolation and yet they were free-spirited and tough, independent women. As they grew older many resolved that they had to fight the injustices heaped upon them in any way they could. These women were not feminists, at least not by any generally accepted definition, but they recognized the plight of women like themselves, and consistently expressed deep-seated anger as they wrote. The wish to express those thoughts evidently motivated them to write.

This essay can discuss only a small slice of the material, primarily those sections relating to family life; analysis of work-related issues will be the subject of other papers. A number of observations emerged from reading the autobiographies. The working-class family's survival and well-being largely depended on the ability of the women in the family to manage the household and contribute to the family's income through paid employment at home or in the factory; most families in no way matched the middle-class ideal. The authors of these autobiographies wanted their readers to understand that it was the combination of work, family/household responsibilities, and terrible living conditions that made their lives so difficult. Many women were unable to stand the strain. By the time they were in their forties, many of them were exhausted and their health was broken. Raising children was a terrible burden. Once a family had more than two children, it was in trouble financially; in fact most families were always on the verge of poverty whether the husband was a low-paid, unskilled worker or higher paid because of a skill he had acquired. There were countless one-parent households headed by an unmarried or widowed woman worker; since women's wages were 20 to 50 percent lower than men's, these families' circumstances were the most marginal. Child care was very difficult. If there were no relatives in the vicinity to care for the children, especially if they were very young, these women often were forced to place their children in foster homes.

The intent here is to reconstruct aspects of these women's daily lives using the autobiographies. Since the space allotted is limited, the emphasis will be on those insights revealed in the autobiographies that would not readily emerge from statistical data. It is appropriate to begin with childhood. Most of the authors spoke bitterly about their youth, and the accounts reveal much about working-class childhood in general. Equally significantly, they expose many facets of the problems parents faced in raising families. Adelheid Popp's painful memories of her early years exemplify the feelings and attitudes of most of these women:

> What I recollect of my childhood is so gloomy and hard, and so firmly rooted in my consciousness that it will never leave me. I knew nothing of what delights other children and causes them to shout for joy—dolls, play things, fairy stories, sweetmeats and Christmas-trees. I only knew the great room in which we worked, slept, ate and quarrelled.[11]

Grinding poverty was the common denominator in the working-class family and putting food on the table was a daily life-threatening challenge when there was little or no money. It was the wife who had to bear that responsibility; if she was not a good manager, the family simply starved.

Often housewives had to keep the food cupboard locked so that the food could be divided up at mealtimes.

Marie Sponer reported that when her father was incapacitated with a lung disease and was unable to work, her mother resorted to an arrangement with a farmer in the vicinity whereby she could grow some potatoes. During that difficult period they lived on potatoes and watery soup.[12] Our nameless waitress described the situation at home when her mother caught typhus and was hospitalized for several weeks. "During the whole time that my mother was in the hospital," she wrote, "we children were left alone since our father was at work all day. In the morning the only concern he showed for us was when he cut a piece of black bread and smeared it with lard. In the evenings it was the same."[13] In ordinary times she recalled that their usual diet consisted of "potatoes [cooked] with their skins on and 20 pfennigs' worth of sausage scraps or one or two herrings and we had to be satisfied with that."[14] They always looked forward to Fridays, when the local butcher let them pick up a pail of broth in which the shop's sausages were cooked. They then ladled out cups of the broth and "prospected" for bits of meat, which were eaten with slices of dry black bread.[15] It is important to understand how absolutely essential it was for the housewife to be on good terms with a butcher or the proprietor of a neighborhood restaurant. They were the only source for such pails of meat broth since meat itself was seldom seen on the tables of unskilled workers, most especially the woman worker. This unearned income was one of the many ways a resourceful housewife was able to supplement wages that were always too low even when both husband and wife worked.

That point can be further illustrated within the context of a larger incident told by our waitress, who remembered her confirmation as one of the most humiliating moments of her childhood.[16] Her mother had left her husband because of his philandering and because of his drinking (his fits of drunkenness usually led to beatings for every member of the family); after that she supported the children entirely on her own. Barely making ends meet, she certainly could not afford for her daughter the nice clothes that were normally worn at confirmation. (The churches never acknowledged the fact that the poor often stayed away from church because they could not dress appropriately.) She approached the local welfare authorities and the pastor but they would not provide used clothing since her husband was still alive, albeit living with another woman. Therefore her daughter had to attend the ceremony in clothes made out of sack cloth and she was tormented by the other children. Moreover, since her mother was ill, this young teenager had to go alone. After that she never attended church again. Nonetheless her mother had wanted to make the occasion as pleasant as possible and so, that evening, she prepared a special dinner of horse meat steak. That was a first for the family, and the daughter recalled that until that night, "I had never seen meat on the table as a child, except when a fly fell in my soup."[17] Though farm people usually ate better than city dwellers, Mrs. Hoffman, the rural woman from East Prussia, expressed similar sentiments when she complained that "in thirty-five years we had a roast for the midday meal only two times. One time there was a birthday in the family and for that reason we had a pork roast."[18]

If the never-ending quest for food was one source of the unpleasant memories of childhood and even adult life, there were certainly a host of others. One chronic debilitating problem was housing. Simply stated, it was caused by the paucity of low-cost dwellings to rent. The meager income of the unskilled worker forced her to live under the most horrendous conditions. These included severe overcrowding because there were many children and too few rooms, small ones at that; cooking, toilet and bathing facilities were limited if they existed at all; rooms were cold either because there were stoves only in one room or because the price of fuel was too high. It is generally assumed that people in the rural areas lived better than their urban counterparts, but that was not necessarily the case. Anna Boschek, an early leader in Austrian Social Democracy, was an advocate of the participation of women in the party and in socialist unions. She traveled extensively to give talks and pass out literature, mainly to groups of workers in rural areas.[19] She described a worker's house where she stayed one night in a small village in northern Bohemia. The worker had not informed the family that he was bringing the speaker home, and his wife was distressed by the prospect of putting up a stranger. Boschek wrote:

> As I saw the surroundings where I was to stay I was quite upset. I had to wait in the hall while the woman went into the room and I heard her say: "Grandmother, get up. Go in the other room, a woman is sleeping with us tonight." Right away I heard small children crying and then an old woman in a nightgown stood half asleep at the doorway with clothes over her arm. She stood opposite me with an astonished look on her face. The wife now called me into the room and showed me my bed, which the old woman had just vacated. A child who had been sleeping with her was put in a second bed where another one was already sleeping. The air in the small room was terrible. I lay down in bed and it was still warm but I could not sleep. In the morning [when it was light] I realized that six children were sleeping in the room where the grandmother had given up her bed. When I saw this poverty, I apologized to the unfortunate woman.[20]

Boschek observed that conditions such as these were widespread.

Verena Conzett's father was an overseer in a paper factory in Zürich and thus earned more than most working men. But with four children all in school they could barely make ends meet. Verena's mother out of necessity was a home worker sewing men's shirts. Through part of Verena's youth they lived on the second floor of a three-story row house in a working-class slum, and she had vivid memories of how hard it was on her mother. The back of the house faced a canal and across it other row houses. Residents dumped their garbage in the canal and huge rats could be seen scurrying after the refuse. Verena described their apartment during a cholera epidemic:

> Never did a ray of sunshine lighten our home, not even a little bit of it. Every morning my mother went through the rooms carrying a shovel full of glowing coals on which she placed juniper berries in order to try and drive out the stinking, musty air. Most people in Zürich lived in small back streets like that in similar or even under worse conditions. No wonder that cholera could find a home under such unhealthy conditions.
>
> On every house where there was cholera there would be a piece of paper attached which said, 'There is cholera here.' Even our house had such a warning as there were people sick with it living above us and below us.[21]

The vicissitudes of overcrowding in urban areas were compounded by the high density of population. Phyllis Knight grew up in Spandau, a working-class neighborhood in Berlin. She provides us with a vivid and dismal picture of conditions in tenement housing (the German word, *Mietskaserne* is best translated literally as renter barracks, to convey the real meaning of the word).[22] She remembered them as brick or greystone buildings, three to five stories high; they were built in a group around a courtyard so tiny that only the garbage was kept there. In her words:

> Depending on the size of the building, there were four or more apartments per floor. There was very little light and the people living in the apartments off the street hardly ever got any direct sunlight in their windows. Most of the year everything was sort of damp and musty. You could actually smell that tenement air, 'Keller Luft' (cellar air) it was called. Although I've read lots of accounts of it, none of them ever really described it. But anyone who grew up in places like that, in Berlin or elsewhere, knows what I mean. People dreamt of the sun.
>
> The drab sort of semi daylight left its mark on you until you died. . . .
>
> Although most tenements were pretty clean and in fairly good repair, kept that way by the people themselves, they all had a sort of drab and closed-in feel to them.[23]

The majority of these tenements contained neither private bathing facilities nor toilets. Knight recalled that generally "there was one toilet per floor and one bath per building. Some didn't even have that, just a row of common toilets, a couple for men and a couple for women, in the courtyard."[24] Of course there was no central heating and only cold running water. Landlords illegally rented their basements and even subbasements to old people. In one building where Knight had lived, an old woman who could barely walk lived in the subbasement and "she spent most of her days in this dank, stonelined room."[25]

The Knight family was luckier than most. They had three rooms and a kitchen—a living room, a bedroom for the parents, and a third room for the five children. Since her sister was ill and her parents both worked, Phyllis was responsible for the housework; her brothers were never asked to help. Most of all, she hated doing the laundry. The laundry vats were located in the attic and she had to carry the coal up four flights of stairs. It took two full days to boil all the clothes and hang them up in the drying room. On the third day they were taken down and folded.

Most working-class families could not afford the luxury of living alone since rents were too exorbitant for their limited budgets. Taking in and caring for lodgers was income-producing work for married women. It meant that there was little or no privacy; but for single or widowed mothers especially, there was no choice in the matter. Lodgers complicated living arrangements. Our waitress lived with her mother, who was forced to rent every bed in the apartment, including her daughter's. She waited on tables until three or four in the morning but could not go home to sleep until 6:00 A.M., when the lodger went to work. She consoled herself with having a warm bed to go home to in the winter.[26] It was also not unusual for parents to take in grown members of the family in time of financial emergency. Phyllis Knight's grandparents had only two rooms but they shared them with a daughter, her husband, and their grandchild when they had nowhere else to go.[27]

Lodgers, whether family or strangers, posed another problem beyond overcrowding, namely, sexual molestation or harassment. When Adelheid Popp was fourteen and still living at home, her brother brought home a lodger, a friend from his job; as a rule that was how such arrangements came about. Adelheid slept with her mother but the lodger's bed was next to theirs. He began to give her candy and presents and then one night, she reported:

> I lay beside my mother, next [to] the wall. I was not quite fast asleep when I suddenly woke with a cry of terror. I had felt a hot breath above me, but in the darkness could not see what it was. My scream had wakened my mother, who immediately struck a light and perceived what it was.[28]

Her brother insisted that he leave but he was allowed to stay until the weekend to avoid disgrace. For the rest of the week, Adelheid wrote, "I was afraid to fall asleep, and when I did I had the most horrid dreams."[29] In the family of the waitress, her mother's sister came to live with them for a time and her father began to make passes at his sister-in-law. That was the last straw for her mother, as he had already confessed to having a mistress and, in addition, had a severe drinking problem. Her mother left her husband and supported the children on her own after that.[30]

The problems that have been discussed thus far are largely the product of low wages. The issues that are the focus of the next section of this essay are in reality best understood within the context of the workers' total environment. It was the cumulative impact of terrible working conditions on the job and marginal, subsistence-level living at home that placed terrible burdens on women's daily lives. In reading and rereading the autobiographies, it became evident to me that these circumstances had an inordinately destructive influence on the health and psychological well-being of the individual and insidious effect on the family as a whole. The workers themselves had a keen appreciation of their predicament. Anna Perthen explained the death of her mother in very straightforward terms:

> As a child of a textile worker I certainly did not have a rosy youth. My father's wages were never adequate and so my mother, despite the nine children she had borne, always had to go to work right after each delivery. We stayed with our grandmother and because we lived out in the country we were far away from a factory. Therefore we worked as home workers sewing on buttons. Since I was the oldest, after school, instead of playing or studying, I had to take care of the other kids, sew on buttons, or collect wood in the forest. Only three of nine children lived. Surely overwork and malnutrition were the causes of my mother's death.[31]

The wife's burden in caring for the family was a common theme reiterated in the autobiographies. The authors marveled that their mothers managed somehow to keep going under such trying conditions.

In sharp contrast, many women had strong negative feelings and unpleasant memories of their fathers. Aurelia Roth said that her father "showed so little concern for the family that my mother had all the responsibilities fall on her."[32] Marie Beutelmeyer remembered that her father "never showed any concern at all for me and my sister. With the exception of a little ability and the fact of my existence, I have nothing for which to thank my father."[33] Adelheid Popp mostly recalled her father's ugly temper. She wrote:

> My father had a hasty temper; when roused he would beat my mother, who often had to flee half clad to take shelter with some neighbour. Then we were some days alone with the scolding father, whom we dared not approach. We did not get much to eat then; pitying neighbours would help us till our mother returned, impelled by anxiety for her children and household. Such scenes occurred nearly every month, and some-

times oftener. My whole heart clung to my mother; I had an unconquer-
able dread of my father, and I never remember to have spoken to him or
to have been addressed by him.[34]

Phyllis Knight expressed similar sentiments:

By the time I could understand things, when I was nine or ten or so, my
father wasn't contributing very much to the household. When he was in
a good mood he might bring home five pounds of the cheapest meat.
That was supposed to take care of his obligations. Sometimes he gave a
few marks for the rent, often nothing. And he treated my mother pretty
rotten.[35]

Thus as a group, these women were consistent in their comments
about their fathers. They commonly complained about indifference and
lack of affection, harsh treatment—beatings of them and their mother—
and minimal concern about the household and the well-being of the
family as a whole. Frequently the immediate cause of these problems was
drinking, and its usual outcome was violence. Adelheid Popp remembered the Christmas Eve that the family had waited for their father to
return from work. They had no presents but they did have a small tree
which they had decorated themselves with homemade ornaments. They
were going to light the candles on the little tree as soon as their father
arrived. But he came home drunk and a fight followed. In his anger he
"cut the Christmas-tree to pieces with a hatchet. I dared not scream;" she
said, "I only wept—wept till I fell asleep."[36] Aurelia Roth described an
analogous incident. Her father drank so much that he seldom had any
money left on payday and when he came home, a family argument always
ensued. Her mother had to provide for the family and so Aurelia, her two
sisters, and her mother worked as home workers when her mother could
not get work in the factory. She recalled one Saturday when the four of
them began working early in the morning. They kept at it all day and did
not finish until midnight; the work had to be done because they had to
make a delivery to the factory the next day. There was no money in the
house and the income from that effort would buy food. Aurelia's father
came home drunk and complained about the children still being awake.
Her mother tried to explain but he would not listen. He took a stick and
destroyed all their work.[37]

Overcrowding and unhappy marriages led many men to hang out in
the streets or to spend most of their free time in local *Kneipen* (bars).
Here is one such scene from a woman's point of view:

One place we lived was directly across a street from a pretty rough
dive where you'd often see women coming to get their husbands before
they drank up all their wages. It was like out of a temperance melo-

drama. But alcohol was a real problem. Most men didn't earn enough to get drunk and still have enough to pay the rent and feed their family.[38]

Alcoholism and alcohol abuse were the bane of the working-class family. For the woman in the family it meant that she would have to feed and house the family with the most limited means.

Family violence that has thus far been discussed was a product of either strangers entering the family as lodgers or it stemmed from alcohol abuse. But violence took many forms and had many causes; another example cited by Marie Wegrainer is worth mentioning here. At age seventeen Marie was called home to live with her mother, really for the first time in her life since she had mostly been under the care of a foster mother. Her mother had finally married at age forty-three and her new step-father insisted that his new wife's children live with them. Marie was in the house but a short time when she was raped by her stepfather. It was a terrible experience for her and it leads one to ask how common rape and incest must have been in the poor family. The question must be considered in further research.[39]

Situations like those described in the preceding pages and low family income in general meant that wives had to shoulder the triple weight of housework, child care, and income-producing work in some form or another. In fact, all the wives and mothers described in these autobiographies worked for pay inside or outside the home. Though this conclusion is based on a rather small sample, it would seem that scholars will have to rethink the general assumption that most women gave up paid employment once they married. That generalization may apply to middle-class women and it may even be valid for some wives of skilled workers but, for families at the bottom of the wage scale, the woman who was only a housewife was relatively uncommon. Married women's employment patterns were quite varied. Some went back to the factory where they had worked as single women. Others would do the same work at home by making arrangements with the factory. Robyn Dasey, in her article on "Women's Work and the Family," maintained that "while workshop seamstresses were almost entirely single women, married women dominated the outwork sector."[40] She also pointed out that "a survey of 1,350 homeworkers in a number of German cities in 1912 revealed that 73 per cent of them were married, widowed or divorced. In 1913 the Hamburg factory inspector reported that of 1,187 outworkers, 53 per cent were married and a further 22 per cent widowed or separated."[41]

Out of dire necessity, women in these three categories were remarkably inventive at finding ways to earn money. Mrs. Hoffman cited examples of how she and other rural women survived. Harvest time was always good, she observed, because one could earn money every day but it was hard work, especially harvesting grain. She often raised a pig and when it was grown, she would sell it to pay the rent. Growing vegetables in a rented garden plot, something city women did also, usually meant a little extra money and more food on the table. She even hauled sand from a pit to earn a few pfennigs.[42] Anna Altmann recalled one winter when her husband could not find work:

> The winter was hard and there were five of us at the table. I realized I had to take the man's place in these circumstances. I was a tireless worker for the family as I did not want them to go hungry. I had to do a great deal of washing and ironing and when my husband was ashamed, I reassured him there would be better times.[43]

Adelheid Popp's mother faced a difficult situation when her husband died, as her only real work experience was domestic service and she could not read or write. At sixty-one, after having given birth to fifteen children, she was forced to sell fruit in the street, among other jobs.[44] The waitress's mother had worked in a paper bag factory as a young single woman, but now with a family she chose to do the same work at home. She and the children had to work from early morning until late at night to glue 10,000 sacks. They earned 20 pfennigs a thousand, or two Marks total. The children had to go to the factory to pick up supplies and also to deliver the finished product. Her mother always waited impatiently for the children to bring the materials as no work could be done until they came home.[45]

When Annelise Rüegg's father died suddenly of a heart attack, her mother faced emotional, economic, and legal problems. Up until about a year before his death, the family had always had a vagabond existence, moving from place to place because Mr. Rüegg drank too much and was always losing his job. He would get drunk on Saturday and Sunday (Saturday was payday) and then do a "blue Monday" and not show up for work. But with the birth of a fourth child and the receipt of a small inheritance, they bought a small house and he stopped drinking. But then he died and Annelise's mother had no income and the local authorities appointed her brother-in-law, a Methodist minister, as guardian. He had legal control over the children but was of no help to the family; he would just eat a big meal when he came to the house. Since they owned their home, the communal authorities would not provide financial assistance and Mrs. Rüegg was still responsible for communal and church taxes. This widow now worked as a home worker, winding silk thread, and all the children had to work. Annelise was first a babysitter, then a domestic, and finally on her fourteenth birthday went to work in a factory. Her mother knew they had survived when the children were finally old enough (fourteen) to take up factory work. Annelise described her mother's attitude:

> We children always had clean clothes. She did not want people to see our poverty. She would rather work all night long [to get things done]. If we received something from the women's organization we were grateful, just as when the authorities paid our doctor bills. But other than that my mother was proud that we could make it without the help of strangers. She often said to us: "I didn't want someone to say later that you were raised by the commune."[46]

Marie Wegrainer's foster mother was a widow who had had five children; all of them were sent into domestic service. When her husband died she had no income and so walked from small town to small town selling nails. Before Marie herself had married she worked as a domestic servant. After marriage she was only a housewife for a while but eventually had to find paid employment when her husband's business failed. Even when her carpenter husband had steady work in a furniture factory, once they had four children she was always out working, generally cleaning and doing laundry since she had no other skill. By the time she was in her forties she was often incapacitated with a life-threatening stomach ulcer. As her husband put it, "To be sure we have grown old, but before our time with all of our problems."[47]

Phyllis Knight's mother sewed dresses for other women (and made clothes for her own family) and she even sold magazines and newspapers. It took a heavy toll on her:

> Sometimes we would find her sitting in a corner staring vacantly across the room. There wasn't the slightest opportunity or place for privacy. It didn't bother us kids too much but it must have been hell for her because she hardly ever got out. She used to sit behind the door sometimes, in a space between the wall and a large wardrobe. There she would sit, still and staring. We kids would open the door quietly and peep in. "Is Mama still sitting there?" "Yes, still there." No supper, no light, nothing. She'd sit there for hours sometimes. Contemplating I don't know what, either mayhem or suicide I suppose. She never said anything about it and it was certainly not one of the things that we kids would ask about.[48]

It is worth noting, even in passing, that quite a number of the autobiographies referred to friends, acquaintances, and family members who ended up in the *Irrenhaus* (the lunatic asylum, a label indicative of contemporary attitudes); the problem of mental stress and mental illness among the poor, both women and men, deserves serious study. In the case of working-class women, it is no wonder they often became ill, given the pressures on them. Moreover, the documents make clear that once they were married most women had all but no free time—perhaps a few hours on Sunday afternoon at the most.

These autobiographies also inform us that the working-class child seldom grew to adulthood without suffering the death of one or both parents and one or more siblings. Death was an ever-present reality and the normal outcome was devastating—a destitute family and an overburdened single parent. When both parents died, or the surviving parent could not care for the family alone, the children were simply parceled out among relatives or even neighbors. The foster child was a regular feature in the lives of these poor families. One woman recalled that her mother had died at 6 o'clock and by 9 o'clock the children had been divided up and given away. The stable nuclear family, so idealized by the middle and upper classes, was almost the exception among the poor, whose very existence was marginal at best. The reaction to death, as expressed in the autobiographies, was a curious mixture of grief for the loss of someone close and fear for the survival of the family with the disappearance of an adult breadwinner.

It was not uncommon for whole families to pass into oblivion within a relatively short period of time. The waitress cited just such a case. Her aunt (who was her father's foster sister) had a husband with a terrible drinking problem and he often beat his wife mercilessly. One day the waitress (who was then a small child) visited them, only the find the husband in the hallway where he had hanged himself. She vividly remembered the body, with his tongue hanging out, and her aunt's immediate reaction. "Thank God that old pig is dead," she said.[49] She was now a widow with three children. Yet his death was a relief since he had treated her so badly and, besides, she had already been supporting the family for some time because of his drinking. The waitress's mother took in the youngest child because he was suffering from a disease of the hip; he died within six months. The second child was then taken. Unfortunately the waitress and her new foster sister found some rotting fruit in the gutter and because they never had fruit at home, they could not resist eating it. Both became deathly ill and this second foster child died. Soon after returning from the cemetery, the aunt herself passed away. Out of a family of five, only one daughter was left alive. She too was taken in, but eventually ended up in a home for juvenile delinquents.[50]

But death was not necessarily the last indignity visited on the poor; scraping together money for a decent burial afforded the family's next crisis. Many had to accept a pauper's funeral from the state. The waitress's aunt begged her sister-in-law to see to it that she had a nice funeral and a good casket when she died. Since there was no money for that, the family went up and down the street asking people to give money;

through the generosity of neighbors, she had her respectable funeral.[51] Ottilie Baader recalled that when her mother died, they too had no money for a funeral. Fortunately, workers at the Borsig factory where her father was employed took up a collection to pay for the burial.[52] Mrs. Hoffmann pointed out that often poor families could not even afford wine or coffee, let alone food, at the reception following the funeral. It was humiliating, but such amenities were just too expensive.[53] A final comment by Phyllis Knight is appropriate:

> Illness, death and madness everywhere. Our family, my relatives and friends weren't at all unusual in that way. Among almost all the families that we knew, including our own, there was always somebody who was suffering.[54]

Some observations on education and work will conclude this essay; it is appropriate that the discussion returns to the question of working-class childhood where it began. As a general rule, work took precedence over the child's education. It is generally believed that the first paid employment for the rural child was domestic service and for the urban child, factory work. The majority of these women began their working life as home workers. Laws requiring elementary education and limiting child labor forbade factory owners from employing very young children as had been the practice in the earlier phases of industrialization. But no such laws regulated work in a child's own home. Home work, done under the supervision of parents, meant that young girls still began working at about age six and they often had to miss school when work was available to the family. Just as rural children might be kept out of school at planting and harvest time, urban children would have to miss school because they had to deliver or pick up supplies. Because home work was seasonal, families had to take work whenever they could find it.

Work and education were the alternate poles of a child's life. School was a welcome relief from the monotony of work. Anna Maier recalled her childhood:

> I am the youngest of twelve children and I learned early what work is all about. When other children were out playing in the street, I would watch them with envy from the window until my mother would slap me to remind me that I had to work. . . . When one thinks that at six, a child has to give up all the pleasures of youth. That is a lot to ask! When I went to school my only desire was to learn. But that desire was an illusion because I had to get up at 5 o'clock, do some spooling and then run off to school poorly dressed. After school I had to run home in order to do some more spooling before lunch. Then after school in the afternoons I had to spool again. I was able to accept that, but not being kept home from school to help with the work. But all the begging and crying in the world didn't help, I had to do what my mother said.[55]

By the turn of the twentieth century more and more working-class children were able to stay in school until the age of fourteen, although some parents ignored the laws when they could. Adelheid Popp described her mother as "an enemy of the 'newfangled laws,' as she called compulsory education."[56] She resented having the state tell her how to care for her family. Since her mother was illiterate, Adelheid would write her own excuses for missing school. But the authorities eventually caught up with them and her mother was arrested. The headmaster at Adelheid's school thought she was a gifted child and urged her mother to let her attend school, but to no avail. Adelheid herself asked, "of what use was it to go to school when I had neither clothes nor food?"[57]

Three generations of Marie Wegrainer's family illustrate how working-class women were trapped in low-paying unskilled jobs because of family circumstances and prevailing social attitudes about women and work. Marie's mother had always worked as a domestic servant and cook. With two illegitimate children she worked to support them until she married at age forty-three. Even though the man she was to marry was known to be a brute, he was a master shoemaker and had a business with five men working for him. His income meant that she would only have to care for the house. But before she married she refused to allow Marie to be an apprentice for some job that would have been better paying, and over Marie's and her foster mother's protests, Marie too went into domestic service. Even in later life she was angry at her mother for not allowing her to become a dressmaker. As a married woman, Marie and her husband scrimped so that their eldest son could have an apprenticeship. It was hoped that once he was a skilled worker he would help support the family. That was not to be. He infuriated his parents by leaving home once he was earning more than his father. A second son trained to be a painter. Both daughters, however, were given little or no training; one became a shopgirl and the other a milliner.[58]

Though a detailed analysis of work experiences will be the subject of another paper, I would point out a common omission in most studies of working-class women. Historians are generally in agreement that all working-class women's jobs had common features. They demanded relatively few skills, hours were long, and pay was low. Scholars also agree that the major occupations open to poorly educated, working-class women were: agriculture, domestic service, factory work (mainly in the textile and garment industries), home work, food products and services, and, of course, prostitution. Given these widely accepted assumptions, there has been a tendency not to ask further questions about how these occupational categories differed from each other, especially in terms of working conditions. Moreover, there has been too little discussion of why women chose one form of employment over another. The autobiographies offer some understanding of these issues which were important to women workers themselves. My reading of the sources leads me to conclude that these assumptions about the working life of women must be challenged. For example, I have argued elsewhere that we must recognize there were really unskilled, semiskilled, and skilled women workers just as in men's work.[59] Of course, skilled women were still paid less than their male counterparts. Moreover, scholars, by describing or categorizing women's work in broad occupational categories have missed the nuances of differences in individual jobs as a they affected women in terms of working conditions, wages, training, health problems, and so forth. It is time to jettison all our stereotypes about women and work and reevaluate this problem from the sources.

Some concluding comments are in order. Though many men would be the first to accept the notion that the family is the woman's "proper sphere," ironically even the writing of family history has placed men at the center of family life. This essay has tried to reverse that equation by making women the focus of family life. In so doing, one arrives at a whole new perspective of women's role in the family. Yet the history of working-class women cannot concentrate solely on the family as this essay has done. All of labor history, especially the history of work, will have to be given its proper due in order that the role of the working woman in modern German economic life is understood. To ignore women's contribution to German industrialization is to ignore almost half the work force. Making use of the autobiographies as this essay has done, and turning to other sources on working-class women, will help make possible a better appreciation of women's impact on the family and society as a whole.

Speaking more specifically to the examples cited in this essay, it must be reiterated how crucial women were to the survival of the working-class family. They contributed to it in every possible way and in most instances their role was greater, if not more important, than that of the men in the family. Often the working-class wife bore the triple burden of household responsibilities, childbirth and child care, and paid employment either inside or outside the home. Ultimately the family's welfare was shaped by a wife's ability to juggle those complex and demanding burdens.

The idea of a stable nuclear family is at best an exaggeration and at worst an illusion. Many working-class women had children without marrying and others, even with common-law husbands, had only a modicum of family life. When there was a real marriage and the husband made a major contribution to it through paid employment, even then the woman was forced to care for the family and work to bring additional income into the family. Women worked for pay during most of their childhood and through most of their adult lives, either single or married. There were times when the wife of a reasonably well paid, skilled worker did not work for pay, often in the early part of the marriage but once there were more than two children, a husband's wages were insufficient. Unskilled workers never earned enough to support a wife, let alone children, and thus wives of male workers at the bottom of the wage scale always worked as housewives and paid workers.

Many factors beyond low pay contributed to the instability of the working-class family. Alcoholism or alcohol abuse was a common problem. Family violence was also common and it took a variety of forms. Most importantly, it was the interplay between the burden of the household and child care on the one hand and the demands of paid employment and terrible living conditions on the other that put so much pressure on working-class women. Many could not stand the burdens and their physical or psychological health (or both) were ruined by the time they were in midlife. It is remarkable that these women survived at all. Finally, such issues as mental illness, broken families, single parent households, and the impact of death will have to be researched, as well as many other fascinating issues raised in the autobiographies.

NOTES

1. For similar sentiments, see Heilwig Schomerus, "The Family Life-Cycle: A Study of Factory Workers in Nineteenth-Century Württemberg," in Richard J. Evans and W. R. Lee, eds., *The German Family* (Totowa, NJ, 1981), p. 175.

2. New work has been appearing at an incredibly fast pace. Some representative works are: Heilwig Schomerus, *Die Arbeiter der Maschinenfabrik Esslingen. Forschungen zur Lage der Arbeiterschaft im 19. Jahrhundert* (Stuttgart, 1977); David F. Crew, *Town in the Ruhr: A Social History of Bochum 1860–1914* (New York, 1979); Mary Nolan, *Social Democracy and Society: Working-Class Radicalism in Düsseldorf 1890–1920* (New York, 1981); Richard J. Evans and W. R. Lee, eds., *The German Family: Essays on the Social History of the Family in Nineteenth- and Twentieth-Century Germany* (Totowa, NJ, 1981); Richard J. Evans, ed., *The German Working Class, 1888–1933* (Totowa, NJ, 1982); Lutz Niethammer, ed., *Wohnen im Wandel. Beiträge zur Geschichte des Alltags in der bürgerlichen Gesellschaft* (Wuppertal, 1979); Jürgen Reulecke and Wolfhard Weber, eds., *Fabrik Familie Feierabend. Beiträge zur Sozialgeschichte des Alltags im Industriezeitalter* (Wuppertal, 1978); Werner Conze and Ulrich Engelhardt, eds., *Arbeiterexistenz im 19. Jahrhundert. Lebensstandard und Lebensgestaltung deutscher Arbeiter und Handwerker* (Stuttgart, 1981). There have been numerous special issues of journals in addition to the numerous essay collections. See,

for example, two issues of *Geschichte und Gesellschaft:* "Soziale Schichtung und Mobilität in Deutschland im 19. und 20. Jahrhundert," vol. 1, issue 1, 1975; "Arbeiterkultur im 19. Jahrhundert," vol. 5, issue 1, 1979.

I should add that these comments do not imply any denigration of the value of a host of works that have contributed so much to our knowledge of German labor history. For example, whether one considers an old classic, Heinrich Herkner's, *Die Arbeiterfrage* (2 vols., 7th rev. ed.; Berlin, 1921), or excellent studies from a more recent period, such as Gerhard A. Ritter, *Die Arbeiterbewegung im wilhelminischen Reich* (2nd rev. ed.; Berlin, 1963), and Vernon L. Lidtke, *The Outlawed Party Social Democracy in German, 1878–1890* (Princeton, NJ, 1966), there are many standard works available to the student of labor history.

3. Thomas Dublin, *Women at Work: The Transformation of Work and Community in Lowell, Massachusetts, 1826–1860* (New York, 1979) and Louise A. Tilly and Joan W. Scott, *Women, Work, and Family* (New York, 1978).

Alice Clark was an early pioneer and her classic, *Working Life of Women in the Seventeenth Century* first appeared in 1919 (now reprinted—Boston, 1982). Many others have since followed, albeit slowly. Also very valuable are Wanda F. Neff, *Victorian Working Women* (London, 1927) and Ivy Pinchbeck, *Women Workers and the Industrial Revolution* (New York, 1932). Of many recent publications, I would mention a few representative examples such as Peter N. Stearns, "Working Class Women in Britain, 1890–1914," in Martha Vicinus, ed., *Suffer and Be Still* (Bloomington, 1972); Marilyn J. Boxer and Jean H. Quataert, eds., *Socialist Women* (New York, 1978); Sheila Lewenhak, *Women and Trade Unions: An Outline History of Women in the British Trade Union Movement* (New York, 1977); three chapters (8, 11, and 12) in Renate Bridenthal and Claudia Koonz, eds., *Becoming Visible: Women in European History* (Boston, 1977)—Richard J. Vann, "Towards a New Lifestyle: Women in Preindustrial Capitalism"; Mary Lynn McDougall, "Working-Class Women During the Industrial Revolution, 1780–1914"; and Theresa M. McBride, "The Long Road Home: Women's Work and Industrialization"; two essays in Mary Hartman and Lois W. Banner, eds., *Clio's Consciousness Raised* (New York, 1974)—Laura Oren, "The Welfare of Women in Laboring Families: England, 1860–1950," and Ruth Schwartz Cowan, "A Case Study of Technological and Social Change: The Washing Machine and the Working Wife"; and Judith R. Walkowitz, *Prostitution and Victorian Society: Women, Class, and the State* (New York, 1980). I would also mention Lee Holcombe, *Victorian Ladies at Work: Middle-Class Working Women in England and Wales, 1850–1914* (Hamden, CT, 1973).

4. Gisela Losseff-Tillmanns, *Frauenemanzipation und Gewerkschaften* (Wuppertal, 1978); Sabine Richebächer, *Uns fehlt nur eine Kleinigkeit. Deutsche proletarische Frauenbewegung 1890–1914* (Frankfurt, 1982); Edith Rigler, *Frauenleitbild und Frauenarbeit in Österreich vom ausgehenden 19. Jahrhundert bis zum Zweiten Weltkrieg* (Munich, 1980); Josef Ehmer, "Frauenarbeit und Arbeiterfamilie in Wien. Vom Vormärz bis 1934," *Geschichte und Gesellschaft,* 7 (1981), pp. 438–73; Jean H. Quataert, *Reluctant Feminists in German Social Democracy, 1885–1917* (Princeton, NJ, 1979); Robyn Dasey, "Women's Work and the Family: Women Garment Workers in Berlin and Hamburg before the First

World War," in Richard J. Evans and W. R. Lee, eds., *The German Family;* Regina Schulte, "Dienstmädchen im herrschaftlichen Haushalt. Zur Genese ihrer Sozialpsychologie," in *Zeitschrift für Bayerische Landesgeschichte,* 41 (1978), pp. 879–920; and Peter Schneck, "Die gesundheitlichen Verhältnisse der Fabrikarbeiterinnen. Ausgewählte Aspekte der Situation in der sächsischen Oberlausitz im ausgehenden 19. Jahrhundert," *Jahrbuch für Wirtschaftsgeschichte,* 16 (1975), pp. 53–72. See also Ingeborg Weber-Kellermann, *Die deutsche Familie. Versuch einer Sozialgeschichte* (6th edition; Frankfurt, 1981) and Michael Mitterauer und Reinhard Sieder, eds., *Historische Familienforschung* (Frankfurt, 1982). For additional citations readers are urged to consult the introduction to this book and the bibliography at the end of this volume.

5. For an important historical and introductory definition of women's history see, Gerda Lerner, "Placing Women in History: Definitions and Challenges," in *Feminist Studies,* 3, (1/2), 1975/6, pp. 5–14.

6. Carlos Ginzburg in the introduction to his fascinating study, *The Cheese and the Worms: The Cosmos of a Sixteenth-Century Miller* (Baltimore, 1980), posed the question of "what relevance the ideas and beliefs of a single individual of his social level can have." He admitted that "to undertake a narrow investigation on a solitary miller may seem paradoxical or absurd, practically a return to hand-weaving in an age of power looms." Yet he maintained, to ignore such material would be equally absurd. Even the solitary individual can be representative of a class or the statistical majority. Ginzburg also argued that too many social scientists have advocated only the use of extensive quantitative research. Such individuals as his miller can shed light on the oblique character of statistical information. Autobiographical details give clues that lead researchers to important new areas of inquiry (pp. xx–xxii). There is in fact a long history of speculation about the value of autobiographical materials. See: Adelbert Koch, "Arbeitermemoiren als sozialwissenschaftliche Erkenntnisquelle," *Archiv für Sozialwissenschaft und Sozialpolitik* 61 (1929), pp. 128–67; Cecilia Trunz, *Die Autobiographie von deutschen Industriearbeitern* (Dissertation: Universität Freiburg: Freiburg, 1934); Wolfram Fischer, "Arbeitermemoiren als Quelle für Geschichte und Volkskunde der industriellen Gesellschaft," *Soziale Welt,* 9 (1958), pp. 288–98; Ursula Münchow, "Das Bild des Arbieters in der proletarischen Selbstdarstellung," *Weimarer Beiträge,* 19 (1973), pp. 110–35; R. P. Neumann, "German Workers' Autobiographies as Social Historical Sources," *Newsletter European Labor and Working Class History,* 7 (1975), pp. 23–27; Jean Peneff, "Autobiographies de Militants Ouvriers," *Revue Française de Science Politique,* 29 (1979), pp. 53–82.

The above have tended only to speculate on the use of workers' autobiographies; some newer works have actually used autobiographies to write working-class history. See: David Vincent, *Bread, Knowledge, and Freedom: A Study of Nineteenth-Century Autobiography* (New York, 1981); Otfried Scholz, *Arbeiterselbstbild und Arbeiterfremdbild zur Zeit der Industriellen Revolution. Ein Beitrag zur Sozialgeschichte des Arbieters in der deutschen Erzähl- und Memoirenliteratur um die Mitte des 19. Jahrhunderts* (Berlin, 1980); Margarete Flecken, *Arbeiterkinder im 19. Jahrhundert. Eine sozialgeschichtliche Unter-*

suchung ihrer Lebenswelt (Weinheim, 1981). Even these most recent works are male-centered.

7. These sources are: *Im Kampf ums Dasein. Wahrheitsgetreue Lebenserinnerungen eines Mädchens aus dem Volke als Fabrikarbeiterin, Dienstmädchen und Kellnerin* (Stuttgart, 1908); Annelise Rüegg, *Erlebnisse einer Serviertochter. Bilder aus der Hotelindustrie* (Zurich, 1915); Doris Viersbeck, *Erlebnisse eines Hamburger Dienstmädchens* (Munich, 1910); Marie Wegrainer, *Der Lebensroman einer Arbeiterfrau,* von ihr selbst geschrieben (Munich, 1914); *Aus der Gedankenwelt einer Arbeiterfrau,* von ihr selbst erzählt [Frau Hoffman], ed. by C. Moseik, Pfarrer (Berlin, 1909); Adelheid Popp, *The Autobiography of a Working Woman,* translated by E. C. Harvey (Chicago, 1913); Phyllis Knight and Rolf Knight, *A Very Ordinary Life* (Vancouver, 1974); Verena Conzett, *Erstrebtes und Erlebtes. Ein Stück Zeitgeschichte* (Zurich, 1929); Ottilie Baader, *Ein steiniger Weg. Lebenserinnerungen* (Berlin, 1921); *Die zwanzigjährige Arbeiterinnen-Bewegung Berlins und ihr Ergebniss,* beleuchtet von einer Arbeiterin [Adeline Berger] (Berlin, [Im Selbstverlage der Verfasserin], 1889); "Geschichte eines Berliner Dienstmädchens," in Oscar Stilich, *Die Lage der weiblichen Dienstboten* (Berlin, 1902); *Gedenkbuch 20 Jahre österreichische Arbeiterinnenbewegung,* Im Auftrage des Frauenreichskomitees, ed. by Adelheid Popp (Vienna, 1912); "Ein Stück soziale Frage. Briefe eines dienenden Mädchens vom Lande an Lina Scheible," *Das Land* 1 (1893), pp. 84–86, 103–6.

8. Viersbeck, pp. 3–5. See Schulte, pp. 886–89.

9. It should be pointed out that the autobiographies are different in some ways. The socialist ones do emphasize these women's involvement in unions or the party. On the other hand, the nonsocialist autobiographies talk a bit about religion and some have a low level of political consciousness and for those reasons were probably ignored by the socialist press. Otherwise I eventually came to the conclusion that they should not be differentiated in terms of their usage and value. I must also add that one cannot tell how truthful any one account is and certainly some may have been doctored by the editors, Mrs. Hoffman's for example, but I have tried to cite examples that are the general rule rather than exceptions. I believe as a group they are very valuable and they have been ignored just because they were written by women.

Recently published document collections now have made excerpts (short ones) of many of these works readily available. See: Wolfgang Emmerich, ed., *Proletarische Lebensläufe* (2 vols.; Reinbek, 1974–75); Friedrich G. Kürbisch and Richard Klucsarits, eds., *Arbeiterinnen kämpfen um ihr Recht* (2nd ed.; Wuppertal, 1981); Eleanor S. Riemer and John C. Fout, eds., *European Women: A Documentary History 1789–1945* (New York, 1980). In the case of the latter, see document numbers 5, 24, and 30 especially. See also, Gisela Losseff-Tillmanns, ed., *Frau und Gewerkschaft* (Frankfurt, 1982).

Some recent reprints on English women are useful. See Margaret Llewelyn Davies, ed., *Life as We Have Known It by Cooperative Working Women* (New York, 1978) and Women's Cooperative Guild, ed., *Maternity: Letters from Working Women* (New York, 1978). See also, John Burnett, ed., *Annals of Labour: Autobiographies of British Working-Class People, 1820–1920* (Bloomington, 1974).

I would also add that another rich source on Austrian working-class women is *Die Arbeits- und Lebensverhältnisse der Wiener Lohnarbeiterinnen* (Vienna, 1897). I have relied heavily on it though I have not quoted it here. See my forthcoming article, "The Viennese Enquête of 1896 on Working Women" to be published by Indiana University Press in the proceedings of an international conference held at the University of Minnesota on April 17, 1983. It dealt with women in Germany in the Eighteenth and Nineteenth Centuries. Many essays are on working-class women. See especially, Mary Jo Maynes, "Feminism in Working-Class Autobiographies."

10. I would put another valuable autobiography in that category. See Lena Christ, *Erinnerungen einer Überflüssigen* (Munich, 1970).

11. Popp, *Autobiography*, pp. 15–16.

12. Marie Sponer, "Aus Nordböhmen," in Popp, *Gedenkbuch*, p. 140.

13. *Im Kampf ums Dasein*, pp. 17–18.

14. Ibid., p. 31.

15. Ibid., pp. 31–32.

16. Ibid., 45–48.

17. Ibid., p. 47.

18. *Aus der Gedankenwelt*, pp. 20–21.

19. Anna Boschek, "Aus vergangenen Jahren," in Popp, *Gedenkbuch*, pp. 89–102.

20. Ibid., p. 100.

21. Conzett, p. 19. See also pages 18–26.

22. Knight, pp. 5–12. My thanks to Prof. Diana Brown for lending a copy of the Knight autobiography to me.

23. Ibid., p. 7.

24. Ibid.

25. Ibid., p. 8. See also, Lutz Niethammer (unter Mitarbeit von Franz Brüggemeier), "Wie wohnten Arbeiter im Kaiserreich?" *Archiv für Sozialgeschichte* 16 (1976), pp. 62–134; Franz Brüggemeier and Lutz Niethammer, "Schlafgänger, Schnapskasinos und schwerindustrielle Kolonie. Aspekte der Arbeiterwohnungsfrage im Ruhrgebiet vor dem Ersten Weltkrieg," in Reulecke and Weber. See also Josef Ehmer, "Wohnen ohne eigene Wohnung. Zur sozialen Stellung von Untermietern und Bettgehern," and Heilwig Schomerus, "Die Wohnung als unmittelbare Umwelt. Unternehmer, Handwerker und Arbeiterschaft einer württembergischen Industriestadt 1850 bis 1900," in Lutz Niethammer, ed., *Wohnen im Wandel*.

26. *Im Kampf ums Dasein*, p. 163.

27. Knight, p. 16.

28. Popp, *Autobiography*, p. 41.

29. Ibid., p. 42.

30. *Im Kampf ums Dasein*, pp. 34–37.

31. Anna Perthen, "Der Anfang in Bodenbach," in Popp, *Gedenkbuch*, p. 113.

32. Aurelia Roth, "Eine Glasschleiferin," Ibid., p. 52.

33. Marie Beutelmeyer, "Aus Oberösterreich," Ibid., p. 70.

34. Popp, *Autobiography*, p. 16.

35. Knight, p. 5.

36. Popp, *Autobiography*, pp. 16–17.

37. Roth in Popp, *Gedenkbuch*, pp. 53–54.

38. Knight, p. 19.

39. Wegrainer, pp. 33–38, 50–51.

40. Dasey, p. 243.

41. Ibid.

42. *Aus der Gedankenwelt*, pp. 6–7, 14, 22.

43. Anna Altmann, "Blätter und Blüten," in Popp, *Gedenkbuch*, p. 29.

44. Popp, *Autobiography*, pp. 20, 46.

45. *Im Kampf ums Dasein*, pp. 18–19, 32–33.

46. Rüegg, pp. 15–16, 22–23.

47. Wegrainer, pp. 6, 9, 155–63, 166.

48. Knight, p. 5.

49. *Im Kampf ums Dasein*, p. 14.

50. Ibid., *passim.*, pp. 13–22.

51. Ibid., p. 16.

52. Baader, p. 9.

53. *Aus der Gedankenwelt*, pp. 19, 24, 115–17.

54. Knight, p. 50.

55. Riemer/Fout, p. 94. In the original, Anna Maier, "Wie ich reif wurde," in Popp, *Gedenkbuch*, p. 107.

56. Popp, *Autobiography*, p. 20.

57. Ibid., pp. 28–29.

58. Wegrainer, pp. 10–11, 33–35, 156–66, 180–86.

59. See my forthcoming "The Viennese Enquête of 1896 on Working Women."

The Civilizing Tendency of Hygiene

Working-Class Women under Medical Control in Imperial Germany*

UTE FREVERT

In recent years, many scholars have stressed the important, if not to say decisive, influence that the medical profession had on the self-esteem and role performance of middle-class women in the nineteenth century. In France, Great Britain, and the United States, historians, mostly women, have pointed out to what extent physicians were concerned with women's pathology, in a practical sense and theoretically.[1] Consequently, medical doctrines which claimed the female body suffered from physiological deficiencies (and was in fact inferior) were used as a justification for excluding women from certain professions and spheres of action. At the same time, however, medical opinions which espoused the notion of "character due to sex"[2] held out elements of identification which women were eager to accept. If their physical constitution was so frail indeed, making women the victims of the uterus and the vicissitudes of the menstrual cycle, they could take advantage of those arguments and at least temporarily escape from their daily household and conjugal duties by claiming they were too ill.[3] Moreover, health propaganda opened up a new and highly esteemed field of endeavor for the wives of the bourgeoisie. Considering themselves responsible for implementing the new rules of health in their homes, they upgraded their domestic and

*My thanks to Ute Daniel and Claudia Huerkamp for critical suggestions.

educational work, which was now recast on a modern and scientific basis. Surely these women enjoyed having the approval and help of the "medical friend of the family."[4]

This privileged alliance between doctors and housewives proved to be an essential component in the lives of middle-class women in France, Great Britain, and the United States. In Germany too, from the late eighteenth century onward, the family doctor now took the part of counselor, controller, and confidant in the bourgeois household formerly played by the priest. As a result, rules of conduct based on religion were gradually replaced by rationally founded and medically approved modes of behavior. Medical norms for body hygiene, cleanliness, healthy food, and responsible child care were increasingly adopted by the "educated classes."

Since the history of middle-class women's "sphere" in Germany in the nineteenth century has not been written, we have very little concrete knowledge about the relationship between medicine, the health movement, and homemaking. Yet, the overwhelming and in fact lasting success of the medical profession's attempts at education came to light when women's organizations and "charitable ladies" began to pass on their newly acquired knowledge to the "lower classes." From midcentury, middle-class women, together with doctors, businessmen, churches, and local government, thus sought to regulate the health standards of their proletarian sisters.

This paper seeks to investigate the process of the "hygienic civilization" of the working-class family. Beginning in the 1860s, "hygiene" became a marvelous slogan for solving social problems; its goal was to reintegrate social outcasts and to reform society as a whole. It encompassed a host of rules, "the application of which was aimed at maintenance of the health of the individual and society, as well as at morality, the destruction of the causes of illness, and the refinement of the physical and moral virtues of human beings."[5] In the second half of the century, a massive educational campaign was begun to implement these rules in the social strata most needing "refinement." It was directed primarily to working-class wives and daughters, as they were to play a key role in the adoption of middle-class values and habits and the mental integration of the working classes into capitalist society and economy. This essay will attempt to explain the appearance of and the driving forces behind that process of controlling the health behavior of the working-class family. It will be more difficult to assess the real impact of those normative models. Though doctors, local government officials, and women's organizations readily explained the motives, aims, and procedures of their educational campaign, working-class women did not reveal their experiences. Therefore only tentative hypotheses can be put forward about the impact of the health movement on the workers themselves—especially in terms of how they perceived it and if it affected their behavior.

THE DISEASES OF THE WORKING-CLASS FAMILY AND WOMEN'S HEALING POWER

"Good health" had become an issue of general social concern in Germany since the late eighteenth century. Thanks to the untiring efforts of doctors, the idea was accepted by more and more people, especially in the middle strata of society. From the very beginning, "good health" was closely associated with bourgeois culture and its values. In this connection, health meant discipline, success, good morals, and social integration. Conversely, illness became synonymous with poverty, corruption, decadence, and mental degeneration. Of course, these analogies were not "invented" in the late eighteenth or early nineteenth century. What was new was the notion that good health, just as ill health, was not a matter of fate. Rather, the individual could control it in either a negative or a positive way. Physicians, in the last third of the eighteenth century, claiming to speak in the name of the Enlightenment, informed their middle-class readers, especially their female readers, of the most important rules which needed to be observed to maintain good health.[6] For those who obeyed the rules, a long life and good health would be guaranteed. Disobedience would mean indisposition, suffering, and an early death.

Consequently, it was up to the individual to lead a healthy life, and if one did, it would bring a bourgeois life of happiness and success. In terms of the sexual division of labor, however, it was up to women to look after the health needs of the family, including proper hygiene and diet. Although the medical profession was extremely skeptical of the "notorious inclination of the gentle sex to play dangerous games with Aesculapius's snake"[7]—and though they never tired of warning women to keep their hands off therapy—doctors still considered women to be their closest allies. They would be the most competent partners in anything connected with family hygiene, healthy food and lodging, the proper care of children, and the proper care of the body. They were granted full authority in these areas as long as they followed the doctors' advice. The same held true for nursing, since it seemed to be particularly suited to the female character. Given those special abilities, women would be the best possible assistants for male doctors.[8] As conscientious mothers who carefully obeyed the doctors' orders, middle-class women turned out to be the most important constituency for medical health propaganda in the period since the late eighteenth century. Without their cooperation, the physicians' dream of a society that worked, ate, slept, danced, bore children, and died according to the rules established by the medical profession would never have come about.

This dream, however, encountered almost insurmountable obstacles in those social strata which were alienated from middle-class work and cultural standards, because these people resisted the medical, clerical, and pedagogical appeals to become more efficient, more caring for the future, and more rational in terms of economic behavior. Nevertheless, they had to be "enlightened" and accustomed to the new norms and rules since they were the soldiers and workers without whom neither an expanding economy nor a state striving to gain military power could flourish. "Irrational" health behavior could have fatal results by undermining physical strength, increasing the mortality rate, and turning those families impoverished by disease and death into paupers. It was thus far more important to achieve the systematic *Medikalisierung* of the lower classes—i.e., the extension of hygienic standards and medical care—than it was for the "educated classes."

Health propaganda was first addressed to the rural population, but by the 1840s the urban working classes were the focus, since they were thought to be the most "socially morbid" group in society. In a prosperous middle-class setting, side by side with cultivated, civilized academics, civil servants, merchants, and entrepreneurs, a rapidly growing group of people had emerged whose values and behavior did not seem to fit in the new social order. They were aliens and carriers of disease and they constituted a permanent danger for their bourgeois surroundings. In the lodgings of journeymen, day laborers, and factory workers, typhus and cholera were all too common and newborn children died like flies. In 1835, J. L. Casper, a professor of medicine in Berlin, demonstrated statistically that out of 1,000 children in poor families, only 598 would live to the age of ten, 486 would live until their thirty-fifth birthday, and not more than 226 would live to sixty. For the gentry, corresponding figures were 938, 735, and 398. Astonished by his findings, Casper wrote: "Mere accident meant that a child born on a rich man's cushions would live eighteen years longer than a child born on a beggar's straw mattress."[9] In another survey done twenty years later by a Frankfurt physician, W. C. de Neufville, the average age at death of different occupational groups was compared and the life expectancy of tailors, shoemakers, and masons, for example, lagged far behind that of middle-class occupations such as merchants, academics, and officials. That observation was confirmed by F. Oesterlen in 1851 when he estimated that the life expectancy of the proletariat on the average was two-thirds or even one-half that of well-to-do people. In 1877, J. Conrad, a professor of economics, proved that, compared to poor people, the "upper classes" were considerably better off in terms of infant and adult mortality. There were important differences in the causes of death as well. For example, in Halle between 1855 and 1874, 3.8 percent of the adult males of the educated classes died of cholera, but among the working classes, 12.4 percent of the adult males died of the disease.[10]

Various explanations were given for the fact that the working class was more prone to disease. A relatively small group of physicians was convinced that work itself was responsible for the poor health of the workers. Long working hours, the increasing pace of the work, the crowded factories, and dangerous materials and machines put a heavy burden on the human body and weakened its natural resistance to diseases. Most other doctors argued that the problem was not the work itself, rather there was an indirect cause which was more important, namely, low wages. Salomon Neumann, for example, who took care of working-class patients in Berlin, argued in 1854 that general living conditions had a decisive impact on health. In terms of the "common, everyday" diseases, "social conditions, especially housing and nutrition," were far more important than occupational status.[11] Insufficient food and damp, dark, overcrowded apartments made workers more vulnerable to illness, especially to such diseases as scrofula, rickets, and tuberculosis.

Nearly all contemporaries agreed, however, that low wages was not the only cause of misery. Rather, the standard of living of the working class was largely dependent on their moral qualifications, they argued. Even under the worst conditions, austerity, moderation, and thrifty housekeeping would accomplish miracles. Again and again, doctors pointed out that working men's wives spent the family income on the wrong things. Instead of buying healthy and nourishing food and preparing wholesome meals, they put bread and potatoes on the table. Instead of milk, they drank weak coffee—and, believe it or not, the money these people should have spent on badly needed protein and fat was in fact spent on alcohol. Naturally the consumption of alcohol undermined the health of working men as much as the lack of cleanliness in their dwellings made them susceptible to illness.[12]

Thus if the lower classes at least shared the responsibility for their poor state of health, it was evident that this kind of deviant behavior could be altered with the help of suitable training programs. Once they had developed a sound attitude about health, cleanliness, sobriety, and adequate provision for future needs, they would have taken a decisive step toward social and cultural integration. Not only the workers but the economy would benefit from increased physical strength because there would be higher productivity. Last but not least, it was expected that proper health education could relieve society of the threat of political change. Once the working man appreciated a "healthy, sober, and ordered way of life," wrote a Breslau physician, Dr. H. Friedberg, and had "healthy housing and clothing," a sense of efficiency and a desire for thriftiness would follow. Likewise, he would then "avoid criticizing many of the things which otherwise have made him dissatisfied with his lot in life, namely, work, his employer, the government, and social conditions."[13] In other words, the promotion of good health would pacify the *classes dangereuses* by focusing their energy on practical "social reforms."

But how would such an ambitious educational program be instituted? What means could be used to teach good health standards to the lower classes and at the same time guarantee that gradually those standards would be observed in working-class households? Clearly, the appeal had to be made to working-class women and their confidence had to be won. Whether or not the household functioned properly depended on them and they were responsible for both the physical and moral welfare of the family.

Contemporaries who witnessed the enormous economic and social changes that were coming about as a result of industrialization believed that the family was the crucial focal point for their efforts. In 1851, the conservative writer Wilhelm H. Riehl published his book *Die bürgerliche Gesellschaft (Middle-class Society)*, and in it he characterized the "proletarians of material work" as having a complete lack of a sense of family. Only seven years before, his colleague Constantin Frantz had recommended that family ties be strengthened as a "remedy for pauperism."[14] Riehl considered the modern factory worker to be a man without family and *Heimat* (homeland), without commitments, and extremely vulnerable to revolutionary propaganda and communist dreams. Strengthening the family was the only way to cope with these problems. Riehl wrote: "Family life is the best protection against social aberrations and if such aberrations are occurring with increasing frequency, that is a sure sign that the sanctuary of the home must have been stunted in some respects."[15] In the family, workers would find the *Heimat* they had lost; there they would be able to relax after working and there they would find a substitute for a way of life they had been familiar with before it was destroyed by industrialization and urbanization.

As a matter of fact, the working class in the nineteenth century was a long way from leading the kind of family life that was modeled on that of master craftsmen. Although the majority of factory workers, journeymen and day laborers were married and had children, relationships between family members lacked the intimacy and solidarity one allegedly still could find among guildsmen. Paternal authority was weakened when women and children had to contribute to family income by selling their labor for wages. Domestic concerns were inevitably neglected as women working in the factories or at home industry simply did not have the free time to do housework. As one Prussian government official put it in 1845, when "men, women, and children have to work all day in the factories of industrial entrepreneurs, and sometimes even at night, and they only use their apartments as a place to sleep or a place to spend a little time on holidays," family life could never mean very much.[16]

Even though there were many people who supported the idea of factory work for the whole family, emphasizing particularly the fact that factory children could stay with their parents and were kept off the streets, which were nothing but "playgrounds for misbehaved children," public opinion gradually came around to accepting the idea that the out-of-house wage labor of women and children was an evil, irrespective of how necessary it might be. In the long run, it would undermine the reproductive capacity of the working class and produce a generation of weak, feeble, and disabled men and women unable to cope with life's burdens and likely to die at an early age.[17] Both the conspicuously high rate of infant mortality and the poor results of military conscription in industrialized regions were taken as proof of this gloomy prognosis.[18] Just as alarming was the apparent moral decay of the "fourth estate." The workers' inclination for drinking and living a dissolute life, together with spiritual degeneration, was obviously the result of a lack of home life and family ties, which in turn was the consequence of the factory work of women and children.

Yet the employment of married women in the factories was by no means as extensive as these middle-class observers suggested. In Germany in 1875 only 20 percent of all women factory workers were married and by 1907 that figure had grown to 27 percent.[19] Factory inspectors reported unanimously that skilled workers tried to avoid sending their wives to work whenever possible because the better-paid workers thought it was insulting if their wives were engaged in paid employment outside the household.[20] It was with this "labor aristocracy" that a family type developed which most closely resembled middle-class norms. Quantitatively, however, this group was not really important. In Vienna in the late nineteenth century, for example, only 10 to 20 percent of the working-class wives were able to devote themselves fully to housekeeping and the rearing of their children; 40 percent had full-time employment; and the other 40 percent had part-time jobs.[21] During the period under investigation, the majority of women workers seem to have left the factory after the birth of the first child—at the latest after the second.[22] That is not to say, however, that they gave up wage work altogether. Household budgets of working-class families tell us that nearly all wives augmented the family income with their earnings. They were home workers, they rented beds to lodgers, they cooked, cleaned, washed, and ironed for middle-class families because the family depended on the income from such popular forms of work for married women, especially where there were little children.[23]

Although the great majority of working-class wives did not spend ten to eleven hours each day in the factory, their life style hardly matched the ideal of a wife and mother who had self-fulfillment through caring for her family. In the eyes of middle-class observers, they spent too much time earning money *and* they lacked the fundamental knowledge which was indispensable for the well-being of a household and its members. They did not know how to be "economical," nor "did they understand how to keep linen and clothing in order and to prepare a decent meal."[24] In terms of child care, they were completely ignorant, leaving room for many to suggest that their behavior was an important cause of the high rate of child mortality among working-class families. In other words, working-class women were seen as an object for education; in dire need of hints and rules from an outside source.

It was indeed middle-class women's organizations, which had come into being in many towns since midcentury, which dedicated themselves with missionary zeal to the task of educating working-class women.[25] In 1856, for example, in the small industrial town of Hörde, situated in the Ruhr Valley, a group of well-meaning women founded a school for daughters of local workers; the girls could attend the school without paying fees. From the age of eight, they would be "taught skills and given knowledge which would make them good housewives later on in life." On two afternoons a week, these patrons taught their pupils how to knit, sew, and do other kinds of needlework and at the same time they read "appropriate stories to shape the girls' intellectual, religious, and moral education." "A love for cleanliness, industry, and order" ranked foremost among the virtues to be learned there.[26]

"Charitable" institutions such as this one soon existed in nearly all of Germany's industrial towns, and they could not complain about lack of attendance.[27] The women's organizations worked closely with the local clergy or factory owners who financed these projects in the hope that they would have a positive impact on the reliability and discipline of the work force.[28] The collaboration of doctors was also welcomed and they gave lectures on hygiene and health issues. Textbooks on housekeeping were published in large numbers by the end of the century, which illustrates how crucial this activity had become in turning working-class girls and women into "proper housewives." Following the suggestion of a weaving-mill owner in Mönchen-Gladbach, a "manual" for "working-class women" was compiled in 1881. It contained "complete instructions for good housekeeping, along with cooking lessons," and within a year, the eleventh edition of this approximately 200-page booklet had been published.[29] Its teachings had been worked out and tested in a local residence hall for women workers run by the Catholic Church. It also had been examined by a physician who contributed a chapter giving advice on healthful food that would prevent disease.

At every turn, the housewife's responsibility for the good health of all family members was stressed; it was her "diligence," her "thriftiness," her "cleanliness," and her "orderliness" which would make her husband and children healthy and happy. To achieve this goal, however, the wife was asked to make sacrifices. When there was not enough money to put meat on the table for everyone in the family, then "it is up to you to do without it. Give it to your husband because he works hard and needs it." Any longings for "fancy clothes" had to be postponed and warm underwear should be bought instead; otherwise, the wife "commits a grave sin as far as the family's health is concerned, because she has herself to blame if she sees her husband or her children getting sick."[30]

Of course, hygienic housekeeping must begin and end with utmost cleanliness and that included both a clean house and a clean body. The living room and bedrooms should be swept once or twice a day and they should be scrubbed weekly with oily soap and sand. Every week the stove should be polished and every two weeks the windows should be washed. The "big housecleaning," which lasted two or three weeks, was done twice a year, and every Monday the clothes should be washed. All members of the family should be provided with "fresh, clean clothes" often and regularly because that would mean greater "health and happiness," which in turn would bring greater "domestic bliss."[31]

Even more specific information on the required degree of cleanliness could be found in health manuals and encyclopedias which were published in large numbers in the second half of the nineteenth century; often several editions would be published in a very short time. The authors were generally doctors who sought to promote good standards of health among the common people. Along with publications which were explicitly addressed to middle-class readers, for whom "education had made life more worthwhile and family welfare a sacred duty,"[32] many booklets were published from the 1860s onward that were addressed "to the people."[33] In actual fact, of course, "the people" was a term synonymous with the urban working-class and again the focus was on the female segment of that population. In colloquial terms, the "honest housewife" was offered a "system of hygiene" to which she was advised to adhere with total dedication.

Like the textbooks on housekeeping, these health manuals described the characteristics of the ideal housewife who could "carry out her domestic concerns with conviction," as the physician and medical professor Rudolf Virchow put it in 1865.[34] The effort which she put into her housework, such as cooking, cleaning, washing, sewing, and ironing, paid off because the household budget was stretched further that way. An even more important result of the additional "coziness" and "homelike atmosphere" was the husband's increased efficiency at the workplace. Everything considered, the working-class family could thus become a bastion of middle-class respectability, guaranteeing greater interest in work, discipline, reliability, and continuity. When a worker "finds he has proper meals, cleanliness, and a smiling face at home, he is less likely to spend his money at a local pub on games and drink which he does when domestic contentment is absent." That visit to the local bar "was for many men nothing but the first step toward drunkenness and crime."[35]

Next to "tasty and nutritious food," cleanliness was necessary for both a satisfying and a healthy family life. Therefore, "a worker's wife should see to it that her ordering and cleaning hands are everywhere."[36] Even unpleasant places could be made "to be comfortable." All the authors of these manuals believed that poverty was not an excuse for filth and disorder, "since with the poor, run-down housing is largely the result of ignorance, indifference, and laziness, because even a miserable apartment can easily be kept clean and healthy when there is good will."[37] It was that sense of good will which working-class women were lacking, and the textbooks sought to create it. Housework, done according to proper scientific standards, was to be praised as a profession *and* a duty of love.[38] Conversely, neglect of duty was equated with moral lapse and sin.

This well-meaning advice of course ran counter to an economic reality that was completely different from what doctors, social reformers, and women's organizations thought it to be. Since most working-class women had to earn money, there was never enough time to do all the daily housework that was required. Moreover, housing conditions made it impossible to apply all the doctors' health rules. Proper maintenance of health requirements stipulated that the kitchen and pantry should be separated from the living room, that everyone should have his own bedroom, and that there be a special room for the children.[39] But that was a joke because few working-class families could afford a three-room apartment. Even the dwellings that Friedrich Krupp built for his workers in the 1870s did not meet all the requirements established by the hygienists.[40] Generally, unskilled and home workers could afford only a one-room dwelling had to accommodate the whole family. Skilled workers earning higher and more regular wages could more easily afford a larger dwelling but they often had to share it with a lodger to help with the rent.[41] Therefore, a dwelling that met minimal requirements—that is, an apartment with a living room, bedroom, and kitchen for one family without lodgers—was for most working-class families a dream.

Despite these difficulties, the middle-class alliance of women's or-

ganizations, doctors, entrepreneurs, teachers, and priests kept on pro-
claiming that it was women's duty to live up to good health rules. Even
the Social Democrats lined up behind those who believed that the "social
question" could be alleviated with good health care for the individual.
Workers' newspapers reviewed health manuals such as the ones by Friedrich and Reich and warmly recommended them to their readers. Workers'
educational associations organized lectures by physicians on the maintenance of good health. The club members' wives were particularly urged
to attend.[42] The *Krankenkassen* (health insurance organizations), which
even before the Health Insurance Law of 1883 insured half the industrial
work force in Prussia, also participated in the effort to make working-class
families healthier. Nearly all of them excluded those members whose
illnesses resulted from uncleanliness, alcoholism, or "sexual excesses."
Health insurance organizations also institutionalized regular contact between the individual and academic doctors. The insurance fund of a Duisburg steel works, for example, stipulated that male workers had to show
up for their medical examinations "with a clean, well-washed body."[43]
Physicians employed by factories or *Krankenkassen* not only wrote out
prescriptions during their office hours; they also made recommendations
about proper care of the body and a good diet. Visiting their patients at
home gave them the opportunity to gain some insight into family life and
remind wives of their *Liebespflichten* (duties of love). Beginning in the
1890s, the *Krankenkassen* often invited their members to medical lectures which discussed hygienic ways to perform household tasks and the
basics of family health care.[44]

Last but not least, the children were used to help facilitate the intrusion of rules of health into the daily life of common people. If a woman
worker wanted to put her baby in a nursery or her child in a day-care
center, she was obliged to bring the child in "well scrubbed and combed
with clothes which were as neat as possible." The director had the right
"to make the mothers respect the regulations and to send the children
home if, despite repeated requests, the child was not dressed warmly
enough or was not dressed in clean clothes."[45] Even the schools served as
agents of cleanliness norms, either through the intervention of teachers
and school doctors or through the addition of specific lessons on hygiene
to the curriculum.[46]

Hence from all sides working-class women were confronted with and
socialized by the rules of good hygiene.[47] Housework, which hitherto had
been done in a more or less haphazard fashion, was now characterized as a
"full-time job" on which the physical and moral health of all family members depended. Naturally few women were in a position to live according
to these norms and act as perfect, reliable housewives and mothers versed
in all the rules of good health. While middle-class women could profit

from these developments—improved health for the family and "scientific" housework—because it was personally meaningful and it increased their power and status within the family,[48] health regulations put enormous pressure on working-class women who could not devote all their time to housework. Without domestic servants or cleaning women, on which middle-class women could rely, hygienic housework for the working-class woman had become a heavy burden. Moreover, when proletarian women accepted the sacrificial attitude which had them neglect their own needs for those of their husbands and children, a situation arose which the Zentralverband der Baugewerblichen Hülfsarbeiter Deutschlands (Central Organization of Unskilled Construction Workers) described in 1908 as follows:

> That is the way it is in the working-class family: the husband, who has to go out to work, gets the biggest share of all the food available and the children too get as much as possible. Whatever is left over is for the mother and she contents herself with just tasting and she lives on bread, coffee, and potatoes. The worker's wife sacrifices herself daily for the family. She is satisfied when the others are full even if she is still hungry. No wonder that the wives of unskilled construction workers do not live as long as their husbands.[49]

While men and children were better off because of cleaner apartments, decent meals, and clean clothes, working-class women paid the price for that progress through their increased work load which in turn had a negative impact on their own health. Presumably this contributed to the conspicuously higher mortality rates of middle-aged married women in comparison to their husbands.[50]

INFANT MORTALITY AND WOMEN'S RESPONSIBILITIES

Although the mortality rate among working-class women was notoriously high, health educators and social reformers ignored this phenomenon altogether. In fact, there were numerous accounts of the catastrophic dangers of factory work for the female worker, and doctors were among the most ardent supporters of rigorous protective measures at the workplace. When they demanded prohibition of night work or maternity leave before and after the birth of the baby, however, they were not concerned about the health of the women as women, but rather about the implications for population policy. Therefore, considering the prohibition of certain kinds of work for women or the establishment of maternity leave meant saving the unborn children, who, as the physician L. Hirt put it, were "sometimes already sick at birth," "badly fed," and "poorly developed."[51] It was obvious that these babies had only a slight chance of surviving. Hirt reported that, on the average, 65 percent of all the children whose mothers worked in mirror factories in Fürth died in their first year.[52] Even with occupations that were less dangerous to women's health, doctors observed a close connection between the factory work of mothers and a higher rate of infant mortality. Nevertheless, it was thought that this was due not to the character of the work itself but rather to the fact that those babies were thoroughly neglected. "A lack of motherly care" was characteristic behavior for women factory workers and was "endemic to the lower classes in general."[53] Likewise, women who were not regularly employed in factories also did not care for their children in the way physicians expected. Thus even working at home (in home industry) did not guarantee improved "child care." Although mother and children were together all day and working hours were more flexible, those children were neither healthier nor more likely to survive.[54]

Diagnoses of this kind were stated quite regularly in the medical and sociopolitical debates in Imperial Germany and the public gradually became alarmed. To be sure, infant mortality rates had always been high; 15 to 17 percent of all children born to even better-off parents died in their first year at the end of the nineteenth century. Yet mortality rates in working-class families were particularly high. For example, infant mortality in families of unskilled workers in the 1890s was 46 percent higher than in families of Prussian civil servants.[55] At that time in Prussia, on the average one child in five died during the first twelve months of life and statisticians and politicians considered that an unbelievable loss of the "nation's wealth and strength."[56]

Earlier generations had accepted the notion that it was a "natural law" that infants were always on the brink of death.[57] Now, in the nineteenth century, physicians fought very hard to change that attitude in all social classes. Since the late eighteenth century, popular medical literature sought to inspire middle-class female readers with the idea of "rational child care." Pedagogical novels of the time insisted on reminding educated bourgeois women of their "vornehmste Mutterpflichten" ("most noble duties of motherhood").[58] One hundred years later the focus of public concern had clearly shifted. Although the situation for the wealthy was not excellent, the lower classes were far worse off, as "excessive infant mortality" prevailing there foreshadowed gloomy things to come. A successful society could not afford such a loss of human beings over a long period of time. Many were concerned about how to maximize all the resources needed for economic and military purposes at a time when demands for the increased quality of these resources had risen. In 1879 the physician F. Erismann summed up the problem this way: "This situation cannot go on for very long. Time moves on and the demands on each individual are increasing rapidly. We need strong and intelligent workers and healthy citizens." Whether these "demands" could be met depended certainly on the breeding and educational capacities of women. "They must contribute to the solution of this problem. They must give up their vegetable-like existence and overcome their narrow views and it is up to men to give them all the support they need."[59]

Thus the education of women, especially those belonging to "the common people," was crucial for the survival of the state and the economy, given the level of international competition. Child care was very important because ignorance and neglect were widespread and responsible for "injurious health practices and for the numerous deaths of newborn children."[60] Breast feeding was essential, as this "natürliche Liebespflicht" ("natural duty of love")[61] had the advantage of being sterile and immunized the child against dangerous infectious diseases. Moreover, mother's milk was easiest to digest, whereas artificial substitutes like thinned cow's milk or meal pap could cause serious stomach troubles which often proved fatal. Contemporary investigations showed that in the case of artificial feeding, infant mortality was six times higher than with breast feeding.[62]

So, in 1869, the physician H. Wasserfuhr told the members of the German Association for Public Health Care that it was necessary for "as many mothers as possible to breast-feed their babies."[63] In the following years doctors, health associations, local governments, and women's clubs orchestrated something like a propaganda campaign supporting breast feeding. When statisticians realized that the birth rate had been falling since the 1880s while the rate of infant mortality had stagnated at a very high level,[64] even government agencies started to react to the problem. In 1904, the Empress herself became involved and she headed a movement fighting infant mortality. A pamphlet put out by the Vaterländische Frauenverein (Patriotic Women's Association) and sent to all birth registries in the Empire was explicitly praised. Every person reporting a live birth at these offices would receive a copy of the pamphlet to instruct them on proper child care and feeding during the first year.[65]

In addition, the Vaterländische Frauenverein, with its 1,200 local branches, organized public lectures where doctors acquainted their female listeners with all the rules of hygienic baby care. Special courses were designed to intensify and practice these rules. It was also thought that the best possible training was on an individual basis. According to an 1874 law, all babies had to be vaccinated for smallpox. Doctors therefore were instructed to take advantage of that contact with mothers and urge them to breast-feed their children.[66] Public maternity hospitals and baby nurseries, most of which were locally administered, also participated in the breast-feeding campaign; as a condition for admission, they demanded that mothers breast-feed their babies.[67] The impact of these institutions was fairly limited, however, as they had relatively few beds and were frequented only by "fallen women." Normally most births were at home, even in the poorest families, usually with a midwife present.[68] In the opinion of many doctors, it was the fault of the midwives that breast feeding was on the decline. It was they who reinforced women's reluctance to breast-feed. They were all too willing to certify that a woman was incapable of doing it and willing to recommend various kinds of artificial feeding. Therefore, information needed to be made available and state intervention was necessary. A governmental edict in 1905 ruled that health officials were to require midwives under their control to insist that their maternity patients breast-feed their babies. In Aachen, for example, midwives were asked to insist with "total conviction" that mothers breast-feed their children for three months at least. In the case of any irregularity a doctor had to be consulted, since only he was able to decide if the woman in question really was unable to breast-feed or if she was simply trying to avoid it.[69]

One problem was that poor families seldom consulted a doctor. To pay a midwife was a real strain on a tight budget, let alone pay a doctor. The *Krankenkassen*, which by the turn of the twentieth century insured ten million workers, did not always cover the cost of family members' medical bills.[70] Even in the cases where women and children were insured and were therefore eligible for free medical care, it did not necessarily mean they took advantage of that opportunity. On the one hand, the doctors employed by the *Krankenkassen* often had insufficient knowledge of pediatrics and no time "to be concerned with the care and feeding of their patients' children." Moreover, these working-class people were unaccustomed to asking for prophylactic medical advice; the Berlin welfare doctor G. Tugendreich shrewdly explained it this way: "Their day-to-day struggle leaves them little opportunity to think about the future." Furthermore, an old saying was common among these people who traditionally shunned doctors: "You really own your child only after its first year; before that it is only on loan."[71]

To counter this skepticism about doctors and to convince mothers that the health of their children was under their control, new methods were needed. Lectures, courses, and pamphlets had not done the job adequately. It was important, therefore, to connect them with a long-term educational process which had institutional support and which was addressed to a specific group of people. In the first decade of the twentieth century, so-called *Säuglingsfürsorgestellen* (baby-care centers), modeled on the French *consultations de nourissons*, which in France were part of maternity hospitals, were established in most German towns and cities, primarily in working-class areas. Most of them came under the control of local government, although they were generally instituted and run by women's or welfare organizations.[72] Their purpose was to inform women who had or were expecting children about healthy and "rational" child care and to urge them to breast-feed their babies. Working-class women, because they were poorly educated to begin with, were the reformers' target.

The campaign, however, did not take into account the fact that working-class women breast-fed their children far more frequently than middle-class women (a fact that had, to be sure, already been confirmed by investigations). A survey done in Berlin at the turn of the century showed that of 1,000 babies in working-class families, 607 were breast-fed; for merchants 376, lawyers 202, and doctors 164. Other medical authorities also reported that mothers in poorer families breast-fed their babies simply because it was much cheaper.[73] Yet despite this striking asymmetry, it was still thought to be necessary to teach working-class women about good health because their babies died at a much higher rate than those of wealthier families.[74] One factor was the poor quality of food substitutes, which, according to the survey quoted above, were used for 40 percent of the working-class babies. Good substitutes for mothers' milk were offered by industrial firms but they were too expensive. Sterilized cow's milk was also available in local milk kitchens but working-class women would not buy that either unless it was subsidized by the state. Some cities began establishing such subsidized milk kitchens as early as the 1880s, and by the beginning of the twentieth century they existed nearly everywhere.[75] Preparing that milk, however, was quite troublesome and risky for working-class families, as "there were no places to keep the milk cool." The poor also lacked "the necessary number of clean bowls, they failed to keep the bottles and nipples sufficiently clean, they lacked the firewood to heat the milk, and sometimes there was not enough milk. For those reasons, poor mothers were obliged to use all kinds of dubious substitutes."[76]

Given these circumstances, "natural feeding" was of course easier and the Säuglingsfürsorgestellen did their best to convince their clients that there were real advantages to breast feeding. Naturally the first problem was getting those clients. Tugendreich stated that the movement in Berlin "could not count on a positive response from the people it benefited; rather the public had to be educated to that end."[77] When two centers opened in Nuremberg in 1905, less than fifty women showed up and "most of those stopped coming after a short while."[78] It was not until the city established another six centers two years later, and promised a premium to all mothers who breast-fed their babies, that they had some success. All mothers whose husbands did not earn over 100 marks a month were entitled to an allowance of from 20 to 40 pfennigs a day if they were willing to breast-feed their children.[79] Indeed, this premium was the lure that enticed women to visit the centers regularly. They had to show up once a week so that a doctor could examine and weigh the baby. Dr. I. Steinhardt, a Nuremberg physician who was in charge of one of the centers, described the premium for breast feeding as "the most fundamental aspect of modern infant welfare upon which the whole system depended." He was not the only one who realized that "only those mothers who get something for bringing in their babies regularly will do so—and only as long as they get something."[80] When the support stopped the women withdrew from medical supervision and vanished. In any case, the centers did not limit themselves to teaching their clients proper child care and paying premiums. They maintained strict controls to ensure that the mothers were properly breast-feeding and following medical instructions. Nurses assisted the doctors by showing up at the mother's residence without warning. They then also inspected "domestic conditions," gave advice on improving housekeeping, and criticized inadequate provisions for proper hygiene.

With the help of the *Säuglingsfürsorgestellen,* urban working-class women were to be educated to be mothers conscious of good health, who would gradually adopt a "rational" way of caring for their newborn children. In individual conversations with the doctors who ran those centers, they learned about the necessity for breast feeding. In an "informal discussion," doctors acquainted them with health standards and explained the new rules they were to follow. For centuries it had been customary to feed the children whenever and as often as they cried for food. Now they were supposed to be fed according to the rhythm of the clock. Every two or three hours the baby was supposed to be put to the mother's breast, but only for a short time, to get accustomed, with *"pedantische Regelmässigkeit"* ("precise regularity"), to eating quickly. Every week the baby was weighed at the center to control how much weight it gained. Every day it was to be bathed in warm water; only after nine months could that be cut to every second or third day.[81]

To the women who visited the centers to get their premiums, these instructions must have sounded very strange, taxing both the readiness and the strength of the young mother to fulfill her duties with precision. It took strong nerves and even greater patience not to immediately suckle a crying baby; instead the mother was to wait until the prescribed feeding time established by the doctor. Moreover, they also had to feed the baby at night when they hoped to get some sleep, and that was an additional burden, along with the complicated hygienic procedures they were to follow in the interests of the baby. No wonder these women reacted with skepticism and reluctance to medical conditioning. Doctors and nurses had "to speak very convincingly" and sometimes they spoke "very harshly"—or they could threaten to cut off the premiums. "Mothers who had already been taught," and who were present during the consultations, were very helpful too, because "they supported the doctors from a woman's point of view; they attested to the correctness of the instructions on the grounds that their own children were healthy."[82]

Besides the general medical education, which was designed to make working-class women into "good housewives" for the benefit of the male work force, both the idea and the conception of *Säuglingsfürsorge* was particularly well suited to smooth the way for the "medicalization" and "hygienization" of the working-class family. If doctors succeeded gradually in spreading their influence among the urban working class, it was because their consultations at the centers were very influential.[83] There they came in contact with women who under normal conditions would not have sought medical advice. Moreover, the doctors used the opportunity to prove their competence in matters of child care. This "contact" was by no means insignificant, as the growth in the number of clients indicates. In 1906, 12,441 babies were brought to the Berlin centers; in 1908, the number was 18,114. The number of nurses' home visits rose from 20,677 to 34,388. In 1914–15, the doctors in Charlottenburg (an area in Berlin) could claim to have treated two-thirds of the babies born there.[84]

This evidence shows that the *Fürsorgebewegung* (welfare movement) had come very close to achieving its goal of gaining a foothold among the lower classes. Nearly all the women who visited the centers were "poor"; their husbands were skilled or unskilled workers who had in most cases lost their jobs and were therefore interested in the financial support; in this way they would not be stigmatized, as they would if they went on welfare.[85] On the average, each mother went to a center eight times, where she allowed the doctors "to inculcate her with principles of health and hygiene."[86]

We can only make some assumptions about the long-term impact of that "vigorous agitation" (Dietrich). There was evidently not a direct impact on breast-feeding behavior, as the trend continued downward, at least in Berlin. On the other hand, it does not seem likely that the educational efforts fizzled out entirely. Even if the women only visited the centers for as long as they could collect the money—six months was the maximum time—they were taught some basics about medicine and hygiene, which the medical profession, the state, and the charity organizations wanted them to have as mothers in the interest of "maintaining public health, securing strong offspring and strengthening the nation."[87] It is difficult to assess whether women met their expectations. In return for the premiums they received, and because they feared they would be cut off, these women would have been anxious to meet all the requirements established by the doctors—at least for a few months they also had to fear the visits by the nurses and the charity "ladies" and they had to appear to be following the health rules.

Unlike the hygiene propaganda disseminated by the schools, through public lectures, and through journals and pamphlets, the close contact with the middle-class health missionaries and the financial rewards had a much greater influence on both the norms and the habits of working-class women. Even if the new standards were in conflict with actual living conditions, they must have had some impact on the outlook of working-class families. Above all, it was the wives of skilled laborers who increasingly took an interest in the new teachings on health and hygiene, especially those who had worked as domestic servants in middle-class households before they were married and thereby had gained some experience. At the beginning of the twentieth century, in that group, both infant mortality and frequencies of birth declined.[88] This can be at least partially explained by the work the middle-class health movement put into disseminating information and establishing new controls. In turn, that work was taken up and supported by the Social Democratic workers' movement.

NOTES

1. For France, see Y. Kniebiehler, "Les Médecins et la 'nature féminine' au temps du Code Civil," *Annales E.S.C.*, 31 (1976), pp. 824–45; A. McLaren, "Doctor in the House: Medicine and Private Morality in France, 1800–1850," *Feminist Studies*, 2 (1975), pp. 39–54; J.-P. Peter, "Entre Femmes et médecins. Violence et singularités dans les discours du corps et sur le corps d'après les manuscrits médicaux de la fin du XVIIIe siècle," *Ethnologie Française*, 6 (1976), pp. 341–48; J.-P. Peter, "Les Médecins et les femmes," in *Misérable et glorieuse la femme du XIXe siècle*, ed. by J.-P. Aron (Paris, 1980), pp. 79–97. For England, see K. Figlio, "Chlorosis and Chronic Disease in Nineteenth-Century Britain," *Social History*, 3 (1978), pp. 167–97; J. L'Esperance, "Doctors and Women in Nineteenth-Century Society: Sexuality and Role," in *Health Care and Popular Medicine in Nineteenth-Century England*, ed. by J. Woodward and D. Richards (New York, 1977), pp. 105–27. For the United States, see A. Douglas Wood, "'The Fashionable Diseases': Women's Complaints and Their Treatment in Nineteenth-Century America," *Journal of Interdisciplinary History*, 4 (1973), pp. 25–52; R. Morantz, "The Lady and Her Physician," in *Clio's Consciousness Raised*, ed. by M. S. Hartman and L. Banner (New York, 1974), pp. 38–53; R. Morantz, "Making Women Modern: Middle-Class Women and Health Reform in 19th Century America," *Journal of Social History*, 10 (1977), pp. 490–507; B. Ehrenreich and D. English, *For Her Own Good: 150 Years of the Experts' Advice to Women* (London, 1979).

2. K. Hausen, "Die Polarisierung der 'Geschlechtscharaktere.' Eine Spiegelung der Dissoziation von Erwerbs- und Familienleben," in *Sozialge-*

schichte der Familie in der Neuzeit Europas, ed. by W. Conze (Stuttgart, 1976), pp. 363–93.

3. See B. Heintz and C. Honegger, "Zum Strukturwandel weiblicher Widerstandsformen im 19. Jahrhundert," in *Listen der Ohnmacht*, ed. by B. Heintz and C. Honegger (Frankfurt, 1981), especially pp. 41 ff.

4. J. Donzelot, *Die Ordnung der Familie* (Frankfurt, 1980), pp. 30 ff.; G. Heller, *"Propre en ordre"* (Lausanne, 1979), pp. 141–216.

5. E. Reich, *System der Hygiene*, 1 (Leipzig, 1870), p. xvi. See also C. Reclam, *Das Buch der vernünftigen Lebensweise* (Leipzig, 1863).

6. See, J. A. Unzer, *Der Arzt* (6 vols.; Hamburg, 1769); J. C. Tode, *Der unterhaltende Arzt über Gesundheitspflege, Schönheit, Medicinalwesen, Religion und Sitten* (4 vols.; Copenhagen, 1785–89); C. W. Hufeland, *Makrobiotik oder die Kunst, das menschliche Leben zu verlängern* (Berlin, 1796; reprinted, Munich, 1978); F. A. May, *Medicinische Fastenpredigten, oder Vorlesungen über Körper- und Seelen-Diätetik* (2 pts.; Mannheim, 1792–94); Mezler, *Diätetik für bürgerliche Mädchenschulen, zunächst für die zu Habsthal* (Karlsruhe, 1810); see also U. Frevert, *Krankheit als politisches Problem* (Göttingen, 1984).

7. *Berliner Medizinische Zeitung*, 1 (1832), p. 56.

8. U. Frevert, "Frauen und Ärzte im späten 18. und frühen 19. Jahrhundert. Zur Sozialgeschichte eines Gewaltverhältnisses," in *Frauen in der Geschichte II*, ed. by A. Kuhn and J. Rüsen (Düsseldorf, 1982), pp. 177–210, especially 183 ff.

9. J. L. Casper, *Die wahrscheinliche Lebensdauer des Menschen, in den verschiedenen bürgerlichen und geselligen Verhältnissen* (Berlin, 1835), pp. 185 f.

10. W. C. de Neufville, *Lebensdauer und Todesursachen zweiundzwanzig verschiedener Stände und Gewerbe* (Frankfurt, 1855); F. Oesterlen, *Handbuch der Hygiene für den Einzelnen wie für eine Bevölkerung* (Tübingen, 1851), p. 763; J. Conrad, *Beitrag zur Untersuchung des Einflusses von Lebensstellung und Beruf auf die Mortalitätsverhältnisse* (Jena, 1877), p. 155.

11. S. Neumann, "Die Fragestellung in der Krankheits-Statistik, mit besonderer Beziehung auf die arbeitenden Klassen," *Deutsche Klinik*, (1854), pp. 216 f.

12. Oesterlen, pp. 76 ff.

13. H. Friedberg, *Über die Geltendmachung der öffentlichen Gesundheitspflege* (Erlangen, 1873), pp. 24 f.

14. W. H. Riehl, *Die bürgerliche Gesellschaft* (Frankfurt, 1976), pp. 239 ff; C. Frantz, *Versuch über die Verfassung der Familie* (Berlin, 1844).

15. Riehl, p. 243.

16. Hoffmann, "Bemerkungen über die Ursachen der entsittlichenden Dürftigkeit oder des sogenannten Pauperismus," *Medicinische Zeitung*, 14 (1845), p. 239.

17. *Mitteilungen des Industrievereins für das Königreich Sachsen*, 4 (1841), pp. 112–24, especially pp. 117 f.

18. See Blümlein, "Die Samt- und Seidenstoff-Weberei in ihrem Einflusse auf den Körper- und Geistes-Zustand der Weber," *Vierteljahrsschrift für gerichtliche und öffentliche Medicin*, 15 (1859), p. 204.

19. *Ergebnisse der über die Frauen- und Kinder-Arbeit in den Fabriken auf Beschluss des Bundesraths angestellten Erhebungen* (Berlin, 1877), p. 15;

W. Weinberg, "Der Einfluss der sozialen Lage auf Krankheit und Sterblichkeit der Frau," in *Krankheit und soziale Lage*, ed. by M. Mosse and G. Tugendreich (Munich, 1913; reprinted, Göttingen, 1977), p. 258; R. Otto, *Über Fabrikarbeit verheirateter Frauen* (Stuttgart, 1910), pp. 83–105.

20. Otto, p. 116; F. Wörishoffer, *Die soziale Lage der Fabrikarbeiter in Mannheim und dessen nächster Umgebung* (Karlsruhe, 1891), p. 74.

21. J. Ehmer, "Frauenarbeit und Arbeiterfamilie in Wien," *Geschichte und Gesellschaft*, 7 (1981), p. 451.

22. E. Beyer, *Die Fabrik-Industrie des Regierungsbezirkes Düsseldorf vom Standpunkt der Gesundheitspflege* (Oberhausen, 1876), p. 133.

23. H. Rosenbaum, *Formen der Familie* (Frankfurt, 1982), pp. 402 ff.

24. *Ergebnisse*, pp. 56, 60; Blümlein, "Medicinische Topographie des Kreises Kempen," *Vierteljahrsschrift für Gerichtliche Medicin und Öffentliches Sanitätswesen*, 28 (1878), p. 307.

25. M. Twellmann, *Die deutsche Frauenbewegung* (Kronberg, 1976), pp. 129 ff.

26. Hoesch Archive, Dortmund: Acta of the Hörder Bergwerks- und Hüttenverein, Nr. 1841.

27. In Berlin, for example, there were ten schools teaching cooking and housekeeping in 1908 run by the local branch of the Vaterländische Frauenverein. Here young girls from poor families learned in a six months' course "simple cooking and preparation of sick diets" (*Bericht über den XIV. Internationalen Kongress für Hygiene und Demographie*, 4 [Berlin, 1908], p. 183).

28. Many firms even organized their own schools or courses on housekeeping for their female workers. See K. Emsbach, *Die soziale Betriebsverfassung der rheinischen Baumwollindustrie im 19. Jahrhundert* (Bonn, 1982), pp. 623–25.

29. *Das häusliches Glück. Vollständiger Haushaltungsunterricht nebst Anleitung zum Kochen für Arbeiterfrauen* (Mönchen-Gladbach, 1882; reprinted, Munich, 1975). Between 1881 and 1910, large firms such as Krupp distributed 200,000 copies of the pamphlet. See K. Saul et al., eds., *Arbeiterfamilien im Kaiserreich* (Königstein, 1982), p. 23.

30. *Häusliches Glück*, pp. 8, 98.

31. Ibid., p. 17.

32. H. Klencke, *Hauslexikon der Gesundheitslehre für Leib und Seele. Ein Familienbuch* (Leipzig, 1865), p. iv. See also Klencke, *Die physische Lebenskunst oder praktische Anwendung der Naturwissenschaften auf Förderung des persönlichen Daseins* (Leipzig, 1864); E. v. Russdorf, *Die Diätetik. Bearbeitet für gebildete Frauen* (Berlin, 1854); K. W. Ideler, *Handbuch der Diätetik für Freunde der Gesundheit und des langen Lebens* (Berlin, 1855); C. E. Bock, *Das Buch vom gesunden und kranken Menschen* (Leipzig, 1859); H. v. Wyss, *Populäre Vorträge über Gesundheitspflege insbesondere für Frauen* (Leipzig, 1887). The two-volume book of Dr. Anna Fischer-Dückelmann was first published in 1901. Seven years later, the book had already sold half a million copies. See Dr. Anna Fischer-Dückelmann, *Die Frau als Hausärztin* (Stuttgart, 1901).

33. E. Friedrich, *Gesundheitspflege für das Volk* (Berlin, 1864); O. Schraube, *Gesundheitslehre für Jedermann aus dem Volke* (Berlin, 1866);

E. Reich, *Volks-Gesundheits-Pflege* (Coburg, 1862); L. Hirt, *Gesundheitslehre für die arbeitenden Klassen* (Berlin, 1891); Reclam.

34. R. Virchow, "Über die Erziehung des Weibes für seinen Beruf," *Allgemeine Deutsche Arbeiter-Zeitung*, no. 117 (1865), p. 606.

35. Friedrich, p. 49; F. Erismann, *Gesundheitslehre für Gebildete aller Stände* (Munich, 1879), p. 109.

36. Friedrich, p. 130.

37. Erismann, p. 220.

38. See G. Bock and B. Duden, "Arbeit aus Liebe—Liebe als Arbeit. Zur Entstehung der Hausarbeit im Kapitalismus," in *Frauen und Wissenschaft* (Berlin, 1977), pp. 118–99.

39. Erismann, p. 120; E. Wernicke, "Die Wohnung in ihrem Einfluss auf Krankheit und Sterblichkeit," in Mosse and Tugendreich, pp. 45–120, especially p. 51.

40. Beyer, "Die Arbeitercolonien der Gussstahlfabrik von Friedrich Krupp zu Essen," *Deutsche Vierteljahrsschrift für Öffentliche Gesundheitspflege*, 6 (1874), pp. 615–23.

41. L. Niethammer, "Wie wohnten Arbeiter im Kaiserreich?" *Archiv für Sozialgeschichte*, 16 (1976), pp. 61–134; F. J. Brüggemeier and L. Niethammer, "Schlafgänger, Schnapskasinos und schwerindustrielle Kolonie," in *Fabrik, Familie, Feierabend*, ed. by J. Reulecke and W. Weber (Wuppertal, 1978), pp. 135–75; J. Ehmer, "Wohnen ohne eigene Wohnung," in *Wohnen im Wandel*, ed. by L. Niethammer (Wuppertal, 1979), pp. 132–50; J. Wietog, "Der Wohnungsstandard der Unterschichten in Berlin," in *Arbeiterexistenz im 19. Jahrhundert*, ed. by W. Conze and U. Engelhardt (Stuttgart, 1981), pp. 114–37.

42. *Allgemeine Deutsche Arbeiter-Zeitung*, 30 (1863), p. 180.

43. *Die unter staatlicher Aufsicht stehenden gewerblichen Hülfskassen für Arbeitnehmer . . . im preussischen Staate* (Berlin, 1876), p. 288.

44. P. Kampffmeyer, *Die Mission der deutschen Krankenkassen auf dem Gebiete der öffentlichen Gesundheitspflege* (Frankfurt, 1903).

45. *Die Einrichtungen für die Wohlfahrt der Arbeiter der grösseren gewerblichen Anlagen im preussischen Staate*, pt. 2 (Berlin, 1876), pp. 37 f.

46. At the beginning of the twentieth century, in most German cities, local authorities had established "housekeeping schools" (combined with the *Volksschulen*), which girls were obliged to attend. See E. v. Mumm, "Die Pflichtfortbildungsschule des weiblichen Geschlechts in hygienischer Beziehung," *Centralblatt für Allgemeine Gesundheitspflege*, 26 (1907), pp. 44 f.

47. See the autobiographical accounts in Saul, pp. 62, 196 ff.

48. Donzelot, pp. 32 ff.

49. *Lebenshaltung und Arbeitsverhältnisse der Deutschen Bauhülfsarbeiter*, ed. by the Hauptvorstand des Zentralverbandes der Baugewerblichen Hülfsarbeiter Deutschlands (Hamburg, 1908), p. 48.

50. See A. E. Imhof, "Die Übersterblichkeit verheirateter Frauen im fruchtbaren Alter," *Zeitschrift für Bevölkerungswissenschaft*, 5 (1979), pp. 487–510; A. E. Imhof *Die gewonnenen Jahre* (Munich, 1981), pp. 141–58; Weinberg, pp. 237 ff.

342   UTE FREVERT

51. L. Hirt, *Die Krankheiten der Arbeiter*, 3 (Leipzig, 1875), p. 154.

52. Ibid., p. 155.

53. *Ergebnisse*, p. 58.

54. Ibid., p. 53. See also R. Beier, "Zur Geschichte weiblicher Lebenschancen. Alltagsleben, gewerkschaftliche Organisation und Streik Berliner Bekleidungsarbeiterinnen 1870–1914," in Kuhn and Rüsen, pp. 211–44.

55. Calculated from R. Spree, "Strukturierte soziale Ungleichheit im Reproduktionsbereich," in *Geschichte als politische Wissenschaft*, ed. by J. Bergmann et al. (Stuttgart, 1979), table 4, p. 73.

56. P. Selter, "Warum und wie sollen wir Säuglingsfürsorge treiben?" *Centralblatt für Allgemeine Gesundheitspflege*, 26 (1907), pp. 205 f; Dietrich, "Die Säuglingssterblichkeit in Preussen, ihre Ursachen und ihre Bekämpfung," *Zeitschrift für Säuglingsfürsorge*, 1 (1906), p. 43.

57. J. Möser, *Anwalt des Vaterlandes* (reprinted, Leipzig, 1978), p. 327.

58. See, for example, C. G. Salzmann, *Carl von Carlsberg oder über das menschliche Elend*, 1 (Leipzig, 1784), pp. 84 ff; C. W. Hufeland, *Guter Rath an Mütter über die wichtigsten Punkte der physischen Erziehung der Kinder in den ersten Jahren* (Berlin, 1803); L. A. Gölis, *Vorschläge zur Verbesserung der körperlichen Kinder-Erziehung in den ersten Lebens-Perioden* (Vienna, 1811); F. A. v. Ammon, *Die ersten Mutterpflichten und die erste Kindespflege* (Leipzig, 1827). See U. Ottmüller, "'Mutterpflichten.' Die Wandlungen ihrer inhaltlichen Ausformung durch die akademische Medizin," *Gesellschaft, Beiträge zur Marxschen Theorie 14* (Frankfurt, 1981), pp. 97–138.

59. Erismann, p. 304.

60. Ibid., p. 303.

61. Klencke, *Hauslexikon*, p. 493.

62. Dietrich, "Hygiene des frühen Kindesalters; Säuglingspflege und Haltekinderwesen," in *Das preussische Medizinal- und Gesundheitswesen in den Jahren 1883–1908*, ed. by O. Rapmund (Berlin, 1908), p. 219.

63. H. Wasserfuhr, "Über die Sterblichkeit der Neugeborenen und Säuglinge in Deutschland," *Deutsche Vierteljahrsschrift für Öffentliche Gesundheitspflege*, 1 (1869), p. 549.

64. See the statistical evidence in Dietrich, "Hygiene," p. 217. For the reaction of the public, see U. Linse, "Arbeiterschaft und Geburtenentwicklung im Deutschen Kaiserreich von 1871," *Archiv für Sozialgeschichte*, 12 (1972), pp. 211 ff.

65. The Frauenverein's leaflet is printed in Brugger, *Die Bekämpfung der Säuglingssterblichkeit* (Leipzig, 1906), pp. 44–47.

66. Dietrich, "Hygiene," p. 224.

67. Nesemann, "Die Entwicklung der Säuglingsfürsorge und deren Stand Ende 1907," *Deutsche Vierteljahrsschrift für Öffentliche Gesundheitspflege*, 40 (1908), pp. 472f; Dietrich, "Säuglingsernährung und Wöchnerinnen-Asyle," *Centralblatt für Allgemeine Gesundheitspflege*, 22 (1903), pp. 46–53.

68. See F. Winckel, "Beiträge zur geburtshülflichen Statistik und zur Kenntniss des Hebammenwesens im Königreich Sachsen," in *Berichte und Studien aus dem Königl. Sächs. Entbindungs-Institute in Dresden über die Jahre 1874*

und 1875, ed. by F. Winckel, 2 (Leipzig, 1876), pp. 242–98. According to this survey, only 5.2 percent of all home deliveries were attended by a doctor (p. 273).

69. Brugger, p. 21.

70. A survey in the Köln district in 1904 found that not more than 20 percent of the sick funds (encompassing, however, about 25 percent of all insured workers) granted family insurance. See F. Tennstedt, "Sozialgeschichte der Sozialversicherung," in *Handbuch der Sozialmedizin*, ed. by M. Blohmke et al. (3 vols.; Stuttgart, 1976), p. 388.

71. B. Salge, "Milchküchen und Beratungsstellen," *Zeitschrift für Säuglingsfürsorge*, 1 (1906–7), p. 315; G. Tugendreich, "Bericht über die Säuglingsfürsorgestellen der Schmidt-Gallischstiftung in Berlin," ibid., 2 (1908), pp. 68 f.; W. Brenner-Schaeffer, *Zur oberpfälzischen Volksmedizin* (Amberg, 1861), p. 14; W. R. Lee, *Population Growth, Economic Development and Social Change in Bavaria, 1750–1850* (New York, 1977), pp. 94 f.

72. For the Austrian case, see B. Bolognese-Leuchtenmüller, "Unterversorgung und mangelnde Betreuung der Kleinkinder in den Unterschichtenfamilien als soziales Problem des 19. Jahrhunderts," in *Wirtschafts- und sozialhistorische Beiträge*, ed. by H. Knittler (Munich, 1979), especially pp. 420 f.

73. Dietrich, "Hygiene," p. 219; E. Hirschberg, *Die soziale Lage der arbeitenden Klassen in Berlin* (Berlin, 1897), pp. 42 ff.; Spree, especially pp. 88–93; H. Wasserfuhr, "Die Sterblichkeit der Kinder im ersten Lebensjahre in Stettin," *Vierteljahrsschrift für Gerichtliche und Öffentliche Medicin*, 22 (1862), table on p. 110; A. Bluhm, "Die Stillungsnot, ihre Ursachen und die Vorschläge zu ihrer Bekämpfung," *Archiv für Soziale Medizin*, 3 (1908), pp. 170 ff; Brenner-Schaeffer, p. 5; K. Seutemann, *Kindersterblichkeit sozialer Bevölkerungsgruppen, insbesondere im preussischen Staate und seinen Provinzen* (Tübingen, 1894), p. 15.

74. G. Heimann, Die Säuglingssterblichkeit in Berlin," *Zeitschrift für Socialwissenschaft*, 7 (1904), pp. 242 f.; Wasserfuhr, *Stettin*, pp. 116 f.

75. V. Ohlen, "Die Bekämpfung der Säuglingssterblichkeit durch öffentliche Organe und private Wohlthätigkeit mittels Beschaffung einwandfreier Kindermilch unter specieller Berücksichtigung Hamburger Verhältnisse," *Zeitschrift für Hygiene und Infektionskrankheiten*, 49 (1905), pp. 199–281; C. Fraenkel, "Die Bekämpfung der Säuglingssterblichkeit durch die Gemeinden," *Technisches Gemeindeblatt*, 6 (1903), pp. 17–22.

76. O. Heubner, *Säuglingsernährung und Säuglingsspitäler* (Berlin, 1897), pp. 30 f.

77. Tugendreich, p. 69.

78. I. Steinhardt, "Über moderne Säuglingsfürsorge," *Deutsche Vierteljahrsschrift für Öffentliche Gesundheitspflege*, 41 (1909), p. 660.

79. See F. Rott, *Umfang, Bedeutung und Ergebnisse der Unterstützungen an stillende Mütter* (Berlin, 1914).

80. Steinhardt, p. 666; Tugendreich, p. 71; Bluhm, pp. 382 f.; Rott, pp. 54 ff.

81. See Erismann, pp. 288, 301 f.; Friedrich, p. 209; Steinhardt, pp 664 ff.

82. Steinhardt, p. 665.

83. On the whole, the physicians' attitude toward the "infant-welfare centers" was rather ambivalent. Many professional organizations vigorously protested

against the centers, which were seen as dangerous competitors. See Salge, "Milchküchen," p. 316. Others supported the welfare centers because they expected them "to restore doctors' authority over the health and diets of the children of the lower classes." See G. Tugendreich, "Bericht über die Säuglingsfürsorgestellen der Schmidt-Gallischstiftung in Berlin," *Zeitschrift für Säuglingsfürsorge,* 4 (1910), p. 109.

84. Tugendreich, "Bericht 1908," p. 78; Tugendreich, "Bericht 1910," p. 110. B. Bendix, "Zehn Jahre Säuglingsfürsorge in Charlottenburg," *Zeitschrift für Säuglingsfürsorge,* 8 (1915), p. 318. For the widespread influence of the infant-welfare movement, see A. Castell, "Unterschichten im 'Demographischen Sübergang,'" in *Vom Elend der Handarbeit,* ed. by H. Mommsen and W. Schulze (Stuttgart, 1981), pp. 386 f.

85. For the mothers' social backgrounds, see Tugendreich, "Bericht 1908," p. 70; J. Trumpp, "Die Milchküchen und Beratungsstellen im Dienste der Säuglingsfürsorge," *Zeitschrift für Säuglingsfürsorge,* 2 (1908), p. 122; H. Helbich, "Jahresbericht der städtischen Säuglingsfürsorgestelle in Berlin-Schöneberg für das Etatsjahr 1912/1913," in ibid., 7 (1914), p. 326.

86. A. Japha and H. Neumann, "Die Säuglingsfürsorgestelle I der Stadt Berlin," ibid., 1 (1906), p. 166.

87. Dietrich, "Hygiene," p. 237.

88. See Castell, pp. 393 f.; Linse, pp. 218 ff.; Spree, pp. 99–106.

The Female Victim

Homicide and Women in Imperial Germany

RANDOLPH E. BERGSTROM AND ERIC A. JOHNSON

The female role in criminal activity in Germany and in other societies has received very little scholarly attention.[1] Perhaps this is because of a perception that women have always been exceptionally law-abiding.[2] In the case of Imperial Germany this perception seems correct, at least if we place any faith at all in German court records. In the period 1871–1918, women were convicted of any type of criminal offense (that is, any *Verbrechen*, felony, or *Vergehen*, misdemeanor) only one-fifth as often as were men; the women's crime rate was far more stable than was the men's crime rate; and the more serious the crime, the less likely that women were involved in wrongdoing. Thus, in 1882, the first year that criminal statistics were published for all of Germany, only 379 out of every 100,000 women of criminally liable age (twelve or older) were convicted of any type of criminal offense; in this same year, however, 1,667 out of every 100,000 men of criminally liable age were convicted. In 1913 the women's rate had fallen slightly to 359, but the men's rate had fluctuated upward to 2,043. In homicide offenses (*Mord*, premeditated murder, and *Totschlag*, non-premeditated murder) women were usually even less likely to be guilty of criminal wrongdoing than were men, and the rate of females convicted for either premeditated or non-premeditated homicide was dropping precipitously. Whereas 73 German women were convicted of homicide in 1882, only 41 German women were convicted of homicide in

1913. The number of men convicted of homicide, on the other hand, grew from 247 in 1882 to 326 in 1913.[3]

If Germans had little need to worry about women as criminal offenders, this does not mean that they did not have to worry about them as the victims of criminal wrongdoing, particularly when heinous criminal activities such as homicide were involved. The record left by German writers and journalists, in fact, shows that Germans were particularly concerned about female homicide victims.[4] Whereas the homicide of German men was usually given only a few scant lines in any German newspaper, it was not rare to see huge and almost lurid stories whenever a woman was killed.[5] German society's concerns over the role females played as homicide victims seemed justified when the first empirical study of murder victims was published in 1938. In his "Mörder und ihre Öpfer" ("Murder and Its Victims")[6] E. Roesner examined all murder trials which ended in convictions between 1928 and 1930. In these trials the murderers were overwhelmingly male, but the victims were more often than not females. Thus, of 169 convicted murderers, 151 or 89.3 percent, were males and only 18, or 10.7 percent, were females; but of the 187 murder victims, only 81, or 43.3 percent were males, and 106, or 56.7 percent were females. Hence, it appeared that German women were much more likely than German men to become victims of homicide.

In 1948 a German criminologist, Hans von Hentig, was the first to put crime victims in a theoretical perspective.[7] In his work *The Criminal and His Victim,* von Hentig offered a general typology of people most likely to become victims and a typology of the victims' psychological traits. Of the major types of people apt to become victims, "The Female" came second only after "The Young," and preceded "The Old," "The Mentally Defective and Other Mentally Deranged," and "Immigrants, Minorities and Dull Normals."[8] According to von Hentig, what united women with these others groups and made women and the others especially good victims, specifically in homicide cases, was weakness. Although he admitted that women's physical weakness vis-à-vis men was not a real issue,[9] his discussion of the psychological traits of victims and of some victim statistics makes it apparent that he believed women were likely to become homicide victims because they were psychologically weak and because they were weaker than men in social and economic position.[10]

Although we do not dispute that German women were in a relatively weaker social and economic position than were men,[11] and even though von Hentig's argument that people in a weak position are easy prey makes some intuitive sense, our evidence does not support him. We disagree with von Hentig even at the most basic level because we found that women are actually much less likely to become murder victims than men.

But how is this possible given the fact that even before von Hentig's work Roesner had shown that women were more often victims than were men in German homicides? It is possible because we used different figures. Our data, of course, came from a different time period, Imperial Germany rather than Weimar, but this is not the major difference between our figures and we do not think that it causes the major difference between our and von Hentig's argument. If one studies homicide trials in Imperial Germany, one would probably also find that women were more often the victims than were men. But this would not prove that women were more often murdered than men.

By using court statistics on which to base their arguments, both Roesner and von Hentig were on shaky grounds. German courts prosecuted only a small minority of the murderers, and, hence, one who uses court statistics for a victimological study would only have information about a minority of homicide victims. Is it not likely that this minority of victims would not be a random minority as well? Were not German courts more likely to prosecute one for murder if one killed a female? If the victim died as a result of a heated dispute, would it not be easier to prosecute the murderer for a lesser charge if the victim were male than if the victim were female? We do not have evidence to prove directly that German courts acted in these ways, but several studies have shown that German courts in Imperial Germany and in Weimar were increasingly trying people for ever milder offenses.[12]

The figures we prefer to use are coroners' reports, and they tell a very different story. Table 1 lists figures for four different ten-year periods spanning the years of Imperial Germany.[13] Here we see that in the state of Prussia, which by population and size represented about three-fifths of the entire German Reich, the number of homicide convictions was a small and declining fraction of the number of homicide deaths reported by German coroners. In the period 1873–84 there were an average of 478 homicide deaths reported each year but there were only an average of 182 court convictions for homicide. Of course, it is possible that 182 murderers could kill 478 victims, but this is not likely given Roesner's figures which showed that 169 murderers in 1928–30 killed only 187 victims. In the period 1905–13 the number of homicide victims reported by German coroners had risen to 779 per year, whereas the number of people convicted of homicide had declined to 169. Thus, over these years it appears that the actual number of homicides increased but the number of homicide convictions decreased; in the earlier period there were about three times more homicide cases reported by the coroners than there were court convictions for homicide, and in the later period the ratio had grown to about five to one. If one controls for the growth of the German population, one finds that in Imperial Germany the coroners' reports

TABLE 1

Average Yearly Figures and Rates per Million People for Homicide Deaths in Prussia and Berlin in Selected Periods

Period	REPORTED DEATHS DUE TO MURDER AND MANSLAUGHTER*				CONVICTIONS FOR PREMEDITATED AND NON-PREMEDITATED MURDER†			
	Average Yearly Total		Average Yearly Rate (per million pop.)		Average Yearly Total		Average Yearly Rate (per million pop.)	
	Prussia	Berlin	Prussia	Berlin	Prussia	Berlin	Prussia	Berlin
1873–84	478	12	17.5	10.2	182	4	6.7	3.2
1885–94	419	16	14.0	10.1	150	5	5.0	3.1
1895–1904	596	30	17.0	16.4	139	4	4.0	2.1
1905–13	779	38	19.4	18.3	169	8	4.2	3.8

*Based on coroners' reports. The coroners' statistics come from a variety of sources, the most important of which is the Prussian government series *Preussische Statistik*, under the yearly volume headings *Die Sterblichkeit nach Todesursachen und Altersklassen der Gestorbenen*.

†Based on court statistics found in annual volumes of criminal statistics (*Kriminalstatistik*), which are part of the German government's series *Statistik des Deutschen Reichs*.

recorded a growth in the actual rate of homicide (e.g., 17.5 per million in 1873–84 and 19.4 per million in 1905–13), but the courts showed a decline in convictions (6.7 per million in 1873–84 and 4.2 per million in 1905–13). So which was it? Was homicide on the rise or on the decline? We think it was on the rise; and, therefore, we think that the court statistics are completely misleading.

By basing our argument on coroners' reports instead of on court records, we observe in Table 2 that German women in every year throughout the entire period of Imperial Germany were far less likely to be murdered than were men. In the years 1873–1907 in the entire state of Prussia, which, again, we take to be a good approximation of the trends for the entire nation, there were 12,767 men murdered and only 5,052 women; in other words, men were murdered about two and one-half times as often as women. We take these figures to be sufficient proof to call into question von Hentig's entire argument that women are particularly good murder victims. We will soon present other evidence which calls into question his argument as to why women were good victims, that is, we will challenge his argument that female weakness leads to homicide.

Our purpose in this essay is, however, more to describe the patterns of female homicide in Imperial Germany than it is to build a general theory about murder victims. We wish to describe what kind of German women were murdered in terms of their age, religion, and marital status. We also wish to describe how they were murdered; in what kinds of environments they were murdered, urban or rural; and in which geographical locations they were most likely to meet with a homicide death. Finally, we would like to point out, if possible, some trends in female homicide deaths. If we can accomplish these tasks, then we will have served our main purpose. But even though description is our major purpose, we would be remiss not to relate our findings to the major theoretical arguments which involve our subject.

Other than von Hentig's there have been very few empirical and theoretical studies which treat women explicitly, and we are not aware of any historical studies at all.[14] But the few studies, mostly sociological works on American women since World War II, which do exist seem to agree on the major theoretical premise that the more that women are involved in what Durkheim referred to as "collective life," the more they are likely to be murdered. As Margaret Zahn, the author of several of these studies, put it, "Long-standing theory and recent research suggests that as people become more involved in collective life, their risks of becoming a homicide victim increase."[15] Unfortunately, what she means by collective life is not entirely clear, but we take it to mean life that involves intimate and frequent contact with family and friends, which

TABLE 2
Yearly Figures for Homicide Deaths by Sex
in Prussia and Berlin

Year	PRUSSIA					BERLIN		
	Total	Male	% Male	Female	% Female	Total	Male	Female
1873	516	394	76.4	122	23.6	9	6	3
1874	556	424	76.3	132	23.7	2	1	1
1875	547	386	70.6	161	29.4	24	5	19
1876	471	357	75.8	114	24.2	10	6	4
1877	543	416	76.6	127	23.4	22	11	11
1878	471	354	75.2	117	24.8	9	6	3
1879	455	341	74.9	114	25.1	2	1	1
1880	470	340	72.3	130	27.7	7	2	5
1881	432	299	69.2	133	30.8	8	2	6
1882	444	328	73.9	116	26.1	21	11	10
1883	406	281	69.2	125	30.8	12	7	5
1884	419	298	71.1	121	28.9	13	6	7
1885	446	340	76.2	126	23.8	10	4	6
1886	432	307	71.3	124	28.7	12	4	8
1887	374	258	69.0	116	31.0	17	10	7
1888	377	264	70.0	113	30.0	23	15	8
1889	320	215	27.2	105	32.8	11	7	4
1890	275	191	69.5	84	30.5	20	9	11
1891	442	298	67.4	144	32.6	24	13	11
1892	485	365	75.3	121	24.7	17	9	8
1893	516	358	69.4	158	30.6	12	5	7
1894	517	374	72.3	143	27.7	18	10	8
1895	471	324	68.8	147	31.2	17	10	7
1896	587	429	73.1	158	26.9	27	13	14
1897	524	365	69.7	159	30.3	28	7	21
1898	534	381	71.3	153	28.7	17	7	10
1899	569	441	77.5	128	22.5	29	16	13
1900	684	493	72.1	191	27.9	27	15	12
1901	664	497	74.8	167	25.2	46	31	15
1902	580	410	70.7	170	29.3	27	14	13
1903	691	473	68.5	218	31.5	39	20	19
1904	708	524	73.9	185	26.1	38	21	17
1905	697	486	60.7	211	30.3	41	23	18
1906	696	491	70.5	205	29.5	33	11	22
1907	788	574	72.8	214	27.2	41	20	21
1908	?	?	?	?	?	?	?	?
1909	?	?	?	?	?	?	?	?
1910	800	570	71.3	230	28.7	?	?	?
1911	?	?	?	?	?	?	?	?

TABLE 2 (continued)

Year	PRUSSIA					BERLIN		
	Total	Male	% Male	Female	% Female	Total	Male	Female
1912	804	533	66.3	271	33.7	?	?	?
1913	889	609	68.5	285	31.5	?	?	?
1914	1,459	1,094	75.0	365	25.0	?	?	?

Totals (through 1907)	12,767	5,052	358 355
Female Homicide as % of Male	39.6		99.2
Female Homicide as % of Total	28.4		49.8

Durkheim thought was more characteristic of traditional village and rural society than of the more anomic life of the metropolis. After demonstrating that in Philadelphia in 1969–73 a much larger proportion of women than men were killed in their homes and by their spouses, relatives, and friends, an observation which jibed with figures which von Hentig provided in his discussion of murder victims, she concluded that "traditional domestic, especially marital contexts, then, still prove the most lethal for women."[16]

Although our evidence does not permit us to say anything about who actually killed the women listed in the German coroners' reports and although we would not doubt that we would probably find that most of the women were killed by family and friends, we will argue that Zahn's theoretical argument was no more supported by our data than was von Hentig's. We find that by and large German women were not in great danger of being murdered if they lived in "traditional domestic, especially marital contexts." We find, on the other hand, that German women who lived in the city were more likely to be murdered than women who lived in the countryside. Since we would expect that urban women were probably less involved in traditional domestic life than were rural women, and probably more likely to be standing on their own, and, by Durkheim's classical argument, more likely to be involved in anomic as opposed to collective life, then we have even less reason to support Zahn's, Durkheim's, or von Hentig's theoretical positions. Rather, what we find is that the more traditional the life circumstances of German females, the less likely they were to become murder victims. We also find that the patterns of female homicide victims were much different from the patterns of male homicide victims, for whom the collective-life argument might possibly apply. Rural and married women were in less danger than urban and

TABLE 3

Homicide Deaths in Prussia and Berlin in Selected Periods*

	PRUSSIA							BERLIN				
	Average Yearly Total					Average Yearly Rate (per million)		Average Yearly Total			Average Yearly Rate (per million)	
Period	Total	Male	% Male	Female	% Female	Male	Female	Total	Male	Female	Male	Female
1873–82	460	333	72.4	127	27.6	26.2	9.7	11	5	6	10.2	12.4
1883–92	400	282	70.5	118	29.5	20.2	8.1	15	8	7	12.6	10.2
1893–1902	564	407	72.2	157	27.8	26.0	9.6	25	13	12	16.0	13.6
1903–14	836	594	71.1	242	28.9	32.2	12.8	38	19	19	19.2	18.3

*These figures were computed by summing the data in Table 1 and by dividing by population figures for Prussia and Berlin.

single women. In Imperial Germany, as more and more women entered the work force,[17] more women moved into urban areas away from traditional domestic settings and they probably became stronger and not weaker, in a social and economic sense at least;[18] but more women were killed. Although the rate of men who were murdered also showed some increases during this period of tremendous urban growth and industrial expansion, the male murder rate did not increase nearly as quickly as did the female murder rate, and the urban setting and the growing urbanization of the society did not seem to put them in as much danger. Nevertheless, men were always in more danger than women. What seemed to make the most difference for men was the religious background from which they came; Catholic men were in greater jeopardy than Protestant or Jewish men. For females, however, religion did not seem to make much of a difference. For confirmation of these statements we now turn directly to our evidence.

In Table 2 and Table 3 we observe that in Imperial Germany men were killed far more often than females, but with the passage of time, women represented a somewhat higher percentage of all people killed. In the 1870s and 1880s women usually comprised about 25 percent of the total number of people murdered, but in later years women often made up more than 30 percent. For both males and females there was no tremendous growth, however, in their murder rates until after the mid-1890s (and in the 1880s there was actually a decline in both male and female homicide rates). After the mid-1880s especially, there was rapid urban growth and the changing ratio of women's to men's homicide seems, then, to have been associated with the process of urbanization. The more urbanized Germany became, the more females vis-à-vis men were murdered. Why the murder rates of both males and females grew so dramatically after the mid-1890s is certainly not clear. One possible explanation is that the rate of murder corresponded with changes in the business cycle. After the mid-1890s, the long depression in agricultural prices ended and there was a general rising trend in the prices of nearly all commodities. Although there are various arguments and counterarguments about what the impact of this was on people's real wages,[20] the inflationary price trend in the late 1890s and continuing on up to the war must have hurt many people, particularly those who lived at the fringes of society, and this may have resulted in more murders. One thing is certain: the rate of female homicide was rising much quicker than the rate of male homicide. Whereas the male homicide rate only grew by about 23 percent, the female homicide rate grew by about 33 percent; this is true either when we compare the decade of the mid-1870s to the mid-1880s with the last decade of Imperial Germany or when we compare this last decade with the decade immediately preceding it (see Table 3). There-

TABLE 4
Zero-Order Correlations Between Homicide Rates and Socioeconomic Variables in Prussia, 1904–6

DEPENDENT VARIABLE	MEN'S HOMICIDE DEATH RATE, 1904–6	% URBAN POPULATION	WEALTH (INC. TAX)	ETHNICITY	% CATHOLIC
Women's Homicide Death Rate, 1904–6	.25	.36	.48	–.13	.10
Men's Homicide Death Rate, 1904–6	—	–.20	–.06	.29	.64

fore, these figures seem to show that women were more affected than men by the changes in the business cycle and by the process of urbanization.

The figures in Tables 2 and 3 also demonstrate some marked differences between Berlin and the rest of Prussia in the patterns of male and female homicide deaths. Whereas Berlin females were in far greater danger than were females in the rest of Prussia, Berlin males were actually much less likely to be murdered than males elsewhere. In all of Prussia, as we have shown earlier, males were roughly two and one-half times as likely to be murdered as females; but in Berlin males and females had almost exactly the same chance of being murdered. Between 1873 and 1907 only three more males were murdered than females, 358 to 355. When we control for the male and female population, we find that in Berlin in the period between 1903 and 1914 the yearly male murder death rate was 19.2 per million males and the female rate was 18.3 per million females; in the rest of Prussia the male rate was, however, much higher and the female rate much lower (32.2 to 12.8). Hence, as Berlin was the largest city in Prussia, these figures suggest strongly that the urban woman was in far more peril than her rural counterpart, but that urban environments were relatively safe for men.

Another way to demonstrate the important differences between urban and rural settings in the homicide deaths of females and males is by employing the results of a correlation analysis (see Table 4). In this analysis the rates of male and female homicide victims in the period 1904–6 for each of Prussia's 36 *Regierungsbezirke* (large governmental administrative districts) were correlated with various social and economic indicators.[21] With the exception of Berlin, each of these districts contained both rural and urban districts. A rate for urban population was computed by dividing the number of inhabitants in each district who lived in cities of more than 20,000 by the total number of inhabitants of the district. Some districts, such as those in the Prussian northeast, had urban rates that were less than 25 percent, but others, such as Düsseldorf, Cologne, and Berlin, had rates which were higher than 50 percent. The remaining districts fell in between these extremes. When we compare the correlations between the male and female homicide rates and the rates of urban population, we find a stark contrast. The rate of urban population showed a mild but still significant correlation with the female homicide rate ($r = .36$), but a negative though weaker correlation with the male homicide rate ($r = -.20$). These correlations are not terribly strong, but they do add support to our contention that the urban environment posed much greater dangers to women than to men. Other significant differences between the homicide deaths of males and females come into view when we consider wealth, ethnic, and religious factors relating to the homicide

TABLE 5
Homicide Victims by Religion and Sex in Prussia, 1904–6

RELIGION	MALE	MALE YEARLY RATE (PER MILLION MALES)	FEMALE	FEMALE YEARLY RATE (PER MILLION FEMALES)	FEMALE AS % OF MALE
Protestant	704	21.5	320	9.8	.45
Catholic	682	37.5	188	10.3	.28
Jewish	10	17.0	3	5.1	.30
Unknown	105	–	90	–	.86

victims. The correlations show that women were more often murdered in wealthier districts (r = .48) than in poorer ones, but that the wealth of the district made no difference for the homicide patterns of males (r = −.06). This, of course, does not mean that wealthy women were killed more often than poor women; but it does mean that women who resided in relatively poor communities were probably in less danger of being murdered than women who lived in richer ones. Whereas communities with a large number of ethnic inhabitants in Germany (mainly Poles and Lithuanians residing in the Prussian northeast) have been shown to have particularly high rates of crime, the ethnic homogeneity or heterogeneity had no significant influence on the homicide deaths of females.[22] The negative sign of the correlation coefficient even suggests that the greater the ethnic concentration of a community, the less the danger of homicide for females. But the ethnicity of the community had a different effect on the homicide of males; the positive correlation (r = .29) between the male homicide rate and the percentage of ethnic inhabitants in a district demonstrates that the more ethnic the community, the greater the number of homicide deaths of male inhabitants. Even more significant in differentiating the female from the male homicide patterns is the religion of the community. The strong, positive correlation between the male homicide rate and the percentage of Catholics in a district makes it plain that Catholic communities were lethal for German males. The religion of the district did not, however, have much of an influence on female homicide deaths.

The importance of religious differences in the homicide patterns of German males and females comes into greater relief with the information presented in Table 5. In this table all known homicide victims in Prussia 1904–6 are classified by sex and religion.[23] Here we found that slightly more Protestant males were murdered than Catholic males (704 to 682) but that many more Protestant females were murdered than Catholic females (320 to 188). In the case of Jewish people, there were almost no murders of either males or females. When we consider that Protestants made up about two-thirds of all Prussians and that Catholics made up almost all of the other third, with Jews and other religions comprising less than 2 percent of the Prussian population, we begin to appreciate the great differences that religion made. As the correlation figures suggested and these figures confirmed, Catholic males were the most likely people to be murdered in German society.[24] With a yearly homicide death rate of 37.5 Catholic men per million, Catholic men were about twice as likely to be murdered as Protestant or Jewish males (their rates were 21.5 and 17.0, respectively), who were themselves between two and four times as likely to be murdered as any type of female. Again, as the correlation figures suggested, Catholic and Protestant females were murdered in

Table 6

Children Under 1 Year Old as Percentage of Homicide Victims in Prussia and Berlin in Two Periods, 1887–91 and 1902–7

	Total Number of Homicides		Homicides of Children, 0–1 Year		Children as % of Total Homicides	
	Male	Female	Male	Female	Male	Female
Prussia						
1887–91	1,226	562	277	237	22.6	42.2
1902–7	2,958	1,203	465	419	15.7	34.8
Berlin						
1887–91	54	41	28	23	51.8	56.1
1902–7	109	110	38	44	34.8	40.0

about the same proportion to the total number of Catholic females or Protestant females in the country (the Catholic female rate was 10.3 and the Protestant female rate was 9.8). One also observes from these figures that Catholic women were far less in danger of being murdered than their men, as more than three times as many Catholic men were murdered than women. Protestant women, on the other hand, had more parity with their men in that only about two Protestant men for every Protestant woman were murdered in these years.[25]

Age and marital status are other factors which bore heavily upon the homicide deaths of German females. In Table 6 we compare the male and female homicide deaths of infants and people over one year old in Prussia and Berlin in two separate five-year periods, 1887–91 and 1902–7. In both periods, in both Prussia and Berlin, female infants made up a large but declining proportion of all female homicide deaths. In the years 1887–91, over half of all female homicide deaths in Berlin were of infants (56.1 percent) and in the same period infants comprised nearly half of all female homicide deaths in all of Prussia (42.2 percent). But after the turn of the century, the percentage of female homicide deaths made up by infants had dropped in Berlin to 40 percent and in Prussia to 34.8 percent. In that we know from our earlier discussions (see Table 3) that in the later period the overall female homicide rate increased markedly, these figures demonstrate that German society was clearly becoming more dangerous for adult German women as time went on. This was true also in the case of men, as the percentage of homicide deaths made up of male infants in both Berlin and Prussia was declining over time as well. But with the exception of Berlin, this was not quite as important a development for males as for females, as a much smaller proportion of male homicide deaths was made up of infants (22.6 percent in the earlier period and 15.7 percent in the later).

In Table 7 we are able to determine at which ages males and females were murdered and how age made a major difference between the sexes. As children, males and females shared a nearly equal chance of being murdered and for very young children this danger was extremely great. Between the ages of 5 and 15, however, not many children of either sex were murdered, but there were even a few more female children than male children murdered. Between the ages of 15 and 40, males were in increasingly more danger of being murdered than females, but after this age women started to catch up with men once again. It was not until truly old age, however, that women reached the parity with men that they shared as children. These figures clearly show, then, that as young and middle-aged adults, women were far safer than men, but that as infants and old people, women got no preferential treatment.

Table 8 presents figures relating to the influence that marriage had on

TABLE 7
Homicide Deaths by Age and Sex of Victims
in Prussia, 1904–6

AGE	NUMBER MALE	NUMBER FEMALE	FEMALE AS % OF MALE
0–5 Years	291	234	80
5–10	27	28	104
10–15	14	18	129
15–20	120	44	37
20–25	223	58	26
25–30	230	39	17
30–40	268	49	18
40–50	170	52	31
50–60	85	33	39
60–70	44	19	43
70–80	14	14	100
Over 80	14	12	86

the homicide death rate of Prussian females. They suggest clearly that marriage was in fact not the type of lethal context for women that some people have argued. On the contrary, they demonstrate that marriage served to protect women from harm. Most women married sometime in their twenties: between the ages of 15 and 20, less than 1 percent of women were married; between the ages of 20 and 25, slightly more than a quarter of all women were married; between the ages of 25 and 30, over two-thirds of all women were married; and eventually almost all women married. With the exception of the 15–20 age group, when very few women were married, married women had considerably lower homicide rates than did single women, and if we recall the figures presented in Table 3 which showed that women of any age in this period had a homicide rate of 12.8 per million women, it turns out that married women after the age of 20 had lower rates of homicide than women in general. Married women between the ages of 20 and 25 had a homicide rate of 8.1, but single women of this group had a homicide rate of 13.8. Between the ages of 25 and 30, when most women were now married, the married women's homicide rate was again only about one-half that of the single women's homicide rate (7.5 to 13.0). After the age of 30, when nearly 90 percent of all women were married, the married women's rate was 7.6 whereas the single women's rate was 11.6. Why young married women between the ages of 15 and 20 diverged from this pattern by having much higher homicide death rates than single women in this age group is uncertain. A possible explanation might be that these women were acting in an

TABLE 8
Female Homicide Deaths by Marital Status and Age in Prussia, 1904–6

Age	Percent Married	Percent Single	No. of Homicides Married	No. of Homicides Single	Percent Homicides Married	Homicide Rate* Married	Homicide Rate* Single	Homicide Rate* All Women
15–20	0.7	99.3	6	38	13.6	77.6	4.0	4.6
20–25	28.4	71.6	11	47	19.0	8.1	13.8	12.4
25–30	64.5	35.5	20	19	51.3	7.5	13.0	9.4
Over 30	87.7	12.3	106	20	84.1	7.6	11.6	8.0

*Homicide rates are per million women per year.

Note: The homicide rate for widowed and divorced women was 11.9.

361

TABLE 9
Means of Homicide by Sex in Prussia and Berlin, 1904–6

Means	PRUSSIA				BERLIN			
	All Homicide		Victim over 15 Years Old		All Homicide		Victim over 15 Years Old	
	Male	Female	Male	Female	Male	Female	Male	Female
Hanged	16	16	3	3	0	3	0	3
Strangled	64	60	11	31	4	1	0	0
Smothered	60	70	3	5	1	7	0	1
Drowned	93	60	9	6	8	5	0	0
Shot	169	120	156	108	7	16	6	14
Stabbed	497	54	491	47	8	2	7	2
Throat Slit	25	35	13	24	0	2	0	1
Burned	1	3	1	2	0	0	0	0
Poisoned	23	23	4	0	6	8	0	0
Pushed Down Stairs	10	7	6	4	2	1	1	1
Beaten	382	84	357	65	6	3	6	3
Buried Alive	4	4	0	0	0	0	0	0
Other Means	61	19	38	9	2	1	0	0
Unknown	96	46	87	17	5	0	4	0

extraordinary way by getting married and that their youth may have increased the strains of marriage. And, as is often the case with exceptionally young couples today, their family economy may have been quite precarious. Of course, this is only conjecture, and, in that there were only 6 married women who were murdered in this age group in these three years, this extremely high rate of murder might have been an aberration. But if we take all of these results at their face value, it appears that women who followed the traditional pattern of getting married at a normal time seemed to be in less danger of being murdered than if they broke with tradition either by getting married at a young age or by not getting married at all.

Before we conclude, there are a few observations we would like to make about the means by which our victims were killed. Table 9 presents figures which show that women were usually killed by different means than were men, except when they were children. Most children of both sexes were murdered either by drowning, smothering, or, to a lesser extent, poisoning or beating. Adult men were most often murdered by being stabbed or beaten. Women, on the other hand, were more than twice as likely to be shot than to be murdered by any other means. Although more men were shot than women, less than one-half as many men were killed in this manner as by being beaten, and less than one-third as many men were shot as stabbed. These findings might suggest that men were often killed in the course of some kind of struggle. As there is less of a chance that one will survive being shot than being stabbed or beaten, there may have been more finality about the way women were murdered. These figures might also suggest that women might have a particular reason to fear guns and to advocate their control.

In conclusion we should first state that we are aware of the many limitations of this study. The figures we have used are, we think, better than those used by some that have based their observations about female homicide victims on court statistics. By using coroners' reports we were able to consider a much larger number of women who actually were murdered than the scanty proportion of cases that actually went to trial. But German coroners were no doubt not without their biases and we have no way of knowing how many of our victims really were suicide or accident deaths. Using coroners' reports instead of court statistics made it impossible for us to make any statements about the important relationship between the murderer and the victim, and our coroners' reports also did not permit us to make any statements about the motive of the murderer. Finally, many of our observations relied on information from the years 1904–6 and it is possible that the religious, marital, and demographic trends we reported might have been different in other years.

Certainly there is considerable work left to be done both in Germany and in other societies on the issue of female homicide. Our findings, nevertheless, permit some interesting and important observations. First, we have no reason to believe that women are particularly good victims, either because they are weak or because they they often accept traditional social roles. In an interesting study which treats interfamilial violence in Victorian England, Nancy Tomes has argued recently that "in 1890, working-class women were far less likely to experience physical violence at the hands of a man than they were in 1840."[26] Her argument was that English working-class women had actually by this time experienced a decline in their economic and social status, but that they less often worked, and more often resigned themselves to traditional roles, and thus they acted subserviently to their men and allowed their men to act as their protectors. If Tomes is correct, it appears that English women were like German women in that women who accepted a traditional role were less likely to be harmed than women who did not. Most people think that German women in the years we have studied were much more traditional-minded than women in England or many other societies. Our study shows that German women were much less likely to be murdered than were German men. And since both German men and German women in comparison with men and women in other societies had low homicide death rates, most German women were, therefore, relatively safe from homicidal violence.[27] But women who broke away from traditional roles, either by getting married at an early age, by not getting married at all, or by moving off to the city, were in more danger of getting murdered than those who followed a traditional life style. In Imperial Germany more and more women did go off to the city to seek employment and opportunity and perhaps more and more women sought parity with men. In relation to homicide, at least, women were making some headway, but they would probably have preferred to forsake this particular kind of parity.

NOTES

1. There are, of course, some exceptions. See, for example, Caesar Lombroso and William Ferrero, *The Female Offender* (New York, 1895), and Otto Pollak, *Criminality of Women* (New York, 1961). Pollak's work even mentions some German studies dealing at least partially with the role of German women in criminality, such as George von Mayr's *Statistik und Gesellschaftslehre* (Tübingen, 1917). Recently there have been several major studies which investigate the patterns of crime in nineteenth- and early-twentieth-century Germany,

but none of them mentions women except in passing. See Dirk Blasius, *Kriminalität und Alltag. Zur Konfliktgeschichte des Alltagslebens im 19. Jahrhundert* (Göttingen, 1978); Howard Zehr, *Crime and the Development of Modern Society: Patterns of Criminality in Nineteenth Century Germany and France* (London, 1976); and Vincent E. McHale and Eric A. Johnson, "Urbanization, Industrialization and Crime in Imperial Germany: Parts I and II," *Social Science History*, 1 (1976–77), pp. 45–78, 210–47.

2. Germans certainly had this perception. The important criminologist Ludwig Fuld explained that in Imperial Germany women themselves seldom committed crimes but they often enticed men into criminal acts, especially in love squabbles. Ludwig Fuld, "Aus der Kriminalpsychologie des weiblichen Geschlechtes," *Vom Fels zum Meer*, 3 (October 1885–March 1886).

3. *Statistik des Deutschen Reichs*, 370 (1930), pp. 45–46.

4. Crime was not a major subject in the social literature of Imperial Germany except in the trashy *Trivialliteratur*, which often contained lurid tales of female victims. For an excellent discussion of this literature, see Rudolf Schenda, *Volk ohne Buch. Studien zur Sozialgeschichte der populären Lesestoffe 1770–1910* (Frankfurt, 1970). See also Rolf Engelsing, *Analphabetentum und Lektüre. Zur Sozialgeschichte des Lesens in Deutschland zwischen feudaler und industrieller Gesellschaft* (Stuttgart, 1973). Although homicide stories were rare in the more serious social literature, female homicide victims did concern naturalist authors like the important playwright Gerhart Hauptmann. Both *Hannele* and *Die Ratten* treat this theme.

5. For a discussion of crime in Imperial German newspapers, see Eric A. Johnson's forthcoming *The Rechtsstaat: Crime and Criminal Justice in Imperial Germany*, especially chap. 3, "Crime and Popular Opinion: Magazines and Newspapers."

6. E. Roesner, "Mörder und ihre Öpfer," *Monatsschrift für Kriminalbiologie und Strafrechtsreform*, 29 (1938), pp. 161–85, 209–28.

7. Hans von Hentig, *The Criminal and His Victim: Studies in the Sociobiology of Crime* (New York, 1979) (first published, New Haven, Conn., 1948).

8. Ibid., pp. 404–19.

9. Ibid., p. 407.

10. Ibid., pp. 390–404, 419–38.

11. See Eda Sagarra, *A Social History of Germany 1648–1914* (London, 1977), pp. 405–24.

12. Franz Exner, *Studien über die Strafzumessungspraxis der deutschen Gerichte* (Leipzig, 1931). Rupert Rabl, *Strafzumessungspraxis und Krimininalitätsbewegung* (Leipzig, 1936).

13. The coroners' homicide statistics combine deaths due to both *Mord* (premeditated murder) and *Totschlag* (non-premeditated murder). They have been taken from the yearly volumes entitled *Die Sterblichkeit nach Todesursachen und Altersklassen der Gestorbenen* contained in the huge Prussian governmental statistical series *Preussische Statistik*. The conviction statistics for homicide were found in the yearly *Kriminalstatistik* volumes of the major Reich governmental statistical series *Statistik des Deutschen Reichs*. Rates were computed by dividing the homicide statistics by population figures found in the latter statistical series.

14. The closest thing to a truly historical study of female victims is Nancy Tomes's recent article on interfamilial violence in working-class families in Victorian England: Nancy Tomes, "'A Torrent of Abuse': Crimes of Violence Between Working Class Men and Women in London, 1840–1875," *Journal of Social History*, 11 (1978), pp. 328–45. Perhaps the leading sociologist in the field of victimology is Marvin Wolfgang. See, for example, his "Victim Precipitated Homicide," *Journal of Criminal Law, Criminology, and Police Science*, 48 (1957), pp. 1–11. For other studies which deal with female victims of homicide and violence, see Paul C. Holinger, "Violent Deaths Among the Young: Recent Trends in Suicide, Homicide, and Accidents," *American Journal of Psychiatry*, 136 (1979), pp. 1144–47; Holinger, "Violent Deaths as a Leading Cause of Mortality: An Epidemiologic Study of Suicide, Homicide, and Accidents," *American Journal of Psychiatry*, 137 (1980), pp. 472–76; Murray Strauss, "Sexual Inequality, Cultural Norms, and Wife Beating," in *Victims and Society*, ed. by Emilio Viano (Washington, D.C., 1976), pp. 543–59; Pawel Horoszowski, "Homicide of Passion and Its Motives," in *Victimology: A New Focus*, ed. by Israel Drapkin and Emilio Viano, (Lexington, Mass., 1975), pp. 3–23.

15. Margaret A. Zahn, "The Female Homicide Victim," *Criminology*, 13 (1975), p. 401.

16. Ibid., p. 413.

17. Throughout the period most women who did work worked in agriculture, in the textile industry, or as domestic servants, but growing numbers found employment in factory production. Patricia Branca cites figures which show that between 1891 and 1911 the number of women working in industrial occupations increased at faster rates than the number of men. See Patricia Branca, *Women in Europe Since 1870* (New York, 1978), especially pp. 47–51.

18. It should be noted, however, that most observers consider German women to have been far more traditional-minded and resigned than women from England and some other countries. See Peter N. Stearns, "Working-Class Women in Britain, 1890–1914," in *Suffer and Be Still: Women in the Victorian Age*, ed. by Martha Vicinus, (Bloomington, 1972), p. 119. Eda Sagarra argues that women in Imperial Germany gained in economic strength but may have lost ground psychologically; they seemed to become "backward-looking in their image of themselves." Sagarra, p. 422.

19. In 1871 nearly two-thirds of the population lived in communities with fewer than 2,000 inhabitants, but by 1910 fewer than 40% lived in such places. For a recent discussion of Prussian urban and economic growth see Gerd Hohorst, *Wirtschaftswachstum und Bevölkerungsentwicklung in Preussen, 1816 bis 1914* (New York, 1977).

20. For a good bibliography and for a discussion of some of them, see Frank E. Tipton, *Regional Variations in the Economic Development of Germany During the Nineteenth Century* (Middletown, Conn., 1976), pp. 42–44. The most detailed discussion of prices and wages, though, is found in Gerhard Bry, *Wages in Germany, 1871–1945* (Princeton, 1960).

21. We use the *Regierungsbezirke* as the level of analysis because there are so few female homicide deaths that correlation figures would be meaningless for lower levels of aggregation. A correlation analysis of homicide figures with socio-

economic variables using *Kreise* data can be found in Eric A. Johnson, "The Roots of Crime in Imperial Germany," *Central European History, 15 (1982), pp. 351–76*. But in this analysis female and male homicide deaths are lumped together.

22. Johnson, "The Roots of Crime."

23. This time period has been chosen because data are not available for earlier or later periods.

24. Emile Durkheim argues that Catholics had higher homicide rates than Protestants in both Germany and other countries in the nineteenth century. Using conviction statistics, he points out that predominantly Catholic countries like Italy and Spain had homicide rates of approximately 70 per million inhabitants but that Protestant-dominated countries like Germany, England, and Denmark had homicide rates of only about 3 per million inhabitants. Durkheim, *Suicide: A Study in Sociology*, trans. by John A. Spaulding and George Simpson (New York, 1951), p. 353.

25. When we compare the murder rates of females in different parts of Germany, it turns out that areas with mostly Catholic inhabitants had much higher murder rates of males than females. In 1904–6 there were 41 men murdered in Westphalia but only 9 women; in Posen there were 29 men murdered and 9 women. In Protestant areas the rate of female homicide deaths was much closer to that of male homicide deaths. Thus, in Schleswig-Holstein in the years 1904–6, 16 males and 8 females were murdered. In Brandenburg, 20 males and 11 females were murdered, and in Saxony, 21 males and 14 females were murdered.

26. Tomes, p. 342.

27. According to Durkheim's figures, the homicide rate in Germany ranked eleventh out of twelve European countries. Only Holland had a lower rate. See *Suicide*, p. 353.

An English-Language Bibliography on European and American Women's History

JOHN C. FOUT

Perhaps at no point in the history of academic interchange has there been such a healthy recognition of scholarship being done on the opposite sides of the Atlantic as there is today in feminist scholarship. It is for that reason that this bibliography has brought together literature on both European and American women's history even though this essay collection itself is concerned specifically with German women. It is hoped that this bibliography will be useful to undergraduate students, historians, and a variety of students and scholars in other disciplines.

Although there is a chronological emphasis in this bibliography on the nineteenth century, many works were cited that range in time from the Renaissance to the present. The large corpus of new works, as well as the extensive reprinting and translating of sources and standard works, has made it a challenge even for the specialist in the field of women's history of the modern era to keep current with the literature. Therefore, I sought to incorporate most of the important works—documents, monographs, and scholarly periodical articles—that have been published primarily, but not exclusively, in the last twelve to fifteen years, at least in the English language. Some older standard works that are not available in reprint have also been included. A fairly complete list of recent German-language studies, mostly on the history of German women, is to be found in the text of the introduction and in the notes of the articles that comprise this book. The bibliography is cross-disciplinary, as is the discipline of women's history, and it is comparative. For that latter reason, and because of the constraints of space, it has been subdivided along national boundaries. Only the first three parts, "Anthologies of Original Sources," "Bibliographies," and the "General European" section are exceptions to that rule. As the table of contents indicates, additional subcategories on individual women follow four of the large sections. That resulted from the publication of reprints of their works and recent biographical studies rather than any systematic attempt to order the bibliography in that way.

All book citations list the place of publication, publisher, and copyright date. In most cases, if there was both a British and an American edition, the latter was chosen. Whenever possible, for books that have been reprinted, the date of the reprinting is followed by the original publication date (in parenthesis) and the most recent or revised edition of any work is the one cited. In the case of journal articles, author and title of a given article are followed by the name of the journal, the volume number, the year (in parenthesis), and inclusive pages. For example: Stansell, Christine. "Women, Children, and the Uses of the Streets: Class and Gender Conflict in New York City, 1850–1860," *Feminist Studies*, 8 (1982), pp. 309–35. When a journal does not use volume numbers, the specific number of the issue is used instead. Otherwise, issue numbers are not noted, unless, as is the case with a handful of journals, issues within a volume are not numbered consecutively; then the issue number follows the volume number (in parenthesis). Hopefully the effort that went into providing these complete citations will pay off by making it possible for students and faculty even in small college libraries to locate these works easily through interlibrary loan.

ANTHOLOGIES OF ORIGINAL SOURCES

Agonito, Rosemary. ed. *History of Ideas on Woman: A Source Book.* New York: Putnam, 1977.

Bauer, Carol, and Ritt, Lawrence. eds. *Free and Ennobled: Source Readings in the Development of Victorian Feminism.* Elmsford, NY: Pergamon, 1979.

Bell, Susan G. ed. *Women: From the Greeks to the French Revolution.* Belmont, CA: Wadsworth, 1973.

Brownlee, Elliot W., and Brownlee, Mary H. eds. *Women in the American Economy: A Documentary History 1675–1927.* New Haven: Yale University Press, 1976.

Buhle, Mari Jo, and Buhle, Paul. eds. *The Concise History of Women's Suffrage: Selections from the Classic Work of Stanton, Anthony, Gage and Harper.* Urbana: University of Illionis Press, 1978.

Burdett-Coutts, Baroness Angela. ed. *Woman's Mission: A Series of Congress Papers on the Philanthropic Work of Women by Eminent Writers.* London: Low, Marston, 1893.

Burnett, John. ed. *Annals of Labour: Autobiographies of British Working-Class People 1820–1920.* Bloomington: Indiana University Press, 1974.

Cott, Nancy F. ed. *Root of Bitterness: Documents of the Social History of American Women.* New York: Dutton, 1972.

Cross, Barbara M. ed. *Educated Women in America: Selected Writings of Catherine Beecher, Margaret Fuller and M. Carey Thomas.* New York: Teachers College Press, 1965.

Davies, Margaret Llewelyn. ed. *Life as We Have Known It.* by Co-operative Working Women. New York: Norton, 1975 (1931).

Dublin, Thomas. ed. *Farm to Factory: Women's Letters, 1830–1860.* New York: Columbia University Press, 1981.

DuBois, Ellen. ed. *Elizabeth Cady Stanton–Susan B. Anthony: Correspondence, Writings, Speeches.* New York: Schocken, 1981.

Eisler, Benita. ed. *The Lowell Offering: Writings by New England Mill Women (1840–1845).* New York: Lippincott, 1977.

Foner, Philip S. ed. *The Factory Girls: A Collection of Writings on Life and Struggles in the New England Factories of the 1840's.* Urbana: University of Illinois Press, 1977.

Giffin, Frederick C. ed. *Woman as Revolutionary.* New York: Mentor, 1973.

Goulianos, Joan, et al. eds. *By a Woman Writ: Literature From Six Centuries by and about Women.* Baltimore: Penguin Books, 1974.

Hellerstein, Erna Olafson; Hume, Leslie Parker; and Offen, Karen M. eds. *Victorian Women: A Documentary Account of Women's Lives in Nineteenth-Century England, France and the United States.* Stanford, CA.: Stanford University Press, 1981.

Hollis, Patricia. ed. *Women in Public 1850–1900: Documents of the Victorian Women's Movement.* London: Allen & Unwin, 1979.

Hourwich, Andrea T., and Palmer, Gladys L. eds. *I Am a Woman Worker: A Scrapbook of Autobiographies.* Salem, NH: Arno, 1974 (1936).

Jenness, Linda. ed. *Feminism and Socialism: An Anthology.* New York: Pathfinder Press, 1972.

Katz, Jonathan. ed. *Gay American History: Lesbians and Gay Men in the U.S.A.* New York: Crowell, 1976.

———. *Gay/Lesbian Almanac A New Documentary.* New York: Harper & Row, 1983.

Kraditor, Aileen Selma. ed. *Up from the Pedestal: Selected Writings in the History of American Feminism.* Chicago: Quadrangle Books, 1968.

Lane, Ann J. ed. *Mary Ritter Beard: A Sourcebook.* New York: Schocken, 1977.

Lerner, Gerda. ed. *The Female Experience: An American Documentary.* Indianapolis: Bobbs-Merrill, 1977.

Levy, Darlene Gay; Applewhite, Harriet Branson; and Johnson, Mary Durham. eds. *Women in Revolutionary Paris, 1789–1795: Selected Documents.* Urbana: University of Illinois Press, 1979.

Marcus, Jacob P. ed. *The American Jewish Woman: A Documentary History.* New York: KTAV, 1981.

Murray, Janet H., and Stark, Myra. eds. *The Englishwoman's Review of Social and Industrial Questions.* New York: Garland, 1979.

Myres, Sandra L. ed. *Ho for California: Women's Overland Diaries from the Huntington Library.* San Marino, CA: Huntington Library, 1980.

O'Faolain, Julia, and Martines, Lauro. eds. *Not in God's Image: Women in History from the Greeks to the Victorians.* New York: Harper, 1973.

Pachmuss, Temira. ed. *Women Writers in Russian Modernism: An Anthology.* Urbana: University of Illinois Press, 1978.

Riemer, Eleanor S., and Fout, John C. eds. *European Women: A Documentary History 1789–1945.* New York: Schocken, 1980.

Rossi, Alice S. ed. *The Feminist Papers: From Adams to de Beauvoir.* New York: Columbia University Press, 1973.

Schneir, Miriam. ed. *Feminism: The Essential Historical Writings.* New York: Random House, 1972.

Stein, Leon, and Baxter, Annette K. eds. *Women of Lowell: An Original Anthology.* Salem, NH: Arno, 1974.

Travitsky, Betty. ed. *The Paradise of Women: Writings by Englishwomen of the Renaissance.* Westport, CT: Greenwood Press, 1981.

Trescott, Martha M. ed. *Dynamos and Virgins Revisited: Women and Technological Change in History: An Anthology.* Metuchen, NJ: Scarecrow, 1979.

The Woman Question: Selections from the Writings of Karl Marx, Friedrich Engels, V. I. Lenin and Joseph Stalin. New York: International, 1970 (1951).

Wortman, Marlene Stein. ed. *Women in American Law. From Colonial Times to the New Deal.* New York: Holmes & Meier, 1984.

BIBLIOGRAPHIES

Aldous, Joan, and Reuben, Hill. eds. *International Bibliography of Research in Marriage and the Family 1900–64.* Minneapolis: University of Minnesota Press, 1967.

Ballou, Patricia K. "Bibliographies for Research on Women," *Signs,* 3 (1977), pp. 436–50.

Borrow, Margaret. *Women Eighteen Seventy to Nineteen Twenty-eight: A Select Guide to Printed and Archival Sources in the United Kingdom.* New York: Garland, 1981.

Bullough, Vern, et al. eds. *An Annotated Bibliography of Homosexuality.* 2 vols. New York: Garland, 1976.

Cantor, Aviva, et al. eds. *The Jewish Woman: 1900–1980 Bibliography.* 2nd ed. New York: Biblio, 1982.

Catalogue of the Library of the International Archives for the Women's Movement, Amsterdam. 2 vols. Boston: Hall, 1980.

Eichler, Margrit. ed. *An Annotated Selected Bibliography of Bibliographies of Women.* Pittsburgh: Know, 1973.

Ende, Aurel. "Bibliography on Childhood and Youth in Germany from 1820–1878: A Selection," *Journal of Psychohistory,* 7 (1979–80), pp. 283–87.

Fout, John C. ed. *German History and Civilization 1806–1914: A Bibliography of Scholarly Periodical Literature.* Metuchen, NJ: Scarecrow, 1974.

Frey, Linda; Frey, Marsha; and Schneider, Joanne. eds. *Women in Western European History: A Select Chronological, Geographical, and Topical Bibliography.* 2 vols. Westport, CT: Greenwood, 1982–1984.

Haber, Barbara. *Women in America: A Guide to Books 1963–1975.* Urbana: University of Illinois Press, 1981.

Harrison, Cynthia E. *Women in American History: A Bibliography.* Santa Barbara, CA: ABC-Clio, 1979.

Hinding, Andrea, et al. eds. *Women's History Sources: A Guide to Archives and Manuscript Collections in the United States.* 2 vols. New York: Bowker, 1979.

Jacobs, Sue-Ellen. *Women in Perspective: A Guide to Cross-Cultural Studies.* Urbana: University of Illinois Press, 1974.

Kanner, Barbara S. ed. *The Women of England from Anglo-Saxon Times to the Present: Interpretive Bibliographical Essays.* Hamden, CT: Shoe String, 1979.

————. "The Women of England in a Century of Social Change, 1815–1914: A Select Bibliography," in Vicinus, Martha, ed. *Suffer and Be Still.* Bloomington: Indiana University Press, 1972.

————. "The Women of England in a Century of Social Change, 1815–1914: A Select Bibliography, Part II," in Vicinus, Martha, ed. *A Widening Sphere.* Bloomington: Indiana University Press, 1977.

Kelly, Joan, *Bibliography in the History of European Women.* 4th rev. ed. Bronxville, NY: Sarah Lawrence College, 1976.

King, Judith D. *Women's Studies Sourcebook: A Comprehensive Classified Bibliography of Books.* Allendale, MD: Grand Valley State College Library, 1976.

Krichmar, Albert, et. al. eds. *The Women's Rights Movement in the United States, 1848–1970: A Bibliography and Source Book.* Metuchen, NJ: Scarecrow, 1972.

Lazar, Robert E. "The International Ladies' Garment Workers' Union Archives," *Labor History* 23 (1982), pp. 528–33.

Lerner, Gerda. *Bibliography in the History of American Women.* Bronxville, NY: Sarah Lawrence College, 1975.

Offen, Karen M. "The 'Woman Question' as a Social Issue in Nineteenth Century France: A Bibliographical Essay," *Third Republic,* no. 3/4 (1977), pp. 238–99.

Palmegiano, Eugenia M. "Women and British Periodicals, 1832–1867: A Bibliography," *Victorian Periodicals Newsletter,* 9 (1976), pp. 3–36.

Parker, William. "Homosexuality in History: An Annotated Bibliography," in Licata, Salvatore J., and Petersen, Robert M. eds. *Historical Perspectives on Homosexuality.* New York: Haworth Press, 1981.

Radcliffe College, The Arthur and Elizabeth Schlesinger Library on the History of Women in America. Manuscripts Inventory and the Catalogs of Manuscripts, Books, and Pictures. 3 vols. Boston: Hall, 1973.

Sharistanian, Janet, et. al. eds. "The (Dr. Aletta H. Jacobs) Gerritsen Collection The University of Kansas," *Feminist Studies,* 3 (3–4) (1975–76), pp. 200–6.

Soltow, Martha J., and Wery, Mary K. *American Women and the Labor Movement, 1825–1874: An Annotated Bibliography.* Metuchen, NJ: Scarecrow, 1976.

Sowerwine, Charles. "Women, Socialism, and Feminism, 1872–1922: A Bibliography," *Third Republic,* no. 3/4 (1977), pp. 300–66.

Stineman, Esther. ed. *Women's Studies: A Recommended Core Bibliography.* Littleton, CO: Libraries Unlimited, 1979.

Weinberg, Martin, and Bell, Alan. eds. *Homosexuality: An Annotated Bibliography.* New York: Harper, 1972.

GENERAL EUROPEAN

Addams, Jane, et al. *Women at The Hague: The International Congress of Women and Its Results.* New York: Garland, 1972 (1915).

Anderson, Adelaide Mary. *Women in the Factory: An Administrative Adventure, 1893 to 1921*. New York: Dutton, 1922.

Ankarloo, B. "Agriculture and Women's Work: Directions of Change in the West, 1700–1900," *Journal of Family History*, 3 (1979) pp. 111–20.

Ariès, Philippe. *Centuries of Childhood: A Social History of Family Life*. New York: Vintage, 1962.

Bachofen, Johann J. *Myth, Religion and Mother Right*. Princeton: Princeton University Press, 1967.

Bailey, D. S. *Homosexuality and the Western Christian Tradition*. London: Longmans, Green, 1955.

Baker, Elizabeth. *Technology and Women's Work*. New York: Columbia University Press, 1964.

Banks, Olive. *Faces of Feminism: A Study of Feminism as a Social Movement*. New York: St. Martin's, 1981.

Banner, Lois W. "On Writing Women's History," *Journal of Interdisciplinary History*, 2 (1971), pp. 347–58.

Behnke, Donna A. *Religious Issues in Nineteenth Century Feminism*. Troy, NY: Whitson Press, 1982.

Berk, Sarah F. ed. *Women and Household Labor*. Beverly Hills, CA: Sage, 1980.

Berkin, Carol R., and Lovett, Clara M. eds. *Women, War and Revolution*. New York: Holmes & Meier, 1980.

Blackwell, Elizabeth. *Pioneer Works in Opening the Medical Profession to Women*. New York: Schocken, 1977.

Bloch, Ruth H. "Untangling the Roots of Modern Sex Roles: A Survey of Four Centuries of Change," *Signs*, 4 (1978–79), pp. 237–52.

Bodek, Evelyn Gordon. "Salonières and Bluestockings: Educated Obsolescence and Germinating Feminism," *Feminist Studies*, 3 (1976), pp. 185–99.

Boulding, Elise. *The Underside of History: A View of Women Through Time*. Boulder, CO: Westview Press, 1976.

Boxer, Marilyn J., and Quataert, Jean H. eds. *Socialist Women: European Socialist Feminism in the Nineteenth and Early Twentieth Centuries*. New York: Elsevier, 1978.

Branca, Patricia. "A New Perspective on Women's Work: A Comparative Typology," *Journal of Social History*, 9 (1975), pp. 129–53.

———. *Women in Europe Since 1750*. London: Croom Helm, 1978.

———. "Women's History: Comments on Yesterday, Today, and Tomorrow," *Journal of Social History*, 11 (1978), 375–79.

Bridenthal, Renate, and Koonze, Claudia. eds. *Becoming Visible: Women in European History*. Boston: Houghton Mifflin, 1977.

Brink, Jeanie R. ed. *Female Scholars: A Tradition of Learned Women Before 1800*. Montreal: Eden Press, 1980.

Browning, Hilda. *Women Under Fascism and Communism*. London: Lawrence, 1934.

Bullough, Vern. *History of Prostitution.* Secaucus, NJ: University Books, 1964.

―――. *Subordinate Sex: A History of Attitudes Toward Women.* Urbana: University of Illinois Press, 1981.

Carroll, Berenice A. ed. *Liberating Women's History: Theoretical and Critical Essays.* Urbana: Unviersity of Illinois Press, 1976.

Chauncey, George Jr. "From Sexual Inversion to Homosexuality: Medicine and the Changing Conceptualization of Female Deviance," *Salmagundi,* 58–59 (1982), pp. 115–46.

Damon, Gene; Watson, Jan; and Jordan, Robin. eds. *The Lesbian in Literature.* 2nd ed. Weatherby Lake, MO: Naiad Press, 1975.

Davies, Mel. "Corsets and Conception: Fashion and Demographic Trends in the Nineteenth Century," *Comparative Studies in Society and History,* 24 (1982), pp. 611–41.

Davis, Natalie Z. "'Women's History' in Transition: The European Case," *Feminist Studies,* 3 (3/4), (1975–76), pp. 83–103.

Degen, Marie L., and Cook, Blanche Wiesen. eds. *History of the Women's Peace Party.* New York: Garland, 1972.

De Grand, A. "Women Under Facism," *Historical Journal,* 19 (1976), pp. 947–68.

Delamont, Sara, and Duffin, Lorna. eds. *The Nineteenth-Century Woman: Her Cultural and Physical World.* New York: Barnes & Noble, 1978.

Deutsch, Regina. *The International Woman Suffrage Alliance: Its History from 1904–1929.* London: Board of the Alliance, 1929.

Engels, Friedrich. *The Origin of the Family, Private Property and the State.* New York: International, 1942.

Evans, Richard J. *The Feminists: Women's Emancipation Movements in Europe, America and Australasia 1840–1920.* New York: Barnes & Noble, 1978.

―――. "The History of European Women: A Critical Survey of Recent Research," *Journal of Modern History,* 52 (1980), pp. 656–75.

―――. "Modernization Theory and Women's History," *Archiv für Sozialgeschichte,* 20 (1980), pp. 492–514.

Faderman, Lillian. "The Morbidification of Love Between Women by Nineteenth-Century Sexologists," *Journal of Homosexuality,* 4 (1978), pp. 73–90.

―――. *Surpassing the Love of Men: Romantic Friendships and Love Between Women from the Renaissance to the Present.* New York: William Morrow, 1981.

Fairchild, Cissie. "Female Sexual Attitudes and the Rise of Illegitimacy: A Case Study," *Journal of Interdisciplinary History,* 8 (1977–78), pp. 627–67.

Follet, Joyce Clark. "Margaret Fuller in Europe 1846–1850," *History Today,* 29 (1979), pp. 506–15.

Forbes, Thomas Roger. *The Midwife and the Witch.* New Haven: Yale University Press, 1966.

Foucault, Michel. *The History of Sexuality: An Introduction.* New York: Pantheon, 1978.

Frenkel, F. E. "Sex Crime and Its Socio-Historical Background," *Journal of the History of Ideas,* 25 (1964), pp. 333–52.

Fryer, Peter. *The Birth Controllers.* New York: Stein & Day, 1965.

Griffiths, Naomi E. S. *Penelope's Web: Some Perceptions of Women in European and Canadian Society.* Toronto: Oxford University Press, 1976.

Hartman, Mary S. "Crime and the Respectable Woman: Toward a Pattern of Middle-Class Female Criminality in Nineteenth-Century France and England," *Feminist Studies,* 1 (1) (1974–75), pp. 38–56.

—— and Banner, Lois. eds. *Clio's Consciousness Raised: New Perspectives on the History of Women.* New York: Harper, 1974.

Heinsohn, Gunnar, and Steiger, Otto. "The Elimination of Medieval Birth Control and the Witch-Trials of Modern Times," *International Journal of Women's Studies,* 5 (1982), pp. 193–214.

Hess, Thomas B., and Nochlin, Linda. eds. *Women as Sex Object: Studies in Erotic Art 1730–1970.* London: Allen Lane, 1973.

Himes, Norman E. *Medical History of Contraception.* New York: Schocken, 1970 (1936).

Horseley, Richard A. "Who Were the Witches? The Social Roles of the Accused in the European Witchcraft Trials," *Journal of Interdisciplinary History,* 9 (1979) pp. 689–715.

Ireland, Norma. ed. *Index to Women of the World from Ancient to Modern Times; Biographies and Portraits.* Westwood, MA: Faxon, 1970.

Kahne, Hilda. "Economic Research on Women and Families," *Signs,* 3 (1977–78), pp. 652–65.

Kaplan, Temma E. "Female Consciousness and Collective Action: The Case of Barcelona, 1910–1918," *Signs,* 7 (1982), pp. 545–66.

——. "Spanish Anarchism and Women's Liberation," *Journal of Contemporary History,* 6 (1971), pp. 101–10.

Kelly, Joan. "Early Feminist Theory and the Querelle des Femmes, 1400–1789," *Signs,* 8 (1982), pp. 4–28.

——. "The Social Relation of the Sexes: Methodological Implications of Women's History," *Signs,* 1 (1975–76), pp. 809–23.

Kors, Alan C. *Witchcraft in Europe 1100–1700.* Philadelphia: University of Pennsylvania Press, 1972.

Kraditor, Aileen Selma. *The Ideas of the Woman Suffrage Movement 1890–1920.* New York: Columbia University Press, 1965.

Kunzle, David. *Fashion and Fetishism: A Social History of the Corset, Tight-Lacing and Other Forms of Body Sculpture in the West.* Totowa, NJ: Rowman and Littlefield, 1981.

Laslett, Peter. *The World We Have Lost.* New York: Scribner's, 1965.

————— and Wall, R. eds. *Household and Family in Past Time.* New York: Cambridge University Press, 1972.

Lauritsen, John, and Thorstad, David. *The Early Homosexual Rights Movement.* New York: Times Change Press, 1974.

Leadbetter, Rosanna. *History of the Malthusian League 1877–1927.* Columbus: Ohio State University Press, 1976.

Lewenhak, Sheila. *Woman and Work.* New York: St. Martin's, 1980.

Lougee, Carolyn C. "Modern European History," *Signs,* 2 (1976–77), pp. 628–50.

MacCurtain, Margaret, and O Corráin, Donncha. eds. *Women in Irish Society: The Historical Dimension.* Westport, CT: Greenwood, 1979.

MacLean, I. *The Renaissance Notion of Woman:* New York: Cambridge University Press, 1980.

Manheimer, Joan. "Murderous Mothers: The Problem of Parenting in the Victorian Novel," *Feminist Studies,* 5 (1979), pp. 530–46.

McBride, Theresa. *The Domestic Revolution: The Modernization of Household Service in England and France 1820–1920.* New York: Holmes & Meier, 1976.

McLaren, Angus. "Women's Work and Regulation of Family Size," *History Workshop,* no. 4 (1977), pp. 70–81.

Medick, Hans. "The Proto-industrial Family Economy: The Structural Function of Household and Family during the Transition from Peasant Society to Industrial Capitalism," *Social History,* 1 (1976), pp. 291–315.

Minge-Kalman, Wanda. "The Industrial Revolution and the European Family: The Industrialization of Childhood as a Market for Family Labor," *Comparative Studies in Society and History,* 20 (1978), pp. 469–82.

Mitchell, Juliet. *Psychoanalysis and Feminism.* New York: Vintage, 1974.

Mobius, Helga. *Woman in the Baroque Age.* Totowa, NJ: Allanheld, Osmun, 1983.

Monter, William E. ed. *European Witchcraft.* New York: Wiley, 1969.

Okin, Susan Moller. *Women in Western Political Thought.* Princeton: Princeton University Press, 1979.

Osborne, Martha L. *Woman in Western Thought.* New York: Random, 1979.

Padgug, Robert A. "Sexual Matters: On Conceptualizing Sexuality in History," *Radical History Review,* 20 (1979), pp. 3–24.

Peel, J., and Dowse, R. E. "The Politics of Birth Control," *Political Studies,* 13 (1965), pp. 181–97.

Putnam, Emily James. *The Lady: Studies of Certain Significant Phases of Her History.* Chicago: University of Chicago Press, 1970 (1910).

Ramas, Maria. "Freud's Dora, Dora's Hysteria: The Negation of a Woman's Rebellion," *Feminist Studies,* 6 (1980), pp. 472–510.

Riemer, Eleanor S., and Fout, John C. "Women's History: Recent Journal Articles," *Trends in History* 1 (1979), pp. 3–22.

Roberts, Helen. ed. *Doing Feminist Research.* London: Routledge and Kegan Paul, 1981.

Robertson, Priscilla. *An Experience of Women: Pattern and Change in Nineteenth-Century Europe*. Philadelphia: Temple University Press, 1982.

Rowbotham, Sheila. *Hidden from History*. New York: Pantheon, 1974.

———. *Woman's Consciousness, Man's World*. Harmondsworth: Penguin, 1973.

———. *Women, Resistance and Revolution*. New York: Pantheon, 1972.

———. *Women's Liberation and Revolution*. Bristol, England: Falling Water Press, 1973.

Ruether, Rosemary. ed. *Sexism and Religion: Images of Women in the Jewish and Christian Traditions*. New York: Simon and Schuster, 1974.

Scott, Joan W., and Tilly, Louise. "Women's Work and the Family in 19th Century Europe," *Comparative Studies in Society and History*, 17 (1975), pp. 36–64.

Shorter, Edward. "Female Emancipation, Birth Control and Fertility in European History," *American Historical Review*, 78 (1973), pp. 605–40.

———. "Illegitimacy, Sexual Revolution and Social Change in Modern Europe," *Journal of Interdisiplinary History*, 2 (1971), pp. 232–72.

———. *The Making of the Modern Family*. New York: Basic, 1975.

———. "Writing the History of Rape," *Signs*, 3 (1977), pp. 471–82.

———, Knodel, John, and Van de Walle, Etienne. "The Decline of Non-marital Fertility in Europe, 1880–1940," *Population Studies*, 25 (1971), pp. 375–93.

Slaughter, Jane, and Kern, Robert. eds. *European Women on the Left: Socialism, Feminism, and the Problems Faced by Political Women, 1880 to the Present*. Westport, CT: Greenwood Press, 1981.

Stanton, Theodore. ed. *The Woman Question in Europe*. New York: Irvington, 1974.

Stearns, Peter, N. ed. *The Rise of the Modern Woman*. Arlington Heights, IL: Forum Press, 1978.

Stimpson, Catharine, and Person, Ethel Spector, eds. *Women: Sex and Sexuality*. Chicago: University of Chicago Press, 1980.

Stock, Phyllis. *Better than Rubies: A History of Women's Education*. New York: Putnam, 1978.

Symonds, John Addington. *A Problem in Modern Ethics*. London: n.p., 1896.

Tilly, Louise A., and Scott, Joan W. *Women, Work, and Family*. New York: Holt, Rinehart & Winston, 1978.

———, ———, and Cohen, Miriam. "Women's Work and European Fertility Patterns," *Journal of Interdisciplinary History*, 6 (1976), pp. 447–76.

Vicinus, Martha. "Sexuality and Power: A Review of Current Work in the History of Sexuality," *Feminist Studies*, 8 (1982), pp. 133–56.

Watkins, Susan Cotts. "Regional Patterns of Nuptiality in Europe, 1870–1960," *Population Studies*, 35 (1981), pp. 199–215.

Women's Work Under Labour Law: A Survey of Protective Legislation. Geneva, International Labour Office. 1932.

Ellen Key (1849–1926)

Key, Ellen. *The Century of the Child.* New York: Putnam, 1909.

———. *The Renaissance of Motherhood.* New York: Source Book Press, 1970 (1914).

———. *War, Peace and the Future.* New York: Garland, 1972 (1916).

———. *The Woman Movement.* Westport, CT: Hyperion, 1976 (1912).

Nystrom-Hamilton, Louise. *Ellen Key: Her Life and Her Work.* New York: Putnam, 1913.

FRANCE

Abray, Jane. "Feminism in the French Revolution," *American Historical Review,* 80 (1975), pp. 43–62.

Backer, Dorothy. *Precious Women.* New York: Basic, 1974.

Berlanstein, Lenard R. "Illegitimacy, Concubinage, and Proletariatization in a French Rural Town, 1760–1914," *Journal of Family History,* 5 (1980), pp. 360–74.

Bidelman, Patrick Kay. "Maria Deraismes, León Richer, and the Founding of the French Feminist Movement 1866–1878," *Third Republic,* no. 3/4 (1977), pp. 20–73.

———. *Pariahs Stand Up! The Founding of the Liberal Feminist Movement in France 1858–1889.* Westport, CT: Greenwood Press, 1982.

———. "The Politics of French Feminism: Léon Richter and the Ligue Française pour les Droits des Femmes, 1882–1892," *Historical Reflections,* 3 (1976), 93–120.

Boxer, Marilyn J. "Foyer or Factory: Working Class Women in Nineteenth Century France," *Proceedings of the Western Society for French History,* 2 (1974), 194–206.

———. "French Socialism, Feminism, and the Family," *Third Republic,* no. 3/4 (1977), pp. 128–67.

Brinton, Crane. *French Revolutionary Legislation on Illegitimacy, 1789–1804.* Cambridge, MA: Harvard University Press, 1936.

Clark, Francis I. *The Position of Women in Contemporary France.* Westport, CT: Hyperion, 1981 (1937).

Clark, Linda L. "The Molding of the Citoyenne: The Image of the Female in French Educational Literature," *Third Republic,* no. 3/4 (1977), pp. 74–103.

———. "The Socialization of Girls in the Primary Schools of the Third Republic," *Journal of Social History,* 15 (1982), pp. 685–98.

Clinton, Katherine. "Femme et Philosophe: Enlightened Origins of Feminism," *Eighteenth Century Studies,* 8 (1975), pp. 283–98.

Darrow, Margaret H. "French Noblewomen and the New Domesticity 1750–1850," *Feminist Studies,* 5 (1979), pp. 41–65.

Davis, Natalie Z. *Society and Culture in Early Modern France.* Stanford: Stanford University Press, 1975.

Dobson, Austin. *Four Frenchwomen.* Salem, NH: Arno, 1972 (1893).

Dubois, Elfrieda T. "The Education of Women in Seventeenth-Century France," *French Studies,* 32 (1978), pp. 1–19.

Flandrin, Jean-Louis. *Families in Former Times: Kinship, Household and Sexuality in Early Modern France.* New York: Cambridge University Press, 1978.

Goldstein, Leslie F. "Early Feminist Themes in French Utopian Socialism: The St. Simonians and Fourier," *Journal of the History of Ideas,* 43 (1982), pp. 91–108.

Goncourt, Edward L. *The Woman of the Eighteenth Century.* Westport, CT: Hyperion, 1981 (1927).

Greenbaum, Louis S. "Nurses and Doctors in Conflict: Piety and Medicine in the Paris Hôtel-Dieu on the Eve of the French Revolution," *Clio Medica,* 13 (1979), pp. 347–68.

Gullickson, Gay L. "The Sexual Division of Labor in Cottage Industry and Agriculture in the Pays de Caux: Auffay, 1750 to 1850," *French Historical Studies,* 12 (1981), pp. 177–99.

Hause, Stephen C. "The Rejection of Women's Suffrage by the French Senate in November 1922: A Statistical Analysis," *Third Republic,* no. 3/4 (1977), pp. 205–37.

———. "Women Who Rallied to the Tricolor: The Effects of World War I on the French Women's Suffrage Movement," *Proceedings of the Western Society for French History,* 6 (1979), pp. 371–78.

———. and Kenny, Anne R. "The Development of the Catholic Women's Suffrage Movement in France, 1896–1922," *Catholic Historical Review,* 67 (1981), pp. 11–30.

———. "The Limits of Suffragist Behavior: Legalism and Militancy in France, 1876–1922," *American Historical Review,* 86 (1981), pp. 781–806.

———. "Woman's Suffrage and the Paris Elections of 1908," *Laurels,* 51 (1980), pp. 21–32.

Hedman, Edwin R. "Early French Feminism from the Eighteenth Century to 1848," Ph.D. dissertation, New York University, 1954.

Hellerstein, Erna O. "French Women and the Orderly Household, 1830–1870," *Proceedings of the Western Society for French History,* 3 (1975), pp. 378–89.

Horvath, Sandra A. "Victor Duruy and the Controversy over Secondary Education for Girls," *French Historical Studies,* 9 (1975), pp. 83–104.

Hufton, Olwen. *The Poor of Eighteenth Century France 1750–1789* New York: Oxford University Press, 1975.

———. "Women and the Family Economy in Eighteenth-Century France," *French Historical Studies,* 9 (1975), pp. 1–22.

———. "Women in Revolution 1789–1796," *Past and Present,* no. 53 (1971), pp. 90–108.

Hunt, Persis. "Feminism and Anti-clericalism under the Commune," *Massachusetts Review,* 12 (1971), pp. 418–31.

———. "Teachers and Workers: Problems of Feminist Organizing in the Early Third Republic," *Third Republic,* no. 3/4 (1977), pp. 168–204.

Jacobs, Eva. *Woman and Society in Eighteenth Century France: Essays in Honour of John Stephenson Spink.* Atlantic Highlands, NJ: Humanities, 1979.

Jones, Colin. "Prostitution and the Ruling Class in Eighteenth-Century Montpellier," *History Workshop,* no. 6 (1978), pp. 7–28.

Kanipe, Esther S. "Working-Class Women and the Social Question in Late 19th-Century France," *Proceedings of the Western Society for French History,* 6 (1979), pp. 298–306.

Kaplow, Jeffry. *The Names of Kings: The Parisian Laboring Poor in the Eighteenth Century.* New York: Basic, 1972.

Kavanagh, Julia. *French Women of Letters: Biographical Sketches.* 2 vols. Darby, PA: Darby Books, 1982 (1862).

———. *Women in France During the Eighteenth Century.* 2 vols. New York: Putnam, 1893.

Kline, Rayna. "Partisans, Godmothers, Bicyclists and Other Terrorists: Women in the French Resistance and under Vichy," *Proceedings of the Western Society for French History,* 5 (1977), pp. 375–83.

Levy, Darline, et al. eds. *Women in Revolutionary Paris, 1789–1795* Urbana: University of Illinois Press, 1979.

Lewis, H. D. "The Legal Status of Women in Nineteenth-Century France," *Journal of European Studies,* 10 (1980), pp. 178–88.

Litchfield, H. B., and Gordon, D. "Closing the Tour: A Close Look at the Marriage Market, Unwed Mothers, and Abandoned Children in Mid-Nineteenth Century Amiens," *Journal of Social History,* 13 (1980), pp. 458–73.

Longfellow, David. "The Silk Weavers and the Social Struggle in Lyon during the French Revolution, 1789–1794," *French Historical Studies,* 12 (1981), pp. 1–40.

Lougee, C. C. *Salons and Social Stratification in Seventeenth-Century France.* Princeton: Princeton University Press, 1976.

Lytle, Scott H. "The Second Sex, September 1793," *Journal of Modern History,* 27 (1955), pp. 14–26.

McBride, Theresa M. "A Woman's World: Department Stores and the Evolution of Women's Employment, 1870–1920," *French Historical Studies,* 10 (1978), pp. 664–83.

———. Women's Work: Mistress and Servant in the Nineteenth Century," *Proceedings of the Western Society for French History,* 3 (1975), pp. 390–97.

McCloy, Shelby T. "Charity Workshops for Women, Paris, 1790–1795," *Social Science Review,* 11 (1937), pp. 274–84.

McLaren, Angus. "Abortion in France: Women and the Regulation of Family Size 1800–1914," *French Historical Studies,* 10 (1978), pp. 461–85.

——. "Doctor in the House: Medicine and Private Morality in France, 1800–1850," *Feminist Studies,* 2 (1974–75), pp. 39–54.

——. "Sex and Socialism: The Opposition of the French Left to Birth Control in the Nineteenth Century," *Journal of the History of Ideas,* 37 (1976), pp. 475–92.

——. *Sexuality and Social Order: The Debate over the Fertility of Women and Workers in France, 1770–1920.* New York: Holmes & Meier, 1983.

——. "Some Secular Attitudes Toward Sexual Behavior in France: 1760–1860," *French Historical Studies,* 8 (1973–74), pp. 604–25.

McMillan, James. *Housewife or Harlot: The Woman Question in France under the Third Republic.* New York: St. Martin's, 1981.

May, Gita. *Madame Roland and the Age of Revolution.* New York: Columbia University Press, 1970.

Maza, Sara C. *Servants and Masters in Eighteenth-Century France.* Princeton: Princeton University Press, 1984.

Meyers, Peter V. "From Conflict to Cooperation: Men and Women Teachers in the Belle Epoque," *Historical Reflections,* 7 (1980), pp. 493–505.

Michelet, Jules. *The Women of the French Revolution.* Philadelphia: Baird, 1855.

Moreau, Thérèse. "Revolting Women: History and Modernity in Jules Michelet," *Clio,* 6 (1977), pp. 167–80.

Offen, Karen M. "Introduction: Aspects of the Woman Question during the Third Republic," *Third Republic,* no. 3/4 (1977), pp. 1–19.

——. "A Survey of Current Research in French History Related to Women, the Family, and Society," *Contemporary French Civilization,* 1 (1977), pp. 266–81.

Okin, Susan Moller. "Rousseau's Natural Woman," *Journal of Politics,* 41 (1979), pp. 393–416.

Phillips, Roderick. *Family Breakdown in Late Eighteenth Century France: Divorces in Rouen, 1792–1803.* New York: Oxford University Press, 1981.

——. "Women and Family Breakdown in Eighteenth Century France: Rouen 1780–1800," *Social History,* 1 (1976), pp. 197–218.

——. "Women's Emancipation, the Family and Social Change in Eighteenth-Century France," *Journal of Social History,* 12 (1979), pp. 553–67.

Pope, Barbara Corrado. "Maternal Education in France, 1815–1848," *Proceedings of the Western Society for French History,* 3 (1975), pp. 368–77.

Racz, Elizabeth. "The Women's Rights Movement in the French Revolution," *Science and Society,* 16 (1951–52), pp. 151–74.

Ravenel, Florence Leftovich. *Women and the French Tradition.* New York: Macmillan, 1918.

Rollet, Catherine. "Infant Feeding, Fostering and Infant Mortality in France at the End of the Nineteenth Century," *Population,* 33 (1978), pp. 1189–1204.

Rowan, Mary M. "Seventeenth Century French Feminism: Two Opposing Attitudes," *International Journal of Women's Studies,* 3 (1980), pp. 273–91.

Shaffer, John W. "Family, Class, and Young Women: Occupational Expectations in Nineteenth Century Paris," *Journal of Family History,* 3 (1978), pp. 63–77.

Shaktini, Namascar. "Displacing the Phallic Subject: Wittig's Lesbian Writing," *Signs,* 8 (1982), pp. 29–44.

Smith, Bonnie G. *Ladies of the Leisure Class: The Bourgeoises of Northern France in the Nineteenth Century.* Princeton: Princeton University Press, 1981.

Sokolnikova, Halina. *Nine Women: Drawn from the Epoch of the French Revolution.* Philadelphia: West, 1977 (1932).

Sowerwine, Charles. "The Organization of French Socialist Women, 1880–1914: A European Perspective for Women's Movements," *Historical Reflections,* 3 (1976), pp. 3–23.

———. *Sisters or Citizens? Women and Socialism in France since 1876.* New York: Cambridge University Press, 1982.

———. "Women Against the War: A Feminine Basis for Internationalism and Pacifism?" *Proceedings of the Western Society for French History,* 6 (1979), pp. 361–70.

———. "Women and the Origins of the French Socialist Party: A Neglected Contribution," *Third Republic,* no. 3/4 (1977), pp. 104–27.

———. "Workers and Women in France before 1914: The Debate over the Couriau Affair," *The Journal of Modern History,* 55 (1983), pp. 411–41.

Spencer, Samia I., and Millman, Mary M. "French and American Women in the Feminine Press: A Cross-Cultural Look," *Contemporary French Civilization,* 5 (1981), pp. 179–203.

Stephens, Winifred. *Women of the French Revolution.* London: Chapman & Hall, 1922.

Strumingher, Laura S. "L'Ange de la maison: Mothers and Daughters in Nineteenth Century France," *International Journal of Women's Studies,* 2 (1979), pp. 51–61.

———. *What Were Little Girls and Boys Made Of? Primary Education in Rural France, 1830–1880.* Albany, NY: S.U.N.Y. Press, 1982.

———. *Women and the Making of the Working Class: Lyon 1830–1870.* St. Albans, VT: Eden Press, 1978.

Sullerot, Evelyne. *Woman, Society and Change.* New York: McGraw-Hill, 1971.

Sussman, George. "Parisian Infants and Norman Wet Nurses in the Early Nineteenth Century: A Statistical Study," *Journal of Interdisciplinary History,* 7 (1977), pp. 637–54.

———. *Selling Mothers' Milk: The Wet-Nursing Business in France.* Urbana: University of Illinois Press, 1982.

———. "The Wet-Nursing Business in Nineteenth Century France," *French Historical Studies,* 9 (1975), pp. 304–28.

Thomas, Edith. *The Women Incendiaries.* New York: Braziller, 1966.

———. "Women of the Commune," *Massachusetts Review,* 12 (1971), pp. 409–17.

Tilly, Louise A. "Women's Collective Action and Feminism in France, 1870–1914," in Tilley, Louis A., and Tilley, Charles. eds. *Class Conflict and Collective Action.* Beverly Hills, CA: Sage, 1981.

Van de Walle, Etienne. *The Female Population of France in the Nineteenth Century.* Princeton: Princeton University Press, 1974.

Watson, Paul B. *Some Women of France.* Freeport, NY: Books for Libraries Press, 1969 (1936).

Wexler, Victor G. "'Made for Man's Delight': Rousseau as Antifeminist," *American Historical Review,* 81 (1976), pp. 266–91.

Whale, Winifred. *Women of the French Revolution.* New York: Dutton, 1922.

Wilkins, Wynona H. "The Debate over Secondary and Higher Education for Women in Nineteenth Century France," *North Dakota Quarterly,* 49 (1981), pp. 13–25.

———. "The Paris International Feminist Congress of 1896 and Its French Antecedents," *North Dakota Quarterly,* 43 (1975), pp. 5–28.

Simone de Beauvoir (1908–)

Ascher, Carol. *Simone de Beauvoir: A Life of Freedom.* Boston: Beacon Press, 1981.

Beauvoir, Simone de. *Memories of a Dutiful Daughter.* New York: Harper, 1959.

———. *The Second Sex.* New York: Knopf, 1952.

Evans, Mary. *Simone de Beauvoir.* Brighton, England: Harvester, 1982.

Marks, Elaine. *Simone de Beauvoir: Encounters with Death.* New Brunswick, NJ: Rutgers University Press, 1973.

Whitmarsh, Anne. *Simone de Beavoir and the Limits of Commitment.* New York: Cambridge University Press, 1982.

George Sand (1804–76)

Barry, Joseph. *Infamous Woman: The Life of George Sand.* Garden City, NY: Doubleday, 1976.

Cate, Curtis. *George Sand: A Biography.* Boston: Houghton Mifflin, 1975.

Edwards, Samuel. *George Sand: A Biography of the First Modern Liberated Woman.* New York: McKay, 1972.

Maurois, André. *Lélia: The Life of George Sand.* New York: Harper, 1953.

Sand, George. *The George Sand–Gustave Flaubert Letters.* Chicago: Academy Chicago, 1979 (1921).

———. *In Her Own Words.* Joseph Barry, ed. New York: Quartet Books, 1979.

———. *The Intimate Journal of George Sand.* Marie Jenny, ed. Chicago: Cassandra, 1977 (1929).

———. *My Life.* New York: Harper, 1979.

Sandars, Mary F. *George Sand.* London: Holden, 1927.

Seyd, Felizia. *Romantic Rebel: The Life and Times of George Sand.* New York: Viking, 1940.

Thomson, Patricia. *George Sand and the Victorians: Her Influence and Reputation in Nineteenth-Century England.* New York: Columbia University Press, 1977.

Winegarten, Renee. *The Double Life of George Sand, Woman and Writer: A Critical Biography.* New York: Basic, 1978.

Renée Vivien (1877–1909)

Vivien, Renée. *At the Sweet Hour of Hand-in-Hand.* Weatherby Lake, MO: Naiad Press, 1979.

———. *The Muse of the Violets.* Weatherby Lake, MO: Naiad Press, 1977.

———. *A Woman Appeared to Me.* Weatherby Lake, MO: Naiad Press, 1979.

GERMANY TO 1914

Albisetti, James C. "Could Separate Be Equal: Helene Lange and Women's Education in Imperial Germany," *History of Education Quarterly,* 22 (1982), pp. 301–17.

———. "The Fight for Female Physicians in Imperial Germany," *Central European History,* 15 (1982), pp. 99–123.

———. *Secondary School Reform in Imperial Germany.* Princeton: Princeton University Press, 1983.

Allen, Ann Taylor, "Sex and Satire in Wilhelmine Germany: 'Simplicissimus' Looks at Family Life," *Journal of European Studies,* 7 (1977), pp. 19–40.

Allen, Richard M. "Rebellion within the Household: Hans Sach's Conception of Women and Marriage," *Essays in History,* 19 (1975), pp. 43–74.

Anthony, Katharine. *Feminism in Germany and Scandinavia.* New York: Henry Holt, 1915.

Arendt, Hannah. *Rahel Varnhagen: The Life of a Jewish Woman.* New York: Harcourt Brace Jovanovich, 1974.

Bach, Matthew G. *Wieland's Attitude toward Woman and Her Cultural and Social Relations.* New York: A.M.S. Press, 1966 (1922).

Bainton, Roland H. *Women of the Reformation in Germany and Italy.* Minneapolis, MN: Augsburg, 1971.

Bajohr, Stefan. "Illegitimacy and the Working Class: Illegitimate Mothers in Brunswick, 1900–1913," in Evans, Richard J. ed. *The German Working Class 1888–1933: The Politics of Everyday Life.* Totowa, NJ: Barnes & Noble, 1982.

Bebel, August. *Women Under Socialism.* New York: Schocken, 1971.

Bernstein, George, and Bernstein, Lottelore. "Attitudes towards Women's Education in Germany, 1870–1914," *International Journal of Women's Studies,* 2 (1979), pp. 473–88.

————. "The Curriculum for German Girls' Schools 1870–1914," *Paedagogica Historica*, 18 (1978), pp. 275–95.

Binion, Rudolph. *Frau Lou: Nietzsche's Wayward Disciple*. Princeton: Princeton University Press, 1968.

Bottigheimer, Ruth B. "Tale Spinners: Submerged Voices in Grimm's Fairy Tales," *New German Critique*, no. 27 (1982), pp. 141–50.

————. "The Transformed Queen: A Search for the Origins of Negative Female Archetypes in Grimm's Fairy Tales," *Amsterdamer Beiträge*, 10 (1980), pp. 1–12.

Carlebach, Julius. "Family Structure and the Position of Jewish Women," in Mosse, Werner E., et al. eds. *Revolution and Evolution: 1848 in German-Jewish History*. Tübingen: Mohr, 1981.

————. "The Forgotten Connection: Women and Jews in the Conflict between Englightenment and Romanticism," *Leo Baeck Institute Year Book*, 24 (1979), pp. 107–36.

Cocalis, Susan L., and Goodman, Kay. eds. *Beyond the Eternal Feminine: Critical Essays on Women and German Literature*. Stuttgart: Akademischer Verlag Hans-Dieter Heinz, 1982.

Crompton, Louis. "The Myth of Lesbian Impunity: Capital Laws from 1270 to 1791," in Licata, Salvatore J., and Petersen, Robert M. eds. *Historical Perspectives on Homosexuality*. New York: Haworth Press, 1981.

Dasey, Robyn. "Women's Work and the Family: Women Garment Workers in Berlin and Hamburg Before the First World War," in Evans, Richard J., and Lee, W. R. eds. *The German Family*. Totowa, NJ: Barnes & Noble, 1981.

Dawson, Ruth P. "The Feminist Manifesto of Theodor Gottlieb von Hippel (1741–96)," *Amsterdamer Beiträge*, 10 (1980), pp. 13–32.

Dentler, Clara Louise. *Katherine Luther of Wittenberg Parsonage*. Philadelphia: Philadelphia Book Co., 1924.

Dohm, Hedwig. *Women's Nature and Privilege*. Westport, CT: Hyperion, 1976 (1876).

Drewitz, Ingeborg. "Bettine von Arnim: A Portrait," *New German Critique*, no. 27 (1982), pp. 115–22.

Ende, Aurel. "Battering and Neglect: Children in Germany, 1860–1978," *Journal of Psychohistory*, 7 (1979–80), pp. 249–79.

Eriksson, Brigitte. trans. "A Lesbian Execution in Germany, 1721: The Trial Records," in Licata, Salvatore J., and Petersen, Robert M. eds. *Historical Perspectives on Homosexuality*. New York: Haworth Press, 1981.

Evans, Richard J. "Feminism and Female Emancipation in Germany 1870–1945: Sources, Methods, and Problems of Research," *Central European History*, 9 (1976), pp. 323–51.

————. *The Feminist Movement in Germany 1894–1933*. Beverly Hills, CA: Sage, 1976.

————. "German Social Democracy and Women's Suffrage 1891–1918," *Journal of Contemporary History*, 15 (1980), pp. 533–57.

————. "Liberalism and Society: The Feminist Movement and Social Change," in Evans, Richard J. ed. *Society and Politics in Wilhelmine Germany*. New York: Barnes & Noble, 1978.

————. "Politics and the Family: Social Democracy and the Working-Class Family in Theory and Practice Before 1914," in Evans, Richard J., and Lee, W. R. eds. *The German Family*. Totowa, NJ: Barnes & Noble, 1981.

————. "Prostitution, State and Society in Imperial Germany," *Past and Present*, no. 70 (1976), pp. 106–29.

Faderman, Lillian, and Eriksson, Brigitte. eds. *Lesbian-Feminism in Turn-of-the-Century Germany*. Weatherby Lake, MO: Naiad Press, 1980.

Fleischer, Manfred P. "'Are Women Human'—The Debate of 1595 Between Valens Acidalius and Simon Gedicus," *Sixteenth Century Journal*, 12 (1981), pp. 107–20.

Fontane, Theodor. *Effi Briest*. Baltimore: Penguin, 1976.

————. *Jenny Treibel*. New York: Ungar, 1977.

Frank, Miriam. "Ricarda Huch: Myth and Reality," in Cocalis, Susan L., and Goodman, Kay. eds. *Beyond the Eternal Feminine*. Stuttgart: Akademischer Verlag Hans-Dieter Heinz, 1982.

Frederiksen, Elke. "German Woman Writers in the Nineteenth Century: Where Are They?" in Cocalis, Susan L., and Goodman, Kay. eds. *Beyond the Eternal Feminine*. Stuttgart: Akademischer Verlag Hans-Dieter Heinz, 1982.

Fromm, Katherine Barber. "German Women in the 1882 Occupational Census." M.A. Thesis, Iowa State University, 1983.

Gluckel of Hameln. *The Memoirs of Gluckel of Hameln*. New York: Schocken, 1977.

Goodman, Kay. "The Impact of Rahel Varnhagen on Women in the 19th Century," *Amsterdamer Beiträge*, 10 (1980), pp. 125–54.

————. "Poesis and Praxis in Rahel Varnhagen's Letters," *New German Critique*, no. 27 (1982), pp. 123–40.

Green, Lowell. "Education of Women in the Reformation," *History of Education Quarterly*, 19 (1979), pp. 93–116.

Guinsburg, Arlene Miller. "The Counterthrust to Sixteenth Century Misogyny: The Work of Agrippa and Paracelsus," *Historical Reflections*, 8 (1981), pp. 3–28.

Hackett, Amy. "Feminism and Liberalism in Wilhelmine Germany, 1890–1918," in Carrol, Berenice A. ed. *Liberating Women's History*. Urbana: University of Illinois Press, 1976.

————. "The German Women's Movement and Suffrage, 1890–1914: A Study of National Feminism," in Bezucha, Robert J. ed. *Modern European Social History*. Lexington, MA: Heath, 1972.

————. "The Politics of Feminism in Wilhelmine Germany, 1890–1918," Ph.D. dissertation, Columbia University, 1976.

Harrigan, Renny. "The Limits of Emancipation: A Study of Fontane's Lower Class Women," *Monatshefte* 70 (1978), pp. 117–28.

Harris, Edward P. "From Outcast to Ideal: The Image of the Actress in Eighteenth-Century Germany," *German Quarterly,* 54 (1981), pp. 177–87.

Hausen, Karin. "Family and Role-division: The Polarisation of Sexual Stereotypes in the Nineteenth Century—An Aspect of the Dissociation of Work and Family Life," in Evans, Richard J., and Lee, W. R. eds. *The German Family.* Totowa, NJ: Barnes & Noble, 1981.

Hertz, Deborah. "Salonières and Literary Women in Late Eighteenth Century Berlin," *New German Critique,* 5 (1978), 97–108.

———. "The Varnhagen Collection Is in Krakow," *American Archivist,* 44 (1981), pp. 223–28.

Hippel, Theodor Gottlieb von. *On Improving the Status of Women.* Timothy F. Sellner, ed. Detroit: Wayne State University Press, 1979.

Honeycutt, Karen. "Clara Zetkin: A Left-Wing Socialist and Feminist in Wilhelmian Germany," Ph.D. dissertation, Columbia University, 1975.

———. "Clara Zetkin: A Socialist Approach to the Problem of Woman's Oppression," *Feminist Studies,* 3 (3/4) (1975–76), pp. 131–44.

———. "Socialism and Feminism in Imperial Germany," *Signs,* 5 (1979–80), pp. 30–41.

Hoverland, Lilian. "Heinrich von Kleist and Luce Irigaray: Visions of the Feminine," *Amsterdamer Beiträge,* 10 (1980), pp. 57–82.

Imhof, Arthur E. "Historical Demography as Social History: Possibilities in Germany," *Journal of Family History,* 2 (1977), pp. 305–32.

———. "Women, Family and Death: Excess Mortality of Women in Childbearing Age in Four Communities in Nineteenth-Century Germany," in Evans, Richard J., and Lee, W. R. eds. *The German Family.* Totowa, NJ: Barnes & Noble, 1981.

Joeres, Ruth-Ellen Boetcher. "The Ambiguous World of Hedwig Dohm," *Amsterdamer Beiträge,* 10 (1980), pp. 255–76.

———. "Ein Dichter: An Introduction to the World of Luise Büchner," *German Quarterly,* 52 (1979), pp. 32–49.

———. "Louise Otto and Her Journals: A Chapter in Nineteenth Century German Feminism," *Internationales Archiv für Sozialgeschichte der deutschen Literatur,* 4 (1979), pp. 100–29.

———. "The Triumph of the Woman: Johanna Kinkel's *Hans Ibeles in London* (1860)," *Euophorian,* 70 (1976), pp. 187–207.

Johnson, Eric A., and McHale, Vincent E. "Socioeconomic Aspects of the Delinquency Rate in Imperial Germany, 1882–1914," *Journal of Social History,* 13 (1980), pp. 384–402.

Johnson, Richard L. "Gabriele Reuter: Romantic and Realist," in Cocalis, Susan L., and Goodman, Kay. eds. *Beyond the Eternal Feminine.* Stuttgart: Akademischer Verlag Hans-Dieter Heinz, 1982.

———. "Men's Power over Women in Gabriele Reuter's *Aus Guter Familie,*" *Amsterdamer Beiträge,* 10 (1980), pp. 235–54.

Kaplan, Marion A. "The Acculturation, Assimilation and Integration of Jews in Imperial Germany: A Gender Analysis," *Leo Baeck Institute Yearbook,* 27 (1982), pp. 3–35.

———. *The Campaign for Women's Suffrage in the Jewish Community in Germany.* New York: Yivo, 1976.

———. "German-Jewish Feminism in the Twentieth Century," *Jewish Social Studies,* 38 (1976), pp. 39–54.

———. The Jewish Feminist Movement in Germany: The Campaigns of the Jüdischer Frauenbund 1904–1938. Westport, CT: Greenwood Press, 1979.

———. "Women's Strategies in the Jewish Community in Germany." *New German Critique,* 5 (1978), pp. 109–18.

Kennedy, Hubert C. "The 'Third Sex' Theory of Karl Heinrich Ulrichs," in Licata, Salvatore J., and Petersen, Robert M. eds. *Historical Perspectives on Homosexuality.* New York: Haworth Press, 1981.

Key, Ellen, *Rahel Varnhagen.* Westport, CT: Hyperion, 1976 (1913).

Klein, Mina C., and Klein, H. Arthur. *Käthe Kollwitz: Life in Art.* New York: Schocken, 1975.

Knodel, John E. *The Decline of Fertility in Germany 1871–1939.* Princeton: Princeton University Press, 1974.

———. "Natural Fertility in Pre-industrial Germany," *Population Studies,* 32 (1978), pp. 481–510.

———. "Malthus Amiss: Marriage Restrictions in Nineteenth Century Germany," *Social Sciences,* 27 (1972), pp. 40–45.

——— and De Vos, Susan. "Preferences for the Sex of Offspring and Demographic Behavior in Eighteenth- and Nineteenth-Century Germany: An Examination of Evidence from Village Genealogies," *Journal of Family History,* 5 (1980), pp. 145–66.

——— and Maynes, Mary Jo. "Urban and Rural Marriage Patterns in Imperial Germany," *Journal of Family History,* 1 (1976), pp. 129–68.

LaFleur, Ingrun. "Five Socialist Women: Traditionalist Conflicts and Socialist Visions in Austria, 1893–1934," in Boxer, Marilyn J., and Quataert, Jean H. eds. *Socialist Women.* New York: Elsevier, 1978.

Lange, Helene. *Higher Education of Women in Europe.* New York: Appleton, 1901.

Lee, W. R. "Bastardy and the Socio-economic Structure of South Germany," *Journal of Interdisciplinary History,* 7 (1977), pp. 403–25.

———. "Family and 'Modernisation': The Peasant Family and Social Change in Nineteenth-century Bavaria," in Evans, Richard J., and Lee, W. R. eds. *The German Family.* Totowa, NJ: Barnes & Noble, 1981.

———. "Medicalisation and Mortality Trends in South Germany in the Early Nineteenth Century," in Imhof, Arthur E. ed. *Mensch und Gesundheit in der Geschichte.* Husum: Matthieson Verlag, 1980.

———. "Past Legacies and Future Prospects: Recent Research on the History of the Family in Germany," *Journal of Family History,* 6 (1981), pp. 156–76.

————. *Population Growth, Economic Development and Social Change in Bavaria, 1750–1850*. New York: Arno, 1977.

————. "Primary Sector Output and Mortality Change in Early Nineteenth Century Bavaria," *Journal of European Economic History*, 6 (1977), pp. 133–62.

Lenk, Elisabeth. "Indiscretions of the Literary Beast: Pariah Consciousness of Women Writers Since Romanticism," *New German Critique*, no. 27 (1982), pp. 101–14.

Lindemann, Mary. "Love for Hire: The Regulation of the Wet-Nursing Business in Eighteenth-Century Hamburg," *Journal of Family History*, 6 (1981), pp. 379–95.

McClain, William H., and Joeres, Ruth-Ellen Boetcher. "Three Unpublished Letters from Robert Schweichel to Louise Otto," *Monatshefte*, 72 (1980), pp. 39–50.

Marholm, Laura. *Studies in the Psychology of Women*. Georgia S. Etchison, ed. Chicago: Herbert S. Stone, 1899.

Matenko, Percy. "Ludwig Tieck and Rahel Varnhagen," *Leo Baeck Institute Yearbook*, 20 (1975), pp. 225–46.

Maynes, Mary Jo. "Theory and Method in Recent German Historical Studies," *Journal of Interdisciplinary History*, 10 (1979), pp. 311–17.

Meyer, Alfred G. "Lily Braun," *Signs*, 6 (1980–81), pp. 355–58.

Meyer, Marsha. "*Wally, die Zweiflerin* and *Madonna:* A Discussion of Sex-Socialization in the Nineteenth Century," in Cocalis, Susan L., and Goodman, Kay. eds. *Beyond the Eternal Feminine*. Stuttgart: Akademischer Verlag Hans-Dieter Heinz, 1982.

Midelfort, H. C. Erik. *Witch Hunting in Southwestern Germany 1562–1684*. Stanford, CA: Stanford University Press, 1972.

Monter, E. William. "Women in Calvinist Geneva (1550–1800)," *Signs*, 6 (1980–81), pp. 189–209.

Neuman, Allen R. "The Influence of Family and Friends on German Internal Migration, 1880–85," *Journal of Social History*, 13 (1979), pp. 277–88.

Neuman, Robert P. "Industrialization and Sexual Behavior: Some Aspects of Working Class Life in Imperial Germany," in Bezucha, Robert J. ed. *Modern European Social History*. Lexington, MA: Heath, 1972.

————. "The Sexual Question and Social Democracy in Imperial Germany," *Journal of Social History*, 7 (1974), pp. 278–81.

————. "Working Class Birth Control in Wilhelmine Germany," *Comparative Studies in Society and History*, 20 (1978), pp. 408–28.

Petschauer, Peter. "Improving Educational Opportunities for Girls in Eighteenth-Century Germany," *Eighteenth-Century Life*, 3 (1976), pp. 56–62.

Pickle, Linda Schelbitzki. "Self-Contraditions in the German Naturalists' View of Women's Emancipation," *German Quarterly*, 52 (1979), pp. 442–56.

Popp, Adelheid. *Autobiography of a Working Woman*. Chicago: Browne, 1913.

Prelinger, Catherine M. "Religious Dissent, Women's Rights, and the Hamburger

Hochschule für das weibliche Geschlecht in Mid-Nineteenth Century Germany," *Church History*, 45 (1976), pp. 42–55.

Quataert, Jean H. "Feminist Tactics in German Social Democracy, 1890–1914: A Dilemma," *Internationale wissenschaftliche Korrespondenz zur Geschichte der deutschen Arbeiterbewegung (IWK)*, 13 (1977) pp. 48–65.

———. "The German Socialist Women's Movement 1890–1918: Issues, Internal Conflicts and the Main Personages," Ph.D. dissertation, University of California, 1974.

———. *Reluctant Feminists in German Social Democracy, 1885–1917*. Princeton: Princeton University Press, 1979.

———. "Unequal Partners in an Uneasy Alliance: Women and the Working Class in Imperial Germany," in Boxer, Marilyn J., and Quataert, Jean H. eds. *Socialist Women*. New York: Elsevier, 1978.

Radycki, J. Diane. ed. *The Letters and Journals of Paula Modersohn-Becker.* Metuchen, NJ: Scarecrow Press, 1980.

Reissner, H. G. "Henriette Mendelssohn: Unresolved Conflicts of Interpretation," *Leo Baeck Institute Yearbook*, 21 (1976), pp. 247–58.

Russell, Alys. "On Social Democracy and the Woman Question in Germany," in Russell, Bertrand. *German Social Democracy*. London: Longmans, Green, 1896.

Safley, Thomas Max. "Marital Litigation in the Diocese of Constance, 1551–1620," *Sixteenth Century Journal*, 12 (1981), pp. 61–77.

Salomon, Alice. *Labour Laws for Women in Germany*. London: Women's Industrial Council, 1907.

Sanford, Jutta Schroers. "The Origins of German Feminism: German Women 1789–1870," Ph.D. dissertation, Ohio State University, 1976.

Schirmacher, Kaethe. *The Modern Woman's Rights Movements*. Westport, CT: Hyperion, 1976 (1912).

Schneider, Joanne. "An Historical Examination of Women's Education in Bavaria: Mädchenschulen and Contemporary Attitudes about Them, 1799–1848," Ph.D. dissertation, Brown University, 1977.

Schreiber, Sara Etta. *The German Woman in the Age of Enlightenment: A Study in the Drama from Gottsched to Lessing*. New York: Kings Crown Press, 1948.

Scott, Marilyn. "Laura Marholm (1854–1928), Germany's Ambivalent Feminist," *Women's Studies*, 7 (1980), pp. 87–96.

[Scott-]Jones, Marilyn. "Laura Marholm and the Question of Female Nature," in Cocalis, Susan L., and Goodman, Kay. eds. *Beyond the Eternal Feminine*. Stuttgart: Akademischer Verlag Hans-Dieter Heinz, 1982.

Shorter, Edward. "Bastardy in South Germany: A Comment," *Journal of Interdisciplinary History*, 8 (1978), pp. 459–76.

Stark, Gary D. "Pornography, Society, and the Law in Imperial Germany," *Central European History*, 14 (1981), pp. 200–29.

Steakley, James D. *The Homosexual Emancipation Movement in Germany*. New York: Arno, 1975.

————. ed. *Lesbianism and Feminism*. New York: Arno, 1975.

Stearns, Peter N. "Adaptation to Industrialization: German Workers as a Test Case," *Central European History*, 3 (1970), pp. 313–31.

Strain, Jacqueline. "Feminism and Political Radicalism in the German Social Democratic Movement, 1890–1914," Ph.D. dissertation, University of California, Berkeley, 1964.

Taylor, Paul, and Rebel, Hermann. "Hessian Peasant Women, Their Families and the Draft: A Social-Historical Interpretation of Four Tales from the Grimm Collection," *Journal of Family History*, 6 (1981), pp. 347–78.

Thönnessen, Werner. *The Emancipation of Women: The Rise and Decline of the Women's Movement in German Social Democracy 1863–1933*. London: Pluto Press, 1973.

Wagner, Maria M. "A German Writer and Feminist in Nineteenth-Century America: An Archival Study of Mathilde Franziska Anneke," in Cocalis, Susan L., and Goodman, Kay. eds. *Beyond the Eternal Feminine*. Stuttgart: Akademischer Verlag Hans-Dieter Heinz, 1982.

Waldstein, Edith. "Bettine von Arnim and the Literary Salon: Women's Participation in the Cultural Life of Early Nineteenth-Century Germany." Ph.D. dissertation, Washington University, 1982.

Weisner, Merry E. "Early Modern Midwifery: A Case Study," *International Journal of Women's Studies*, 6 (1983), pp. 26–43.

————. "Paltry Peddlers or Essential Merchants? Women in the Distributive Trades in Early Modern Nuremberg," *Sixteenth Century Journal*, 12 (1981), pp. 3–13.

Zucker, Stanley. "German Women and the Revolution of 1848: Kathinka Zitz-Halein and the Humania Association," *Central European History*, 13 (1980), pp. 237–54.

GERMANY 1914–45

Arnothy, Christine. *I Am Fifteen and I Don't Want to Die*. New York: Dutton, 1956.

Blauel, Hans Peter. *Sex and Society in Nazi Germany*. Philadelphia: Lippincott, 1973.

Bock, Gisela. "Racism and Sexism in Nazi Germany: Motherhood, Compulsory Sterilization, and the State," *Signs*, 8 (1983), pp. 400–21.

Bridenthal, Renate. "Beyond *Kinder, Küche, Kirche:* Weimar Women at Work," *Central European History*, 6 (1973), pp. 148–66.

———— and Koonz, Claudia. "Beyond *Kinder, Küche, Kirche:* Weimar Women in Politics and Work," in Carroll, Berenice A. ed. *Liberating Women's History*. Urbana: University of Illinois Press, 1976.

"The Employment of Women in Germany under the National Socialist Regime," *International Labour Review*, 44 (1941), pp. 617–59.

Evans, Richard J. "German Women and the Triumph of Hitler," *The Journal of Modern History*, 48 (1976), pp. 123–75.

Fessenden, Patricia K. "More Than a Question of Numbers: Women Deputies in the German National Constituent Assembly and the Reichstag, 1919–1933," in Goodman, Kay, and Sanders, Ruth H. eds. *Proceedings of the Second Annual Women in German Symposium*. Oxford, OH: Miami University, 1977.

Grossman, Atina. "Abortion and Economic Crisis: The 1931 Campaign Against #218 in Germany," *New German Critique*, 5 (1978), pp. 119–37.

––––––. "The New Woman and the Rationalization of Sexuality in Weimar Germany," in Snitow, Ann; Stansell, Christine; and Thompson, Sharon. eds. *Powers of Desire: The Politics of Sexuality*. New York: Monthly Review Press, 1983.

Grunberger, Richard. *The Twelve Year Reich: A Social History of Nazi Germany, 1933–1945*. New York: Holt, Rinehart and Winston, 1971.

Grünfeld, Judith. "Mobilization of Women in Germany," *Social Research*, 9 (1942), pp. 476–94.

Haeberle, Erwin J. "'Stigmata of Degeneration': Prisoner Marking in Nazi Concentration Camps," in Licata, Salvatore J., and Petersen, Robert M. eds. *Historical Perspectives on Homosexuality*. New York: Haworth Press, 1981.

Hannah, Gertrud. "Women in the German Trade Union Movement," *International Labour Review*, 8 (1923), pp. 21–37.

Harrigan, Renny. "The Stereotype of the Emancipated Woman in the Weimar Republic," in Goodman, Kay, and Sanders, Ruth H. eds. *Proceedings of the Second Annual Women in German Symposium*. Oxford, OH: Miami University, 1977.

Hillesum, Etty. *An Interrupted Life: The Diaries of Etty Hillesum 1941–1943*. New York: Pantheon, 1983.

Holland, Carolsue, and Garett, G. R. "The 'Skirt' of Nessus: Women and The German Opposition to Hitler," *International Journal of Women's Studies*, 6 (1983), pp. 363–81.

Kirk, Robert, *Women in Hitler's Germany: The Limits of Misogyny*. Chicago: Academy Chicago Ltd., forthcoming.

Kirkpatrick, Clifford. *Nazi Germany: Its Women and Family Life*. New York: Bobbs-Merrill, 1938.

Koonz, Claudia. "Conflicting Alliances: Political Ideology and Women Legislators in Weimar Germany," *Signs*, 1 (1975–76), pp. 663–83.

––––––. "Mothers in the Fatherland: Women in Nazi Germany," in Bridenthal, Renate, and Koonz, Claudia. eds. *Becoming Visible*. Boston: Houghton Mifflin, 1977.

––––––. "Nazi Women Before 1933: Rebels Against Emancipation," *Social Science Quarterly*, 56 (1976), pp. 553–63.

Laska, Vera. ed. *Women in the Resistance and in the Holocaust: The Voices of Eyewitnesses.* Westport, CT: Greenwood Press, 1983.

Lautmann, Rüdiger. "The Pink Triangle: The Persecution of Homosexual Males in Concentration Camps in Nazi Germany," in Licata, Salvatore J., and Petersen, Robert P. eds. *Historical Perspectives on Homosexuality.* New York: Haworth Press, 1981.

Leber, Annelore. "The Contribution of Women," in *Germans Against Hitler: July 20, 1944.* Bonn: Press and Information Office of the Federal Republic of Germany, 1969.

McIntyre, Jill R. "Women and the Professions in Germany, 1930–1940," in Nicholls, Anthony, and Matthias, Erich. eds. *German Democracy and the Triumph of Hitler.* New York: St. Martin's, 1971.

Mason, Tim. "Women in Germany, 1925–1940: Family, Welfare and Work," *History Workshop,* no. 2 (1976), pp. 5–32.

———. "Women in Nazi Germany," *History Workshop,* no. 1 (1976), pp. 74–113.

Neff, Hildegarde. *The Gift Horse: Report on a Life.* New York: McGraw-Hill, 1971.

Nicholls, Anthony, and Mattias, Erich. eds. *German Democracy and the Triumph of Hitler: Essays in Recent German History.* New York: St. Martin's, 1971.

Pauwels, Jacques R. "German Women University Students, National Socialism and the War, 1939–1945," in Goodman, Kay, and Sanders, Ruth H. eds. *Proceedings of the Second Annual Women in German Symposium.* Oxford, OH: Miami University, 1977.

Peterson, Brian. "The Politics of Working-Class Women in the Weimar Republic," *Central European History,* 10 (1977), pp. 87–111.

Pore, Renate. *A Conflict of Interest: Women in German Social Democracy, 1919–1933.* Westport, CT: Greenwood Press, 1981.

Puckett, Hugh Wiley. *Germany's Women Go Forward.* New York: Columbia University Press, 1930.

Rupp, Leila J. "'I Don't Call That Volksgemeinschaft': Women, Class, and War in Nazi Germany," in Berkin, Carol R., and Lovett, Clara M. eds. *Women, War, and Revolution.* New York: Holmes & Meier, 1980.

———. *Mobilizing Women for War: German and American Propaganda, 1939–1945.* Princeton: Princeton University Press, 1978.

———. "Mother of the *Volk:* The Image of Women in Nazi Ideology," *Signs,* 3 (1977–78), pp. 362–79.

Schoenbaum, David. *Hitler's Social Revolution: Class and Status in Nazi Germany 1933–39.* Garden City, NY: Anchor, 1966.

Scholl, Inge. *Students Against Tyranny: The Resistance of the White Rose.* Middletown, CT: American Education Publications, 1970 (1952).

Scholtz-Klink, Gertrud. *Tradition Is Not Stagnation But Involves a Moral Obligation: Women's Conference at the National Congress of Greater Germany.* Nuremburg: Deutsches Frauenwerk, 1938.

Sender, Toni. *The Autobiography of a German Rebel.* New York: Vanguard, 1939.

Shelton, Regina Maria. *To Lose a War: Memories of a German Girl.* Carbondale: Southern Illinois University Press, 1982.

Staden, Wendelgard Von. *Darkness Over the Valley.* New Haven, CT: Ticknor and Fields, 1981.

Stephenson, Jill. "Girls' Higher Education in Germany in the 1930s," *Journal of Contemporary History,* 10 (1975), pp. 41–69.

———. *The Nazi Organization of Women.* Totowa, NJ: Barnes & Noble, 1981.

———. *Women in Nazi Society.* New York: Barnes & Noble, 1975.

———. "Women's Labor Service in Nazi Germany," *Central European History,* 15 (1982), pp. 241–65.

Thomas, Katherine. *Women in Nazi Germany.* London: Gollancz, 1943.

Tillion, Germaine. *Ravensbruck: An Eyewitness Account of a Women's Concentration Camp.* Garden City, NY: Anchor, 1975.

Wheeler, Robert. "German Women and the Communist International: The Case of the Independent Social Democrats," *Central European History,* 8 (1975), pp. 113–39.

Zassenhaus, Hiltgunt. *Walls: Resisting the Third Reich—One Woman's Story.* Boston: Beacon Press, 1974.

GREAT BRITAIN

Alaya, Flavia. "Victorian Science and the 'Genius' of Woman," *Journal of the History of Ideas,* 38 (1977), pp. 261–80.

Anderson, Michael. *Family Structure in Nineteenth Century Lancashire.* New York: Cambridge University Press, 1970.

Anderson, Olive. "Did Suicide Increase with Industrialization in Victorian England?", *Past and Present,* no. 86 (1980), pp. 149–73.

———. "The Incidence of Civil Marriage in Victorian England and Wales," *Past and Present,* no. 69 (1975), pp. 50–87.

Andre, Caroline S. "Some Selected Aspects of the Role of Women in Sixteenth Century England," *International Journal of Women's Studies,* 4 (1981), pp. 76–88.

Austin, Sarah Taylor. *Two Letters on Girls' Schools, and on the Training of Working Women.* London: Chapman & Hall, 1857.

Banks, Joseph. *Prosperity and Parenthood: A Study of Family Planning Among the Victorian Middle Classes.* London: Routledge & Kegan Paul, 1954.

——— and Banks, Olive. *Feminism and Family Planning in Victorian England.* New York: Schocken, 1964.

Bayne, Powell. *Housekeeping in the Eighteenth Century.* London: Murray, 1956.

Beattie, J. M. "The Criminality of Women in Eighteenth-Century England," *Journal of Social History,* 8 (1975), pp. 80–116.

Becker, Lydia. *The Rights and Duties of Women in Local Government.* Manchester: Ireland, 1879.

Beeton, I. M. *The Book of Household Management.* London: Ward and Lock, 1899.

Behlmer, George K. "Deadly Motherhood: Infanticide and Medical Opinion in Mid-Victorian England," *Journal of the History of Medicine and Allied Sciences,* 34 (1979), pp. 403–27.

Besant, Annie. *The Law of Population.* London: Butts, 1878.

Black, Clementina. ed. *Married Women's Work.* London: Bell, 1915.

Blackburn, Helen. *A Handbook for Women Engaged in Social and Political Work.* Bristol: Arrowsmith, 1895.

————. *Women's Suffrage: A Record of the Women's Suffrage Movement in the British Isles.* New York: Source Book Press, 1970 (1902).

———— and Vynne, Nora. *Women under the Factory Acts.* London: Williams and Norgate, 1903.

Blakeley, Brian L. "Women and Imperialism: The Colonial Office and Female Emigration to South Africa, 1909–1910," *Albion,* 13 (1981), pp. 131–49.

Blease, W. Lyon. *The Emancipation of English Women.* Salem, NH: Arno, 1977 (1910).

Bondfield, Margaret. *A Life's Work.* London: Hutchinson, 1948.

Boone, Gladys. *The Women's Trade Union Leagues in Great Britain and the United States.* New York: Columbia University Press, 1942.

Boos, Florence, and Boos, William. "Catharine Macaulay: Historian and Political Reformer," *International Journal of Women's Studies,* 3 (1980), pp. 49–65.

Bostick, Theodora P. "Women's Suffrage, the Press and the Reform Bill of 1867," *International Journal of Women's Studies,* 3 (1980), pp. 373–90.

Boucé, Paul-Gabriel, ed. *Sexuality in Eighteenth-Century Britain.* Totowa, NJ: Barnes & Noble, 1982.

Boyd, Elizabeth F. *Bloomsbury Heritage: Their Mothers and Their Aunts.* New York: Taplinger, 1976.

Boyd, Nancy. *Three Victorian Women Who Changed Their World: Josephine Butler, Octavia Hill, Florence Nightingale.* New York: Oxford University Press, 1982.

Branca, Patricia. *Silent Sisterhood: Middle Class Women in the Victorian Home.* Pittsburgh: Carnegie-Mellon University Press, 1975.

Braybon, Gail. *Women Workers in the First World War: The British Experience.* Totowa, NJ: Barnes & Noble, 1981.

Brennan, Teresa, and Pateman, Carole. "'Mere Auxiliaries to the Commonwealth': Women and the Origins of Liberalism," *Political Studies,* 27 (1979), pp. 183–200.

Bristow, Edward. *Vice and Vigilance: Purity Movements in Britain Since 1700.* Dublin: Gill and Macmillan, 1977.

Brittain, Vera. *Lady into Woman: A History of Women From Victoria to Elizabeth II.* New York: Macmillan, 1953.

Brown, P. S. "Female Pills and the Reputation of Iron as an Abortifacient," *Medical History,* 21 (1977), pp. 291–304.

Browne, Stella F. W. "Women and Birth Control," in Paul, Eden, and Paul, Cedar. eds. *Population and Birth Control.* New York: Critic and Guide, 1917.

Burnet, John. *Plenty and Want: A Social History of Diet in England from 1815 to the Present Day.* London: Penguin, 1966.

Burstyn, Joan. *Victorian Education and the Ideal of Womanhood.* Totowa, NJ: Barnes & Noble, 1980.

Bythell, Duncan. *The Sweated Trades.* New York: St. Martin's, 1978.

Calder, Jenni. *Women and Marriage in Victorian Fiction.* New York: Oxford University Press, 1976.

Carlton, Charles. "The Widow's Tale: Male Myths and Female Reality in Sixteenth and Seventeenth Century England," *Albion,* 10 (1978), pp. 118–29.

Chamberlain, Mary. *Fenwomen: A Portrait of Women in an English Village.* London: Virago, 1977.

Chandresekhar, Sripati. ed. *A Dirty Filthy Book: The Writings of Charles Knowlton and Annie Besant on Birth Control and Reproductive Physiology and an Account of the Bradlaugh-Besant Trial.* Berkeley: University of California Press, 1981.

Clark, Alice. *Working Life of Women in the Seventeenth Century.* New York: Kelly, 1968.

Colby, Vineta. *The Singular Anomaly: Women Novelists of the Nineteenth Century.* New York: New York University Press, 1970.

Cole, Margaret I. *Women of To-day.* Freeport, NY: Books for Libraries Press, 1968 (1938).

Crafts, N. F. R. "Average Age of First Marriage for Women in Mid-Nineteenth-Century England and Wales: A Cross-Section Study," *Population Studies,* 32 (1978), pp. 21–25.

Crangle, John V., and Baylen, Joseph O. "Emily Hobhouse's Peace Mission, 1916," *Journal of Contemporary History,* 14 (1979), pp. 731–44.

Crow, Duncan. *The Edwardian Woman.* New York: St. Martin's, 1978.

Cunningham, C. W. *English Women's Clothing in the Nineteenth Century.* London: Faber and Faber, 1952.

Davidoff, Leonore. *The Best Circles: Women and Society in Victorian England.* Totowa, NJ: Rowman and Littlefield, 1973.

———. "Class and Gender in Victorian England: The Diaries of Arthur J. Munby and Hannah Cullwick," *Feminist Studies,* 5 (1979), pp. 87–141.

Davies, Cella. ed. *Rewriting Nursing History.* Totowa, NJ: Barnes & Noble, 1980.

Davies, Emily. *The Higher Education of Women.* London: Strahan, 1866.

Davies, Margaret Llewelyn. *The Women's Co-operative Guild 1883–1904.* Westmoreland: Kirkby Lonsdale, 1904.

Davin, Anna. "Imperialism and Motherhood," *History Workshop*, no. 5 (1978), pp. 9–65.

Dingwall, Robert W. J. "Collectivism, Regionalism and Feminism: Health Visiting and British Social Policy 1850–1975," *Journal of Social Policy*, 6 (1977), pp. 291–315.

Dowling, Linda. "The Decadent and the New Woman in the 1890's," *Nineteenth-Century Fiction*, 33 (1979), pp. 434–53.

Drake, Barbara. *Women in Trade Unions*. London: Labour Research Department, 1924.

———— and Cole, Margaret I., eds. *Our Partnership by Beatrice Webb*. New York: Longmans, Green, 1948.

Dunbar, Janet. *The Early Victorian Woman: 1837–1857*. London: Harrap, 1953.

Dyhouse, Carol. *Girls Growing Up in Late Victorian and Edwardian England*. London: Routledge and Kegan Paul, 1981.

————. "Working-class Mothers and Infant Mortality in England, 1895–1914," *Journal of Social History*, 12 (1978), pp. 248–67.

Edelstein, T. J. "They Sang 'The Song of the Shirt': The Visual Iconology of the Seamstress," *Victorian Studies*, 23 (1980), pp. 183–210.

Ellis, Katherine. "Paradise Lost: The Limits of Domesticity in the Nineteenth-Century Novel," *Feminist Studies*, 2 (1975), pp. 55–63.

Engel, Arthur. " 'Immoral Intentions': The University of Oxford and the Problem of Prostitution, 1827–1914," *Victorian Studies*, 23 (1979), pp. 79–107.

Fair, John D. "The Political Aspects of Women's Suffrage During the First World War," *Albion*, 8 (1976), pp. 274–95.

Fassler, Barbara. "Theories of Homosexuality as Sources of Bloomsbury's Androgyny," *Signs*, 5 (1979–80), pp. 237–51.

Fawcett, Millicent Garrett. *What I Remember*. Westport, CT: Hyperion, 1976 (1924).

Fee, Elizabeth. "The Sexual Politics of Victorian Social Anthropology," *Feminist Studies*, 1 (3/4) (1972–73), pp. 23–39.

Ferguson, Neal A. "Women's Work: Employment Opportunities and Economic Roles, 1918–1939," *Albion*, 7 (1975), pp. 55–68.

Fernando, Lloyd. *"New Women" in the Late Victorian Novel*. University Park: Pennsylvania State University Press, 1977.

Ford, Isabella. *Women as Factory Inspectors and Certifying Surgeons*. London: Women's Co-Operative Guild, 1898.

Fulford, Roger. *Votes for Women*. London: Faber & Faber, 1957.

Fussell, G. E., and Fussell, K. R. *The English Countrywoman: A Farmhouse Social History, A.D. 1500–1900*. Salem, NH: Arno, 1966 (1953).

Gardener, Dorothy. *English Girlhood at School: A Study of Women's Education Through Twelve Centuries*. London: Humphrey Millford, 1929.

Gathorne-Hardy, Jonathan. *The Rise and Fall of the British Nanny*. New York: Dial, 1973.

Gillis, John R. "Sexual Relations, and the Risks of Illegitimacy in London, 1801–1900," *Feminist Studies*, 5 (1979), pp. 142–73.

Gittins, Diana G. "Married Life and Birth Control Between the Wars," *Journal of the Oral History Society*, 3 (1975), pp. 53–64.

Goldfarb, Russell M. *Sexual Repression and Victorian Literature*. Cranbury, NJ: Bucknell University Press, 1970.

Goldsmith, Margaret. *Seven Women Against the World*. London: Methuen, 1935.

Gorham, Deborah. "The 'Maiden Tribute of Modern Babylon' Re-examined: Child Prostitution and the Idea of Childhood in Late-Victorian England," *Victorian Studies*, 21 (1978), pp. 353–79.

———. *The Victorian Girl and the Feminine Ideal*. Bloomington: Indiana University Press, 1982.

Grundy, Isobel. "The Politics of Female Authorship: Lady Mary Wortley Montagu's Reaction to the Printing to Her Poems," *Book Collector*, 31 (1982), pp. 19–37.

Gunn, Peter. *Vernon Lee: Violet Paget, 1856–1935*. New York: Arno, 1975 (1964).

Haldane, Elizabeth. *Mrs. Gaskell and Her Friends*. New York: Appleton, 1931.

Hamilton, Mary Agnes. *Mary MacArthur: A Biographical Sketch*. Westport, CT: Hyperion, 1976 (1926).

Hammerton, A. James. *Emigrant Gentlewomen: Genteel Poverty and Female Emigration 1830–1914*. Totowa, NJ: Rowman and Littlefield, 1979.

Harrison, Brian. *Separate Spheres: The Opposition to Women's Suffrage in Britain*. New York: Holmes & Meier, 1978.

Hartman, Mary S. *Victorian Murderesses*. New York: Schocken, 1978.

Hecht, J. Jean. *The Domestic Servant Class in Eighteenth Century England*. Westport, CT: Hyperion, 1981 (1956).

Heeney, Brian. "The Beginnings of Church Feminism: Women and the Councils of the Church of England 1897–1919," *Journal of Ecclesiastical History*, 33 (1982), pp. 89–109.

Helsinger, Elizabeth, et al. eds. *The Woman Question: Society and Literature in Britain and America*. New York: Garland, 1981.

Helterline, Marilyn. "The Emergence of Modern Motherhood: Motherhood in England 1899 to 1959," *International Journal of Women's Studies*, 3 (1980), pp. 590–614.

Hewitt, Margaret. *Wives and Mothers in Victorian Industry*. London: Rockliff, 1958.

Hill, Georgiana. *Women in English Life: From Medieval to Modern Times*. 2 vols. London: Richard Bentley, 1896.

Holcombe, Lee. *Victorian Ladies at Work: Middle Class Working Women in England and Wales 1850–1914*. Hamden, CT: Archon, 1973.

———. *Wives and Property: Reform of the Married Women's Property Law in Nineteenth Century England*. Toronto: University of Toronto Press, 1982.

Hole, Christina. *The English Housewife in the Seventeenth Century.* London: Chatto and Windus, 1953.

Holtzman, Ellen M. "The Pursuit of Married Love: Women's Attitude toward Sexuality and Marriage in Great Britain, 1918–1939," *Journal of Social History,* 16 (1982), pp. 39–52.

Horn, Pamela. *The Rise and Fall of the Victorian Servant.* New York: St. Martin's, 1975.

How-Martyn, Edith, and Breed, Mary. *The Birth Control Movement in England.* London: Bale & Danielsson, 1930.

Hughes, Mary Vivian. *A London Family 1870–1900.* London: Oxford University Press, 1958.

———. *A Victorian Family.* 3 vols. New York: Oxford University Press, 1979.

Hume, Leslie P. *The National Union of Women's Suffrage Societies 1897–1914.* New York: Garland, 1982.

Humphries, Jane. "The Working Class Family: Women's Liberation, and Class Struggle—The Case of Nineteenth Century British History," *Review of Radical Political Economics,* 9 (1977), pp. 25–41.

Hutchins, Elizabeth Leigh. *Women in Modern Industry.* London: Bell, 1915.

Jenkins, Isobel. "The Yorkshire Ladies' Council of Education, 1871–91," *Publications of the Thoresby Society,* 56 (1978), pp. 27–71.

John, Angela V. *By the Sweat of Their Brow: Women Workers at Victorian Coal Mines.* Cheshire, CT: Biblo and Tannen, 1980.

———. "Colliery Legislation and Its Consequences: 1842 and the Women Miners of Lancashire," *Bulletin of John Rylands University Library,* 61 (1978), pp. 78–114.

Kamm, Josephine. *Hope Deferred: Girls' Education in English History.* London: Methuen, 1965.

———. *Rapiers and Battleaxes; The Women's Movement and Its Aftermath.* London: Allen and Unwin, 1966.

Kapp, Yvonnac. *Eleanor Marx.* New York: International, 1973.

Kinnaird, Joan K. "Mary Astell and the Conservative Contribution to English Feminism," *Journal of British Studies,* 19 (1979), pp. 53–75.

Klein, Viola. *Britain's Married Women Workers.* New York: Humanities, 1965.

Knight, Patricia. "Women and Abortion in Victorian England," *History Workshop,* no. 4 (1977), pp. 57–69.

Lance, Keith Curry. "Strategy Choices of the British Women's Social and Political Union, 1903–18," *Social Science Quarterly,* 60 (1979), pp. 51–61.

Langer, William I. "Origins of the Birth Control Movement in England," *Journal of Interdisciplinary History,* 5 (1975), pp. 669–86.

Lee, Vernon. (pseud. Violet Paget.) *Gospels of Anarchy.* New York: Brentano's, 1909.

Legates, Marlene. "The Cult of Womanhood in Eighteenth-Century Thought," *Eighteenth-Century Studies,* 10 (1976), pp. 21–39.

Leranbaum, Miriam. "'Mistresses of Orthodoxy': Education in the Lives and Writings of Late-Eighteenth-Century Women Writers," *Proceedings of the American Philosophical Society,* 121 (1977), pp. 281–301.

L'Esperance, J. "Doctors and Women in Nineteenth-Century Society: Sexuality and Role," in Woodward, J., and Richards, D. eds. *Health Care and Popular Medicine in Nineteenth Century England: Essays in Social History.* New York: Holmes & Meier, 1977.

Lewenhak, Sheila. *Women and Trade Unions: An Outline History of Women in the British Trade Union Movement.* New York: St. Martin's, 1977.

Liddington, Jill, and Norris, Jill. *One Hand Tied Behind Us: The Rise of the Women's Suffrage Movement.* London: Virago Press, 1978.

Linklater, Andro. *An Unhusbanded Life: Charlotte Despard: Suffragette, Socialist and Sinn Feiner.* London: Hutchinson, 1980.

Longford, Elizabeth. *Eminent Victorian Women.* New York: Knopf, 1981.

Love, Rosaleen. "'Alice in Eugenics-Land': Feminism and Eugenics in the Scientific Careers of Alice Lee and Ethel Elderton," *Annals of Science,* 36 (1979), pp. 145–58.

Lutyens, Lady Emily. *A Blessed Girl: Memoirs of a Victorian Girlhood Chronicled in an Exchange of Letters 1887–1896.* Philadelphia: Lippincott, 1954.

MacKenzie, Norman, and MacKenzie, Jeanne. eds. *The Diary of Beatrice Webb.* Vol. 1: *"Glitter Around and Darkness Within," 1873–1892.* Cambridge: Harvard University Press, 1982.

Malcolmson, Patricia A. "Laundresses and the Laundry Trade in Victorian England," *Victorian Studies,* 24 (1981), pp. 439–62.

Marcus, Jane. "Transatlantic Sisterhood: Labor and Suffrage Links in the Letters of Elizabeth Robins and Emmeline Pankhurst," *Signs,* 3 (1978), pp. 744–55.

Marcus, Steven. *The Other Victorians: A Study of Sexuality and Pornography in Mid-Nineteenth Century England.* New York: Basic, 1966.

Marshall, Dorothy. *The English Domestic Servant in History.* London: G. Philip, 1949.

———. *The English Poor in the Eighteenth Century: A Study in Social and Administrative History.* London: Routledge and Kegan Paul, 1969.

Mayhew, Henry. *London Labour and the London Poor.* 4 vols. New York: Dover, 1968 (1851).

McDorman, K. "Leftists, Ladies and Lenin: English Women Respond to Bolshevism," *Social Science Journal,* 16 (1979), pp. 31–40.

McGregor, Oliver Ross. *Divorce in England: A Centenary Study.* London: Heinemann, 1957.

McHugh, Paul. *Prostitution and Victorian Social Reform.* New York: St. Martin's, 1980.

McLaren, Angus. "Abortion in England, 1890–1914," *Victorian Studies,* 20 (1977), pp. 379–400.

————. *Birth Control in Nineteenth Century England.* New York: Holmes & Meier, 1978.

————. "Contraception and the Working Classes: The Social Ideology of the English Birth Control Movement in its Early Stages," *Comparative Studies in Social History,* 18 (1976), pp. 236–51.

McLaren, Barbara. *Women of the War.* London: Hodder & Stoughton, 1917.

Menefee, Samuel P. *Wives for Sale: An Ethnographic Study of British Popular Divorce.* New York: St. Martin's, 1981.

Middleton, Lucy. ed. *Women in the Labour Movement: The British Experience.* Totowa, NJ: Rowman and Littlefield, 1977.

Mitchell, David J. *The Fighting Pankhursts: A Study in Tenacity.* New York: Macmillan, 1967.

Mitchell, Hanna. *The Hard Way Up: The Autobiography of Hanna Mitchell, Suffragette and Rebel.* London: Virago Press, 1977.

Mitchell, Sally. "Sentiment and Suffering: Women's Recreational Reading in the 1860s," *Victorian Studies,* 21 (1977), pp. 29–45.

Morgan, David. *Suffragists and Liberals: Politics of Woman Suffrage in England.* Totowa, NJ: Rowman and Littlefield, 1975.

Muggeridge, Kitty, and Adam, Ruth. *Beatrice Webb: A Life, 1858–1943.* London: Secker & Warburg, 1967.

Murray, Janet Horowitz. *Strong-minded Women and Other Lost Voices of Nineteenth-Century England.* New York: Pantheon, 1982.

Myrdal, Alva, and Klein, Viola. *Women's Two Roles: Home and Work.* 2nd ed. London: Routledge and Kegan Paul, 1968.

Neff, Wanda F. *Victorian Working Women.* New York: A.M.S. Press, 1966 (1927).

Newberry, Jo Vellacott. "Anti-War Suffragists," *History,* 62 (1977), pp. 411–26.

————. "Women and War in England: The Case of Catherine E. Marshall and World War I," *Peace and Change,* 4 (1977), pp. 13–17.

Norton, Caroline. *English Laws for Women in the Nineteenth Century.* Westport, CT: Hyperion, 1981.

Oakley, Ann. *The Sociology of Housework.* New York: Pantheon, 1975.

————. *Woman's Work: The Housewife, Past and Present.* New York: Vintage, 1976.

Olcott, Teresa. "Dead Centre: The Woman's Trade Union Movement in London 1874–1914," *London Journal,* 2 (1976), pp. 33–50.

Outhwaite, R. B. ed. *Marriage and Society: Studies in the Social History of Marriage.* New York: St. Martin's, 1982.

Pankhurst, Christabel. *Unshackled: The Story of How We Won the Vote.* London: Hutchinson, 1959.

Pankhurst, Emmeline. *My Own Story.* London: Virago Press, 1979 (1914).

Pankhurst, Estelle Sylvia. *The Life of Emmeline Pankhurst: The Suffragette Struggle for Women's Citizenship.* London: T. W. Laurie, 1969 (1935).

————. *The Suffragette: The History of the Women's Militant Suffrage Movement, 1905–1910.* New York: Sturgis & Walton, 1911.

————. *The Suffragette Movement.* London: Virago Press, 1977 (1931).

Parkes, Bessie Rayner. *Essays on Women's Work.* 2nd ed. London: Strahan, 1865.

Pederson, Joyce Senders. "The Reform of Women's Secondary and Higher Education: Institutional Change and Social Values in Mid and Late Victorian England," *Higher Education Quarterly,* 19 (1979), pp. 61–91.

————. "School Mistresses and Headmistresses: Elites and Education in Nineteenth Century England," *Journal of British Studies,* 15 (1975), pp. 132–62.

————. "Some Victorian Headmistresses: A Conservative Tradition of Reform," *Victorian Studies,* 24 (1981), pp. 463–88.

Pethick-Lawrence, Emmeline. *My Part in a Changing World.* Westport, CT: Hyperion, 1976 (1938).

Pinchbeck, Ivy. *Women Workers and the Industrial Revolution.* New York: Crofts, 1930.

———— and Hewitt, Margaret. *Children in English Society.* 2 vols. Toronto: University of Toronto Press, 1970–73.

Poovey, Mary. "My Hideous Progeny: Mary Shelley and the Feminization of Romanticism," *Proceedings of the Modern Language Association,* 95 (1980), pp. 332–47.

Post, J. B. "A Foreign Office Survey of Veneral Disease and Prostitution Control, 1869–70," *Medical History,* 22 (1978), pp. 327–34.

Prochaska, F. K. *Women and Philanthropy in Nineteenth Century England.* Oxford: Clarendon Press, 1980.

Raeburn, Antonia. *The Militant Suffragettes.* London: Joseph, 1973.

Reeves, Maud Pember. *Round About a Pound a Week.* London: Virago Press, 1979 (1913).

Richardson, Joanna. "The Great Revolution: Women's Education in Victorian Times," *History Today,* 24 (1974), pp. 420–27.

Roberts, Barbara. "Daughters of the Empire and Mothers of the Race: Caroline Chisholm and Female Emigration in the British Empire," *Atlantis,* 1 (1976), pp. 106–27.

Roberts, Helene E. "The Exquisite Slave: The Role of Clothes in the Making of the Victorian Woman," *Signs,* 2 (1976–77), pp. 554–69.

Roe, Jill. "Modernisation and Sexism: Recent Writings on Victorian Women," *Victorian Studies,* 20 (1977), pp. 179–92.

Roebuck, Janet, and Slaughter, Jane. "Ladies and Pensioners: Stereotypes and Public Policy Affecting Old Women in England 1880–1940," *Journal of Social History,* 13 (1979), pp. 105–14.

Rogers, Katharine M. *Feminism in Eighteenth Century England.* Brighton, England: Harvester, 1982.

————. "Inhibitions on Eighteenth-Century Women Novelists: Elizabeth Inchbald and Charlotte Smith," *Eighteenth-Century Studies*, 11 (1977), pp. 63–78.

Rose, June. *Elizabeth Frey: A Biography.* New York: St. Martin's, 1981.

Rosen, Andrew. "Emily Davies and the Women's Movement, 1862–1867," *Journal of British Studies*, 19 (1979), pp. 101–21.

———. *Rise Up, Women! The Militant Campaign of the Women's Social and Political Union, 1903–1914.* London: Routledge and Kegan Paul, 1974.

Ross, Ellen. "'Fierce Questions and Taunts': Married Life in Working-Class London 1870–1914," *Feminist Studies*, 8 (1982), pp. 575–602.

Rover, Constance. *Love Morals and the Feminists.* London: Routledge and Kegan Paul, 1970.

———. *Women's Suffrage and Party Politics in Britain 1866–1914.* London: Routledge and Kegan Paul, 1967.

Rowbotham, Sheila. *A New World for Women: Stella Browne, Socialist Feminist.* London: Pluto, 1977.

——— and Weeks, Jeffrey. *Socialism and the New Life.* London: Pluto, 1977.

Sackville-West, Victoria. *The Dark Island.* Garden City, NY: Doubleday, 1934.

Satre, Lowell J. "After the Match Girls' Strike: Bryant and May in the 1890s," *Victorian Studies*, 26 (1982), pp. 7–31.

Sauer, R. "Infanticide and Abortion in Nineteenth-Century Britain," *Population Studies*, 32 (1978), pp. 81–93.

Schmiechen, James A. *Sweated Industries and Sweated Labor: The London Clothing Trades, 1867–1914.* Urbana: University of Illinois Press, 1984.

———. "Sweated Industries and Sweated Labor: A Study of Industrial Disorganization and Worker Attitudes in the London Clothing Trades, 1867–1909," *Journal of Economic History*, 36 (1976), pp. 283–86.

Schupf, Harriet Warm. "Single Women and Social Reform in Mid-Nineteenth Century England: The Case of Mary Carpenter," *Victorian Studies*, 17 (1974), pp. 301–17.

Senf, Carol A. "'Dracula': Stoker's Response to the New Woman," *Victorian Studies*, 26 (1982), pp. 33–49.

Shklonik, Esther Simon. "Petticoat Power: The Political Influence of Mrs. Gladstone," *Historian*, 42 (1980), pp. 631–47.

Showalter, Elaine. *A Literature of Their Own: British Women Novelists from Brontë to Lessing.* Princeton: Princeton University Press, 1977.

———. "Victorian Women and Insanity." *Victorian Studies*, 23 (1980), pp. 157–81.

Silverstone, Rosalie. "Office Work for Women: An Historical Review," *Business History*, 18 (1976), pp. 98–110.

Smith, Harold. "The Issue of 'Equal Pay for Equal Work' in Great Britain, 1914–19," *Societas*, 8 (1978), pp. 39–51.

Smith, Hilda. "Gynecology and Ideology in Seventeenth Century England," in

Carroll, Berenice, ed. *Liberating Women's History*. Urbana: University of Illinois Press, 1976.

———. *Seventeenth Century English Feminists*. Urbana: University of Illinois Press, 1982.

Snell, K. D. M. "Agricultural Seasonal Unemployment, the Standard of Living and Women's Work in the South East: 1690–1860," *Economic History Review*, 34 (1981) pp. 407–37.

Soldon, Norbert C. *Women in British Trade Unions 1874–1976*. Totowa, NJ: Rowman and Littlefield, 1978.

Soloway, Richard Allen. *Birth Control and the Population Question in England, 1877–1930*. Chapel Hill: University of North Carolina Press, 1982.

Spenceley, G. F. R. "The English Pillow Lace Industry 1840–80: A Rural Industry in Competition with Machinery," *Business History*, 19 (1977), pp. 68–87.

Spring Rice, Margery. *Working Class Wives*. London: Virago Press, 1981 (1939).

Staves, Susan. "British Seduced Maidens," *Eighteenth-Century Studies*, 14 (1980–81), pp. 109–34.

Stebbins, Lucy. *London Ladies*. New York: A.M.S. Press, 1952.

Stenton, Doris Mary. *The English Woman in History*. New York: Schocken, 1977 (1957).

Stephen, Barbara. *Emily Davis and Girton College*. Westport, CT: Hyperion, 1975 (1927).

Stetson, Dorothy M. *A Woman's Issue: The Politics of Family Life Reform in England*. Westport, CT: Greenwood, 1982.

Stone, Lawrence. *The Family, Sex and Marriage in England 1500–1800*. New York: Harper, 1977.

Stopes, Marie. *Married Love*. New York: Putnam, 1939.

———. *Wise Parenthood*. London: Fifield, 1919.

Strachey, Ray. *The Cause: A Short History of the Women's Movement in Great Britain*. London: Virago Press, 1978.

Stubbs, Patricia. *Women and Fiction: Feminism and the Novel, 1880–1920*. Brighton, England: Harvester, 1982.

Taylor, Barbara. *Eve and the New Jerusalem: Socialism and Feminism in the Nineteenth Century*. New York: Pantheon, 1983.

———. "'The Men are as Bad as Their Masters . . .': Socialism, Feminism and Sexual Antagonism in the London Tailoring Trade in the Early 1830's," *Feminist Studies*, 5 (1979), pp. 7–40.

Thane, Pat. "Women and the Poor Law in Victorian and Edwardian England," *History Workshop*, no. 6 (1978), pp. 29–51.

Thomis, Malcolm I. *Women in Protest 1800–1850*. New York: St. Martin's, 1982.

Thompson, E. P. *The Making of the English Working Class*. New York: Vintage, 1963.

Thomson, Patricia. *The Victorian Heroine: A Changing Ideal 1837–1873*. Westport, Ct: Greenwood, 1978 (1956).

Tickner, Frederick W. *Women in English Economic History*. Westport, CT: Hyperion, 1980 (1923).

Tomes, Nancy. "A 'Torrent of Abuse': Crimes of Violence Between Working-Class Men and Women in London, 1840–1875," *Journal of Social History*, 11 (1978), pp. 328–45.

Trudgill, Eric. *Madonnas and Magdalens: The Origins and Development of Victorian Sexual Attitudes*. New York: Holmes & Meier, 1976.

Trumbach, Randolph. *The Rise of the Egalitarian Family: Aristocratic Kinship and Domestic Relations in Eighteenth Century England*. New York: Academic Press, 1978.

Tweedie, Ethel B. *Women and Soldiers*. London: John Lane, 1918.

Twining, Louisa. *Workhouses and Pauperism and Women's Work in the Administration of the Poor Law*. London: Methuen, 1898.

———. *Workhouses and Women's Work*. London: Longmans, 1858.

Vicinus, Martha. ed. *Suffer and Be Still: Women in the Victorian Age*. Bloomington: Indiana University Press, 1972.

———. ed. *A Widening Sphere: Changing Roles of Victorian Women*. Bloomington: Indiana University Press, 1977.

Walkley, Christina. *The Ghost in the Looking Glass: The Victorian Seamstress*. Atlantic Highlands, NJ: Humanities, 1981.

Walkowitz, Judith R. "Male Vice and Feminist Virtue: Feminism and the Politics of Prostitution in Nineteenth Century Britain," *History Workshop*, no. 13 (1982), pp. 79–93.

———. "Notes on the History of Victorian Prostitution," *Feminist Studies*, 1 (1/2), (1972–73), pp. 105–14.

———. *Prostitution and Victorian Society: Women, Class, and the State*. New York: Cambridge University Press, 1980.

Webb, Beatrice. *My Apprenticeship*. New York: Longmans, Green, 1926.

Webb, Catherine. *The Woman with the Basket: The History of the Women's Cooperative Guild, 1883–1927*. Manchester: Cooperative Wholesale Society, 1927.

Weeks, Jeffrey. *Coming Out: Homosexual Politics in Britain, from the Nineteenth Century to the Present*. New York: Quartet Books, 1977.

———. *Sex, Politics and Society: The Regulation of Sexuality Since 1800*. New York: Longmans, 1981.

Weintraub, Rodelle. ed. *Fabian Feminist: Bernard Shaw and Women*. University Park: Pennsylvania State University Press, 1977.

Wicks, George. *The Amazon Letters: The Life and Loves of Natalie Burney*. New York: Popular Library, 1978.

Williamson, Marilyn L. "Who's Afraid of Mrs. Barbauld? The Bluestockings and Feminism," *International Journal of Women's Studies*, 3 (1980), pp. 89–102.

Josephine Butler (1828–1906)

Butler, Josephine. *An Autobiographical Memoir.* Bristol: Arrowsmith, 1909.

———. *The Education and Employment of Women.* London: Macmillan, 1868.

———. *Personal Reminiscences of a Great Crusade.* Westport, CT: Hyperion, 1976 (1911).

———. ed. *Woman's Work and Woman's Culture: A Series of Essays.* London: Macmillan, 1869.

Petrie, Glen. *A Singular Inquiry: The Campaigns of Josephine Butler.* New York: Viking, 1971.

Radclyffe Hall (1886–1943)

Brittain, Vera. *Radclyffe Hall: A Case of Obscenity?* South Brunswick, NJ: Barnes, 1969.

Dickson, Lovat. *Radclyffe Hall at the Well of Loneliness.* New York: Scribner's, 1975.

Hall, Radclyffe. *The Well of Loneliness.* New York: Avon, 1981 (1956).

Harriet Martineau (1802–76)

Martineau, Harriet. *Harriet Martineau's Autobiography.* 3 vols. London: Smith, Elder, 1877.

Pichanick, Valerie Kossew. *Harriet Martineau: The Woman and Her Work 1802–76.* Ann Arbor: University of Michigan Press, 1980.

Webb, R. K. *Harriet Martineau: A Radical Victorian.* New York: Columbia University Press, 1960.

John Stuart Mill (1806–73)

Caine, Barbara. "John Stuart Mill and the English Women's Movement," *Historical Studies,* 18 (1978), 52–67.

Goldstein, Leslie. "Mill, Marx and Women's Liberation," *Journal of the History of Philosophy,* 18 (1980), pp. 319–34.

Hayek, Friedrich August von. ed. *John Stuart Mill and Harriet Taylor: Their Correspondence and Subsequent Marriage.* Chicago: University of Chicago Press, 1951.

Hughes, Patricia. "The Reality *versus* the Ideal: J. S. Mill's Treatment of Women, Workers, and Private Property," *Canadian Journal of Political Science,* 12 (1979), pp. 523–42.

Mill, John Stuart. *The Subjection of Women.* Cambridge, MA: M.I.T. Press, 1970.

——— and Mill, Harriet Taylor. *Essays on Sexual Equality.* ed. by Alice S. Rossi. Chicago: University of Chicago Press, 1970.

Florence Nightingale (1820–1910)

Allen, Donald R. "Florence Nightingale: Toward a Psychohistorical Interpretation," *Journal of Interdisciplinary History*, 6 (1975), pp. 23–45.

Showalter, Elaine. "Florence Nightingale's Feminist Complaint: Women, Religion, and *Suggestions for Thought*," *Signs*, 6 (1980–81), pp. 395–412.

Smith, F. B. *Florence Nightingale: Reputation and Power.* New York: St. Martin's, 1982.

Woodham-Smith, Cecil. *Florence Nightingale: 1820–1910.* London: Reprint Society, 1952.

Olive Schreiner (1855–1920)

Berkman, Joyce Aurech. *Olive Schreiner: Feminism on the Frontier.* Montreal: Eden Press Women's Publications, 1980.

Hobman, D. L. *Olive Schreiner: Her Friends and Times.* London: Watts, 1955.

Schreiner, Olive. *Woman and Labour.* London: Fisher Unwin, 1911.

Virginia Woolf (1882–1941)

Bazin, Nancy T. *Virginia Woolf and the Androgynous Vision.* New Brunswick, NJ: Rutgers University Press, 1973.

Bell, Quentin. *Virginia Woolf: A Biography.* New York: Harcourt Brace Jovanovich, 1972.

Carroll, Berenice A. "'To Crush Him in Our Own Country': The Political Thought of Virginia Woolf," *Feminist Studies*, 4 (1) (1978), pp. 99–131.

DeSalvo, Louise. "Lighting the Cave: The Relationship between Vita Sackville-West and Virginia Woolf," *Signs*, 8 (1982–83), pp. 195–214.

Marcus, Jane. ed. *New Feminist Essays on Virginia Woolf.* Lincoln, NE: University of Nebraska Press, 1981.

Marder, Herbert. *Feminism and Art: A Study of Virginia Woolf.* Chicago: University of Chicago Press, 1968.

Proudfit, Sharon L. "Virginia Woolf: Reluctant Feminist in 'The Years,'" *Criticism*, 17 (1975), pp. 59–73.

Woolf, Virginia. *The Diary of Virginia Woolf.* ed. by Anne Oliver Bell. New York: Harcourt Brace Jovanovich, 1980.

———. *Moments of Being: Unpublished Autobiographical Writings.* New York: Harcourt Brace Jovanovich, 1976.

———. *Mrs. Dalloway.* New York: Harcourt Brace Jovanovich, 1953 (1925).

———. *A Room of One's Own.* New York: Harcourt Brace, 1929.

Mary Wollstonecraft (1759–97)

Bouten, J. *Mary Wollstonecraft and the Beginnings of Female Emancipation in France and England.* Philadelphia: Porcupine Press, 1975.

Flexner, Eleanor. *Mary Wollstonecraft.* Baltimore: Penguin, 1973.

George, Margaret. *One Woman's Situation: A Study of Mary Wollstonecraft.* Urbana: University of Illinois Press, 1970.

Janes, R. M. "On the Reception of Mary Wollstonecraft's *A Vindication of the Rights of Woman*," *Journal of the History of Ideas,* 39 (1978), pp. 293–302.

Korsmeyer, Carolyn W. "Reason and Morals in the Early Feminist Movement: Mary Wollstonecraft," *Philosophy Forum,* 5 (1975), pp. 97–111.

Sunstein, Emily. *A Different Face: The Life of Mary Wollstonecraft.* New York: Harper, 1975.

Todd, Janet M. "Mary Wollstonecraft: A Review of Research and Comment," *British Studies Monitor,* 7 (1977), pp. 3–23.

Tomalin, Claire. *The Life and Death of Mary Wollstonecraft.* New York: Harcourt Brace Jovanovich, 1974.

Wardle, Ralph M. ed. *Godwin and Mary: Letters of William Godwin and Mary Wollstonecraft.* Lawrence: University of Kansas Press, 1966.

———. *Mary Wollstonecraft: A Critical Biography.* Lincoln, NE: University of Nebraska Press, 1951.

Wexler, Alice, ed. "Emma Goldman on Mary Wollstonecraft, Her Tragic Life and Her Passionate Struggle for Freedom," *Feminist Studies,* 7 (1981), pp. 113–33.

Wollstonecraft, Mary. *Mary Wollstonecraft, Posthumous Works.* 4 vols. New York: Garland, 1974.

———. *Letters to Imlay.* New York: Haskell House, 1971.

———. *Thoughts on the Education of Daughters with Reflections on Female Conduct, in the Most Important Duties of Life.* New York: Garland, 1974.

———. *A Vindication of the Rights of Women.* New York: Norton, 1967 (1792).

RUSSIA

Allendorf, Marlies. *Women in Socialist Society.* New York: International, 1976.

Atkinson, D.; Dallin, A.; and Lapidus, G., eds. *Women in Russia.* Stanford: Stanford University Press, 1977.

Babrovskaya, Cecilia. *Twenty Years in Underground Russia: Memoirs of a Rank-and-File Bolshevik.* New York: International, 1934.

Balabanova, Anzhelika. *My Life as a Rebel.* New York: Harper, 1938.

Breshkovskaia, Katerina. *Hidden Springs of the Russian Revolution.* Stanford: Stanford University Press, 1931.

Broido, Eva. *Memoirs of a Revolutionary.* New York: Oxford University Press. 1967.

Broido, Vera. *Apostles into Terrorists: Women and the Revolutionary Movement in the Russia of Alexander II.* New York: Viking, 1977.

Brown, Donald. *Role and Status of Women in the Soviet Union.* New York: Teachers College Press, 1968.

Bryant, Louise. *Six Red Months in Russia*. New York: Doran, 1918.

Chao, Paul. *Women Under Communism: Family in Russia and China*. New York: General Hall, 1977.

Clements, Barbara Evans. "Working-Class and Peasant Women in the Russian Revolution, 1917–1923," *Signs*, 8 (1982–83), pp. 215–35.

Dodge, Norton T. *Women in the Soviet Economy*. Westport, CT: Greenwood, 1977 (1966).

Donald, M. "Bolshevik Activity Amongst the Working Women of Petrograd in 1917," *International Review of Social History*, 27 (1982), pp. 129–60.

Dunham, Vera. "Sex: From Free Love to Puritanism," in Inkeles, A., and Geiger, K., eds. *Soviet Society*. Boston: Houghton Mifflin, 1961.

Edmonson, Linda. "Russian Feminists and the First All-Russian Congress of Women," *Russian History*, no. 2 (1976), pp. 123–49.

Engel, Barbara A. *Mothers and Daughters: Women of the Intelligentsia in Nineteenth-Century Russia*. New York: Cambridge University Press, 1983.

————. "Women Medical Students in Russia, 1872–1882: Reformers or Rebels?" *Journal of Social History*, 12 (1979), pp. 394–414.

———— and Rosenthal, Clifford N., eds. *Five Sisters: Women Against the Tsar*. New York: Shocken, 1977.

Figner, Vera. *Memoirs of a Revolutionist*. New York: International, 1927.

Gasiorowska, Xenia. *Women in Soviet Fiction 1917–1964*. Madison: University of Wisconsin Press, 1968.

Geiger, H. Kent. *The Family in Soviet Russia*. Cambridge, MA: Harvard University Press, 1968.

Halle, Fannina W. *Women in Soviet Russia*. New York: Viking, 1933.

Herr, D. M., and Youssef, Nadia. "Female Status Among Soviet Central Asian Nationalities: The Melding of Islam and Marxism and Its Implications for Population Increase," *Population Studies*, 31 (1977), pp. 155–73.

Johanson, Christine. "Autocratic Politics, Public Opinion, and Women's Medical Education during the Reign of Alexander II, 1855–1881," *Slavic Review*, 38 (1979), pp. 426–43.

Kennedy, Don H. *Little Sparrow* [Sophia Kovalevksy]. Athens: Ohio University Press, 1983.

Knight, Amy. "Female Terrorists in the Russian Socialist Revolutionary Party," *Russian Review*, 38 (1979), pp. 139–59.

————. "The Fritschi: A Study of Female Radicals in the Russian Populist Movement," *Canadian-American Slavic Studies*, 9 (1975), pp. 1–17.

Koblitz, Ann Hibner. *A Convergence of Lives: Sofia Kovalevskaia: Scientist, Writer, Revolutionary*. Boston: Birkhäuser, 1983.

Kovalevskaya, Sofya. *A Russian Childhood*. New York: Springer, 1978 (1895).

Lapidus, Gail W. ed. *Woman, Work and Family in the Soviet Union*. Armonk, NY: M. E. Sharpe, 1982.

————. *Women in Soviet Soviety*. Berkeley: University of California Press, 1978.

Lenin, Vladimir I. *Emancipation of Women*. New York: International, 1970.

Lubin, Nancy. "Women in Soviet Central Asia: Progress and Contradictions," *Soviet Studies*, 33 (1981), pp. 182–203.

McAulay, Alastair. *Women's Work and Wages in the Soviet Union*. Winchester, MA: Allen & Unwin, 1981.

McNeal, Robert H. *Bride of the Revolution: Krupskaya and Lenin*. Ann Arbor: University of Michigan Press, 1972.

———. "Women in the Russian Radical Movement," *Journal of Social History*, 5 (1971–72), pp. 143–63.

Madariaga, Isabel de. *Russia in the Age of Catherine the Great*. New Haven: Yale University Press, 1982.

Madison, Bernice. *Social Welfare in the Soviet Union*. Stanford: Stanford University Press, 1968.

Mandel, William M. *Soviet Women Update*. Palo Alto, CA: Ramparts, 1982.

Massell, Gregory L. *Surrogate Proletariat: Moslem Women and Revolutionary Strategies in Soviet Central Asia 1919–1929*. Princeton: Princeton University Press, 1974.

Mickiewicz, Ellen. "Regional Variation in Female Recruitment and Advancement in the Communist Party of the Soviet Union," *Slavic Review*, 36 (1977), pp. 441–54.

Pachmuss, Temira. "Women Writers in Russian Decadence," *Journal of Contemporary History*, 17 (1982), pp. 111–35.

Polubarinova-Kochina, P. *Sophia Vasilyevna Kovalevskaya: Her Life and Work*. Moscow: Foreign Languages Publishing, 1957.

Satina, Sophie. *Education of Women in Pre-revolutionary Russia*. New York: n.p., 1966.

Schuster, A. "Women's Role in the Soviet Union: Ideology and Reality," *Russian Review*, 30 (1971), pp. 260–67.

Selivanova, Nina Nikolaevna. *Russia's Women*. Westport, CT: Hyperion, 1976 (1923).

Slaughter, Jane M. "Women and Socialism: The Case of Angelica Balabanoff," *Social Science Journal*, 14 (1977), pp. 57–65.

Smith, Jessica. *Women in Soviet Russia*. New York: Vanguard, 1928.

Somerville, Rose M. "The Urban Working Woman in U.S.S.R.: An Historical Overview," in Michel, Andree. ed. *Family Issues of Employed Women in Europe and America*. Leiden: Brill, 1971.

Stites, Richard. *The Women's Liberation Movement in Russia: Feminism, Nihilism and Bolshevism, 1860–1930*. Princeton: Princeton University Press, 1978.

———. "Women's Liberation Movements in Russia 1900–1930," *Canadian Slavic Studies*, 7 (1973), pp. 460–74.

Stuart, Robert S. "Women in Soviet Rural Management," *Slavic Review*, 38 (1979), pp. 603–13.

Trotsky, Leon. *Women and the Family*. New York: Pathfinder Press, 1974.

Vodovozova, Elizaveta. *A Russian Childhood.* London: Faber and Faber, 1961.

Whittaker, Cynthia H. "The Women's Movement in the Reign of Alexander I: A Case Study in Russian Liberalism," *Journal of Modern History,* 48 (1976), pp. 35–69.

Winter, Ella. *Red Virtue: Human Relationships in the New Russia.* New York: Harcourt, Brace, 1933.

Yedlin, Tova. ed. *Women in Eastern Europe and the Soviet Union.* New York: Praeger, 1981.

Zimmerman, Judith E. "Natalie Herzen and the Early Intelligentsia," *Russian Review,* 41 (1982), pp. 249–87

Aleksandra Kollontai (1872–1952)

Clements, Barbara Evans. *Bolshevik Feminist: The Life of Aleksandra Kollontai.* Bloomington: Indiana University Press, 1979.

———. "Emancipation Through Communism: The Ideology of A. M. Kollontai," *Slavic Review,* 32 (1973), pp. 323–38.

Farnsworth, Beatrice. *Aleksandra Kollontai: Socialism, Feminism, and the Bolshevik Revolution.* Stanford, CA: Stanford University Press, 1980.

———. "Bolshevism, the Woman Question, and Aleksandra Kollontai," *American Historical Review,* 81 (1976), pp. 292–316.

Kollontai, Alexandra. *Alexandra Kollontai: Selected Writings.* Alix Holt, ed. Westport, CT: Lawrence Hill, 1978.

———. *The Autobiography of a Sexually Emancipated Communist Woman.* New York: Herder and Herder, 1971.

———. *Communism and the Family.* Sydney, Australia: Young, 1971 (1918).

———. *A Great Love.* New York: Vanguard, 1929.

———. *Love of Worker Bees.* Chicago: Academy Chicago Limited, 1978.

———. *Red Love.* Westport, CT: Hyperion, 1973.

———. *Sexual Relations and the Class Struggle: Love and the New Morality.* Bristol: Falling Water Press, 1972.

———. *Women Workers Struggle for Their Rights.* Bristol, England: Falling Water Press, 1973.

Porter, Cathy. *Alexandra Kollontai: The Lonely Struggle of the Woman Who Defied Lenin.* New York: Dial Press, 1980.

THE UNITED STATES

Aldrich, Mark. "Determinants of Morality Among New England Cotton Mill Workers During the Progressive Era," *Journal of Economic History,* 42 (1982), pp. 847–63.

Andrews, John B., and Bliss, W. D. eds. *History of Women in Trade Unions.* Salem, NH: Arno, 1974 (1911).

Antler, Joyce. "Feminism as Life-Process: The Life and Career of Lucy Sprague Mitchell," *Feminist Studies,* 7 (1981), pp. 134–57.

Aptheker, Betina, ed. *Woman's Legacy: Essays on Race, Sex and Class in American History.* Amherst, MA: University of Massachusetts Press, 1982.

Banner, Lois W. *American Beauty: A Social History.* New York: Knopf, 1983.

———. *Women in Modern America: A Brief History.* New York: Harcourt Brace Jovanovich, 1974.

Baron, Ava. "Women and the Making of the American Working Class: A Study of the Proletarianization of Printers," *Review of Radical Political Economics,* 14 (1982), pp. 23–42.

Basch, Norma. *In the Eyes of the Law: Women, Marriage and Property in the Nineteenth Century.* Ithaca, NY: Cornell University Press, 1982.

———. "Invisible Women: The Legal Fiction of Marital Unity in Nineteenth-Century America," *Feminist Studies,* 5 (1979), pp. 346–66.

Beard, Mary R. *On Understanding Women.* New York: Longmans, Green, 1931.

———. *Woman as Force in History.* New York: Collier Books, 1962.

Beecher, Catherine E., and Stowe, Harriet B. *The American Woman's Home.* Hartford, CT: Stowe-Day, 1975.

Benson, Mary. *Women in Eighteenth Century America: A Study of Opinion and Social Usage.* New York: A.M.S. Press, 1976 (1936).

Benson, Susan Porter. "Business Heads and Sympathizing Hearts: The Women of the Providence Employment Society, 1837–1858," *Journal of Social History,* 12 (1978), pp. 302–12.

———. "The Cinderella of Occupations: Managing the Work of Department Store Saleswomen, 1900–1940," *Business History Review,* 55 (1981), pp. 1–25.

Berg, Barbara J. *The Remembered Gate: Origins of American Feminism: The Woman and the City.* New York: Oxford University Press, 1978.

Berkin, Carol, and Norton, Mary B. *Women of America: A History.* Boston, MA: Houghton Mifflin, 1979.

Bérubé, Allan. "Marching to a Different Drummer: Lesbian and Gay GIs in World War II," in Snitow, Ann; Stansell, Christine; and Thompson, Sharon eds. *Powers of Desire: The Politics of Sexuality.* New York: Monthly Review Press, 1983.

Best, Joel. "Careers in Brothel Prostitution: St. Paul, 1865–1883," *Journal of Interdisciplinary History,* 12 (1982), pp. 597–619.

Biggs, Mary. "Neither Printer's Wife nor Widow: American Women in Typesetting, 1830–1950," *Library Quarterly,* 50 (1980), pp. 431–52.

Biklen, Sari Knopp. "The Progressive Education Movement and the Question of Women," *Teachers College Record,* 80 (1978), pp. 316–35.

Blair, Karen J. *The Clubwoman as Feminist: True Womanhood Redefined 1868–1914.* New York: Holmes & Meier, 1980.

Blewett, Mary H. "The Union of Sex and Craft in the Haverhill Shoe Strike of 1895," *Labor History*, 20 (1979), pp. 241–56.

Bloch, Ruth H. "American Feminine Ideals in Transition: The Rise of the Moral Mother, 1785–1815," *Feminist Studies*, 4 (1978), pp. 101–26.

Bogdan, Janet. "Care or Cure? Childbirth Practices in Nineteenth-Century America," *Feminist Studies*, 4 (1978), pp. 92–99.

Bordin, Ruth. *Woman and Temperance: The Quest for Power and Liberty 1873–1900*. Philadelphia: Temple University Press, 1981.

Breckinridge, Sophonisba P. *Women in the Twentieth Century*. Salem, NH: Arno, 1972 (1933).

Brenzel, Barbara. "Domestication as Reform: A Study of the Socialization of Wayward Girls, 1856–1905," *Harvard Educational Review*, 50 (1980) pp. 196–213.

———. "Lancaster Industrial School for Girls: A Social Portrait of a Nineteenth-Century Reform School for Girls," *Feminist Studies*, 3 (1/2), (1975–76), pp. 40–53.

Brumberg, Joan Jacobs. "Zenanas and Girlless Villages: The Ethnology of American Evangelical Women, 1870–1910," *Journal of American History*, 69 (1982), pp. 347–71.

Buhle, Mari Jo. *Women and American Socialism, 1970–1920*. Urbana: University of Illinois Press: 1981.

Bullough, Vern, and Bullough, Bonnie. "Lesbianism in the 1920s and 1930s: A New Found Study," *Signs*, 2 (1977), pp. 895–904.

Carter, Susan B. "Academic Women Revisited: An Empirical Study of Changing Patterns in Women's Employment as College and University Faculty, 1890–1963," *Journal of Social History*, 14 (1981), pp. 675–700.

——— and Prus, Mark. "The Labor Market and the American School Girl 1890–1928," *Journal of Economic History*, 42 (1982), pp. 163–71.

Chudacoff, Howard P. "The Life Course of Women: Age and Age Consciousness, 1865–1915," *Journal of Family History*, 5 (1980), pp. 274–92.

Clinton, Cahterine. *The Plantation Mistress: Women's World in the Old South*. New York: Pantheon, 1982.

Conrad, Susan P. *Perish the Thought: Intellectual Women in Romantic America 1830–1860*. New York: Oxford University Press, 1976.

Cook, Blanche Wiesen. ed. *Crystal Eastman on Women and Revolution*. New York: Oxford University Press, 1978.

———. "Female Support Networks and Political Activism: Lillian Wald, Crystal Eastman, Emma Goldman," *Chrysalis*, no. 3 (1977), pp. 43–61.

———. "The Historical Denial of Lesbianism," *Radical History Review*, 20 (1979), pp. 60–65.

———. "Women Alone Stir My Imagination: Lesbianism and the Cultural Tradition," *Signs*, 4 (1978–79), pp. 718–39.

Cott, Nancy F. *The Bonds of Womanhood: "Woman's Sphere" in New England, 1780–1835*. New Haven: Yale University Press, 1977.

———. "Passionlessness: An Interpretation of Victorian Sexual Ideology, 1790–1850," *Signs,* 4 (1978–79), pp. 219–36.

Cowan, Ruth Schwartz. *More Work for Mother: The Ironies of Household Technology from the Open Hearth to the Microwave.* New York: Basic Books, 1983.

Cutright, Phillips, and Shorter, Edward. "The Effects of Health on the Completed Fertility of Non-white and White U.S. Women Born between 1867 and 1935," *Journal of Social History,* 13 (1979), pp. 191–217.

Dannenbaum, Jed. "The Origins of Temperance Activism and Militancy Among American Women," *Journal of Social History,* 15 (1981), pp. 235–52.

Dawson, D. A.; Meny, D. J.; Ridley, J. C. "Fertility Control in the United States Before the Contraceptive Revolution," *Family Planning Perspectives,* 12 (1980), pp. 76–87.

Degler, Carl N. *At Odds: Women and the Family in America.* New York: Oxford University Press, 1980.

———. "What Ought to Be and What Was: Women's Sexuality in the Nineteenth Century," *American Historical Review,* 79 (1974), pp. 1467–90.

D'Emilio, John. "Capitalism and Gay Identity," in Snitow, Ann; Stansell, Christine; and Thompson, Sharon. eds. *Powers of Desire: The Politics of Sexuality.* New York: Monthly Review Press, 1983.

———. *Sexual Politics, Sexual Communities: The Making of a Homosexual Minority in the United States, 1940–1970.* Chicago: University of Chicago Press, 1983.

Dietrich, Mabel E., and Purdy, Virginia C., eds. *Clio Was a Woman: Studies in the History of American Women.* Washington, DC: Howard University Press, 1980.

Dobkin, Marjorie Housepian. *The Making of a Feminist: Early Journals and Letters of M. Carey Thomas.* Kent, OH: Kent State University Press, 1979.

Donegan, Jane B. *Women and Men Midwives: Medicine, Morality and Misogyny in Early America.* Westport, CT: Greenwood, 1978.

Douglas, Ann. "'The Fashionable Diseases': Women's Complaints and Their Treatment in Nineteenth Century America," *Journal of Interdisciplinary History,* 4 (1973), pp. 25–52.

———. *The Feminization of American Culture.* New York: Knopf, 1977.

Drachman, Virginia G. "Female Solidarity and Professional Success: The Dilemma of Women Doctors in Late Nineteenth-Century America," *Journal of Social History,* 15 (1982), pp. 607–20.

Drinnon, Richard. *Rebel in Paradise: A Biography of Emma Goldman.* Chicago: University of Chicago Press, 1961.

Dublin, Thomas. "The Hodgdon Family Letters: A View of Women in the Early Textile Mills 1830–1840," *History of New Hampshire,* 33 (1978), pp. 283–95.

———. *Women at Work: The Transformation of Work and Community in Lowell, Massachusetts, 1826–1860.* New York: Columbia University Press, 1979.

————. "Women, Work and the Family: Female Operatives in the Lowell Mills, 1830–1860," *Feminist Studies*, 3 (1975), pp. 40–53.

————. "Women Workers and the Study of Social Mobility," *Journal of Interdisciplinary History*, 9 (1979), pp. 647–65.

DuBois, Ellen Carol. *Feminism and Suffrage: The Emergence of an Independent Women's Movement in America, 1848–1869*. Ithaca, NY: Cornell University Press, 1978.

————. "The Radicalism of the Woman Suffrage Movement: Notes Toward the Reconstruction of Nineteenth-Century Feminism," *Feminist Studies*, 3 (1975), pp. 63–71.

————; Buhle, Mari Jo; Kaplan, Temma; Lerner, Gerda; and Smith-Rosenberg, Carroll. "Politics and Culture in Women's History: A Symposium," *Feminist Studies*, 6 (1980), pp. 26–64.

Eakin, Paul J. "Margaret Fuller, Hawthorne, James, and Sexual Politics," *Southern Atlantic Quarterly*, 75 (1976), pp. 323–38.

Ehrenreich, Barbara, and English, Deirdre. *For Her Own Good: 150 Years of Expert's Advice to Women*. Garden City, NY: Doubleday, 1979.

Elder, Glen H. Jr., and Rockwell, Richard C. "Marital Timing in Women's Life Patterns," *Journal of Family History*, 1 (1976), pp. 34–53.

Ellsworth, Edward W. *Liberators of the Female Mind: The Shirreff Sisters, Educational Reform, and the Women's Movement*. Westport, CT: Greenwood, 1979.

Epstein, Barbara L. *The Politics of Domesticity: Women Evangelism and Temperance in Nineteenth Century America*. Middletown, CT: Wesleyan University Press, 1981.

Erenberg, Lewis A. "Everybody's Doin' It: The Pre-World War I Dance Craze, the Castles and the Modern American Girl," *Feminist Studies*, 3 (1975), pp. 155–70.

Faderman, Lillian. "Emily Dickinson's Letters to Sue Gilbert," *Massachusetts Review*, 18 (1977), pp. 197–225.

————. "Female Same-Sex Relationships in Novels by Longfellow, Holmes, and James," *New England Quarterly*, 60 (1978), pp. 309–22.

————. "Lesbian Magazine Fiction in the Early Twentieth Century," *Journal of Popular Culture*, 11 (1978), pp. 800–17.

Faragher, John Mack. "History from the Inside-Out: Writing the History of Women in Rural America," *American Quarterly*, 33 (1981), pp. 538–57.

Feinstein, Karen Wolk. "Kindergartens, Feminism and the Professionalization of Motherhood," *International Journal of Women's Studies*, 3 (1980), pp. 28–38.

Finnegan, Frances. *Poverty and Prostitution: A Study of Victorian Prostitutes in New York*. New York: Cambridge University Press, 1979.

Flexner, Eleanor. *Century of Struggle: The Women's Rights Movement in the United States*. rev. ed. Cambridge, MA: Harvard University Press, 1975.

Foner, Philip S. *Women and the American Labor Movement: From the First Trade Unions to the Present*. 2 vols. New York: Free Press, 1979–80.

Frankfort, Roberta. *Collegiate Women: Domesticity and Career in Turn of the Century America*. New York: New York University Press, 1977.

Fraundorf, Martha Norby. "The Labor Force Participation of Turn-of-the-Century Married Women," *Journal of Economic History*, 39 (1979), pp. 401–18.

Freedman, Estelle B. "Separatism as Strategy: Female Institution Building and American Feminism, 1870–1930," *Feminist Studies*, 5 (1979), pp. 512–29.

———. *Their Sisters' Keepers: Women's Prison Reform in America 1830–1930*. Ann Arbor: University of Michgan Press, 1981.

Friedan, Betty. *The Feminine Mystique*. New York: Dell, 1974.

Friedman, Jean E., and Shade, William G. eds. *Our American Sisters: Women in American Life and Thought*. 3rd ed. Lexington, MA: Heath, 1982.

Fuller, Margaret. *Woman in the Nineteenth Century*. New York: Norton, 1971 (1855).

Gelb, Joyce, and Palley, Lief. *Women and Public Policies*. Princeton: Princeton University Press, 1983.

George, Carol. ed. *Remember the Ladies: New Perspectives on Women in American History*. Syracuse, NY: Syracuse University Press, 1975.

Goldin, Claudia. "The Changing Economic Role of Women: A Quantitative Approach," *Journal of Interdisciplinary History*, 13 (1983), pp. 707–33.

———. "Female Labor Force Participation: The Origin of Black and White Differences, 1870 and 1880," *Journal of Economic History*, 37 (1977), pp. 87–108.

———. "The Work and Wages of Single Women 1870 to 1920," *Journal of Economic History*, 40 (1980), pp. 81–88.

——— and Sokoloff, Kenneth. "Women, Children, and Industrialization in the Early Republic: Evidence from the Manufacturing Censuses," *Journal of Economic History* 42 (1982), pp. 741–74.

Goldman, Emma. *Anarchism, and Other Essays*. New York: Dover, 1969 (1917).

———. *Living My Life*. 2 vols. New York: Dover, 1970 (1931).

Goldman, Marion S. *Gold Diggers and Silver Miners: Prostitution and Social Change on the Comstock*. Ann Arbor: University of Michigan Press, 1981.

Gordon, Linda. *Woman's Body, Woman's Right: A Social History of Birth Control*. New York: Grossman/Viking, 1976.

Green, Elizabeth Alden. *Mary Lyons and Mount Holyoke*. Hanover, NH: University Press of New England, 1979.

Greenwald, Maurice W. *Women, War, and Work: The Impact of World War I on Women in the United States*. Westport, CT: Greenwood, 1982.

Grotzinger, Laurel. "The Proto-Feminist Librarian at the Turn of the Century: Two Studies," *Journal of Library History*, 10 (1975), pp. 195–213.

Haller, John S., and Haller, Robin M. *The Physician and Sexuality in Victorian America*. Urbana: University of Illinois Press, 1974.

Harris, Barbara J. *Beyond Her Sphere: Women and the Professions in American History*. Westport, CT: Greenwood, 1980.

Hayden, Dolores. "Charlotte Perkins Gilman and the Kitchenless House," *Radical Historical Review*, 21 (1979), pp. 225–47.

———. "Two Utopian Feminists and Their Campaign for Kitchenless Houses," *Signs*, 4 (1978–79), pp. 274–90.

Heilbrun, Carolyn G. *Reinventing Womanhood.* New York: Norton, 1979.

Henry, Alice. *Trade Union Woman.* New York: Burt Franklin 1973 (1915).

Hill, Mary A. *Charlotte Perkins Gilman: The Making of a Radical Feminist 1860–1896.* Philadelphia: Temple University Press, 1980.

Hirata, Lucie Cheng. "Free, Indentured, Enslaved: Chinese Prostitutes in Nineteenth-Century America," *Signs*, 5 (1979), pp. 3–29.

Hunt, Vilma R. "A Brief History of Women Workers and Hazards in the Workplace," *Feminist Studies*, 5 (1979), pp. 274–85.

Hymowitz, Carol, and Weissman, Michael A. *History of Women in America.* New York: Bantam, 1978.

Irwin, Inez H. *Angels and Amazons: A Hundred Years of American Women.* Salem, NH: Arno, 1974 (1934).

Jacoby, Robin Miller. "Feminism and Class Consciousness in the British and American Women's Trade Union Leagues 1890–1925," in Carroll, Berenice A., ed. *Liberating Women's History.* Urbana: University of Illinois Press, 1976.

———. "The Women's Trade Union League and American Feminism," *Feminist Studies*, 3 (1975–76), pp. 126–40.

Jeffrey, Julie Roy. *Frontier Women: The Trans-Mississippi West 1840–1880.* New York: Hill and Wang, 1979.

Jeffrey, Kirk. "Career and Feminine Ideology in Nineteenth-Century America: Reconstructing the Marital Experience of Lydia Maria Child, 1828–1874," *Feminist Studies*, 2 (2/3), 1975–76), pp. 113–30.

Jensen Joan M., and Miller, Darlis A. "The Gentle Tanners Revisited: Approaches to the History of Women in the American West," *Pacific Historical Review*, 49 (1980), pp. 173–213.

Karlsen, Carol F. *The Devil in the Shape of a Woman: Witchcraft in Seventeenth-Century New England.* Forthcoming. New York: Norton, 1985.

——— and Crumpacker, Laurie, eds. *The Jounral of Esther Edwards Burr, 1754–1757.* New Haven, CT: Yale University Press, 1984.

Katzman, David M. *Seven Days a Week: Women and Domestic Service in Industrializing America.* New York: Oxford University Press, 1978.

Kaufman, Polly Welts. *Women Teachers on the Frontier.* New Haven: Yale University Press, 1984.

Kennedy, Susan Estabrook. *If All We Did Was to Weep at Home: A History of White Working-Class Women in America.* Bloomington: Indiana University Press, 1981.

———. " 'The Want It Satisfies Demostrates the Need of It': A Study of Life and Labor of the Women's Trade Union League," *International Journal of Women's Studies*, 3 (1980), pp. 391–406.

Kerber, Linda K. *Women of the Republic: Intellect and Ideology in Revolutionary America.* Chapel Hill: University of North Carolina Press, 1980.

Kern, Louis J. *An Ordered Love: Sex Roles and Sexuality in Victorian Utopias— The Shakers, the Mormons, and the Oneida Community.* Chapel Hill: University of North Carolina Press, 1981.

Kessler-Harris, Alice. *Out to Work: A History of Wage-Earning Women in the United States.* New York: Oxford University Press. 1982.

———. "Women's Wage Work as Myth and History," *Labor History,* 19 (1978), pp. 285–307.

Klotter, James C. "Sex, Scandal, and Suffrage in the Gilded Age," *Historian,* 42 (1980), pp. 225–43.

Kohlstedt, Sally Gregory. "In from the Periphery: American Women in Science, 1830–1880," *Signs,* 4 (1978), pp. 81–96.

Kushner, Howard I. "Nineteenth-Century Sexuality and the 'Sexual Revolution' of the Progressive Era," *Canadian Review of American Studies,* 9 (1978), pp. 34–49.

Leach, William. *True Love and Perfect Union: The Feminist Reform of Sex and Society.* New York: Basic, 1980.

Lebsock, Suzanne D. "Radical Reconstruction and the Property Rights of Southern Women," *Journal of Southern History,* 43 (1977), pp. 195–216.

Lemons, Stanley J. *The Woman Citizen: Social Feminism in the 1920's.* Urbana: University of Illinois Press, 1975.

Lerner, Gerda. *Black Women in White America.* New York: Pantheon, 1972.

———. *The Majority Finds Its Past: Placing Women in History.* New York: Oxford University Press, 1979.

———. "New Approaches to the Study of Women in American History," *Journal of Social History,* 3 (1969), pp. 53–62.

———. "Placing Women in History: Definitions and Challenges," *Feminist Studies,* 3 (1/2) (1975–76), pp. 5–14.

———. "Politics and Culture in Women's History," *Feminist Studies,* 6 (1980), pp. 49–54.

Levine, Susan. "'Honor Each Noble Maid': Women Workers and the Yonkers Carpet Weavers' Strike of 1885," *New York History,* 62 (1981), pp. 153–76.

Lewis, Denslow, M.D. *The Gynecologic Consideration of the Sexual Act.* Weston, MA: M & S Press 1970 (1900).

Licata, Salvatore J. "Homosexual Rights Movement in the United States: A Traditionally Overlooked Area of American History," *Journal of Homosexuality,* 6 (1980–81), pp. 161–89.

Litoff, Judy Barrett. "Forgotten Women: American Midwives at the Turn of the Twentieth Century," *Historian,* 40 (1978), pp. 235–51.

Loveland, Anne C. "Domesticity and Religion in the Antebellum Period: The Career of Phoebe Palmer," *Historian,* 39 (1977), pp. 455–71.

Lumpkin, Katherine D. *The Emancipation of Angelina Grimké.* Chapel Hill: University of North Carolina Press, 1974.

McCarthy, Kathleen D. *Noblesse Oblige: Charity and Cultural Philanthropy in Chicago 1849–1929*. Chicago: University of Chicago Press, 1982.

McConnell, Dorothy. *Women, War and Fascism*. New York: American League against War and Fascism, 1935.

McGaw, J. A. "Good Place to Work: Industrial Workers and Occupational Choice: The Case of Berkshire Women," *Journal of Interdisciplinary History*, 10 (1979), pp. 227–48.

McGouldrick, Paul, and Tannen, Michael. "The Increasing Pay Gap for Women in the Textile and Clothing Industries," *Journal of Economic History*, 40 (1980), pp. 799–814

McLoughlin, William G. "Billy Sunday and the Working Girl of 1915," *Journal of Presbyterian History*, 54 (1976), pp. 376–84.

Magner, Lois N. "Women and the Scientific Idiom: Textual Episodes from Wollstonecraft, Fuller, Gilman and Firestone," *Signs*, 4 (1978), pp. 61–80.

Marrett, Cora Bagley. "On the Evolution of Women's Medical Societies," *Bulletin of the History of Medicine*, 53 (1979), pp. 434–48.

Marsh, Margaret S. "The Anarchist-Feminist Response to the 'Woman Question' in Late Nineteenth-Century America," *American Quarterly*, 30 (1978), pp. 533–47.

Masel-Walters, Lynne. "To Hustle with the Rowdies: The Organization and Function of the American Woman Suffrage Press," *Journal of American Culture*, 3 (1980), pp. 167–83.

Matthews, Jean V. "'Woman's Place' and the Search for Identity in Ante-Bellum America," *Canadian Review of American Studies*, 10 (1980), pp. 289–304.

Matthies, Susan A. "Families at Work: An Analysis by Sex of Child Workers in the Cotton Textile Industry," *Journal of Economic History*, 42 (1982), pp. 173–80.

Melder, Keith E. *Beginnings of Sisterhood: The American Woman's Rights Movement, 1800–1850*. New York: Schocken, 1977.

Millet, Kate. *Sexual Politics*. Garden City, NY: Doubleday, 1970.

Mitchell, Juliet. *Women's Estate*. New York: Vintage, 1973.

Morantz, Regina Markell. "Making Women Modern: Middle Class Women and Health Reform in 19th Century America," *Journal of Social History*, 10 (1977), pp. 490–507.

Neu, Irene D. "The Jewish Businesswoman in America," *American Jewish History Quarterly*, 66 (1976), pp. 137–54.

Nies, Judith. *Seven Women: Portraits from the American Radical Tradition*. New York: Viking, 1977.

Norton, Mary B., ed. *Liberty's Daughters: The Revolutionary Experience of American Women 1750–1800*. Boston, MA: Little, Brown, 1980.

Padgug, Robert A. "Sexual Matters: On Conceptualizing Sexuality in History," *Radical History Review*, 20 (1979), pp. 3–23.

Pearson, Willie Jr., and Clark, Maxine L. "The Mal(e) Treatment of American Women in Gynecology and Obstetrics," *International Journal of Women's Studies*, 5 (1982), pp. 348–62.

Peck, Mary Gray. *Carrie Chapman Catt.* Westport, CT: Hyperion, 1976 (1944).

Peters, Margot. "Biographies of Women," *Biography,* 2 (1979), pp. 201–17.

Pohl, Frances K. "Historical Reality or Utopian Ideal? The Woman's Building at the World's Columbian Exposition, Chicago, 1893," *International Journal of Women's Studies,* 5 (1982), pp. 289–311.

Porter, Jack Nusan. "Rosa Sonneschein and the American Jewess Revisited: New Historical Information on an Early American Zionist and Jewish Feminist," *American Jewish Archives,* 32 (1980), pp. 125–31.

Porterfield, Amanda. *Feminine Spirituality in America: From Sarah Edwards to Martha Graham.* Philadelphia: Temple University Press, 1980.

Pugh, Evelyn L. "John Stuart Mill, Harriet Taylor, and Women's Rights in America, 1850–1873," *Canadian Journal of History,* 13 (1978), pp. 423–42.

Rich, Adrienne. "Compulsory Heterosexuality and Lesbian Existence," *Signs,* 5 (1979–80), pp. 631–60.

Riley, Glenda. *Frontierswomen: The Iowa Experience.* Ames: Iowa State University Press, 1981.

Rosen, Ruth. *The Lost Sisterhood: Prostitution in America 1900–1918.* Baltimore, MD: Johns Hopkins University Press, 1982.

Rosenberg, Rosalind. *Beyond Separate Spheres: Intellectual Roots of Modern Feminism.* New Haven: Yale University Press, 1982.

———. "In Search of Woman's Nature, 1850–1920," *Feminist Studies,* 3 (1975), pp. 141–54.

Rossiter, Margaret W. *Women Scientists in America: Struggles and Strategies to 1940.* Baltimore, MD: Johns Hopkins University Press, 1982.

Rothman, Sheila M. *Woman's Proper Place: A History of Changing Ideals and Practices, 1870 to the Present.* New York: Basic, 1978.

Ruether, Rosemary R., and Kelly, Rosemary S. *Women and Religion in America.* New York: Harcourt Brace Jovanovich, 1982.

Ryan, Mary P. *Cradle of the Middle Class: The Family in Oneida County, New York, 1790–1865.* New York: Cambridge University Press, 1981.

———. *The Empire of Mothers: American Writing on Women and the Family, 1830–1860.* New York: Haworth Press, 1982.

———. "The Power of Women's Networks: A Case Study of Female Moral Reform in Antebellum America," *Feminist Studies,* 5 (1979), pp. 66–85.

———. "Reproduction in American History," *Journal of Interdisciplinary History,* 10 (1979), pp. 319–32.

———. *Womanhood in America: From Colonial Times to the Present.* 2nd ed. New York: Watts, 1979.

Sanger, Margaret. *Motherhood in Bondage.* New York: Brentano's, 1928.

Schlissel, Lillian. *Women's Diaries of the Westward Journey.* New York: Schocken, 1982.

Schlossmann, Steven, and Wallach, Stephanie. "The Crime of Precocious Sexuality: Female Juvenile Delinquency in the Progressive Era," *Harvard Educational Review,* 48 (1978), pp. 65–94.

Scott, Anne F. *The Southern Lady: From Pedestal to Politics 1830–1930*. Chicago: University of Chicago Press, 1972.

Seller, Maxine. "The Education of the Immigrant Woman, 1900–1935," *Journal of Urban History*, 4 (1978), pp. 307–30.

Shiels, Richard D. "The Feminization of American Congregationalism, 1730–1835," *American Quarterly*, 33 (1981), pp. 46–62.

Sklar, Kathryn Kish, "American Female Historians in Context, 1770–1930," *Feminist Studies*, 3 (1975), pp. 171–84.

———. *Catherine Beecher: A Study in American Domesticity*. New York: Norton, 1976.

Sloan, Kay. "Sexual Warfare in the Silent Cinema: Comedies and Melodramas of Woman Suffragism," *American Quarterly*, 33 (1981), pp. 412–36.

Smith-Rosenberg, Carroll. "The New Woman and the New History," *Feminist Studies*, 3 (1975–76), pp. 185–98.

———. "Puberty to Menopause: The Cycle of Femininity in Nineteenth-Century America," *Feminist Studies*, 1 (3/4), (1972–73), pp. 58–72.

———. "Sex as Symbol in Victorian Purity: An Ethnohistorical Analysis of Jacksonian America," in Demos, John, and Boocock, Sarane Spruce, eds. *Turning Points: Historical and Sociological Essays on the Family*. Chicago: University of Chicago Press, 1978.

Snitow, Ann; Stansell, Christine; and Thompson, Sharon, eds. *Powers of Desire The Politics of Sexuality*. New York: Monthly Review Press, 1983.

Spruil, Julia C. *Women's Life and Work in the Southern Colonies*. Tampa, FL: Russell, 1969 (1938).

Stage, Sarah. *Female Complaints: Lydia Pinkham and the Business of Women's Medicine*. New York: Norton, 1979.

Stansell, Christine. "Women, Children, and the Uses of the Streets: Class and Gender Conflict in New York City, 1850–1860," *Feminist Studies*, 8 (1982), pp. 309–35.

Stein, Leon, and Baxter, Annette K., eds. *The Autobiography of a Happy Woman*. Salem, NH: Arno, 1974 (1914).

Steinson, Barbara J. "Sisters and Soldiers: American Women and the National Service Schools, 1916–1917," *Historian*, 43 (1981), pp. 225–39.

Stewart, Abigail J., and Winter, David G. "The Nature and Causes of Female Suppression," *Signs*, 2 (1977), pp. 531–53.

Sticker, Frank. "Cookbooks and Law Books: The Hidden History of Career Women in Twentieth Century America," *Journal of Social History*, 10 (1976), pp. 1–19.

Stimpson, Catharine, and Person, Ethel Spector, eds. *Women: Sex and Sexuality*. Chicago: University of Chicago Press, 1980.

Strasser, Susan. *Never Done: A History of American Housework*. New York: Pantheon Books, 1982.

Strong-Boag, Veronica. "Female Minds, Feminine Experience: The Emerging

Definition of Female Intellect in American History," *Canadian Review of American Studies*, 13 (1982), pp. 97–107.

Swisshelm, Jane G. ed. *Crusader and Feminist: Letters of Jane Grey Swisshelm 1858–1865*. Westport, CT: Hyperion, 1976 (1934).

Tentler, Leslie Woodcock. *Wage-Earning Women: Industrial Work and Family Life in the United States*. New York: Oxford University Press, 1979.

Thomas, Samuel J. "Catholic Journalists and the Ideal Woman in Late Victorian America," *International Journal of Women's Studies*, 4 (1981), pp. 89–100.

Thompson, Eleanor Wolf. *Education for Ladies, 1830–1860: Ideas on Education in Magazines for Women*. New York: King's Crown Press, 1947.

Thompson, Roger. *Women in Stuart England and America: A Comparative Study*. Boston, MA: Routledge and Kegan Paul, 1978.

Thorne, Melvin J. "Fainters and Fighters: Images of Women in the Indian Captivity Narratives," *Midwest Quarterly*, 23 (1982), pp. 426–36.

Walsh, Mary Roth, and Walsh, Francis R. "Integrating Men's Colleges at the Turn of the Century," *Historical Journal of Massachusetts*, 10 (1982), pp. 4–16.

Watkins, Bari. "Women's World in Nineteenth-Century America," *American Quarterly*, 31 (1979), pp. 116–27.

Weiner, Nella Fermi. "Of Feminism and Birth Control Propaganda (1790–1840)," *International Journal of Women's Studies*, 3 (1980), pp. 411–30.

Wertheimer, Barbara M. *We Were There: The Story of Working Women in America*. New York: Pantheon, 1977.

————. *Women and Trade Unions: A Short History of Women in the British Trade Union Movement*. New York: St. Martin's, 1977.

Wertz, Dorothy C. "Social Science Attitudes Toward Women Workers, 1870–1970," *International Journal of Women's Studies*, 5 (1982), pp. 161–71.

Wertz, Richard W., and Wertz, Dorothy C. *Lying-in: A History of Childbirth in America*. New York: Schocken, 1977.

Wilson, Margaret G. *The American Woman in Transition: The Urban Influence, 1870–1920*. Westport, CT: Greenwood, 1979.

Woloch, Nancy. *Women and the American Experience*. New York: Knopf, 1984.

Wright, Mary C. "Economic Development and Native American Women in the Early Nineteenth Century," *American Quarterly*, 33 (1981), pp. 525–36.

Young, Louise M. "Women's Place in American Politics: The Historical Perspective," *Journal of Politics*, 38 (1976), pp. 295–335.

Zickefoose, Sandra. "Women and the Socialist Party of America," *UCLA Historical Journal*, 1 (1980), pp. 26–41.

The Contributors

JOHN C. FOUT is Professor of History at Bard College in New York State, where he has been teaching since 1969. He was a Fulbright Scholar at the University of Heidelberg in 1964–65 and completed his Ph.D. at the University of Minnesota in 1969; he studied there under the direction of Otto Pflanze. He is the editor of *German History and Civilization: A Bibliography of Scholarly Periodical Literature* (Scarecrow, 1974), co-editor of *European Women: A Documentary History, 1789–1945* (Schocken, 1980; Harvester, 1983), and has written articles and reviews for scholarly journals. Professor Fout is currently editing a collection of essays entitled *Politics, Parties, and the Authoritarian State: Imperial Germany, 1871–1918* (Holmes & Meier, 1985). He has completed an article entitled "The Viennese Enquête of 1896 on Working Women" (forthcoming in an essay collection) and he hopes to do a monograph on that topic. He is working on a German/English-language bibliography on nineteenth-century German women and he hopes to edit and translate an anthology of documents on that same topic.

JOANNE F. SCHNEIDER is currently an Assistant Professor of History at Wheaton College, Norton, Massachusetts, and a teaching associate at Brown University in Providence, Rhode Island. She has been teaching for the past six years at such diverse institutions as the University of Montana at Missoula, Stonehill College in North Easton, Massachusetts, and the aforementioned Wheaton and Brown. She received her Ph.D. from Brown University in 1977. Professor Norman Rich directed her German history field and thesis research. Her dissertation is entitled "An Historical Examination of Women's Education in Bavaria: *Mädchenschulen* and Contemporary Attitudes about Them, 1799–1848." She is the co-editor of a chronological, geographical, and topical bibliography entitled *Women in Western European History*, vol. 1: *Antiquity to the French Revolution* (Greenwood Press, 1982), and vol. 2: *The Nineteenth and Twentieth Centuries* (Greenwood Press, 1984). She has plans for a similar work which would collate sources on eastern and northern European and Russian women and their historical experiences. She is also a contributor to *Collier's Encyclopedia Yearbook*.

DEBORAH HERTZ is Assistant Professor of History at the State University of New York at Binghamton. In 1984–85 she will be a Mellon Fellow at Harvard University. She received her Ph.D. from the University of Minnesota in 1979 for a dissertation on the social history of the Berlin salons in the late eighteenth century. She has received grants from the Fulbright Commission, the German Academic Exchange Service, IREX, the National Endowment for the Humanities, and the American Philosophical Society. She is editor of *Briefe an eine Freundin: Rahel Varnhageu an Rebecca Friedländer*, which will be published in 1985 by Kiepenheuer and Witsch in Cologne. She is completing a book, *Mixed Company: The Jewish Salons of Eighteenth-Century Berlin.*

GWENDOLYN E. JENSEN is presently Vice President for Academic Affairs at Western State College of Colorado in Gunnison, Colorado. She received her Ph.D. from the University of Connecticut in 1971 and taught in the History Department at the University of New Haven from 1968 to 1983. She has presented a number of papers and has published articles on early-nineteenth-century German history, including "Official Reform in Vormärz Prussia: the Ecclesiastical Dimension," *Central European History* (1974), and "A Comparative Study of Prussian and Anglican Church-State Reform in the Nineteenth Century," *Journal of Church and State* (1981).

RENATE MÖHRMANN is Professor of Theater, Film, and Television Studies at Cologne University. She studied German, French, philosophy, and the media in Hamburg, Lyon, and New York. In 1972 she completed her doctorate at the City University of New York and afterwards worked for three years at Duisburg University as Assistant Professor of Modern German Literature and Media. In 1977 she was invited to take up a professorship in the Institute of Theater, Film, and Television Studies at Cologne University. She is the author of the following books: *Der vereinsamte Mensch: Studium zum Wandel des Einsamkeitsmotivs im Roman von Raabe bis Musil* (Bouvier, 1974), *Die andere Frau: Emanzipationsansätze deutscher Schriftstellerinnen im Vorfeld der Achtundvierziger-Revolution* (Metzler, 1977), *Frauen im Vormärz. Texte und Dokumente* (Reclam, 1978), *Die Frau mit der Kamera. Filmemacherinnen in der Bundesrepublik Deutschland* (Hanser, 1980); the editor of the series *Studium zum Theater, Film und Fernsehen* (P. D. Lang, 1981); and author of numerous articles and reviews for scholarly journals. At present she is occupied with the completion of a 2,000-page documentation of criticism on the theater at the turn of the century which is being financed by the Deutsche Forschungsgemeinschaft.

CATHERINE M. PRELINGER has served since 1970 at Yale University, currently as Associate Research Editor. She completed her Ph.D. at Yale, where she was a student of Hajo Holborn. She has held numerous research grants, including an NEH Summer Stipend, an American Philosophical Society Research Grant, an NEH-Rockefeller Grant, a grant from Deutscher Akademischer Austauschdienst, and was a holder of a Harvard Divinity School Research Associateship in Women's Studies in 1982–83. She has long been active in women's studies and has in recent years presented over two dozen papers at various historical conferences, with most of those being on German women. She has completed "The Charitable Context: Religious Dimensions of the Mid-Nineteenth-Century German Women's Movement," a book-length manuscript, and she has published numerous articles and reviews in scholarly journals.

STANLEY ZUCKER is Associate Professor of History at Southern Illinois University at Carbondale. He received his Ph.D. from the University of Wisconsin in 1968. His previous work dealt with the history of German political parties, Mainz history, and the Revolution of 1848–49. Some of his publications include: *Ludwig Bamberger: German Liberal Politician and Social Critic* (Pittsburgh, 1975); "Ludwig Bamberger and the Rise of Anti-Semitism in Germany, 1848–1893," *Central European History* (1970); "1848 and the Birth of Politics in Mainz," in *Consortium on Revolutionary Europe, Proceedings 1976* (1978); "Politischer Katholizismus und deutsche Demokratie. Der Fall Philipp Wasserburg," *Historisches Jahrbuch* (1982); and "German Women and the Revolution of 1848: Kathinka Zitz-Halein and the Humania Association," *Central European History* (1980). He is currently working on a monographic study of Kathinka Zitz-Halein.

LIA SECCI is Professor of German Literature and Director of the Institute for Foreign Languages in the Liberal Arts Faculty at the University of Perugia, where she has been teaching for the past fifteen years. She also taught Italian in the Romance Language Department at the University of Heidelberg from 1963 to 1969. She has written numerous scholarly articles on the history of women's emancipation in Germany which were based on literary sources, and she has edited an anthology entitled *Dal salotto al partito. Scrittrici tedesche tra rivoluzione borghese e diritto di voto (1848–1918)* (Roma, 1982). She is also the leader of a research group of German specialists researching the history of women's emancipation in Germany. That research is being funded by an Italian research institute and the Ministry of Culture.

RUTH-ELLEN BOETCHER JOERES is Associate Professor of German and Director of Graduate Studies of the Department of German at the University of Minnesota in Minneapolis. She received her Ph.D. from the

Johns Hopkins University in 1971 after completion of a dissertation on Karl Gutzkow. She is the translator/commentator of Karl Gutzkow's *Wally, die Zweiflerin (Wally the Skeptic)* (Lang, 1974), editor of the annotated catalogue of the history of German women, Gerritsen Collection of Women's History (Microfilming Corporation of America, in press), the author of a monograph on Louise Otto-Peters, *Die Anfänge der deutschen Frauenbewegung. Louise Otto-Peters (The Beginnings of the German Women's Movement)* (Fischer, 1983), and of articles on nineteenth-century German writers in *Modern Language Notes, Monatshefte, The German Quarterly, Internationales Archiv für Sozialgeschichte der deutschen Literatur, Amsterdamer Beiträge,* and *Euphorion.* She was co-director with M. J. Maynes of "Condition and Consciousness," an international, interdisciplinary conference held at the University of Minnesota in April 1983 on the social and literary history of German women in the eighteenth and nineteenth centuries. She has been a recipient of a number of national and international research fellowships.

JULIANE JACOBI-DITTRICH is Assistant Professor in the History of Education at the University of Bielefeld, where she has been teaching since 1975. She received her Ph.D. in the same field at that university in 1976. Family history and the history of childhood have been her special interest and she spent a year in the United States investigating the childhood of German immigrant families in the eighteenth and nineteenth centuries, funded by a Deutsche Forschungsgemeinschafts research fellowship. She is now working on a book entitled "Kinder zwischen Familie, Kirche und Schule am Beispiel deutscher Siedlergruppen in Nordamerika: Pennsylvania (1689–1780)." Her interest in the development of feminist theories led her to edit the writings of Theodor Gottlieb von Hippel (Vaduz, 1980). This expanded edition of his works deals with the question of women's rights. She is also the co-editor (with Eckhard Dittrich) of an article dealing with methodological problems concerning the use of autobiographical material for social history and especially the history of childhood: "Autobiographien als Quellen zur Sozialgeschichte der Erziehung," in *Aus Geschichten Lernen,* ed. by Dieter Baacke and Theodor Schulze, (Munich, 1979).

ALFRED G. MEYER is Professor of Political Science at the University of Michigan, where he has been teaching since 1966. He was born in 1920, emigrated to the United States in 1939, and served in the U.S. Army from August 1941 to December 1945. His M.A. (Slavic languages) and Ph.D. (political science) degrees were obtained from Harvard University in 1946 and 1950. He has published books on Marxist and Communist theory, on Soviet politics, and on German-Soviet foreign relations, in addition to numerous articles, book chapters, and the like. Some of his works are:

Leninism (Cambridge, Mass., 1957), *Marxism: The Unity of Theory and Practice* (Ann Arbor, 1963), *The Soviet Political System* (New York, 1965), and *Communism* (4th ed.; New York, 1983). He has won awards for excellence as a teacher and for outstanding service as a general undergraduate counselor. He is currently working on a biography of Lily Braun and on a volume of translations of her essays on feminist and socialist themes. In the Women's Studies Program at the University of Michigan he teaches a course on "Women and Socialism."

W. R. LEE is currently Senior Lecturer in Economic History at the University of Liverpool, where he has been teaching since 1972. He received his Ph.D. from Corpus Christi College, Oxford. He is the author of *Population Growth, Economic Development and Social Change in Bavaria, 1750–1850* (New York, 1977), editor of *Helmut Böhme: An Introduction to the Social and Economic History of Germany—Politics and Economic Change in the 19th and 20th Centuries* (Oxford, 1978), the editor of *European Demography and Economic Growth* (London, 1979), and co-editor of *The German Family: Essays on the Social History of the Family in Nineteenth- and Twentieth-Century Germany* (London, 1981). He contributed two essays to the latter: "The German Family: A Critical Survey of the Current State of Historical Research" and "Family and 'Modernisation': The Peasant Family and Social Change in Nineteenth-Century Bavaria." He is also the author of numerous other articles on the social and economic history of Modern Germany.

BARBARA FRANZOI is currently the Chairperson of the History Department at the College of St. Elizabeth in Convent Station, New Jersey, where she teaches courses on modern Europe and women's history. She holds her Ph.D. from Rutgers University. She has presented a number of papers on women and industrial work at recent history conferences, and she is currently completing the revision for publication of her doctoral dissertation, entitled "Women and Industrial Work in the German Reich, 1871–1914."

JEAN H. QUATAERT is Associate Professor of European History at the University of Houston–Clear Lake. Prior to that she was an instructor in modern German history at Loyola-Marymount University, Los Angeles. Jean Quataert received her Ph.D. in history in 1974 from the University of California, Los Angeles. She is the author of *Reluctant Feminists in German Social Democracy, 1885–1917* (Princeton, 1979); co-editor with Marilyn J. Boxer of *Socialist Women: European Socialist Feminism in the Nineteenth and Early Twentieth Centuries* (New York, 1978), and has written several journal articles and book chapters. She has been the

recipient of a National Endowment for the Humanities Research Fellowship (1980–81) and an American Council of Learned Societies Grant-in-
Aid and German Academic Exchange Service "Study Visit" Grant
(DAAD) (summer 1982), and currently is working on a book-length project on changes in the work and family lives of women textile and garment
industry workers in Germany, 1806–1914.

UTE FREVERT studied history and sociology at the universities of Münster
and Bielefeld and at the London School of Economics and Political Science. She received her Ph.D. in 1982 and since then has been a lecturer
in the History Department of the University of Bielefeld in West Germany. Her doctoral dissertation is concerned with the health care of the
working class in nineteenth-century Germany. She has published a number of articles on women's history, especially on female white-collar workers in Germany in the 1920s and 1930s, as well as on the relationship
between doctors and women since the late eighteenth century. She is now
working on male-female relationships between 1750 and 1950.

RANDOLPH E. BERGSTROM is presently studying for the Ph.D. at Columbia University.

ERIC A. JOHNSON is presently an Associate Professor of History at Central
Michigan University. He holds his Ph.D. from the University of Pennsylvania. His research interests at this time deal with urbanization and crime
in Imperial Germany, and he has presented a number of papers and has
published a number of articles on that subject, including two articles he
co-authored with Vincent McHale: "Urbanization, Industrialization and
Crime in Imperial Germany," *Social Science History* (1976 and 1977) and
"Socioeconomic Aspects of the Delinquency Rate in Imperial Germany,
1882–1914," *Journal of Social History* (1980). He is currently completing
a monograph to be entitled "The Rechtsstaat: Crime and Criminal Justice
in Imperial Germany." This study will employ quantitative and qualitative
data to examine and describe the German system of criminal justice,
popular and elite attitudes toward crime and criminals, and the causation
of criminal action by means of urbanization, industrialization, ethnicity,
poverty, and social discord.

Index